Social Issues in Sport

THIRD EDITION

Ronald B. Woods, PhD
University of Tampa

Library of Congress Cataloging-in-Publication Data

Woods, Ron, 1943 November 6-
Social issues in sport / Ronald B. Woods. -- Third edition.
pages cm
Includes bibliographical references and index.
1. Sports--Social aspects. 2. Sports--Sociological aspects. I. Title.
GV706.5.W655 2015
306.4'83--dc23

2015002522

ISBN: 978-1-4504-9520-2 (print)

The web addresses cited in this text were current as of June 2015, unless otherwise noted.

Permission notices for photos reprinted in this book from other sources can be found on pages xiii-xiv

Acquisitions Editor: Myles Schrag
Developmental and Managing Editor: Amanda S. Ewing
Copyeditor: Tom Tiller
Proofreader: Jim Burns
Indexer: Andrea Hepner
Permissions Manager: Dalene Reeder
Senior Graphic Designer: Keri Evans
Cover Designer: Keith Blomberg
Photograph (cover): Gian Mattia D'Alberto/LaPresse/Icon Sportswire
Photo Asset Manager: Laura Fitch
Photo Production Manager: Jason Allen
Art Manager: Kelly Hendren
Associate Art Manager: Alan L. Wilborn
Illustrations: © Human Kinetics, unless otherwise noted
Printer: Walsworth

Printed in the United States of America. 10 9 8 7 6 5 4 3 2

The paper in this book was manufactured using responsible forestry methods.

Human Kinetics
Web site: www.HumanKinetics.com

United States: Human Kinetics
P.O. Box 5076
Champaign, IL 61825-5076
800-747-4457
e-mail: info@hkusa.com

Canada: Human Kinetics
475 Devonshire Road, Unit 100
Windsor, ON N8Y 2L5
800-465-7301 (in Canada only)
e-mail: info@hkcanada.com

Europe: Human Kinetics
107 Bradford Road
Stanningley
Leeds LS28 6AT, United Kingdom
+44 (0)113 255 5665
e-mail: hk@hkeurope.com

Australia: Human Kinetics
57A Price Avenue
Lower Mitcham, South Australia 5062
08 8372 0999
e-mail: info@hkaustralia.com

New Zealand: Human Kinetics
P.O. Box 80
Mitcham Shopping Centre, South Australia 5062
0800 222 062
e-mail: info@hknewzealand.com

CONTENTS

Part III Sport as an Institution 121

PREFACE

This book examines contemporary sport both factually and critically, particularly in the United States. As part of this project, the book situates the modern sport world in the context of the historical development of sport. As you will see, sport participation and spectatorship in the United States have changed considerably and now lean toward a corporate model.

In the past 50 years, major changes in U.S. society have spilled over into the world of sport. Racial barriers have given way to dominance by African Americans in basketball and football, and Latinos now account for a third of Major League Baseball players. Women and girls also participate more in sport and advocate for equal opportunities as both participants and spectators. In addition, the Special Olympics and the Paralympic Games have become major sport events for people with intellectual or physical disability. Finally, consumer sport now accommodates a surging population of older adults who look to sport to enhance their personal fitness, quality of life, and social interaction. Each of these changes promotes new sport outlooks and strategies and offers hope for the continued expansion of sport for every person.

At the same time, sport sociology has advanced as a science and created more rigorous and insightful methods of studying sport. The sociology of sport is explored in plentiful university courses, and relevant issues are studied by hundreds of professors and researchers. For its part, this book presents the controversies and the status of sport in a sociological context without dwelling on theoretical constructs. More specifically, the text provides a look at sport by a longtime sport participant, observer, fan, teacher, coach, administrator, and critic who has tried to maintain a balanced approach to sport.

Intended Audience

This book is intended for people who are looking at sport objectively for the first time. It can help you understand sport, its place in society, and possible changes that may be needed if sport is to maintain a positive future. I hope you will become better acquainted with both the historical and the current roles of sport in society. Regardless of your major course of study, if you are a sport participant or fan, you will find the information illuminating—and in some cases surprising.

As you come to understand more about the sport world and its interaction with society at large, you will be better equipped to decide what role sport plays in your life and in the life of your family. Whether you are a competitive athlete, an enthusiastic participant, or a spectator, this book can help you enjoy sport more, appreciate the challenges faced by sport, and better evaluate decisions made by sport leaders. Sport can either help unify or help divide society, and it stands a better chance of being beneficial if more people understand both its value and its limitations.

Although this book is based on research and reflects various social theories, it was not written for academic colleagues, and it does not break new theoretical ground. Rather, it is intended to encourage students to delve more deeply into the issues and contradictions that characterize what for many of us can be a love–hate affair with sport.

Text Organization

Part I of the book presents a framework for studying sport in society. More specifically, chapter 1 defines terms and establishes the purpose and importance of sport study. It also addresses the overall field of sport science and how sport research contributes to knowledge within sport.

Chapter 2 presents sociological methods for studying sport in order to help you understand how knowledge is gathered and analyzed. It describes social theories and the ways in which these theories aid the study of sport. To help you apply these theories, this edition of the book includes sidebars that ask you to analyze a topic from the perspective of one of the social theories presented. These sidebars enhance your understanding of the social theories and pique your interest in applying them to current topics in sport.

Part II examines the scope of modern sport and how it affects society. For example, chapter 3 clarifies the parallels and differences between sport participants and sport spectators. It also compares growth trends in various sports and distinguishes people who participate in recreational sport from those who are devoted to high-performance sport. One critical aspect of this work involves reviewing current research reports and analyzing recent trends in the popularity of various sport and fitness activities.

Chapter 4 addresses the business side of sport at the professional and collegiate levels and discusses the issues involved in spending public funds for private gain. It also considers how finances affect athletes, coaches, owners, and participants, both individually and collectively. These discussions help you appreciate the huge economic investments made in sport and the influence of money on sport policies and programs.

Chapter 5 outlines the powerful symbiotic relationship between media and sport. It acknowledges the influence of sport media personalities and journalism and the continuing challenges of including minorities and females more often in sport media. This chapter also recognizes the dramatic shift from print media to electronic media, thanks to technology undreamed of just a generation ago, and its effect on how we consume both sport itself and news about sport.

Part III looks at sport as an institution and how it functions in relation to other institutions, such as colleges and the Olympics. More specifically, chapter 6 examines youth sport outside of the school setting, which has largely become an adult-organized activity for kids that permeates every community. Next, chapter 7 addresses coaching, a topic that appeared elsewhere in earlier editions of the book but has been moved to this section because coaching is such a key determinant of success for teams at various levels. Therefore, it makes sense to integrate the study of coaching with the study of the institutions of youth, high school, and college sport.

Chapter 8 addresses interscholastic and intercollegiate sport. Interscholastic teams continue to grow and prosper, but they also face the challenges of integrating opportunities for girls in accordance with Title IX and meeting the constant pressure to secure funding. Collegiate teams also struggle to find their way amid the economic pressure to support programs for a relatively few elite athletes who may or may not be comfortable in the academic setting.

Chapter 9 broadens the scope to consider the globalization of sport, which reflects our increasingly connected world. On one hand, international competition has increased as American sports have been exported around the world; meanwhile, soccer has finally begun to take hold in North America. Chapter 10 focuses on the particular international sport phenomenon known as the Olympic movement, which has propelled certain sports to international prominence and taken on an originally unintended economic and political significance. In particular, the inclusion of professional athletes has changed the nature of the Olympic Games and increased attention in countries around the world on developing elite athletes who can compete for gold medals.

Part IV focuses on the interaction between culture and sport and lays out the significance of social issues in the sport world, including good sporting behavior (chapter 11), race and ethnicity (chapter 12), women (chapter 13), and social class (chapter 14). The changing role of women and African Americans in society has revolutionized sport, and ethnicity and social class continue to be powerful factors in who plays and watches sports overall and in particular sports.

Chapter 15 examines the relationship of sport to other particular populations, including those who are aging and those who have a physical or cognitive disability. In particular, the chapter recognizes the effects of major societal changes regarding these populations in the past 25 years. For instance, as baby boomers have aged and life expectancy has increased, population demographics have changed, and more of the population consists of older adults who view sport both as a form of recreation and as a tool for living more healthily. At the same time, since the enactment of the Americans with Disabilities Act of 1990, sport opportunities have been greatly expanded for people with a physical or cognitive disability.

As has been the case for centuries, sport also interacts with religion (chapter 16) and politics (chapter 17). Institutions and individuals in both arenas have affected the growth of sport and used sport to their advantage. Athletes use religion in their sport, and religious organizations use sport to promote their purposes. Governments use sport to promote identity, unity, social values, and nationalism. And as citizens, we rely on government to provide reasonable regulation of sport in order to help us stay safe, in good health, and free from exploitation by unscrupulous promoters of entertainment sport.

Chapter 18 focuses on the use of sport to combat perplexing challenges faced by societies, particularly those characterized by strong socioeconomic barriers. For example, the chapter explores the increasing worldwide emphasis on using sport for the development of peace and understanding among people of various countries. It also examines the use of youth sport programs to help at-risk youngsters with academics, discipline issues, moral development, socialization, and living in a law-abiding manner.

Chapter 19 is the first of two chapters in this edition devoted to deviant behavior. This chapter looks at rule breaking by athletes at various levels of sport. It also examines violence both on and off the field. More specifically, it addresses growing concerns about concussions and debilitating injuries in collision-type sports, as well as off-field violence perpetrated by professional athletes—a timely topic that deserves serious attention.

Chapter 20 explores deviant behaviors such as eating disorders, hazing practices, and sport wagering with an eye toward current trends, education, and the development of strategies and regulations to prevent or minimize the negative effects of these practices. Of course, deviant behavior also includes the use of performance enhancers and doping, which can create questions about whether a given performance was achieved with the help of an illegal aid.

Finally, chapter 21 anticipates future sport trends in North America, where performance sport (played by professionals) continues to compete with participation sport (played by amateurs). In addition, many youth have moved toward extreme sports that suit their needs better than traditional, adult-organized sports do. Older adults, on the other hand, look to sport to enhance their chances for a longer life of higher quality. More broadly, U.S. sport continues to face issues related to finances, opportunities for women, growing minority populations, and access to sport for families of all income levels. Meanwhile, the delivery of sport events and programs continues to be influenced by the fact that spectators increasingly rely on electronic implements in their consumption of sport.

Updates in the Third Edition

This new edition features updated statistics that allow us to freshly analyze sport trends related to topics such as participation, popularity, gender, race, and class. Similarly, current information is used to address the business side of sport, particularly in entertainment or spectator sports. In addition, the discussion of media and sport has been updated to consider the dramatic effects of the electronic media.

This edition also features updated sidebars that reflect key changes in the world of sport over the past five years. These sidebars feature current athletes, trends, and experts in order to bring alive the topics considered in each chapter. In addition, this edition features a new type of sidebar—Applying Social Theory—to help readers grasp the essentials of each theory and apply it to a current issue in sport.

As mentioned earlier, the chapter on coaching has been moved to part III to better integrate it with the chapters on youth, high school, and college sport. Indeed, the success or failure of an athletic team at any level can invariably be traced in large part to the philosophy, training, and skill of the coach. Therefore, it is encouraging to see that the past 10 years have brought significant progress in certification processes and continuing education for coaches; even so, however, standards are still lacking at most levels of sport.

Learning Tools

To aid learning, each chapter begins with a list of key student outcomes and ends with a summary of the chapter's main topics. In addition, key terms are highlighted in boldface and defined in a glossary for easy reference. Throughout the text, various types of sidebar highlight diverse aspects of sport:

"In the Arena With . . . " sidebars highlight key players in sociological change in sport.

"Pop Culture" sidebars discuss current trends in film, books, magazines, and other media that highlight sociological issues in sport.

"Expert's View" sidebars show how experts in sport sociology interpret sport issues; they also raise discussion points for students.

"Activity Time-Out" sidebars give students the opportunity to classify information, engage in friendly debate, and obtain crucial information.

"Applying Social Theory" sidebars ask students to analyze a particular topic from the perspective of one of the six social theories described in chapter 2.

Instructor Resources

Several instructor resources are available to help you use this text in your class. The instructor guide has a sample syllabus and a list of supplemental resources. The test package provides 210 questions in multiple-choice and essay format. The chapter quizzes provides 10 questions per chapter to test students' knowledge of the most important chapter concepts. The Microsoft PowerPoint presentation package has 455 slides outlining the text in a lecture-friendly format. All of these resources are available at www.HumanKinetics.com/SocialIssuesInSport.

Closing Comments

I have spent more than 40 years studying sport and applying that knowledge as a professor, coach, and administrator. I spent nearly 20 of those years on a college campus. Later, I worked in various administrative roles for the United States Tennis Association and spent 8 years on the coaching committee for the United States Olympic Committee, which took on the challenge of improving coaching in all U.S. sports.

For the past 10 years, I have taught a course on sport and society at the University of Tampa. Most of the material in this edition has been vetted by current or former students, who invariably end the semester with a much different understanding of U.S. sport from the opinions they had at the beginning of the course.

I have also been fortunate enough to experience extensive international travel (most recently to China) and in the process have learned a great deal about sport in other countries. These experiences have given me a unique perspective on sport. It is my hope that you will enjoy this perspective while also understanding where it is limited.

ACKNOWLEDGMENTS

I express warm thanks to the hundreds of students who have sparked my interest in evaluating the information available on the sociology of sport. They have challenged me to make the information relevant to *today's* world of sport. In particular, students at the University of Tampa have provided consistent feedback and creative ideas and have clearly articulated their interest in certain topics. My interactions with these students have taught me a great deal about their perceptions of American sport and physical activity; these interactions have also given me the opportunity to share with students my own career and life experiences. Through this sharing process, we have all realized that sport plays a critical role in our lives and in our society, and we hope that sport will similarly entertain future generations of participants, performers, and consumers of sport and physical activity.

I'm indebted to Rainer Martens, who challenged me to accept this project and showed confidence in me to produce a worthwhile product. Likewise, I appreciate the work of Myles Schrag, acquisitions editor, for his guidance in the conception and shaping of the manuscript. Later in the process, developmental editor Amanda Ewing offered insightful advice, helped keep me on target, and made terrific suggestions for revision for this third edition. Both Myles and Amanda have been loyal partners from the original conception of this work and throughout each new edition of it.

I also acknowledge the assistance and friendship of Dr. Tian Ye and Dr. Tian Hui of Beijing, China, who invited me to their country to speak to the China Institute of Sport Science and other distinguished groups in their country. Their hospitality and keen interest in American sport eventually led to their translating this text into Chinese to be used in their universities.

Finally, my wife, Kathy, has been a tireless supporter throughout the project and has encouraged me every step of the way. Without her interest, patience, and personal commitment to sport, it would have been a difficult undertaking.

PHOTO CREDITS

Page 3	Karin Lau/fotolia.com
Page 6	© Human Kinetics
Page 11	© Human Kinetics
Page 17	© Marvin Newman/AGF RM/age footstock
Page 23	© Human Kinetics
Page 27	AP Photo
Page 33	Vincent Curutchet/DPPI/Icon SMI
Page 35	© Human Kinetics
Page 37	© Human Kinetics
Page 39	RÈmy MASSEGLIA/fotolia.com
Page 51	AP Photo
Page 56	Kevin Coloton/Icon Sportswire
Page 59	Brad Schloss/Icon Sportswire
Page 61	Courtesy of the Library of Congress, LC-USZ62-133669
Page 71	© Mira Agron | Dreamstime.com
Page 75	AP Photo
Page 80	AP Photo/John Raoux
Page 84	Photodisc
Page 87	© Human Kinetics
Page 93	© Human Kinetics
Page 95	Frank Micelotta/Invision for NFL/AP Images
Page 99	Matthew Visinsky/Icon Sportswire
Page 101	Icon Sportswire via AP Images
Page 110	© Human Kinetics
Page 111	© Human Kinetics
Page 113	Galina Barskaya
Page 123	© Human Kinetics
Page 125	© Old Visuals/age fotostock
Page 139	ROBERTO MAYA/Mexsport/Fotoarena/Icon Sportswire
Page 144	© Human Kinetics
Page 146	Copyright SWP, Incorporated 2004
Page 150	© Human Kinetics
Page 155	AP Photo, File
Page 162	© Human Kinetics
Page 164	© Human Kinetics
Page 169	© Human Kinetics
Page 178	© Human Kinetics
Page 181	AP Photo/Tony Gutierrez
Page 183	© Aviahuismanphotography/Dreamstime
Page 187	© Human Kinetics
Page 190	AP Photo/PepsiCo Inc.
Page 210	Anton Hlushchenko
Page 213	Sipa via AP Images
Page 215	AP Photo/Darron Cummings
Page 218	The Rucker Archive/Icon Sportswire
Page 225	Daniel A. Anderson/Zuma Press/Icon Sportswire
Page 227	AP-Photo/stf

Page 233 Daniel Stiller/Bildbyran/Icon Sportswire
Page 235 © Brian Jannsen/age fotostock
Page 236 Agencia Estado via AP Images
Page 252 © Human Kinetics
Page 257 AP Photo/Chris O'Meara
Page 259 AP Photo/Kathy Willens, File
Page 261 © Human Kinetics
Page 267 © Human Kinetics
Page 279 Associated Press
Page 288 AP Photo/William Thomas Cain
Page 295 AP Photo/Denis Poroy
Page 302 © Human Kinetics
Page 309 © Dr. Wilfried Bahnmüller/imageBROKER/age fotostock
Page 311 Bettmann/Corbis / AP Images
Page 313 Courtesy of the Library of Congress, LC-USZ62-45888
Page 322 © Laurence Mouton/PhotoAlto/age fotostock
Page 324 AP Photo/Matt York
Page 325 AP Photo/Damian Dovarganes
Page 337 Fotolia Royalty Free
Page 346 Art Explosion
Page 351 Tony Quinn/Icon Sportswire
Page 355 AP Photo/Katsumi Kasahara
Page 357 Sporting News/ZUMA Press/Icon SMI
Page 369 Rex Features via AP Images
Page 373 Doug Murray/Icon Sportswire
Page 384 AP Photo/The Florida Times-Union, Kelly Jordan
Page 390 AP Photo/Frank Franklin II
Page 393 AP Photo/Silvia Izquierdo
Page 395 © Human Kinetics
Page 401 Icon Sportswire via AP Images
Page 409 AP Photo/Pablo Martinez Monsivais
Page 413 Photo courtesy of Boston Police Tennis Program
Page 419 AP Photo/Danny Johnston
Page 427 AP Photo/Elise Amendola
Page 430 Cal Sport Media via AP Images
Page 433 AP Photo/CTK, Jan Koller
Page 449 Sirotti/Action Plus/Icon Sportswire
Page 452 AP Photo/Tony Dejak, File
Page 461 AP Photo/Wilfredo Lee, File
Page 463 Copyright Bettmann/Corbis / AP Images
Page 469 Warren Wimmer/Icon SMI
Page 473 © Human Kinetics
Page 479 Julian Stratenschulte/picture-alliance/dpa/AP Images
Page 484 Fotolia

PART I

Studying Sport in Society

These opening chapters set the stage for studying sport from a sociological perspective by pointing out the integral relationship between sport and society in North America. The first chapter defines key words such as *play, game, sport*, and *work* in terms of purpose, organization, and complexity. As sport moves from *participation sport* (played by amateurs) to *high-performance sport* (played by professional athletes), it also moves away from recreation or leisure-play activities and takes on the characteristics of work.

Chapter 1 examines why people study sport and reviews the sport sciences that enable us to develop the scientific knowledge on which coaching and training are based. Chapter 2 presents typical methods of studying sport. It defines several social theories and gives examples of how they might apply to sport research and interpretation. These social theories, referred to throughout the book, provide a framework for understanding different points of view relevant to the specific topics of each chapter. Therefore, it is critical that you understand these theories so that you can respond effectively to their application in later chapters.

Chapter 2 also describes the emerging field of sport sociology. Whereas sport psychology tends to focus on one individual, sport sociology explores people in groups and how they interact with and affect one another in relation to sport. The chapter also provides information about sociological tools for learning more.

1

STUDENT OUTCOMES

After reading this chapter, you will know the following:

- The definition of sport
- The sport pyramid
- Why you should study sport
- The subdisciplines of sport science

What Is Sport and Why Do We Study It?

What Is Sport and Why Do We Study It?

Like many college students, you may feel that sport plays a significant role in your life. Perhaps you even chose your university partly on the basis of its athletic success. In fact, in the United States, many of us have heard of certain colleges simply because of their prowess in athletics. Though sport plays a relatively minor role in an institution's mission and purpose, college sport teams typically enhance school spirit and serve as a focus of campus social life.

However, if college sport merely produces more spectators—more people who watch other people participating in sport—we might ask whether they really benefit students. More to the point, perhaps the question should be this: How physically active are students in both sport and other activities that contribute to their overall health and well-being?

On Thursday, April 15, 1954, I realized that baseball was important in the world. On that day, Baltimore got its own Major League Baseball team, the Orioles, and opened the brand-spanking-new Memorial Stadium. The formation of the Orioles, spawned from the lowly St. Louis Browns franchise, marked the entry of my home city into the big leagues. Although I was just a kid, I knew that day was special because city hall closed for half the day, most businesses shut down, and, best of all, schools were closed so that everyone could enjoy the citywide parade.

In fact, Baltimore was about to embark on its golden age of sport, which would coincide with my childhood. At first, we rooted for moderately talented sport teams, but soon Hall of Famer Brooks Robinson led the Orioles and the magical arm of Hall of Famer Johnny Unitas guided our football team, the Colts. Having these two superstars in the same city was like having a quarterback such as Peyton Manning or Tom Brady along with an infielder such as Derek Jeter or Evan Longoria as your football and baseball heroes. I knew right then that I was falling in love with sport.

You may have a similar childhood story of your own introduction to sport. Regardless of the details, once we're hooked, many of us never quite let go of our interest in and devotion to our favorite sports and heroes. In fact, the word *fan* derives from *fanatic*—and that's just what many of us have been and continue to be. Furthermore, if you're like me, studying sport is fun and can also help you expand your understanding of the place that sport holds both in North America and in the world. To get a quick sense of this significance, imagine that all sports were banned, as indeed some have been in certain civilizations. Our lives would change, immediately and dramatically, in terms of how we invest our discretionary time, our money, and our emotions.

This scenario is jarring because sport affects our lives every day. Strangers on the street stop to chat about their hometown sport successes—whether they involve a local high school, a college, or a professional team. Entire cities wake up on the morning after an exhilarating win by the home team and feel proud to live where they do—or wake up after a tough loss and sink into mourning. Kids look up to sport heroes, memorize the lifetime statistics of favorite athletes, and dream of making it someday to their own fame and fortune. They may even copy the stance, mannerisms, and clothing of their heroes.

Sport also affects the cultures, traditions, and values of a society. Stories in the sport world help us clarify our stances on a wide range of issues, such as race and gender relations, the rights of senior citizens and persons with a disability, class mobility, youth development through physical activity, and progress toward a better standard of health and fitness for everyone. These issues and others are examined in the coming chapters. For now, let's focus on what sport is and how it differs from play and games.

Sport Through the Ages

Before we can analyze the effect of sport on society (and vice versa), we need to know what sport is and why we should study it. The word *sport* is derived from the Latin root *desporto*, which means "to carry away." The term *sport* has been used through the ages to refer to physical activities that are competitive and organized and that divert people from the everyday business of sustaining life or producing economic gain.

Over the centuries, both sport and game playing have fulfilled various roles in societies. Early Greek civilization used sport and game playing in celebrations, in rituals honoring their gods, and in funeral ceremonies; in fact, as you may be aware, the great Greek poet Homer described sport in his literary classics, the *Iliad* and the *Odyssey*. Typical contests of physical prowess among the ancient Greeks included footraces, chariot races, wrestling, boxing, leaping, and hunting. In the ancient city-state of Sparta, sport and game playing helped young men refine the skills of war. In contrast, the city-state of Athens educated young men in grammar, music, and gymnastics to fully develop their physical and mental capacities. These two approaches established different parties as the beneficiary of sporting skill. In Sparta, sport benefited the state; in Athens, it aided the perfection of the individual man.

Sport and game playing also played a role in other ancient civilizations, as is evidenced in paintings, carvings, and various historical documents. Indeed, every culture has included running, swimming, and jumping competitions and has also had a place for combat-related activities, such as boxing, wrestling, and other martial arts. Ball-oriented games have also been popular in diverse civilizations, including those of the Egyptians and of American and Canadian Indians; various forms of football can be traced to ancient China.

Of course, sport and game playing are still used today, both as forms of celebration and as examples of athletic prowess. But what exactly *is* sport?

Definition of Sport

The **sport pyramid** (figure 1.1) provides a helpful way to think of sport. The pyramid contains four elements of human activity—play, games, sport, and work. These activities are often confused because of the interchange and overlap of ideas. Let's look at each one individually and then examine the interrelationships.

FIGURE 1.1 The sport pyramid.

Play

Play forms the base of the pyramid since it is the physical activity of childhood and continues throughout life in various forms. Play is free activity involving exploration, self-expression, dreaming, and pretending. It follows no firm rules and can take place anywhere. Other than giving pleasure, the outcome of play is unimportant. Over the years, theories of play have been formulated by many people, including Dutch historian Johan Huizinga (1950), who described play as being free of form, separate from ordinary life, and free of specific purpose. He considered games and sport to be specialized forms of play, with more formal rules and purposes and an emphasis on the outcome.

Games

A **game** is an aspect of play that possesses greater structure and is competitive. Specifically, games pursue clear participation goals that can be either mental, physical, or a combination of both; they are governed by either informal or formal rules; they involve competition; they produce outcomes determined by luck, strategy, skill, or a combination thereof; and they result in prestige or status.

Examples of inactive games include board games, such as Monopoly; card games, such as hearts and Texas Hold'em (a kind of poker); and video games, such as Madden NFL and Grand Theft Auto. In contrast, examples of active games include kickball, ultimate, paintball, touch football, and street hockey. As these games have become more mainstream, some people have moved to organize them by means of national rules and competitive events. As a result, they have evolved beyond informal neighborhood or schoolyard games and activities and taken on the characteristics of a sport (described in more detail in the next section).

In the past 20 years, our understanding of games has also been complicated by the rise of the X Games, a commercial sporting event put on by ESPN that features extreme action sports. In fact, these "games"—which include skateboarding, snowboarding, motocross, and in-line skating—are not just games but also sports. To clarify, the category of games is broader than the category of sport. Therefore, a sporting event such as a football or basketball contest is often described as a game; however, when such a game (for example, a college football game) takes place in the context of a league with rules, standings, and sponsors, it is sport.

Unsatisfied with competitive games, some people, such as Dale Le Fevre, have worked to create and popularize what they call New Games, which focus not on competition but on cooperation, participation, creativity, and personal expression. New Games have been and continue to be used to teach team building in physical education classes, youth camps, religious groups, and businesses.

Le Fevre's book, *Best New Games* (2012), is popular around the world. In many of his workshops held over the past 35 years, traditionally adversarial groups have come together to play and have fun—for example, ethnic Arabs and Israelis, competing religious groups in Ireland, and different racial groups in South Africa. The principles of New Games could also be applied today to political trouble spots such as the Ukraine, North Africa, and Iraq, where ethnic, religious, and racial differences continue to cause mistrust, separation within countries, and violent uprisings.

Board games are inactive games that require participants to follow set rules and use a combination of strategy, skill, and luck.

Sport

Sport can be thought of as a specialized or higher order of play and as a kind of game with certain characteristics that set it apart. Many people's definition of sport is influenced by television programming, particularly that of ESPN, which presents an activity such as poker as sport but doesn't broadcast e-sports. However, it isn't reasonable to accept as sport everything that ESPN chooses to broadcast as "sport." To the contrary, sport has been defined over the years by various textbook authors, and, taken as a whole, their ideas point to certain characteristics (Coakley 2004; Leonard 1980; Sage 1998; VanderZwaag and Sheehan 1978).

1. *Physical component.* Perhaps the most critical characteristic of sport is that it involves a physical component. Unlike play and games, which may or may not be physical, sport must include physical movement and skill. More specifically, sport typically involves the use of physical coordination, strength, speed, endurance, and flexibility. According to this definition, chess and checkers are not sports whereas games such as billiards and darts can be classified as sports, though the physical skill required is fairly limited to eye–hand coordination.
2. *Competition.* Sport is also competitive and involves outcomes that are important to participants and often to others, such as family members, fans, sponsoring organizations, and the media. Competition, of course, includes winning and losing, and this reality powerfully motivates participants to train faithfully and give their best effort.
3. *Institutionalized games.* Sports are governed by an outside group or institution that enforces rules and oversees conduct and results. For example, in the United States, professional football is governed primarily by the National Football League (NFL), collegiate sports are governed largely by the National Collegiate Athletic Association (NCAA), and rules for hunting and fishing are set by local game and wildlife commissions. Therefore, whereas a pickup baseball game at a local park is simply a game, a Little League Baseball game—with rules, customs, standards for play, officials, coaches, and win-loss records—is a sport.
4. *Specialized facilities and equipment.* Sport almost always requires specialized facilities and equipment. Although this is less true of certain sports, such as cross country running and distance swimming (across a natural body of water), most sports require a created setting—whether it is a field with set boundaries, a pool, a gymnasium, a court, a golf course, or some other facility. Equipment is particularly important at the professional level, where athletes rely on the precise quality of their sled, skates, vaulting pole, tennis racket, golf clubs, baseball bat, or other specialized gear.

Sport, then, is typically defined in North America as institutionalized competitive activity that involves physical skill and specialized facilities or equipment and is conducted according to an accepted set of rules in order to determine a winner.

sport—Institutionalized competitive activity that involves physical skill and specialized facilities or equipment and is conducted according to an accepted set of rules in order to determine a winner.

The definition of sport in a given society reflects the culture, beliefs, and attitudes of that society toward a variety of concerns, including warfare, gender identity, survival, and the honoring of any gods. For example, a society that emphasized cooperation more than competition would engage in sports that differed from those found in North American society. The definition of sport can also change within a given culture, as illustrated by the rise of alternative sports for youth (see chapter 6).

Most people do not have the option of achieving high sport performance and developing a professional career in sport. Instead, most of us who play a sport do it as a hobby for the love of the game; in other words, we play as **amateurs**—a label that stems from the Latin word for love. We gain intrinsic satisfaction in improving our fitness, refining our physical skills, working as part of a team, or embracing the challenge and excitement

POP CULTURE

Video Games for Physical Activity

For the current generation of youth, video games may occupy a major part of the day—an average of more than five hours daily, according to some studies. Many of these time-consuming video games are sedentary, which means that they reduce kids' amount of physical activity.

There are, however, some exceptions in the form of video games that include physical activity. For example, Xbox Kinect and Wii both offer players a chance to play electronic versions of tennis, golf, baseball, and bowling, all of which involve some degree of physical activity, such as swinging an imaginary racket, club, or bat. Similarly, Dance Dance Revolution helps participants actively burn calories through vigorous dance moves, and adventure-based video games include prompts for players to jump, dodge obstacles, run, and balance their body. In fact, some physical education programs have experimented with using video games to develop physical activity and exercise routines in the hope of attracting kids who seem to shun more traditional sports and games.

Some video games have now been available for years, and their claims of promoting physical activity have received mixed reviews. Some studies have shown that active video games do cause energy expenditure similar to that of moderate walking, but other studies are less enthusiastic. The most common criticism is that kids who play video games spend more time indoors, thus eschewing more vigorous physical activities that contribute more to physical fitness and often keep kids active for longer periods of time.

of testing our skill against nature or other competitors. For amateur athletes, then, the key lies not in the outcome but in the participation itself. Sport participation is recreation, and it differs greatly from work. We participate to rejuvenate the spirit, and we don't need extrinsic rewards for doing so.

Sport can vary to accommodate people with physical or sensory impairment. Program directors who value the inclusion of people with a disability can use modified sports—such as wheelchair basketball, tennis, soccer, and volleyball—to blend people who have a disability with those who do not in sport competition. For a closer look at sport for people with a disability, see chapter 15 on special populations.

Work

Work is purposeful activity that includes physical or mental effort, or both, in order to perform a task, overcome an obstacle, or achieve a desired outcome. Often, people earn their living through work by trading it for compensation that provides for the necessaries of existence. Work appears at the top of the pyramid shown in figure 1.1 because sport can take on the characteristics of work at the professional level. Professional athletes are paid to perform work by training their physical skills to the highest level for competition with other elite athletes. Although all professional athletes begin their lives with childhood play and then participate in games and eventually sport, they may begin to regard sport as work after many years of facing competitive pressure, fighting through injuries, and living up to the expectations of employers, fans, and the media.

At the highest level of organized sport, athletes and coaches may earn millions of dollars for their performances, along with endorsement fees for the right to use their appearance or name in promoting particular products. Once they accept financial remuneration for their athletic performances, they are deemed to be professional athletes who are hired to perform in their sport. If such a person were a collegiate student-athlete, the NCAA would then classify him or her as a sport professional who is ineligible to compete in collegiate sport.

Athletes of any age who aspire to the professional level may be described as **high-performance athletes**. They develop their composite athletic skill so that they can perform at the highest level and perhaps earn a living by doing so. In fact, children as young as age 10 may follow a dream of becoming a star athlete and therefore submit to a regimen of training and competition that prepares them for a professional career. Even at a young age, if the goal is a professional career, playing a sport can take on the characteristics of work, which can lead to burnout and boredom for a child who is more interested in participating in a sport for the fun of it.

In light of this discussion of sport and work, we might represent the top levels of the sport pyramid in the manner shown in figure 1.2.

The reality of the pyramid as shown in figure 1.2 is that much of the attention paid to sport in North America is focused on the highest level of

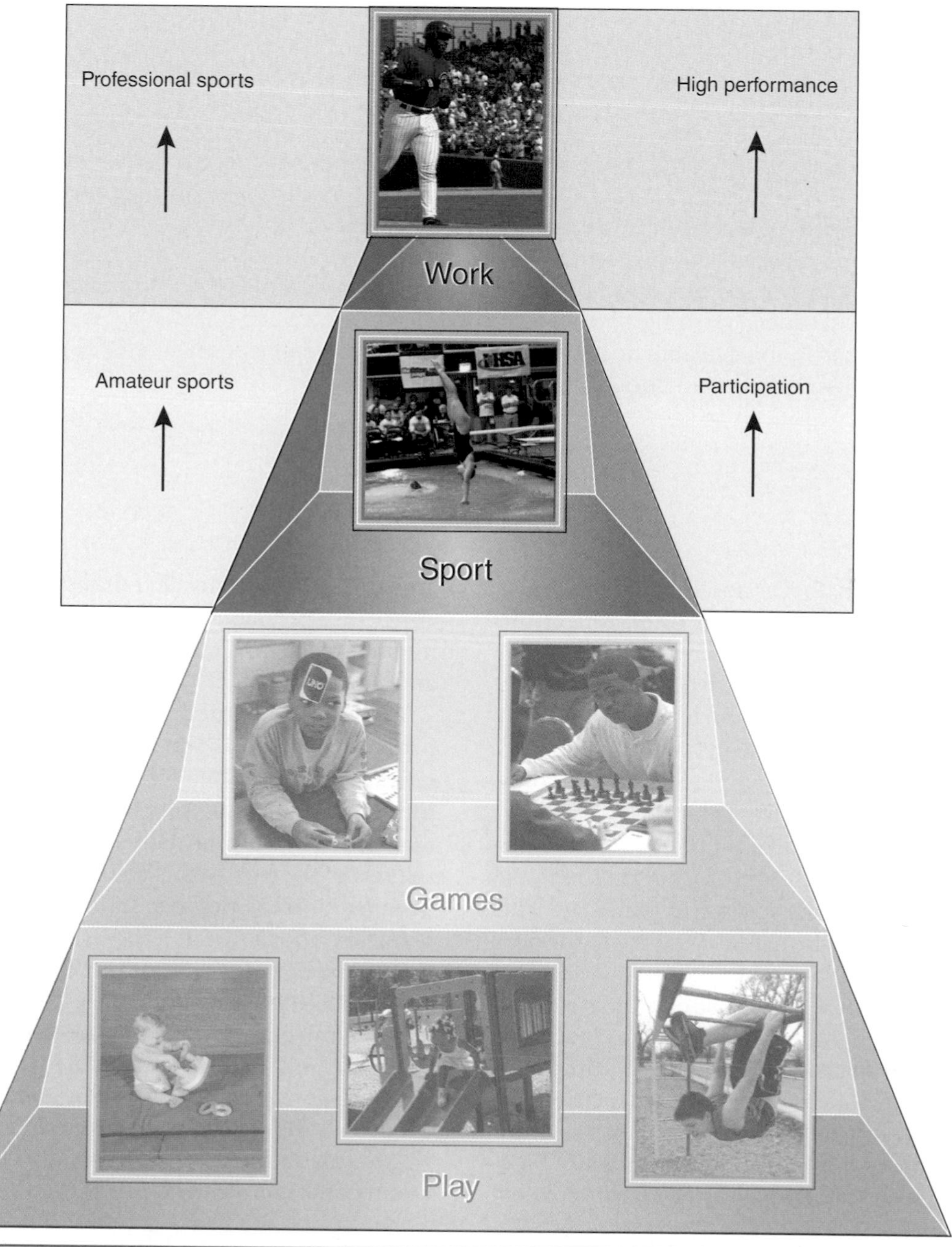

FIGURE 1.2 Detailed sport pyramid.

ACTIVITY TIME-OUT

Sport, Game, or Physical Activity?

How would you classify each of the following endeavors? Test your understanding of the differences between sport, physical activity, and games and then compare your answers with those of other students. Mark S for sport, G for game, and PA for physical activity.

____ Flying a kite	____ Ballroom dancing	____ Fishing
____ Street hockey	____ Cheerleading	____ Bowling
____ Bocce	____ Roulette	____ Skateboarding
____ Throwing a flying disc	____ Rope jumping	____ Riflery
____ Weightlifting	____ Jogging	____ Bicycling
____ Tap dancing	____ Juggling	

If you had trouble classifying some activities, that struggle may relate to the fact that they fit neatly into neither the sport category nor the game category. For one thing, an activity may involve physical activity but be used primarily for entertainment. For example, professional wrestling involves two people who perform carefully choreographed moves that may appear to be competitive but in fact are designed purely for entertainment. Similarly, a Broadway show may entertain you with skillful dancing and singing, but the dancing does not qualify as a sport. With these examples in mind, evaluate an activity against all of the classification criteria before judging whether it fits the definition of sport.

sport performance. Professional sport is a business, and decisions at this level often reflect the goal of earning money. Moreover, the line between professional and amateur becomes blurred at the highest levels of collegiate sport, where universities support their athletic teams with large sums of money, even though the players receive only scholarships in return for their services. Even some youth programs take on the characteristics of professional sport by requiring kids to train year round, specialize in one sport at a young age, and perhaps risk a career-threatening injury in the heat of competition.

Despite the prevalence of sport, only a small percentage of athletes can ever hope to reach the professional level. Despite this focus on the gifted few, the health and welfare of society depend more substantially on the amount of exercise and activity performed by citizens as a whole. Indeed, as the U.S. population ages, as obesity increases, and as health and physical fitness become national concerns, perhaps participation in sport by the masses will command more attention, funding, and publicity.

Only in the United States are the amateur and professional segments of sport defined so specifically. This delineation results largely from the unique presence of thousands of collegiate sport teams that have maintained an amateur label. In the rest of the world, this distinction is unnecessary because universities generally do not field sport teams or offer athletic scholarships. For example, in European countries and in China, Russia, and Africa, children as young as age 10 can sign professional contracts (with parental consent) that provide coaching and training expense money from a sporting goods manufacturer or government sport agency. In the United States, people would say that these athletes have "turned pro," but in their home country no such distinction is even considered.

In 2013, Michael Andrew became the youngest male swimmer in history to turn pro when he did so just after his 14th birthday. What makes Andrew unique is that—with the notable exception of Michael Phelps, who turned pro at age 16—elite male swimmers generally swim collegiately before turning professional. Andrew, however, signed a sponsorship agreement with P2Life, a high-performance nutrition supplement manufacturer, and thus forfeited his opportunity to swim competitively in high school or college.

Other athletes, particularly in individual sports, have turned professional at an early age with varying results. Some have gone on to successful sport careers—for example, golfer Michelle Wie, who turned pro at age 15, and gymnast Gabby Douglas, who turned pro at age 16 and became an Olympic champion. Other talented athletes have had mixed results; examples include soccer player Freddy Adu and Spanish basketball player Ricky Rubio, who competed in a Spanish pro basketball league at age 14.

For the vast majority of people of all ages, the virtue of sport lies in participation as a recreational activity. Playing a sport provides well-documented overall health benefits, keeps us physically fit and strong, and maximizes our personal energy. Recreational sport can also have dramatic effects on our mind and body and allow us to recover from the stress of everyday life. Therefore, as we examine the role of sport in culture, we must always consider the entire spectrum of sport—from the competition of professional sport to the pleasure and fun of pure recreational sport.

Daily participation in physical activity, including recreational sport, is one of the keys to a healthy society.

Average University of Texas Football Players Worth $578,000

Although college football players are not allowed to accept money for their play or use their athletic fame for financial profit, the colleges they play for rake in large amounts of money as a direct result of the players' performances. The only expense to the university is the cost of an athletic scholarship, which has been calculated at about $37,600 per year at the University of Texas. That leaves a net profit for the university of about $540,400 per player or a total revenue for the football program exceeding $42 million (Gaines 2013).

Here's how the folks at *Business Insider* came up with the calculation of fair market value for each University of Texas football player. First, they chose to use the NFL's most recent collective bargaining agreement, in which the players as a whole receive 47 percent of all revenue, then divided that number by the 85 scholarship football players at the University of Texas. Using the same formula, the average value of all football players at the top 25 schools in the country stands at about $190,000. No one is suggesting that players should receive a six-figure salary, but, more reasonably, perhaps they should receive a stipend to assist with general living expenses beyond what their scholarships cover. The NCAA is actively considering such proposals that allow colleges to pay the full cost of attending college; the proposals have developed strong support among the Atlantic Coast Conference, Big Ten, Big 12, Pac-12 and SEC.

Study of Sport

Now that we have established what sport *is*—physical competition according to a set of rules in order to determine a winner—let's consider why it is worthwhile to study sport. In particular, let's explore three major reasons that people seek to learn about sport and physical activity:

- Personal development
- Scholarly study
- Professional practice

Many people enjoy learning about the science of sport and physical activity because they feel attracted to sport and intrigued enough to want to expand their understanding. Every country is home to a large number of sport fans, many of whom are experts at sport trivia, but only a few truly understand sport from a scientific viewpoint.

According to S. Hoffman (2013), academics programs for the study of physical activity are offered at more than 600 colleges and universities in the United States, along with many others worldwide. The growth of interest in studying sport can also be seen in an explosion in the number of scholarly sport journals and societies since 1960; the number of journals has multiplied about eight times, and the number of societies has grown fourfold (S. Hoffman 2013).

Much of the study of sport occurs in universities, which often include departments devoted to specific sport sciences or to the overall field of kinesiology or physical education. At the undergraduate level, most students acquire a general overview of the field. At the graduate level, students seeking a master's or doctoral degree often concentrate their studies in one or two of the field's subdisciplines (discussed later in this chapter).

Professional practice in sport and physical activity has also grown and developed over the years in order to serve others through sport. Many students study the general field of kinesiology in college and later fashion a career by specializing in a subdiscipline or in its application in everyday living. In order to practice legitimately in a given specialty, one must often pass a competency or certification test. Career options can be grouped as follows:

- Teaching and coaching
- Sport management
- Sport research
- Program direction
- Sport promotion and publicity
- Recreation and leisure
- Therapeutic exercise
- Sport business
- Health and fitness

Sport Sciences

In the past, in the United States, the study of physical activity was typically labeled "physical education," and academic programs in physical education were intended mainly to prepare teachers and coaches. In recent years, other labels have been used—such as "exercise and sport science," "health and human performance," "movement science," and "sport and leisure studies"—to more accurately describe the study and function of physical activity.

Happily, many universities have now adopted the term *kinesiology*, leading the trend toward greater unanimity in labeling the field. After extensive study and debate, this term received support from the American Academy of Kinesiology and Physical Education. (In 2010, that organization changed its name to the National Academy of Kinesiology [NAK].) Although you may not include the term *kinesiology* in your typical daily language, it is important to understand who studies physical activity and where to seek information about it. The field of kinesiology addresses both sport and many other forms of movement.

During the last 50 years, the study of sport has changed remarkably as scientific approaches have expanded its base of knowledge. As part of this process, sport study has been divided into subdisciplines, each of which has its own devotees, researchers, and practitioners. The emerging subdisciplines, based on scientific inquiry, have slowly changed the perception of sport and physical activity and given rise to a discipline that is both broader and more concrete. The following discussion is organized to help you understand each of these subdisciplines, how they relate to each other, and how to integrate the information they offer. The subdisciplines of sport science are typically divided into three domains:

- Biophysical
- Psychosocial
- Sociocultural

Biophysical Domain

The **biophysical domain** focuses on physical activity from the viewpoint of the sciences of biomechanics, physiology, and medicine. Areas of study within this domain include the following:

- **Biomechanics** is the study of the structure and function of biological systems through application of principles of physics to human motion. It helps us understand how the body uses gravity, inertia, balance, force, and motion to produce speed, power, and distance.
- **Exercise physiology** is the study of human systems to enhance strength, speed, and endurance in performance in pursuit of the Olympic ideal: "Faster, Higher, Stronger."
- **Nutrition** is sometimes studied as part of physiology to understand how performance is affected by food and drink. It investigates an athlete's diet and hydration habits under varied climates, contest durations, and environmental conditions.
- **Sports medicine** examines the prevention, care, and rehabilitation of injuries caused by participation in physical activity and sport. Research in sports medicine may also affect recommendations for training.

Psychosocial Domain

The **psychosocial domain** focuses on physical activity from the standpoint of the science of psychology. Areas of study within this domain include the following:

- **Sport psychology** is the study of human behavior in sport, including the enhancement of performance and the treatment of disorders affecting optimal performance.
- **Motor learning and behavior** is the study of relatively permanent changes in motor behavior that result from practice or experience. It focuses on how people learn to

perform motor skills and patterns and retain that ability even under pressure. It encompasses the study of human motor development through growth or maturation throughout the life span.

- **Pedagogy** is the study of the art and science of teaching. It focuses on the teacher or coach who creates the learning environment and helps athletes learn sport skills.

Sociocultural Domain

The **sociocultural domain** focuses on physical activity from the perspectives of the sciences of history, philosophy, and sociology. Areas of study within this domain include the following:

- **Sport history** is the study of the traditions and practices of physical activity and sport over time and in different countries, cultures, and civilizations.
- The **philosophy of sport** examines the definition, value, and meaning of sport. Developing a personal philosophy of physical activity can help you create your own coaching style or prescription for participating in sport.
- **Sport sociology** is the study of sport and physical activity in the context of the social conditions and culture in which people live.

This book, of course, focuses on the sociology of sport, which can help you identify the role of sport in your society and world. Whether you are an elite athlete, a recreational athlete, a prospective coach, a prospective athletic trainer, or a sport fan, you can deepen your understanding of the issues and possibilities in the sport world. Studying sport sociology can help you determine what role you want sport to play in your own life, family, and community. Once you clearly understand that role, you can act as a positive force for change, growth, and continuing prosperity for sport.

Broadly speaking, **sociology** is the study of society, its institutions, and its relationships. This field relies on systematic study of the development, structure, interaction, and collective behavior of groups of human beings. Mature societies are likely to be complex; therefore, in a modern society like the one in the United States, sociological analysis of sport is both broad and deep because its focus ranges widely—including, for example, families, sport participants, sport spectators, and even those who gamble on sport.

EXPERT'S VIEW

Who Is the Greatest Athlete of All Time?

Debate rages endlessly about who is or has been the greatest athlete. You might name a basketball player, such as LeBron James or Michael Jordan; Olympic swimmer Mark Spitz; boxer Muhammad Ali; soccer great Pelé; or perhaps your favorite American football player. Some opinions focus on identifying the athlete who has had the largest effect on his or her sport. Others look at his or her number of championships or Olympic gold medals.

From a purely scientific perspective, however, is it possible to fully measure athleticism in terms of categories such as quickness, agility, strength, power, endurance, speed, and durability? What about the ability to perform under pressure? What about exceptional motor skills, such as those demonstrated by golfers Rory McIlroy and Sergio Garcia and tennis players Serena Williams and Maria Sharapova. You can judge what experts say for yourself on any number of sport television shows.

ESPN has been the leader in using sport science to help us search for answers to the popular questions asked by athletes, coaches, and fans. In the recurring ESPN Sport Science feature, host John Brenkus has brought us cutting edge science applied to sport performance. So, the next time you're in an argument about a topic such as the greatest athlete of all time, check out the available video resources on sport science and blow your friends away with facts from the experts.

ACTIVITY TIME-OUT

How Much Physical Activity Is Enough?

Many U.S. residents may be obsessed with sport, but we appear to be more interested in sitting on the couch and watching others play than in participating ourselves. Indeed, you may be alarmed by the following recent statistics from the President's Council on Fitness, Sports, and Nutrition (2015):

- On average, U.S. kids spend more than seven and a half hours per day in front of a screen (such as a TV, video game, or computer).
- Only one in three U.S. children are physically active every day.
- More than 80 percent of U.S. adolescents do not meet the daily guidelines for aerobic activity.
- Fewer than 5 percent of U.S. adults participate in at least 30 minutes of daily physical activity, and only one in three get the recommended amount of physical activity each week.
- More than 80 percent of U.S. adults do not meet the guidelines for both aerobic and muscle-strengthening activities.

Given these facts, what do you expect are the recommendations for physical activity as developed by fitness experts and endorsed by the U.S. government?

1. How much physical activity should a person under age 18 perform daily?
2. How much physical activity should an adult perform in a week?
3. How should activity time be allocated between aerobics, muscular strength development, and endurance and flexibility training?
4. How should participation in physical activity change with age?

Do a little independent research and compare what you find with your classmates' results.

Sociology provides us with tools to better understand sport as it exists in our lives. In order to develop a thorough understanding of how sport operates, we analyze institutions such as schools, colleges, clubs, churches, youth sport organizations, and professional sport organizations. We also study social processes, such as commercialization, institutionalization, mass communication, conflict, and change.

Growth in Sport Sciences

Now that you understand the overall field of sport science, you might imagine its influence on the field's recent growth in volume and complexity. The explosion of knowledge produced by sport science has improved the average person's experience of sport and physical activity. Specifically, the knowledge acquired through sport science allows us to do the following:

- Understand historical precedents in sport and fitness, avoid mistakes of the past, and plan a healthier future
- Enhance competitive performance through better training methods and enable record-setting performances that challenge us all
- Better motivate people by helping them understand the value of physical activity and plan for physical development
- Teach people new activity skills faster and more efficiently and thus better convince them of their ability to succeed at an activity
- Prevent physical injuries and accelerate the recovery process
- Understand the influence of sport on culture and use sport and activity to promote equality, fairness, and success for all

- Help people deal with stress and anxiety through sport
- Promote good health that allows people of all ages to function with high energy
- Understand how training for sport expands and challenges our physical systems and strengthens them to deal with emergencies
- Provide healthy activities for youth that enhance their maturation into productive adults
- Offer a better quality of life in the later years as life expectancy increases

This list gives you an idea of the many ways in which sport science can positively influence our lives. You can also see why the growth of sport science affects the expansion of sport and physical activity. There is a slight risk that some people will take information produced by sport science out of context because it seems daunting to look at the complete picture. To avoid this pitfall, we need to integrate the knowledge gained in the various sport science subdisciplines in order to achieve the best understanding of sport and physical activity.

Chapter Summary

The sport pyramid provides a good way to look at sport. It starts with play—informal, free activity that begins in childhood and continues throughout life. The second level of the pyramid consists of games, which are more structured than play and address specific goals and outcomes through competition. Sport is a higher order of game that is marked by specific characteristics: a physical component, competition to determine a winner and loser, a group or institution that enforces rules and governs conduct and results, and the use of specialized facilities and equipment.

Sport can be divided broadly into two categories: professional and amateur. Professional sport focuses on high performance by athletes who are rewarded extrinsically with money, fame, and prestige. In amateur sport, on the other hand, people compete for the love of the game and value their participation for the resulting excitement, physical exertion, test of skill, and personal health benefits.

Sport is studied for multiple purposes: personal development, scholarly understanding, and professional practice. By studying sport, we can recognize historical precedents in sport, health, and physical activity and advocate for positive changes in society. The 10 sport science subdisciplines each belong to one of three domains: biophysical, psychosocial, or sociocultural. We can best interpret the knowledge produced by these subdisciplines if we do the necessary work to integrate it.

STUDENT OUTCOMES

After reading this chapter, you will know the following:

- Types of research methods and data
- Sociological theories used to analyze sport
- How sociological theories apply to the study of sport
- How to use theories to interpret sport and formulate necessary changes

How Do We Study Sport?

How Do We Study Sport?

Most sport fans hold strong opinions about their favorite teams and players and about sport in general. As a result, sport talk radio shows have grown in popularity, and fans often use them as a way to exchange their opinions with great passion. But when people discuss the burning issues in sport, how many of them can back up their position with solid evidence?

Chances are, multiple research projects have investigated just about any hypothesis you might have, and this research could help you support your opinions and impressions. For example, is it true that sport team owners lose money, as they often claim? Should taxpayers support using public funds to build a new stadium for the home team because the owner cannot afford the expense?

Before you form an opinion about this issue, it might be useful to take a hard analytical look at the costs and benefits of owning a team. Do you want to have your tax dollars spent to enhance the value of a franchise that the owner will likely sell for a healthy profit? Once you understand the types of research that can be done—and how the results can be interpreted—you'll be in a much better position to formulate an informed opinion.

You may have watched, read about, and played a lot of sports during your lifetime. You probably know what it means to be a participant or spectator in a sport setting. But you may not know that you have been asking the same questions that sport sociologists have asked for years.

For example, if your high school athletic program was in danger of losing district funding and you defended it on the grounds that sport teaches a strong work ethic, did you know that you were speaking as a functionalist? Similarly, if you've ever suggested that intercollegiate athletes should be compensated as workers for the millions of dollars they bring to their universities, did you know that you were acting as a critical theorist? And if you've argued that female tennis pros who win a Grand Slam final should be paid the same as the male winners, did you know that you might be considered a feminist? These and many other examples show how sociocultural issues pervade the sport world, both locally and globally.

Chapter 1 establishes the fact that sport involves physical competition that follows a set of rules in order to determine a winner. That chapter also demonstrates that studying sport enables us to recognize trends and apply that information to the current world. But *how* do we study sport? First, we collect data through research, then we analyze the collected data by using any of various social theories, each of which views the world differently.

Research Methods

In order to study sport or physical activity, a research scientist must possess tools for collecting data that can be organized and analyzed. In many cases, a researcher uses more than one tool at a time. A sport sociologist generally uses two types of tool: **quantifiable data**, or facts and figures that can be counted and analyzed statistically, and **qualitative data**, which is collected either through interviews and observations of individuals or groups or through analysis of societal characteristics and trends. Here are some specific research methods:

- **Survey research**, conducted through questionnaires, is popular for determining sport participation and comparing spectators' habits. This method enables researchers to collect large quantities of data, analyze it for trends, and then, if random sampling is used, generalize to the larger population. However, this approach is limited by the fact that it relies on self-reports by athletes or spectators that may or may not be accurate. Furthermore, if the data are not discrete enough to allow identification of responses from different groups of people, they may be misleading. For example, large surveys often combine all age groups to determine trends, when separation by age might produce very different responses. Similarly, data interpretation can also be affected by failing to account for race, gender, ethnicity, or income level. Finally, because surveys limit the possible responses, they may miss the respondents' true feelings.
- **Interviews** with individuals or small groups (called **focus groups**) use more in-depth questioning and can elicit unexpected

answers to open-ended questions. When designed correctly—including sampling from various ethnic groups, geographical locations, income levels, genders, and other variables—an interview can enable more in-depth analysis. However, interviews are time-consuming and expensive, and for these reasons they often rely on small sample sizes. The smaller sample sizes make it more difficult to generalize the results to the population at large.

- **Content research** involves collecting information or pictures—for example, from journal articles, magazines, and video programs—and assigning the data to categories based on a particular theme. For example, in content research, the ideal feminine body type for sport could be inferred from the frequency of photos of various body types appearing in the sport media. One drawback of content research is that the information is not provided directly by athletes but rather is obtained from others reporting about them. Content research has been useful, however, in assessing certain issues, such as the amount of coverage that the media give to females in sport over a specified period.
- **Ethnography**, which is based on observation, addresses data collected by researchers who immerse themselves in an environment and keep recorded conversations or notes. As a result, it is particularly suited to experiential topics such as "life on the pro tour" and "life in the minor leagues." Researchers using this method use detailed notes of their observations, personal interviews, and other sources of data to gather a full picture of their subject. The obvious weakness in this approach involves the large cost, in both time and money, of performing a complete analysis. Yet some of the most intriguing and helpful studies in sport have used this method to provide an inside view of a particular sport or class of athletes.
- **Historical research** involves looking at trends in sport over time. Often, the value of such research lies in the fact that it can be used to compare trends in sport with trends in society. For example, changes in female participation in sport during the second half of the twentieth century closely

EXPERT'S VIEW

Institute for Diversity and Ethics in Sport

Richard Lapchick, director of the University of Central Florida's Institute for Diversity and Ethics in Sport (TIDES), conducts annual quantitative research on the issues of gender and racial diversity in collegiate and professional sport. His work is widely quoted in the news media as the authoritative source for statistics in this field, such as the percentage of players from various racial groups in every collegiate sport and in major professional sports.

For example, if the Advocates for Athletic Equity (AAE), formerly known as the Black Coaches and Administrators Association (BCA), makes headlines decrying the small number of African American football coaches at major colleges, it uses—and the media publish—the actual count from Lapchick's work. Lapchick's research (2014) also revealed that, as of 2014, the percentage of African Americans in Major League Baseball (MLB) had fallen to 8.2 percent, whereas the percentage of Latinos had risen to 28.4 percent. This research helped us understand the changing face of baseball and spurred MLB to develop programs to promote baseball in cities with a significant number of young African American athletes.

Another contribution of the Institute is to show the annual percentage of females at every level of sport competition in terms of athletes, coaches, athletic directors, and other leaders. Do you think that girls and women now have opportunities in sport equal to those of their male counterparts? To be well-informed and accurate, you will need to analyze the most recent data available from TIDES before stating your position.

paralleled the push for equality and women's rights in the United States. While such historical research is helpful, it is usually limited to addressing large societal trends.

- **Societal analysis** uses social theories (described in the next section of this chapter) to examine life from a social point of view. For example, a researcher might apply a critical feminist model to professional sport in order to compare opportunities available to female professional athletes with those available to males, including financial compensation for similar work.

The risk of using only one theory lies in the possibility of overlooking other salient facts, such as race, income level, and historical precedent (S. Hoffman 2013). Regardless of the research method used, once the data are collected, they need to be analyzed, and this process can be performed by using any one of several social theories.

Social Theories

Social theories are used to examine trends in sport through the lens of an overall social theory and thus draw conclusions about whether sport reflects the larger culture or acts as a change agent. Theories of sport sociology help us organize our thoughts about a particular issue. They help us describe existing social situations, analyze them from various perspectives, and formulate beliefs based on the findings. A theory can also be explained to others, who can then compare it with their own analyses. As a theory gains acceptance, it may become the basis for predicting the future or calling for a change in the world of sport.

Analyzing sport through social theory helps us consider the larger picture of how sport exists in society. It forces us to examine all aspects of the sport experience, including the seat of power in a given sport, the values embraced, and the interaction of various groups. When we examine a sport in this way, we can see that it is much more than a competitive season with a beginning and an end. Most social theories are geared toward either enhancing and preserving the status quo or looking at the need for change. Table 2.1 lists the six theories considered in this chapter; let's discuss each of them now.

Functionalist Theory

Functionalist theory looks at sport as a social institution that reinforces the current value system in a society. In this view, sport is seen as maintaining the status quo by positively benefiting a community or nation that is striving to work and play together. In this view, the traditional American values of hard work, discipline, and competition are perpetuated through sport and reinforced as the path to success.

Functionalist theorists see sport as contributing to the smooth functioning of a society by helping people promote common values, which in turn leads to stability in communities and in the nation as a whole. At the same time, as social changes do occur, sport can take a leading role in promoting those changes and thereby reinforce the dominant social value system.

The weakness of functionalist theory lies in the fact that what is good for the architects of sport—often the economically or culturally privileged few—may not benefit society at large. Furthermore, sport may positively benefit many citizens while discriminating against members of certain groups (such as women, Hispanics, or people with a disability) that are typically underrepresented in sport.

A proponent of functionalist theory may embrace the traditional American emphasis on winning at all costs in sport. U.S. society tends to celebrate winners and reward them lavishly—until the next great team or player knocks them out of the winner's circle. In professional sport, the emphasis on winning reflects the business approach to competition. However, when the preoccupation with winning seeps down to collegiate, scholastic, and youth sport programs, the results can be damaging. One recurring result is the overinvolvement of parents in youth sport, which has been well documented in the sport media.

Sports that emphasize high achievement tend to dominate U.S. culture, garner media coverage, and attract in-person spectators and video viewers. However, the majority of Americans who are involved in sport spend most of their time participating in recreational sport rather than seeking high performance. When the values of high performance are applied to the recreational setting, the result often involves confusion and

TABLE 2.1 Social Theories for the Study of Sport

Theory	How it looks at the world	Preferred method of research	Major concerns as it looks at sport	Shortcomings
Functionalist theory	Emphasizes maintenance of the status quo and equilibrium. Change happens only gradually, to adjust to conditions.	Quantitative survey research	Sport is a valuable social institution that helps build character and instill values. Competition is valuable, and high performance is a critical outcome of sport participation.	Tends to overemphasize the positive consequences of sport while ignoring people who are disenfranchised or overlooked, such as women, people in lower socioeconomic classes, certain racial groups, and people with a physical or intellectual disability.
Conflict theory	Sees economic interests as shaping the world. Those who have power exploit those who do not; change is inevitable, and struggle on the part of repressed classes is expected.	Societal analysis	Sport benefits individuals and organizations who hold power, to the detriment of participants and members of the working class. Athletes should have more control over their sport destiny and the quality of their experience.	Relies too heavily on economic factors and ignores the importance of race, ethnicity, gender, and age. Underestimates the effect of groups that empower individuals in a capitalist society. Tends to overlook participation and recreational sport for healthy living.
Critical theory	Views life as complex and diverse. Order is obtained through struggles over ideology and power. The goal is a better life for all citizens. Sport does not simply mirror society; it provides opportunities to change society.	Societal analysis	Sport must change in order to be fair to everyone, more democratic, and sensitive to diversity. Sport can help us improve our outlook on gender and sexual orientation, physical and mental disability, physical talent, race, and ethnicity.	Critical theories are varied and sometimes confusing. They tend to encourage resistance to the status quo in order to protect special interests even when doing so may disadvantage the majority of a group or culture. They work better for specific cases than for forming an overall ideology.
Feminist theory	Views social life as based on a patriarchal ideology and controlled by men in powerful positions. Argues that feminine virtues are ignored or undervalued. Questions the traditional categories of masculine and feminine.	Quantifiable questionnaires, societal analysis, ethnography, and content research	Females lack equal opportunity in sport and are underrepresented in coaching and leadership positions. Traditional masculine traits of competitiveness and aggressiveness conflict with traditional feminine traits such as sensitivity and nurturing.	Feminist theory has weaknesses similar to those of other critical theories. It is also weak in addressing other categories that affect gender, such as age, race, social class, and disability.
Interactionist theory	Views the world from the bottom up rather than from the top down. Focuses on relationships between people. People make conscious decisions about how to respond and act toward the outside world.	Qualitative ethnographic research	People choose to participate in sport in various ways, and the quality of the athlete's experience is important. Sport organizations should be open and democratic. Youth sport should fit the needs and desires of kids rather than those of parents and coaches.	Focuses on the individual to the exclusion of the overall structure of sport. Does not address issues of power in sport as critical theories do.
Figurational theory	Emphasizes connections between people and their interdependence. Examines change over time.	Historical research	Sport exists as part of society and can be viewed historically and over the long term. Sport tends to focus on traditional masculinity and on male power. Developments in sport are seen in the context of global processes.	Devotes little attention to current issues because of its focus on the long term, thus reducing the urgency to press for changes. Has been mostly popular in Europe in mature societies but rarely used in North America.

ACTIVITY TIME-OUT

Using Research Methods

Suppose that you want to know if differences exist between adolescent boys and girls in terms of their participation in sport and physical activity. Specifically, you would like to compare, in some detail, their motivation for engaging in organized competitive sport, casual or pickup sport, and other types of physical activity. Which of the research methods would you use to gather this information, and why?

conflict among players, coaches, and officials (Leonard 1980; Loy and Booth 2004).

Conflict Theory

Conflict theory rejects the status quo as it exists in capitalistic societies such as the United States. Conflict theory is based on the theories of Karl Marx and views sport as built on a foundation of economic power. In a capitalistic society, it is easy to point to the owners of professional sport teams who use their economic wealth and power to benefit financially at the expense of athletes, coaches, and spectators. Those in the upper economic class, such as team owners, are often seen as taking advantage of those in the middle or lower classes by setting the conditions and prices for attending football games or basketball games that are out of reach for the average family. Similarly, many view the bureaucratic organizations that operate sport—such as the National Collegiate Athletic Association, sport-specific governing, and the International Olympic Committee—as promoting sport in order to gain power, status, and money. When this apparent domination is resisted by sport participants or spectators, conflict arises.

Unlike the functionalist theories based on constructing and developing a state of social balance that operates efficiently, conflict theories focus on the disruptive forces that produce instability and disorganization. In other words, they look at sport in relation to changes in society; nothing is as certain in life as the fact of change produced by struggles between groups pursuing different interests. In the middle of the twentieth century, many sport sociologists moved toward the conflict-theory approach and away from the more traditional functionalist point of view that tended to simply reinforce the status quo.

Much of conflict theory is directed at the dominant spectator sports. Advocates of this theory would place more power in the hands of sport participants and promote sport at the local level so that it benefits all classes of people rather than the elite few. The working class would enjoy more influence over sport than the rich. Therefore, conflict theorists favor player unions that confront owners; they also support organizations that guard against using public money to build luxurious stadiums benefiting the owners of professional teams.

Conflict theorists also campaign for athlete representation at all levels of decision making in sport organizations. In this model, for example, Olympians would vote on policy questions concerning the staging of the Games. Similarly, student-athletes would help their colleges in coaching searches, and even athletes in youth sport would provide input into decisions made by league officials and coaches (Leonard 1980; Rigauer 2004).

Critical Theory

Critical theories evaluate culture and determine the source of authority wielded by one group over another. These theories examine how a culture operates and explore its struggles in the search for a better life for all citizens. A critical theorist is especially attuned to combating structural conditions in a society that lead to exploitation, oppression, or social injustice. Rather than simply shifting power to sport participants without question, as conflict theorists advocate, critical theorists agitate to effect change where they find that it is warranted after careful analysis.

Unlike functionalists and conflict theorists, critical theorists conclude that sport does not simply mirror society but instead offers the opportunity to help create society by affecting how people think and feel about social conditions. For example, it is possible that eventually all people will understand the far-reaching benefits of regular physical activity in improving the quality of life well into one's older years. In recent U.S. history, physical activity has often been relegated to the role of fun and recreation, which is indeed a worthy use of leisure time. However, evidence continues to mount that sport and activity should in fact be a regular part of life in order to maximize disease resistance, maintain energy, control body weight, improve appearance, and reduce the cost of health care.

When faced with large expenditures of public funds to promote sport, critical theorists agitate to spend money instead on sport facilities, equipment, and good coaching made widely available to the greatest number of citizens rather than just to elite athletes. Similarly, they would much rather support sport facilities built for participation by the masses than huge stadiums filled with many more spectators than players.

One critical theory of particular interest is **hegemony theory**, which is based largely on the ideas of Italian political theorist Antonio Gramsci. Hegemony theory focuses on dominance—that is, the power that one individual or group holds over others—as in the case of power wielded by coaches. In professional sport, where the goal is winning above all else, an authoritarian coach can usually survive as long as the team makes the playoffs. For example, Bill Belichick, head coach of the National Football League's New England Patriots, clearly controls every decision made regarding his team and his players, who go along with him largely because he is a proven winner. In fact, under his tutelage, the Patriots once won three Super Bowls in a four-year period, and they won it again in 2015.

In many youth sports, the focus is often on encouraging fair play, giving every athlete a chance to play, and not keeping score. A critical theorist would say these are all good things. What do you think?

Analyzing sport with critical theory may lead us to new ways of looking both at sport and at our role in sport. It also helps us understand the plight of others whose sport opportunities may differ from our own. The goal of critical analysis is to make sport more democratic and sensitive to diversity and to provide access to everyone, regardless of ethnic background, social class, or financial status. Viewed in this way, sport can also lead us to new understandings of gender, sexual orientation, and physical talent.

Critical theorists attempt to take an objective view of the conventional wisdom about sport in U.S. society. Using critical thought, we can challenge the status quo, analyze its effects on society, and propose beneficial changes. At the same time, we can look objectively at the weaknesses of our current economic system, including how we treat people who are poor or socially disadvantaged (Hargreaves and McDonald 2004; Sage 1998).

APPLYING SOCIAL THEORY

Critical Theorists and the Education of Dasmine Cathey

How would you respond to the following situation using a critical theorist approach?

Dasmine Cathey was recruited to play football at the University of Memphis, a Division I FBS school, and spent five years there. Despite possessing exceptional athletic skills and good size at 6 feet 4 inches (about 1.9 meters) and more than 200 pounds (about 91 kilograms), Cathey never had much of an impact on the football field. His off-the-field struggle, however, merits scrutiny. The reason? Cathey found himself in college without possessing even a minimal ability to read. Confronted with the challenge of college courses, he realized that he needed to learn to read but was too proud to ask for help. Instead, late at night he shut his dorm room door and began to immerse himself in a series of ten Learn to Read books designed for first graders. Within three years, he taught himself how to read, at least a little bit.

This was a young man who had hated everything about school while he was growing up. Asked to read aloud in front of his peers, he mumbled and faked his way through amid snickers from his classmates. By high school, he had never read a book, but on the athletic field he shined. He was a finalist for Tennessee Lineman of the Year in football and played on a state-champion basketball team. Once he enrolled in college, the football team assigned him to study halls and provided tutors to help him complete his college work. Because of his poor academic record, he was ineligible during his first year, and in subsequent years he barely maintained his eligibility.

With a background in a low-income Memphis suburb, and without parents to support and guide him, Cathey ended up being responsible for extended family members who needed a hand. Eventually, he also fathered several children of his own, with different women, while in college, and he did his best to provide for them.

The University of Memphis is not unique among Division I athletic programs in admitting student-athletes who are underprepared for university work. Like many other schools, Memphis offers a summer program designed especially for athletes who need remedial help before beginning college. Nearly half of those students test at or below a seventh-grade reading level.

Universities have a stake in helping these athletes succeed as students not only to maintain their eligibility but also to ensure that the institution does not lose scholarships or postseason opportunities (a possibility if too many athletes fail to graduate). The academic counseling staff at Memphis includes more than twenty graduate assistants, interns, and tutors, in addition to eight full-time counselors. This staff provides hundreds of hours of assistance to student-athletes with a learning disability or deficiency in basic reading or writing skills.

After five years in college, Cathey's graduation depended on passing three more courses with grades that would push his overall grade point average above the minimum of 2.0. Yet with only three months to go, Cathey hadn't attended any classes in several weeks. With his college eligibility for football used up, he seemed to have lost all interest in school (Wolverton 2012).

Although it would take him several more months after he was permitted to attend his graduation ceremony in June of 2012 to complete his senior project, he did finally receive his degree in interdisciplinary studies after 18 semesters in college, which included attending every summer (Wolverton 2012).

In analyzing this situation as a critical theorist, consider all sides of the story. Who has been hurt? What should be done to resolve similar predicaments, which are widespread in big-time college athletic programs?

Feminist Theory

Feminist theories evolved from dissatisfaction with sociocultural traditions and practices that emphasize males and either ignore females or reduce them to a subservient role. Among other things, feminist analysis of sport forces us to confront our sexuality, rigorously define our expectations of males and females, and openly discuss homophobia.

Feminist theories, of course, help us analyze the status of women in sport. In U.S. society, people may rejoice in the gains that have been made even as they acknowledge the work that remains in order to ensure equal opportunities for both sexes. For example, the dearth of women in coaching deprives half of our youth population of role models of their own sex. Similarly, the scarcity of women in sport leadership positions affects decisions made in sport and disenfranchises a majority of our population.

An obvious weakness of analyzing sport by means of feminist theories is the tendency to overlook the influence of other factors, such as race, religion, ethnicity, and economic class. Clearly, these factors can be equally powerful, and when we ignore them we are doomed to an inadequate evaluation of sport (Birrell 2004; Coakley 2004; Sage 1998).

IN THE ARENA WITH . . .

Women's Boxing at the 2012 Olympic Games

With the addition of women's boxing to the program at the 2012 London Olympics, the International Olympic Committee approved the inclusion of 26 sports available to both men and women for the first time in its history. However, despite the appearance of equality of opportunity for both sexes, female boxers competed in the only three weight classes that were offered, as compared with ten classes for males. In addition, the total number of female fighters was 36, as compared with 250 for men, and only amateur boxers for both men and women were allowed to participate. Male professional boxers will be allowed to compete for the first time in the Olympic Games in Rio de Janeiro in 2016.

For female boxers around the world, however, this competition was a momentous event. Women's boxing is sanctioned in 120 countries, and an estimated 500,000 women participate in the sport. Europe leads the way with 40 countries that sanction female boxing, followed by the Americas with 34, Asia with 22, Africa with 17, and Oceana with 8. Previous efforts to include women in Olympic boxing raised concerns about participant safety, but more than 15 years of data now show that women's Olympic-style boxing is in fact safer than men's.

Once the decision was made to include women in Olympic boxing, another barrier appeared in the form of a proposal from the International Boxing Association (AIBA) that women should be required to wear skirts in the ring. In light of vociferous resistance from most female boxers, the Olympic rules were amended to merely *allow* women to wear skirts—not require it or even recommend it. Still, the hesitancy to approve of women punching each other is famously illustrated by a comment from the Cuban national boxing coach, who opined that "Cuban women should be showing off their beautiful faces, not getting punched in the face" (Bentley 2012; Bearak 2012).

As you might expect, someone with a feminist point of view would wholeheartedly support the inclusion of women in Olympic boxing, but they would likely be dissatisfied with the disparity in the number of participants as compared with men. Look for changes in the near future to reconcile the differences between the male and female competitions.

Interactionist Theory

Those who subscribe to **interactionist theories** view society from the bottom up rather than from the top down. They focus on social interactions between people based on the realities that people choose to accept. In this view, rather than simply responding to our world, we make conscious choices about how we will behave based on the effects that we think our actions will have on ourselves, on other people, and on our society.

Research by interactionists involves extensive interviewing and ethnography to elicit athletes' thoughts and feelings about their sport participation. This approach helps us understand how people choose particular sports and how they define themselves as athletes within the culture of a particular sport. Interactionists also create sport experiences that focus on the athlete rather than on the business, the institution, or leaders. As a result, for example, interactionists put kids' needs first in youth sport rather than allowing sport to be defined by adults who think they know what kids need.

Similarly, interactionists focus on the human experience of African American athletes rather than on their athletic performance. They also confront the exploitation of college athletes who never earn a degree but serve the university's purpose as an athlete for hire. And they encourage women who seek to develop traditional masculine and athletic virtues, such as aggressiveness, that conflict with traditional feminine values.

Interactionist theorists rely on the methods of psychology by probing a person's feelings and understandings rather than by looking at the structured world outside of the individual. They also study subcultures in sport, such as those reported in a classic text by Ball and Loy (1975), which devotes chapters to the subcultures of college coaches, professional baseball players, hockey players, and wrestlers.

Since the 1990s, the interactionist approach has become more popular and productive among sport sociologists because of the rich in-depth analyses that it favors. For example, survey research has long established that more males than females are involved in sport and physical activity, but it was left to the individual researcher to speculate about why this was true. When research was refocused through ethnographic observations, the reasons behind the trends became more understandable (Donnelly 2004).

Figurational Theory

Figurational theories are rooted in Europe, particularly England, and are rarely used in North America. They emphasize interpersonal connections called figurations. The crux of these theories is that we are all connected by networks of people who are interdependent on one another by nature, through education, and through socialization. Over time, the connections change as we mature, move in different circles, and absorb more information. When looking at sport from this perspective, theorists study the historical processes through which people change.

The interrelationships in our lives are dynamic and frequently changing; therefore, figurational theories use long-term analysis to develop rich understandings of social influences. If we are fully engaged in changes in our culture, then our perspectives, including those on sport, change as we age. For example, consider the warm camaraderie among senior athletes who compete furiously but also view their sport differently because their self-concept is not tied exclusively to success or failure in competitive sport as is often the case in youthful athletes.

Figurational theories have helped researchers study the amazing rise of soccer in Europe and around the world. More particularly, they have also studied the rise in violence on the part of both players and spectators, and in the early 2000s figurational theory was used to evaluate reports from officials who had taken bribes to influence the outcomes of soccer matches.

Perhaps the most critical contribution of figurational theories has been a fuller understanding of the global processes at work in a shrinking world. As the connections between people and between nations have strengthened worldwide, sport has prospered in unimaginable ways through international training, competition, and coaching courses.

A weakness of figurational theory is that it tends to reduce the urgency for change. Since it views social problems over the long term, it affords little opportunity to confront social problems in sport in a timely manner. The risk is that by the time we understand what has happened,

Figurational theorists are typically passionate about soccer (or football, as it is referred to internationally). Here, Hong Kong police's organized crime and triad bureau display stacks of cash seized after they launched an operation with counterparts in mainland China to dismantle a cross-border illegal gambling syndicate days before the start of the 2014 World Cup in Brazil.

and perhaps why it happened, new changes have already taken place (Murphy, Sheard, and Waddington 2004).

Summary of Theories

After reviewing these six theories, you may wonder how they all fit into the sociology of sport. Each theoretical approach was developed over time and has helped sport sociology develop as a legitimate academic discipline with a discrete body of knowledge. Each of these theories has also contributed to our understanding of the world of sport and exercise as it presently exists. To help you absorb the significance of each theory, here are some generalizations:

- Most people who extol the virtues of sport as it has traditionally existed use the *functionalist* approach. Although this approach may have been useful in the past, it does not help identify existing social issues or provide any hope of solutions. People who work in existing sport organizations may adopt this approach in the interest of maintaining the status quo.

ACTIVITY TIME-OUT

Applying Social Theories

Which of the social theories does each of the following four statements typify? Explain your answer.

1. The goal for our society should be to produce sports and make them available to all citizens as a source of personal expression, creative energy, and physical health and well-being.
2. You've always loved sport and been an athlete. Nothing would be more satisfying to you than forging a career in sport management. Eventually, it would be your dream to work for the National Football League or perhaps one of its teams.
3. Athletes who dedicate themselves to succeeding in professional sport to the exclusion of education and personal growth exhibit a form of socially deviant behavior. U.S. society should not support such pursuits financially, socially, or morally.
4. Success in sport competition is wedded to material gain, but upward mobility through sport is a mirage. By definition, competition creates classes of winner and losers, much to the detriment of society.

- *Conflict theories* have impressed on us the influence of social class and the power structure in sport. Capitalist society and social structures protect the most powerful among us at the expense of the least powerful. The power of money in sport has only been reinforced by the economic model that has overtaken both the Olympic Games and international professional sport. Conflict theories have pointed out the conflict in sport and have often led to dramatic proposals for change.
- Since the 1970s, *critical theories* have been the most helpful in clarifying the challenges of making sport more accessible to people from all backgrounds and abilities. One specific critical theory, *feminist theory*, has enabled us to understand the issues that women faced before Title IX (for in-depth discussion, see chapter 13) and their ongoing struggle to claim a share of the sporting world and make it people oriented rather than male oriented.
- *Interactionist theories* allow us to look in depth at sport from an athlete's point of view and add a qualitative bent to our analysis. Since the 1990s, North American researchers have adopted this approach more than any other.
- *Figurational theories* have been especially helpful in Europe in long-term analyses of sporting subcultures and in understanding the global expansion of sport.

Current Status of Sport Sociology

Although sociology as a discipline became popular around the turn of the century, it was not applied to sport for another 50 years. In 1965, the International Committee for the Sociology of Sport was created as an outgrowth of the International Council of Sport and Physical Education. This organization, presently named the International Sociology of Sport Association, has published the

POP CULTURE

Sport Magazine Covers

An analysis of *Sports Illustrated* covers from 2000 through 2011 (a total of 716 issues) revealed that only 35 covers (5 percent) featured a female athlete and only 18 featured women as the primary or sole image (Tuggle 2003). The study did not include the annual swimsuit edition, which features scantily clad models but few female athletes.

More recently, *Golf Digest* drew the ire of the Ladies Professional Golf Association and its members, who were outraged that a nongolfer, Paulina Gretzky, was featured on the cover of the sport's premier magazine. Several tour players lamented that they simply receive no respect as female professional golfers and in this case were ignored in favor of a "golf celebrity" whose claim to fame is being the daughter of hockey legend Wayne Gretzky and the fiancée of golf star Dustin Johnson. No doubt her glamorized appearance was intended to promote sales to male golf fans.

Media decisions such as these continue to sexualize and exploit females rather than featuring them as highly skilled successful athletes. Is it any wonder that feminist theorists protest that even though we encourage young girls and women to participate in sport, this encouragement is contradicted by the media's failure to consistently portray strong, skilled female athletes?

International Review for the Sociology of Sport quarterly since 1966. It also meets every year and attracts scholars from around the world.

The second major organization for sport sociology is the North American Society for the Sociology of Sport. Founded in 1978, it holds annual conferences, and since 1984 it has published the *Sociology of Sport Journal*.

As the popularity of sport increases, more researchers are drawn to the relationships between sport and society. Most large universities and many small ones now offer courses such as sport and society, sport sociology, the social science of sport, and social issues in sport. In addition, students from diverse fields of study are drawn to such courses as electives because of their interest in sport.

The media also rely on research in sport sociology for articles and features on athletes and on particular sports. Along with reporting current events, the media provide commentary to help people understand the underlying causes of the behavior, attitudes, and struggles of their sport heroes. Without solid grounding in sociological research, much of this material would be limited to the reporter's or commenter's own experience, knowledge, and bias.

Chapter Summary

This chapter lays out the plan for looking at sport through the methods and theories of sociology. Methods for collecting data include interviews, surveys, content research, historical research, and ethnography. Once data are collected, they can be analyzed with functionalist theories, conflict theories, critical theories, feminist theories, interactionist theories, and figurational theories. The chapter presents the essential elements of each of these theories, compares them, and suggests how each is applied to the world of sport.

In the context of these theories, researchers can analyze data and interpret the resulting evidence. Doing so organizes large amounts of data that can be examined both in detail and from an overall perspective. Using scientific methodology reduces the influence of personal bias and preconceived notions about sport.

PART II

Scope and Effect of Sport on Society

This part of the book begins with chapter 3, which highlights the important distinction between sport participants and sport spectators. Even though these two groups overlap, combining them in order to assess the popularity of a particular sport leads to faulty assumptions. The reason is that participants in a particular sport are likely to be spectators, but spectators are often not participants. Think, for example, of the millions of football fans who watch the sport but do not play it.

The chapter also makes a further distinction between people who participate in sport for recreation and those who strive for high performance. High-performance or elite athletes are usually younger, whereas older adults participate primarily in recreational sport. However, more and more young people are also turning toward recreational models of sport. The chapter closes with a consideration of how sport is marketed to both participants and spectators.

Chapter 4 evaluates sport as a corporate venture and also looks at how sport affects the national economy. The chapter documents the benefits to owners of professional sport teams and discusses the questionable value of financing sport stadiums with public money. In addition, it discusses the laws that allow sport leagues to operate as virtual monopolies and examines the ways in which colleges and universities can profit from sport. It also takes a realistic look at the earning power and job conditions of the athletes who participate in corporate sport.

The section concludes with chapter 5, which examines the close relationship between sport and the media. Television continues to bring sport entertainment to our homes through ever-increasing hours of sport broadcasts. At the same time, the delivery of sport is being affected by advances in technology. Worldwide access to the Internet has changed the delivery of spectator sport and will continue to do so. The role of the print media appears to be rapidly declining as electronic media expand in accessibility, variety, and impact. The explosion of social media provides opportunities to link sport tracking and reporting through services such as Facebook, Twitter, Instagram, Google+, and YouTube, as well as blogs. As a result, athletes can connect more directly with fans, and fans can connect instantly with each other.

Chapter 5 also examines how sport and the media affect each other and how sport influences societal ideology and values through the media. In addition, it describes careers in sport journalism, as well as the substantial challenge of increasing access for women in the sport media. Finally, it explores how the decisions made in the sport media are affected by the imbalance between males and females in the profession.

3

STUDENT OUTCOMES

After reading this chapter, you will know the following:

- Who a sport participant is
- What affects the decision to participate
- Who a sport spectator is
- Trends for both participants and spectators
- How marketing efforts follow participant and spectator trends

Participants Versus Spectators

Participants Versus Spectators

You may still be a bit confused about exactly what *sport* is, especially as you begin to learn about the popularity of various sports. To clarify, it may help you to think for a moment about *all* types of goal-oriented physical activity that involve voluntary movement. For most of us, this general grouping includes physical activities associated in some way with good health and well-being. More specifically, we might think about specific sports or about the broader categories of exercise or skilled movement.

When we look at sport in this context, we see quickly that some sports involve more exercise, whereas others feature more skilled movement. However, these two categories are often combined in research on sport participation (as in some studies cited in this chapter), which, unfortunately, confuses the issue. Furthermore, some activities, such as walking, can either serve simply as informal exercise or be classified as a sport at the highest level (for example, in Olympic competition). Therefore, in order to understand this chapter, hold in mind the fact that the terms *physical activity*, *sport*, and *exercise* are often used by people interchangeably, even though, technically speaking, they can be clearly distinguished from each other.

Participating in sport is quite different from watching sport. Yet in sport studies, these two activities are often lumped together, both statistically and anecdotally. Unfortunately, combining them creates confusion about the value of each, thus leading to suspect conclusions and interfering with attempts to assess the overall influence of sport. For example, if asked, many people would rate tackle football as the most popular sport in the United States, and this is a reasonable conclusion based on spectator interest. However, if we look at participation, football is popular only through high school and only among boys. Beyond age 18, tackle football is not a reasonable option due to the number of players required, the lack of readily available equipment, and the risk of injury. Thus it is more accurate to say that football is the most popular *spectator* sport in the United States but that it rates far down the list in participation.

Some evidence does support the claim that watching sport and playing sport relate significantly to each other. Young people are often attracted to participate in a sport because they see famous athletes on television or perhaps in live action (Harris 2004). In addition, youth who participate in a sport are more likely to watch that sport in later years because they understand it (Kretchmar 1994). Without question, many people who play a sport also watch that sport; in fact, they are likely to watch other sports as well, because their athletic experience helps them empathize with competitors in other sport activities. Sport competitors enjoy observing and admiring athletes as they perform common athletic skills and strategies that cut across different sports.

For years, some have argued that spectators who watch favorite sport performers are more motivated than nonfans to participate in sport themselves. In particular, young people seem to readily imitate their sport heroes in pickup games, on the playground, and in the gym. Perhaps it is not surprising, then, that sports without elite role models, such as men's field hockey in the United States, languish and suffer low participation. On the other hand, watching high-skilled athletes—for example, Olympians—can also discourage an average person who lacks exceptional skill or talent. Indeed, elite athletes tend to make performance look easy, when in fact it results from years of intense practice and instruction.

Sport Participants

To understand **sport participation**, we must look closely at the characteristics of sport participants, their motivation, and the outside factors that influence their decisions.

High-Performance Versus Participation Athletes

As introduced in the sport pyramid (see figure 1.1), people who play a sport can be classified as either a high-performance athlete or a participation athlete. Regardless of age, these two groups differ markedly in their motivation, training, and attitudes toward competition. Athletes who seek high performance (as characterized by the Olympic motto "Faster, Higher, Stronger") train intensively, compete aggressively, and aspire to a professional career that brings **extrinsic rewards**, such as money and fame. In contrast, athletes who value participation are motivated by **intrinsic rewards**, such as fun and fitness; they use sport as a form of recreation in order to enhance their quality of life, escape from work responsibilities, and socialize with family and friends.

In the United States, about 72 percent of people over the age of six integrate at least some participant sport or physical activity into their life. However, only about 34 percent of the population is active at a level that definitely promotes good health—that is, participating at least three times per week in activity that uses a high number of calories (Sports and Fitness Industry Association 2014)—thus making purely recreational sport or exercise the overwhelming dominant group in U.S. society. At the same time, the human preoccupation with excellence, competition, and performance has vaulted high-performance sport to dizzying heights of popularity, fueled by business interests and the media, even though relatively few athletes are elite. Of course, spectator sport feeds off of the popularity of high-performance sport, because people enjoy watching exceptional performers match skills, wits, and courage.

We can also classify athletes by age while also keeping in mind the two tracks that they may follow: high-performance and participation for recreation. At times, these two paths overlap, which can cause confusion for athletes, coaches, parents, and sponsoring organizations. For example, most youth sports are based on participation, but once players join a travel team or sport club, they aim for high performance.

Youth Sport Athletes

Youth sport athletes typically fall between the ages of four and thirteen. Participation opportunities tend to be community driven, seasonal, and oriented toward team sports. Parents encourage their children to play in order to learn the skills of a particular sport, to socialize with other children, and to engage in physical activity. Many parents are also involved as team coaches, chauffeurs, and fans. Most youth sport programs encourage participation by everyone, regardless of skill, and strive to offer low-key competition and generate an interest in sport that will last a lifetime.

How does the motivation and training program of this high-performance athlete differ from yours?

Even so, some parents push their children into sport, hoping that their child will be the next youth superstar. Toward this end, children as young as 10 years old can join specialized high-performance programs that emphasize competition, rankings, travel teams, national events, and specialization in one sport throughout the year. These programs are clearly dedicated to developing elite athletes. Youth sport is covered in more detail in chapter 6.

High School Varsity Athletes

Athletes at this level may participate for reasons similar to those of youth sport athletes; that is, they like to socialize with their peers and want to continue to improve in their sport. The choice to participate is usually made by the athlete rather than his or her parents. Participation can also be motivated by a desire to receive a college athletic scholarship (in one sport or a few sports) or to progress directly into professional play. By definition, high school varsity sport involves competition between schools. Because most teams are limited in size the majority of high school students do not play a varsity sport and therefore must rely on intramural, community-based sport, or informal pickup games.

Some high school sport teams—such as football, basketball, and baseball teams—are high-performance programs that truly prepare athletes for college sport. In other sports, particularly Olympic and individual sports, high school teams are more recreational, and elite athletes must look outside of the school setting and find private developmental programs and competitions sponsored by their chosen sport's national governing body. For further discussion of high school sport, see chapter 8.

College Varsity Athletes

College athletes form an even more select group than high school athletes. Specifically, whereas U.S. high school varsity athletes numbered 7.8 million in recent reports, the number of U.S. college varsity athletes was only about 450,000 (National Collegiate Athletic Association 2012–2013b; National Federation of State High School Associations 2013–2014). It is no surprise, then, that college varsity slots are the subject of intense competition, especially at large institutions. As a result, most high school athletes face the fact that they are not good enough to play at the intercollegiate level and therefore join college intramural programs or club teams that offer recreational competition. In addition, during the summer, many of them turn to community-based sport in their hometown in order to satisfy their competitive and recreational urges.

The most intense high-performance programs are found at the large universities categorized as Division I by the National Collegiate Athletic Association (NCAA). Most athletes in these programs receive a full or partial athletic scholarship and are expected to produce athletically in order to justify the expense to the university. Other colleges compete in NCAA Divisions II and III, where the competition is less intense, the commitment to athletics is more modest, and the financial investment by the institutions is lower. For further discussion of college sport, see chapter 8.

Professional Athletes

Professional athletes compete in sport for extrinsic financial rewards, such as salary, prize money, and product endorsements. Virtually every sport holds professional tournaments or leagues somewhere in the world, including the Olympic Games. Of course, professional athletes may compete in their sport because they enjoy it, but the longer they compete at the professional level, under pressure to perform, the closer their sport participation moves toward work. Except for a few sport prodigies, most athletes do not qualify for professional sport until they are young adults. Furthermore, professional sport careers have limited duration because of the exceptional physical performances they demand. As physical skills decline in the late 20s and 30s, most professional athletes are forced to retire from competition.

Masters Athletes

Although older competitors typically cannot compete with younger competitors who are at the height of their physical prowess, masters athletes may be focused on the highest level of performance for their age group. Masters-level competition is staged in categories beginning as young as 35 and ending up as old as (in some sports) 90 or even beyond. The competition is intense; the athletes train year round, and events are often staged at the local, national, and even international levels. Aided by advancements in health, training regimens, and medical care, masters athletes continue to break records and grow in number. As compared with their younger professional counterparts, masters athletes generally compete for modest, if any, financial reward. Some masters competitions do offer prize money, but most offer only good competition, an opportunity to travel, and an expanded social network.

Adult Participation or Recreational Athletes

At every age, beginning with youth sport, some participants play simply for fun. They enjoy socializing with friends, being physically active, and playing the game. But they may not have the physical or psychological attributes needed to compete at high levels. In fact, we often spend our childhood years testing our physical limits; by the time we reach adulthood, very few of us can compete at the elite levels of sport. Yet more than half of the U.S. population still enjoys playing a sport. As we age, we tend to move away from collision sports (such as football, soccer, wrestling, and boxing) and toward sports that involve less risk of physical injury or stress on the body. In addition, because team sports are more difficult to organize in the adult world, many people turn to sports geared toward individuals or a smaller number of contestants.

Participation athletes spend less time than higher-level athletes in practicing and training for competition. Since their sport time is limited by work and family commitments, most participation or recreational athletes just play when they can. The question of winning or losing does not affect their life as much as it might have at a younger age; nor does it affect their reputation in their field of work.

Don't let age fool you! Masters athletes are just as competitive—and accomplished—in their chosen sport as are younger athletes.

Factors Affecting Sport Participation

Now that you have an idea of who participates in sport, let's look at the factors that influence participation, as well as the conflicts between different levels of participation.

Pursuit of Excellence

Perhaps encouraged by parents and coaches, some youthful competitors are oriented toward producing the best possible physical performance. Indeed, it could be argued that youth sport in general discovers the best potential competitors through a progression of competitions promoting survival of the fittest. Athletes who do well at a young age play on all-star teams, receive advanced training and coaching, and sometimes compete at the national or even the international level. Because of their early success, these athletes often accumulate sport experiences that help them increase their edge over other kids their age.

One of the difficulties with designating athletes as elite at a young age is that their dominance may result simply from maturing early. In such cases, once their peers catch up with them physically, they quickly lose confidence and motivation as kids they used to defeat routinely overtake them.

Of course, the U.S. preoccupation with high achievement spills over into youth sport. Many parents hope that their child will be chosen for the elite, select, or traveling team. In many sports, the number of youngsters chosen for these teams may account for as much as 30 percent of the participants in order to cast a wide net for future superstars. In reality, only about 5 percent of high school athletes are fortunate enough to compete at the collegiate level, and fewer than 1 percent make it to the professional level (NCAA 2013e).

Even so, the quest for high performance in sport is often emphasized by schools, businesses, sponsors, and the media. This quest reflects and reinforces the pioneering spirit that motivates humans to break barriers of existence and performance. In pursuit of this quest, schools and colleges spend huge sums of money to support athletic teams whose primary purpose is to defeat their rivals.

Athletes who sacrifice to perform at the highest level receive rewards that include money, fame, media attention, and hero worship. Their efforts to excel in sport are supported by commercial sponsors, professional teams, college teams, and Olympic organizations.

Recreation Through Sport

Many people take a different attitude toward sport by setting recreation as their ultimate goal, regardless of their level of skill or achievement. This approach is well suited to the masses, because, by definition, very few can reach the elite level. This type of sport participation is founded on the principle that people need diversion from their work and that recreation provides this diversion and recharges their natural energy reserves. In many instances, what we refer to as "participation sport" might also be (and commonly is) called "recreational sport."

Participating in sport in this manner emphasizes the social aspect of activity. For example, people may go fishing or enjoy a friendly game of golf, tennis, or volleyball as a way to spend time with family and friends. Thus, whereas high-performance athletes aim to defeat one another, participation athletes typically root for one another and help each other out whenever they can.

The fact that participation athletes far outnumber high-performance athletes is clearly recognized by the commercial sponsors of sport, who operate facilities, sell sport clothing and equipment, and run sport associations. As a result, in their efforts to attract average people to sport participation, these commercial groups modify sport to make it friendly to people of all ages, skills, and income levels. Here are a few examples:

- Golf is one of the few sports in which players of different skill levels can enjoy competing against each other by altering the scoring system. For instance, in a scramble format, after each shot, all players move their ball to the best location achieved by

POP CULTURE

Faster, Higher, Stronger by Mark McClusky

This bestselling book by a veteran journalist (McClusky 2014) tackles the intriguing topic of how sport science is helping to create a new generation of "superathletes" and what we can learn from them. Conventional wisdom tells us that a champion must practice 10,000 hours in order to achieve greatness, but new research proves that this is not the case. In fact, the kids who dominate youth sport are probably the least likely to end up at the top of their sport at the professional level.

For today's elite athletes, it is simply not enough to have been born with good genes or to put forth 100 percent in order to reach the top level of a sport. These days, an elite athlete must also be aware of the technology and science related to her or his sport; work with a coach who knows how to apply it in training and performance; and remain open to new ideas, products, and training methods—sometimes before they have been fully vetted, as long as they are legal.

This book, then, is a good read packed with insights into athletic greatness. But even if you're not an elite athlete, it provides clues about how you can get more out of your talent than you ever thought possible. For example, did you know what you wear when competing can dramatically affect your performance? Or that what—and how much—you drink might determine how long you can last?

Battling the elements and conquering nature motivates some people to be active, just as trying to win a competition motivates others.

any of the players in the group. Another approach involves awarding points for each hole based on which player reaches the green first or holes out first.

- Tennis can be adjusted for local recreational settings by altering the length of play. For example, the winner might be declared after a certain time limit in order to accommodate indoor play, which is precisely scheduled and purchased by the hour. Shortened sets have also become popular, and tiebreakers may be used at the end of the second set instead of playing a traditional third set to decide the winner.
- Recreational volleyball and softball leagues sponsor co-ed teams that require a set number of females on each team. To reduce softball injuries, players are prohibited from wearing spiked shoes or sliding into bases.
- Soccer can be played by smaller groups, such as teams of three, so that each player gets more action and the game can be played on a smaller field.

Participation and High Performance Tug-of-War

There seems to be a perpetual tug-of-war for resources between supporters of high-performance sport and those who prefer participation sport. National associations and governing bodies often pour their financial resources into developing high-performance athletes, to the detriment of average sport participants. Meanwhile, debates rage about the percentage of resources that ought to be expended for either purpose.

Consider the **Amateur Sports Act of 1978**, in which the U.S. Congress established the United States Olympic Committee (USOC) and outlined its responsibilities. The act listed 12 purposes for the USOC, about half of which address the issue of amateur sport participation. For instance, the sixth purpose is "to promote and encourage physical fitness and public participation in amateur athletic activities." The law was revised in 1998 as the Olympic and Amateur Sports Act, which addressed the needs of elite Paralympic athletes. The law does not prescribe the proportion of time, effort, or budget dedicated to various purposes; those decisions are left to the USOC board of directors (Stevens 2005).

Other common areas of debate include rules, boundaries, equipment, and clothing. New equipment may allow ordinary performers the thrill of better performance and keep them hooked on the sport. However, that same equipment may be illegal for high-performance athletes who must compete according to a particular set of rules. In baseball, for example, amateur college players can use aluminum bats, but professional players must use wooden bats.

Similarly, the PGA Tour has considered using a type of ball that is less lively than its current ball in order to put more of a premium on accuracy rather than power and distance. This proposal has garnered support from golf legends, such as Jack Nicklaus and Arnold Palmer, who believe that the sport has developed into a power game with less emphasis on accuracy and skill. Yet the average weekend player thrills to the whack of a golf ball that flies farther than he or she ever thought possible.

Attitudes toward sport at the youth and high school levels can tilt heavily toward either high performance or participation, depending on the attitude taken by the leaders of the school or league. In such settings, however, it is self-defeating to lean too heavily toward the high-performance model, since doing so limits the number of participants. Because athletics are justified as educational opportunities, shouldn't schools sponsor multiple teams at various skill levels in order to include more students?

More generally, it is often suggested that sport participation improves people's quality of life, helps fight obesity, and keeps people stronger and healthier. As a result, as the population ages and health concerns rise, the balance of spending and public attention may tip more toward sport participation. Indeed, support for emphasizing sport participation is already emerging from the health community, sport organization leaders, organizations that advocate for older people, and youth sport organizations. This support can be seen in the many comments and position statements—which are consistent with the sixth purpose stated in the Olympic and Amateur Sports Act—that appear in the media and are making inroads in the public consciousness.

The conflict between high-performance sport and participation sport is not unique to the United States. In fact, this topic served as the focus for the fifteenth International Olympic Committee World Conference on Sport for All, which was held in

ACTIVITY TIME-OUT

Performance Versus Participation Sport

As you examine the potential for conflict between performance and participation sport, do you think it is possible to support both? If you were responsible for a community budget for youth sport, what proportions of funding would you allocate to high-performance and participation sport? Justify your answer and give specific examples. In making your recommendation, consider that approximately 5 percent of the population qualifies for high-performance sport, and the other 95 percent is relegated to or chooses participation sport. Would it be fair to use those proportions as the basis for allocating funds? How would you account for the fact that high-performance sport is always much more expensive due to the frequency, intensity, and expertise it involves?

Lima, Peru (International Olympic Committee 2013a). This conference issued the following call to action for the world of sport: "Get moving." More than 500 participants from 90 countries attended the conference to explore ways to spread the word that both participation sport and performance sport can reap benefits if their supporters work together. Doing so encourages individuals to enjoy a lifetime of sport and physical activity by being physically active and participating in sport at their own level, whether elite or more ordinary. In this way, rather than competing for time, facilities, and money, the two camps of sport can complement each other and better serve all people.

Social Influences on Sport Participation

People of all ages decide consciously whether or not to participate in sport. If they do choose to participate, they eventually make another decision, either consciously or unconsciously, about whether to continue their participation or drop out. If they decide to continue, they must then choose their level of dedication and performance intensity. This last decision—about whether to participate for fun or for high performance—is influenced not only by internal factors (one's feelings, thoughts, and aspirations) but also by outside factors, including other people. Of course, a person might also change his or her mind due to personal development or a change in external conditions.

When we are young, our families influence us more than outsiders do. For example, if your parents participated in sport, took you to sporting contests, helped you learn basic sport skills, and encouraged you to participate, chances are good that you gave sport a try. Alternatively, you may have been encouraged to participate in sport by other family members, such as grandparents, aunts, uncles, or older siblings. In any case, if you tried a sport, your decision about whether to continue it was influenced by critical factors, including whether you felt comfortable in the environment created by the coach and other athletes. Indeed, coaches, teachers, camp counselors, and older children can powerfully influence us as we try to figure out what is important in life. In addition, your attitude about sport may have been shaped by your own success or failure in competition.

Your environment also influences your choice of a particular sport. For example, certain choices such as stickball, handball, or basketball occur as a natural part of city life. Another factor is access (or lack thereof) to recreational facilities that are affordable and comfortable. Your available choices are also affected by climate, tradition, and even the characteristics of your neighborhood. In addition, your parents and siblings affect both your earliest choices and your later decisions about whether to sustain your chosen pursuits. Another influence, and a pervasive one, comes in the form of your peers, especially as you mature and depend less on your family for decisions and support.

Once you are involved in sport, your decision about whether to stay involved is affected by key factors that include your aptitude and the reinforcement you receive from coaches, friends, and role models. Athletes who experience success are more likely to crave the resulting emotional support and rely on it. Role models and heroes may help kids adjust socially to sport participation. When kids watch their heroes and imitate their behavior, work ethic, and love for sport, they learn what is expected of an athlete. In this way, they often imitate their role models in order to see if a role fits them.

On the other hand, children who struggle in sport often reject it. Who wants to play right field, bat last, get picked last, or ride the bench as a substitute? Coaches can also make a child's sporting experience unpleasant if, for example, they utter insensitive remarks or encourage rough play. Even talented athletes often withdraw from the sport scene if they do not measure up to expectations or, in the case of high-performance programs, if they lack the expected drive and intensity.

As we mature, our decisions about sport participation are affected by new factors. Other facets of life interfere, friends drop out of sport, social cliques develop either within or outside of sport, and the economic costs of continued participation may drain one's resources. Adults also face the challenges of work responsibilities, reduced discretionary time, anxiety about their ability, and difficulty in finding playing partners.

Geography, Age, Gender, and Social Class

In addition to family, friends, and coaches, our decisions about sport participation are influenced by a number of other factors. For one thing, our options are affected by the geography of the area in which we live and the sports that are available in that place. For example, in the United States, winter sports are most popular in the northern parts of the country, and water sports thrive in areas near a lake, river, or ocean.

Even so, some intuitions based on geography and weather do not hold true. For instance, the highest U.S. participation rate in tennis is found not in Florida, Texas, or California (which are the three states most often guessed) but in New York City and its surrounding counties—Westchester County in New York and multiple counties in northern New Jersey and southern Connecticut. The reason? These areas have greater affluence, which correlates more highly than weather does with tennis participation.

Sport participation is also affected by age. As we get older, the demands of many traditional sports become daunting due to weight gain and the reduction of flexibility, strength, and endurance. These physical effects can be mitigated only by people who devote hours to training, and even then only to some degree. As a result, some sports that are popular among young people—such as gymnastics, figure skating, wrestling, tackle football, lacrosse, and track and field—are difficult to sustain after the teenage years. The stress on the body is simply too debilitating for most people.

In addition, popular youth sports tend to be team sports, which present a special problem for adults who are unable to arrange their work schedule around practices and competitions. Therefore, individual sports appeal to adults simply because they are easier to organize and schedule. As a result, participation rates for football, soccer, basketball, and baseball drop sharply after people exit their 20s and move naturally into lifetime sports such as golf, tennis, and swimming.

Sport participation is also affected by gender in various ways, including tradition, interest, and sometimes body structure. For instance, girls generally do not play tackle football, rugby, or other collision sports, although some female athletes have broken down traditional barriers in boxing, wrestling, and weightlifting. Now, in fact, women even participate in these sports in the Olympic Games, though the number of contestants and events are admittedly few compared to those for men in these sports.

In the United States, the Title IX federal legislation enacted in 1972 opened the way for female participation in many sports that traditionally had been male oriented. As a result, for example, soccer, basketball, cross country, and lacrosse are now seen as equally accessible to males and females. Conversely, spirit squads (formerly called cheerleading squads) now include both females and males, though the majority of participants are still female.

Perhaps no factor influences sport participation more powerfully than social or economic class. Indeed, whereas some traditions of participation are based on custom and accessibility, others are simply a matter of economics. Though overall trends have their exceptions, some sport favorites are associated with economic class (Coakley and Donnelly 1999; Eitzen 2003; Gruneau 1999). For example, people with a high income, strong education, and high-status occupation tend to participate in individual sports such as golf, tennis, sailing, and skiing. They can arrange their schedule as needed and can afford the cost of club membership, travel, and appropriate equipment and clothing.

In contrast, people in the middle-income group tend to focus on sports that are publicly accessible at modest cost, are school or community sponsored, and do not require membership in an expensive club. At the lower end of the middle-income group, families of skilled workers often choose sports that tend toward competition, power, and machismo. In this group, males especially often choose sports that are characterized by aggression, violence, and physical risk such as football, wrestling, auto racing, and boxing.

People who struggle to make a living tend to have little time or money for sport or recreation. In addition, their work often involves physical labor, which may leave them with little energy for physical games. As a result of these factors, they often find it difficult to choose any recreational activity. The effects of social class are explored more thoroughly in chapter 14.

At the level of elite competition, particularly in individual sports and many Olympic sports, athletes tend to come from upper-middle-class backgrounds (Coakley 2004). The financial sacrifices required to fund a young athlete's development—for example, in sailing, gymnastics, equestrian events, and skiing, none of which is usually offered in public schools—are simply beyond the reach of the average family. Team sports, on the other hand, are often offered in public schools at little cost to participants; therefore, they are financially feasible for many families, which allows athletes of various social classes to compete in team sports such as track and field, soccer, basketball, baseball, and wrestling.

EXPERT'S VIEW

The Sports and Fitness Industry Association

A number of sport marketing firms compile data about sport participation, but none offers a more comprehensive and detailed analysis of sport and fitness activities in the United States than the Sports and Fitness Industry Association (SFIA), formerly known as the Sporting Goods Manufacturers Association. SFIA is a premier trade association for sporting goods manufacturers, retailers, and marketers in the sport products industry. Its purpose is to serve its members by providing information and conducting research to ensure industry vitality and promote sport, fitness, and an active lifestyle. The sport products industry generates more than $60 billion in the United States and $15 billion internationally.

SFIA offers annual participation surveys for all sport and fitness activities, thus enabling sport organizations, industry leaders, and government officials to analyze trends both yearly and over multiple years. Sometimes the longer view is essential. For example, a single-year high percentage of growth for a sport might be an anomaly, but strong growth over five years clearly indicates a trend. In addition, the researchers contracted by SFIA conduct follow-up interviews and focus groups to determine the causes of various trends, such as the recent decline in team sport participation among youth.

The research presented in this chapter on U.S. participation in sport and fitness activity is often derived from the work of SFIA. That work includes actual participation numbers, the percentage of increase or decrease from the previous year, and trends over a five-year period.

Trends in Sport Participation

Just as trends change over time, the research methodology used to study trends has itself become more sophisticated and more accurate in recent years. Table 3.1 summarizes the most exhaustive and up-to-date information available about sport participation based on data collected in 2014 by the Sports and Fitness Industry Association. The numbers reported include participants of all ages from six years onward. For ease of comparison, similar activities are grouped into categories, such as conditioning activities and individual sports. All numbers reflect *millions* of participants out of the total U.S. population of 287,138,000 over the age of six. The group of respondents includes more than 1 million people and is representative of the U.S. population in terms of gender, age, income, household size, region, and population density.

To collect the report data, researchers carried out a total of 19,240 online interviews, including 7,528 individual surveys and 11,712 household surveys. In order to calibrate the response from ethnic groups that typically under-respond, researchers oversampled those groups. They also balanced the data by means of a weighting technique to accurately reflect the U.S. population in terms of gender, age, income, household size, region, and population density. The level of statistical accuracy of this study is illustrated by the fact that a sport with a participation rate of five percent has a confidence level of plus or minus 0.31 percentage points at the 95 percent confidence level. This calculation translates to plus or minus four percent of participants.

The sheer number of U.S. residents who are inactive has continued to increase steadily since 2007; however, for the first time, the overall *percentage* of inactive people declined slightly in 2013. Although this is a hopeful sign, the percentage of inactive people in 2013 was still higher than five years earlier. This improvement can be attributed to large portions of the adult population. More specifically, the level of inactivity was highest among youth aged 6 to 17 (for whom inactivity was at its highest level in the past six years) and adults aged 25 to 34. Groups that showed improvement in physical activity included college-age persons (18 to 24 years old) and adults of age 35 or older.

TABLE 3.1 Trends in Sport Participation

TOTAL PARTICIPATION (IN MILLIONS OF PARTICIPANTS)					
Activity	**2008**	**2012**	**2013**	**1-year percentage change (2012–2013)**	**5-year average annual percentage change (2008–2013)**
Aerobic activities					
Aerobics (high impact)	11,780	16,178	17,323	7.1	8.1
Aerobics (low impact)	23,283	25,707	25,033	−2.6	1.5
Aerobics (step)	9,423	9,577	8,961	−6.4	−0.7
Aquatic exercise	9,512	9,177	8,483	−7.6	−2.2
Cardio kickboxing	4,905	6,725	6,311	−6.2	5.4
Elliptical motion machine	24,435	28,560	27,119	−5.0	2.3
Running and jogging	41,097	51,450	54,188	5.3	5.7
Stair-climbing machine	13,863	12,979	12,642	−2.6	−1.8
Stationary cycling (group)	6,504	8,477	8,309	−2.0	5.3
Stationary cycling (recumbent)	11,104	11,649	11,159	−4.2	0.1
Stationary cycling (upright)	24,918	24,338	24,088	−1.0	−0.7
Swimming (fitness or competition)	N/A	23,216	26,354	13.5	N/A
Treadmill	49,722	50,839	48,166	−5.3	−0.6
Walking for fitness	110,204	114,029	117,351	2.9	1.3
Conditioning activities					
Abdominal machine	20,172	18,907	18,439	−2.5	−1.8
Pilates	9,039	8,519	8,069	−5.3	−2.2
Rowing machine	8,902	9,975	10,183	2.1	2.7
Stretching	36,235	35,873	36,202	0.9	0.0
Tai chi	3,424	3,203	3,469	8.3	0.5
Yoga	17,758	23,253	24,313	4.5	6.5
Strength activities					
Free weights (barbells)	25,821	26,688	25,641	−3.9	−0.1

Activity	2008	2012	2013	1-year percentage change (2012–2013)	5-year average annual percentage change (2008–2013)
Free weights (dumbbells) over 15 lb. (6.8 kg)	N/A	N/A	32,209	N/A	N/A
Free weights (hand weights) under 15 lb.	N/A	N/A	43,164	N/A	N/A
Home gym exercise	25,169	25,492	25,514	0.1	0.3
Weight and resistance machines	38,844	38,999	36,267	−7.0	−1.3
Individual sports					
Adventure racing	809	1,618	2,095	29.5	21.6
Archery	6,180	7,173	7,647	6.6	4.4
Billiards (e.g., pool)	50,054	34,712	34,538	−0.5	−7.1
Bowling	59,417	48,614	46,209	−4.9	−4.9
Boxing for competition	N/A	959	1,134	18.3	N/A
Boxing for fitness	N/A	4,831	5,251	8.7	N/A
Golf	28,571	25,280	24,720	−2.5	−2.8
Horseback riding	11,457	8,423	8,089	−4.0	−6.7
Martial arts	6,818	5,075	5,314	4.7	−4.6
Roller skating (in-line wheels)	10,211	6,647	6,129	−7.8	−9.7
Roller skating (2×2 wheels)	8,388	7,274	6,599	−9.3	−4.6
Scooter riding (nonmotorized)	6,588	4,636	4,061	−12.4	−9.1
Skateboarding	8,118	6,227	6,350	2.0	−4.7
Trail running	4,537	5,806	6,792	17.0	8.5
Triathlon (off road)	543	1,075	1,390	29.3	21.2
Triathlon (road)	943	1,789	2,262	26.5	19.8
Racket sports					
Badminton	7,148	7,278	7,150	−1.8	0.1
Racquetball	4,611	4,070	3,824	−6.0	−3.6

(continued)

Table 3.1 (continued)

Activity	2008	2012	2013	1-year percentage change (2012–2013)	5-year average annual percentage change (2008–2013)
Squash	659	1,290	1,414	9.6	16.8
Table tennis	16,578	16,823	17,079	1.5	0.8
Tennis	17,749	17,020	17,678	3.9	0.0
Team sports					
Baseball	15,539	12,976	13,284	2.4	−3.0
Basketball	26,108	23,708	23,669	−0.2	−1.9
Cheerleading	3,192	3,244	3,235	−0.3	0.3
Field hockey	1,122	1,237	1,474	19.2	5.9
Football (flag)	7,310	5,865	5,610	−5.8	−5.1
Football (tackle)	7,816	6,220	6,165	−0.9	−4.6
Football (touch)	10,493	7,295	7,140	−2.1	−7.3
Gymnastics	3,975	5,115	4,972	-2.8	4.7
Ice hockey	1,871	2,363	2,393	1.2	5.1
Lacrosse	1,092	1,607	1,813	12.8	10.8
Paintball	5,167	3,528	3,595	1.9	−6.8
Roller hockey	1,569	1,367	1,298	−5.1	−3.4
Rugby	654	887	1,183	33.4	13.8
Soccer (indoor)	4,487	4,617	4,803	4.0	1.5
Soccer (outdoor)	13,996	12,944	12,726	−1.7	−1.8
Softball (fast pitch)	2,321	2,624	2,498	−4.8	1.6
Softball (slow pitch)	9,660	7,411	6,868	−7.3	−6.6
Track and field	4,604	4,257	4,071	−4.4	−2.4
Ultimate Frisbee	4,459	5,131	5,077	−1.1	2.7
Volleyball (beach)	4,025	4,505	4,769	5.9	3.6
Volleyball (court)	7,588	6,384	6,433	0.8	−3.2
Volleyball (grass)	5,013	4,008	4,098	0.3	−3.9
Wrestling	3,335	1,922	1,829	−4.8	−10.9

Activity	2008	2012	2013	1-year percentage change (2012–2013)	5-year average annual percentage change (2008–2013)
Water sports					
Boardsailing (windsurfing)	1,213	1,372	1,324	−3.5	1.9
Jet skiing	7,935	6,996	6,413	−8.3	−4.1
Rafting	4,496	3,756	3,836	2.1	−3.0
Sailing	4,006	3,841	3,915	1.9	−0.3
Scuba diving	3,091	2,781	3,174	14.2	0.7
Snorkeling	9,795	8,644	8,700	0.4	−2.3
Surfing	2,407	2,545	2,658	4.4	2.1
Wakeboarding	3,532	3,368	3,316	−1.6	−1.2
Water skiing	5,756	4,434	4,202	−5.2	−6.1

Adapted, by permission, from Sports and Fitness Industry Association (SIFA) 2014.

The U.S. population has seen an explosion of adults over the age of 50 since the "baby boomers" began hitting the mid-century mark in 1996. Many of this group have been and continue to be keenly interested in their physical health and fitness. The AARP reported that in 2014 there were 108.7 million people over the age of 50 in the United States out of a total population of 317 million; that was nearly 35% of the total population (Gillian 2014). However, whereas in previous generations people in this age group may have looked forward to a life of ease and relaxation in retirement, today's older adults realize that they may live 20 or 30 years longer. In fact, trends suggest that many of them will continue working (at least part-time) for several more years, both in order to secure their financial solvency and to feel useful and engaged in society. Given these realities, many believe that improving their personal health and fitness will enable them to enjoy a better quality of life in their later years, allowing them to live with more energy and fewer health concerns.

As people age, they often make fitness activities their top priority. In fact, fitness activities are the most popular choice of exercise among senior citizens. Taking all age groups together, fitness activities are the most popular physical activity, followed by outdoor sports and individual sports. For kids of ages 6 to 12, outdoor sports are most popular, followed by team sports and individual sports.

In the past year, participation rates remained relatively flat in fitness activities, outdoor sports, racket sports, and winter sports. The largest declines were seen in individual sports (3 percent) and team sports (1 percent). More specifically, golf has declined at a steady rate over the past six years, particularly at private golf clubs, which were hit hard by the economic recession that stretched from late 2007 into mid-2009.

In contrast, two smaller sports have posted large increases in recent years: triathlon (traditional on-road, as well as off-road) and adventure racing. These two sports have grown at an annual average of 21 percent over the past five years. Triathlon is likely familiar to you as a combination of swimming, running, and biking performed as fast as possible over certain distances. The governing body of this Olympic sport in the United States is USA Triathlon, which boasts more than 140,000 members.

On the other hand, adventure racing (also called expedition racing) may be new to you. It includes a combination of two or more disciplines from among the following: navigation, orienteering, cross country running, mountain biking, paddling, climbing, and performing rope skills. Adventure racing is typically co-ed and is performed in teams. You can get started in the sport by visiting the nearest local or national park, but races are scheduled throughout the world in a wide variety of terrains. Each race has its own special character, and the race director often challenges racers with unique and unexpected tasks. A given competition can last for anywhere from two hours to 10 days. According to SFIA (2014), adventure racing registered 2,095,000 participants in 2014 (United States Adventure Racing Association 2014).

Two water sports have also seen significant increases in participation. Kayaking boasts a 10 percent annual increase in each of the past five years, and stand-up paddling has averaged an annual increase of more than 30 percent over the past two years (SIFA 2014).

Interest has also skyrocketed in U.S. health and fitness clubs, whose membership rolls have grown over the past 20 years from 20 million to a record high of 53 million in 2014. That number represents 18 percent of the population, and members visited their club an average of 103 times in 2013 (International Health, Racquet, and Sportsclub Association 2014). Key fitness categories are generally accepted as including the following: aerobic activity, which improves cardiovascular and respiratory function through continuous activity; muscular strength and endurance training; and stretching to improve range of motion in the joints. Participation in these categories far exceeds any single-sport participation rate because they are performed by people of all age groups; in addition, people who participate in sport also use these fitness activities to supplement their sport-specific training.

Here are the raw numbers for specific fitness categories:

Aerobics

Fitness walking	117,351,000
Running or jogging (outside)	54,188,000
Treadmill	48,166,000
Total	219,705,000

Muscular Strength and Endurance Training

Hand weights	43,164,000
Dumbbells	32,209,000
Barbells	25,641,000
Total	101,014,000

Stretching

36,202,000

Team sport activities showed a 1 percent overall decrease, thus continuing a trend of decline over the past five years. Slight drops in participation were seen even in the popular sports of basketball, baseball, softball, soccer, and volleyball. Other sports that declined include paintball, roller hockey, track and field, and wrestling (which has dropped more than 10 percent each year for the past five years). Football has also dropped about 5 percent annually over the past five years in all of its forms—tackle, touch, and flag.

In contrast, some smaller sports increased their participation rates (the increases look particularly large when expressed in terms of percentages due to these sports' lower number of participants). Here are the average annual growth rates (in terms of percentage) for the largest gainers over the past five years:

Rugby	13.8
Lacrosse	10.8
Field hockey	5.9
Ice hockey	5.1
Gymnastics	4.7
Beach volleyball	3.6

In an intriguing footnote to the overall drop in team-sport participation, a recent SFIA report (2013b) finds clear evidence of a trend toward specialization in team sports among youth. Specifically, 15 of the 24 sports tracked showed an increase in the number of "core" participants, whereas only 5 sports showed such an increase in the previous year. A core participant is defined as a regular or frequent participant, as distinguished from a casual participant. In other words, it appears that fewer kids are playing multiple team sports or playing a team sport casually. Thus the overall drop in team-sport participation appears to be influenced by an increase in single-sport specialization at younger ages, as well as dropouts

ACTIVITY TIME-OUT

Trends in Sport and Exercise Participation

Study the chart (shown in table 3.1) about sport and fitness participation for 2013, then identify at least five trends. In particular, note changes that have occurred over five years, since a mere one-year change could be an aberration. You might also combine some activities into a larger category (for example, using free weights of various types). As part of your analysis, suggest factors that might have affected the changes in popularity for certain activities. Among the many possibilities are the aging of the adult population, economic factors, and the availability of new kinds of exercise equipment.

due to overuse injuries, burnout, safety concerns, marginalization of recreational players, and participation costs.

Various researchers and scholars blame the decline in youth physical activity on time spent watching television, as well as the rise of video games and computer use, all of which combine for an estimated average of seven and a half hours per day. In addition, many schools have eliminated recess time and either reduced or eliminated physical education classes due to budget cuts or an emphasis on core academic subjects.

Other equally significant factors include a sharp reduction (over the past 20 years) in unorganized or "pickup" games, an emphasis in youth sport on elite players, and the tendency of parents or coaches (or both) to encourage kids to specialize in one sport at an early age. Among those who do still participate in pickup games, the leading sports are basketball and touch football—perhaps because all you need is a ball, some buddies, and a place to play.

Some of the statistics that point to these trends are presented in table 3.2 (Sporting Goods Manufacturers Association 2009).

TABLE 3.2 Percentage of Play in Organized Sport Versus Pickup Games

Sport	Organized	Unorganized (pickup)	Other
Baseball	52	44	4
Basketball	36	60	4
Ice hockey	48	46	6
Football (touch)	19	77	4
Football (tackle)	49	49	2
Football (flag)	48	48	4
Soccer (indoor)	70	27	3
Soccer (outdoor)	60	36	4
Softball (slow)	62	35	3
Softball (fast)	76	19	5

Reprinted, by permission, from Sporting Goods Manufacturers Association, 2009, *Organized sport play dominates team sport market*. Available: www.sgma.com/press/153_Organized-Sport-Play-Dominates-Team-Sports-Market

While participation has declined in traditional pickup games, there has been a rise in the relatively new category called "extreme sport," which are also referred to as "action sport" or "adventure sport." Generally, these sports involve some amount of perceived danger to the participant due to speed, height, high exertion, or spectacular stunts. Extreme sport is usually the purview of relatively younger participants rather than adults. The competitions are somewhat uncontrolled due to environmental variables, such as weather and terrain.

This type of sport has been popularized by television and other media sources, especially in the form of the X Games, which were first held in the United States in 1995. Their attraction for most youth participants lies in the fact that they typically involve individual competition in which athletes are not restricted to following the rules and directions of a coach. For a closer look at extreme sports, see chapter 6.

Sport Spectators

Watching sport has become part of the American way of life. Since the 1920s, commercial sport has steadily attracted more and more **sport spectators**, primarily because people generally now have more leisure time and more money to spend. The number of people who watch sport rises each year, and the money generated from sport spectatorship, sponsorship, advertising, and product sales has increased dramatically.

Unlike participating in sport, watching or listening to sport doesn't take much effort or talent. It is a form of entertainment that appeals to millions of people for a variety of reasons. For example, a spectator may enjoy the particular sport itself, may play or have played the sport, or may simply enjoy the competition and drama inherent in the spectacle of superior athletes demonstrating their prowess.

The number of spectators who watch live events continues to increase, but the most significant growth around the world results from the availability of sport via television and the Internet. Sport broadcasting began in the United States in the late 1940s, when there were fewer than 190,000 TV sets in the country. At that time, NBC broadcast the baseball World Series, heavyweight boxing matches, and the Army–Navy football game. In the early years of televised sport, viewer growth was enormous, and, as broadcast provid-

IN THE ARENA WITH . . .

Tough Mudder

Tough Mudder is the latest craze among outdoor adventure enthusiasts, who are typically in their 20s and 30s. This endurance event tests participants physically, mentally, and emotionally as they navigate obstacle courses based on the 10- to 12-mile (about 16- to 19-kilometer) military courses designed for British special forces. Each Tough Mudder course features 20 to 25 obstacles that play on common human fears, such as fire, water, electricity, and heights. Participants are encouraged to work in teams to overcome the obstacles, and there are no time limits. Typically, about three-quarters of participants finish a given course, albeit a little worse for wear—and definitely muddy.

Tough Mudder was founded by two Englishmen living in New York and one of them, Will Dean, developed the idea while attending Harvard Business School and came up with the idea as part of a business plan competition. It didn't win the contest, but soon afterward, in 2010, the pair founded the organization and held three events. That number grew to 35 events (in four countries) in 2012 and then to 53 events in 2013, putting the organization's total number of registrants over a million in just three years. Tough Mudder supports a military charity in each location where it holds an event, and participants have donated more than $6 million to the U.S. Wounded Warrior Project. The organization is now worth $70 million and has partnered with companies including Under Armour, Degree, Bic, Wheaties, Dos Equis, Advil, Clif Bar, and CamelBak (Tough Mudder 2014).

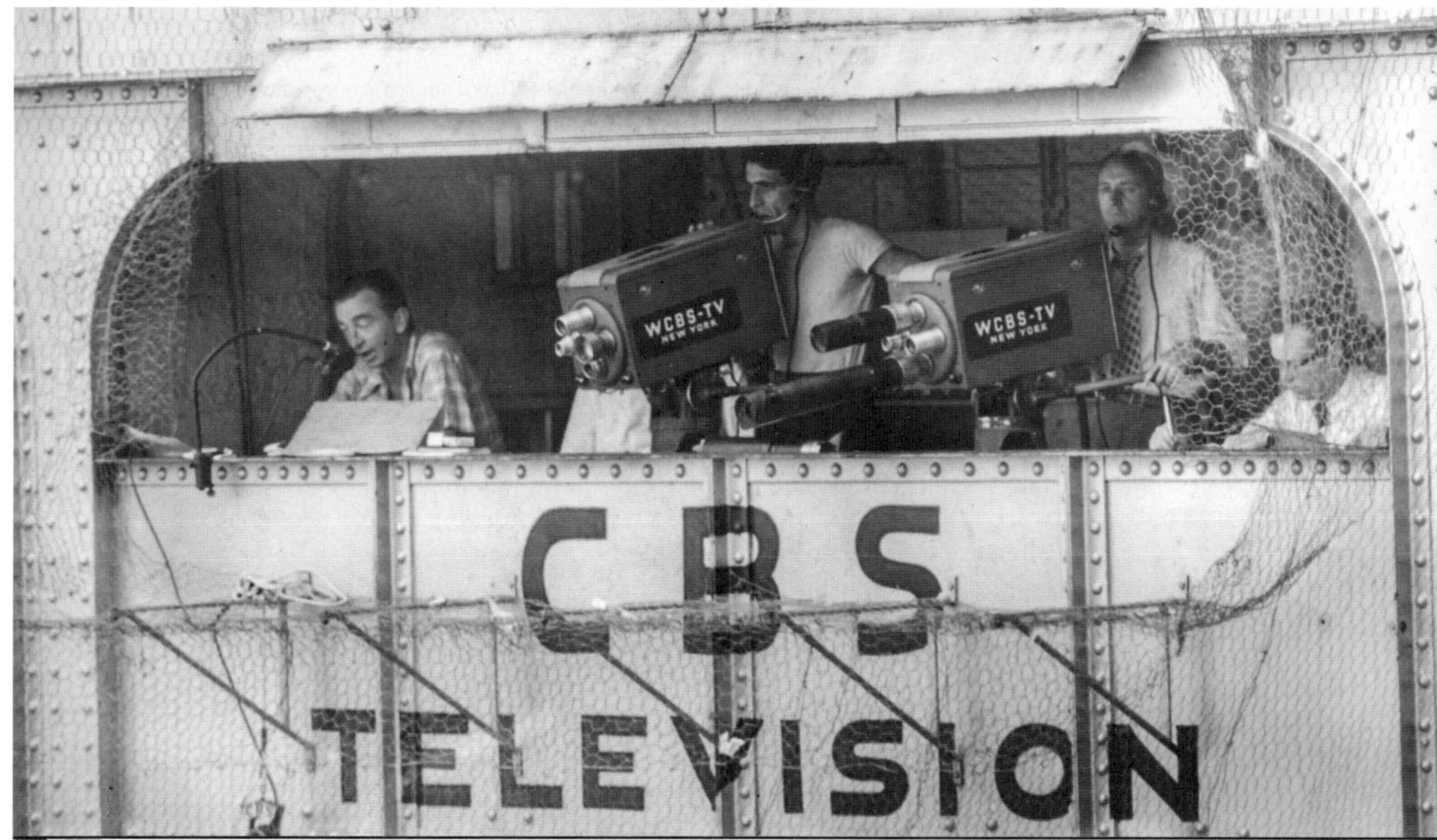

Early sport broadcasts, such as this one in 1947 of a baseball game between the Brooklyn Dodgers and the St. Louis Cardinals, reached a very limited audience. Today, a single sporting event can reach millions of people through TV and Internet viewership.

ers improved their technical presentation, the popularity of sport continued to explode. As more people watched, advertisers spent more money to reach a sport audience that consisted primarily of young men. Great moments in sports were shared by millions of viewers and became the topic of discussion at work. In fact, televised sport not only promoted sport viewing but also helped the television industry grow to heights unimagined in its early days.

In the most recent two decades, viewing of network sport broadcasts has generally declined in the United States, as all-sport and other cable channels have begun to offer more choices and as viewer interest has expanded to include a wider variety of sports. Overall, however, despite a sharp drop in baseball viewing and the relatively flat viewing statistics for football, sport entertainment on television continues to thrive. These days, events are televised nationally in college sport, high school sport, and even youth sport. Fans can tune in to a variety of sporting events at almost any hour or check up-to-the-minute scores on the web.

As the sport audience grows, so does the willingness of commercial sponsors to pay for an advertisement during events such as the Super Bowl. For the 2015 Super Bowl, the average price for a 30-second commercial was about $4.5 million depending on the placement of the ad during the game and the number of spots that the marketer purchased. That average price of $4.5 million marks a 75% increase over the last 10 years, but during that same period the size of the TV audience has nearly doubled (Tadena 2015).

Social class and economic status affect spectatorship, as they do participation. Most white-collar workers are college graduates and therefore are natural supporters of college sport teams. Long after graduation, many of them assiduously follow their college team, donate money to its athletic programs, and buy tickets to major sport events. In contrast, people who do not attend college tend to feel little affinity for college sport and focus instead on professional sport.

In addition to college sport, the most affluent spectators tend to identify with sports such as polo, yachting, sailing, sport car racing, and thoroughbred racing. In contrast, members of the upper-middle class tend to enjoy tennis, golf, sailing, and skiing, whereas members of the working class often lean toward auto racing, wrestling, bowling, pool, boxing, demolition derby, and roller derby.

The relatively high cost of attending many popular sporting events discourages families with modest means from attending more than once a year. The expense for a family of four (two parents and two children) to attend a major professional game likely includes something like the following: four moderately priced tickets, four soft drinks, two beers, four hot dogs, two programs, parking, and two adult-sized caps. If we total up the cost of these items, National Football League (NFL) games are by far the most expensive at $459.65 per family.

Similar costs can be estimated for the National Basketball Association (NBA) at $315.66 and for the National Hockey League (NHL) at $354.82. Strikingly, the comparable cost for a Major League Baseball (MLB) game is $207.80—a real bargain as compared with the other sports (Team Marketing Report 2013). Remember that these figures each represent a league-wide average for moderately priced tickets. Tickets cost more in larger cities where the cost of doing business is higher—for example, New York, Los Angeles, and Chicago.

Professional baseball, which is often thought of as a working person's game, actually attracts spectators from all social classes, and this mass appeal may have contributed to its long-held reputation as America's national pastime. Likewise, professional football attracts spectators of all incomes. Perhaps the fact that baseball and football stadiums can accommodate fans of all economic levels adds to their appeal. Affluent spectators can ply their guests with food and drink in luxury suites that cost thousands of dollars per game; alternatively, they might choose to sit right by the action, either behind home plate or on the 50-yard line. Meanwhile, at the same game, spectators who are less affluent can use saved-up funds to purchase a more modestly priced seat in the bleachers, the end zone, or the upper rows.

The general socioeconomic trends just described refer to live attendance at sporting events. If we factor in sport television viewing—which mitigates the expense of sport viewing for most people—spectators choose their sports not by expense but by interest, history, and familiarity. For example, people may watch sports with which they identify through previous participation; they may also focus on performers with whom they feel a connection. Television has brought spectator sport and the performances of the world's finest athletes to nearly every home in the United States. As a result, today's commercial sponsors reach audiences that include both rich and poor, both male and female, and both young and old.

The growing interest shown by girls and women in watching sport has caused a major shift in the cross section of sport spectators. That growth has resulted in part from the tremendous increase in female sport participation as a result of Title IX. This landmark legislation has produced a new generation of women who enjoy watching sport, can identify with the athletes, and generally include sport in their life. Gone are the days when the men retired to the den to watch sport while women retired to the kitchen or living room.

Starting in the 1960s, the goals of the second wave of the women's movement in the United States were to grant expanded freedom to women, equal opportunity, and control over their lives. More specifically, higher education became available in virtually every field, and the place of women in the workforce and politics was acknowledged and rewarded. The traditional feminine role of women was forever changed (Napikoski 2015). As part of this process, the more traditional feminine traits of nurturance and support were joined by other traits, such as vigor, strength, competitiveness, and poise under pressure. The feminist movement reveled in seeing women display athleticism, grit, and courage in competitive sport on television. Hundreds of thousands of women donned sneakers and workout clothes to exercise, sweat, and improve their body image and athletic skills, thus modeling the exceptional athletes they admired on television.

Spectators are also influenced by racial background. Certain races have traditionally participated in particular sports, thus producing heroes with whom other members of their race can identify. For example, Hispanics are proud of their superstars in boxing and MLB, while African

Americans love to see their heroes dominate in professional basketball and football. Of course, nontraditional heroes sometimes emerge, such as Tiger Woods in golf and the Williams sisters in tennis, or Dirk Nowitzki or Steve Nash in basketball, thus attracting nontraditional spectators who want to follow their struggles and achievements.

Trends in Spectator Sports

Spectator sports can be divided into two major categories: those watched live and those followed through media (such as TV, Internet, and radio). As a result, accurately counting a sport's total number of watchers is somewhat more difficult than merely tracking attendance at a sporting event, particularly a professional event. Organizers of amateur sports, such as youth sports and most high school sports, do not charge admission and therefore cannot provide attendance records.

One overall statistic is clear: Sport watching has grown steadily over the years, and the availability of sport on television has contributed to that growth. More specifically, certain sports have enjoyed a recent boost in popularity, including figure skating and women's college basketball. Of course, sport interest is also boosted by the televised Olympics, which alternate between the Summer and Winter Games every two years.

Let's take a look now at trends in the choice of favorite spectator sport (table 3.3). In a study released by Harris Polls in 2013, more than 2,000 adults were asked, "If you had to choose one, which one of these sports would you say is your favorite?" In a similar 2013 Gallup Poll, the responses were to the question, "Which is your favorite sport to watch?" The third column shows the result for 2013 by Global Sports Media where respondents were allowed to pick their three or four top sports rather than just one, thus producing higher percentages for most sports.

No other sport than those listed was chosen by more than 1 percent of respondents. Professional football not only ranked first but also has shown a 10 percent increase in popularity over the past 20 years.

TABLE 3.3 Percentage of Americans Who Picked Each Sport as Their Favorite

Sport	Harris Poll	Gallup Poll	Global Sports Media
Football	34 (professional)	39 (college and professional)	51 (college and professional)
Professional baseball	13	14	33
College football	11	N/A	N/A
Auto racing	8	21	14
Men's basketball	7 (professional)	12 (college and professional)	29 (college and professional)
Professional ice hockey	5	3	12
Men's college basketball	3	N/A	N/A
Tennis	2 (men's)	3 (men's)	9 (men's and women's)
Golf	2 (men's)	2 (men's)	12 (men's and women's)
Soccer	2	4	8
Swimming	2	<1	N/A

Data from Harris Poll 2015; Gallup Poll 2013; Global Sports Media 2013.

We can also rank differences in what is being watched by gender (see table 3.4) and other demographic differences. The differences highlighted in table 3.5 involve age, race, geographic location, education, and political inclination (Harris Polls 2013).

As shown in table 3.6, the number of people attending major sporting events in person continues to climb. In the most striking example of growth, women's college basketball has increased its attendance figures four times over.

TABLE 3.4 Fans of Various Sports (Percentage of U.S. Population by Gender)

Men		Women	
Professional football	77	Figure skating	60
College football	70	Professional football	60
Professional baseball	58	Professional baseball	46
College basketball	49	College football	39
Professional basketball	42	Professional basketball	36
Professional golf	40	College basketball	32
Auto racing	39	Professional tennis	25
Professional ice hockey	28	Auto racing	22
Professional tennis	24	Professional golf	20
Figure skating	21	Professional ice hockey	18
Professional wrestling	14	Professional wrestling	7

TABLE 3.5 Demographic Variations Among Sport by Percentage of Indicated Population Group

Sport	All adults	Highest	Lowest
Pro football	32%	43% Generation X 37% Easterners 35% Moderates	25% Millennials 25% Post-graduates 26% Liberals
Baseball	16%	23% Easterners 22% Liberals 20% Baby boomers	10% Adults with children 12% Millennials 12% Midwesterners
College football	10%	22% Post-graduates 16% Southerners 16% Conservatives	3% Easterners 6% Urban adults 6% Income $34,900 or less
Auto racing	7%	12% High school or less 12% Income $34,900 10% Southern, conservatives, rural areas	2% College graduates 2% Income above $75,000 4% Millennials

Adapted, by permission, from Harris Polls 2015. www.harrisinteractive.com/NewsRoom/HarrisPolls/tabid/447/ctl/ReadCustom%20 Default/mid/1508/ArticleId/1546/Default.aspx

TABLE 3.6 In-Person Attendance at Sporting Events (in Millions)

Sport	1990	1994	2001	2007	2008	2010
Baseball (MLB)	55.5	71.2	73.2	80.8	79.9	74.4
Football (NFL)	17.6	14.8	20.5	22.2	21.8	21.1
Football (college)	35.3	36.5	40.4	48.7	48.8	49.6
Basketball (NBA and WNBA)	18.5	19.3	21.4	23.6	21.9	N/A
Basketball (college men)	28.8	28.3	28.9	32.8	33.3	32.8
Basketball (college women)	2.8	4.6	8.8	10.8	11.1	11.1
Ice hockey (NHL)	12.3	15.7	20.3	20.8	21.2	20.9

Data do not include TV viewers.

Reprinted from U.S. Census Bureau, 2012, *Statistical abstract of the United States*. Available: www.census.gov/compendia/statab/2012/tables/12s1244.pdf

If you study the table closely, you might notice that Major League Baseball clearly draws the most spectators per year, but consider the fact that it relies on a schedule of 162 games per year per team. In contrast, college football is typically limited to 11 or 12 games per year, but attendance at the games involving high-prestige football programs averages more than 100,000 fans per game.

While professional football is the most popular sport with fans overall, in-game attendance for college football is clearly more robust, partially because it includes more than 100 major college programs and many more Division II and Division III programs. In the southern region of the United States, the popularity of big-time college football surpasses even that of professional football.

APPLYING SOCIAL THEORY

Conflict Theorists and Participant-Versus-Spectator Trends

Now that you have analyzed participation trends in sport and physical activity, as well as trends in sport spectatorship, assume the perspective of a conflict theorist. From that point of view, what is your overall assessment of the trends in participation versus spectatorship? Does the United States show growth and interest in raising its citizens' level of physical activity? Or is it becoming a nation of watchers of elite athletes rather than people who participate in activity for their own health, recreation, and well-being. Once you have taken a position, suggest possible causes of these trends from the perspective of a conflict theorist.

Marketing to Participants and Spectators

The business of sport generates considerable income for a variety of parties, including educational institutions, the U.S. Olympic Committee, national sport governing bodies, the media, and corporate sponsors. Cities pour millions of dollars into facilities for professional teams, as well as facilities for use by their residents. Manufacturers of sporting goods produce equipment, uniforms, and footwear. The clothing industry designs casual apparel that can be worn on the street and is also acceptable for physical activity.

All of these groups have a strong interest in promoting their products and services to either sport participants, spectators, or both. As a result, the money they spend on marketing has increased dramatically over the years as the popularity of sport has ballooned. In fact, some universities now offer degrees in sport business and emphasize sport marketing as a career path.

Sport marketing must adapt as various sports rise or fall in popularity, new classes of potential participants or spectators emerge, and demographic patterns shift. One example of the changing marketplace is the growing opportunity to globalize sport marketing. Soccer is currently the most popular sport in the world, followed by tennis. The global reach of these sports exposes the products of their sponsors worldwide. Similarly, the leaders of U.S. sports such as football, basketball, and baseball have worked hard to expand into overseas markets in order to increase revenue. Satellite television and the Internet have allowed events to be seen around the world, thus helping popularize particular sports and their athletes and attracting huge amounts of sponsorship money.

Organizations intending to market their sport or product to sport participants need to accomplish multiple tasks. Specifically, they must care-

Best Buy receives great advertising through its use of signage in baseball stadiums.

fully research the historical perspective of people who have tended to participate, identify potential customers, and launch marketing campaigns targeting those audiences. For example, not long ago, many sport advertisements almost exclusively featured male athletes, and organizations that wanted to attract potential female consumers had to change their advertising by including females in their portrayals of athletes as role models.

As a result, a number of female athletes have capitalized on their athletic credentials and marketability—for example, Maria Sharapova, Danica Patrick, Lindsey Vonn, Serena Williams, Candace Parker, and Swin Cash. Male athletes who currently top the marketability list include LeBron James, Roger Federer, Phil Mickelson, Kobe Bryant, and Dale Earnhardt Jr. In fact, these athletes and other top professionals often earn more money from commercial endorsements than they do from their athletic performances.

Consider Kevin Durant of the NBA's Oklahoma City Thunder, who was voted league MVP in 2014 and has led the league in scoring four times. When Durant was offered a 10-year, $285 million deal by Under Armour to ditch his endorsement deal with Nike, Nike countered with a new deal worth more than $300 million and retained his endorsement. In contrast, Durant's two-year basketball contract at that time paid him "only" about $41 million (Money 2014).

Another change in sport marketing involves the efforts by leaders in golf and tennis to reach out to African Americans. The success of Tiger Woods and Serena and Venus Williams has provided the perfect opportunity for officials in these sports to demonstrate openness to people of all racial backgrounds and to actively recruit them by means of advertising. In a former generation, Zina Garrison, an African American who ranked number four in women's tennis, couldn't command a clothing endorsement contract for most of her career. Instead, she chose to wear fellow player Martina Navratilova's signature line until eventually Reebok offered her a contract near the end of her career. Twenty years ago, companies saw little value in positioning Garrison as a role model for advertising their clothes because few African Americans were interested in tennis.

Sponsors support the sports that attract participants or spectators who most closely parallel the target consumers of their product. Thus, for example, Mercedes and Lincoln sponsor professional tennis to promote their luxury cars, Chevrolet sponsors auto racing to promote its trucks, and Miller and Budweiser sponsor professional football to promote their beers. Similarly, manufacturers of women's products naturally select women's sports as a way to reach their intended market. At the same time, advertising in sports (such as football) that attract a strong male audience tends to feature attractive women in sexually suggestive ads in an attempt to pique the interest of male viewers.

In trying to present an inclusive message, advertisers are careful to design ads that feature members of various ethnic and racial groups, both genders, and various ages. Showing this range of diversity can be tricky in the advertising business, because visual images of one or two athletes tend to be more powerful than collages of many smaller images.

In addition, television ads for sport products tend to use music and speech patterns that match those of the potential customer. For example, an ad targeting young people is likely to use styles, sounds, and performers that a youthful audience recognizes and admires. Similarly, if a marketing campaign for fitness activities is intended to reach people around the age of 50, the models in the ads must look like the people in this particular audience—or at least look how members of this audience would like to look. Watching a buff model who is, say, 25 years younger does not speak to an older person where he or she lives.

Chapter Summary

Sport participants range from youth league athletes to Olympic athletes. People at each level of play participate for certain reasons. In spite of the fact that the overwhelming number of participants play simply to have fun, the majority of attention and funding is lavished on the relatively small number of athletes who make it in high-performance sport.

Trends in U.S. adult sport participation show that fitness-oriented activities are now more popular than competition activities. Trends in U.S. youth sport participation show that a significant number of youth drop out of sport by their teenage years and that participation in extreme sports is increasing. For most sports, organized play attracts more participants than casual or pickup (unorganized) games.

Sport spectators come from all ages, races, and economic backgrounds. College graduates are more likely to support their college teams, whereas those who did not attend college tend to support professional teams. Working-class spectators often enjoy violent sports, whereas people with higher incomes are more drawn to sports that are traditionally supported at private clubs and are more expensive to watch or play.

Professional and college football are the top spectator sports in the United States. Baseball ranks second, and basketball trails by a significant margin in third place. If we separate fans by gender, women rank figure skating as their top spectator sport, followed closely by professional and college football. In the past 20 years, the number of U.S. sport spectators has nearly doubled in many sports, but in the past five years many of the numbers have been stable or even declined slightly, probably due to economic circumstances.

Finally, trends in sport marketing are based on multiple factors: the changing demographics of society, sport preferences, and the separation between marketing to potential participants and marketing to potential spectators.

STUDENT OUTCOMES

After reading this chapter, you will know the following:

- The powerful economic influence of sport
- How professional sport affects national and local economies
- How collegiate athletic programs profit

Business of Sport

Business of Sport

Would you like to own a National Football League (NFL) team? Are you kidding? According to *Forbes* magazine, the average NFL team is worth $1.43 billion. Just over a decade ago, when Forbes first valued NFL teams, the average franchise was worth "only" $288 million. By 2014, the highest-value teams were estimated at $3.2 billion (Dallas), $2.6 billion (New England), and $2.4 billion (Washington) (Ozanian 2014).

Do you know of any other financial venture in which you could essentially triple your money, especially during a period of economic uncertainty? As the most popular U.S. sport league, the NFL enjoys strong television contracts, rabid fan support, and a plethora of new stadiums designed to maximize on-site profit. What does the NFL do with all of this money? For one thing, it follows a philosophy set by former NFL commissioner Pete Rozelle in which revenue is shared among the franchises to help enable success for every team—and thus provide hope for fans in every city that next year could be "their year."

Sport is big business, both in the United States and around the world. In 2013, Americans spent about $34.3 billion on spectator sport, and the total sport industry for 2014 was estimated to include $485 billion in spending (Plunkett Research 2014). Since the business of sport involves entertainment, we pay for the right to watch it, root for our team, forget about work or other weighty matters, and just enjoy life. Some of us also participate directly in sport, and sporting goods manufacturers value our use of their products, venues, and programs. Other people simply observe athletes performing, and most of us thrill to witness compelling athletic feats, especially in the midst of pressurized competition at events such as the Super Bowl, the World Series, and the Olympic Games.

By every measure, the money generated by sport events, spent by sport consumers, and allocated for sport sponsorship has increased dramatically in recent years. Of course, the amount of money spent on recreational sport is modest as compared with the amount generated by professional sport. For that reason, most of this chapter focuses on the business of professional sport, which is sometimes referred to as **corporate sport**. At the same time, though collegiate athletics is reputedly an amateur venture, its business aspects at large Division I universities are undeniable. Therefore, the chapter also considers the business of college sport. In addition, it looks at career opportunities produced in recent years by the rapid economic growth of sport.

Sport and the Economy

One primary role of both participation sport and spectator sport has always been to entertain people during their time off from work. However, though sport entertainment in the past was usually casual and relaxed, today's sport is often organized, mechanized, marketed, and administered as a business. Indeed, commercial interests influence virtually every decision made in both collegiate and professional sport. As a result, events are rated by television audience share, ticket sales, website hits, concession sales, sponsor revenue, and media coverage. In this environment, wins and losses are viewed as important in no small part because they influence these other standards of measurement.

How did this happen? When did commercialization begin to take over sport? In the nineteenth century, almost 90 percent of U.S. workers were farmers or skilled tradespeople. As U.S. society became industrialized, many workers quit self-employment to join larger companies. In this new model, each worker was merely one piece of a larger machine, helping to produce whatever goods or services the company provided (Leonard 1980; Rice, Hutchinson, and Lee 1958; Spears and Swanson 1978). In other words, the worker was fitted into the overall hierarchy of the larger corporation.

As sport grew more businesslike, the corporate model crept into the organization of every sport franchise and governing body. Athletes were encouraged to provide their services for the good of the larger entity, to contribute to the bottom line, and to share in the profits with the head or owner of their sport organization. Coaches became the supervisors of athletes, who were sometimes asked to go against their personal choices for the good of the team or organization. Players who demonstrated a good work ethic, exemplary moral character, and a willingness to sacrifice for the good of the team were admired and held up as role models. Those who deviated from that path were labeled as malcontents and given only limited playing time or cut from the team.

As the sport industry grew in economic power, it attracted commercial interests that could benefit from that power by influencing its organization. As the industry continued to develop, the role of the athlete increasingly became that of serving the organization. The growth of commercial sport would not have occurred without the presence of various conditions that supported rapid expansion, such as the following.

- In order to watch or participate in sport, people need time away from work. The life of a farmer left little time for activities outside of work, but industrialization changed the average worker's opportunity for leisure time.
- People also need money to spend on sport. Therefore, in order for sport business to succeed, society must create an economic environment in which the majority of its people can afford to be sport consumers.
- People must live in relatively concentrated areas in order to use sport facilities, travel to sport events, and identify with a local professional sport team. Small cities and rural areas can rarely support a professional team, so they focus instead on local college or high school sport.

Athletes such as Billy Orr, Herb Pennock, Weldon Wyckoff, Joe Bush, Bob Shawkey, and Amos Strunk of the 1914 Philadelphia Athletics played baseball during a time that coincided with a shift toward more industry in the United States.

- Media outlets (whether print, audio, video, or digital) must provide access to sport and to athletes in order to sustain spectators' interest in professional sport.
- Facilities for presenting professional sport must be constructed, financed, and refurbished in order to maintain sport revenue streams.

Ownership in Professional Sport

For the most part, U.S. professional sport franchises are owned by extremely wealthy people (overwhelmingly male) who benefit from ownership both personally and financially. They may use their team to directly increase their personal wealth or to provide a tax advantage that helps offset other business gains.

Originally, owners of professional sport teams were people who loved the game. They spent much of their personal time and money promoting the game and strengthening their team and league as profitable businesses. The next wave of owners were similarly dedicated to sport and did not use their professional teams to promote other businesses. Examples include Tom Yawkey of the Boston Red Sox (owner from 1933 to 1976), Phil Wrigley of the Chicago Cubs (1932 to 1977), and August "Gussie" Busch Jr. of the St. Louis Cardinals (1953 to 1989). As this generation of owners died off, however, a new breed of ownership emerged.

These days, more and more owners are corporate conglomerates that purchase sport franchises in order to help them market and promote their other products. There are some exceptions; for

IN THE ARENA WITH . . .

The Irsay Sisters

The National Football League is essentially run by millionaire white men, and there have been only a few exceptions in the history of the league. Currently, only two principal team owners are female: Martha Ford of the Detroit Lions and Virginia McCaskey of the Chicago Bears. However, a fresh new trio of young women, daughters of Indianapolis Colts owner Jim Irsay, recently stepped into leadership roles in the wake of their father's legal troubles and struggle with addiction. After pleading guilty to driving under the influence in 2014, Jim Irsay was suspended from by the NFL for six games and fined $500,000.

The Irsay women, in birth order, are Carlie Irsay-Gordon, Casey Foyt, and Kalen Irsay. They have previously been active with the Colts, serving first as interns, then working in administrative positions, and, since 2012, each holding the title of vice chair and owner. During their father's absence, Carlie Irsay-Gordon, the oldest of the three, took the lead role in making decisions and representing the team in NFL meetings. She is a graduate of Skidmore College and is working on her PhD in psychology. The middle sister, Casey, graduated from Indiana University with a sport marketing degree and has focused on marketing and community relations with the Colts. The youngest sister, Kalen, is also a graduate of Indiana and has a background in sport management; she is involved in corporate sales and community outreach for the Colts.

Although the Irsay women have stepped into leadership positions, future ownership of the team remains a bit hazy. In order to succeed their father as team owners, they will have to address serious tax hurdles. According to experts in wealth transfer, Irsay's daughters might owe upwards of $400 million in taxes as a result of inheriting the team at its current franchise value. That's a large challenge to overcome, but don't count out these three talented women who plan to make their mark in the "old boys club" of the NFL (Schoettle 2014; Wells 2014).

example, the Green Bay Packers football club is owned by members of the general public, who hold shares in the team. More generally, however, club owners have evolved into corporate managers who may or may not consider the welfare of the team or the host city in making their decisions, which tend to focus on the bottom line. Thus the guiding forces behind ownership decisions today involve issues such as player depreciation, capital gains tax laws, and potential income.

This change in the character of ownership has led to some dramatic moments in the sport business. For example, in 1984 the Baltimore Colts, a proud and storied franchise, were surreptitiously moved to Indianapolis to benefit the owner, Robert Irsay, in the form of financial inducements and a new stadium. Twelve years later, Baltimore retaliated by enticing Art Modell and the Cleveland Browns to forsake Cleveland and move to Baltimore to become the Baltimore Ravens.

In some cases, individual club owners still own a professional sport franchise, perhaps in order to find fun and excitement, boost their ego, or gain a sense of power. Others simply enjoy being around famous athletes. Some owners are actively involved in day-to-day operations, standing on the field with athletes and consulting with coaches about decisions. Others leave the sport itself to professional coaches and managers and stick to the business side of the franchise.

Making Money From Professional Sport

Virtually all professional sport franchises make money, despite some owners' claims of losing money and their requests for cities to bear the brunt of the cost of building new sport facilities. The NFL is by far the most lucrative league, taking in more than $9 billion annually, an amount driven largely by $5 billion in television contracts. In comparison, Major League Baseball (MLB) brings in $8 billion with only $1.5 billion from TV, the National Basketball Association (NBA) generates $5 billion with just under $1 billion from TV, and the National Hockey League (NHL) takes in $3.3 billion including $600 million from TV (ESPN 2013a; Forbes 2013; USA Today 2014; Yglesias 2014).

Let's look now at the ways in which an owner might make an investment in a sport franchise worthwhile. Not all team owners take advantage of all of these factors, but many do.

Investment

Professional team franchises experience **appreciation**, growing in value every year. As a result, a club that was once purchased for hundreds of thousands dollars might now be bought for hundreds of millions. No sport owner of a major sport franchise has ever lost money on the initial capital investment, and putting money into a professional team has always paid off in the long run. In addition, if an owner can get a new venue built with funding sources other than his or her own money, the value of the franchise is increased by $30 million to $40 million.

To give you some idea of how the value of an NFL franchise can grow, consider that Jerry Jones purchased the Dallas Cowboys in 1989 for $150 million. The estimated value of the franchise in 2014 was $3.2 billion, which means that the Cowboys have been a pretty good investment for Jones. The most recent sale of an NFL franchise was that of the Buffalo Bills to Terry and Kim Pegula at a reported price of $1.1 billion even though the Forbes magazine estimated the team's worth at $935 million, ranking it 31 out of 32 teams in the league (Isidore 2014).

Taxes

Though some owners may see a loss in their franchise's bottom line at the end of a given year, they usually go into that particular year expecting such an outcome. In fact, they may balance those losses against significant profits made in their other businesses, thereby saving money by reducing their overall tax liability. For example, if an owner earns a profit of $1 million in another business, such as a manufacturing company, he or she can subtract the losses in the sport franchise from the $1 million in other profits and pay taxes only on the remainder. The resulting savings can be considerable.

Though losing money each year in order to gain a tax write-off might seem like bad business, remember that the value of the franchise steadily increases year by year, and once the owner sells, he or she will see a significant profit. With this in mind, don't be fooled by owners who claim that they are losing money on their team. If they really see the team as a loss, they'll sell it. In fact, the only

NFL team that has lost money in recent years is the Detroit Lions, which lost $3.5 million in 2012, the fourth consecutive year in which the franchise lost money (Ozanian 2013).

In 2013, the Houston Astros were baseball's worst team but also its most profitable ever. Despite losing more than two-thirds of their games, the Astros were projected to earn $99 million in operating income (total revenues minus operating expenses) for the year (Alexander 2013). To give you some perspective, that amount is estimated to be nearly as much as the *combined* operating income for the previous six World Series championship teams.

This happy state of affairs for Astros owner Jim Crane was accomplished by crafting a payroll that is the lowest in all of Major League Baseball while also generating healthy cable-television revenues. The regional sport channel, Comcast SportsNet Houston, pays the franchise an average of $80 million per year to broadcast Astros games—about $50 million more than the team's previous deal. Ostensibly, Crane has invested wisely and generously in his club's farm system in hopes of developing future superstars. He's also saving his pennies to invest in higher salaries in future years as the talent development merits more generous compensation.

The Astros are not the only team capitalizing on a lucrative television deal. In fact, big-market teams in New York and Los Angeles not only have huge contracts with their regional cable networks but also own a big piece of the networks themselves. As network owners, they get low-cost entertainment programming for their viewers, and as baseball owners they get a huge share of the profits. Any way you look at it, television has become the economic driver of professional sport.

Depreciation

Depreciation has always been a mainstay of American business. Assets such as equipment, tools, and (in sport) athletes have a limited life expectancy, and the annual decrease in their business value is referred to as *depreciation.* Because U.S. tax law allows businesses to reduce the book values of their capital assets each year, businesses can show depreciation as a loss against their profits and thus reduce their tax liability even if the actual value of their **capital assets** has increased.

Depreciation may be one of the least understood facets of owning a professional sport franchise. The players who are under contract to a given team are valued at a certain level each year. Because their value decreases over time as they age and their careers wind down, federal laws allow each club to annually depreciate the value of its stable of players.

Here's how a sport franchise owner might depreciate players in order to gain tax benefits. Suppose that a franchise breaks even in yearly income versus yearly expenses and that the owner can depreciate the value of his players by $1 million. If the owners' other businesses show a profit of $2 million, then she or he can apply the depreciation of $1 million against that profit and pay tax only on the remaining $1 million.

Revenue Sharing

The NFL and MLB differ sharply in both the structure and the amount of money shared among the league's teams. Although the total annual revenues for baseball ($8 billion) and football ($9 billion) are comparable, the sharing formula is not. In the NFL, more than 80 percent of league revenue is divided evenly between all 32 teams. As a result, market size has little to do with the revenue base of a football franchise.

In contrast, MLB teams share less than 25 percent of their total revenue. In other words, more than 75 percent of the revenue generated by a given team stays there; in other words, the bulk of the money goes to teams in large markets with a history of strong brand and competitive success. As a result, a given team's finances for a particular year can be dramatically affected by winning or losing (which can increase or decrease attendance), ticket sales, luxury suite rentals, and local broadcast ratings. For example, whereas the New York Yankees generated nearly $400 million in 2007, one of their division rivals, the Tampa Bay Rays, made barely $100 million—yet still faced pressure to pay players a competitive salary (Dubner 2007).

At the risk of oversimplifying the situation, it appears that the NFL is truly a national league in which power is held by the owners, who share the revenue generated by national broadcast television rights. In contrast, MLB teams face more revenue risk, depending on their local market. Even so, the past few years have seen some changes in the NFL's revenue-sharing plan that may sow seeds of discontent among smaller-market teams. Newly constructed NFL stadiums feature large box seats that are leased to corporations, and revenue from those seats is not shared. Other revenues that are not shared include those derived from the sale of venue naming rights, team sales of their own licensed products, and other stadium-generated revenues, such as those brought in by concerts, other special events, and associated restaurants.

In addition, a league's revenue-sharing arrangement affects how its individual teams respond to the league's rules for limiting player salaries. For example, the NFL salary cap (the limit on the total salary that can paid to a given team's athletes) is calculated as a percentage of the total revenue generated by all league teams. However, whereas teams in the top third of NFL markets (such as New England, Washington, Dallas, Philadelphia, Chicago, and New York) generate revenues averaging $256 million, teams in the lower third (such as Cincinnati, Minneapolis, Jacksonville, and Buffalo) generate an average of only about $177 million. Thus the difference in revenue between some large and small markets may be $100 million.

Since the salary cap is determined based on *all* teams' revenue, the small-market teams simply do not have the cash to spend up to the cap limit, because they have less unshared revenue on hand from luxury boxes, venue naming rights, local media, and local sponsorships. As a result, one study found that large-market teams were paying an average of 47 percent of their revenue to players, whereas for small-market teams (such as the Cincinnati Bengals) the figure was 68 percent (Curnutte 2007).

Other leagues, such as MLB and the NBA, use softer caps that do not prohibit teams from exceeding a certain salary level but do penalize them for doing so. In this model, some teams simply decide to exceed the league-established limits; for example, the New York Yankees have done so numerous times. Rather than worry about the financial penalty for going beyond the limit, teams like the Yankees, who play in large markets and have deep pockets, simply pay the so-called "luxury tax" and move on.

As a result, at the end of the 2013 season, the Yankees owed the league $28 million, and the Los Angeles Dodgers had to cough up more than $11

POP CULTURE

Moneyball

The 2011 film *Moneyball* was nominated for six Academy Awards, including best actor and best picture. Adapted from Michael Lewis' 2003 nonfiction bestseller of the same title, this drama follows the 2002 Oakland Athletics baseball season as the franchise's innovative and controversial general manager Billy Beane works to field a competitive team in an unfavorable financial situation. The film illustrates the challenges faced by small-market professional teams trying to compete with large-market clubs in any professional sport.

As the story goes, Billy Beane (played by Brad Pitt) meets Peter Brand (played by Jonah Hill), a young Yale economics graduate with revolutionary ideas about using a kind of statistical analysis (called "sabermetrics") to assess player value. Brand advises Beane to select players based on their on-base percentage to the exclusion of almost all other data. As a result, Beane assembles a team of undervalued players to make a valiant run at the championship.

Early in the season, things do not go well for Beane's new approach, and the critics are gathering. Eventually, however, the A's not only improve but also fashion a 20-game winning streak that puts them in the thick of the championship race. Although they end up losing in the first round of the postseason, Beane feels validated in having demonstrated the value of this new approach. Indeed, the owner of the Boston Red Sox is so impressed with Beane's creative approach that he offers Beane a record-setting contract to join the Red Sox as their general manager. Beane turns him down to stay in Oakland, and other (mostly small-market) teams begin to find similar success with the sabermetric approach to evaluating players.

million. In the NBA, the Lakers owed $29 million, and at the end of the 2013–2014 season the Brooklyn Nets were expected to owe more than $70 million on top of their player payroll, which totaled about $100 million in itself. In the wake of such penalties, the Yankees have threatened to cut their payroll in order to stay under the salary limit, but most pundits scoff at this threat. The reason? In the past, when the Yankees have needed a player, they have simply opened their pocketbook and bought him (Zillgitt 2013; ESPN 2013c).

Ticket Sales

In the NFL, the total money paid for seats (on average, about $2.5 million per game) is split between the home and visiting teams on a 60-to-40 basis. Total ticket sales are affected by a variety of factors, including the stadium's seating capacity, seat prices, and, of course, attendance numbers. Many NFL teams with winning traditions routinely sell out their games and even have a waiting list of customers who want to purchase season tickets.

In MLB, a game rarely sells out, simply because a baseball team plays 162 games per year, whereas a football team plays only 16. Baseball's national broadcasts generate just 20 percent of its overall sales; the largest proportion of other revenue comes from money spent at the ballpark and money brought in through local broadcasts. MLB teams that have their own stake in a cable network—for example, the New York Yankees, New York Mets, and Boston Red Sox—can earn huge revenues that they do not have to share with other teams in the league (Jacobson 2007).

Venue Revenues

Venue revenues include income from luxury boxes, general ticket sales, concessions, and parking. Luxury boxes, typically the most expensive seats available, can be found in all recently built venues; they often include food service, offer private restrooms, and feature televisions showing the game in progress. Most luxury boxes are bought by corporations and are deducted as a business expense since the firms use them to entertain clients. The appeal of luxury boxes is that they are paid for in advance and thus are guaranteed income. Another source of venue revenue is the relatively new category of "naming rights," which allow a sponsor to put its name on a facility for a cost that generally ranges from $2 million to $10 million per year (Sports Venues 2014).

The food and souvenir concessions at most ballparks and arenas also generate considerable profits for the home team. Most venues ban outside food and beverage, thus forcing fans who wish to eat or drink to patronize the concession stands during the game. Parking also produces revenue, since most fans drive to the venue and like to park nearby.

To get an idea of such revenues in the NFL, we can turn to the Green Bay Packers franchise, which, because it is publicly owned (the only such team in the NFL), must release its financial figures annually. The Packers reported local revenue of $136 million for 2013, which included ticket sales, advertising, and merchandise sales. Of course, teams located in a larger market can earn considerably more local revenue (Yglesias 2014). The local franchise typically retains these stadium revenues, but in the case of publicly financed stadiums, the sponsoring agency (such as the city) may get some of the money in return for financing the stadium in the first place.

Media Revenues

Media revenues include income from radio, television, and pay-per-view broadcasts. They constitute the largest single source of income for the NFL, accounting for about half of all NFL revenue. Happily for most NFL franchises, that revenue (as discussed earlier in the chapter) is shared equally by all 32 teams. **Revenue sharing** among teams in the league enhances their total bargaining power and helps balance the differences in various markets due to size, tradition, and competition from other recreational activities.

Beginning in 2014, NFL teams divvied up nearly $7 billion per year in media money, which works out to more than $200 million per team before the sale of a single ticket, beer, or piece of team merchandise. For most NFL teams, this guaranteed TV money essentially covers the expense of their complete player payroll for the year. Although television income generates about 55 percent of each NFL team's revenue, the figure in other major sports is only about 18 percent. Figures for 2012–2013 are listed in table 4.1.

Licensing Fees for Team Merchandise

Professional sport franchises sell team jerseys, caps, T-shirts, and every other imaginable souvenir. The NFL became the leader in capitalizing on such merchandise by establishing NFL Properties

TABLE 4.1 2014 Television Income for Major Sport Teams

Sport	Total revenue ($)	TV revenue ($)	TV % of total
NFL	9 billion	5 billion	55
MLB	8 billion	1.5 billion	18
NBA	5 billion	930 million	18
NHL	3.3 billion	600 million	18

Data from Forbes 2013; USA Today 2014; ESPN 2013a; Gretz 2012.

to market the league and license its merchandise. The revenue from these sales was shared equally among all NFL teams until 1995. Some team owners balked at this arrangement, particularly if their team traditionally generated more sales than other, less popular teams did. In spite of the success of NFL Properties, owner Jerry Jones of the Dallas Cowboys sued the NFL for the income generated by Nike and Pepsi deals he negotiated for the Cowboys and won; he also won the right to keep the revenue from his team merchandise sales, which is about $80 million annually.

The sizes of these revenue streams vary greatly from team to team, city to city, and sport to sport. Some leagues, such as the NFL, practice some degree of revenue sharing among all teams, whereas others allow each franchise to keep what it generates or cap the earnings and penalize franchises for exceeding the cap. The NFL and its franchises generate about $9 billion annually, including about $5 billion from national TV contracts. That money, along with the money from licensing product sales, is distributed evenly between the NFL's 32 teams.

In contrast, MLB teams made $8 billion overall in 2013 but generated a much more modest amount of national TV revenue at $1.5 billion, which amounted to less than 20 percent of MLB's total income. National TV income is shared equally among all 30 MLB teams, along with funds from league merchandise sales. In addition, each MLB franchise must place 34 percent of its locally produced revenue (much of it from local TV) in a pot to be shared by all 30 teams. Each team's share is calculated based on its market size, its revenue generated, and its performance on the field (Juliano 2013).

Payoff for Reaching the Postseason

On average, an MLB team can earn an additional $20 million to $30 million dollars just by making the playoffs. For example, when the underdog Kansas City Royals scrapped their way to the 2014 World Series, they raked in more than $1 million for each playoff game they hosted. In addition, reaching the postseason guarantees higher earnings for the next several seasons. Typically, playoff teams increase their in-season attendance, which increases their local revenue, concessions revenue, and broadcast revenue. Local sponsorship of the team should also jump, and the Royals expect an increase of $6 million to $7 million in revenue in 2015 from new team sponsors. As you might expect, the Royals have also enjoyed a huge spike in the popularity of their team merchandise; however, because those revenues are split evenly among all 30 major league teams, the direct financial impact for the Royals is considerably reduced.

It is quite revealing to compare the playoff bonanza for the small-market Royals with the situation of the Los Angeles Dodgers, who play in one of the league's largest markets. For the 2014 season, the Dodgers spent $235 million in payroll, which resulted in 94 wins, a division crown, and the opportunity for 11 more wins in the postseason. In contrast, the Kansas City team spent $92 million for 89 wins, a home wild-card game, and the potential for 11 additional wins. In the end, however, the benefit to both teams is a likely increase of 20 percent to 25 percent in revenue relative to their own market, which of course is much larger in Los Angeles.

The key to maximizing a team's financial profit from reaching the playoffs is to reinvest the money in team development, increase player payroll, and hopefully increase the odds of reaching future playoffs. Consider that one trip to the World Series for the Royals may transform them from a team that competed in the 2011 season with a $36 million payroll (the lowest in MLB) to a team flirting with a $100 million payroll for 2015 (Mellinger 2014; Rieper 2014; Barmasse 2014).

Naming Rights

Another major source of income—for cities and teams—is the sale of **naming rights** for their athletic venues. In the past, venues were typically named after a former owner, a celebrity, or the local city. This is no longer the case. For example, the former Joe Robbie Stadium in Miami, which honored the one-time Miami Dolphins owner, was replaced by Pro Player Stadium and is now Sun Life Stadium. Similarly, Connie Mack Stadium, named for a former manager of the Philadelphia Athletics, has been replaced by Lincoln Financial Field. As a result of this shift, we are now accustomed to names such as Raymond James Stadium, American Airlines Arena, Pepsi Center, Tropicana Field, Safeco Field, and Bank of America Stadium. The largest naming-rights deals are shown in table 4.2.

A new or refurbished venue increases the value of a professional sport franchise. As a result, if outside public or private funding finances a new venue, a team owner may see his or her franchise appreciate by $30 million or $40 million without spending a dime. The owner then pockets the increased value upon selling the franchise.

Venue Financing

The financing of stadiums and other athletic arenas has been the subject of public debate for years, and the discussion is sure to continue. Because of the need for constant refurbishments, upgrades, and redesigns, constructing a new facility is often a better option than remodeling an old one. Still, building a new facility easily costs several hundred million dollars, if not more, which makes the source of that funding a point of contention. As a result, many creative minds have developed various financial packages to support these new facilities. Let's look at some of them.

The percentages of **public funds** and **private funds** used for construction vary by the situation. Between 1991 and 2004, 78 venues (an average of nearly 6 per year) were either built new or substantially renovated, at a total cost of $26 billion, of which 61 percent came from public funds (Fischer-Baum 2012). Public sources include sales taxes, proximity and beneficiary taxes, general obligation and revenue bonds, and tax increment financing. Private sources include owner contributions, league contributions, bank loans, loans from local businesses, and personal seat licenses

More recent analysis reveals that in 2010 the 121 sport facilities used by the NFL, MLB, NBA, and NHL cost the taxpaying public about $10 billion more than had been previously reported. The difference is due to hidden subsidies (such as land), infrastructure (such as road improvements), operations, and of course lost property

TABLE 4.2 Top Prices Paid for Venue Naming Rights

Venue name	Sponsor	Team name	Annual revenue
Citi Field	Citigroup	New York Mets	$21 million
Barclays Center	Barclays	Brooklyn Nets	$20 million
MetLife Stadium	MetLife	New York Jets, New York Giants	$19 million
AT&T Stadium	AT&T	Dallas Cowboys	$19 million
Levi's Stadium	Levi Strauss & Co.	San Francisco 49ers	$11 million

Data from K. Schaul and K. Belson, 2013, "Playing the Stadium Name Game," *The New York Times*.

taxes. When these hidden costs are factored in, the average split for the cost of sport facilities is 78 percent from public funds and 22 percent from private funds (Long 2012).

The majority of venues are publicly owned, either by local governments or by special venue or sport authorities. These groups oversee operation of the facility, negotiate leases with the sport teams that use it, and may also supervise nearby ancillary construction, such as shops, restaurants, and other amenities. A few venues—for example, Bank of America Stadium and Gillette Stadium—were privately financed and are privately owned. Bank of America Stadium, home of Carolina Panthers football, was completed in 1996 at a cost of $248 million (Ballparks 2006a). Gillette Stadium has been home to the New England Patriots since 2002 and was funded entirely by owner Robert Kraft at a price of $325 million (Ballparks 2006b). The inducement for the owner to fund the facility is the ability to depreciate the asset. Over several years, the tax savings from such depreciation can be sizable.

When the economic recession hit in 2007, publicly financed venues became a tougher sell to taxpayers, thus forcing more private financing. As a result, recently completed venues for the Dallas Cowboys, New York Yankees, New York Giants, New York Jets, and Brooklyn Nets were built mostly with private financing; specifically, of the combined cost of $5.4 billion, 83 percent ($4.5 billion) came from private sources (Fischer-Baum 2012).

For years, Florida has assessed a **bed tax** on hotel guests from out of state. For every room night, $1 goes into a special fund to help finance public sport venues around the state. The state government decides which sport in which city is due for support and allocates a portion of the bed tax revenue for that project. As you might suspect, these funds are the subject of intense lobbying by leaders in football, basketball, baseball, tennis, and other sports. The beauty of this plan is that residents are mollified regarding the use of public money, since it comes from the pockets of out-of-state tourists and businesspeople. Of course, some might wonder what other uses the money could be put to, such as education, housing for poor residents, hurricane relief, and coastline refurbishing.

Another financing option comes in the form of **personal seat licenses (PSLs)**, wherein fans pay for the right to purchase specific seats in a venue. If the owner of a certain seat decides not to purchase the seat for a particular game, the seat can be sold to the general public. This plan has been popular and has raised significant capital in 11 of the 20 new NFL stadiums built since 1995. According to John Vrooman, sport economist at Vanderbilt University, "the advantage of PSLs is that they shift the cost of new stadiums to the fans who actually directly benefit from the team as opposed to the general state, local, or federal taxpayers who will never benefit from the project." However, requiring PSLs also puts the cost of tickets out of the financial reach of many middle class families. The amount that a team can raise in this manner varies widely, depending on the market history and the economy. For instance, the sale of PSLs raised $800 million to pay for MetLife Stadium, new home of the New York Giants and New York Jets, whereas the Seattle Seahawks raised only $17 million by offering a limited number of PLSs at Quest Field (Zremski 2014).

The Dallas Cowboys offered what they call "seat options" in their new stadium in Arlington at a cost ranging from $16,000 to $150,000 per year for 30 years, depending on the location of the seats. These fees are by far the most expensive in sport history. Add the cost of the ticket itself, at roughly $350 per seat per game, and you begin to see the expense to the fan (Marta 2008).

Public tax funds provide funding for construction and maintenance of most professional sport venues. In addition, the public financing may derive from tax-free public bonds, thereby depriving the government of a source of revenue that critics of such financing argue could be better applied toward improved living conditions for residents, especially those who are most in need. In many cases, the city taxes ticket sales, refreshment sales, and parking fees, although each of these possibilities depends on the agreement negotiated with the sport franchise. If a facility was built with public money, most cities also charge the team a rental fee that ranges from several hundred thousand dollars a year to a nominal one dollar. Again, the size of the fee depends on the agreement negotiated by city officials with the sport franchise.

APPLYING SOCIAL THEORY

Critical Theorists and the Financing of Sport Venues

How would a critical theorist respond to the public financing of sport venues? Explain your answer. Here's an example to ponder.

As of 2015, the NFL's Minnesota Vikings franchise is building a new stadium worth about $1 billion with substantial help from the state of Minnesota (contributing $348 million) and the city of Minneapolis (contributing $150 million). The remaining cost of $526 million is being covered by the football team and private contributions. As things tend to go, it's not a bad deal for taxpayers, who on average tend to pay about three-quarters of the cost of sport venues. But let's take a step back and ask if this is the best investment that a city could make.

Proponents of public financing often point out that new venues bring jobs, economic activity, and tourist dollars to the area. But critics, such as sport economist Victor Matheson of the College of Holy Cross, point out that if local people spend discretionary money to see a ballgame, they don't spend it at other local businesses, such as restaurants and movie theaters. In fact, most sport economists agree that, in the final analysis, new sport facilities generate little economic benefit for the surrounding area (Matheson 2010, 2014; Long 2012). In addition, the jobs they create involve primarily seasonal and low-wage employment.

Matheson sums it up this way: "If someone says a sports team is a great amenity for local people and something that makes them happy, fine. We do have flat out evidence that sports makes people happy. Just don't claim that it's going to make us rich" (Nohlgren 2013).

In Atlanta, they finally said no to the Atlanta Braves, who wanted a new baseball stadium. The Braves announced in 2013 that they were moving to nearby Cobb County, an affluent Atlanta suburb, because the financial opportunity was simply too good to pass up. No city mayor wants to be blamed for losing a sport team, but Atlanta mayor Kasim Reed had already committed to a deal to help pay for a new stadium for the Atlanta Falcons football team. His reasoning was that the Falcons would be a revenue generator for the city and would be funded through a hotel-motel bed tax. Even better, the city won't be on the hook for the $1.2 million debt for the football stadium. However, the bed-tax money has a limit, and the city simply couldn't afford to build a stadium for the Braves.

In U.S. cities with tight budgets and aging infrastructure—including roads, bridges, sidewalks, schools, and green spaces—many taxpayers don't see the sense in dedicating money to sport venues. Of course, fans of professional sport teams may be more willing to pay the price, but the drama is playing out across the land as more cities struggle with these costs. Is it worthwhile to saddle the city with long-term debt in order to enrich sport franchises that are uniformly owned by millionaires?

So what is a fair split between public and private funds? Sport economist Judith Grant Long says that such deals may be reasonable for cities if they stick to providing land and some infrastructure, such as road and sewer improvements (Long 2012). In this view, given that infrastructure expenses usually account for about 25 percent of a venue's total cost, a reasonable deal would be in the range of a 25-75 split between public and private funding. Unfortunately, that split is just the reverse of the typical pattern up to this point.

You might wonder how cities or states justify spending public funds to build stadiums and arenas that clearly benefit team owners. Here are the major justifications that are typically presented to the taxpayers:

- The general public benefits from the presence of a professional sport team, which helps the area be regarded as "major league," increases real estate values, and allows residents to take pride in their team identity and enjoy the recreational value of following the team.

- The city gains revenue from tourists who attend games, restaurants and hotels gain customers, and the city government realizes tax revenue on all the money spent locally, which goes back into city coffers.
- The city and region see priceless publicity that attracts potential residents, especially potential businesses that are looking to either relocate offices and groups of employees or establish new operations, which will provide jobs for local residents.
- National media attention attracts tourism, and local businesses flourish because of exposure and a chance to sell their products nationally or at least regionally.
- Special events, such as playoffs and championships, may provide further benefits (such as additional exposure), and the revenue generated from just one such event can easily be $50 million or more.
- The sport franchise creates jobs and income for local people who work, whether directly or indirectly, for the team. For example, ushers, ticket takers, refreshment stand workers, cleanup crews, and maintenance workers all derive income from the facility.

Detractors of public financing for such facilities argue just as vehemently that the promised benefits are modest when compared with the true cost to the city and its taxpayers. Over the years, various opposing groups have mounted campaigns to block public financing by drawing attention to other ways in which the funding might be used to improve the quality of life for a city's residents. Alternatives include housing for poor people, educational services, public infrastructure improvements, medical research and care, and many other services.

Should public money be spent on stadiums, which create jobs and revenue for a city, or on projects such as public housing that improve the quality of life for a city's poorer population?

Who wins the debate usually depends on the amount of money spent on the campaign for public support. Sport team owners spend considerable money hiring the best "spin doctors" to present their case to the public. They are often aided by local politicians, business leaders, and members of the media who happily support the new proposal by reporting its supposed benefits to the public. Opposition forces, on the other hand, are often led by a small group of active local citizens with limited financial resources to publicize their point of view.

Sport owners may also subtly or not so subtly threaten to simply move their team to another city if the residents don't want the team enough to finance it. Although such threats might be said to constitute a form of blackmail, they have carried the day in many cities around the country. Furthermore, the actions of Art Modell in Cleveland, Robert Irsay in Baltimore, and Al Davis in Oakland prove that such threats are not just idle chatter (Turco and Ostrosky 1997).

Organizations as Owners

Many sporting events and even some professional sport teams, such as the Green Bay Packers, are owned by a group or organization. The dynamics of group ownership differ considerably from those of individual ownership, since decisions have to be made by group members or at least by the elected board of directors. In addition, if the group is a public corporation, its financial records are open to public scrutiny—an unpalatable prospect for professional sport leagues that would prefer to keep their finances private.

One of the most successful stories of group ownership of a professional sport event can be found in the United States Open Tennis Championships, held annually in Flushing Meadows, New York. The two-week tournament is owned and operated by the United States Tennis Association (USTA), which was appointed by the U.S. Olympic Committee as the national governing body for U.S. tennis under the Amateur Sports Act of 1978. The USTA has a membership of about 770,000 people, each of whom pays a modest yearly dues fee (about $44 for an adult membership). The real moneymaker for the USTA is the U.S. Open, which provides about 80 percent of the organization's annual revenue. In 2014, the total revenue for the U.S. Open was $260 million. At the same time, the economic benefit to the greater New York City

EXPERT'S VIEW

Judith Grant Long

Judith Long is associate professor of urban planning at the Harvard University Graduate School of Design. Her research interests include infrastructure mega-projects; public–private partnerships for urban development; and the intersection of tourism, historic preservation, and city branding strategies. She is the author of *Public-Private Partnerships for Major League Sports Facilities* (Long 2012). During her research on the topic, she discovered that the financial arrangements for most sport facilities cost the average taxpayer much more than is commonly admitted. In fact, she calculates that the split for more than 100 facilities in use in 2010 was 78 percent public funds and just 22 percent private money.

Long's current book project, tentatively titled *Olympic Urbanism: From Rome to Rio*, analyzes the claims of the International Olympic Committee that hosting the Olympic Games serves as a catalyst for urban redevelopment. She bases this work both on archival information and on field research conducted in 15 host cities, ranging from Rome (1960) to Rio de Janeiro (2016). Long also compares host cities' plans in their bid packages to the actual results after the Olympic Games are concluded in terms of the post-Games use of sport venues, athlete villages, ceremonial parks, transportation upgrades, security networks, and media communication. As you might suspect, once the excitement of the Olympic Games subsides, many host cities find themselves saddled with facilities and aspects of infrastructure that are no longer useful.

area exceeded $720 million, along with 13,000 seasonal jobs (Kaplan 2014).

By constitution and bylaws, the USTA is a not-for-profit organization that must spend the money it takes in each year on activities that promote tennis. It does so by operating tennis leagues for adults and kids, developing community tennis programs, supporting elite junior players who promise to be successful professionals, and fulfilling its traditional role as a tournament organizer for men and women of every possible age group and ability level.

In the late 1990s, the facilities at the USTA National Tennis Center in New York, the home of the U.S. Open, received a total face-lift at a cost exceeding $250 million. The USTA bore the total cost of that expense, with no expenditure of public funding. Compared with other sport owners who have their facilities built for them, the USTA stands alone as self-supporting. Another major face-lift is currently in progress. With a projected total cost of about $500 million, it will add a roof to Arthur Ashe Stadium, build a new stadium to replace the aging Louis Armstrong Stadium, and build another new stadium, along with a wide pedestrian walkway to accommodate the extra 100,000 fans the Open hopes to attract. Once again, the costs are being financed by the USTA (Kaplan 2014).

The only New York sport team that earns more money than the U.S. Open is the New York Yankees, who accumulate their earnings over a season of 81 home games. During its two-week tournament, the U.S. Open earns more than the Jets, Giants, Knicks, Rangers, or Islanders. How does the USTA do it?

The U.S. Open derives its income about equally from three sources: the sale of tickets, food, beverages, and merchandise; corporate sponsors; and worldwide television rights. Other professional tennis events around the country operate similarly, though on a much smaller scale. Some are owned by groups, such as IMG, a sport organization founded by Mark McCormack that represents players and also owns tennis events. Other tournaments are owned by individuals or local sporting groups that secure the sanction of the men's or women's professional tour in order to ensure that their event is not scheduled at the same time as another tour event.

Sport as Monopoly

Some people argue that professional sports in the United States are unique in that they clearly constitute monopolies and that no other U.S. business operates under the same favorable set of rules. Let's examine this argument, beginning with a historical review. In the 1890s, President Grover Cleveland grew concerned about the influence of the Standard Oil Company on the economy and influenced the U.S. Congress to pass the Sherman Antitrust Act, which made illegal "every contract, combination in the form of trust or otherwise, or conspiracy in restraint of trade or commerce among the several states or with foreign nations" (Michener 1987, 386).

Although this bill did not directly target baseball, it did affect the sport. Professional baseball was conducting interstate commerce and restrained trade, since players couldn't move from one team to another and the owners conspired to keep players' salaries at a desired level. Over the next 30 years, various interests challenged the Sherman Antitrust legislation; in 1922, however, Supreme Court Justice Oliver Wendell Holmes declared that baseball was not in violation of the Sherman laws. Numerous court suits have been filed since, and minor changes have been made in this momentous decision. Naturally, other professional sports fell into the same favorable position due to the similarity of their businesses.

How have professional sports used this favorable ruling to operate as monopolies? Here are a few of the ways:

- Team owners formed leagues like the NFL to control how teams compete against each other for fans, players, media revenues, sales of licensed merchandise, and sponsorships.
- The leagues—including MLB, the NBA, the NFL, and the NHL—also work together to eliminate potential competition from new leagues that try to cash in on their sport.
- Using a draft system for hiring players, owners force players to negotiate only with the team that drafts them, thereby limiting athletes' salaries.

- New or expansion teams cannot join the league without paying substantial fees to all of the other owners, and one owner cannot relocate his or her team to another city without the approval of other owners.
- Owners of individual teams cannot sell merchandise associated with their team. In professional football, NFL Properties markets all NFL business properties as a unit and therefore has been wildly successful in negotiating sponsorships, licensing agreements, and television contracts. However, Jerry Jones, owner of the Dallas Cowboys, the most popular team in America, wanted to merchandise Cowboys paraphernalia himself. He didn't see why he should support other franchises with revenue from the sale of Cowboys hats, jerseys, and so on. Jones forced the NFL to modify the monopolistic stance under which it had operated for years, though the league still retains the majority of its power.

For most teams, television revenue is a huge source of income, but the potential revenue for each major league baseball team depends on the size of its market. The NFL restricts individual teams from negotiating local TV contracts, but MLB does not. Hence, the New York Yankees can sell their local TV rights for $75 million a year, whereas the former Montreal Expos were lucky to command $1 million. Among other things, this inequity in potential income helped convince the Expos to relocate to Washington, DC, in 2005. You can see the disparity that different markets create between teams, which throws the teams' power and competitiveness off balance. The NFL, however, remains a true monopoly by negotiating as one entity. The NFL model for distribution of TV revenue is just one of several strategies the league has used to ensure the financial sustainability of each franchise and thus minimize the differences between small, medium, and large markets.

Management Versus Labor

Team owners restrict the options available to the workforce in their sport. First, they limit the choice of teams with whom a player can sign. Each league conducts an annual draft, in which each player is

ACTIVITY TIME-OUT

Should the NFL Be a Tax-Exempt, Not-For-Profit Organization?

It's a little-known fact that the NFL is classified by the Internal Revenue Service as a 501c (6) not-for-profit organization and thus owes no taxes to the federal government (*Tampa Bay Times* 2013). This classification is intended to be used by trade or industry associations whose primary purpose is to further the industry or profession they represent. This status is also claimed by the NHL, the Professional Golfers' Association (PGA), and the Association of Tennis Professionals (ATP). As a result, millions of dollars of potential tax revenue are lost, and critics of such arrangements claim that rich sport organizations are unjustifiably avoiding federal taxation and therefore sticking it to the average U.S. workers who do pay taxes on their modest salaries.

In September 2013, U.S. Senator Tom Coburn (Republican of Oklahoma) introduced a bill in Congress that would strip the NFL of its tax-exempt status. In response, the NFL pointed out that only the league office claims such status and that each of its 32 franchises are for-profit entities and thus pay taxes on all income. Under similar criticism in 2007, MLB gave up its tax-exempt status and now claims that the change was revenue neutral. Standing alone among professional sport leagues is the NBA, which has always been a for-profit organization.

It remains to be seen whether or not the U.S. Congress will delve into this issue. If you had a chance to vote, would you favor requiring the NFL to pay taxes? Why or why not?

selected by one team. As a result, a player who grew up in California and thrives in warm weather may be drafted by the Green Bay Packers and therefore have no choice but to go to Green Bay if he wishes to play in the NFL. This process also eliminates each player's potential negotiating leverage with other teams and therefore limits the size of player salaries.

To put this process in perspective, imagine the following scenario: A young lawyer just out of school is drafted by a law firm and assigned to work there regardless of her or his preferences or the salary offered. That's how professional athletes in the major U.S. sports go into their work. Those who support athletes' rights would say that athletes who spend their whole lives preparing to play professionally ought to have the same rights as other citizens, who can offer their services to the highest bidder. In contrast, team owners argue that a league draft fairly distributes sport talent and allows every team a shot at signing the best players. Since the draft begins with the team that had the worst record in the previous season, it allows that team, at least in theory, to strengthen itself by hiring the best new talent. This argument may make more sense in basketball—where one 7-foot (about 2-meter) player can dominate the court—than in other sports.

From the outset, team owners also benefited from owning the services of their athletes for life if they so wished. This option, referred to as the reserve clause, was first challenged by baseball player Curt Flood in 1969 when he refused his trade to the Phillies by the St. Louis Cardinals and simply sat out the next season. He sued MLB and lost in the courts, but by 1976 the reserve clause was dead. Flood changed the sport forever at great sacrifice to his personal career since he never played again in major league baseball. Now, after a certain amount of time, baseball players can become free agents and bargain with other teams for their services.

Curt Flood forever changed sport when he challenged the reserve clause and fought for the right to play for a different baseball team.

Football and basketball have at various times used an option clause, which requires a player to play one more year after his contract expires, typically at 90 percent of his previous year's salary, before he becomes a free agent able to sell his services to another team. Each new collective bargaining agreement between a sport's owners and the players union sets the terms of option clauses for the length of that agreement. Of course, when a player and his agent negotiate a contract, they also have the right to agree to an option clause in exchange for other favorable provisions, such as a sizable signing bonus. Many teams try to trade a player once he announces that he is playing out his option, because they figure it's better to get something in return than to lose the player's services without any compensation at all. For this reason, you sometimes see established players with solid careers traded for fringe players, future draft choices, or the famous "player to be named later."

Over the years, other changes favorable to athletes have been brought about thanks to strong leadership from union officials and former athletes. For example, minimum pay levels have been established for rookies and veterans, options have been set for players who cannot agree on a contract with the team that drafts them, and freedom has been established for players who fulfill their original contract to negotiate with other teams for their services.

The owners gave in only grudgingly to each of these player demands, arguing, for example, that allowing players to sign with the highest bidder at any time would upset the balance of competitiveness. Large-market teams, such as the New York Yankees, would pay the highest salaries, attract the best players, and thereby field the best teams year in and year out. Small-market teams would be left with lesser players, see their attendance figures tumble, and face economic risk. The final irony would be that large-market teams with deep pockets would eventually have no other teams to play, and the sport as a whole would put itself out of business.

The Yankees already contend for the championship nearly every year, often beating up on their competition. In 2013, the Yankees' total payroll was listed at more than $200 million, the second highest in MLB. In contrast, division rival Tampa Bay was ranked 28th in payroll at just over $55 million. In fact, New York paid just three players (Alex Rodriguez, C.C. Sabathia, and Mark Teixeira) a total of about $76 million—more than Tampa's total payroll (Petchesky 2013).

Player Compensation and Taxes

Let's look now at the yearly compensation of athletes in the United States. Keep in mind that the following statistics include all sports and all athletes, even those in the so-called minor leagues. According to the U.S. Bureau of Labor Statistics (2013b), in 2010 the median annual salary for athletes was $43,740, although of course many of the highest-paid athletes earned much more. Statistics also show that all levels of U.S. professional sport combined provide about 21,000 jobs for athletes. Therefore, though you see headlines about the multimillion-dollar contracts signed by top athletes, thousands more struggle to make ends meet in the minor leagues, hoping for a chance at the big leagues. Competition is intense in the effort to reach the highest level of any professional sport, and the average length of a professional sport career is only about three and a half years due to debilitating injuries and age.

Once athletes in major sports such as baseball, football, and basketball reach a certain level of performance, they are rewarded with a contract that may extend for multiple years (as many as eight or ten in the case of some superstars). Since these athletes fall into a high tax bracket, their earnings are reduced significantly by federal, state, and local taxes. In fact, many athletes are required to pay state taxes both in the state where their team is based and in the states where their team competes, even if their residence is in a different state. As a result, they face the daunting task of accounting and filing returns in many states.

Even in the relatively safe sport of tennis, the average career length is only about seven years. If an athlete wants this income to last a lifetime, he or she must invest wisely in order to grow a nest egg. You might suggest that an athlete can find another job once his or her career ends; however, professional athletes often fall victim to relying on their athletic prowess and therefore end up with no other marketable skills. Some sport-related jobs are available—for example, in officiating, coaching, scouting, and front-office work—but these positions are limited in number and demand specific training and experience. In addition, the income potential of these jobs is modest—much less than what the athlete may have learned to live on.

ACTIVITY TIME-OUT

Taxes Paid on Winnings

In July 2013, Phil Mickelson won his first British Open, one of golf's four biggest tournaments. Soon thereafter, he realized that the majority of his prize money would be staying in Great Britain, thanks to a whopping 61 percent tax, which reduced his earnings of nearly $2.2 million to a take-home amount of about $850,000. In fact, after figuring in his expenses for the two weeks (which include giving 10 percent of the prize money to his caddie and paying airfare, hotel and meal costs, and agent fees) his true take-home pay was closer to 30 percent of his initial winnings. In addition, nonresident athletes such as Mickelson can also be taxed in the United Kingdom on their endorsement income. And when he arrived home, the state of California taxed his winnings at a rate of 13 percent (Blumenfeld 2013).

If you were Phil Mickelson, would you compete in the British Open again, knowing how much of a tax hit you'd take on your winnings? Or would you compete elsewhere and consider joining many of your fellow golfers in making your home in Florida, which does not tax personal income?

Of course, some of the most successful athletes move into television reporting or broadcasting. This work can be very lucrative, but the competition is intense for the available spots, and sustaining such a job requires excellent skills. The challenge is increased by the fact that, during their 20s and early 30s—when most of us are carving a niche for ourselves in our chosen profession, honing our craft, and perhaps seeking additional education—professional athletes are focused completely on their sport career.

The top wage earners in football, baseball, and basketball are shown in table 4.3; the top wage earners in all of sport are shown in table 4.4. These salaries are extremely generous as compared with the median household income ($52,250 in 2013) in the United States (U.S. Bureau of Labor Statistics 2013b), but athletes are not ordinary people. Indeed, their athletic talents are extraordinary, and if they combine that talent with good business sense, they can earn double and triple their salary in endorsements, appearances, and other activities. As an example, Tiger Woods was the world's highest paid athlete for a string of ten years before dropping to number 3 on the list in 2012, nearly two years after a sex scandal frightened off several of his sponsors. However, Woods was back on top of the list by 2013, with total earnings of $78 million, including $65 million in sponsorship (Badenhausen 2013).

The average fan may feel disgusted by the exorbitant pay of top athletes, particularly when an athlete doesn't play up to expectations. This reaction is understandable; at the same time, professional athletes face extreme competition simply to make it in their sport, and that competition rarely goes away. In addition, in some sports, such as professional tennis and golf, players must earn prize money in tournaments; as a result, if they suffer an injury or don't play well, their income stops even as their expenses continue. Thus there are no guarantees in professional tennis and golf, and athletes must prove themselves at every event, year after year.

In addition, the day-to-day work of any professional athlete is extremely demanding, even during the off-season. Athletes are constantly challenged at their physical and mental limits. They also often travel extensively and spend long periods away from family. Furthermore, if an athlete is traded, he or she is forced to uproot the family and start life in a new city.

Media coverage of athletes is also intense, and sportswriters often harshly criticize performances that they judge as wanting. Indeed, very few occupations or performances are subjected to such intense public scrutiny, especially on a daily basis. As a result, athletes must develop thick skin in order to deal with constant criticism. With this in mind, one fair way to look at athletes'

TABLE 4.3 Top Wage Earners in U.S. Football, Baseball, and Basketball for 2014

Athlete	Team	Salary ($ millions)	Endorsement income ($ millions)	Total income ($ millions)
Pro football				
Aaron Rodgers	Packers	40	5.8	45.8
Peyton Manning	Broncos	25	12	37
Tom Brady	Patriots	31	4	35
Mathew Stafford	Lions	31	1	32
Joe Flacco	Ravens	30	2	32
Pro basketball				
LeBron James	Heat	19	38	57
Kobe Bryant	Lakers	30	20	50
Derrick Rose	Bulls	17	17	34
Kevin Durant	Thunder	17	13	30
Dwyane Wade	Heat	18	10	28
Pro baseball				
Zack Greinke	Dodgers	28	—	28
Robinson Cano	Mariners	24	3	27
Ryan Howard	Phillies	25	1	26
Albert Pujols	Angels	23	2.5	25.5
Cliff Lee	Phillies	25	.2	25.2

Data from D. Roberts, 2014, "50 highest earning American athletes," *Fortunate 50*. Presented by FORTUNE and Sports Illustrated. Available: http://fortune com/fortunate50/

compensation is to regard them as entertainers who happen to work in the sport industry. When their earnings are compared with the earnings of entertainers in music, stage, and film, the figures are not so amazing. Here is a list of the top 10 celebrities in earnings (in millions of U.S. dollars) from June 2012 to June 2013 (Pomerantz 2013):

1.	Madonna	125
2.	Steven Spielberg	100
3.	E.L. James	95
4.	Howard Stern	95
5.	Simon Cowell	95
6.	James Patterson	91
7.	Glenn Beck	90
8.	Michael Bay	82
9.	Jerry Bruckheimer	80
10.	Lady Gaga	80

Limits on Athlete Earnings

After years of wildly escalating salaries, professional sport owners decided to take steps to limit players salaries. One approach involves setting a **total salary cap** that limits how much each team

TABLE 4.4 World's Highest-Paid Athletes for 2013 and 2014

Name	2013 ranking	2014 ranking	Sport	Total earnings (US$ millions)		Endorsements (US$ millions)	
				2013	2014	2013	2014
Tiger Woods	1	6	Golf	78.1	61.2	65	55
Roger Federer	2	7	Tennis	71.5	56.2	65	52
Kobe Bryant	3	5	Basketball	61.9	61.5	34	31
LeBron James	4	3	Basketball	59.8	72	42	53
Drew Brees	5	66	U.S. football	51	21	11	11
Aaron Rodgers	6	55	U.S. football	49.2	22	6	7.5
Phil Mickelson	7	8	Golf	48.7	53.2	44	48
David Beckham	8	Didn't make the list	Soccer	47.2	—	42	—
Cristiano Ronaldo	9	2	Soccer	44	80	21	28
Lionel Messi	10	4	Soccer	41.3	64.7	21	41.7
Tom Brady	11	Didn't make the list	U.S. football	38.3	—	7	—
Derrick Rose	13	13	Basketball	37.4	36.6	21	19
Joe Flacco	13	Didn't make the list	U.S. football	36.8	—	0.9	—
Floyd Mayweather Jr.	14	1	Boxing	34	105	0	0
Manny Pacquiao	15	11	Boxing	34	41.8	8	.8

Note: In 2014, Beckham, Brady, and Flacco did not make the top 100 where the cutoff was $17.3 million per year.

Based on Badenhausen 2013; Mughal 2014.

can spend on player salaries, thus letting teams save money and facilitate competitive balance in the league. The NFL enforces the toughest version of salary limitation, whereas baseball allows some wiggle room. When a baseball team goes over the cap, it must pay a luxury tax on the amount by which it exceeded the cap. As already mentioned, the New York Yankees routinely exceed the cap and pay the fine.

Because of these salary-limiting measures, every team employs experts who figure out the implications of every player contract and how it will affect the team cap in upcoming years. As a result, veteran players sometimes agree to renegotiate their contract and postpone earnings in order to free cap space so that the team can sign a desirable free agent who might help the team win now. In other cases, a team might retire a veteran player with a big contract in order to avoid having to count his or her entire salary in its cap total.

Team administrators compile all available data, scout for the best players, sign them to contracts while (presumably) staying under the cap, and try to keep everybody happy. In reality, it is rare that everyone is happy, due to the competitiveness of the athletes, their agents, and team officials.

Collegiate Sport as Moneymaker

Born out of student activities, college sport has evolved into big business on many university campuses. In the 2012–2013 academic year, the total estimated revenue from college sport in all divisions of the NCAA was $913 million (Plunkett Research 2014). Particularly in major or **revenue-producing sports**, such as football and basketball, the amount of money that major universities earn and spend on sport makes the operation of the athletic department a meaningful business endeavor. Although the department's specific purpose may not be to make money, it certainly is not allowed to lose money. Amateur sport has become such a big business for several reasons:

- The student body enjoys having high-profile athletic teams on campus for entertainment and recreation purposes.
- The university administration recognizes the power of the free publicity that schools competing at high levels receive in the sport media.
- Sport publicity helps universities recruit more applicants, which increases competition for admission, thus improving the institution's student profile.
- Alumni enjoy identifying with their alma mater through sport, especially if they take pride in the athletic achievements of their schools' teams. They are also more likely to return to campus to attend athletic events.
- Alumni are more likely to donate significant sums of money to their university if they are excited about its sport teams. Some alumni restrict their gifts to the athletic program, others donate to the general fund used at the administration's discretion, and still others earmark their money for specific campus projects.
- Revenue from a high-profile sport, such as football, can support a complete athletic program that provides a full complement of offerings for both men and women.

A successful athletic program can even affect an institution's overall reputation. For example, the University of Connecticut (UConn), a small

Collegiate sport is big business and can bring prestige to a university. By winning its tenth NCAA championship in 2015, the most in the history of women's collegiate sport, the UConn basketball team is now tied with John Wooden's UCLA teams that won 10 NCAA men's championships.

regional university that was not even widely regarded as the best state university in New England, moved into national prominence by dominating college basketball. Concurrently, the state of Connecticut invested a billion dollars over five years to refurbish the campus, build new facilities, and generally upgrade the school environment. Both the men's and women's basketball teams aided the emergence of UConn as a nationally competitive university. During the late 1990s, both teams steadily won titles, including a national championship. In 2004, both teams won the national championship in basketball, making UConn the first university to achieve that feat. Afterward, the number of applications for admission exploded, standards for admission were upgraded, and pride soared among alumni and students.

College athletic departments collect revenue from myriad sources. Big universities sell tickets to football games in stadiums that seat more than 100,000 fans. They add to their income through parking fees, concessions, souvenirs, and luxury boxes available for a substantial fee to alumni or businesspeople who want to entertain clients.

Television rights can also be a bonanza, provided the team is good enough. Notre Dame has been so well known in football for so long that it negotiates its own TV package for football and refuses to join a league and share its profit with other football teams. Most schools, however, benefit from league membership and receive revenue from all televised league games. Playoffs and bowl games provide additional income for the schools that earn those opportunities.

In addition, most colleges charge every student an athletic fee that helps support the sport program. Athletic departments also charge many of their expenses to other university programs, budgets, or cost centers, thus making it difficult to track the actual cost for university athletics. For example, a new weight training facility may be built as part of a general fitness facility and therefore not charged directly to athletic programs. Similarly, football stadiums and basketball arenas at large state universities are often financed with public funds or tax-free bonds available for public purchase.

Licensing fees for merchandise can also serve as a major source of income, particularly if a school's athletic teams are successful. College bookstores, which are supposedly filled with books, are in fact often filled with sweats, caps, shirts, running gear, souvenirs, and any other item that can be adorned with the university name or mascot. Indeed, the books are often an afterthought, located in the back of the store.

Corporate sponsors also contribute to big-time college sport, either in the form of cash or in donations of clothing, equipment, or services. In addition, local physicians often donate medical services in return for the publicity they receive for being associated with the team.

A quick perusal of table 4.5 may surprise you with its estimates of the monetary value of the top college football teams. Forbes ranked the listed teams on the basis of their value to their school's athletic department, which they often support entirely; their value to the local economy in which they are situated; the revenue they generate for their conference; and the financial benefit they provide to academic programs at their school. For example, the University of Florida Gators football team contributed more money to academic programming on its campus than any other team except Notre Dame. Specifically, the Gators gave $7.2 million back to the university, including $1.5 million earmarked for nonathletic scholarships (C. Smith 2013).

Note the conference affiliations of these programs. It is no accident that the traditionally powerful Southeast Conference (SEC) led in 2013, with four schools in the top 10, followed by three from the Big Ten, and two from the Big 12. Furthermore, the next ten schools listed by Forbes include five more from the SEC (Arkansas, Auburn, South Carolina, Tennessee, and Texas A&M), three more from the PAC 10 (Washington, Oregon, and Southern California), and two more from the Big Ten (Wisconsin and Penn State). In 2014, the SEC lost one school (Florida) from the top 10 but gained two others in Auburn and Tennessee.

This list makes clear which college teams are likely to be in the running for a national football championship year in and year out. Teams that have built a fan base, a mammoth stadium, loyal alumni donors, corporate sponsors, and sizable television revenue are assured, at the very least, of being competitive year after year. Of course, the two teams that competed for the 2013 national championship, Florida State (winner) and Auburn, were not in the top 10, and Florida State did not even make the top 20. 2014 was the first year of a playoff between the top four teams (Alabama, Florida State, Ohio State, and Oregon), and in

TABLE 4.5 Top 10 Most Valuable College Football Programs for 2013 and 2014

School	2013 ranking	2014 ranking	Conference	Value (in US$ millions)		Revenue (in US$ millions)		Profit (in US$ millions)	
				2013	2014	2013	2014	2013	2014
Texas	1	1	Big 12	139	131	109	113	82	74
Notre Dame	2	2	None (independent)	117	122	78	81	46	48
Alabama	3	4	Southeastern	110	107	89	95	47	53
Louisiana State	4	5	Southeastern	104	103	74	88	48	50
Michigan	5	3	Big Ten	104	117	81	91	58	65
Auburn	—	6	Southeastern	—	97	—	75	—	39
Tennessee	—	7	Southeastern	—	94	—	70	—	49
Florida	6	—	Southeastern	94	—	75	—	49	—
Oklahoma	7	8	Big 12	92	93	70	71	45	43
Georgia	8	10	Southeastern	91	83	66	66	40	39
Ohio State	9	9	Big Ten	83	87	61	66	38	39
Nebraska	10	—	Big Ten	80	—	61	—	35	—

Florida and Nebraska dropped out of the top ten in 2014 and were replaced by Auburn and Tennessee both of the Southeastern Conference.

Data from C. Smith 2013; C. Smith 2014.

the championship game the victory went to Ohio State over Oregon.

High-profile athletic programs receive so much publicity that many people assume they are typical. However, a closer look at the statistics reveals that such programs are operated by a relatively small number of universities. Specifically, of the 120 Division I Football Bowl Subdivision (FBS) overall athletic programs, only 23 reported positive net revenue in 2012. Those that made money showed a median profit of $5.4 million, whereas the majority (the other 97) suffered a median loss of $14.6 million.

Of course, the majority of revenue comes from football and men's basketball, and in recent years 50 percent to 60 percent of programs in these two sports at FBS institutions have shown a profit. In contrast, the only women's sport to show a profit is basketball, and that happened only once (in 2012) at just one school. Overall, FBS institutions show median per-school revenues of $40,581,000, median expenses of $56,265,000, or a difference of more than $15,000,000, which the university then has to subsidize. At the Football Championship Subdivision (FCS) level, which generally includes smaller programs, the median loss per school was $10,217,000, and for schools in Division I without football teams the median loss was $9,809,000 (NCAA 2013f).

Annual budgets for college athletics vary from a couple hundred thousand dollars to more than $100 million. Highly competitive athletic programs are designated as Division I, whereas less competitive programs fall into either Division II or Division III. Of the 1,200 active NCAA member institutions in the United States in 2013, only 339 met the qualifications for Division I. Those 339 were further subdivided: 120 schools had FBS football programs; 119 schools had FCS programs, which are smaller in terms of stadium size and average attendance; and 100 schools without football had Division I programs that concentrated on basketball (NCAA 2014a).

The top 10 athletic programs in terms of spending (see table 4.5) are operated by schools that are familiar to sport fans. The only way to generate a budget of this size is to establish a top-grade football program that makes more than half of the total revenue by itself. The top five schools in 2013 in terms of profit from their football teams were, in order, Texas, Michigan, Florida, Louisiana State, and Alabama. However, just as the revenue from big-time football seems to keep increasing, so do the expenses involved in operating these programs. In fact, a majority of programs had to increase their budgets by a double-digit percentage in fiscal years 2010 through 2012, and at least 17 of the 52 Division I FBS programs reported increasing their budget by more than 15 percent. The only apparent way to counter these increases is for schools to chase even more revenue from television contracts—an issue that is analyzed in more detail in chapter 8 (M. Smith 2011; NCAA 2013f).

In spite of the continued increase of collegiate athletic budgets, the total amount spent by NCAA universities at all levels of education for all students was about $330 billion in 2010-2011. The $12 billion spent on intercollegiate athletics represents just over 3.5% of that total figure.

As you can see, a great deal of money is invested in college sport. Large programs offer athletic scholarships to attract the best athletes in hopes of producing winning teams that please students, fans, alumni, and administrators. However, not all college athletic programs fit the high-profile model, and we must clarify the level of any given program rather than lumping all of college sport together. In fact, hundreds of colleges approach sport simply as a diversion from studies, and they attract athletes who play for the fun and experience.

One such school is Swarthmore College, a highly selective liberal arts school located in Pennsylvania, founded by Quakers, and renowned for its academics. Students at this college even made it a point of pride when their football program lost game after game. The losses symbolized to students the fact that football was not overemphasized on their campus. Of course, the players

ACTIVITY TIME-OUT

Are College Coaches' Salaries Out of Control?

You may read about, but gloss over, the amount of money paid to high-profile football and basketball coaches at major Division I FBS schools. As an increasing number of coaches hit the salary range of $3 million to $4 million per year—not to mention performance bonuses and built-in increases—many students, parents, and athletic program supporters are questioning the idea of paying such an exorbitant salary to a coach at what is purported to be a primarily academic institution.

In 2013, FBS football coaches averaged $1.8 million annually, a 10 percent increase over the previous year. In fact, coaching salaries for big-time programs have increased 90 percent since 2006. Moreover, three coaches—Nick Saban (Alabama), Mack Brown (Texas), and Bret Bielema (Arkansas)—each earned more than $5 million in 2013 (*USA Today* 2012). In this environment, coaches' salaries dwarf not only the money paid to professors but even the salaries of college presidents.

What is your opinion of this situation? Should there be a limit on coaches' salaries at universities? Should the decision be left to each school? Justify your answer.

on that team did not have much fun or a positive experience; losing year after year makes a player wonder if the effort is worth it. Swarthmore ended up dropping the football program in 2000 after fielding a team for 120 consecutive seasons (Longman 2000).

We look further at collegiate sport in chapter 8. It has been mentioned here because some major athletic programs truly are big business.

How much money have these sailors contributed to the business of sport?

Recreational Sport as a Business

The economic effect of recreational sport is measured in terms of the sales of sport equipment, such as golf clubs, tennis rackets, balls, boats, and fishing rods. Sales also include athletic footwear and clothing, which often serve the dual purposes of activewear for sport participation and leisure wear. Of the estimated $485 billion generated by the U.S. sport industry in 2014, $44 billion was generated from retail sporting goods stores and $22 billion from health and fitness clubs (Plunkett Research 2014).

Another way to measure expenditures for sport recreation is to tally the amount of land in natural settings that is used for boating and fishing, sport fields, public parks, and private sport facilities throughout the country. When the national economy thrives, people have more discretionary income to spend on recreation, and facilities are constructed and maintained to meet this demand. In fact, every community spends a portion of its annual budget maintaining public recreational areas, often at significant expense to its citizens.

Even public facilities often charge a user fee to help cover their operating costs. As municipal budgets are squeezed, recreational service funds are often among the first to be reduced and replaced by fees in order to support facility maintenance and operation. For example, golf courses (whether public or private) charge green fees and cart fees and sell golf merchandise to help support their operations. In addition, many public park systems have remained solvent by treating their operations like a business, which may mean, among other things, leasing their facilities to private contractors who guarantee an agreed-upon rate of return.

Another facet of local recreational activities involves youth sport and the facilities needed for such activities as youth soccer, swimming, tennis, football, baseball, and basketball. Virtually every town maintains community facilities to allow its kids to participate in sport for a modest user fee. Arguments occasionally spring up about the priorities—for example, whether to create playing fields for kids or preserve undisturbed, passive parkland for nature lovers—but the public foots the bill for either choice.

At the next levels, middle school and high school, the sport facilities in some towns look like miniature versions of professional complexes. In football-crazy towns, for instance, it is common to see football fields with lights, artificial turf, and commodious grandstands. More generally, immaculate playing fields grace many suburban communities, and school-based athletic facilities may be used to support community sport programs in the summer.

Let's look now at how an individual consumer might contribute to the business of sport. I recall getting my first baseball glove, smacking it to build the pocket, oiling it to make the leather supple, and sleeping with it just to get used to the feel of it. Next came my very own baseball bat, a football, a basketball, a soccer ball, uniforms, sneakers, a bicycle, roller skates, a plastic ball and bat, swim gear (flippers and a mask), soccer and baseball shoes with spikes, a tennis racket, and finally golf clubs. Children of families with at least modest incomes go through a similar progression of sport equipment, and over a lifetime a family may spend thousands of dollars on toys and equipment for sport and recreation.

As this discussion illustrates, recreational sport generates revenues through services provided to people of all ages, incomes, and skill levels. Program administrators and coaches can earn a living by using their skills to organize and implement recreational sport programs. Rental fees for sport facilities and equipment are collected at the community level in order to maintain current facilities and in some cases build new ones.

Sport clubs and other commercial sport facilities also charge fees for use by recreational participants. In fact, golf courses, tennis centers, bowling alleys, fitness clubs, shooting ranges, swimming pools, equestrian facilities, skating rinks, and country clubs take in millions of dollars for recreational sport and provide employment and income for the people who work in them.

Chapter Summary

This chapter examines the economics of sport in U.S. society. Owners of professional sport franchises tend to be wealthy people who have been successful in another business and purchase a team in order to minimize their tax liability, to associate with athletes, or to enjoy the excitement and high visibility of ownership. Some sport teams are owned by groups, conglomerates, or, in the case of the Green Bay Packers, the public. Franchise owners often tell the public that their team "loses money" in a given year, when in fact the franchise's increase in value alone compensates the owner handsomely if he or she ever sells the team.

To ensure the quality of their team's facilities, franchise owners often upgrade or replace facilities in order to create a state-of-the-art venue. Venue financing often involves major contributions from public funds even though the public may receive little direct benefit from the deal. Meanwhile, the value of the sport franchise increases considerably with a new venue, thus making the franchise a solid investment. Some organizations, such as the United States Tennis Association, own and operate professional sport events.

In addition, the chapter explores issues related to athletes' monetary compensation and working conditions. In the tenuous relationship between athletes (that is, labor) and sport owners, the owners seem to hold most of the leverage, though in recent years athletes have acquired some control over their professional sport careers. The chapter also compares player compensation with that of others in the workforce in terms of longevity and earnings spread over a lifetime. It then looks at the working conditions of professional athletes and the odds of making it to the big leagues. Though a career in sport is very attractive to young people, the odds of cashing in on a big sport contract are long indeed.

Collegiate sport programs at the major institutions classified as NCAA Division I FBS operate as another form of professional sport, except that they compensate athletes for participation only through athletic scholarships. Of the roughly 2,500 colleges in the United States, only about 100 operate their athletic program as a big business. However, these schools get most of the media attention and notoriety.

Finally, the chapter addresses the business side of recreational sport. The amount of money spent on recreational sport has escalated rapidly in recent years as more people have participated in athletic activities. In fact, the total annual cost of sporting goods purchases and health club memberships has exceeded $70 billion. In 2013, spectator sport accounted for $34.3 billion in revenue, and millions more have been spent in providing facilities and services to average citizens who participate in sport for leisure (Plunkett Research 2014).

STUDENT OUTCOMES

After reading this chapter, you will know the following:

- The evolution of media in presenting sport
- How the media affect sport and how sport affects the media
- How sport affects ideology
- Careers in sport media

Media and Sport

Media and Sport

Even when we attend a game in person, we still depend on the media to help present the game. We're curious about what others think, how they saw the same plays, and what they think it all meant. After a game, have you ever turned on the postgame summary to hear about what happened? Have you watched replays of key plays or events? Listened to coaches' or other experts' opinions about the game? Read about the game the next day on a sport news website? Checked Twitter to see what your friends thought and what they're feeling? Read personal blogs by athletes who participated in the event? It's almost enough to make us wonder if maybe a sporting event doesn't exist unless the media report it and we share it with somebody.

It makes sense to follow a discussion about the business of sport (chapter 4) with an analysis of the role that the mass media play in sport. In fact, the media exert tremendous influence on sport by generating revenue through free publicity and advertisements. Equally substantial is the influence of sport programming on the media; in fact, sport is the reason that some media outlets exist, and it serves as a healthy source of revenue for many others. Clearly, then, the economic effects of the sport–media relationship are significant to the overall business of sport. For consumers of sport, sport media fulfill a number of functions.

- They help create excitement leading up to sport events, describe the action during the event, and offer analysis and criticism afterward.
- They convey to fans the significance of the game, the players, the history, and the individual matchups. In fact, we rely on the media to give us the information that makes each of us a quasi expert on the game—able to discuss it with friends and strangers who also are quasi experts with their own opinions.
- Personal emotional attachments are developed through media features about athletes, coaches, and teams leading up to a season or a specific contest. We pick our favorite performers based on our own interests and experiences. Athletes with compelling personal stories, such as a struggle to overcome injury, often capture fans' imagination and develop large fan clubs. Underdogs are typically favorites, as are rookies, aging veterans, and athletes with a knack for delivering peak performance under pressure.
- For many people, preoccupation with sport is a healthy form of recreation and entertainment that helps them escape from everyday life. Rooting for their favorite team or player often provides emotional excitement and drama.

The media that cover sport usually fit into two broad categories: electronic and print. **Electronic media** are by far the largest media sources and deliver their content via the Internet, television, or radio; **print media** include printed newspapers, magazines, and books. In addition, these days, nearly all traditional print media sources (especially magazines and newspapers) have a web presence as well. For example, *Sports Illustrated* delivers its content both electronically and in a weekly print edition. Moreover, the World Wide Web is just one kind of Internet use. As you are no doubt aware, access to the Internet is not limited to traditional computers but is also now available through smartphones and tablets. This environment has enabled rapid growth and expanding options in electronic peer-to-peer communication.

Each of us has an inclination toward certain media that we enjoy and feel comfortable with, but all of us are also exposed to sport coverage in various types of media as technological advances encourage integration across media types. In the 1920s and 1930s, sport news was delivered by print media and radio. In the 1950s, television began to dominate sport delivery, and it maintained that position through the end of the 20th century. Around the turn of the century, the Internet began to open up new ways to relay sport news, and nowadays electronic news, entertainment, and social media services make up the primary delivery system for sport around the world. As a harbinger of today's reality, the 2010 World Cup was the first international event to use Twitter to keep the world informed of its results in real time.

As consumers of professional sport, we can be categorized as either *direct* or *indirect* spectators.

Direct spectators attend a live sporting event at a stadium, arena, or other venue. **Indirect spectators** listen to or watch sport through radio, television, or the Internet. Although direct spectators continue to increase in record numbers, that increase is relatively modest as compared with the increase in indirect spectators. Indeed, electronic coverage, particularly video, has opened up sport viewing to millions of fans around the world. Major sporting events are now broadcast live across time zones and to people in diverse cultures who often rearrange their sleep patterns or daily activities to catch a live telecast of an event such as the Super Bowl or the Olympic Games.

Consider, for example, the power of the 2014 Super Bowl, which attracted 82,529 direct spectators and 111.5 million U.S. indirect spectators, and was viewed in more than 53 million homes. In addition, over the course of the game, 5.6 million people in the United States sent a total of 25.3 million tweets about the game (Nielsen 2014a). Even the halftime show, featuring Bruno Mars and the Red Hot Chili Peppers, drew 115.3 million viewers and broke the previous record of 114 million set by Madonna in 2012 (Huffington Post 2014).

To put the 2014 Super Bowl's viewership into perspective, we have to go back to 1983, to the final episode of the classic TV series *M*A*S*H* (a military comedy set during the Korean War), which set the standard for most-watched television show in U.S. history with 105 million viewers. That record survived until 2010, when the New Orleans Saints claimed Super Bowl XLIV with a 31-17 win over the Indianapolis Colts in a game that drew 106.5 million viewers. Since 2010, every Super Bowl has surpassed the *M*A*S*H* record. In fact, the top 21 viewer events in U.S. television history are all Super Bowls when calculated by "total audience"

POP CULTURE

NFL Films

In 1960, pro football was the fourth most popular spectator sport in the United States, trailing baseball, college football, and boxing. Over the next decade, however, it exploded into first place, and it has continued its upward trajectory in the years since. Part of the reason for this rise is found in NFL Films, founded by Ed Sabol as a family business, which helped transform professional football into the sport media juggernaut it is today. For his contribution to professional football, Ed Sabol was inducted into the Pro Football Hall of Fame. His son Steve inherited the business and used his lifelong love of movies to develop a way of filming and presenting football that set the standard for every network—and continues to do so.

Indeed, the mundane business of filming sport highlights has now become an art form. The Sabols integrated classical music, poetic scripts, creative techniques, and voiceover narration by announcer John Facenda (whose rich tones were hailed as the "voice of God") to thrill and inspire a generation of football fanatics. Over the years, NFL Films also won critical praise, as represented by an amazing 35 Emmy Awards.

Each year, NFL Films carefully sought to capture the essence of that season in the form of breathtaking tackles, throws, and catches interspersed with scenes of heartbreak and jubilation. The crew filmed elements such as coaches' inspirational pregame speeches, snorts of linemen in the trenches, a flip of the hair from a cheerleader, and raucous reactions from fans who were either pleased or dismayed by the performance of the home team. The annual year-in-review digest powerfully portrayed this violent yet intriguing sport that rapidly captured the hearts of many Americans.

Sports Illustrated magazine once referred to NFL Films as "perhaps the most effective propaganda organ in the history of corporate America." Steve Sabol passed away from a brain tumor in 2012 at age 69, but his legacy and that of NFL Films lives on in today's television presentations of football that use similar creative techniques and wizardry (*Tampa Bay Times* 2012).

(which counts anyone who watched any part of the game, whereas "average audience" indicates the average number of viewers for the entire event). The viewership numbers quoted in this paragraph refer to average number of viewers (Posnanski, 2014; Deans 2010).

Because television stations are owned by corporations, sport and large corporations are inextricably linked through the media. The complex relationships that arise as a result of this link influence decisions about which sports and events to present and how to present them. This chapter looks at these relationships—how the media affect sport, and how sport affects the media. It also examines careers in sport media, as well as some of the challenges faced by women in this field.

Evolution of Sport Media

Growing up in the 1950s, I relied on news of professional sport from two major sources: newspapers and radio. A few times a year, I convinced my dad to purchase tickets to a live game, where I was thrilled to see my favorite players perform in person. Nothing compared to being at a game, but for most of the year I was entertained by poring over the daily sport pages for game results, writers' opinions, and team or individual statistics. Games were broadcast regularly on radio, and families and groups of fans gathered around to listen to the play-by-play description. I also spent many nights alone in my room, listening to radio broadcasts of a seemingly endless season of baseball games through the spring, summer, and fall.

Without radio and newspaper, few members of my generation would have become avid sport fans. These media provided our link to each game, stimulated our dreams and conversations, and helped form our attitudes toward both sport and life. Professional sport boomed in popularity through this exposure, and advertisers took advantage of that popularity to sell their wares.

Radio coverage of sport events began in the 1920s, which just happened to be the golden age of sport; in turn, sport helped make the late 1920s and early 1930s the golden age of radio. In the United States, the roaring '20s were also called the golden age of sports as more workers had increased leisure time, and a wide array of sports both collegiate and professional were flourishing. National sport heroes abounded led by Babe Ruth and Lou Gehrig in baseball, Bill Tilden and Helen Wills in tennis, Bobby Jones in golf, Jack Dempsey in boxing, Johnny Weissmuller in swimming, and Red Grange in football (Hoffman, 2013). By the end of the twentieth century, radio stations in the United States broadcast more than half a million hours of sport events annually. Many stations converted to an all-sport format, and by 1998 there were 160 such stations. In addition to broadcasting live action, sport stations began to provide talk shows that sparked exchanges of opinion, particularly about local teams and well-known athletes (Sage 1998).

The first sport pages in newspapers appeared sporadically in the second half of the nineteenth century in big-city dailies. The first modern sport section is credited to William Randolph Hearst, publisher of the *New York Journal*. As Hearst acquired newspapers in other cities, he spread the sport section to Los Angeles, San Francisco, Boston, and Chicago, and sport pages thrived in newspapers during the 1920s. As professional baseball and football rose in popularity, as horse racing and boxing thrived, and as golf and tennis gained an audience, the public thirst for sport news demanded more and more information. Virtually every major newspaper created a sport section staffed by a small army of researchers, beat writers, columnists, features editors, photographers, and design editors.

During the 1950s, television became a fact of life in homes throughout the United States; indeed, by 1955, 67 percent of U.S. homes had a television set. Just five years later, that figure had jumped to 87 percent, and by 2000 it had risen to 98 percent (Neuman 2005). In 2011, for the first time in two decades, the number of homes with a television set decreased, by more than 1.2 million. According to Nielsen reports, there were essentially two reasons: First, the switch from analog to digital broadcasting made television too expensive for some poorer households, who simply opted out. Second, other consumers were increasingly foregoing a TV set in favor of viewing video content on desktop computers, laptops, and electronic tablets (Caulfield 2011).

The advent of television changed U.S. sport forever. Indirect consumers of sport—those who watched by means of television—gradually became the pacesetters among fans. Millions of fanatics sat glued to their TV sets, watching live-action sport. The end of the 1950s was marked by what many consider the "greatest game ever played," the 1958 National Football League (NFL) championship between the Baltimore Colts and the New York Giants. It was the first overtime championship in NFL history, and the Colts' dramatic win propelled professional football to an unprecedented run of popularity that has endured for more than 50 years.

Television networks latched on to sport in order to fill up weekends with programming that they did not have to invent or stage. At the same time, workers and their families, who were looking for entertainment and relaxation, often sat down in front of the TV. As a result, advertisers lined up to sponsor sport events in order to reach the attractive audience of males who often acted as the decision makers for their families and businesses.

With this mix, it seemed that television couldn't broadcast enough sport events to satisfy the demand. Then, in 1979, ESPN (initially known as the Entertainment and Sports Programming Network) was born as the first full-time sport station. All day, every day, ESPN made sport events available on its family of stations. More recently developed all-sport networks include FoxSports and regional networks, such as Madison Square Garden (MSG) and Sun Sports. The last few decades have also seen the development of channels devoted to a single sport, such as golf or tennis, that cater to niche audiences.

The mass media disseminate information to large numbers of geographically dispersed people. Through television, for example, people across the country and around the world can view sport contests in real time. They learn about the sport, the specific game, and the players through the live telecast itself; through the announcers, who provide play-by-play descriptions; and through "color commentators," who point out highlights and background information. The plethora of cable channels, specialized sport networks, and sport packages has also contributed to a diffusion of the television audience. Those who want to watch sport all day (or night) can do so thanks to the 24-7 availability of sport programming.

New ways to watch television programs are also changing the business model for the industry; typically, that business model has involved scheduling programs and events at certain times and expecting a mass audience to view them. In effect, networks have "pushed" viewers to watch events and shows at times chosen by the networks. However, technological advances, such as digital video recorders (DVRs), now allow people to record any program and replay it at their convenience; in addition, recording services are available from the likes of TiVo, Netflix, and Hulu, which also offers free live streaming. This phenomenon, referred to as "time shifting," has complicated the process of calculating TV ratings because many people don't watch their saved programs until a week or more later. As a result, viewership tracking companies, such as Nielsen, cannot gauge viewership by using their traditional methods.

The model of the future seems to be one in which viewers "pull" TV programs from storage at a time that is convenient for them. Time shifting also allows viewers to skip advertisements if they wish, thus fracturing the television business model that has been in place for more than 50 years. Sport, however, is much less affected by time shifting than other television programming because most viewers prefer to watch live broadcasts of sport. In fact, according to an official at Disney, which owns ESPN, 99.4 percent of sport is watched live (Badenhausen 2012b, 3).

In spite of the enormous influence of TV on sport viewing since the 1950s, fewer people than ever are watching television. Just as TV eventually forced newspapers and magazines to the fringes of the media world, multimedia electronics such as computers and smartphones are pushing television into the background. In fact, according to Nielsen's Total Audience Report, about 2.6 million U.S. households are now "broadband only," meaning that they neither subscribe to cable nor use a broadcast signal; moreover, that number doubled between 2013 and 2014.

On a daily basis, viewers in the United States watched about 12 minutes less television in 2014 than they did a year earlier. Overall, viewers spend about 14.5 hours per month watching video on their phones and tablets—or about a tenth of a tenth of the time they spend watching TV (Luckerson 2014). Here are some additional changes in U.S. TV viewing according to two articles in *Business Insider* (Blodget 2012; Edwards 2013):

- Fewer households have a physical television set.
- Fewer people are watching TV.
- Broadcast ratings have been declining even for some major TV events like the World Series.

IN THE ARENA WITH . . .

ESPN

ESPN, which bills itself as "the worldwide leader in sports," was founded as an all-day sport television station in 1979 in Bristol, Connecticut, by Bill Rasmussen, his son Scott Rasmussen, and Ed Eagan. Original funding for the new venture was provided by Getty Oil Company. The rest, as they say, is history. ESPN's signature telecast, SportsCenter, aired its 50,000th episode on September 13, 2012.

ESPN is now worth an estimated $50 billon and claims the title of the world's most valuable media property (Badenhausen 2014b). Currently owned by Disney (80 percent) and the Hearst Corporation (20 percent), ESPN generates the most significant portion of annual income for Disney, without which Disney might not even exist. In fact, as former Disney CEO Michael Eisner once put it, "the protection of Mickey Mouse is ESPN" (Starkman 2013, 2).

From just one television station, the ESPN family has grown to include more than a dozen related channels, franchises, and business units. Perhaps the best known are ESPN2, ESPN3, ESPNU, and ESPNClassic, along with the Longhorn Network (focused on the University of Texas) and the SEC Network (focused on the Southeastern Conference). In addition, espnW is a relatively new venture begun in 2009 to connect young women with sport. It is the first national digital media business designed for female athletes, and ESPN hopes for it to become the premier sport media home for girls and women.

Still, not all is rosy for this sport media power. It has been the subject of criticism for biased coverage, conflicts of interest, and various controversies involving individual broadcasters and analysts. Perhaps no criticism is more difficult to shake than that of suffering from a conflict of interest. This criticism hinges on the fact that ESPN holds substantial financial interests in various leagues and sport organizations that it covers. For example, ESPN will receive more than $15 billion to broadcast NFL football games through 2021 (Starkman 2013). It also holds contracts with the college football playoffs, Major League Baseball (MLB), the National Basketball Association (NBA), and various college sport leagues, including the Pac-12, the Big Ten, the Big 12, and the SEC.

It would be a stretch to imagine ESPN broadcasting program content that might reflect badly on any of these entities. In fact, when the NFL asked ESPN to join its study of head injuries, ESPN originally agreed to do so but eventually backed out. In a sense, the NFL was hoping that ESPN would help the league put its best face on a topic that has increasingly drawn damaging criticism of the league (Starkman 2013).

ESPN also acts as a unique power broker in college football. Its broadcast agreements with the power conferences have caused a wholesale migration of top college football teams who want their share of guaranteed TV dollars before a game is even played. In addition, ESPN influences which games are scheduled, sets game times to maximize its viewing audience, and affects which college football conferences thrive and which ones fold over the long run. On a more specific basis, when ESPN hosts its College GameDay broadcast at a given campus, it provides that institution with advertising exposure that it could never afford on its own.

And finally, even though some people have little or no interest in sport, if they wish to subscribe to cable television they must still pay a premium price due in part to the cost of including ESPN in the channel lineup. They may resent subsidizing sport for the rest of us, but there's little they can do about it.

- Fewer viewers watch shows when they are broadcast (except live sport).
- Viewers increasingly do not watch shows with ads, even on a DVR.
- Viewers watch a lot of TV and movie content—but mostly on demand via Netflix, iTunes, or HBO.
- People tend to get their news from the Internet (except when a major crisis occurs).
- People watch on various screens for convenience (for example, TV, laptop, smartphone, or tablet).

Another change came about in 2014 when CBS, following the lead of HBO, announced the interactive streaming CBSN—the first live-anchored news network across all leading digital platforms. The next network to offer a stand-alone online TV service may well be Starz. This development means that viewers are no longer locked into a cable or satellite subscription service that offers hundreds of channels in which they have no interest; instead, they can choose channels they will actually watch (Cheredar 2014).

Just as television changed how families in the 1950s interacted with sport, the Internet gives twenty-first-century fans another way to experience sport. It provides sport fans with virtual access to sport on demand and in real time and allows them to create personal, specific methods of interaction. For example, people can visit the website of a favorite team, check scores, listen to games in progress, order tickets, browse for stories, read sport blogs, and enter chat rooms to discuss event results.

In fact, we can now go online to track the progress of sport events anywhere in the world and access perspectives from sport newsrooms around the world. The administration of U.S. president Barack Obama has poured billions of dollars into expanding the reach of the Internet, and today nearly 98 percent of U.S. homes have access to some form of high-speed broadband service. Even so, roughly 20 percent of the U.S. population still does not use the Internet—chiefly elderly people and those in low income brackets (Wyatt 2013).

Another milestone was reached in 2013, when for the first time a majority (56 percent) of the U.S. populace owned a smartphone of some kind. In the United States, 92 percent of adults own some type of cell phone, but one third of them (35 percent) have some other type that is not a smartphone. Demographic research reveals that smartphone ownership is slightly higher among men than women (59 percent to 53 percent) and slightly higher among black and Hispanic people (64 percent and 60 percent, respectively) than among white people (53 percent). In terms of age groups, the 18-to-34 category has the highest smartphone ownership rate at 80 percent, and the rate drops steadily from there on, to just 18 percent of the 65-plus age group.

Smartphones, tablets, and other electronic devices have changed the way in which sport fans access the media.

Smartphone ownership is also affected by education level. Specifically, people with the highest levels of education own these devices at nearly double the rate of people with less than a high school diploma. Similarly, higher-income Americans are more likely to own a smartphone, and nearly 60 percent of those who live in an urban or suburban area own such a device, as compared with just 40 percent of rural folks (A. Smith 2013).

Some people use the Internet to supplement televised sport and print media coverage, but for the majority of people in the United States, the Internet is now the primary source for both general news and sport news. Fans who follow their sport via **social media** report using the following platforms: Facebook (89 percent), Twitter (33 percent), YouTube (65 percent), and Google+ (18 percent). Other options—including Instagram, Flickr, and blogs—have also opened up possibilities for sport news and discussion (Laird 2012).

Beyond simply reporting the news, social networking sites link sport fans with each other and with professional athletes to enable the sharing of ideas and images at lightning speed around the world. In 2012, 26 percent of sport fans reported using social media to follow leagues, teams, and players and to access late-breaking sport results. That was an increase from just 15 percent the year before, and the trend is clearly heading upward at a rapid pace (Laird 2012).

The Internet also enables a wide variety of programming by video streaming in real time, which, for example, allows fans to watch their alma mater play a football game in another time zone or follow their daughter's college volleyball game. Even high school sport has gotten into the business of streaming, both locally and nationally, and the National Federation of State High School Associations streams all types of high school sport across the country. As a result, you can use the organization's website to watch a state championship tennis match in Wisconsin or an ice hockey match in North Dakota. You can also access live streaming of sport events for free at SportLemon, Stream2Watch, WatchESPN, FirstRow Sports, and Wiziwig.

Major League Baseball established its advanced media site (MLBAM) in 2000, and the result is an entity that generates $620 million per year. This Internet company operates the league's official website and the 30 MLB club websites via MLB.com, which draws four million hits per day. Its most successful venture is MLB At Bat, which can be used to track or watch on devices such as the iPhone, iPad, Xbox, and Amazon Kindle (*Wharton Alumni Magazine* 2007; NYConvergence 2012).

Similarly, the National Collegiate Athletic Association (NCAA) began to tap into new media formats and services in 2010, beginning with an on-demand website for its Division I men's basketball tournament in cooperation with CBS. On the first day of the tournament, the website generated the largest-ever single-day volume of Internet traffic for a live sport event; specifically, 3.4 million hours of live video and audio streaming were consumed by 3 million unique viewers (Osborne 2010). That was the beginning of a new era for the NCAA in providing live video coverage of what has become known as "March Madness."

In 2014, NCAA.com (managed by Turner Sports) introduced a new NCAA sport app that provides an extensive viewing experience with broader social integration. The app for iPhone and iPod Touch was redesigned to offer exclusive live streaming video for more than 65 NCAA championships and more than 350 live events. The app provides access to scores and schedules, custom scoring alerts, and team hubs featuring a user's favorite schools. In addition, Turner Sports and CBS Sports together provided live coverage of all 67 games of the Division I men's basketball tournament, including the Final Four on TBS and the championship game on CBS. The women's basketball championship was covered from the regional games through the championship game (Reynold 2013; NCAA 2014e).

If you search for "sports" or "athletes" on YouTube, you'll find countless hits, including sport blooper videos, commercials, athlete interviews, videos about women in sport, profiles of athletes at every level of competition, and many more results. The three most popular sport channels on YouTube are Sports (general) with 77.2 million subscribers, the National Basketball Association with 5.9 million subscribers and 2.47 billion views, and World Wrestling Entertainment (WWE) with 4.6 million subscribers and 2.33 billion views; no other sport channels even come close to these leaders (VidstatsX 2014).

Fantasy sports have also cornered a significant share of the Internet marketplace. According to a survey by the Fantasy Sports Trade Association (FSTA), an industry organization representing more than 110 companies, some 33 million Ameri-

Did you know that there are award shows for fantasy leagues? Here, Le'Veon Bell of the Pittsburgh Steelers accepts the 2015 NFL.com fantasy player of the year award.

can adults participate in fantasy sports, and this activity generates more than $1 billion in revenue per year. About 85 percent of gamers play fantasy football, and 40 percent play fantasy baseball. The most typical player is a white male between the ages of 18 and 49 with an above-average education; he also possesses above-average income, which makes him a marketer's dream.

The average cost to the player per year is about $150. Fantasy sports are not regulated by gambling rules, since the outcome of games has been judged to be based more on participants' skill and knowledge than on chance. Fantasy sports participants spend an average of 17 hours per week consuming sport entertainment, of which 8.5 hours involve fantasy sport (Fantasy Sports Trade Association 2013).

Recent years have also seen a meteoric rise in e-sport or video game competition. Early in 2014, e-sport reached a critical mass by attracting more than 70 million viewers worldwide, roughly half of them from the United States. This means that there is a sufficient number of players to make e-sports self-sustaining. The average e-sport viewer watches 19 times per month for a session lasting 2.2 hours. These competitions have become extremely popular on some college campuses, including Harvard University and Florida State University, and they have been dominated by West Coast schools such as the University of Washington (SuperData Research 2014).

In 2014, Robert Morris University in Chicago even created an official video game team in its athletic department and offered scholarships to team members. The fact is, however, that e-sports are not sports nor are they even about sports; rather, they are games played on video devices. For his part, ESPN boss John Skipper has declared that e-sports "are not a sport" and pointed out that no physical activity is involved. What e-sports do involve is competition for prize money (US$25 million in 2013) and more than 70 million viewers in 2013 (SuperData Research 2014; Tassi 2014; Wingfield 2014).

The rise of the Internet is one cause of the declining print circulation of major newspapers. In fact, newspaper circulation has been falling slowly since the 1980s, but that descent now seems to be moderating. Since the recession of 2007, newspapers have found some grounds for optimism. For one thing, companies have adjusted by making major organizational changes and experimenting with a variety of new revenue streams. Digital pay plans have been or are being adopted at nearly half of the country's daily newspapers, including large, midsize, and even small papers.

Thanks to these changes, as well as price increases and in some cases reduced printing frequency (for example, three times per week), revenues have stabilized in spite of a continuing drop in advertising revenue. Still, however, the newspaper industry is now only about half the size it used to be. Moreover, digital advertising has been slow to develop and will likely never approach the level of previous print advertising because of the number of choices now available including social media. Instead, newspapers are hoping to offset the loss of advertising revenue with increases in digital subscribers.

The *Wall Street Journal* remains number one in total circulation of combined print and digital at 2.3 million, followed by the *New York Times* at 1.8 million, *USA Today* at 1.6 million, and the *Los Angeles Times* at 610,000. In an exception to the norm, the *New York Times* boasts 1.1 million digital copies daily versus just 731,000 print copies, whereas the other papers have about twice as many print copies as digital copies (Beaujon 2013).

As technology improves and access to the Internet increases, websites continue fighting to win consumers. Media corporations enter the fray and try to entice consumers by offering exclusive data and entertainment on their sites. Eventually, Internet access may allow us to design our own sport entertainment by giving us access to novel event presentations with unique camera angles, favorite announcers, instant replay on demand, and player and coach interviews. The interactive nature of such experiences will draw us closer to the action and make us more involved than the average spectator if we choose.

Even though sport fans love the opportunity to connect with sport figures via social media, athletes and coaches themselves are often pulling back. Too many athletes have tweeted in the heat of the moment without thinking through the possible repercussions and ended up embarrassing themselves or their team. At the collegiate level, the NCAA sets no rules or policies regarding social media, instead leaving the matter to individual universities. Most collegiate athletes are expected to conform to school or team policies regarding cell phones, Twitter, and other social media.

Some coaches and schools even require athletes on scholarship to sign a contract pledging their adherence to school policy regarding social media. Such regulation is most common among high-profile teams, such as football and basketball, where fan interest is the most intense and extensive. Generally, players are expected to avoid the use of cell phones and social media during team activities, such as meetings, practices, study halls, and of course competitions. Most universities also caution players about the content of their social media comments and offer suggestions and guidance. Some have expressed concern that such restrictions may exceed the authority of a university, especially a public one, by unfairly restricting athletes' free speech. As of yet, this issue is not subject to any court decisions that might provide guidance (Santos 2014).

In contrast, professional athletes are generally encouraged by their leagues and teams to be active on social media in order to generate interest and loyalty by interacting with fans. However, all of the major pro leagues have leaguewide policies and individual team policies about when and what athletes can communicate through social media. For example, the NFL, NBA, and MLB all make it clear that when players are "at work"—which means during team meetings, practices, games, and in the times immediately before and after a game—they should not be on social media. These three leagues leave it up to individual teams or the commissioner to discipline players for inappropriate use of social media. The National Hockey League (NHL) is the only major professional league with a collectively bargained social media policy. Essentially the policy prohibits the use of social media during a blackout period on game days, makes it clear that players can be held responsible for their communications on social media, and can be disciplined by the league for comments deemed to be prejudicial to the NHL, the sport, a member club, or the officials (Friedman, 2012).

Internet-enabled TV sets are relatively new and do not currently constitute much of a factor, but

APPLYING SOCIAL THEORY

Interactionist Theory and Athletes on Social Media

The perspective of an interactionist theorist is one that tends to view society from the bottom up rather than from the top down. From this point of view, consider the dilemma of a professional athlete who is encouraged by his employers to use social media to interact regularly with fans as a way of promoting the sport and stoking fans' interest and loyalty. The athlete, however, is wary of revealing too much about his personality or personal beliefs to the public. He's also concerned about the negative effects that casual statements might have on potential endorsement contracts. The employer expects the athlete's cooperation, but the athlete feels a responsibility to himself to project the best possible professional image. From the perspective of interactionist theory, does the professional athlete have a responsibility to his employer to be available via social media—and if so, to what extent?

predictions are that they will exert the greatest effect of any medium on sport consumption. At the present time, however, live sport programming is very rare on the Internet. The NBA offers some games for streaming, but they are not the ones shown on broadcast television. ESPN3 also offers Internet access to live programming not carried on broadcast TV. In addition, for the most part, Internet-enabled televisions do not yet offer the same quality of big-screen, high-definition experience that makes sport so compelling on broadcast or cable television.

As we approach the middle of the decade, an Internet-enabled television is a good choice for streaming videos from YouTube, updating a Twitter account, checking the weather, monitoring the news, or streaming high-definition movies (for example, from Netflix). However, in the next decade, the possibilities on your TV may be endless in terms of live streaming of sports of every kind, at every level, and available when you want to watch them (Pishardy 2013).

Interplay of Sport and Media

Professional spectator sports depend on the media for survival. Ticket sales to live events simply cannot generate enough money to make professional events profitable without media support. The overwhelming bulk of revenue that sport generates from the media comes from television fees.

For example, the two most valuable Major League Baseball franchises are the New York Yankees at $2.5 billion and the Los Angeles Dodgers at $2 billion. A major part of that valuation depends on the guaranteed revenue from their regional sport networks, YES for the Yankees and SportsNet LA for the Dodgers, in which they each have a controlling interest. For 2014, each team received $84 million in rights fees and more than $100 million in dividends from their TV network. As you might suspect, these TV deals allow both teams to spend on player rosters that are the highest paid in Major League Baseball at $235 million for the Dodgers and $204 million for the Yankees in 2014 (Ozanian 2014).

Amateur sport other than NCAA football and basketball has a much more casual link with the media. For the most part, the media restrict their attention to occasionally featuring certain amateur events, particularly those that provide a public service, or to reporting on local amateur sport events in order to encourage local readership.

Let's look now at the ways in which sport and media affect each other.

How Television Affects Sport

In his seminal book *Sports in America* (1987), James Michener estimated that television expended more than $200 million annually on sport. That amount seemed unbelievable then, but it is far exceeded by today's annual rights fees. For example, for its 2014 season, the NFL negotiated agreements with ESPN, NBC, CBS, Fox, DirecTV, and its own NFL Network that generated a total of more than $6 billion for the league. Though the NFL is not required to release this financial information, one of its franchises—the Green Bay Packers—is required to do so because it is a public company. As one of 32 NFL franchises, the Packers received 1/32 of the TV money, or about $200 million for the year (Rovell 2014).

The NFL's $6 billion in TV money far surpasses the amounts for the other professional leagues in the United States, which as of 2014 stood at $1.6 billion for MLB, $0.9 billion for the NBA, and $0.6 billion for the NHL (Gaines 2014). Virtually every major sport relies on television contracts for the majority of its income, and TV money far surpasses revenue from ticket sales to people who attend the contests in person.

Television viewing can be expanded dramatically through effective marketing, event presentation, outreach to new audiences, expansion to include more female fans, and general worldwide expansion (as U.S. sports gain popularity in other parts of the world and as internationally popular sports are broadcast in North America). Technology has helped expose U.S. sports in other countries and fueled the expansion of baseball, basketball, and American football. The major U.S. professional leagues have all experimented with playing some games overseas in order to expand their revenue base with varying degrees of success.

The Olympic Games have also grown into a huge moneymaker through expanding television coverage around the world. In 1980, the broadcast rights for the Summer Olympic Games in Moscow cost $87 million for the U.S. rights. That figure grew to $793 million for the 2004 Games in Athens. By 2012, the television rights fees for the United States alone grew to $2 billion. In fact, for the four-year cycle or quadrennium that includes both the Winter and Summer Games, the International Olympic Committee (IOC) broke the $8 billion barrier in total revenue due largely to a 52 percent increase since the previous cycle in the value of the Games' media rights. This dramatic increase is attributed largely to the maturing of new television markets, particularly in China; to increased competition between networks in mature markets such as the United States; to the increasing role of pay-television, for example in Italy; and to the developing market for broadband and mobile rights (Murray 2012).

Broadcasts of the 2012 Summer Olympics from London are presently the most watched event in history, with a global reach of 3.6 billion people in 220 countries, which amounted to 76 percent of the potential global audience. In the United States alone, more than 219 million people tuned in, and the viewing audience during prime time averaged 31.1 million. When the Olympics were last held in London, in 1948, TV coverage was broadcast only to about 500,000 people, who lived within a 50-mile radius of the city.

In addition, the 2012 London Games marked the first time that the number of viewers using Internet, mobile, and other digital platforms exceeded the number of traditional television viewers. Altogether, official broadcast partners delivered more than 1.9 billion video streams globally on more than 170 digital platforms or websites (IOC 2014b).

Perhaps the most important factor affecting revenue in professional sport is the potential marketplace provided by televised sport. Part of the reason is the fact that revenue from live attendance can grow only so much, both because only a certain number of spectators can attend any given event and because ticket prices can be raised only so much without cutting into demand. With this reality in mind, let's review what television means to sport:

- Television networks pay sizable fees for broadcast rights to professional sport leagues, organizations, and franchises.
- Advertisers pay for the right to advertise their products to viewers during sport events.
- Sport owners and leagues can afford to pay athletes huge salaries due to the guaranteed income provided by television coverage.
- Ticket sales and other game-day revenues pale in comparison with the income derived from the sale of television rights.
- Money is the most significant link between the media and professional sport. As rights fees increase, professional sport relies even more heavily on television for its revenue stream. As a result, television's influence on sport grows, and the television industry increasingly affects how sport events are presented to viewers.

How the Media Affect Sport

Few people would dispute the assertion that the media can positively affect sport even beyond guaranteeing income through television rights. For example, the media can

- affect the popularity of sport,
- provide free publicity for local teams, and
- present player personalities and build fan allegiance to teams and individual players.

In fact, the popularity of both collegiate and professional sport exploded as more and more U.S. homes gained access to television. Even people who had little or no interest in sport couldn't help but catch bits of games as they surfed the channels. They didn't even have to leave their chairs to see the games. Sport announcers hyped each contest to draw viewers in, and once they caught viewers' attention, they enthusiastically and concisely described the game, making it exciting to watch.

Expert commentators work hard to strike a delicate balance by educating viewers who know little about the sport without insulting diehard fans. For people who enjoy history, statistics, individual matchups, and record-setting performances, TV presentations offer all that and more. You don't need to lift a finger to find out more about a particular event than you ever wanted to know. You can just sit back, relax, and let the game come to you. And now, options such as DVR allow you to view games on your own schedule, so you can even decide *when* you want to spend time watching sport. Thus the media have expanded the popularity of sport by making sport spectatorship accessible, fun, and convenient for the masses.

Free publicity for the local professional team is a major contribution from all media outlets. Imagine what it would cost team owners to purchase all the publicity they receive from blogs, tweets, social media postings, and print and broadcast news stories—and the larger the market, the higher the

ESPN's GameDay provides publicity to the school where each broadcast is held—in this case, SMU. This is just one example of how the media can affect sport.

number of media outlets and the larger the potential audience. Local businesses further publicize sport by advertising their support of local teams in hopes of attracting customers who are fans.

Individual players also depend on the media for publicity. Star players are given a public face in their community, receiving recognition for their sport performances and perhaps also kudos for visiting local schools or supporting local charities. Fans develop heroes, seek their autographs or pictures, follow their careers, join their fan clubs, and wear their jersey numbers. Kids imitate their style of play.

In addition, a star player's life is often scrutinized, and athletes dedicated to their family are praised and held up as role models. Of course, those who appear in the news for less attractive reasons quickly find out that the media can also be harsh critics. Without the media's presentation of athletes, however, fans would have little opportunity to relate to them; indeed, uniforms tend to make one player look like all the rest.

In newspapers across the country (in both their electronic and print versions), local headlines feature the fortunes of the local team on the front page. Similarly, local radio talk shows invite callers to comment on the home team. Interviews with coaches and top athletes on television and social media help local fans understand a team's attitude toward a game before, during, and after the contest. The local media, unabashedly rooting for the home team, nourish hometown pride and spirit.

At the same time, the media can negatively affect sport by changing the way in which it is presented to the audience. Traditionalists generally oppose *any* change in sport, claiming that changes ruin the integrity of the game. Depending on your point of view, however, you may see changes as negative developments or simply as signs of progress. Let's look now at how sport has changed over the last 25 years.

Rule Changes

Sport events that are unpredictable in length wreak havoc with television schedules. As a result, broadcasters have pressured sports to revise their format in order to ensure that contests finish in a predictable amount of time. In response, collegiate football instituted an overtime format in which the teams try to score from each other's 25-yard line. The excitement generated by this approach has been a pleasant by-product of the attempt to regulate game times. Even the more conservative NFL has introduced some revised overtime rules to limit the number of games that end in a tie.

The NFL has also adopted instant replay in order to ensure that officials' calls are correct; even though each coach is limited to two challenges, the time spent reviewing challenged plays has lengthened NFL games. College football has also begun to use instant replay, though on a more limited basis. The halftime break has also been modified by the NFL by reducing the time from 15 minutes to 12 minutes, while college football still allocates 20 minutes. Both moves were an effort to shorten the length of the game overall and to keep the viewer glued to the game by including game summaries, features, and analyses rather than the traditional marching bands that lose much of their entertainment value on television.

In tennis, a tiebreaker was instituted to decide sets in which the players are tied at six games each; in the tiebreaker, the first player to win 7 points and be ahead by 2 points wins the set. This change ensured that a set would end after the equivalent of 13 games rather than go on and on, as sometimes happened under the old rules. Thus the tiebreak contributes to the predictability of match lengths, which helps television producers plan their programming accordingly. Of course, from the spectator's point of view, the excitement generated by the critical tiebreak turned out to be a positive thing for the sport as well.

Tennis also scrapped its traditional "white clothing only" policy for bright colors, changed the color of tennis balls from white to yellow, and, more recently, changed tennis courts that were traditionally green to blue—all to make TV viewing more attractive. High-definition broadcasts further improved the product by allowing even older viewers to track the tennis ball moving at speeds upwards of 130 miles (210 kilometers) per hour. Finally, the newest change in tennis involves the use of electronic line-calling equipment for professional tournaments. By installing electrodes beneath the court surface, it is now possible to determine whether a ball is inside or outside the boundary or on the line. No longer does tennis need to rely solely on the unreliable eyesight or judgment of human umpires.

Golf has moved almost exclusively to medal play (in which the golfer with the lowest shot score wins), rather than match play (in which each hole earns 1 point for the winner of that hole). The dif-

At the start of the 2015 season, MLB instituted a pitching time limit rule in an effort to speed up the pace of the game.

ference between the two systems is that medal play tends to leave the outcome in doubt until later in the contest, perhaps even until the final hole. As a result, familiar players are more likely to be in the running on the final weekend, which pleases both fans and sponsors.

In basketball, the three-point shot was adopted to put more emphasis on long-range shooting and thereby reduce the dependence on large bodies pounding the ball inside to score. In addition, the size of the lane or key under the basket was expanded to help push big players out, thus opening up the game for more scoring with athletic moves. A shot clock was also instituted, requiring the team with the ball to shoot within a prescribed amount of time, in order to prevent the tactic of just holding onto the ball when leading near the end of a game. These changes have helped make basketball a more exciting sport for audiences who love high-scoring games and watching dramatic action.

Major League Baseball revised the strike zone and, in the American League, instituted the designated hitter in order to add more offense to the sport. Whereas purists may enjoy low-scoring pitchers' duels, the average television fan is more interested in seeing hitting and a barrage of home runs. Baseball also moved the majority of games to the evening in order to fill prime-time slots and attract the most viewers, especially during the playoffs.

Not all changes are pleasing to viewers, however. Perhaps the most annoying change for television viewers is the use of frequent time-outs to allow for television commercial breaks. These breaks can interrupt rallies and cause momentum to be lost just because the network is obliged to fulfill its promise to commercial sponsors. Indeed, watching football sometimes seems like watching a series of time-outs with a little action squeezed in between.

However, when you calculate the financial benefit of commercial time-outs, you can see why they have become standard practice. During the 2014 Super Bowl, for example, a 30-second ad cost commercial sponsors as much as $4 million (an all-time high), depending on the ad's placement during the game (Steinberg 2013). Of course, most NFL games do not produce that kind of income, but they still generate critical revenue.

Curiously, some sports have not adapted well to television. Notably, ice hockey moves so fast that the action is difficult to follow, and tracking the hockey puck is almost impossible. As a result, in the mid-1990s, the NHL experimented with a "smart puck" containing a microchip that transmitted a signal to a computer, which superimposed a blue and red halo around the puck on the screen, thus making it easier to track. However, the cost per puck was more than $50,000, and after a year of experimentation the NHL abandoned the effort (Mancini 2013).

The world's most popular sport—soccer—has also failed to catch on widely with U.S. television viewers due to the scarcity of scoring and the absence of time-outs for commercial breaks. The common complaint from potential viewers goes something like, "Why would I watch a sport where the score can end up 0-0?" With this sentiment in mind, both the NFL and the NBA have modified their rules to enhance scoring and thus give fans what they want. Soccer aficionados, however, say that low scoring is part of what makes the game so fascinating, because even one goal carries huge importance and the outcome is nearly always in doubt. Perhaps more significant is the fact that U.S. networks would rather broadcast football or basketball games, which accommodate the frequent breaks in the action when they can show commercials and thus make their money (Hershberger 2014).

Attendance Declines Due to Televised Sport

In some markets, the presentation of games on television has affected attendance in the stadium or arena. As a result, the NFL adopted a blackout rule, according to which a game cannot be broadcast within a range of roughly 150 miles (240 kilometers) of the venue unless all tickets are sold. Owners contend that without this rule, many fans would simply stay home to watch games on television rather than buy a ticket. The blackout rule was suspended for the 2015 season to see if eliminating blackouts negatively affected ticket sales.

Of course, when a game is blacked out, free access is also denied to the millions of fans who cannot afford to buy tickets or who prefer not to deal with the hassles of parking, uncertain weather, traffic, and so on. Diehard fans get around blackouts by purchasing games on a pay-per-view basis, which still creates revenue for the media and the teams, or by signing up for satellite programs that provide access to all NFL games on a given day. Blackout policies have been in effect for decades, but as times change and the majority of revenue comes from television, the NFL seems to be gradually phasing out these rules.

Professional sport is so accessible on television that fans become spoiled by watching superior athletes and thus often lose interest in the athletes who perform on local minor league, college, or high school teams. For a case in point, consider the decline of minor league baseball. In 1939, attendance at minor league games exceeded that of MLB games (15 million for the minors and 11 million for the majors). Many medium-sized cities across the country sponsored local teams, and local fans supported them.

Then came television, which offered an easy way to watch the top players in the country. Attendance dropped quickly for minor league franchises, and the number of minor league teams fell from nearly 500 in 1950 to about 150 just 25 years later. Today, there are only 17 minor league teams that are affiliated with MLB teams, and together they employ approximately 8,000 players. By comparison, the number of MLB players was 1,304 in 2013. Eventually, the role of player development that had been traditionally assigned to minor league baseball teams was filled largely by collegiate teams, who stepped up as the training ground for aspiring players (Leonard 1980).

Of course, minor league baseball was not the only victim of televised sport. Local college and high school sport teams also lose spectators to professional teams on television. Similarly, the relatively few colleges with big-time football teams whose games are broadcast on TV often draw fans away from the hundreds of other colleges that operate smaller football programs. High school games have avoided some of the conflict by scheduling football games on weeknights and Friday nights—times that do not conflict with professional sport and maximize the opportunity for fans to attend games in person.

As the reach of televised sport has increased and the technology has improved the product, many households contain a "man cave," where family members can watch multiple sport events on huge screens in high definition with realistic sideline sound. As the cost of attending a sport event has skyrocketed, thus putting attendance out of reach for a middle-class family, more fans seem to lean toward watching on television.

Scheduling Conflicts

Games are often scheduled based not on the interests of players or spectators but on the interests of television broadcasters. Here are a few examples:

- World Series games are typically scheduled on October nights in order to attract the maximum television audience on both coasts. Selling out the ballpark for a World Series game is not a problem, since only about 45,000 fans are needed; thus the largest fan base and income potential involve the television audience. Night baseball is not popular with most players, but they are accustomed to such games throughout the regular season. Late starting times on the East Coast mean that many potential fans, particularly children, are unable to watch because they have to go to bed. However, the late start allows people on the West Coast to get home from work or school and watch the game, which balances the loss of fans on the East Coast.
- *Monday Night Football* suffers from the same dilemma—the second half starts after bedtime for many East Coast fans, but starting late would not allow many fans on the West Coast to watch the game. Here's how NFL nighttime broadcasts fared in

EXPERT'S VIEW

Society of Professional Journalists

In 2014, the Society of Professional Journalists approved a new code of ethics replacing an earlier edition that was adopted in 1996. A lot has changed since 1996 including the dominance of the Internet, citizen journalists, and the explosion of social media. In order to maintain trust from both readers and sources, journalists understand their responsibilities to the public and to the people they cover.

Some of the critical issues discussed in debates among sports journalists included what role the reporter plays in regard to the team she covers. Most experts believe she should not function as a team publicist but simply report the facts, regardless of whether or not they reflect favorably on the team's image. However, that strategy has to be balanced so as not to lose the trust or the team or a team's players and thus become shut out of future news.

The trend of sports media to express opinions that lack factual basis or logical reasoning just to gain publicity and attention is a questionable practice and does not align with the ethics expected of a professional journalist. Separating fact from fiction is one of the most valuable insights a journalist can provide; this includes citing sources whenever possible or explaining the reasons for anonymity.

Similarly, the code of ethics encourages journalists to only print what is ethical, rather than what might be legal, and to consider the possible harm, discomfort, or damage the article might cause. When writing about a professional athlete's personal life, consider whether the information is relevant to the sport or her sport performance. The code also instructs journalists to "avoid conflicts of interest, real or perceived" and when that is not possible, make a full disclosure to the readers.

The full code of ethics is available at this website: www.spj.org/ethicscode.asp.

2013: Sunday averaged 22 million viewers, Monday 13.7 million, and Thursday only 7.1 million (Kissel 2014). The NCAA men's and women's basketball championships also start after 9 p.m. on the East Coast, thus shutting out young people—and many adults as well.

- The U.S. Open schedules tennis matches through negotiations between four main parties: tournament officials, representatives of the men's and women's tours, and television broadcasters. Guess who wields the most leverage in deciding which match to feature at what time? Players' preferences are largely ignored, and tournament officials know that the money from the TV rights pays their bills. Therefore, a match featuring a well-known U.S. player is likely to be scheduled in a prime-time spot instead of a matchup between two lesser-known international players. That's just the logical schedule for television programming.
- Olympic telecasts provide a critical source of income for the IOC, and events are therefore broadcast in such a way as to attract the maximum audience in various countries. Featured events such as gymnastics, swimming, and track and field—and, recently, women's and men's team sports, such as soccer and basketball—get the prime spots in the United States. In recent years, when the Olympic Games were broadcast from other parts of the world, U.S. broadcasts were typically tape-delayed to appear in the U.S. prime-time hours. As a result, eager fans who used the Internet or social media sites to follow the progress of certain events or athletes already knew the results before the events were shown on television.

Gambling

Gambling has always been part of the sport world. The posting of odds for each game in various media outlets increases the interest in finding out the winners and losers, the point spreads, and possible upsets. There is no way to tell how much local betting occurs between neighbors and friends, at bars, or in office pools; however, at playoff time, it's rare for an office not to have at least one betting pool.

More serious betting is aided by media reports on odds set in Las Vegas by bookmakers, picks provided by experts, daily reports about player injuries, and articles predicting outcomes. Those who worry about the unhealthy influence of gambling in society wish the media did less to accommodate those who do gamble. Sport gambling is examined in detail in chapter 20.

Free Publicity for Some Universities

Media attention raises the public's awareness of a relatively few colleges based on their football success thanks to the broadcasting of big-time games and the endless publicity provided by weekly rankings, bowl speculation, and awards for best performances. This free publicity typically translates into more student applications, which allows these institutions to be more selective in their admissions. Therefore, although football success is unrelated to academic excellence or to the many other important factors in choosing a college, football-related publicity helps universities that have top-ranked teams.

During a televised game, the two competing schools get a spot on television to trumpet their virtues. They also get appearance money for being on TV, which is often split with the other teams in their conference. Games are scheduled according to TV commitments, and schedules are often changed to accommodate TV networks.

College Football Realignment

As the competition for television dollars continues to mount in big-time college football, we have witnessed a continual realignment of leagues in Division I FBS in an effort to generate the maximum profit from television rights for each league school. As a result, league alignment no longer hinges on traditional rivalries or geography; instead, it's a question of the size of the television market that a school can bring to a league.

During just 18 months of frenzied activity, between May 2011 and the end of 2012, 34 universities changed athletic conferences—some more than once. All of these moves resulted directly from seeking more guaranteed television revenue based on a leaguewide package. The Big Ten, Pac-12, and SEC each expect to have their own league network generating millions of dollars for each school, based primarily on televised football games.

Increased TV exposure helps the schools recruit athletes, and students in general, and gives them the opportunity to feature less popular sports supported by the league. Elite college football is now limited to just five conferences: the three just mentioned, as well as the ACC and the Big 12. Some experts predict that those five will someday be consolidated into a smaller number of even larger leagues in order to sell their media rights for more money because they cover a wider geographic audience (Staples 2012).

The fallout from this realignment is clear: The rich get richer, and the poor get poorer. Schools that are not fortunate enough to be part of the new super leagues fall further behind in the race to generate revenue and the ability to compete at the national level. As a result, look for the NCAA to realign in the near future to reflect this new reality gap dividing the 120 schools in the Division I Football Bowl Subdivision.

How Sport Affects the Media

As the preceding discussion has documented, the media have served as a primary support for the rapid expansion of big-time college and professional sport. However, this relationship has not been a one-way street. Sport has also provided the media with enormous, predictable audiences that are attractive to advertisers both in the United States and around the world. Indeed, the revenue generated by sport coverage has been a major source of income for various media, especially newspapers, television broadcasters, and specialty magazines.

Just who are the sport fans and media consumers in the United States? About 70 percent of the adult population, or 168 million people, claim to follow sport. Of those fans, 55 percent are male and 45 percent female. In terms of age, each of five groups—beginning with the 18 to 25 range and continuing up through the 55-plus category—accounts for approximately 20 percent of the fan base. The top three sports followed are football (49 percent), baseball (31 percent), and basketball (28 percent). The next most popular sports, which lag considerably, are ice hockey and NASCAR (15 percent each), golf (13 percent), tennis (10 percent), and soccer (9 percent).

Here are some other key statistics about U.S. sport fans (Perform Sports Media 2014):

- 68 percent consume sport online.
- 57 percent read sport news online.
- 50 percent read sports in print.
- 45 percent use a second screen (such as a smartphone) while watching sport on television.
- 31 percent watch sport video highlights online.

These sport fans are changing the ways in which sport affects the media.

For more than a century, newspapers have thrived on comprehensive sport sections. For many readers, reading the sport pages is the first priority—and may be the primary reason—for purchasing a newspaper. Even though they watch sport contests in person or on television, many fans also love to read accounts in the next day's paper, evaluate the opinions of the sportswriters, and search for inside information to which they might not otherwise have access.

Most major newspapers in North America devote more space to sport than any other topic,

ACTIVITY TIME-OUT

Advertising to the Target Audience

Watch at least one full college football game and one NFL game on television. For each game, make a list of each advertisement shown and note when ads are repeated. Then see if you can accurately judge the specific audience targeted by the ads. Be as specific as possible in terms of gender, age, race, income level, and any other relevant audience characteristic.

including business, politics, and world news. They have found that formula to be popular with readers and therefore attractive to advertisers. The primary audience for the sport pages has typically consisted of males between the ages of 25 and 50 who have an above-average income (Coakley 2004). Advertisers for products targeted to that demographic have seized the opportunity to reach potential customers in newspaper sport sections.

Newspapers also publicize local professional teams. They may not derive advertising income directly from providing this publicity, but the number of readers they attract is heavily influenced by the public's interest in local teams. Thus covering local teams is one way to guarantee a core group of faithful readers.

Newspapers can also attract readers by publishing stories about social concerns related to sport, which stimulate readers' thinking and maintain their interest in lively debates. In contrast, sport pages that simply print event results and basic accounts of contests may not hold readers' interests, particularly as more people seek to find out results by means of television or the Internet. Sport-related social issues debated in newspapers include the following:

- Racism among coaches, players, or organizations
- The economics of sport, including owner profits, union demands, club payroll comparisons, extravagant player compensation, and public financing of facilities
- Moral issues, such as gambling on sport events, fan behavior at events, beer and cigarette sponsorship, and athletes as role models
- Gender bias, equal pay for women, appropriate attire for women when promoting their sport, and attitudes of female athletes toward competition
- Changes in technology, such as improved surfaces, equipment, and apparel, as well as their effects on the integrity of sport
- Training regimens, equipment, and the effect of training on injury prevention
- Performance enhancing aids, drugs, drug testing, and penalties for those who fail drug tests

As these topics suggest, whereas television thrives on presenting live game-day action, newspapers are more suited to providing in-depth analysis of social topics that require considerable research, clear presentation, and a frame that challenges readers to think.

Magazines that cover sport have responded to growing interest in particular sports. In fact, most general news magazines rarely cover sport unless a major human interest story is involved. Instead, magazine publishers have found that appealing to fans of a specific sport guarantees a more stable audience of subscribers who are likely to support that magazine for a length of time. Indeed, a quick check of the website Mags on the Net finds more than 200 specific-sport magazines offered for subscription; examples include *Golf Digest* and *Tennis*.

In contrast, a few general sport magazines—such as *Sports Illustrated*, *SportingNews*, and *ESPN The Magazine*—seek to attract committed fans. These publications cover the major sports for their bread and butter but also include stories about less popular sports for varied interest and to broaden their readers' horizons. The growing general interest in overall health and fitness has also spurred the growth of *Men's Health* and, for women, *Self*.

Because magazines are published monthly or several times a year, they lend themselves to stories that take time to develop; as a result, stories that examine social issues and trends in sport provide them with prime fodder. In addition, the in-depth analysis typical of a monthly sport magazine cannot be easily adapted to the Internet, just because of the background research that must be done before the writer weaves a story.

On the other hand, because of their infrequent publication and their lead time of several months, magazines are poor sources of information for up-to-the-minute news. By the time the reader receives a magazine in the mail, the news it contains might well be out of date. For example, players might have been traded, franchises remade, predictions proved false, and players released or injured. Keeping readers happy under these conditions requires an astute editorial staff.

Of course, no media form has been affected by sport more than television. From its beginnings in the 1950s, television has included sport coverage as a critical part of its programming. In the beginning, the camera angles were crude, replay did not exist, and many sports had not yet adjusted to television; however, the foundation was laid for a happy and profitable relationship.

ACTIVITY TIME-OUT

The Survival of Sports Illustrated

First published in 1954, *Sports Illustrated (SI)*, which is published weekly, has long been one of the most treasured possessions of U.S. male sport fans. However, during its long history, times have changed around it. Previously owned by Time Warner, it was spun off in 2013 along with *Time*, *Fortune*, and *Money* into an independent company. It appears that Time Warner executives had lost faith in the future of these once coveted properties. *SI's* decline was marked by a 56 percent drop in newsstand sales from 2007 to 2013 (Travis 2013).

Competitors such as *ESPN The Magazine* and the online *Bleacher Report* have challenged *SI* to get with the times. Another competitor, the *Sporting News*, which has been around for well over 100 years, has already left the print arena and gone to a digital format. Therefore, it appears that *SI* may simply be "a dead magazine walking" (Travis 2013).

Sport journalism is so ubiquitous today that its presence on the Internet and television is nearly unavoidable. Therefore, there is no need to wait for a weekly magazine. At the same time, the thoughtful, in-depth pieces that characterized *SI* through the years have fallen victim to the "fast food" era of superficial sport news coverage that lacks research and depth. As a result, *SI* should still be able to find an edge in investigative reporting, thorough research, and substantive engagement with issues in sport—for example, women's sport, drugs, violence, gambling, and gene doping, to name but a few.

With this context in mind, what would *you* do to keep *SI* alive? Would you simply convert to an online-only format? Or perhaps half-print and half-digital, as the *Wall Street Journal* and *New York Times* have done? Are there enough advertising dollars to support such a project? Could *SI* adopt ESPN's Grantland model, which presents a popular sport blog including serious and well-written articles for a niche audience? Organize your thoughts and share them with your classmates in oral or written form.

Television executives figured out that fans would watch TV on weekends when looking for relaxation and diversion. Fortunately for the executives, hours of ready-made weekend programming could be had by securing the rights to sport events and recouping the costs (and then some) from corporate sponsors. The executives learned that sport events minimized production costs, garnered predictable ratings, and could be used to advertise the next event to the target audience. Soon televised sport included *Monday Night Football*; college football on Saturdays; and special events such as the Olympics, tennis tournaments, golf tournaments, and the NCAA basketball championships.

In the United States, sport has typically dominated all other types of programming, especially on weekends, since the invention of television. In 2012, for example, nine of the ten largest TV audiences were drawn by sporting events; only the Grammy Awards sneaked onto the list (see table 5.1). As is typical, professional football took the top eight spots, and the Olympic Games scored ninth in a year of the Summer Games (Nielsen 2012). In 2013, the only nonsport show that placed in the top 10 was the Academy Awards, which landed in seventh place (Nielsen 2013a).

The largest worldwide audience every four years is typically attracted by the Summer Olympic Games, which features both men and women competing in about 30 sports. More than 4.7 billion people watched the 2008 Beijing Olympic Games—about 76 percent of the potential global audience (International Olympic Committee 2014b). Even so, the Olympic Games hasn't drawn the largest audience ever. Though it may surprise U.S. residents, the largest television audience in the world has been drawn by World Cup soccer. This fact makes sense, however, when you consider that soccer is easily the most popular sport worldwide.

TABLE 5.1 Top 10 U.S. Television Programs in 2012 and 2013 (Single Telecast)

Rank	Telecast	Network	Total viewers (millions)
2012			
1	Super Bowl XLVI	NBC	111.3
2	Super Bowl pre-kick	NBC	84.2
3	Super Bowl postgame	NBC	76.8
4	Super Bowl kick-off	NBC	67.0
5	NFC championship	FOX	57.6
6	AFC championship	CBS	48.6
7	NFC playoff	FOX	45.1
8	AFC wildcard playoff	CBS	42.3
9	Summer Olympics opening ceremony	NBC	40.6
10	Grammy Awards	CBS	39.9
2013			
1	Super Bowl XLVII	CBS	108.6
2	Super Bowl (delay)	CBS	106.5
3	Super Bowl postgame	CBS	63.2
4	Super Bowl kick-off	CBS	63.0
5	AFC Championship	CBS	47.7
6	NFC Championship	Fox	41.9
7	The Oscars	ABC	40.3
8	NFC wildcard	Fox	38.0
9	AFC Divisional Playoff SU	CBS	37.6
10	AFC Divisional Playoff SA	CBS	35.2

Adapted from Nielsen 2012; Nielsen 2014a.

In nations on every continent, fans of every economic level flock to live soccer games and follow them on television.

In the United States, the popularity of soccer has been fueled by the rapid growth of youth, high school, and college soccer in response to the federal Title IX legislation, which requires equal sport opportunities for males and females. Girls and young women have flocked to the sport, and the U.S. women's team captured the imagination of the whole country by winning the gold medal in the 1996 Olympics and then winning the 1999 World Cup. Superstars on that team included Mia Hamm, Brandi Chastain, and Kristine Lilly, who provided outstanding role models for aspiring female athletes.

Moreover, the U.S. women's team is the only member of the Confederation of North, Central American, and Caribbean Association Football (CONCACAF) to win all three major worldwide women's soccer (football) events: the World Cup (twice), the Olympics (four times), and the Algarve Cup (nine times). In addition, in 2014, U.S. forward Abby Wambach was named CONCACAF Female Player of the Year. She is also the team's all-time leading scorer, with 177 goals in 232 career appearances (U.S. Soccer 2014).

It has taken longer for men's soccer to flourish in the United States, but the U.S. men's team has begun to become a factor in world competition. The team's inspiring play in the 2010 World Cup captured the attention of U.S. sport fans for the first time. Having earned first place in their group, the U.S. men moved through to round 16 with high hopes but lost to Ghana. They had not won a game in a World Cup for the previous eight years, and their top group finish was their first since the original World Cup in 1930. What's more, Landon Donovan, Clint Dempsey, and goaltender Tim Howard emerged as legitimate stars on the world soccer stage.

In the 2014 World Cup, the U.S. men's team defeated Ghana 2-1, tied with Portugal 2-2, and lost to eventual World Cup champion Germany 1-0 in group play. They were eliminated in the round of 16 with a 2-1 loss to Belgium despite a World Cup record-setting performance by goalkeeper Howard, who made 16 saves. The 2014 team was led by Howard and team captain Dempsey, and Howard was named CONCACAF Goalkeeper of the Year for the second consecutive year (U.S. Soccer 2014).

Soccer claims three spots among the world's ten most watched sporting events, including the UEFA Champions League final, the UEFA European Championship, and of course the World Cup. More than 3.2 billion viewers—46 percent of the world population—tuned in to the 2010 World Cup for at least one minute (International Federation of Association Football 2010).

It is difficult to collect accurate worldwide statistics on sport viewing because of the inconsistency of reporting in many less-developed countries. However, educated estimates from sport observers make it clear that soccer generally dominates worldwide and that every four years the Summer Olympic Games draw the world's attention. Beyond those two, the list is rounded out by the Winter Olympics, the Super Bowl of American football, Wimbledon tennis, and the rugby and cricket World Cups. Of course, some of these events last several weeks, whereas others are one-day affairs. Here is the full list of power rankings for the world's most-viewed sporting events (Pumerantz 2012):

1. FIFA World Cup
2. Olympics
3. 24 Hours of Le Mans
4. The Super Bowl
5. The Grand National
6. Masters Golf Tournament
7. Polo championship
8. Wimbledon
9. Kentucky Derby
10. NBA Finals
11. Cricket World Cup
12. World Series

As we've seen, the more people watch sport, the more the media cover sport. Of course, this dynamic holds true not only for men's sport but also for women's sport, and the media have slowly begun to reach out to female viewers. For decades, sport was viewed as a man's world, and television presentations showed a strong bias toward male viewers. Eventually, however, the networks realized that more than half of the population was female and that many females were embracing sport. As a result, the networks began to devote more programming hours to sports that were popular with women, such as figure skating, gymnastics, tennis, and women's soccer. Currently, the most popular sports on television for female viewers are, in order, the Summer Olympic Games, the Winter Olympic Games, the Kentucky Derby, the Super Bowl, the Women's World Cup soccer tournament, and the U.S. Open women's tennis finals.

Women have also made strides behind the microphone in sport coverage. Female announcers have gradually become included in broadcast teams, and efforts have been made to present sport in a style that is friendlier to female viewers. For instance, broadcasters have toned down—though not eliminated—the gratuitous shots of female cheerleaders, the sexist beer commercials, and the endless parade of commercials for pickup trucks. In addition, women's golf and tennis have been featured in prime-time hours to attract larger audiences.

As more women's sport has appeared on television, young girls in youth sport have begun to identify with their athletic heroes and model their behavior. Women's soccer, for example, has helped grow women's collegiate soccer and youth soccer. Similarly, the emergence of Venus and Serena Williams in tennis has opened up the sport to a new generation of black females, who might otherwise never have considered giving tennis a try. With the rise of the Williams sisters, inner-city high schools with predominantly African American populations suddenly had 50 girls trying out for the tennis team.

Venus Williams has helped to increase both tennis viewership and participation.

In golf, Michelle Wie, who at 14 years of age competed in selected professional golf events for men, suddenly became a constant story on sport pages. Not only did she achieve amazing success among women in professional golf, but also her challenge to qualify for male events also made her story riveting. Although the Ladies Professional Golf Association does not typically grant full membership to players under age 18, multiple young players—including Lydia Ko and Lexi Thompson—have recently won professional golf tournaments before turning 17.

Ideology of Sport Through the Media

The media emphasize certain sport-related behaviors that affect the next generation of athletes and spectators. More specifically, the presentation of sport in the media tends to emphasize behaviors that demonstrate certain values, attitudes, and beliefs that reflect the history of sport and help maintain the status quo. Generally, the sport media are owned and operated by six large conglomerates (Warner 2013):

- Disney (e.g., ABC, the ESPN family of stations)
- Comcast (e.g., NBC, NBC Sports, Golf Channel)
- Time Warner (e.g., TNT, TBS, the CW)
- News Corporation (e.g., Fox, Fox Sports 1, Fox Sports 2, regional Fox Sports networks)
- CBS Corporation (e.g., CBS Sports Network)
- Al Jazeera Media Network (e.g., beIN Sports)

In the pay-TV arena, all of these media corporations owe their power and influence to the practice of "bundling," which simply means grouping dozens of channels together to offer subscribers the illusion of greater value. In this way, they offer dozens of niche channels and have subscribers pay for them all even though there is relatively little interest in any given one of them.

Here's how it works. If you are a sport fan, you certainly want ESPN and are willing to pay for it. But you must also pay for all the other Disney channels, along with A+E Networks. Similarly, you probably want to have Fox Sports 1 and 2, but to get them you must also pay for Fox News, Fox Business, FX, and National Geographic. As you can see, these mammoth companies have a sweet deal, and efforts to dispense with bundling and allow viewers to make à la carte choices have been slow to develop. Many predict that such online options are the shape of the future, but as of 2014 only HBO and CBSN had established them.

These media conglomerates are dedicated to maintaining their powerful position and are unwilling to venture into controversial positions. In addition, some conglomerates have bought and sold professional sport franchises. There was a time, in the 1990s, when it made sense for companies that owned television networks to buy sport franchises in order to ensure available programming and to benefit from the synergy between the two ventures. However, in more recent years, that trend has been reversed, and most corporations have transferred franchise ownership to individuals.

In order to appeal to mass audiences, the U.S. sport media tend to reflect the opinions of the majority of U.S. viewers in order to curry their support. Social scientists would classify this media approach to sport as *functionalism* (as described in chapter 2). In other words, the media tend to reinforce commonly held values. As a result, mainstream media productions tend to avoid controversy, cutting-edge opinions, and creative discussion.

Some of the cultural values held by media executives, team owners, and league administrators clash with those held by athletes. Moreover, issues of race, gender, and sexual preferences are often at the root of different attitudes toward both sport and life. However, because the media realize that their audience and benefactors generally hold fairly mainstream values, they tend to present and reinforce those same values. Let's look now at some of the general themes delivered by sport media.

A few significant ideologies that pervade North American sport are worth pointing out. For example, winning is worshipped in the sport media, and the excitement generated by sport media is generally focused on that objective. As a result, athletes who advance to the finals of a championship event but then lose are regarded as losers.

For example, in the U.S. Open tennis championships, 128 men and 128 women start out contending for first place. Of these players, 127 men and 127 women are destined to be losers, according to the media, and all attention is focused on the one winner in each group. Similarly, professional football players and coaches who reach the Super Bowl, even several times, are branded as losers until they win the big game. This emphasis has a predictable effect on youth sport, future athletes, and armchair quarterbacks: Kids may give up and drop out of a sport when they realize they are not going to win the big game.

Even very young athletes feel pressure to win. If that pressure becomes too overwhelming, it can lead an athlete to drop out of sports.

In another common theme, athletes who act as cooperative team players receive reinforcement from the media and are praised as leaders and role models. In addition, individual athletes who deliver clutch individual performances are idolized and revered for their fortitude and success under pressure. On the other hand, the media harshly criticize athletes who question coaching decisions, celebrate individual achievements over team performance, or do not cooperate with the media.

The media also revere the history, traditions, and past heroes of a given sport. Coaches emphasize hard work and discipline, and the media reinforce those values. Players who persevere and play even while injured are labeled as courageous competitors and team players.

One example is NFL quarterback Peyton Manning, now nearing the end of his career, who has been a go-to guy for both the NFL and the media that cover it. Recently, when his contract expired and the Indianapolis Colts chose not to retain his services in light of the fact that he was coming back from a possible career-threatening injury in 2012, Manning took control of the Denver Broncos and led them to the playoffs—all while maintaining his squeaky-clean image. In fact, he was the only NFL player to land in the top 10 of highest-paid athletes, primarily due to the fact that his attractive image as a role model allowed him to earn more than $10 million in endorsement fees.

Manning's image contrasts sharply with that of NBA star Metta World Peace, who was born Ronald William Artest Jr. and raised in the Queensborough projects in Queens, New York. This was a rough neighborhood, as he emphasized in relating his memory of a fellow player who died when he was stabbed in the back with a broken table leg during a YMCA-sanctioned basketball game. World Peace went on to play college basketball at nearby St. John's University and was selected with the 16th pick of the NBA draft in 1999. Known primarily as a formidable defensive force, he won an NBA championship (2010) and a Defensive Player of the Year award (2004) and was selected for the NBA All-Star Team (2004).

Between 1999 and 2014, however, World Peace played for six NBA teams and caused disruptions at each stop due to his abrasive personality. His most famous incident in the NBA involved an altercation among players and fans during a Pacers–Pistons game in November 2004. For his role in the brawl, World Peace was suspended for the rest of the season and missed 86 games—the longest suspension in NBA history.

That was the start of a series of bizarre incidents, conflicts with other players, and more suspensions, and World Peace was traded several times. It seemed like he carried a "chip on his shoulder," as revealed in one quote where he explained a conflict with teammate Yao Ming by saying, "I don't think he's ever played with a black player that really represents his culture as much as I represent my culture" (Feigen 2008, 3).

Even so, World Peace went on to win the NBA championship as a member of the Los Angeles Lakers in 2010, when he starred in the playoffs. Remarkably, in 2011 he won the NBA's J. Walter Kennedy Citizenship Award and changed his name to Metta World Peace. He chose "Metta" as his first name because it is a traditional Buddhist word that means loving kindness and friendliness toward all. Similarly, he chose "World Peace" to inspire and bring youth together around the world. Signs of a changed man seemed to appear, but the next season he arrived in training camp out of shape and was relegated to a reduced role as a sub. Then, another on-court incident resulted in another suspension at a critical time in the season.

World Peace's personal life has included an arrest for domestic violence, a six-year marriage to Kimsha Hatfield that produced three children, and another son with his former high school girlfriend. Clearly, then, he has given the media ample opportunity to criticize his behavior and hold him up as an anti–role model for youngsters. Nearing the end of his career, he landed with the New York Knicks in a city that can be brutal to "bad boy" athletes due to constant scrutiny and no-holds-barred criticism. Yet a smaller host city might not be able to absorb World Peace into its sport family, simply because trouble seems to follow him wherever he goes.

Participation in Sport and Physical Activity

The importance of physical activity for everyone is well documented. With the alarming increases in obesity in the United States recently reported in the media for both youth and adults, you might guess that the media would take a strong stance regarding sport participation as an antidote for excess body weight. Instead, the majority of sport broadcasts urge viewers to tune in to watch more sports rather than actually playing a sport. Research to date does not support the idea that watching sport on television affects a person's own sport participation one way or the other; rather, the evidence is mixed.

On one hand, many people who are already active report that their interest is heightened by watching great athletes perform, and many young people want to emulate their sport heroes on the playground or ball field. For example, in a poll taken in London after the city hosted the 2012 Olympic Games, one in five people reported that watching the Games inspired them to play sport. More specifically, increases in participation were reported in the sports of cycling and rowing shortly after the Games. Similarly, after the 2008 Beijing Olympics, participation increased in the United States in Olympic sports such as table tennis, triathlon, beach volleyball, running, badminton, cycling, and gymnastics (Sports and Fitness Industry Association 2012).

On the other hand, increases in sport participation following the Olympic Games appear to be merely short-term effects. As reported by Sport England, one year after the conclusion of the 2012 London Games, 20 of 29 sports showed decreasing participation rates, and the number of people exercising one to three times weekly also fell. More generally, sport scholars report that hosting the Olympic Games has never led to a lasting increase in participation in the host country. In fact, some viewers are put off by watching the world's greatest athletes perform feats that seem unimaginable to an average person. In fact, the only group that seems to be truly inspired by watching superior athletes perform are those who are already physically active in sport or another fitness activity (Watson 2012).

The menu of sports shown in the United States on television is dominated by American football, basketball, and baseball. This is where heredity becomes a huge factor, since so few of us have the body size or type necessary to be successful at a professional level in those sports. In addition, more than half of the population is female, which means that they are rarely seeing sport role models of the same sex, except perhaps in basketball.

Moreover, our fascination as spectators with professional athletes who are almost "freaks of nature" in size and talent makes it hard to identify with the athletes we watch. If we are truly serious about helping more people become physically active for a lifetime, then there has to a better contribution that television can make. Simply attracting an increasingly large audience of spectators is certainly not the answer.

After the Olympic Games, there is an increase in recreational participation in many of the Olympic sports, though that increase is often short term.

Traditional Values

Certain traditional values have become part of our North American culture. We generally invest in the ideal of individualism—that one person can make a difference. As a result, even team achievements are sometimes traced back to the success or failure of key players. At the same time, we expect players to work cooperatively, and we extol the virtues of team chemistry and working cohesively as a unit. Therefore, players who put their own welfare first quickly fall out of favor with owners, coaches, and fans. In some cases, the ideals of individual achievement and teamwork clash with each other, thus creating conflict for players.

Harry Edwards, an influential sport critic and prominent sport sociologist in the 1970s, reviewed various media publications and identified dominant social values attributed to sport. His work listed the following key values:

- Character building
- Religiosity
- Nationalism
- Discipline
- Mental fitness
- Competition
- Physical fitness

The place of each of these values in North American sport has been discussed since the 1970s, and generally these values have stood the test of time. Other behaviors that are more specific have been added over the years by other researchers, but Edwards' classic list covers the broad categories (Edwards 1973).

More recent research has revealed that people who participate in sport show higher levels of various elements of social character, including teamwork, loyalty, work ethic, and perseverance. However, when moral character is considered—including traits such as honesty, integrity, and responsibility—athletes fare poorly as compared with nonathletes. In fact, the longer one participates in competitive sport, the more one's ability for sound moral reasoning seems to decline, possibly due to the emphasis on winning at all costs at the highest levels of competition (Rudd and Stoll 2004).

Winners and Losers

U.S. society looks for winners, builds them up, showers them with praise for at least a day, and then looks to the next year. Fame is fickle, and the message is clear—if you haven't won the big one, you don't count for much in sport. Historically, some of our greatest athletes and coaches have failed to win the ultimate contest and are therefore considered failures or lesser athletes. Other athletes who are less talented and productive over the course of their career have been considered successful because they won a big game. Never mind that the win may have been due to luck, teammates, or an inferior opponent—they won. As a result, Super Bowl heroes who were never heard from before (or perhaps after) their one shining moment go down in history as winners.

For some fans, the preoccupation with winners grows tiresome. Veteran fans prefer to watch a well-played and exciting contest, and they feel discontent with one-sided games, predictable outcomes, defensive struggles with little scoring, and sloppy play. Television producers look for ways to minimize the chances of such disappointment by emphasizing possible upsets, possible rallies, and the possible need for exciting tiebreakers.

Yet the beat goes on. Even athletes who deliver an illegal hit are lionized for their competitive spirit as long as they are not caught or the penalty poses only a minor inconvenience to their team. Other athletes who reenter a game after a concussion or other painful injury or in spite of obvious exhaustion are lauded for their courage. As a result, young people who watch professional sport may come to believe that winning is more critical than good health or common sense.

In addition, the fallout from the preoccupation with winning in sport functions as a negative factor if we want to promote full participation in sport for a lifetime. Indeed, many young people drop out of sport because they cannot resolve the conflict between deriving satisfaction from winning and simply benefiting from the sheer act of participation and giving full effort (Weinberg and Gould 2015). The preoccupation with winning at the professional level makes some sense because it involves an athlete's job and livelihood; however, when fans carry that attitude over into youth sport, it functions more as an obstacle to healthy enjoyment of sport.

Gender

In terms of gender, the sport media have predominantly portrayed hegemonic masculinity, revering and reinforcing the traditional masculine characteristics of power, dominance, and violence. This focus is not surprising in light of the fact that male athletics predated the rise of female athletics. However, as women's sport gained a foothold in the 1970s and continued to grow in the following years, one might have expected a change in the traditional sport media's worship of everything traditionally male. Since males have continued to be in positions of power at every television network and dominate production and commentary as well, perhaps more interest in women's sports was unrealistic.

Media coverage of sport can shape the perception of the role played by sport in the life of girls and women—and, by extension, can shape attitudes about the potential of females to be strong, competitive, confident, and highly skilled in sport. As boys grow up seeing their sport heroes perform on television and grab the spotlight on social media, many of them can't help but wish that they too could be so admired. Unfortunately, girls receive very few such messages from the media. In fact, the primary message from the media about female athletes is that they should be feminine and attractive, especially in swimwear. This emphasis has sometimes reached the point that the Women's Sports Foundation felt compelled to develop guidelines for how female athletes should be portrayed in the media (Women's Sports Foundation 1995).

Outside of the Olympic Games and women's World Cup soccer, which occur only every four years, women's sport has traditionally taken a backseat to men's sport in media coverage. Granted, the women's sports that were initially deemed more socially acceptable—such as gymnastics, figure skating, tennis, and golf—have continued to get media attention, and women's soccer and basketball have also begun to tip the balance slightly toward more equal media attention to both female and male athletes. Even so, statistics reveal an ongoing imbalance between sport coverage of men and sport coverage of women.

In fact, since 2000, overall television coverage of women's sport has declined. As a result, the percentages of stories and airtime devoted to women's sport are nearly as low now as they were in 1990, when women's sport received approximately 5 percent of the coverage. In 1999, women's coverage nearly reached 9 percent, but in 2004 it declined back to 6 percent (Duncan and Messner 2005).

In addition, a 20-year study released in 2010 (by University of Southern California and Purdue University sociologists Michael Messner and Cheryl Cooky) reported that in 2009 men received 96 percent of all sport news coverage. Even worse, women's sport accounted for less than 2 percent of coverage shown on network news and ESPN SportsCenter. These figures seem particularly surprising in light of the fact that women's overall sport participation has exploded during the past 20 years (Jenkins 2010). In a 2013 follow-up, the same researchers found that coverage of women's sport had fallen to an all-time low of 1.3 percent to 1.6 percent (Cooky et al. 2013).

According to CNN sport journalist Amanda Davies, the three weeks of the 2012 Summer Olympics were "like no other in [her] career as a sports journalist. Never before have we seen so much coverage of women's sports" (Davies 2013). These headlines focused in part on Sarah Attar, who became the first Saudi Arabian woman to represent that country's flag on the track at the Olympics, thus breaking yet another barrier for women in the world.

More generally, on the fields, in the swimming pool, and in the gyms of the 2012 Games, women delivered riveting performances of power, skill, and determination for the world to watch. In fact, Team USA for these Olympics included 269 women and 261 men—the first time that women outnumbered men on the team. Moreover, the U.S. women delivered the goods by earning 100 medals, as compared with 59 for the men. Regrettably, the excitement and media attention paid to women's sport during the Games faded quickly after the closing ceremonies and indeed returned to the previous lower levels of coverage.

To be fair, ESPN has continued to set a positive example by filling airtime on its ancillary networks (such as ESPNU) with plenty of live coverage of women's sport—more than 1,300 hours in 2012. In fact, the network showed all 63 games of the NCAA women's collegiate basketball tournament on either ESPN or ESPN2. The 12 women's tournament games that aired on the network's main outlet averaged 1.8 million viewers in 2012, and the title game—in which Baylor, led by player of the year Brittney Griner, defeated Notre Dame—drew a viewing audience of 4.2 million (Porter 2012).

These developments demonstrate at least a small shift in emphasis toward more equality of coverage between men's and women's sport. The scheduling and availability of games showing women's college basketball have essentially mirrored the attention given to men, but the media accounts presented in most daily newspapers might lead one to believe that the women's games hold little interest for readers. In spite of the apparent equality with men in television time, women's games still command relatively little attention in many newspapers.

In contrast, professional women's tennis has been well established for some years, and the televising of the women's matches is nearly identical to that of men's matches at Grand Slam events. Other sports, however, can claim no such parity. For instance, women's soccer, professional basketball, golf, and softball are televised only sporadically in comparison to the corresponding men's sports.

Similarly, as discussed in the following section about careers, women are vastly underrepresented in the sport media.

If you want to track the ongoing coverage of women's sport, monitor mentions of it in the main sport pages of the *New York Times*, *USA Today*, and the *Washington Post* on a daily basis. You might also be interested in a novel women's sport channel dedicated to featuring 100 percent female athletic coverage. Janet TV, launched in 2013, operates on a 24-hour schedule and covers both traditional mainstream women's sports and newer action sports, such as surfing, snowboarding, and motocross. Janet TV aspires to spark a reimagination of TV sport, a reinvention of how girls and women see themselves as athletes, and a reset of how the world views female athletes (Bradstreet 2013).

Race and Ethnicity

Viewers' ideas about race and ethnicity can also be influenced by what they see and hear in sport media coverage. Most sport journalists are careful to avoid language that could be interpreted as racist, and the few incidents that have occurred recently have been dealt with quickly. Yet some argue that racism in the media exists in less overt ways—for example, that stories about black athletes focus too often on their rise from poverty to wealth.

Historically, many black athletes have felt belittled by the media's constant portrayal of them as physically talented, whereas white teammates are often praised for cool, strategic play. Those stereotypes have been diminished, yet many black quarterbacks in the NFL resent the emphasis on their running ability and want to be recognized for their leadership, courage in standing in the pocket, and coolness under fire—like their white counterparts. In the 2013 NFL season, nine African Americans started at quarterback, and seven had been drafted in the previous three years. In addition, college football currently features a handful of black quarterbacks at major programs who are likely to join the NFL very soon.

For many years, black football players who specialized on offense were largely limited to the positions of running back and wide receiver. However, high school football coaches figured out that if they could put the ball in the hands of their best athletes on every play, then good things were likely to happen. Nowadays, like white players, black players have been throwing the football since their time in youth leagues, and by the time they complete their college career, their passes are polished, powerful, and accurate. The most prominent example of the coming wave of black quarterbacks at the upper levels of the sport is found in Florida State quarterback Jameis Winston, who won the 2013 Heisman Trophy for best collegiate football player even though it was only his first year at that level; he was also the first choice in the 2015 NFL draft.

The prevalence of black athletes in the NFL and NBA has given rise to discussions of their influence on members of younger generations. Though it is good to be represented in sport, some African Americans cringe at the thought of so many young black people believing that sport is their cultural destiny. This issue and others involving sport and race are covered in greater detail in chapter 12.

Ethnic insensitivities have always existed in sport, and, though many have been eliminated, some persist. For example, the use of Native American nicknames, chants, and cheers in sport has become more offensive to the general population, yet it continues, albeit at a reduced level. In addition, stereotypes of Asians also abound in descriptions of athletes, such as Michelle Kwan (figure skating), Yao Ming (basketball player), Michelle Wie (golfer), and Ichiro Suzuki and Daisuke Matsuzaka (baseball players). In the United States, Asians are often stereotyped as smart competitors but, in spite of their achievements, not as superior athletes. Instead, comments are often made about their self-discipline, intelligence, and methodical approach to sport, even though such descriptions do not necessarily apply to all Asian athletes.

Finally, racial overtones are present in the media's consistent presentation of African Americans as violent. For their part, the sport media have done much to portray the violent black athlete in football and basketball. Stories about domestic beatings, drugs, and arrests after a fight at a nightclub often feature black athletes. The public's impression is that black men are to be feared or avoided. There are feelings in some quarters that the overwhelming number of white sport reporters contributes to this tendency of highlighting the actions of black athletes who get in trouble. In 2012, 90 percent of sport editors, 84 percent of sport columnists, and 86 percent of sport reporters were white (Lapchick 2012a). More discussion is provided about race and violence in chapter 19.

Careers in Sport Media

Sport journalism careers have evolved to keep pace with the changes in sport media. In the past, most sport reporters and editors worked in print media for newspapers and magazines. However, as online media have developed and print media have retrenched, sport journalism and reporting have increasingly migrated to websites, blogs, e-magazines, and e-newspapers.

The required skills are similar, but the approach to providing sport coverage has changed in order to fit the new delivery system. Online media thrive on "scoops" and immediate delivery of news. As a result, the skills of conducting thorough research and developing sport stories over a period of days or even weeks has largely become a thing of the past. Even journalism schools have had to retool their curriculums in order to prepare professionals who can adapt to today's sport media platforms and be equipped to continue adapting to changes yet to come. As of 2013, the average annual salary for a sportswriter in the United States was $49,000 (Suttle 2014).

Sport announcers on radio and television play a much different role from reporters and therefore must develop a different set of skills. Their job is to excite listeners or viewers through their description of the game. Although they need to report play-by-play information, it is critical that they also prepare audience members for what they will see or hear and provide quick analysis after a play. They must also bring energy, wit, and a thorough understanding of the sport.

Many networks hire former athletes as announcers in order to establish the credibility of their commentary. The public expects a former player in the sport to understand the game, as well as the athletes' struggles. And indeed, some athletes have done remarkably well even with little training as sportcasters. Another fertile source of sport announcers is found in the ranks of former coaches, who can share an expert viewpoint and often possess better communication skills than well-known athletes simply because of their years of practice.

There is also a breed of professional sport announcer who has developed the skills of the craft, paid his or her dues by fulfilling modest assignments, and risen to the top of the field. These people, mostly males, often make their reputation in one sport and then branch out to others. For example, Howard Cosell, Brent Musburger, Dick Enberg, Jim Nance, and Bob Costas all made their mark in sport announcing and eventually came to earn considerable money. Although announcers' personalities and styles vary, they all study sport and prepare thoroughly before each event so that they can convey the complete package to viewers.

The median annual salary for a TV sport anchor is $45,000 in the United States versus an average salary of $60,000. That compares with the $60,000 median salary for a TV weathercaster versus an average salary of $70,500. Of course, the salary varies depending on the size of the local market; in fact, sportcasters in large urban markets can earn as much as $650,000 (Papper 2012).

There is a certain tension between sport journalists and the athletes they cover. In looking for a story, many sport journalists probe an athlete's personal life, and they sometimes share the less flattering aspects. Sport journalists may also be critical of teams, owners, coaches, and players in order to stimulate readership. This approach often causes athletes to mistrust the media and resort to stock answers when queried. Consider how many clichés you've heard from athletes during interviews. Here are some you might recognize:

- It's just another game to us.
- We play them one game at a time.
- She leaves it all out there on the field.
- We're focused on the next game, not our record or the playoffs.
- My teammates deserve this award for giving me opportunities.
- We just didn't get it done.
- We came out a little flat and just never recovered.
- We need to get everyone on the same page.
- My serve let me down today.
- You've got to give them credit for their performance today.
- He gives 110 percent and has his game face on today.
- We beat a great team today. They really brought their A-game.
- No single player was responsible for this loss.

As women's sport has risen dramatically in both participation and publicity, you might expect a concomitant growth in the number of women

IN THE ARENA WITH . . .

Robin Roberts

Robin Roberts is one of the most familiar faces and voices on television—a role model for millions of girls and women and a passionate crusader for the value of sport and physical activity for girls. She got her start as an athlete at Southeastern Louisiana on a tennis scholarship but became a record-setting basketball player and one of the finest in school history. She is one of only three female basketball players at Southeastern Louisiana University to score more than 1,000 points and collect more than 1,000 rebounds. She was inducted into the Women's Basketball Hall of Fame in 2012 in recognition of her influence on the game as both a player and a broadcaster.

After Roberts graduated cum laude in 1983 with a degree in communication, her love of sport led her into sport broadcasting at local TV stations in Mississippi, Tennessee, and Georgia. Eventually, she landed at ESPN, where she became the first female African American anchor. Roberts was a familiar face on ESPN's *SportsCenter* and a featured reporter for ABC's *Good Morning America* (both ESPN and ABC are owned by Disney). In 2005, she was named co-anchor of *Good Morning America* and, along with partner George Stephanopoulos, led the show back to the top of the ratings by 2012, beating out NBC's *Today* show, which had held that spot for the previous 16 years.

At the height of her career success, Roberts also became a role model for millions of women by fighting breast cancer, enduring both chemotherapy and radiation treatment. Just four years later, she was diagnosed with a myelodysplastic syndrome (MDS), a disease of the bone marrow. She received a bone marrow transplant and became a spokesperson for Be The Match, thus inspiring hundreds of potential bone marrow donors to register and raising awareness of the need for even more donors. In 2013, ESPN awarded Roberts its Arthur Ashe Courage Award.

Roberts is also forthright about other aspects of her personal life. She makes no secret that she is a practicing Christian, and in December 2013 she used Facebook to reveal her longtime love relationship with Amber Laign, a massage therapist who provided much emotional support during her physical illnesses. Roberts' acknowledgement of her same-sex relationship, while no surprise to many, captured national headlines both on TV and in print.

In addition to Roberts' professional success and her facing of personal health challenges in the public eye, she continues to be a steadfast and inspirational advocate of sport for girls and women. She is the producer of ESPN's *Nine for IX,* a series of female-directed documentaries recognizing the passage of the Title IX legislation that changed the sport world by mandating equal opportunities for females in sport. In 2009, in recognition of her contributions to sportcasting, Roberts was named third on the all-time list of female sportcasters by the American Sportscasters Association (Onslow 2013).

who report on sport. Indeed, between 1994 and 2000, the Association for Women in Sports Media (AWSM) doubled its membership to more than 850. The number of current members for AWSM exceeds 600 (AWSM 2014). Likewise, within months of its founding, the Female Athletic Media Relations Executives (FAME) organization claimed more than 200 members (College Sports Information Directors of America 2001). In spite of these advances, however, the percentage of women working in the sport media remains alarmingly small.

The authors of the 2012 Racial and Gender Report Card for the Associated Press Sports Editors (APSE) calculated the number of females employed at APSE-affiliated websites and newspapers. As the main finding of the report, APSE newspapers and websites were given a grade of F for their gender hiring practices related to the key positions covered in the study. This was the third consecutive time that this biannual report had assigned an overall F grade to the industry on this concern (Lapchick 2012a).

Even so, as stated in the report by Richard Lapchick, founder of the Institute for Diversity and Ethics in Sport (TIDES), "In spite of the failing grade for gender, I think it is encouraging that the APSE has continued to request the report even though the news has been not good." Specific statistics for 2012 showed that males accounted for 90 percent of sport editors, 83 percent of assistant sport editors, 90 percent of sport columnists, 88 percent of sport reporters, and 80 percent of sport copyeditors and designers (Lapchick 2012a).

ESPN has been a leading advocate of hiring female sportcasters, and were it not for that organization the percentage of females working in the field would be even lower. Fortunately, ESPN has also been one of the few news organizations still hiring (most print media operations have been slashing staff positions just to survive financially).

For many years, female reporters were banned from male locker rooms, and even after they gained access they were mercilessly taunted and ridiculed for their efforts. Perhaps the most well-known case of sexual discrimination involved reporter Lisa Olson, who was sexually harassed by three New England Patriots football players during the 1990s. Adding insult to injury, *Playboy* magazine not only carried a story about Olson's experience but also offered to feature her in a pictorial layout. The typical experience of female sportcasters in male locker rooms gained widespread publicity with the publication of an article titled "Never Let the Bastards See You Cry" by Toni Bruce (2000). Bruce's narrative is a fictional account of a female sportswriter's treatment by male athletes who taunt her, make lewd comments, and caution her against any "feminist crap."

Women still often find it difficult to secure positions in sport journalism; furthermore, if they do manage to break down the barriers and get in, the challenge is not over. Once they are hired, they may face harassment or isolation in a sport environment populated mostly by males. In addition, they are often compensated at a lower rate than their male colleagues and may find it difficult to secure promotions. Eventually, they may turn to other journalistic fields, where the odds for advancement and success are more favorable (Dodds 2000). As Johnette Howard, then a *Newsday* sport columnist, observed, "I used to get mail saying 'You're a dumb broad and you don't know anything about sports.' Now they just say, 'You're a dumb broad.' I'd say that's progress" (McNamara 2000).

In spite of the barriers, a growing number of female television reporters have earned respect in recent years for covering a wide variety of both male and female sports. In 2009, the American Sportscasters Association voted CBS veteran Lesley Visser the number one female sportcaster of all time. Others included in the list are shown here in order of selection (American Sportscasters Association 2009):

Andrea Kremer	NBC
Robin Roberts	ABC, ESPN
Michele Tafoya	ESPN
Hannah Storm	CBS, ESPN, NBC
Mary Carillo	HBO
Linda Cohn	ESPN
Andrea Joyce	ABC, ESPN
Suzy Kolber	ABC, ESPN
Phyllis George	CBS
Bonnie Bernstein	ESPN
Pam Oliver	FOX
Donna de Varona	ABC
Judy Rankin	ABC, ESPN
Ann Meyers Drysdale	NBC

Chapter Summary

This chapter examines how the media affect sport fans by increasing their knowledge, excitement, and interest in sport at all levels, particularly the professional level. The media and big-time sport are inextricably intertwined; in fact, the money and interest generated by television has been instrumental in generating new league structures for big-time college football. It also continues to be the number one revenue source for NFL teams and nearly guarantees their success even before the season's first kickoff.

The chapter also examines how publicity generated by the media can affect the popularity of specific athletes, teams, and sports. The sport media have also driven some dramatic changes in the presentation of sport, particularly on television, which serves as a major revenue source for professional sport.

The chapter then looks at the media–sport relationship from the opposite point of view—that is, how sport has affected the media. For example, the media turned to sport because it is nearly guaranteed to produce interest and revenue.

Millions of people worldwide thirst for the instant gratification of watching professional sport on television, and most of them also enjoy reading articles, blog postings, and social media postings about what they watch.

Sport and the sport media also have the potential to affect a society's ideology in their presentation of key values. In this vein, the chapter explores the effect of spectatorship on sport participation, as well as attitudes about gender, sexuality, race, and ethnicity. Since sport and sport media have been almost exclusively the domains of white males, the values presented by sport media have typically been oriented toward that same demographic and therefore have not provided fair treatment of minority athletes or females. Although both minorities and women have seen rapid gains as athletes in the past 50 years, their treatment by the media has still lagged depressingly behind that of white males.

Finally, the chapter examines careers in sport journalism, as well as the status of the profession. Changes in the composition of sport staffs are slowly occurring, yet women still lag far behind their male cohorts in sport journalism opportunities.

PART III

Sport as an Institution

This section begins with chapter 6, which examines the steady increase in organized youth sport programs in the United States over the past 20 years. Of particular note is the rapid growth in participation by females following the passage of the landmark Title IX legislation. However, as organized youth sport has grown, pickup games and other informal kinds of sport activity that were popular in previous generations have declined dramatically due to transportation issues, safety issues, and competition from sedentary pursuits. This chapter examines the positives and negatives of youth sport programs organized by adults and presents problem areas—for example, the lack of well-trained volunteer coaches—as well as potential solutions.

Chapter 7 addresses coaching, a topic that in earlier editions of this text appeared as the next-to-last chapter of the book. However, it makes sense to consider coaching in concert with the other chapters presented here in part III because the institutions that deliver sport are led by coaches; as a result, their expertise, or lack thereof, affects the sport experience for athletes at all levels. This chapter explores both the positive and negative influences of coaches, as well as the status of various personalities, philosophies, and styles of coaching—both past and present. It also explores professional issues, including coach certification and development.

Chapter 8 addresses the fact that sport conducted within the educational system in North America has developed differently from sport in any other place in the world. Although sport is designated as an extracurricular activity, it often serves schools and colleges in a fundamental way by unifying students, alumni, and fans. At universities, sport also helps attract more applicants, encourages alumni to donate funds, and generates considerable publicity for the school.

Although interscholastic and collegiate sports have traditionally been extolled for their virtues, many of these claims are not based on solid research. Moreover, the percentage of students who make high school or college teams is relatively small, even though the per-student cost to the institution is considerable.

Title IX has affected both high school and college sport by requiring equal opportunities for females and males. The result has been a vast improvement in sport opportunities for girls. At the same time, budget allocations continue to be a source of debate and agony as costs escalate at schools trying to offer equal opportunities to students of each sex.

Chapter 9 examines sport from an international perspective and shows how sport is expanding worldwide. As advances in media technology help shrink the world, sport spreads quickly from one country to another. As a result, favorite U.S. sports—such as football, basketball, and baseball—have gained considerable popularity throughout the world; in fact, the United States no longer dominates world competition in basketball or baseball. At the same time, soccer is finally beginning to gain a toehold in the United States after several decades of rapid growth in youth soccer, especially among females. The most popular sports worldwide may surprise you, and the chapter will help you understand the reasons for the popularity of each sport.

Many have touted the potential of using sport competition to further relationships between countries. Indeed, evidence suggests that international understanding can be promoted through athlete exchange programs between nations, world amateur competitions, and professional leagues that span the globe. However, claims that sport globalization may dramatically alter political processes or governments seem to be based more on wishful thinking than on reality.

As discussed in chapter 10, no other sporting event has had a worldwide effect comparable to that of the Olympic Games. Steeped in the tradition of amateur athletes competing for the love of sport, the Olympics has evolved into a very big business. The inclusion of professional athletes has helped the Games popularize events and attract huge amounts of television coverage and commercial sponsorship. As part of this process, the nationalism that characterized the Games for the last 50 years has been giving way to an economic model of sport.

All countries that compete seriously in the Olympic Games operate organized national programs to help their best athletes succeed. However, the United States Olympic Committee has recently struggled with this role. Unlike programs in most other countries, it receives no government funding; instead, it relies on private sponsors and donations. In contrast, in countries with a government-funded Olympic program, Olympic sport is an affordable and accessible pursuit for any talented athlete.

STUDENT OUTCOMES

After reading this chapter, you will know the following:

- The history of youth sport
- The current organization of youth sport
- Current participation in youth sport
- The distinction between athlete-organized sport and adult-organized sport
- Reasons that young people participate in sport
- Future modifications that may benefit youth sport

Youth Sport

Youth Sport

Perhaps you grew up in a household like this: Your mom, like other moms in your neighborhood, spent a large portion of her day driving you and your brother and sister to various youth sport activities. Between you three kids (aged about 6 to 13), someone always had soccer, Little League Baseball, swim lessons, tennis, or dance. It was up to Mom to coordinate the daily sport schedules for practices and games, and Dad pitched in on weekends. Dinners as a family were few and far between because there were few nights when everyone was home at the same time. Instead, snacks and reheated dinners were the norm, followed by homework.

If so, your mom was a "soccer mom," to use a term that became popular in the United States in the 1990s—and even became a prized demographic for U.S. politicians Bill Clinton and Bob Dole as they competed for votes in the presidential election of 1996. The *Wall Street Journal* described soccer moms both as swing voters who would decide the election and as key consumers in the marketplace. According to other major newspapers, soccer moms typically lived in the suburbs; were swing voters; were busy, harried, and stressed out; worked outside the home; drove a minivan or sport utility vehicle; were part of the middle class; and were married and white. As you read this chapter, you'll see that the soccer mom typifies the mothers of the majority of kids who play youth sport.

How did U.S. culture move from one in which parents told kids aged 8 to 12 to "go out and play but be sure to be back in time for dinner" to one in which sport and other activities for children are highly organized affairs? Adult-organized sport for kids, as this type of activity is called, has exploded in the past 30 years for a variety of reasons, which are considered in this chapter. Some critics lament the more casual days of the past, but the demand for organized youth sport programs seems to continue growing.

Youth sport affects the development of young people simply because of the large amount of time they spend participating in sport. Whether they choose to play informal games with their peers or join an organized program, almost all children experiment with sport between the ages of 6 and 12. Those who are successful may continue their sport involvement through the teenage years; others may try different sport activities or drop out of sport completely.

The number of young people who participate in organized sport programs continues to grow, and girls' participation in particular has shown large increases as compared with participation from 30 years ago. Part of the reason can be found in the larger number of families in which both parents work outside the home, which has created a need for scheduled, supervised children's activities after school. Sport has emerged as a natural child care activity and offers the added advantage of delivering multiple benefits, such as increasing a child's physical activity and fitness levels, helping the child learn physical skills, and encouraging the child to socialize with peers.

However, before we congratulate ourselves on the continuous growth of organized youth sport, we must reckon with the fact that a closer look reveals a steep decline in youth sport (particularly team sport) that is not organized at school or in the community (Sporting Goods Manufacturers Association 2009). In other words, kids no longer leave the house to spend the day playing pickup games in neighborhood parks or on school playing fields as they once did. Some observers attribute this decline to hesitancy on the part of today's parents to allow their children the freedom to roam unsupervised. Others point the finger at video games, the Internet, and television (Cauchon 2005).

In addition, as adult-organized youth sport has grown, so too have criticisms of programs that emphasize winning and early specialization in one sport, overschedule kids' time, overinvolve adults in structuring the program, and cost a lot of money. With all of these concerns in mind, it's time to look closely at the current organization of youth sport and consider what changes should be made in order to enhance the role of youth sport in the development of young people.

Popular opinion about youth sport varies and depends somewhat on the influence of the media. Although the media may criticize excesses in youth sport, they also celebrate the successful performances of local teams and broadcast the Little League World Series into every home with a television. Parents decry the negative influences exerted by some coaches such as the use of negative criticism of young players, and training and certification of youth sport coaches is indeed spotty. The good news is that they are improving, in both accessibility and quality.

For example, coaching education has been greatly expanded through modestly priced online courses, and high-quality content is offered by pioneering organizations such as the National Alliance for Youth Sports and Human Kinetics Coach Education. However, their impact is limited to communities that require their coaches to become certified. Sadly, a survey of 43,000 households in 2013 revealed that only one in five coaches of youth teams for kids under age 14 say they have been trained in motivational techniques and just one in four in sport-specific skills and tactics (Aspen Institute 2014). In addition, though organizers often recruit young people to play by stressing how much fun they will have, the actual experience is often structured to teach conformity to rules and instructions and to reward winning teams and athletes for exceptional performance.

The Youth Sports National Report Card was released in 2005 by the Citizenship Through Sports Alliance, a national coalition of sport organizations that includes, among others, the four major professional leagues in the United States (for baseball, basketball, football, and ice hockey); the National Collegiate Athletic Association (NCAA); and the United States Olympic Committee (USOC). The report card issued grades ranging from A to F in five categories and included some harsh criticism of youth sport. Here are a few details:

Child-centered philosophy	D
Coaching	C–
Health and safety	C+
Officiating	B–
Parental behavior	D

The ratings, given by youth sport experts from across the country, focused on community-based sport for children aged 6 to 14. Specific findings

In the past, children would spend hours outdoors playing youth-organized games and sports. Now, most youth sport is adult-organized. What has led to this change?

of the report included the conclusion that youth sport had lost its focus on the child; suffered from the actions of overinvested parents; failed to recruit and train high-quality coaches; focused too much on early sport specialization; and failed to listen to the voice of the child who wanted to participate in sport for fun, friendship, fitness, and skill development.

History of Youth Sport

One hundred years ago, lower-class children competed in youth sport under adult supervision, whereas their upper-class counterparts were more likely to be found occupied by noncompetitive activities, such as music lessons and dancing, that were usually conducted at home under the tutelage of a private teacher. Some children from the higher social classes were also schooled in certain sports, such as equestrian, sailing, golf, tennis, and skiing. Children's athletic competitions typically took the form of athletic tournaments staged in big cities that were populated by poor immigrant families.

After World War II, youth sport—at least for boys—became popular in middle-class communities across the land, especially in baseball, football, and basketball. It wasn't until the 1970s that youth sport for both sexes was embraced by upper-middle-class communities, where parents came to believe that competitive youth sport was a requirement if their kids were to be successful. As a result of these developments, youth sport programs have become a huge factor in U.S. society over the past 60 years.

Before then, however, few programs existed, and most children organized their own games. Children who grew up in cities spent hours playing variations of baseball such as stickball, wireball, and Wiffle ball. They also filled time by jumping rope, playing hopscotch, and shooting baskets. Children who lived in rural areas were more likely to choose recreational activities that took advantage of the woods, lakes, mountains, and back roads of their local environment. Popular outdoor pursuits among these children included hunting, fishing, boating, hiking, mountain climbing, bicycling, and running.

In the years following World War II, youth sport programs were dominated by Little League Baseball, which was founded in 1939 in Williamsport, Pennsylvania. It was a community-based program in which the teams were funded by local businesses. In addition to teaching baseball skills and strategy, Little League was looked upon by parents and organizers as a way to teach young boys important life skills, proper values, discipline, and adherence to rules.

In other words, along with the Boy Scouts, youth sport programs were invested in training the boys of the nation for adulthood (Little League 2015). Indeed, youth sport in the 1950s and 1960s was intended primarily for boys and was heartily endorsed by most people, particularly those in the middle class, as a worthy use of time to learn athletic and social skills. Community leaders asserted that young men would learn the lessons of life on the ball field during competition.

Perhaps the most dramatic change in U.S. youth sport programs in the last 30 years has been the explosion of sport opportunities for girls that resulted from the passage of the Title IX federal legislation in 1972. Before Title IX, girls were expected to be cheerleaders, pompon girls, or majorettes or perhaps to participate in a few "ladylike" sports, such as gymnastics, figure skating, equestrianism, swimming, and tennis. Once Title IX was passed, however, girls showed up in record numbers at softball fields, basketball courts, field hockey and lacrosse fields, and soccer fields.

Since the 1970s, family life in North America has undergone many changes and that in turn has resulted in significant changes to youth sports. One significant change involves an increase in the number of mothers who work outside the home—from 40 percent in the 1970s to 71 percent in 2012 (U.S. Bureau of Labor Statistics 2012a). As mentioned earlier, this change means that kids need someplace safe to go after school, and sport fills that void. It also helps kids get exercise; improve their self-confidence; and learn life lessons in winning, losing, and good sporting behavior.

A second factor in the change in youth sports since the 1970s is an increase in child abductions and sexual predators, which of course frightens parents and makes them fear for their children's safety (Cauchon 2005). When their children are actively engaged under adult supervision in a sport program, however, parents can feel some comfort that they are safe.

A third factor is the belief, particularly in areas of high crime, that children are more likely to stay out of trouble if they are participating in an organized sport program. In such areas, many children are exposed to drugs, sex, and crime on

POP CULTURE

Stoop Ball in the City

My favorite childhood game in the 1950s was "stoop ball," which was probably invented in Brooklyn, New York, and was exported to various major urban settings shortly after World War II. I spent many afternoons with my buddies in Baltimore throwing a ball against our front stoop and trying to catch it on the rebound. All we needed in order to play was a rubber ball, variously called a pinky, a spaldeen, a pimple ball, or an old tennis ball. The ball was pink, a bit smaller than a baseball, and inexpensive (just five cents).

We played in front of our single-family, inner-city row house, which, like all the others, had a "stoop"—a small porch with steps. (The word comes from the Dutch for sidewalk.) The front steps were typically made of wood, concrete, brick, or, in Baltimore, marble, which had to be washed daily. Parents and families often perched on their front stoops to watch the world go by, supervise kids playing in the street, or catch a break from the summer heat.

Although the rules of stoop ball could vary, the favorite version in my neighborhood was a version of baseball. The "batter" stood a few feet from the steps of the stoop and threw the ball overhand against the steps, trying to hit a "pointer" (edge of a step). The ball then flew toward the street, where an opponent or two tried to catch the ball in the air for an out. A foul ball—one that landed outside the boundary marked by a streetlight, parked car, or garbage can—was also an out.

Areas were marked to indicate a single, double, or triple for a ball not caught cleanly by the fielders. Of course, a ball thrown against the actual edge of the step flew unpredictably far and usually earned a home run. Players had to keep the base positions and scores in their head, and time-outs were called to make way for passing cars who dared to intrude on our narrow one-way street.

Stoop ball and other city street games kept us occupied and physically active near our homes and under the watchful eyes of the neighborhood moms, who never interfered except to call us in for meals. These games were fun, safe, and cheap, and they helped shape a sense of neighborhood, especially in working-class areas populated by Irish, Italian, Dutch, and Jewish immigrants. Best of all, everyone got to play, and we kids got to set our own rules and settle disputes without adult intervention (Anastasio 2000).

the streets before the age of 10. In contrast, if they have a safe haven after school, children who live in dangerous neighborhoods can participate in sport free of worry; in many programs, they also spend time completing homework assignments.

Finally, the emergence of specialized training for high-performance sport at very young ages has encouraged parents to go to great lengths to give their child a chance to become a great athlete. As a result, these kids are encouraged at an early age to commit completely to one sport, train hard in it every day, and focus on it year round. Such parents feel a sense of guilt if they do not support their child's one chance to be famous and make millions, so they sacrifice money, time, and sometimes even family happiness in the pursuit of athletic excellence.

Sponsors of Youth Sport

The rise in youth sport occurred in large part because certain organizations gave it their support. The following list summarizes them in broad categories:

- Public community and parks programs
- Community organizations, such as the YMCA and YWCA, the Police Athletic League, and the Boys & Girls Clubs of America

- Church organizations, such as Catholic youth organizations (CYOs)
- Nonprofit sport organizations, such as Little League Baseball and Softball, Pop Warner (football), the United States Tennis Association, the Amateur Athletic Union, and Youth Soccer.
- Corporate sponsors, including national, regional, and local businesses
- Commercial sport and fitness clubs
- Private sport organizations and clubs that rent public facilities at schools and parks

One question often raised about youth sport is who should pay for it. When schools disengaged from sponsoring sport programs for young children, communities looked for other sources of funding. One solution uses public funds to support community sport programs, often at local parks or playgrounds. The rationale here is that taxpayer money is well spent if it keeps children busy, out of trouble, and physically active. Most of these programs are offered during the summer, when school is not in session. They are often free of charge or provided for only a nominal charge. Sport programs delivered through this model tend to be introductory, recreational, and moderately organized.

When public funds are not available, other organizations—such as YMCAs, YWCAs, the Boys & Girls Clubs of America, and churches—step in to fill the void. The process involves raising funds (from public or private sources) and establishing modest memberships fees. In addition, youth sport programs clearly have a social component and are often targeted toward populations at risk. As a result, in some programs, tutoring and academic enrichment are combined with athletic activity.

Nonprofit sport organizations began sponsoring youth programs in order to expose kids to their chosen sport, build a solid base of fans, scout talent, and help develop elite players who might one day play professionally. These organizations largely finance youth leagues, but they do charge

EXPERT'S VIEW

Long-Term Athlete Development Plan

National Olympic Committees and national sport governing bodies have wrestled for years to create a sport development model that would both maximize their results in international competition and help produce a citizenry that is committed to lifelong physical activity. One such model, the Long-Term Athlete Development (LTAD) plan, provides a program for training, competition, and recovery that is based on each athlete's developmental age—that is, on each individual's maturation level—rather than on chronological age. It is athlete centered, coach driven, and supported by sport administrators, sport science experts, and sponsors. Athletes are guided in developing an individual plan that is specific to their unique developmental needs.

"Following this LTAD guide will ensure that children develop physical literacy, which is the development of fundamental movement and fundamental sport skills, that permits them to move confidently and with control in a wide range of physical activity, rhythmic (dance), and sport situations. Physical literacy also includes the ability to read what is going on in an activity setting and react appropriately to those events. The goal of physical literacy in all children, from early childhood to late adolescence, is quality daily physical activity and a coordinated approach to developing physical abilities" (M. Robinson 2010, 189).

The model is structured on the basis of stages and rough chronological-age guidelines, but of course children differ in the rate at which they move through the stages. Table 6.1 presents a brief summary of the stages relevant to youth sport. Analyze the plan and compare it with your own progression through youth sport. Is it similar or different? Be specific in your comments and share your assessment with classmates.

TABLE 6.1 Stages in the LTAD Plan

1. FUNdamentals stage	2. Learning-to-train stage
Chronological age/developmental age Males, 6–9 Females, 6–8 Characteristics Fun and participation Learning overall movement skills Integrated mental, cognitive, and emotional development Developing locomotor skill Developing general motor ability Introducing basic sport skills Introducing basic rules of ethics Daily physical activity along with multiple sports	Chronological/developmental age Males, 9–12 Females, 8–11 Characteristics Overall sport skill development Major skill learning Integrated mental, cognitive, and emotional development Introduction to mental preparation Talent identification Narrow focus to three sports Single or double periodization Sport-specific training three times per week Other sport participation three times per week
3. Training-to-train stage	**4. Training-to-compete stage**
Chronological/developmental age Males, 12–16 Females, 11–15 Characteristics Specific sport skill development Major fitness development Integrated mental, cognitive, and emotional development Developing mental preparation Introducing strength training Developing ancillary capacities Narrow focus to two sports Single or double periodization Sport-specific training six to nine times per week, including complementary sports	Chronological/developmental age Males, 16–23 Females, 15–21+/– Characteristics Sport-, event-, and position-specific physical conditioning Sport-, event-, and position-specific tactical preparation Sport-, event-, and position-specific technical and playing skills under competitive conditions Integrated mental, cognitive, and emotional development Advanced mental preparation Developing ancillary capacities Specialization in one sport Single, double, or triple periodization Sport-specific technical, tactical, and fitness training 9 to 12 times per week

Based on Balyi et al. 2005.

participants a modest fee to help cover the costs. Programs operated by these organizations tend to lean more toward skill instruction, greater emphasis on winning and losing, and development of elite performers.

Commercial sponsors of youth sport got involved because they saw an opportunity to influence children and their families to consider using their products. Local businesses know that sponsoring a team promotes goodwill in the community even as it allows them to advertise their business on player uniforms and ballpark signs. A few national sponsors have also gotten involved in some programs—for example, the National Football League's Punt, Pass, and Kick competition.

Privatization of Youth Sport

When public parks and schools have struggled with funding issues, organized youth sport programs have often been eliminated or reduced in scope. In addition, since the 1970s, a segment of the public has embraced the philosophy that government is more the problem than the solution to societal issues. Rather than support strong public schools and other programs for youth development, this ideological perspective seeks to transfer the responsibility to individuals and families. A parallel line of thought holds that the best source of economic growth is unregulated self-interest and that the key to personal motivation is competition

(Coakley 2010). In response to such challenges to public support of youth sport, the private sector stepped quickly into the void.

For example, private coaches and entrepreneurs quickly realized that there was money to be made in the youth sport market. In response, they organized competitive travel teams or clubs in a variety of sports, including soccer, basketball, baseball, and softball. Some teams used public facilities at schools or parks, and others built their own facilities or converted warehouses or health clubs to meet their needs.

Commercial sport clubs have also become a mainstay of the youth sport market. Local clubs offer swimming, tennis, dance, gymnastics, soccer, and basketball at prices that are typically affordable only to the middle and upper classes. Programs are oriented toward high performance and geared toward serious young athletes who, at the very least, are pursuing a college scholarship, if not a professional career.

Summer sport camps specialize in one or two sports and draw thousands of youngsters from families who can afford to send their children to camp for weeks or even an entire summer. These camps mix traditional camp activities with a heavy dose of sport instruction, drilling, and supervised play. Private lessons are also recommended by the coaches, who love working one-on-one with young athletes to improve their sport skills, such as their tennis stroke, their baseball swing, or their goaltending ability. The financial rewards for the coaches allow many of them to coach youth sport not merely as a source of supplemental income but as a full-time job.

Perhaps the logical extreme of this approach is seen in local sport "academies" that offer up to six hours of sport instruction and training per

IN THE ARENA WITH . . .

IMG Academy

In Bradenton, on Florida's west coast, sits one of the most famous youth sport academies in the world. It began over 30 years ago as the Nick Bollettieri Tennis Academy and has since expanded to offer more than a dozen sports, including tennis, golf, soccer, basketball, football, baseball, softball, swimming, and lacrosse. Young people of all ages can come for weekend training or summer camps or live as full-time residents. Participants train in their sport every day under the watchful eyes of expert coaches; they engage in regular competitive play and receive advice from various sport science experts and performance trainers, including sport psychologists. A typical day at the academy is divided into two parts; about half the day is spent in academic schooling at the on-site private school, and the other half is spent in sport training.

The primary customers for this commercial enterprise are young players who aspire to play at a high college level or eventually turn pro. About 80 percent of academy graduates go on to play collegiate sport, most of them with the aid of an athletic scholarship. The academy helps students locate colleges that would be a good fit—tailored to them and their athletic ability.

The cost to attend the academy averages about $1,500 to $2,000 per week for training camps, depending on how many extras players want to tack on. Fees are added for individual coaching, athletic training, and sessions with a private sport psychologist. Full-time residents pay between $65,000 and $70,000 while day students are charged between $53,000 and $56,000 for sports training only.

School tuition is treated as an additional expense, and public schools usually are not an option because of training schedule demands, so IMG students must attend a private school or receive at-home education arranged by their family. Private school tuition costs about $16,000. The bottom line, then, is that attending IMG Academy costs more than $70,000 for a resident for the 2015-2016 school year. That price tag exceeds the cost of even the most expensive colleges in the United States. Of course, some financial aid is made available through scholarships, but it is risky to count on receiving one (IMG Academy 2015).

day. This work is organized around the young athlete's schooling, which may take the form of home schooling or private school. Some academies, such as the IMG Academy in Bradenton, Florida, go a step further by offering a residential program so that kids from anywhere in the country can train, go to school, and live at the sport academy—assuming their family can afford a financial tab that typically exceeds $50,000 for a September-to-June experience.

This shift toward privatization quickly changed the culture and character of youth sport. The new philosophy focused on excellence, skill development, and competition and thus required year-round training, more emphasis on fitness development, and intense competitive experience that often involves extensive travel. Once private programs attract kids to their program, they want to keep them year round in order to support program facilities, as well as administrative and coaching staff.

Current Status of Youth Sport

With participation in youth sport at an all-time high, it would appear that things are rosy in the sporting world of kids. But participation statistics are helpful only if they are considered in relation to the possible number of youth sport consumers. In 2013, according to the U.S. Bureau of Labor Statistics (2013a), the United States was home to about 25 million children aged 6 to 11 and another 25 million aged 12 to 17, for a total of about 50 million. Yet another 25 million were younger than 6, but relatively few in that age group participated in organized sport activity.

So, we can assume a round number of about 50 million potential youth sport participants in order to gain some perspective on national studies about youth sport participation. One study, conducted by the Sports and Fitness Industry (SFIA), showed that about 22 million kids participated in sport in 2011 (Kelley and Carchia 2013). A similar study, conducted for the Women's Sports Foundation and using a smaller sample size, estimated the number of youth sport participants as about 29 million (Women's Sports Foundation 2008).

Therefore, whichever of these statistics we use, the bottom line is that about half of U.S. kids are actively engaged in organized sport programs. Equally significant, of course, is the fact that the other half are not. Whether you see the cup as half full or half empty depends on your point of view, but the sheer fact is that half of U.S. children are not physically active.

A related study revealed that team sport participation peaks at age 11. Basketball remains the most popular team sport, primarily because it is played by both boys and girls, and participation in sport by girls has never been higher. Still, the rate of *frequent* participation in team sport is declining among both boys and girls. Moreover, a closer look reveals a host of problems. Perhaps most alarming, some estimates say that more than 70 percent of participants drop out of youth sport programs along the way to high school. Speculation is rampant as to the cause, but no clear pattern has yet emerged. Possible causes include the following (Cary 2004):

- Weeding out (By high school, many kids realize that they have little chance to succeed in higher levels of competitive sport. In many sports, high school teams can accommodate only a set number of athletes and therefore select only the best for inclusion, thus leaving out many willing and enthusiastic participants. Those who are cut simply drop out of sport altogether unless they find a recreational league in their community.)
- Overemphasis on winning, which increases pressure to achieve
- Stress on high performance, which translates into longer hours of practice, longer seasons, and specialization in one sport at an early age
- Participation expenses—for travel teams, sport camps, sport academies, coaching, and equipment—that are out of reach for middle-class families
- Increased injury incidence due to inordinate demands on young bodies
- Increased participation in alternative or extreme sports by young people who are turned off by traditional adult-organized programs
- Lack of training for youth coaches and resulting frustration among kids who take orders from well-intentioned but misguided adults
- Earlier starts in youth sport (sometimes as young as age three or four), which can lead children to simply grow bored with sport after a number of years

Go Out and Play, a study sponsored by the Women's Sports Foundation (2008), investigated U.S. youth participation in exercise and organized team sport. The study found that 72 percent of youth were participating or had participated in a sport during the past 12 months, whereas 12 percent had dropped out of sport and 15 percent had never played a sport. Perhaps more revealing were the statistics showing that gender, race, and location significantly affected kids' likelihood of sport participation.

In terms of gender, boys were more likely to be involved in sport at every age, more likely to play multiple sports, and more likely to be avid participants. Girls tended to enter sport later than boys (at 7.4 years old as compared with 6.8 years for boys) and drop out sooner and in greater numbers. In addition, girls were more likely than boys to take part in nontraditional sports, including cheerleading, dance, competitive rope jumping, and volleyball; for their part, boys tended to stick with more traditional sports (Women's Sports Foundation 2008).

In suburban communities, the sport participation rates of boys and girls are comparable; in rural and urban communities, however, girls participate at much lower rates than boys do. In one particularly telling statistic, 84 percent of urban girls and 68 percent of rural girls have no physical education classes at all in the 11th and 12th grades. In contrast, 48 percent of girls in suburban schools do not participate in physical education.

In her book *Playing to Win: Raising Children in a Competitive Culture*, psychologist Hilary Friedman points out the need for kids (particularly girls) to develop "competitive capital." She tracked the lives of upper-middle-class parents who enrolled their kids in competitive youth programs in soccer, dance, and chess. She noted five central themes in the programs she observed: (1) internalizing the importance of winning, (2) bouncing back from a loss to win in the future, (3) learning how to perform within certain time limits, (4) learning how to succeed in stressful situations, and (5) performing in front of an audience (Friedman, 2013a.)

Indeed, the world of sport has been latched onto as a rite of passage by many upper-middle-class parents who want their children, especially girls, to be able to function as part of a team, become leaders in their occupation, and succeed in a competitive world. In the past, girls from similar backgrounds often focused on learning the arts and refining their appearance in the hope of marrying well, which for many people at that time defined female success. In this age of working women, however, different skills and assets are needed in order to get a job and thrive in the competitive business world. Consider the results of

ACTIVITY TIME-OUT

Burning Issues in Youth Sport

Visit the websites of three sport organizations listed here (or others of your own choosing) and see what catches your eye about the issues of concern to these groups. List at least five topics discussed on more than one of the sites and summarize each topic in a paragraph. Cite the websites and the particular articles from which you gleaned your information.

- National Alliance for Youth Sports, a nonprofit organization that emphasizes making sport safe and positive for young people
- Institute for the Study of Youth Sports at Michigan State University, which sponsors research and provides educational materials
- MomsTeam, an information gateway for parents of youth sport participants
- Human Kinetics Coach Education, a premier site for youth sport coaches
- National Council of Youth Sports, which represents more than 200 youth sport organizations and corporations

one study by the Oppenheimer Foundation, which found that 82 percent of executive businesswomen participated in organized sport in middle and high school and 80 percent of female executives identified themselves as competitive "tomboys" during childhood (Oppenheimer/MassMutual Financial Group 2002).

In terms of race and ethnicity, youth sport is diverse; in fact, at many ages, boys of color participate at higher rates than white boys do. However, the picture for girls of color is not encouraging. They seem to be hit by both gender and racial discrimination, and their participation levels fall significantly below those of white girls. The reasons for this difference involve a combination of culture, family responsibilities, income level, and living locations (Women's Sports Foundation 2008). The Hispanic/Latino and African-American cultures seem to discourage girls from playing sports and typically expect them to help care for younger siblings and help their mothers around the house.

Let's take a closer look now at some trends in youth sport. In 1975, the most popular sports among youth included traditional male sports, such as basketball, football, baseball, track, and swimming—and perhaps skiing, wrestling, bowling, and gymnastics. Now that girls are much more involved in sport, the category of popular sport activities has broadened to include volleyball, soccer, cycling, lacrosse, field hockey, ultimate, cheerleading, double Dutch, and stepping. Table 6.2 shows the most popular physical activities by gender (Women's Sports Foundation 2008).

Dropping out of youth sport and physical activity continues to be a concern, especially since a majority of youth withdraw during the middle school years. Primary reasons cited typically include structure (which includes tryouts), a smaller number of teams, emphasis on competitive results, length of season, required level of commitment, and boredom. This topic is addressed further in a later section of this chapter (Why Kids Participate—and Stop Participating—in Sport).

Decreased Physical Activity

In 2010, the Kaiser Family Foundation published a report that confirmed earlier studies in finding that U.S. kids spend just about every waking moment outside of school using a smartphone,

TABLE 6.2 Most Frequent Physical Activities for Girls and Boys

Physical activity	% participation
Girls	
Dancing	61
Swimming or diving	56
Basketball	55
Jogging or running	53
Volleyball	47
Bowling	47
Soccer	40
Baseball or softball	38
In-line skating	33
Camping or hiking	29
Ultimate	29
Boys	
Basketball	71
Football	65
Soccer	51
Jogging or running	49
Swimming or diving	48
Baseball or softball	48
Bowling	48
Weight training	42
Cycling or mountain biking	33
Skateboarding	29
Ultimate	29

computer, television, or other electronic device (see figure 6.1). More specifically, kids aged 8 to 18 years now spend an average of more than seven and a half hours per day on electronic devices—up more than an hour from a study done just five years earlier by the same group. And because so many kids are multitasking—for example, surfing the web while listening to music—they are really packing almost eleven hours of media into those seven and a half hours each day.

In this light, it is not surprising that more than two-thirds of kids have a TV in their bedroom and about one-third have a computer with Internet access in their home. The heaviest media users are black and Hispanic kids and "tweens" (those aged 11 to 14) of any race. As kids move into the 16- to 18-year-old age bracket, their use of video games and TV recedes and their use of music and audio entertainment rises. Heavier use of all media is associated with behavioral problems; lower grades; and a higher chance of reporting boredom, sadness, or trouble at school (Kaiser Family Foundation 2010).

So when are kids physically active? It seems to happen only in households where parents limit the use of electronics and physically take their children to participate in sport. When given a choice, the vast majority of today's youth seem more likely to rely on physically passive electronic entertainment.

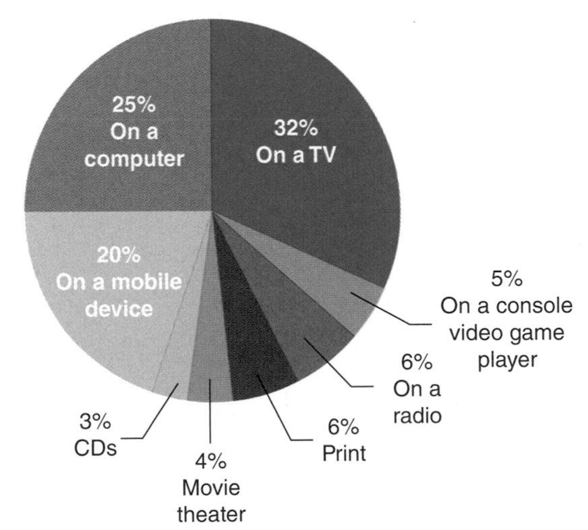

FIGURE 6.1 Percentage of media time spent on specific platforms by children aged 8 to 18 years.

Victoria J. Rideout, Ulla G. Foehr, and Donald F. Roberts, *Generation M2, media in the lives of 8- to 18-year-olds*. The Henry J. Kaiser Family Foundation, 2010, Available: http://kaiserfamilyfoundation.files.wordpress.com/2013/01/8010.pdf.

Is it any wonder, then, that the rate of youth obesity is rising? Gone are the days when children left early in the day for outside play and the only requirement was that they return in time for dinner. Suburban living has divided friends by miles, and parents fear for their children's safety if they go out to play without adult supervision. In addition, the presence of air conditioning in most homes now negates the need to head for the local swimming spot in order to cool off in the heat of summer.

According to a recent SFIA report (2013a), which addressed sport and fitness patterns from 2007 through 2012, participation among the youngest age groups (6 to 12 and 13 to 18) declined consistently (see figure 6.2). Overall participation numbers in team sport are simply not as strong as they once were, and this trend seems to be driven by several factors.

- The recent economic recession reduced the number of families who can afford to pay fees for their children to play on local teams, especially the more expensive travel teams.
- The increased popularity of developing sports—such as lacrosse, rugby, ultimate, and of course extreme sports—has siphoned off kids who might once have played traditional team sports.
- Pickup or sandlot play has continued to decline overall, though certain sports have seen an increase in pickup play even as they have lost participants in more formally organized settings. Currently flourishing pickup sports include basketball, ice hockey, field hockey, touch football, lacrosse, and grass and beach volleyball.
- Athletes who play multiple team sports are a fading breed. Most youth now specialize in one sport at a young age in hopes of becoming successful in that sport; by doing so, however, they miss out on the variety of experience available in other sports. Pressure from coaches and parents to focus on one sport year round may also backfire as kids tire of the sport and lose enthusiasm for it.

Increase in Overweight and Obesity

In the past few decades, childhood obesity has more than doubled among young children and quadrupled among adolescents. For example, among

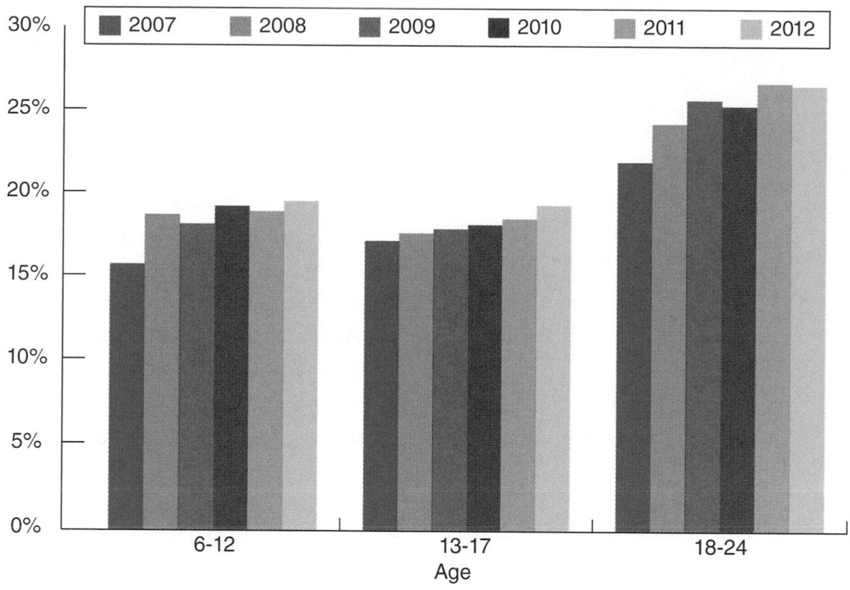

FIGURE 6.2 Increases in inactivity among youth and young adults (ages 6 and up) from 2007 to 2012.
Adapted from Sports Fitness Industry Association 2013a.

kids aged 6 to 11, obesity rose from 7 percent in 1980 to 18 percent in 2012. During the same period, the percentage of adolescents (aged 12 to 19) who were obese rose from 5 percent to 21 percent. Overall, more than one-third of U.S. children are now overweight or obese.

The statistics were particularly alarming for African American adolescent girls, who showed a 43 percent prevalence of obesity (as compared with 37 percent for boys of the same race)—the highest of any age group by gender, race, or ethnicity. In addition, Latino kids aged 2 to 19 are more likely to be overweight or obese than their non-Hispanic white or black peers. The prevalence of overweight and obesity is 39 percent for Hispanic youth as compared with 35 percent for black youth and 29 percent for white youth (Leadership for Healthy Communities 2014a, 2014b; Centers for Disease Control and Prevention 2014).

These disturbing trends can be countered primarily through healthy diet and exercise. However, specific cultures and communities are also affected by economic conditions, family traditions, and recreational opportunities or lack thereof (including lack of physical education and athletic facilities). Certain residential locations have also been clearly identified as correlating with lack of physical activity in both urban and rural settings (Lee, McAlexander, and Banda 2011).

Increasing Cost of Sport

In 2013, 54 percent of parents reported that they had to pay an extra fee for their kids to participate in a school sport, and 57 percent indicated that the cost had risen during the past year. The largest subgroup (27 percent) paid more than $200 in fees, and the next largest group (25 percent) paid between $100 and $200. Of course, these same parents also support school sport through local taxes; as a result, some of them see sport fees as a form of double taxation. Parents also projected significant spending increases for sports and activities not associated with school (Sports and Fitness Industry Association 2013b). Here are the percentage of average increases they expect:

Team sport (outside of school)	12 percent
Travel for sport	10 percent
Lessons, instruction, and sport camps	12 percent
Gym membership fees	12 percent
Individual sport events (e.g., tournaments)	14 percent
Outdoor recreation activities	15 percent
Sport-related footwear	8 percent

Extreme Sport

Extreme sport, also called action or adventure sport, continues to grow in popularity and provide alternative forms of competitive physical activity for youth—primarily males between the ages of 12 and 30. Although no precise definition exists for extreme sport, most activities in this group involve a fairly high level of inherent danger or risk of injury. They typically include challenges replete with speed, height, and exertion and require specialized equipment and gear.

Action sport tends not to be school sanctioned (due to the risk), and competitors tend to participate more individually than as part of a team. Extreme athletes also seem to prefer to practice on the own, at least in the initial stages, rather than rely on a coach, and they are often seen as rebels against more traditional youth sports. The range of extreme sports has continued to increase, but typical categories include the following:

- Board sports
- Cycling
- Flying (e.g., gliding, hang gliding, paragliding, speed flying)
- Free falling
- Motorsports
- Mountaineering
- Orienteering
- Roller sports (e.g., roller skating, in-line skating, freestyle scootering)
- Skiing
- Water sports

Studies conducted a few years ago by the Sporting Goods Manufacturing Association (2005) and the National Sporting Goods Association (2009) showed a dramatic shift among teens and preteens away from mainstream sports (such as basketball and football) and toward extreme or action sports (see table 6.3). More specifically, from 1990 to 2005, participation in football, baseball, and basketball dropped by more than 30 percent among 6- to 17-year-olds. Meanwhile, participation in action sports (such as snowboarding, skateboarding, and in-line skating) increased by more than 600 percent.

More recent research conducted by SFIA in 2013 (SFIA 2013a) showed that extreme or action sports were not a temporary fad but are now clearly established as popular options for youth in the United States. However, as with most other activities, participation levels have leveled off; in fact the majority of extreme sports suffered single-digit decreases in the six years from 2007 to 2012. The most precipitous declines affected in-line skating, paintball, and skateboarding, which had dominated the category for 10 years. The extreme sports that have continued to grow at better than a 5 percent annual increase include (in order) cardio kickboxing, trail running, and ultimate. If you examine table 6.3, you can see that the participation of millions of kids in action sports has likely contributed to the decline of some traditional team sports.

You may be curious about the shift toward action or extreme sport. Why has it happened? Here's a view from skateboarding legend Tony Hawk, a promoter of the X Games (an extreme sport competition): "Kids like the freedom of what we do, no strict practice regimen, no coaches, and it's an artistic pursuit as much as sport. It has constant action, no standing in the outfield waiting for something to happen" (Scheiber 2005, C8).

Whatever the reason, the rise is undeniable. A decade ago, there were about 100 skate parks,

ACTIVITY TIME-OUT

Your Extreme Sport Profile

Review the list of sports presented in table 6.3 and check off the ones in which you have ever participated, then double-check the ones you do regularly. Next, describe to your classmates why you were attracted to the ones you've tried and how you felt about them once you did. Finally, predict whether action sports will continue to grow and give reasons for your answer.

according to Ryan Clements, general manager of Skate Park of Tampa: "Skateboarding used to be punk. Now it's normal" (Scheiber 2005, C8). Indeed, summer 2005 marked the 11th anniversary of the X Games, which are no longer a novelty but part of mainstream youth culture; in fact, they are now featured on ESPN. Another breakthrough was made with the agreement by NBC Sports and USA Network to televise 32 hours of the 2005 Dew Tour, which was the first season-long professional competition involving action sport.

The X Games feature wakeboarding, which evolved from waterskiing and surfing; motocross, which came from motorcycles and cross country running; surfing; BMX, or bicycle motocross, which includes racing and jumping; and skateboarding. These sports often share certain features in common, such as racing, jumping, specialized lingo, and an emphasis on creativity and athleticism. Action sports were once viewed as pursuits for outsiders, rebels, and geeks, but all of that has changed; they're mainstream sports now. Participants say they pursue these sports for fun, for the associated fashion and lifestyle, and for the chance to express themselves.

Changes in Sport Preference

Over the past decade, several changes have occurred in youth sport preferences. As discussed earlier, the most popular youth sports used to be baseball and football—and they are still popular—but other sports have made more dramatic gains. More generally, team sport has always been the most popular type of sport for youth, and that has

TABLE 6.3 Most Popular Extreme Sports in the United States

Extreme sport	Participants in 2007 (approximate millions)	Participants in 2012 (approximate millions)	Average annual growth or loss
1. In-line skating	10.8	6.6	−9.2%
2. Skateboarding	8.4	6.2	−5.8%
3. Mountain biking	6.9	7.3	+0.8%
4. Snowboarding	6.8	7.4	+1.6%
5. Paintball	5.5	3.5	−8.3%
6. Cardio kickboxing	4.8	6.7	+7.0%
7. Climbing (indoor, sport, boulder)	4.5	4.4	−0.7%
8. Trail running	4.2	5.8	+6.6%
9. Ultimate	4.0	5.1	+5.0%
10. Wakeboarding	3.5	3.4	−0.9%
11. Mountain or rock climbing	2.1	1.9	−1.6%
12. BMX bicycling	1.9	1.9	−0.1%
13. Roller hockey	1.8	1.4	−3.8%
14. Boardsailing (windsurfing)	1.1	1.4	+4.3%

Includes participants age six or older.

Reprinted, by permission, from Sports and Fitness Industry Association, 2013, *2013 sports, fitness and leisure activities topline participation report* (Silver Spring, MD: SFIA).

not changed. However, the majority of team sports have barely maintained their past levels of participation, and most have declined. Indeed, you may be surprised to see which team sports grew the most and which lost the most from 2008 to 2013 (Sports and Fitness Industry Association 2014):

Team Sport Growth

Rugby	15 percent
Lacrosse	11 percent
Field hockey	6 percent
Ice hockey	5 percent
Gymnastics	5 percent
Volleyball (Beach)	4 percent

Team Sport Decline

Wrestling	−11 percent
Paintball	−7 percent
Softball (slow-pitch)	−7 percent
Football (all types)	−6 percent
Baseball	−3 percent

The dramatic growth in some sports is due in part to the fact that their total numbers have historically been much smaller. As a result, a modest increase pushes their growth *percentage* considerably higher, whereas the larger sports typically maintain a degree of equilibrium in their numbers.

Among team sports, basketball has the highest participation total (about 24 million), largely because it is played in significant numbers by both males and females. Baseball and touch football rank next in total number of participants, but they both typically attract mostly males. However, if we combine the related sports of baseball and softball, the total number of participants of both sexes is about 23 million, which stands second only to basketball. Football can be subdivided into its flag, touch, and tackle versions; even when these three are combined, however, football draws a total participation of about 19 million, which still ranks third behind basketball and the combination of baseball and softball. Soccer comes next, with about 18 million participants, and volleyball follows with about 15 million (Sports and Fitness Industry Association 2014).

These popular sports are also marked by differences in frequency of participation. Casual participants are defined as those who play fewer than 12 times per year, whereas core participants play more than 30 times per year. Basketball and baseball are weighted toward core participants over casual participants by a ratio of about 2 to 1, and tackle football is also weighted toward core participants at a ratio of 3 to 2. In contrast, soccer, flag football, and touch football are evenly balanced between core and casual players.

Basketball

Basketball has become the most popular team sport for kids (Sports and Fitness Industry Association 2014; Kelley and Carchia 2013). It appeals to both sexes, can be highly competitive, and is hugely popular as a recreational or pickup sport. In addition, courts are fairly accessible, which is particularly important in urban settings where space is at a premium, and player costs are minimal. Basketball peaks in popularity at age 13 (as compared with age 7 or 8 for baseball and soccer) but continues to be popular throughout the teenage years; in fact, it has the highest number of high school teams of any sport for both boys and girls. In contrast, tackle football rates only fourth in the number of high school teams, though football ranks first in number of participants for boys, due to the large number of players required to form a team (National Federation of State High School Associations 2013-2014).

Today's generation of young basketball players has been inspired by sport heroes including Tim Duncan, Dwyane Wade, Kobe Bryant, and LeBron James. In addition, as women's college and professional basketball have gained a solid foothold, young basketballers have been able to find female role models in players such as Candace Parker, Diana Taurasi, Sue Bird, Elena Delle Donne, Breanna Stewart, Skylar Diggins, and Brittney Griner.

Soccer

Soccer has grown at an unprecedented rate in the United States over the past 30 years and now ranks second only to basketball in participation, especially among younger children. In the past 10 years, however, U.S. soccer participation has leveled off, showing little gain or loss. Although soccer participation peaks at the relatively young age of eight, it still attracts the fifth-highest number of participants of all sports in high school, and that participation is spread evenly between girls and boys.

The major impetus for soccer's U.S. growth has come from community-based programs affiliated

Tim Howard (right) gained national attention for his performance at the 2014 World Cup.

with U.S. Youth Soccer, as well as the influence of Title IX and the liberation of girls to play soccer. That happy circumstance led to the resounding success enjoyed in world competition by the U.S. women's national team, led by Mia Hamm, Kristine Lilly, Brandi Chastain, Abby Wambach, and a core group of others who starred at the professional level for over a decade. Young girls now have female role models to emulate in sport, and these women have been outstanding citizens, athletes, and promoters of their sport.

On the men's side, U.S. goalkeeper Tim Howard became a national hero for his dramatic play in the 2014 World Cup. With the American team locked in an epic overtime struggle against Belgium to avoid elimination in the round of sixteen, Howard set a World Cup record with 16 saves, sometimes deflecting the ball with his feet or leaping to punch it harmlessly over the crossbar. Eventually, Belgium prevailed 2-1 but not before facing a mighty challenge.

Howard is a quiet man off the field but yells a lot during games, mixing instruction and encouragement for his teammates. He has become the latest role model for U.S. kids who play soccer. Despite having Tourette's syndrome—a neurological disorder characterized by physical and vocal tics—Howard stands tall among both his peers and his fans (Fox News Latino 2014).

Soccer has some built-in advantages over other sports. No certain size or body type is required for success, and the skills needed to play at the beginning level are somewhat modest. In contrast, other sports that are popular in the United States do put a premium on size—for example, basketball (height) and football (height and weight)—thus eliminating most aspiring young athletes from higher levels of play. Although youth soccer is often marked by a swarm of players moving toward the ball, players still get multiple benefits: good exercise; basic balance, running, and kicking skills; and camaraderie with their teammates. In addition, the cost per player is modest, since putting 22 kids on one field is a cost-effective use of both space and personnel.

Soccer programs also benefit from the fact that they start as early as age four, thus snatching up kids before other sports have a chance to recruit them. In order to play soccer, kids need only be able to run and kick a ball, whereas more complicated skills are required for many other sports. Recreational leagues are plentiful, and most communities also offer travel teams, which are the next step up in competition. Up to 30 percent of soccer participants are identified as elite players and offered advanced training and coaching. We know this number is inflated, but at a young age many players show the potential to develop, and parents eagerly support their children's attempts to develop their talent.

Football

Even as football has continued to grow in popularity—it is the top U.S. spectator sport—it has experienced a steady decline in participation. To help us understand the full picture of football participation, the SFIA's 2014 sport participation report breaks football participation into three categories: tackle, touch, and flag. A further drill-down categorizes participants as either casual or core participants based on their frequency of play. The bottom line regarding football participation is that since 2008 it has decreased in every category—in some cases by a percentage exceeding 7 percent (Sports and Fitness Industry Association 2014).

The nation's largest youth football program is the Pop Warner organization, which was founded in 1929 and, according to the National Football League (NFL) Players Association gave 60 to 70 percent of all NFL players their start in football. Overall, about 250,000 boys annually play youth football on Pop Warner teams, but participation declined by 10 percent from 2010 to 2012. A closer look at the statistics reveals a loss of nearly 24,000 players in that two-year period, which is thought to be the largest decline since the organization began keeping statistics several decades ago (Fainaru and Fainaru-Wada 2013). Another source (Sports and Fitness Industry Association 2014) reports an average annual decline in tackle football participation of nearly 5 percent from 2008 to 2013—or, in sheer numbers, a total drop in participation from 7.8 million players to 6.1 million.

Pop Warner's chief medical officer, Dr. Julian Bailes, whose 10-year-old son plays Pop Warner football, attributes the decline primarily to concerns about head injury as the crisis that began in the NFL filters down to youth sport. Bailes believes that unless changes are made, kids will keep dropping out of the sport. In 2012, in response to the decline, Pop Warner leagues cut down on the amount of tackling permitted during practices and renewed efforts to teach tackling techniques thought to minimize injuries. In 2013, Pop Warner joined efforts headed by the NFL to consider other rule changes that could minimize head trauma, along with encouraging manufacturers to continue using advanced engineering to improve the safety features of helmets (Fainaru and Fainaru-Wada 2013).

Baseball and Softball

Baseball, once considered America's pastime, has begun to play a more modest role in the culture. A number of reasons have been suggested to explain this decline, but no clear answers have emerged. Some people blame it on Major League Baseball (MLB) itself—in particular, on the bitter feuds between professional players and owners that have resulted in strikes and lockouts. Others say the game is too slow, even boring. In addition, the sport's steroid controversy, which exposed many stars as users of illegal substances, continues to generate negative publicity (for more discussion of performance enhancement and doping, see chapter 20).

Baseball also faces other challenges in its attempts to attract participants at the youth level. For one thing, more than any other sport, baseball at the youth level has relied on parents to serve as coaches and team administrators. In many families, however, both parents are now active in the workforce and therefore have limited time for such activities. In addition, fields are expensive to develop and maintain, particularly in urban settings. Youth baseball has even been touched by scandals in which players lied about their age in order to compete in divisions for which they were too old or lied about their legal place of residence.

For the last 20 years, baseball has also experienced a considerable decline in the number of African Americans who count themselves as fans or players. As a result, young black males see fewer black role models in MLB. They are also more likely to lack ready access to baseball fields and youth leagues, and they often lack a male father figure to introduce them to the sport. The overriding issue is the cost of playing baseball, particularly in the inner city where basketball courts are ubiquitous while landscaped baseball diamonds are rarely found (Solomon 2014).

Another factor in baseball's decline is the relative lack of opportunities for college scholarships, since Division I universities are limited to just 11.7 scholarship equivalents for baseball and therefore rarely award a full scholarship to one player. Compare that number with the 85 full scholarships allowed for football and you can see why so many young men choose football (Cook 2013; Solomon 2014).

All of these factors are often mentioned as reasons for the decline in baseball participation, which dropped from 15.5 million in 2008 to 13.2 million in 2013—an average annual decline of 3 percent. Of course, few girls play organized baseball, but more play softball, which of course closely resembles baseball. Therefore, when comparing baseball with other team sports, it seems reasonable to combine baseball with softball (which is also favored by many older men). If we combine all participants in baseball, fast-pitch softball, and slow-pitch softball, the total comes to nearly 23 million—very close to basketball, which at nearly 24 million is the most popular participatory team sport (Sports and Fitness Industry Association 2014).

Individual Sports

Participation in individual sports that traditionally have been popular—for example, ice skating, skiing, golf, tennis, and gymnastics—have had their ups and downs over the past five years. Gymnastics and skiing have been trending upward, tennis and ice skating have been flat, and golf has been declining (SFIA 2014). The primary obstacle to growth for these sports lies in the expense of practicing and competing. Some affordable community programs are available for young people just starting out, but athletes who aspire to higher performance must participate in an elite program. Therein lies the catch. According to experience-based estimates by various families, supporting one child in an elite program costs \$20,000 to \$25,000 per year, depending on the sport and the amount of travel required. That figure includes expenses for coaching, equipment, and travel to competition, for both the child and for a parent chaperone.

For those select few who attend a sport academy away from home, the tab can exceed \$75,000 a year for room and board and schooling—and that's in addition to the expenses just mentioned. For example, at IMG Academy in Bradenton, Florida, training is offered in baseball, basketball, tennis, football, golf, lacrosse, soccer, and track and field. In addition, academic education is provided on-site at the academy's private school. For the academic year beginning in 2015, the cost for a high school boarding student at IMG Academy exceeds \$70,000 depending on the sport pursued (day students pay \$56,000).

Clearly, these costs are out of reach for the average family, which means that only a select few young people can attend such high-performance programs without risking the family finances (see chapter 14 for more on sport and social class). Even so, some parents are so consumed by the lure of a pot of gold in professional sport that they risk everything in hopes that their child will reach the big payday. Just imagine the pressure these children feel when the family finances depend on them (IMG Academy 2015).

The high price of attending elite academies typically causes middle-class and minority families to be underrepresented in these programs. In turn, this exclusionary effect tends to produce artificial social environments for players who associate only with other players from families like their own.

Organized Youth Sport

Sport at the youth level is organized by one of two groups: youths or adults. Both approaches have grown in recent years, and the question is whether one will dominate the other over the long run. The two approaches can differ considerably in intent, application of traditions and rules, social influences, and financial cost. Sports organized by adults tend to be more reflective of adult and professional models of sport. They offer kids a glimpse into the adult world of sport and socialize them into a system that prepares them for continued play in high school, college, and beyond. In contrast, sport programs organized by young people are more likely to be accepted as an end in themselves, to offer an opportunity to simply have fun and enjoy competition, and to allow participants to control their level of involvement and dedication.

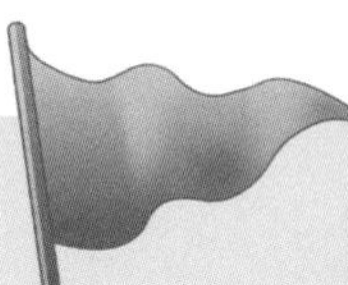

IN THE ARENA WITH . . .

i9 Sports

i9 Sports has become the largest and fastest-growing U.S. youth sport league franchise, and it's built on hugs. Founded in 2002 in the suburbs of Tampa, Florida, i9 now boasts more than 100 franchises serving 500 communities scattered across 28 states from New York to Hawaii. More than 10,000 kids have run its field in Tampa, and 650,000 kids are customers nationwide.

Seeing a need created by underfunding of school athletic teams and public recreational leagues, i9 stepped in with a unique concept to privatize youth sport by answering parents' calls for a different kind of youth sport program. Going back to the 1970s, the prevailing model for adult-run youth sport had emphasized learning the rules and skills of the game in an increasingly competitive structure that often adopted the principles and practices of adult professional sport. However, parents thought there might be a better way, and i9 responded to that market. Their organization's programs are marked by inclusive, low-conflict sport play where participation is king and competitiveness is low key.

Many parents had also grown tired of putting in endless volunteer hours at the concession stand, carrying out candy-bar fundraisers, and tolerating overbearing parents who cursed at coaches and officials. As i9 founder Frank Flume puts it, "Parents know their kid is not going to be the next Peyton Manning, but they want their kids to have fun, a great experience, and be physically active." Flume points out that youth sport is the greatest secret in U.S. small business. You just have to make it attractive to kids and easy for parents.

In the i9 approach, every team in every sport is co-ed, and each week involves just one practice and one game. Every kid gets to play the same amount, regardless of ability, and most children end up playing every position at some point. In addition, every week emphasizes a new principle of good sporting behavior—for example, hustle, teamwork, or helping a buddy. There are no MVPs, but everyone gets a participant award and plenty of hugs when they need them.

Some critics will say that this is just another example of the coddling of U.S. kids, wherein everyone gets a gold star and is a dirty word. Not so, says Flume, who quickly points out that "too much of sports today is over-aggressive and burn-out inducing, focusing on earning college scholarships or a pro career. That's just not realistic for 99 percent of kids, and parents know it."

This approach to privatizing youth sport works as a business model too. Consider that i9 Sports has 800 employees, more than 2,000 independently contracted officials, and a slew of volunteer coaches. In 2015, it expects to add 375 positions and 33 new locations. Local owners invest $40,000 to $60,000 to launch their own franchise and can earn revenues of $200,000 to $500,000 per year. They are expected to follow the corporate playbook, marketing plan, and program philosophy.

In addition, the conduct of coaches, parents, and players is strictly monitored and must remain consistent with the values and philosophy of the corporation. Thus i9 Sports is selling youth sport in a way that allows time for other things in life, keeps kids safe, and improves their self-esteem. And the kids are having fun (Harwell 2014a).

Athlete-Organized Sport

Athlete-organized sport involves sports and games that develop naturally as children go outside to play. Free from school, parents, and other adult supervision, children choose an activity, agree on the rules, and settle disputes among themselves. Games begin and end by mutual agreement or when the child who provided the equipment decides to go home.

Sides are chosen by natural leaders, who are often the best players or the oldest kids. The hurt feelings of those chosen last are ignored, and kids learn where they stand in the minds of their peers. The most popular games provide lots of action for every player and flexible rules to mitigate imbalances due to size, age, or level of experience. For example, younger children who might often strike out in baseball-type games are often given a chance to bat until they actually hit the ball.

Disputes are solved creatively by one side's giving in, negotiation between team leaders, or allowance of a certain number of gimmes or do-overs during a game. In playground basketball, for example, the team with the ball can often call a foul on the opposing team without the foul's being open to question. Rules are agreed upon before play begins but may be changed by agreement during play. They also often change from game to game, depending on the participants. For example, in "make-it-take-it" pickup basketball, the side that scores a bucket keeps the ball for another possession. Similarly, some sandlot football games are tackle, some are touch, some are two-hand touch, and some are flag.

The problem of uneven numbers between teams is often solved by having one player serve both teams in the role of pitcher, catcher, or some other position. Girls are accepted as part of pickup games and are typically treated no better or worse than their male counterparts. More skilled athletes typically choose active positions that are crucial to the game—for example, pitcher, shortstop, quarterback, receiver, goalkeeper, and point guard—but positions are often shifted during the game to balance out the action.

Youth-controlled activity offers multiple advantages. For example, young people learn how to negotiate group dynamics, make decisions, and get along with their peers. As players come and go, lopsided scores develop, or bad feelings arise, players are forced to be creative and flexible if the game is to go on.

As discussed earlier in the chapter, a recent trend toward athlete-centered sport has occurred in the rapid rise of alternative sport—for example, in-line skating and snowboarding. Indeed, these activities appeal to participants in part because they involve only limited adult supervision. Although these sports do involve some inherent danger, young people are flocking to them as an alternative to traditional sport.

Adult-Organized Sport

At about age six, many children begin playing soccer, munchkin tennis, tee ball, biddy ball (a form of basketball), or flag football in an adult-organized program. Parents are often heavily involved in both practices and games, serving as coaches, partners, pitchers, or base coaches. The rules are modified to suit the ability of the players so that their introduction to the sport is successful. Rules are also established to protect the safety of each child, ensure fair allotment of playing time, and control game length.

Since physical development proceeds at different rates, many children are not ready or able to perform precise skills when they enter an organized sport program. In such cases, frustration and lack of confidence can easily turn off a child for life when pushy parents force them into a no-win situation. Granted, we often read about champion athletes who started in their sport at age three or four, but clearly they are the exceptions. Moreover, who knows what their sport beginnings looked like? They may have been simply hitting a tennis ball against a wall or playing a game of catch with parents or peers.

Adult-organized sports are primarily concerned with teaching kids the following:

- Skills of the game
- Rules of the game
- Proper playing of positions
- Obedience to adult directions, strategy, and training methods

Adult coaches and parents are usually the key figures who determine the success of the experience. They set the tone and the level of competitiveness, arbitrate rule infractions, determine who plays where and when, and offer encouragement or disapproval. Since their role is so important, several national organizations have been established to offer training for coaches and parents involved in youth sport. Examples include the National Alliance for Youth Sports, Human Kinetics Coach Education, and the Institute for the Study of Youth Sports. Such organizations tackle a big challenge given that every season brings a new crop of adults to train and educate.

When coaches or parents go untrained, young athletes are put at great risk. They can be seriously harmed if the adults in charge lack necessary knowledge about sport safety, healthy competition, and the emotional needs of children. In addition, an inability to teach sport-specific skills can slow down the learning process and lead to frustration for the aspiring players. Fortunately, great strides have been made in coach and parent education, but the task remains daunting—and nothing is more crucial to ensure a positive experience for kids in adult-controlled youth sport. Coaching is covered in more detail in chapter 7.

Since many kids are used to adult instruction and judgment at home and at school, the athletic field may seem little different to them. To be successful, they need to please the adults, conform to the rules of the game, stay in position, and follow the strategy set by the coaches. Failure to do these things usually results in reprimand or punishment (for example, benching).

The adults in charge of adult-organized sport for youth need to be aware of the multiple motivations that may drive kids' participation in sport. For some kids, sport participation mainly offers a way to spend time with friends, and postgame trips for pizza and ice cream may be more important to these kids than the outcome of the game. At the same time, celebrating success with friends generates enthusiasm, reinforces effort, and tends to keep players coming back. A team that rarely comes out on top needs a wise, creative leader to salve wounded egos and help participants cultivate a healthy approach to competition.

If former NFL commissioner Pete Rozelle were still around to share his wisdom, he would probably advise youth sport leaders to aim for competitive balance—as he did in the NFL—so that every team contends for honors until the end of the season. Parity among teams produces some wins and losses for every team and helps kids learn to deal with both situations. Too much winning often produces cockiness and unrealistic expectations. Too much losing undermines confidence, encourages finger pointing, and may instill a defeatist attitude.

Key Role of Parents

Youth sport has the potential to be either a terrific, positive influence on family life or a divisive, painful experience for all. To maximize their kids'

The most effective coaches at the youth sport level are warm, caring individuals who have completed training to be a youth sport coach.

chances of having a positive sport experience, parents can read educational materials, attend orientation sessions, and talk with other parents in order to understand the sport philosophy, policies, and expectations of local sport programs before their children begin to participate. Then, when their children come home and say they want to sign up for soccer because their friends are doing so, parents will be armed with accurate and helpful information.

If parents get involved as coaches, league officials, or chaperones, they are likely to get a better picture of the experience and be better prepared to counsel their child when a problem arises. However, once a practice or game is over, parents need to let it go and resume normal family life. Kids don't need to feel constant pressure from family about their performance on the ball field. Parents can deliver a message of strong parental interest and support simply by attending home games as fans, providing transportation to away games, and joining in team celebrations. These activities also allow parents to meet their child's friends, those kids' parents, and the team's coaches.

Watching kids play their chosen sport gives parents insight into the type of child they have raised. Rarely do they get to watch their child at school, but on the athletic field they see their child in his or her peer environment. Many opportunities arise for shaping and reinforcing children's attitudes toward teammates, opponents, and adult coaches and officials, as well as good sporting behavior.

If a family includes more than one child, time and money must be balanced so that each one gets a fair share. By nature, some activities are more expensive than others, but kids need to understand the general expense and appreciate the family commitment.

Parents who take a relaxed view of the importance of competition can relieve the pressure on kids. Parents need to set expectations for good effort, improvement in skill or strategy, healthy physical activity, and cooperation with coaches and teammates. By reinforcing positive actions in these areas, they send a powerful message about what is important in sport—and in life.

Most parents whose children have been through the experience of youth sport would counsel parents approaching those years to have fun with them. Before they know it, those precious hours of growth and challenge will be gone for their kids, and they won't get the chance for a do-over. In order to fulfill their supporting role effectively, most parents need some direction and counseling. Coaches who are experienced and well trained may be able to provide parental guidance, both in writing and during required preseason meetings. However, some communities prefer to have program administrators provide parent education to ensure that a consistent philosophy is shared with every family.

Why Kids Participate—and Stop Participating—in Sport

Most kids are first attracted to sport because their friends are involved. The chance to spend time with peers, make new friends, and escape from the adult world (and maybe school or boredom) all factor into the attraction of sport. In addition, kids seem to enjoy the physical challenge of games and activity. In the typical suburban household, friends are separated by geography, and sport offers friends an opportunity to spend time together. There is little doubt that if a child's parents have a favorable attitude toward sport, as most parents do, then the child is more likely to be encouraged to join a team or program. Once a child is involved, if parents initiate positive interactions, support, and encouragement—and avoid pressuring the child—then he or she is more likely to embrace challenges and display greater intrinsic motivation (Fraser-Thomas and Cote 2006).

In virtually every survey investigating why kids participate in sport, they say they enjoy it—especially if they get to play regularly and not sit on the bench. In fact, they would rather play for a team that loses most games if they get to play than be on a team that wins a championship while they ride the bench (Harris Interactive 2004). When sport ceases to be fun, youth are likely to drop out. But what does fun mean to a typical kid? Adults ascribe all types of motivation to young people and tend to try to convince them that having fun means playing like the pros; wearing sharp uniforms; and displaying hard work, dedication, and a commitment to success. But conversations with young people tell a different story.

In 1990, the largest study ever conducted of youths' feelings about sport was sponsored by the Athletic Footwear Association and conducted by the Institute for the Study of Youth Sports (ISYS) at Michigan State University. The results, from

Why do kids like to participate in sport? Because it's fun!

some 10,000 students aged 10 to 18, showed once again that the number-one reason young people play sport is to have fun. The top ten reasons also included improving their skills, staying in shape, doing something they're good at, experiencing the excitement of competition, and being part of a team. In fact, for many respondents, these factors were also part of the fun (Ewing and Seefeldt 1990).

There are also deeper reasons for sport participation. One recent study, for example, suggests that benefits of participation include growth and maturation, improved self-worth, increased social competence, and enhanced moral development (Malina and Cumming 2003). In addition, Gould (1993) suggested that young athletes' perception of their own competence or ability is crucial. If they see their own competence as low in comparison with that of their peers, they tend to become discouraged and drop out of sport.

The most critical time for youth in relation to dropping out of sport is the onset of adolescence at about age 11 or 12. By then, youth have evaluated their own skill competence, decided whether an activity is fun, and drawn conclusions about how they respond to competition and coaching. The major reasons they drop out of sport include changing interests, interest in another activity, feeling that the sport is no longer fun, or feeling that the coach is a poor teacher or plays favorites (Seefeldt, Ewing, and Walk 1992). Another study identified the following extensive list of key reasons that kids stop participating in sport (Women's Sports Foundation 2008):

I was not having fun. (38%)

I wanted to focus more on studying or grades. (31%)

I had health problems or injury. (28%)

I did not like or get along with the coach. (20%)

I wanted to focus more on other clubs or activities. (19%)

I did not like or get along with other players on the team. (17%)

I was not a good enough player. (16%)

My family worried about me getting hurt or injured. (13%)

I had a job. (13%)

I had a problem traveling to practices. (12%)

I had to care for a younger brother or sister. (11%)

My mother or father said I could not play. (10%)

In another survey, young people reported having a variety of negative experiences in sport at the hands of coaches, parents, or teammates (Harris Interactive 2004). Here is the prompt and a selection of responses:

Which of the Following Experiences Have You Had During Your Participation in Youth Sport?

Saw parents yelling at or arguing with umpires, referees, or officials. (31%)

Didn't get to play as much as I wanted. (30%)

Saw parents yelling at or arguing with coaches. (28%)

Heard coaches or parents use bad language. (27%)

Had coaches who were too focused on winning. (23%)

Had teammates who insulted me. (21%)

Had too many practices. (18%)

Felt sports were too competitive for me. (15%)

Felt pressure to play when I was hurt. (14%)

Had coaches who insulted me. (11%)

Felt pressure to focus on only one sport. (9%)

Had too much travel to get to games. (9%)

Was physically hit by an adult. (2%)

Burnout in Youth Sport

Burnout is simply a natural reaction to chronic stress. Kids who have burned out in a sport seek to reduce the stress by withdrawing from the sport. If they know that their parents and coaches will be disappointed in them, the stress is heightened, and they may feel forced to take drastic measures, such as faking an injury or illness. In fact, the pressure they feel may even produce an illness.

At the same time, stress isn't all bad; in fact, we often learn valuable life lessons from dealing with stressful situations. Consider, for example, the stress of being the last batter in a baseball game when your team is behind and runners are on base. Sure, the batter and the pitcher both feel stress, but the one who comes out on top gains confidence. In addition, the one who loses may learn from his mistake, and—assuming that his friends, teammates, and coaches respond constructively—he'll also learn that they still value him.

Still, youth sport can be the scene of too much stress, which may eventually cause kids to burn out and then drop out. Athletes at particular risk for burnout include those who worry too much about game outcomes, experience performance anxiety or low self-esteem, or believe that their parents attach too much importance to games. In addition, an athlete may come to feel that sport is no longer fun if he or she is subjected to year-round sport programs, single-sport specialization at a young age, overdone physical training, overly long practices, too many games without days off, or an overemphasis on winning.

With these risks in mind, parents and coaches need to learn how to listen to kids and address potential burnout symptoms before they become irreversible. According to Waldron (2000), the signs of burnout can take the form of feelings, thoughts, behaviors, or physical symptoms. Specifically, observers may notice that players feel anxious or moody; often mention thoughts about mental errors or lack of attention; cry easily or bite their nails; or experience physical symptoms, such as headache, upset stomach, or a racing pulse. Youth sport organizers and coaches must become sensitive to the signs of burnout by learning about the effects of stress on youngsters; in addition, they must either be prepared to deal with the causes or refer the child to someone with more training.

The scars from a negative sport experience can turn a happy, well-adjusted kid into a withdrawn, unhappy kid. Therefore, parents also need to learn to recognize when their kids show signs of burnout, which may include avoiding practice or games, never smiling, frequent physical ailments, lack of caring about performance, emotional outbursts, or other behavior that is atypical for that child. Once burnout is suspected, intervention

ACTIVITY TIME-OUT

Keeping Kids in the Game

In the United States, it seems that we entice the majority of young people to try youth sport, but we are not very successful in keeping most of them active through their teenage years and beyond. To the contrary, it seems that only the most intense and dedicated kids stick with sport as they get older. What strategies would you suggest to keep kids involved in sport or otherwise physically active throughout their teenage years and early adulthood?

by trained professionals may be necessary to plot a path back to normalcy, which may or may not include the sport in which the child burned out.

The best source of help is likely to be a sport psychologist who is trained to address youth sport problems. Sport psychologists can teach athletes, parents, and coaches specific strategies to combat burnout if the damage is not too extensive. They can also help young athletes reassess their reasons for playing a sport and work toward a healthier approach that includes physical activity and perhaps other sports (Gould 1993; R. Smith 1986; Weinberg and Gould 2015).

Early Specialization in One Sport

Youth sport is increasingly characterized by specializing in just one sport at an early age, to the exclusion of participation in other sports. The result has been an increasing number of kids who simply drop out of that one sport and do not replace it with another physical activity. It need not be this way. Simply stated, research shows that both elite athlete development and lifelong sport participation are best promoted when kids play informal games in childhood and then participate in multiple sports until about age 15.

So why the trend toward specialization? This approach has become popular as part of the seemingly ubiquitous quest for excellence—keeping up with the competition—and the trend toward privatization of youth sport. For example, kids are often subjected to intense pressure for exclusive specialization in a program that depends on year-round income to pay for facilities and coaches. Many coaches justify encouraging kids to focus on one sport by saying that it is just a fact of life if they want to make their high school team or perhaps earn a college scholarship.

Unfortunately, specialization puts kids at risk of suffering an overuse injury, growing bored due to repetition, overemphasizing the importance of success in competition, and resenting the time commitment that precludes most other activities. Parents, too, often feel the pressure—in their case, to attend contests, provide transportation, help raise funds, and keep writing checks to pay for it all.

Indeed, parents who seek to encourage excellence in their kids who show unusual talent in music, art, or sport often feel conflicted about the time investment required to reach an elite level. Various widely quoted experts (Gladwell 2008) have expressed the opinion that it takes about 10,000 hours, or 10 years of deliberate practice, to excel in a sport. Their definition of deliberate practice involves high-quality, high-concentration practice that is not usually inherently enjoyable; rather, it must become increasingly complex over time, and the primary goal must be to improve performance.

In reality, there is little research to support this assertion; in fact, some studies show that elite performance after age 20 can be achieved with 3,000 to 4,000 hours of sport-specific training. In addition, even the proverbial 10,000-hour threshold has been presented as an average, thus implicitly acknowledging that some people can train much less and some must train much more, depending on other relevant factors (Ericsson 2012).

The National Association for Sport and Physical Education (now SHAPE America) turned to experts to formulate a position statement on youth sport specialization. Their collective position asserts that programs lasting longer than three months in any given sport are often counterproductive, especially when they also include one-sport summer camps and clinics, private lessons, or year-round practices. Indeed, if our goal is to nurture intrinsic motivation in kids so that they sustain sport participation throughout a lifetime, we can help them thrive by giving them sport experiences that develop their love of sport, their self-esteem and self-efficacy, and their sense of self-mastery. To this end, engaging in a variety of sport activities widens their social network of friends and role models (SHAPE 2010).

Dropping Out Due to Burnout

Burnout often leads young athletes to drop out of sport. According to Ronald Smith, professor of psychology at the University of Washington, "The No. 1 reason kids drop out of sports is: It's not fun. The next five reasons all have to do with parents' or coaches' behaviors" (Condor 2004, 2). Drawing from sources cited previously in this chapter, here are a few common mistakes made by parents that lead children to burn out and potentially drop out of sport:

- Choosing a sport that the parents like rather than allowing the child to decide after trying several activities
- Insisting that a child follow one sport season with another, when the child may just want a little free time for a change

- Putting too much emphasis on the results of competition (for example, asking "Did you win?"—a question that says winning is the most important thing)
- Forcing a child to compete even at the risk of overuse injury
- Becoming overinvolved in the game or team (possible indicator: "*We've* got a game tomorrow.")
- Arguing with officials, parents from opposing teams, or coaches
- Failing to reinforce the positive experiences that children are looking for in sport, such as learning new skills, staying active, being with friends, achieving independence, and improving self-confidence
- Pushing children to the next level of competition even when they resist

Poorly trained coaches can also contribute to burnout in young participants. Youth sport coaching positions may be occupied by paid professionals, parents, or other volunteers. Given this mix, one major concern about youth coaching involves the lack of standardized training; a second concern involves the rapid turnover of coaches and, in turn, the continual need to train new coaches.

Based on recommendations from Human Kinetics Coach Education and other youth sport organizations (such as the Institute for the Study of Youth Sports at Michigan State University), here are some common mistakes for youth coaches to avoid:

- Emphasizing winning rather than building skills and improving performance
- Spending more time on—and allocating more playing time to—more skilled athletes at the expense of average or below-average players
- Expecting kids to absorb rules and strategy that may be too advanced for their level of development in terms of understanding or skill
- Using physical punishment (running laps or push-ups) as discipline
- Arguing with officials or parents in inappropriate ways
- Neglecting to create an atmosphere of fun for practices and games
- Expecting families to sacrifice time, money, and priorities for the sport team
- Encouraging kids to specialize in one sport at an early age to the exclusion of other sports or school-related activities
- Using an authoritarian coaching style or imitating the coaching style of coaches of professional athletes

In addition to coaches, youth sport administrators include league organizers, publicity staff, governing board members, officials, and sponsors. All of these people play important roles in the success of a youth sport league; conversely, they can have a detrimental effect if their vision is not appropriate and clear or if league policies are not set in writing for everyone to see. According to multiple experts (Ewing and Seefeldt 1990; Weinberg and Gould 2015), typical problems involving league-affiliated adults include the following:

- Failing to establish a philosophy for the league from which policies naturally follow
- Failing to communicate the philosophy and policies to parents, coaches, and players through training days, newsletters, and websites
- Putting too much emphasis on winning, playoffs, and all-star squads rather than on creating a healthy program for all kids
- Requiring an unrealistic financial commitment from families, particularly those who have several children competing at the same time
- Extending seasons by having preseason, postseason, and off-season programs that force kids to choose between one sport and other activities
- Lacking proper safety procedures, training for coaches, and support from medical personnel to deal with emergencies and chronic health problems of players
- Failing to provide safe, clean, and attractive facilities for practices and games
- Adopting a casual attitude toward the hiring and training of league coaches and officials
- Failing to balance the level of competition between teams in order to facilitate excitement and fair competition

Elite Teams and Burnout

In 2004, *U.S. News and World Report* published an article titled "Fixing Kids' Sports: Rescuing Children's Games from Crazed Coaches and Parents" (Cary 2004). The article relied heavily on an interview with Fred Engh, founder of the National Alliance for Youth Sports, who has spent a lifetime trying to educate youth sport leaders about the need to make team sport "less pressurized, safer, and more child friendly." He created a training manual for coaches, and his organization has certified more than three million volunteer coaches. But Engh realizes that his accomplishments aren't enough, and he continues to extol the virtues of training everyone involved, including parents, administrators, and officials.

One way to prevent burnout in young athletes is to encourage them to try various sports rather than focusing exclusively on one.

One of the major problems described in the article is the phenomenon of so-called travel teams, in which kids who are judged to be above average are placed on club, select, or elite teams that travel to nearby towns for games or tournaments. These teams often practice twice a week, play two games a week, and absorb participants' time during every weekend. Parents usually provide the transportation by carpooling.

The pitch to families is that if kids don't join one of these elite teams, their chance of making a high school varsity team is diminished considerably. In other words, if they fall behind their peers in skill development, they'll never catch up. Of course, basketball great Michael Jordan and many more like him have proved that you don't even have to make your high school team to go on to play professionally. Jordan got cut from his high school team in the tenth grade!

In reality, playing just one sport can lead to miserable kids. In the misguided attempt by league officials and parents to make their kids more competitive, traditional seasons are extended into year-round programs. Baseball is extended into fall and winter seasons in warm climates; basketball is played year round; tennis and golf are stocked with one-sport athletes; and swimmers hit the pool for workouts regardless of the month. The potential results of this overspecialization at a young age include the following (Wendel 2005):

- Kids lose interest due to overexposure and no longer have fun playing.
- When kids hit a performance barrier in their sport of choice, they have no other sport to turn to for activity.
- Kids' friends tend to be limited to those with whom they associate on a daily basis in their sport.
- The single-sport focus neglects complementary athletic skills that might be developed by cross-training.

- Kids are not exposed to a variety of coaching and training methods.
- Overuse injuries can occur due to the repeated stress demands of one sport.

Pressure builds on kids and families to commit time, money, and long seasons and off-seasons to one sport. Private instruction and summer sport camps add to the pressure and the expense. In addition, if more than one sibling is involved, families are forced to juggle time, transportation, and finances.

Some parents justify their actions by saying something like the following: "I know the chances of my kid making the pros are small. I just want to give them a chance to earn a college scholarship." However, if you pay between $10,000 and $20,000 per year, as many families do, for one child in swimming, tennis, skating, or another sport, wouldn't it make more sense to invest that money in a college savings plan? There's no guarantee that athletic scholarships will even be available in the sport in the next 10 years as colleges trim budgets and support scholarships only for revenue-producing sports.

Reforms for Youth Sport

Now that we have traced the history of youth sport and considered some current issues, perhaps you think that changes should be made. It's natural to try to improve an experience for children, whether it involves education or recreation. Kids need to be able to adjust to the world they will live in—not the one we lived in the past. As a result, they will need different skills in order to embrace new experiences, and they should be provided with opportunities for positive social experiences through sport activity.

Kids want to participate in sport programs that are designed to be a fun, positive experience in which they can invest energy and enthusiasm. In 1979, with this end in mind, two leaders in youth sport training—Rainer Martens and Vern Seefeldt—developed the Bill of Rights for Young Athletes (see figure 6.3) as a response to growing concern about abuse of young athletes (Martens and Seefeldt 1979). This seminal work is still used and is available from many sport organizations.

As made clear by this bill of rights, there are some concerns that must be addressed in youth sport. Earlier in the chapter, for example, we reviewed typical characteristics of adult-controlled youth sport, some of which obviously conflict with the bill of rights presented here. Realistically, many local sport programs probably do not exhibit all of the characteristics of either adult-centered sport or athlete-centered sport; rather, they fall somewhere between the two. One thing, however, is certain: If the young athlete's bill of rights is accepted and implemented, the experience of youth sport will be enhanced for all children.

The keen interest in youth sport in the United States has spawned various organizations to provide educational services to coaches, parents, and officials. For example, the National Council of Youth Sports (NCYS) represents more than 200 organizations and corporations, as well as 60 million registered participants, or 44 million actual participants some of whom play more than one sport. By its estimates, the total number of coaches involved in youth sport is 2.4 million, and the number of volunteers has ballooned to 7.6 million. Altogether, then, more than 55 million kids and adults are involved together in youth sport programs (NCYS, 2010).

Perhaps the most inclusive organization is the National Alliance for Youth Sports (NAYS), a multisport corporation established to foster the continued education of youth sport administrators and to support the growth and development of young people through participation in organized youth sport. Building on past work, NAYS developed the National Standards for Youth Sports (2008). These standards—available to all youth sport programs, parents, and participants—address key issues affecting the delivery of youth sport programs. Here are the nine standards:

- Quality sports environment
- Sports participation should be fun and a portion of a child's life.
- Training and accountability
- Screening process
- Parents' commitment
- Sportsmanship
- Safe playing environment
- Equal play opportunity
- Drug, tobacco, alcohol, and performance enhancer–free environment

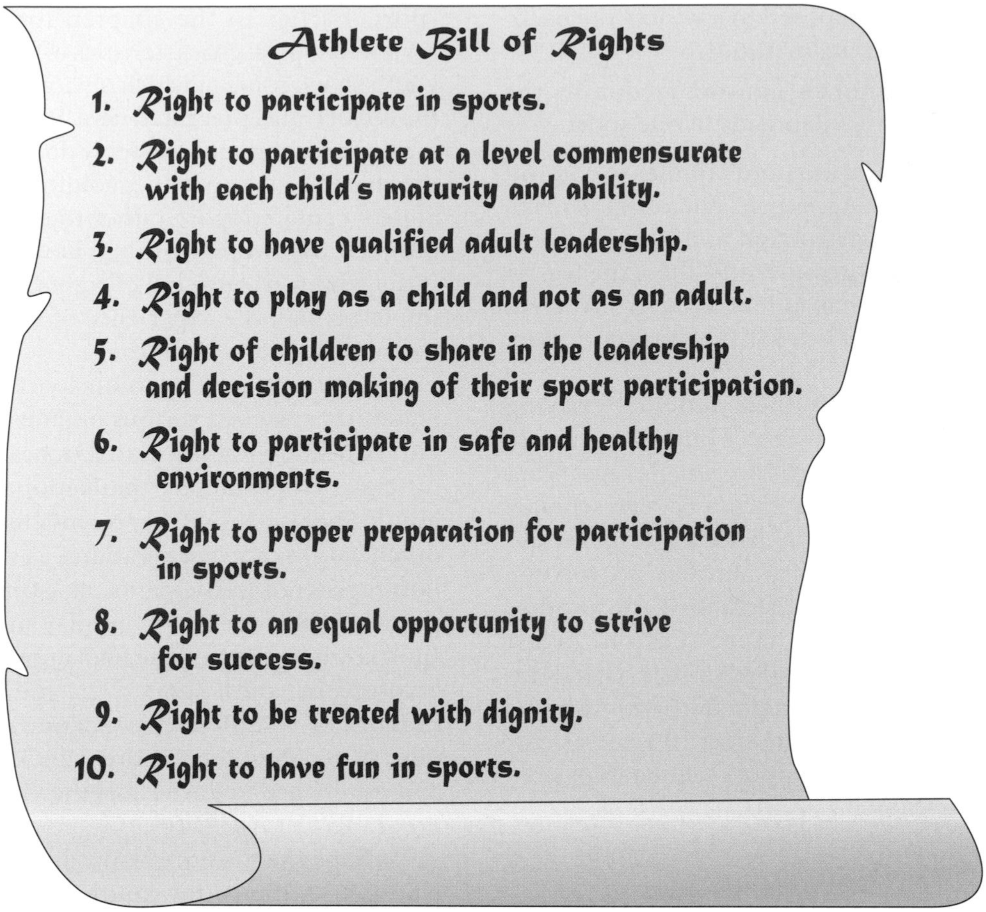

Athlete Bill of Rights

1. Right to participate in sports.
2. Right to participate at a level commensurate with each child's maturity and ability.
3. Right to have qualified adult leadership.
4. Right to play as a child and not as an adult.
5. Right of children to share in the leadership and decision making of their sport participation.
6. Right to participate in safe and healthy environments.
7. Right to proper preparation for participation in sports.
8. Right to an equal opportunity to strive for success.
9. Right to be treated with dignity.
10. Right to have fun in sports.

FIGURE 6.3 The Bill of Rights for Young Athletes.

From R. Martens and V. Seefeldt, 1979. Reprinted with permission from the Society of Health and Physical Educators (SHAPE America), 1900 Association Drive, Reston, VA 20191, www.shapeamerica.org.

Finally, you should be aware of Human Kinetics Coach Education (formerly the American Sport Education Program). Established in 1981, this program develops and implements coaching education courses and resources. The program's leadership in offering online educational courses and certification for coaches provides a delivery system that reaches out nationwide to youth sport programs and coaches.

Based on research about current issues in youth sport, here are some modifications to consider:

- Increase public funding of open fields and other facilities to support youth sport activities.
- Use community funding to supplement organizations that sponsor youth sport in order to provide after-school programs that are safe, affordable, and supervised by knowledgeable adults.
- Limit specialization in one sport at an early age; instead, encourage kids to sample several sports when they are young in order to broaden their athletic development and therefore the activity choices that will be available to them as they mature.
- Insist on continuous coaching certification programs for volunteers and paid coaches alike.
- Offer and support sport programs at various levels of skill, commitment, and intensity, thus allowing parents and children to choose the level that fits the child.
- Offer affordable high-performance programs to kids who demonstrate athletic

APPLYING SOCIAL THEORY

Interactionist Theorists and Changing Youth Sport

An interactionist theorist would view youth sport primarily from the point of view of kids. What needs and wants do kids have at various ages that can be satisfied by sport? Using this perspective as your point of departure, research the topic and develop a paper setting forth five key changes that you would make to youth sport programs as they exist today. Explain your reasons for each change as an interactionist theorist would be likely to do.

talent and want a more intense program. Currently, these programs are largely limited to athletes from more affluent families.

- Provide funding to make sport programs available to children of all economic, racial, and ethnic backgrounds.
- Ensure equal opportunities for girls and boys.

Recent headlines have often decried the lack of physical activity and the rise in obesity among people of all ages. Although we seem to get many children started in the right direction for lifetime fitness, we tend to shut down their progress just as they enter adolescence. Youth sport seems to be more of an elimination process, selecting the most talented kids for later sport participation in high school and relegating the rest to a life without organized sport.

Should we be organizing and promoting community-based activities that attract youths who do not play interscholastic sport? Should these programs be oriented toward lifetime activities, such as self-defense, tennis, volleyball, aerobic fitness, golf, and swimming? Offering these sports as co-ed activities would certainly increase their appeal for many kids.

Chapter Summary

This chapter examines the relatively recent historical development of youth sport and the reasons for its growth. It also considers the current status of youth sport in terms of participation and popularity. The organizations that sponsor youth sport are identified and differentiated.

The chapter also describes the characteristics and popularity of sport programs that are organized by adults as compared with those organized by young athletes themselves. Regardless of the type of organization, many programs have problems and shortcomings that need to be dealt with.

In addition, the chapter lays out differences between various sports and examines the popularity trends for each sport. It also explores the recent increase in alternative sport in the form of extreme or action sports, as well as reasons for their rapid rise. Although overall youth sport participation continues to increase, troubling questions persist about affordability, time requirements, dropout rates, and coaches' training in youth sport.

What kids say they want out of sport programs—and what they need—often differs from the offerings of adult-designed programs. One major theme that has emerged from kids' comments is the fact that they want sport to be fun. However, it seems that *fun* can mean quite different things to different people, depending on their motivation for participation and their individual needs.

Finally, the chapter considers whether changes to youth sport are needed, what challenges it is likely to face in the coming years, and what effective solutions might look like. Overall, youth sport programs seem to retain the approval of most parents, coaches, and players. However, this favorable status does not mean that significant improvements cannot be made, starting with putting more priority on children's need for—and right to—healthy physical activity and recreation.

7

Coaching Sport

STUDENT OUTCOMES

After reading this chapter, you will know the following:

- Commonly observed negative and positive influences of coaches
- Standards, certification programs, and continuing education for coaches
- Differences in coaching at various levels of sport
- Keys to coaching personality, social orientation, and leadership style
- Challenges for the future of coaching

Coaching Sport

When John Wooden died in 2010, he left a legacy that is likely to go unmatched in the world of coaching. He was the most successful coach in the history of college basketball and the first person to be elected to the Basketball Hall of Fame as both a player and a coach. He retired from coaching in 1975 with a 40-year head-coaching record of 885 wins and 203 losses. Most remarkably, during his 27 years of coaching at UCLA, his teams won 10 national championships in a 12-season stretch from 1964 through 1975. In addition, from 1971 to 1974, UCLA won 88 consecutive games—still the National Collegiate Athletic Association (NCAA) record for a men's basketball team.

Even so Wooden's most enduring legacy is not his win-loss record but the lessons he taught about coaching. His famous Pyramid of Success features 15 conceptual building blocks, including traits (such as industriousness, alertness, and poise) held together by faith and patience. Long after retirement, Wooden shared the pyramid's concepts in speeches to large crowds of coaches and others. Indeed, he viewed himself more as a teacher than as a coach, perhaps because he treasured a message from his father that he carried with him always: "Be true to yourself. Make each day a masterpiece. Help others. Drink deeply from good books, especially the Bible. Make friendship a fine art. Build a shelter against a rainy day. Pray for guidance and count and give thanks for your blessings every day."

The following words of tribute to Wooden came from Hall of Famer Kareem Abdul-Jabbar, who led UCLA to three national championships before starring in the National Basketball Association (NBA): "Coach always said that basketball was a simple game, but his ability to make the game simple was a part of his genius. . . . There was no ranting, no histrionics or theatrics. To lead the way Coach Wooden led takes a tremendous amount of faith. He enjoyed winning, but he did not put winning above everything. He was more concerned that we became successful as human beings, that we earned our degrees, that we learned to make the right choices as adults and parents. In essence, he was preparing us for life" (Litsky and Branch 2010).

Here are three of Wooden's many famous quotes:

"Success comes from knowing you did your best to become the best that you are capable of becoming."

"Be more concerned with your character than your reputation, because your character is what you really are, while your reputation is merely what others think you are."

"I don't coach basketball; I coach young men who play basketball."

In looking at sport as an institution, we've examined youth sport participants (see chapter 6). Before we look at other groups of participants, let's take a quick detour and examine a group that fills a critical role in sport: coaches. No matter the level of competition, coaches affect the experience of both athletes and spectators.

If you ask former athletes about their sport experience, they often mention important coaches in their career. More than team owners, sport organizers, and parents, coaches stand in the spotlight of athletic competition. They often help young people mature, set priorities, establish goals, learn sport skills, and develop self-discipline. Moreover, because coaches typically work with young athletes who are going through critical stages of personal development, they have a golden opportunity to influence those young people. Of course, their potential influence is also heightened by the fact that they are often perceived as the keepers of the keys to athletic success.

Influence of Coaches

The following quotation captures something of the responsibilities and joys of coaching. It was adapted by Tom Crawford, former director of coaching education for the U.S. Olympic Committee (USOC), from Haim Ginott, a prominent psychologist and author, who wrote two 1960s bestsellers—*Between Parent and Child* and *Between Parent and Teenager*. In the following quotation, Crawford substituted the word *coach* for *teacher*, *student* with *athlete*, and *classroom* with *playing field* (qtd. in Mills 1997):

I have come to a frightening conclusion. I am the decisive element on the playing field. It is my personal approach that creates the climate. It is my daily mood that makes the weather. As a coach, I possess the tremendous power to make an athlete's life miserable or joyous. I can be the tool of torture or an instrument of inspiration. I can humiliate or humor, hurt or heal. In all situations, it is my response that decides if a crisis will be elevated or de-escalated, and an athlete humanized or dehumanized.

Many of us who have participated in sport would heartily agree. Coaches have been our heroes, role models, confessors, disciplinarians, mentors, teachers, leaders, and often our beloved friends. Their influence on us is incalculable, and we know how important they have been in our lives.

Like teachers, coaches have the opportunity to affect young people who are in the process of becoming adults. The uncertainty faced by young people opens doors for coaches to suggest appropriate behaviors and attitudes. At the same time, the questioning of authority figures by teenagers presents coaches with opportunities to respond with patience and reason in order to influence rebellious minds. The battle with emotions in a young athlete uncovers feelings of inadequacy and the inability to manage feelings. Coaches can help athletes embrace these challenges; they can also suggest sensible courses of action and reinforce good decision making.

Perhaps contrary to expectations, outstanding former athletes do not always make the best coaches. If they learned skills easily and demanded much of themselves, they may be impatient with lesser athletes. Yet the public often seeks top former athletes to coach their children, even when they possess little training or experience in coaching. The only way to combat this mistaken bias is to educate the general public about what good coaching really involves.

Similarly, coaching awards are almost always handed out to those who win championships. However, the winning coach may win simply because his or her team has the best talent, the best facilities, or the most money. It may be easier to judge win-loss records than to assess the more intangible results of coaching, but this bottom-line approach to evaluation reinforces an unhealthy emphasis on winning.

Positive Influences

It is impossible to describe successful coaching without comparing coaching results with expectations for the position. Obviously, for example, success is defined differently for coaches of Little League teams than for managers of Major League

POP CULTURE

Life as an NFL Coach

If you want an insider's view of the life of a National Football League (NFL) coach, check out *Coaching Confidential: Inside the Fraternity of NFL Coaches* by Gary Myers (2012). The book presents interviews with more than 20 current and former NFL head coaches, including familiar names such as Bill Parcells, Mike Holmgren, Tony Dungy, Sean Payton, Dick Vermeil, and Brian Billick. The coaches share their experiences and philosophies, open up about the professional and personal challenges of the job, and share insights about topics including the player draft, training camp, coach–owner dynamics, the X's and O's of coaching, and the pressure of the postseason.

Sure, these guys have earned a lot of money doing something they love, but they have also faced personal crisis and burnout. At the end of the day, the NFL is just a business with two interrelated objectives: winning and making money. And at some point, the pressure cooker atmosphere has gotten to every one of these coaches in one way or another (Myers 2012).

Baseball (MLB) teams. Though public assessment of coaching typically uses the win-loss record as the measuring stick, we know that the best record does not always represent the best coaching performance. Let's consider the criteria by which a coach might be judged more fairly. We begin with professional and high-performance sport, where competition outcomes are viewed as an acceptable standard of measurement. What other standards should be considered for coaches at these levels?

For a more accurate indicator of coaching ability, we look for coaching success sustained over several years and characterized by consistency of performance, regardless of the particular athletes participating in any given year. You may have heard coaches say that they were prouder of their 20-year record than of the number of conference championships they have won. These coaches realize that consistency over time is the real mark of excellence in coaching.

Another valuable contribution is made by innovative coaches who change their sport through their training methods, strategies, or other visible influences. Regardless of these coaches' win-loss record, the results of their innovation endure. One striking example can be found in Hall of Fame basketball coach Dean Smith, who retired from the University of North Carolina as the winningest coach in men's NCAA basketball history, won two national titles and the 1976 Olympic gold medal, and coached numerous great athletes, including Michael Jordan. One of Smith's trademark strategies was the Four Corners, a time-melting strategy used to protect a lead by spreading the offense and retaining possession of the ball while making no attempt to score—an approach that frustrated both opponents and fans. The eventual result was the introduction of a shot clock to speed up the game and prevent the use of the Four Corners strategy by counting down a limited number of seconds in which a team must shoot the ball.

In addition, coaches may be judged ultimately by the loyalty of their athletes, even after those athletes' careers are over. In fact, many former athletes keep in touch with coaches who made a difference in their life and continue to rely on their counsel and support.

Leadership skills are critical for coaches at every level of competition. Successful leaders learn to adapt their skills both to the group of athletes on a given team and to each team member as an individual. This balancing act requires not relying on a single, fixed coaching or leadership skill but tailoring one's approach to fit the athletes. Coaches must also develop leadership ability in multiple areas of focus: training athletes' physical and technical skills, applying appropriate strategy, and setting a framework for the team to operate in a way that benefits the athletes both as a group and as individuals.

Coaches who have been highly successful in college coaching do not always shine at the professional level. For example, Steve Spurrier of the University of South Carolina and Nick Saban of the University of Alabama are both great college football coaches who managed only a short tenure in the NFL before returning to the college level. In contrast, Chip Kelly came from the University of Oregon to the NFL's Philadelphia Eagles and brought with him a high-powered "spread offense" that uses a no-huddle, up-tempo style of play. Critics wondered if this "college offense" would work in the vaunted NFL with its uniformly great athletes. A few years later, it is clear that Kelly has adapted his offense to the NFL, and some rival coaches are tinkering with their own offenses and adopting some of Kelly's principles.

Some coaches use a democratic approach that allows athletes to play a larger role in setting group goals, arranging team practices, and plotting team tactics. This approach can foster growth, especially among younger players. However, it also involves some risk on the part of the coach, who must allow the group to make certain decisions. The democratic approach can be especially beneficial to coaches in sports that require a great deal of independence in athletes. Participants in team sports, on the other hand, generally seem to prefer a more autocratic approach, in part because of the nature of the sport, the complexity of player interactions, and the dynamics of group interdependence (Riemer and Chelladurai 1995).

Coaches who work in an educational setting should be measured according to their contribution to the overall education of the young people in their charge. The task is much easier for the coach if the school district or university clearly delineates expected outcomes for student-athletes. Of course, coaches can pay attention to more than athletic instruction; for example, they can focus on enhancing each athlete's self-concept, self-awareness, and personal development. Coaches in this setting fill the role of both adviser and supporter as athletes explore their potential through sport.

As part of this process, coaches can help athletes make good decisions, figure out strategies, set performance goals, and learn from their mistakes.

Coaches who have a reputation for good sporting behavior can also contribute to the development of integrity in their athletes. These coaches

EXPERT'S VIEW

A Coaching Code of Ethics

Virtually all sport organizations have established a code of ethics that coaches must read, understand, and abide by. With this in mind, you might want to check out the code of ethics for your particular sport as posted by its national governing body. Alternatively, you might review the USOC's Coaching Ethics Code (USA Coaching 2010). The following code was developed by the National Federation of State High School Associations (2014a):

"The function of a coach is to educate students through participation in interscholastic competition. An interscholastic program should be designed to enhance academic achievement and should never interfere with opportunities for academic success. Each student-athlete should be treated as though he or she were the coaches' own, and his or her welfare should be uppermost at all times. Accordingly, the following guidelines for coaches have been adopted by NFHS board of directors.

The coach shall be aware that he or she has a tremendous influence, for either good or ill, on the education of the student-athlete and, thus, shall never place the value of winning above the value of instilling the highest ideals of character.

The coach shall uphold the honor and dignity of the profession. In all personal contact with student-athletes, officials, athletic directors, school administrators, the state high school athletic association, the media, and the public, the coach shall strive to set an example of the highest ethical and moral conduct.

The coach shall take an active role in the prevention of drug, alcohol, and tobacco abuse.

The coach shall avoid the use of alcohol and tobacco products when in contact with players.

The coach shall promote the entire interscholastic program of the school and direct his or her program in harmony with the total school program.

The coach shall master the contest rules and shall teach them to his or her team members. The coach shall not seek an advantage by circumvention of the spirit or letter of the rules.

The coach shall exert his or her influence to enhance sportsmanship by spectators, both directly and by working closely with cheerleaders, pep club sponsors, booster clubs, and administrators.

The coach shall respect and support contest officials. The coach shall not indulge in conduct which would incite players or spectators against the officials. Public criticism of officials or players is unethical.

The coach should meet and exchange cordial greetings with the opposing coach to set the correct tone for the event before and after the contest.

The coach shall not exert pressure on faculty members to give student-athletes special consideration.

The coach shall not scout opponents by any means other than those adopted by the league and/or state high school athletic association."

point out the requirements for moral behavior, allow athletes to make moral decisions, and help them analyze the results of their choices.

Negative Influences

For all the positive influence that coaches can have on athletes, there is another side. Coaches who are inadequately prepared to coach, or who coach for the wrong reasons, can damage young lives. Well-known sport psychologist Terry Orlick (1974) put it this way:

> *For every positive psychological or social outcome in sports, there are possible negative outcomes. For example, sports can offer a child group membership or group exclusion, acceptance or rejection, positive feedback or negative feedback, a sense of accomplishment or a sense of failure, evidence of self-worth or lack of evidence of self-worth. Likewise, sports can develop cooperation and a concern for others, but they can also develop intense rivalry and complete lack of concern for others.*

There are many positive coaches who set a good example; there are also coaches who set a negative example. In fact, many coaches negatively influence young athletes, but the reasons they do so vary considerably. For instance, volunteer coaches who have little or no training may inadvertently make errors in judgment due to their lack of preparation for coaching. No matter how well intentioned they are, they may harm their athletes due to their lack of understanding of players or of the coaching process. In order to minimize this risk, parents, players, and communities must raise expectations for coaches who accept the challenge of working with youth. Parents have the right to expect that coaches possess a basic understanding

IN THE ARENA WITH . . .

Coaching Scandals

There is no shortage of prominent coaches who have been embarrassed, disciplined, or fired for transgressions that include rule breaking, cheating, verbal and physical abuse, and a host of other behaviors that might charitably be called unethical. From the NFL to big-time college football and basketball, coaches at every level face daily challenges in trying to conduct themselves and their programs in a way that brings honor and distinction for the good that they do for young people. Here are just a few of the most notable and most publicized coaching scandals in recent years:

- Bill Belichick, New England Patriots: fined for "Spygate" scandal that involved illegal videotaping of an opponent's defensive signals
- Sean Payton, New Orleans Saints: suspended for one year for "Bountygate" scandal in which staff coaches paid bounties to players who injured opposing players
- Joe Paterno, Penn State: fired after 46 years of coaching for apparent cover-up of child sexual abuse by former assistant Jerry Sandusky
- Jim Tressel, Ohio State: fired for scandal in which players received illegal benefits
- Bobby Petrino, Arkansas: fired for extramarital affair with football staff member
- Mike Rice, Rutgers: fired for verbal and physical abuse of players

And then there were the scandals at the University of Miami (for impermissible benefits paid by a team booster), the University of Southern California (for illegal money paid to star player Reggie Bush), and the University of North Carolina at Chapel Hill (for academic fraud and illegal payments made to players by sport agents). Each of these scandals hurt the young people involved, besmirched the reputation of the team and university, and cast doubt on the integrity of coaches in general.

of coaching, attend training sessions, and access appropriate distance-learning resources online.

A negative environment can also be created by coaches who are certified or have some level of experience. Perhaps the most common conflict in this situation occurs when a coach's philosophy clashes with an athlete's reasons for participating in sport. For example, if the coach is focused on winning, some of his or her decisions will seem unfair or simply illogical to athletes who are more interested in the sheer joy of playing.

Another common source of conflict is the routine use of physical punishment with young athletes to discourage bad behavior, poor performance, or lack of effort. Kids who are disciplined by being made to run laps or do push-ups soon learn to avoid physical activity whenever they can. Coaches who instill an aversion to physical activity in young athletes are setting those children up for a lifetime of inactivity.

As a result, physicians, educators, school boards, and sport psychologists all advise teachers and coaches to avoid using physical punishment. Instead, they recommend emphasizing what students or athletes are doing right and reinforcing that behavior. In contrast, negative feedback and punishment are generally recommended only to prevent behavior that is unsafe or emotionally abusive to others. The National Association of State Boards of Education (2008) states, "Teachers shall aim to develop students' self-confidence and maintain a safe psychological environment free of embarrassment, humiliation, shaming, taunting, or harassment of any kind. Physical education staff shall not order performance of physical activity as a form of discipline or punishment."

Youth sport can also involve conflicts between coaches and parents. For example, parents may misunderstand the coach's intentions or question the coach's methods (sometimes with justification) or allocation of playing time. The solution is for coaches to share their philosophy before the season starts, meet regularly with parents to discuss issues, and try to find common ground with parents. Without the support of the parents, the coach's role is considerably more difficult and may even become impossible.

Coaches who work at higher levels of competition may face many of the same issues as those who work with younger athletes. In addition, coaches whose employment depends on posting a winning record often make decisions that do not please every athlete on the team. Therefore, athletes who accept the competitive challenge of joining a team that is clearly focused on winning must expect the coach to build a system that in the coach's judgment will produce the best results.

Because coaches are human beings with certain beliefs, prejudices, and personality quirks—just like anyone else—athletes need to evaluate coaching behavior within the overall context of the situation. If the coach's philosophy and behavior are simply at odds with the athlete's reasons for playing, then the athlete may prefer to change sports, schools, or programs and find a situation in which she or he feels more in tune with the program and the coaching personality.

The negative extreme of coaching behavior takes the form of verbal, physical, or psychological abuse of athletes. **Abuse** involves willful infliction of injury, pain, mental anguish, intimidation, or punishment, and it can exist in the workplace, at home, in the government, and even in religious organizations. Adults who hold power over younger people sometimes fall prey to the urge to use their power inappropriately, and the result can constitute abuse.

Awareness of sexual abuse has increased in part due to the increase of females in sport and the fact that more than half of their coaches are male. The Women's Sports Foundation has led the way in educating coaches, players, and parents about how to minimize the chances for sexual abuse through background checks, clear policy statements that delineate unacceptable behaviors, and clear processes for reporting and dealing with abuse if it occurs.

In one dramatic example, USA Swimming, the U.S. governing body for swimming, made headlines in 2010 when it released the names of 46 coaches who had been banned from or permanently quit the organization, mostly for sex-related offenses. Most prominent among them was Everett Uchiyama, former director of the national team, who was accused by a woman (who remains anonymous) of having had a relationship with her soon after she started swimming for him at 14 years of age. He hastily resigned as national team director for USA Swimming without explanation.

Uchiyama was permanently banned from USA Swimming a few days later, but that did not stop him from securing a job as aquatics director at a nearby country club in Colorado. However, he resigned from that position on the same day that the list was released by USA Swimming. Club representatives said they had received a positive recommendation for Uchiyama from USA Swimming and had known nothing about the allegations against him. USA Swimming had come under increasing scrutiny for its handling of sexual abuse cases, and some critics charged that it covered up wrongdoing by prominent coaches. The organization admitted that it must do more to educate athletes, parents, coaches, and club leaders about what they can do to help (ESPN 2010).

Verbal and physical abuse have always been difficult issues in sport, but athletes today are less tolerant of it and more likely to strike back or report it to authorities. In addition, most educational institutions now prohibit the use of racist remarks, profanity, and public sanctioning or embarrassment. Offenders can lose their jobs.

The key to avoiding abuse and negative behaviors in coaching is for athletic organizations to delineate their expectations for coaches in writing and secure agreement from prospective coaches before hiring them. In addition, coaches should be trained in implementing the policies and should be given specific examples of inappropriate behavior. The organization should also spell out a procedure for filing complaints against coaches and explain it to coaches, parents, and athletes so that situations can be resolved effectively and everyone's rights protected in the process. Finally, the consequences for a coach who exhibits abusive behavior should be spelled out and applied in situations in which the charges are clearly proven.

Most youth sport coaches in the United States are either volunteers or receive very little pay. How do you think this reality influences their coaching decisions?

Status of Coaching

The number of young athletes who participate in sport has been estimated recently at about 40 million in the United States, which includes more than half of all kids aged 5 to 10 years. To serve these young athletes, more than three million coaches work at all levels of ability, and more than 500,000 of these coaches work in high school programs with varsity athletes. The U.S. Bureau of Labor Statistics (2014a) expects job opportunities for coaches to grow faster than the average for all occupations through 2022—specifically, to increase by 15 percent due to rising participation in high school and college sport. The median annual wage for a coach as of May 2012 was $28,360.

Coaching varies greatly depending on the level of athletes being coached, their reasons for playing, the sponsoring organization, and the remuneration provided to coaches. Recognizing these differences, an International Sport Coaching Framework was developed in 2013 through a partnership between the International Council for Coaching Excellence, the Association of Summer Olympic International Federations, and Leeds Beckett University in Great Britain. This group's continuing work is likely to affect coaching standards in the United States as countries openly share knowledge and best practices with each other.

Coaches of college and professional athletes are more likely to have professional preparation for coaching than those who work with younger athletes. In most cases, they have graduated from college sport programs and served some time as an apprentice coach with other experienced coaches. However, at the professional level, many coaches are former athletes who may have been outstanding sport performers but who have little background in coaching. As a result, their coaching methods are more likely the result of watching former coaches and imitating qualities that they admired.

When considering the history of coaching, its current status, and its future, we may find it helpful to distinguish between those who coach high-performance athletes and those who coach athletes more focused on participation. Coaches of high-performance athletes tend to have the most preparation for coaching. Because coaching is their chosen full-time occupation, their career success depends on their coaching knowledge and competence. As a result, they are highly motivated to seek every last bit of knowledge that might influence their chances for success—for example, through formal coaching education, as well as mentoring from more experienced coaches. Because these coaches work with elite athletes, only a limited number of positions are available; as a result, the vast majority of coaches never work with high-performance athletes.

Coaches of athletes who are more interested in participation than performance include almost all youth sport coaches and many at the high school level. These coaches enjoy sport and being around young people. At the youth level, they are typically volunteers; at the high school level, they may be paid a modest stipend. As a result, almost all of these coaches receive income from other work that represents their true profession. This group also includes some individuals who work for sport organizations, private clubs, and public parks.

Admittedly, some coaches blend the goals of participation and performance when working with adolescent or adult athletes. This group is likely to have some coaching preparation, and the demands of their competitive athletes force them to continue to upgrade their coaching skills. For example, high school coaches in highly competitive sports, such as football and basketball (especially in sport-crazy communities), usually lean toward the performance model of coaching by virtue of the demand for winning teams.

Without drawing a sharp line between these two major groups of coaches, it is still helpful to consider the significant differences between them. As we consider various topics, keep in mind that we don't want to lump the two groups together, especially where they differ in major ways.

Coaching Compensation

We often hear about coaches who make several million dollars per year for coaching professional players or elite football or basketball players at the college level. But these coaches account for only a small percentage of the hundreds of thousands of coaches working in various levels of sport. In addition, these elite coaches' salaries are determined by the market at the highest-profile, most pressurized level of competition. If their teams don't win, they are gone.

In contrast, most college coaches of a nonrevenue sport earn a modest salary; the median income is $39,550. At the high school level, many coaches are employed full time by the school system, either as a teacher or in another position. As a result, their salary for the school year is typically set by a union contract negotiated with the school board. If they take on a coaching responsibility beyond their regular teaching or staff assignment, they receive additional compensation, which can range from about $1,000 for smaller sports (such as cross country, golf, and tennis) to $10,000 for a large sport (such as football).

The level of pay also depends on the location and wealth of the school district. For example, you may have heard that some high school football coaches in Texas earn more than $100,000 per year. Keep in mind, however, that their coaching pay typically supplements a regular salary for serving as a teacher or filling a combined administrative position, such as athletic director, along with their coaching duties.

Coaches who work in youth sport may be paid, but they often serve as volunteers. Paid coaches are typically compensated at a modest level unless they also teach and coach at a private club or large public facility. At the high end of this spectrum, coaches who work in golf, tennis, skiing, or swimming may earn a solid middle-class living over the course of a career (U.S. Bureau of Labor Statistics 2014a).

Coaching as a Profession

Although we often refer to coaching as a profession, it is very difficult to make the case that this is true. A profession is an occupation that does the

Do you think there should be standards for coaching education at the collegiate level?

following (Martens, Flannery, and Roetert 2002; S. Hoffman, 2013):

- Dedicates itself to providing beneficial services to people
- Is based on a generally accepted scientific body of knowledge
- Requires a rigorous course of study to transmit knowledge and skills
- Requires certification, achieved by demonstrating mastery of knowledge and ability to use appropriate skills, and controls membership by licensing after testing
- Establishes an accepted public code of ethics
- Monitors itself to sanction or remove those who do not live up to the expectations of the profession
- Provides and expects continuing education of members to ensure up-to-date knowledge and skills
- Establishes an organization to implement standards, certification, and member education

Generally speaking, this set of standards is not met by coaching in the United States, where many youth sport coaches serve as volunteers, are untrained, and coach only as a hobby. If volunteers were required to submit to more rigorous standards, their numbers might simply decline, resulting in a huge coaching shortage for youth sport programs. At the same time, some studies have shown that 85 percent of youth sport coaches prefer to coach in a league that requires training, and 72 percent of them feel encouraged to continue coaching. Other studies report that some prospective coaches are hesitant to coach due to a lack of confidence in their coaching skills and abilities—and that they would welcome required training (National Council for Accreditation of Coaching Education 2013).

At the high school and college levels, many coaches are hired on a part-time basis and must rely on teaching or another occupation as their primary source of income. Therefore, their time is limited, and the financial reward is modest. Even so, more schools are requiring some level of coaching education in order to provide a safer sport experience for their students and to reduce their liability resulting from negligent behavior by coaches.

Full-time professional coaches who work at their craft would likely benefit in both their career and their compensation if coaching became a true profession. Raising the standards for coaching would likely improve coaches' skills and knowledge and garner greater public recognition of the quality of the athletic experience. The casual, uncontrolled manner in which many coaches are currently hired simply does not merit public acceptance or regard for coaching as a profession when compared, for example, with the fields of law, medicine, engineering, or religion. There is no reason not to work toward making coaching a profession.

Coaching Standards

Standards for youth sport coaching are set primarily by local communities. Depending on the organizing group, coaches may be expected to have playing experience, coaching experience, or some level of coaching certification or training. On the other hand, organizations may simply accept a willing volunteer. Thus the level of expertise varies widely from sport to sport, community to community, and possibly year to year.

Due to the great need for youth sport coaches, most communities are only too happy to welcome volunteers, and they often have to persuade hesitant parents to coach. Without volunteer coaches, sport teams simply cannot operate, and children lose a great opportunity. As a result, parents who lack the time, experience, or skill that is necessary for good coaching may agree to coach anyway just to be sure that their kids can play on a team.

This situation creates two perplexing concerns. One is the lack of experience and training among coaches. The second is that even if the community sponsors coaching education or training for volunteer coaches, the turnover rate is extremely high and the training must be repeated every year. Most volunteer coaches continue to coach only while their own children are in the program. This is understandable, because if they want to continue to spend time with their own child in sport, they either move to a higher level or become a spectator as their child progresses.

High school coaching standards have suffered from a similar dilemma. In the 1970s, the demand for competent high school coaches skyrocketed due to the passage of Title IX, which ensured equal opportunities for girls in sport. Suddenly, high schools were faced with a critical coaching shortage. The situation was exacerbated by declining enrollment, a depressed economy, and thus a decline in job openings for classroom teachers who might be coaching candidates. Matters were further complicated by the fact that, as teaching staffs aged, many teachers kept their teaching jobs but retired from coaching. As a result, principals were forced to change or reduce their standards for coaches just to find available bodies to staff their athletic programs.

It wasn't until 1995 that the first set of national coaching standards for high school coaches was crafted. Today, led by SHAPE America, more than 140 sport organizations have agreed that these standards represent the core body of knowledge for coaching expertise. Referred to as the National Standards for Sport Coaches (NSSC), they were developed through review and adaptation of scientific knowledge, practical coaching experience, and examination of the content of existing coaching education programs. Now in its second edition, the NSSC consists of forty standards divided into the following eight domains of knowledge and competency (SHAPE America 2006):

- Philosophy and ethics
- Safety and injury prevention
- Physical conditioning
- Growth and development
- Teaching and communication
- Sport skills and tactics
- Organization and administration
- Evaluation

The goal is for this document to serve as a blueprint for coaching education programs and certification processes. In 1990, to further this effort, the coaching education task force of the National Federation of State High School Associations (NFHS) joined with the American Sport Education Program (ASEP, now known as Human Kinetics Coach Education) to take the lead in recommending that interscholastic coaches be required to participate in ongoing professional development programs. By 2004, the organizations provided the opportunity for 35 states to offer coaching education courses that were accessible online (American Sport Education Program 2010).

Perhaps the most important contribution of these standards lies in the fact that they identify the vast breadth of knowledge required of competent coaches. As they become more publicized and more familiar to sport administrators, school personnel, parents, and the general public, it is hoped that more will be expected of athletic coaches. However, in order to be realistic about coaches at the high school level, we must remain mindful of the fact that coaching is a supplementary income source for them rather than their primary profession.

The NFHS Coach Education Program was started in 2007 and has been adopted by all 51 state associations (including Washington, D.C). By the end of 2014, nearly 2.5 million courses had been completed, thus benefiting some 18,500 high schools and 11 million students (NFHS 2014a). Because these courses are available online, they reduce the required time and expense, which often challenged coaching education advocates in the past. Current prices for the online courses range from free to $75.

The first level of national certification offered to coaches through NFHS—accredited interscholastic coach (AIC)—was introduced in 2009. Since then, this certification has been obtained by more than 13,000 individuals. This level of certification requires coaches to complete four courses: Fundamentals of Coaching; First Aid, Health, and Safety for Coaches; Concussions in Sports; and one sport-specific course. In 2014, a second level of certification was launched—certified interscholastic coach (CIC). This level requires coaches to complete the AIC training and seven additional courses: Creating a Safe and Respectful Environment; Engaging Effectively with Parents; Sportsmanship; Strength and Conditioning; Teaching and Modeling Behavior; and two other courses of choice (NFHS 2014a).

In the last 15 years, the USOC has encouraged each of its national governing bodies to identify the coaching competencies needed for its sport. National models were developed that were similar to the NASPE standards but were tailored specifically to volleyball, soccer, tennis, swimming, and other Olympic sports. By sharing information with each other, the national governing bodies created a more developed model for coaching education and certification programs within the Olympic family. For further information, visit the USOC website and navigate to the page for a specific sport (for example, USA Hockey or USA Volleyball) to review its programs and standards for coaching certification and education.

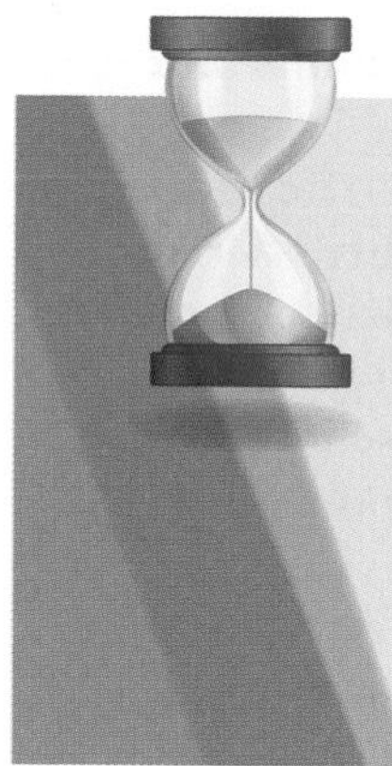

ACTIVITY TIME-OUT

Domains of Coaching Knowledge

Interview a coach of your choice and ask him or her to rate the eight domains of coaching knowledge from most important (a rating of 1) to least important (a rating of 8). Ask why the coach rated certain domains high and others low based on his or her coaching experience and practical life experience. Analyze the coach's responses with an eye toward the level of athletes with whom he or she works. Share your findings with your classmates and see what conclusions you can draw as a group.

Coaching Education Expectations

Requirements vary greatly for athletic coaches in school settings. According to SHAPE America, 22 states require coaches to possess state teaching credentials, and 6 states recommend that they do so. Of course, this means that nearly half do not require teaching credentials. In addition, though a teaching credential may set a reasonable minimal standard, it may not include specific knowledge or training in athletic coaching methods. In fact, only 9 states require specific coaching education, and half of those allow some flexibility as to the requirement.

A strong movement has arisen to address this undesirable situation since 2006, when the national coaching standards were revised by NASPE (now part of SHAPE America) and supported by dozens of other organizations. Specifically, the movement would use the revised standards to upgrade the coaching profession at all levels. In fact, we can now say that there is a national movement toward certification of high school coaches, as evidenced by the fact that 50 states and the nation's capital have adopted, recommended, or required one of two national certification programs: the NFHS program or Human Kinetics Coach Education.

Here are some key facts about the state of coaching education in high school sport (NASPE 2008):

- The number of sport opportunities and the scope of sport in high schools are both at their highest point ever, therefore creating great demand for high-quality coaching across all sports.
- Coaching education most frequently requires a first aid course, CPR (cardiopulmonary resuscitation) training, and a course in fundamentals of coaching. Some states or schools also require training in sport rules, and training in sport-specific skills is typically offered as an elective.
- States now include non-education-based requirements for coaching, such as background checks and health screenings.
- Coaching education is typically delivered through online courses, weekend workshops, and formal academic courses.
- Few if any continuing education requirements exist for coaches once they have met the initial standards; as a result, coaches have little external incentive or reward to periodically update their knowledge and skills.

In most colleges and universities across the United States, the minimal standard for an athletic coach is a college degree, since these coaches work with college athletes and operate in a college setting. Beyond that, the requirements vary widely and may include athletic experience in the relevant sport, coaching experience at the high school or college level, or certification by a national governing body or other sport-specific agency. Some coaches work their way into college coaching by serving as a volunteer assistant coach, intern, or graduate assistant in order to gain experience and a foothold in the profession.

Coaching in professional sport differs markedly from coaching in the educational system. In professional sport, the required background can range from experience as a player at that level to years of successful coaching at a lower level of competition. Educational qualifications are typically not critical, since a professional team simply emphasizes winning. However, lack of preparation for coaching weighs on many professional coaches who are limited to drawing on their own personal experiences in sport. For example, most coaches of professional tennis are excellent former players who rely on the coaching methods used by their coaches—perhaps a decade earlier. As a result, without firsthand knowledge of current coaching science, they may use coaching methods and information that are hopelessly out of date.

Coaching Certification

Now that standards for coaching have been developed, publicized, and disseminated, you might expect that pathways would be established for prospective coaches to gain certification. Indeed, there are at least three avenues to pursue, depending on the sport, the level of coaching, and the depth of coaching education that one seeks.

Nearly 180 institutions of higher education offer an undergraduate major or minor in coaching education or a graduate degree in coaching. Most college programs are offered by state universities, though a few are offered by private colleges. At a minimum, the typical undergraduate program requires six to eight courses, including principles of coaching, some sport science, and sport-specific courses, as well as practical experience in coaching. Virtually every curriculum also requires a course in prevention, care, and treatment of injuries. Many students minor in coaching while majoring in physical education, kinesiology, sport studies, or sport and exercise science. These coaching major or minor programs are the logical track for prospective coaches who hope to find employment at the high school or college level.

A second way to approach coaching certification is to investigate the requirements that apply in your chosen sport. Most national governing bodies operate a certification program that evaluates coaching knowledge and competence. Such a program may specify various levels of competence for beginning coaches while also providing opportunities for coaches to advance through additional study, experience, and demonstration of higher levels of coaching expertise. Certification programs may also be tailored in other ways—for example, geared toward youth coaching, private coaching, or high-performance coaching. For example, professional tennis coaches are certified as having the skills to work at tennis clubs and public facilities.

A third possibility is to seek certification through a national program that is neither offered by an educational institution nor affiliated with a particular sport. These programs are primarily targeted toward coaches of youth, high school athletes, Special Olympics participants, and athletes with a disability.

Human Kinetics Coach Education, founded by Rainer Martens in 1976, is committed to improving amateur sport by encouraging coaches, officials, administrators, parents, and athletes to embrace a philosophy of "athletes first, winning second." To put this philosophy to work, the program has produced excellent training materials, courses, and videos. The remaining challenge for many coaches and program administrators is simply finding the time to use them. Human Kinetics Coach Education has helped solve that problem by developing online courses for coaches to take at their leisure. The program works with about 40 states to directly deliver programs for high school coaches and many youth coaching organizations.

Certification is also offered by the National Youth Sports Coaches Association (NYSCA) in partnership with many community organizations, such as the Police Athletic League, Catholic youth organizations, Jewish community centers, the Boys & Girls Clubs of America, National Park and Recreation Association, and state and local parks and recreation departments. NYSCA also offers an introductory instructional video, one-day clinics, and a web-based course.

Coaching certification is usually awarded after the prospective coach demonstrates competence through written tests of knowledge and understanding, a face-to-face course of instruction, or evaluation of his or her coaching or teaching ability. For beginning coaches, certification typically focuses on introductory aspects of coaching philosophy, first aid, basic coaching principles, and ethics.

Certification standards vary from program to program and typically measure only a small fraction of the competencies required for successful coaching. If you are uncertain about the quality or relevance of a particular certification program, consider consulting the National Council for Accreditation of Coaching Education (NCACE), which is affiliated with SHAPE America. NCACE provides independent review of coaching education programs to ensure that they meet recommended national standards.

Continuing Education for Coaches

Once coaches enter the profession, they have an obligation to expand their knowledge and keep up with new developments. To understand the importance of staying current in the field, imagine how much coaching methods have changed due to advances in nutrition, physiology, sport psychology, sport equipment, and injury prevention and treatment. Even when the strategy and tactics of a sport remain relatively constant, preferred approaches to teaching them may evolve. In fact, technique often changes as athletes invent new ways of performing, and in some sports athletes now use skills that may have been undreamed of in the past.

Fortunately for interested coaches, many self-education resources are available. Here are a few of the options:

- Follow social media sites that offer coaching instruction.
- Watch online videos.
- Purchase books and videos to build a personal coaching library.
- Review information resources, such as courses, coaching discussion groups, and networks (some of them international in scope) of coaches who are eager to exchange ideas.
- Attend coaching conferences sponsored by national governing bodies, state high school sport associations, and college sport associations; these events may be held locally or at the state or national level. Experts in every imaginable area will tutor you, and informal conversations with other coaches can provide a wealth of knowledge.
- Subscribe to relevant newsletters and periodicals—for example, *Coach and Athletic Director* magazine or publications from coaching or sport-specific organizations—that deliver current coaching tips and information on a regular basis. The information is typically screened by a panel of experts and written by experienced coaches.
- Join a professional coaching organization in your sport, such as the United States Professional Tennis Association. Such organizations offer workshops, materials, and regular mailings to help you stay on the cutting edge of your sport.
- Attend a coaching school offered by the national governing body in your sport for a few weeks of intensive study and practical experience.
- Volunteer to assist an expert coach whom you admire.
- Take graduate courses in coaching education at a nearby college or university.
- Take a coaching course offered by Human Kinetics Coach Education or another national coaching program.
- Watch sport on television and observe the coaches' behavior.

How do the skills of this collegiate swim coach need to differ from those of a youth sport coach?

- Consult specialists in fields about which you know little. For example, a sport psychologist might be willing to help you learn about the basics of mental toughness.
- Read books that chronicle the careers of successful coaches.
- Rent movies that feature coaches, such as *Friday Night Lights*, *Remember the Titans*, *Hoosiers*, *Glory Road*, and *When the Game Stands Tall*.
- Listen to interviews with coaches whom you admire to see how they handle questions, criticism, victory, and defeat.

Like most people, coaches have to work at their profession. Imagine how horrified you would be if your personal physician did not keep up with advances in medicine. My own doctor just spent two weeks away from his office studying and taking examinations to renew his board certification in internal medicine. This recertification is required every five years and helps ensure that doctors stay current in their field. Not only must they give up office appointments during that process, but also they must pay the recertification costs of several thousand dollars out of their own pocket. Coaching should be no different. It demands a lifetime of continuing education; fortunately, continuing education for coaches typically costs much less than for doctors!

Coaching at Different Levels of Sport

It is unfair to lump all coaches together when considering what skills and competencies they ought to have. Different types of coaching skill are needed for working with athletes in different sports and of different ages, skill levels, and commitment levels. The following sections look closely at coaching at each level of participation and what enables a coach to succeed at that level.

Professional Sport

At the highest performance levels, coaches typically have personal competition experience at the relevant level. They also need to understand and accept the business aspect of sport, the required commitment to winning, and the criticism they will face if their team does not win. In addition, since the athletes may make several times more than the coach, motivation is sometimes a challenge unless the athlete is in the final year of his contract. In addition, years of athletic training have inured some professional athletes to advice from coaches. And although these athletes are adults, they are often susceptible to lifestyle habits that interfere with their performance.

Another challenge for coaches at this level involves a perplexing conundrum: Although these athletes have reached the highest levels of sport, their fundamental skills may be lacking. As a result, coaches of professional athletes must be skilled at teaching fundamentals to athletes who are typically resistant to change.

On the other hand, coaches at the professional level typically enjoy an advantage in having access to experts in many fields, including sport psychologists, nutritionists, physical trainers, sports medicine experts, and physical therapists. As a result, rather than rely on their limited knowledge in these areas, a wise professional coach can tap available experts to become part of the coaching team when necessary.

Finally, coaches at this level must be prepared to help professional athletes deal with the length of the season, the physical injuries, and the intensity of competition—all of which take a toll. Coaches need to be well versed in the mental skills and strategies that can help athletes deal with constant challenges to maintaining a healthy psyche.

High-Performance Amateur Sport

Some children begin specializing before the age of 10 with the goal of reaching the highest levels of sport, whether that means the Olympics, other international competition, or professional sport. Those who coach these young athletes must be able to help them learn fundamental skills that will stand up against top competition as they age and gain experience.

Coaches of young athletes also need to possess a firm understanding of the growth and development of prepubescent athletes. Their charges will be going through significant physical, emotional, and mental changes as they experience puberty. In addition, they need to understand the mental side of performance, since their athletes must handle competitive pressure even at a young age. Therefore, coaches must help them learn not only physical skills but also psychological skills that enhance performance. In addition, burnout is common in intense competitive training, and coaches need to recognize warning signs and know how to deal with related problems.

At elite amateur levels of sport, physical training and conditioning are quite intense and can be harmful if not properly designed and monitored. For example, injuries from overuse are common unless steps are taken to minimize them. Other essential components of high-performance training include diet, nutrition, and strength development.

Finally, coaches of athletes with high aspirations must deal with parents and agents who also have opinions about the athlete's training and competition schedule. Even if their motives are noble, they may be less informed than the coach. Therefore, it falls to the coach to provide steady and responsible guidance and, when necessary, to bring in expert specialists to bolster their position.

Intercollegiate Sport

The requirements for college coaches vary depending on the sport, the college, and the level of competition (NCAA Division I, II, or III or other classifications). These factors affect expectations, facilities, athlete skill levels, and compensation. Many smaller colleges hire part-time coaches who are paid several thousand dollars per season. In contrast, large universities with highly competitive programs employ many full-time coaches who devote their time year round to recruiting, off-season training, preseason training, and of course in-season practices and games.

The NCAA publishes and enforces a set of rules that college coaches must follow. Coaches must spend a significant amount of time verifying that their actions fall within the rules in order to avoid embarrassing mistakes that could cost their employer dearly in penalties.

Coaches at this level also help their athletes build size, strength, and endurance because they are capable of making huge gains at this point in their development. Year-round training is expected, especially for Division I athletes, though NCAA rules limit off-season contact with coaches.

IN THE ARENA WITH . . .

Muffet McGraw

Muffet McGraw has been the women's basketball coach at Notre Dame for 27 seasons, during which she has compiled a record of 662 wins and 217 losses (for a winning percentage of .753). Her team won the national championship in 2001 against Purdue and has reached the Final Four six times. In 2014, Notre Dame compiled a record of 37-1, losing only to the University of Connecticut (undefeated at 40-0) in the national championship game. In recognition of her team's performances in 2013 and 2014, McGraw was named national coach of the year by the Associated Press, the Women's Basketball Coaches Association, espnW, the Naismith Awards, and the U.S. Basketball Writers Association.

Born in Pennsylvania, Ann "Muffet" McGraw played basketball at and graduated from Saint Joseph's University in Philadelphia, then briefly played professionally in the WNBA for the California Dreams. She began her coaching career at a high school in Philadelphia, then served as an assistant coach at her alma mater and as head coach at Lehigh University before settling in at Notre Dame in 1987.

At Notre Dame, McGraw took over a low-profile program at a university known for football and built the women's basketball program into a national power that now typically plays before a sold-out crowd. She is perfectionistic and detail oriented and demands excellence of her players. Yet she is not a yelling, screaming, in-your-face coach but a calming, analytical presence who is masterful at nurturing the leadership qualities of her student-athletes and melding them into a unified force (Bradford 2014).

High School Sport

Coaches of high school athletes need to possess both a wide breadth of coaching knowledge and a keen understanding of young adults. Skills and strategy expertise are a must, and athletes who have developed bad habits need special care to learn new skills. Coaches at this level must also be reasonably well versed in various areas of practical sport science, such as injury prevention, physical training, and sport psychology (which can be extremely helpful, for example, in teaching gifted athletes and addressing psychosocial issues).

Generally, high school coaches are former athletes who may also have played college sport. They are hired to teach in the school system and offered a supplemental contract to coach after school. Young teachers may coach several seasons of sport and thus earn supplemental pay during each season. However, teaching a full day and then adding coaching duties can be both challenging and exhausting. As a result, many retire from coaching as their own families mature and they no longer enjoy the intense schedule.

Coaching education for high school coaches is spotty, and aspiring coaches must seek out coaching clinics, workshops, and conferences on their own. Some sports offer easy access to education through books, videos, and seminars, but others are poorly organized. Few states have established rigorous standards for high school coaching, and many athletes have suffered under the tutelage of so-called "warm-body" coaches who accept the job under pressure but have minimal expertise or interest and are poorly paid for their time. Fortunately, through the leadership of NFHS and Human Kinetics Coaching Education, the majority of states now offer coaching education programs that are gradually becoming more robust and easily accessible online.

A typical high school coach usually likes kids, knows how to organize and administer a team, and is able to serve as a helpful adult role model during the critical adolescent years. It is less common for high school coaches to possess a broad and deep knowledge of coaching or of their chosen sport. If they do, greener pastures often beckon at the collegiate level.

High school coaches who are dedicated to their sport often also get involved at the community level to help develop youngsters as a feeder system for the high school team. They track potential athletes from an early age, offer advice, coach them in high school, and help them choose a college. For many dedicated coaches, this is a lifelong pursuit, and they gain so many friends and supporters over the years that a run for mayor is not out of the question. I've known more than one coach who easily "retired" to the position of mayor or town council member.

As athletes enter their preteen and teenage years, their coaches need to be strong, both technically and strategically. Exceptional athletes often turn to high-performance sport programs outside of school to supplement their high school experience and benefit from coaches who are more highly qualified or experienced. Whether affiliated with a school or not, coaches of adolescent athletes need to empathize with kids experiencing puberty and be sensitive to the huge physical and emotional changes that characterize this stage of life. In addition, instilling the value of discipline and hard work enables athletes to develop their individual talents. At the same time, coaches must help young athletes balance their dedication to sport with their responsibilities to family, friends, and school.

Youth Sport

When kids are young and first exposed to sport, they need coaches who understand them, why they play, and what they expect out of sport. Coaches are worth their weight in gold when they are able to be sensitive to youngsters' needs, concerned for each child's welfare, and supportive of each child's success. Coaches of young beginners also need to be well schooled in teaching the basic strategy and skills of the sport so that children develop sound fundamentals.

In addition, coaches of young athletes must help them learn how to approach sport—how to understand the rules of the game, practice good sporting behavior, learn basic skills and strategies, and have fun. If coaches don't make sport attractive to children, even talented athletes will drop out since they haven't yet invested much time or effort. Moreover, unlike at other levels, coaches may also need to educate parents about the philosophy of the program. When athletes are young and malleable, it is critical for coaches to help parents understand the chosen sport and support the program's goals. It is particularly important for coaches to help parents develop good attitudes about winning and losing and embrace and guide their youngsters' efforts regardless of competition results.

For the young athletes themselves, it is critical that they learn from a coach who is fun, warm, and engaging. Kids want to enjoy time with their friends, test their skills, and celebrate games with a trip to the ice cream or pizza parlor regardless of whether they have won or lost. Therefore, coaches should love to spend time with kids and enjoy their foibles without judging them or their parents.

Of course, even within youth sport, situations can vary at different levels of competition. For example, very young high-performance athletes—for example, talented gymnasts, tennis players, and swimmers who compete nationally and internationally—present a very challenging coaching dynamic. Their parents spend huge amounts of money and sometimes uproot the family to seek better competition; as a result, these kids may feel tremendous pressure to succeed. Given this intense atmosphere, it takes a coach with special training and a special personality to work with these young athletes and their families while also handling the pressure to achieve immediate success against the best competition in the world.

Coaching for Male or Female Athletes

Since the passage of Title IX, opportunities have expanded for female athletes and coaches. During the ensuing years, research has focused less on female coaches' methods and more on tracking the number of women in the coaching ranks. This focus may have resulted partly from the fact that so many men have taken over women's teams. In any case, female athletes agree that they prefer a coach who is a good person and role model and who is assertive, cooperative, determined, respected, willing to help, dedicated, responsible, energetic, and cool under pressure. They also prefer a coach who has a great personality. These are essentially the same traits valued by male athletes (Holbrook and Barr 1997).

At the same time, there are some indications that boys and girls react differently to coaching styles and that coaches should tailor their coaching methods to maximize the athletic experience for members of both sexes. Craig Stewart (2005) has summarized the research on the need for different approaches in coaching female and male athletes. According to Stewart, girls are more intrinsically motivated than boys by self-improvement and goals related to team success. Girls are also more motivated by a cooperative, caring, and sharing team environment. Indeed, some female athletes are turned off by coaches who overemphasize winning, and they seem to approach competition somewhat differently than male athletes do (Garcia 1994).

APPLYING SOCIAL THEORY

Feminist Theorists and the Lack of Women Coaches

Some 40 years after the passage of Title IX ensured equal opportunities for girls in sport, female participation has mushroomed. As a result, there are more coaching opportunities today than ever before in sport, but the vast majority of coaches are males. In 1974, just after Title IX was passed, the percentage of women coaching women's teams at the college level was more than 90 percent, but that percentage has fallen to about 40 percent. Moreover, in youth sport, fewer than 20 percent of coaches of girls' teams are female (LaVoi 2009). These trends are somewhat perplexing because many girls and women have now had the requisite athletic experience to qualify and motivate them to enter coaching.

Indeed, advocacy groups such as the Women's Sports Foundation believe that having more women in the coaching profession would provide a rich opportunity to challenge stereotypes about gender roles and provide girls and women with visible role models of leadership. Taking the position of a feminist theorist, research possible reasons for the low percentage of female coaches and suggest strategies for improving the situation. In other words, what is the cause, and what are some possible solutions?

For example, girls seem to place more emphasis on playing fair, and they tend to blame themselves for a poor performance. Boys are more likely to break rules, strive to win at any cost, and blame their defeats on other people or on factors such as the weather or lucky breaks. It is not clear whether these differences result from cultural expectations or relate to innate traits (Stewart 2005). It is quite possible that girls who are exposed to male coaches and compete at highly competitive levels will be more likely to exhibit traits similar to those exhibited by boys simply because of their training and competitive experience. Nevertheless, it is important for coaches to recognize that differences exist and that coaching styles should fit the needs of the athletes.

Coaching Personality

It may be unfair to lump all coaches together in a single group and attempt to describe their personalities, beliefs, and orientations. However, in every occupation, certain similarities among practitioners give the impression of a certain type that has some basis in fact. Furthermore, coaches are not immune to being stereotyped. Movies, television, and books often present a coach in a baseball cap wearing a whistle around his or her neck and shouting profanities at hapless young athletes. Of course, these representations are unfair when applied to an entire group, but they are based in part on years of observation by athletes, parents, and spectators.

In fact, researchers have revealed that, historically, male coaches have typically manifested certain personality traits. Sport psychologists Tom Tutko and Bruce Ogilvie and sport sociologist George Sage collected information in the 1970s suggesting that coaches tended to be moderately conservative; that is, they tended to value loyalty to tradition, respect authority, expect obedience, follow standards of conduct accepted as normal, and have a strong religious orientation. In highly competitive environments, coaches in traditional team sports still tend to exhibit these characteristics because that style of authoritarian coaching fits with the so-called professional model of coaching (Lombardo 1999; Sage 1973).

In fact, athletic coaches tend to be more conservative on most matters than the college students they coach—a situation that has often led to conflicts. However, when compared with some other adult groups, such as businesspersons and farmers, coaches are more in the middle of the road. Still, as compared with other teachers at both the high school and college levels, coaches tend to be among the most conservative. Historical reasons for this tendency toward a conservative personality include the following (Lombardo 1999):

- Coaches are typically former athletes who have seen their own coaches operate in a conservative manner, and they tend to perpetuate that style.
- Coaches often have clear concepts of right and wrong based on strong religious and cultural backgrounds.
- Coaches often come from working-class families that emphasized traditional values and respect for tradition and authority.
- Because most coaches are held accountable for their team's performance, they like to seize control of the team even if doing so means coaching in an authoritarian style.
- In the past, many coaches had a strong military background, which influenced their attitudes, beliefs, and habits. However, this influence may have declined since the United States instituted a volunteer army and, as a result, fewer current coaches have had military experience.

Since this research by Lombardi was conducted, sport has changed, and in many instances the changes mirror shifts in society. Women are now more engaged in competitive sport as athletes; significant progress has been made in racial integration in sport; and scientific research on sport has added to the existing knowledge base for coaches. However, there is still significant progress to be made in each of these areas.

Active coaches today have certainly been affected by their own athletic experiences, mentors, and life experiences. However, if they simply model their coaching behavior on past experiences, they will likely encounter difficulties. Young athletes today have grown up in a world much different from the one their coaches grew up in. They have more personal freedom, are more likely to question authority, tend to make decisions without parental knowledge or support, and often rely on peers for advice and counsel. These changes have resulted in part from the decline in stable two-parent families, as well as general societal trends toward a more permissive environment, such as the fact that many families have both parents employed outside the home, thus giving kids a lot of independence.

In this atmosphere, young athletes expect to enjoy their sport experience, and if they don't they often simply withdraw. They expect coaches to be attentive and interested in them as people rather than just as sport performers. As a result, though authoritarian coaches may succeed in certain situations, they have generally been forced to modify their coaching behaviors to adjust to today's athletes. Many coaches of women's teams also have learned to adapt to the specific needs of their female athletes, which can differ from the needs of male athletes.

An in-depth look at characteristics of coaches today is likely to reveal patterns that differ from those of the past. In addition, coaches in certain individual sports may have different views than traditional team coaches. Consider, for example, the role of a tennis or golf coach who deals with only six or eight athletes, as compared with a football coach who presides over a squad with more than a hundred athletes. Naturally, with such a large squad, the opportunities for close interpersonal relationships are limited, and the coach may be forced to adopt a role similar to that of the CEO of a small company.

Another factor is the shifting emphasis even in professional sport from autocratic coaches to those who can manage a sizable business with the acumen of a savvy businessperson. In addition, the exorbitant contracts of star players and their influence on the success of the team have shifted the balance of power from coaches to outspoken players.

One case in point is the breakup of the Los Angeles Lakers dynasty after the 2004 season,

IN THE ARENA WITH . . .

Nick Saban

You can talk about winning all you want, but really the goal is for our guys to go out there and play to the best of their ability in terms of their effort, toughness, and a discipline-to-execute standpoint.

Nick Saban, during a press conference before the 2013 BCS National Championship Game

This quote expresses a key part of the coaching philosophy of Nick Saban, head football coach at the University of Alabama. We should pay attention because Saban is probably the most successful college football coach of our day—and certainly the highest paid at more than $5.6 million per year. His overall career record as a head coach at four universities is 165-57-1, and he has been named national coach of the year six times.

Saban coached the Louisiana State Tigers to the BCS National Championship in 2003 and has tacked on three more championships at Alabama (2009, 2011, and 2012). Saban is known as an outstanding leader, motivator, organizer, and tactician whose attention to detail is legendary. Except for a brief two-year foray into the NFL as head coach of the Miami Dolphins, he has dedicated his life to college football and compiled a record of achievement that few can match.

In spite of his success, or perhaps because of it, Saban doesn't let his life be defined by wins and losses. To paraphrase his words, "Success to me is being all you can be at what you're trying to do. Focus on being a relentless competitor, play every play like it has a history and life of its own. Be the best you can be. That guarantees you the best result" (Pillion 2011). In other words, Saban believes that if he can get his players to focus on the process and execute to the best of their ability, the outcome will take care of itself (O'Keefe 2012).

which included the firing of Phil Jackson, one of the most celebrated coaches in NBA history. Because star player Kobe Bryant was unhappy with his role as compared with that of Shaquille O'Neal, both Jackson and O'Neal were let go. Eventually, O'Neal was traded to the Miami Heat, and Jackson was rehired by the Lakers for the 2005 season. This dynamic—in which one superstar wields an inordinate amount of power and influence—has been played out repeatedly in the NBA. Imagine the diplomatic skills required of the coach when an athlete believes that he has the right to decide what is best for him and the rest of the team.

It is dangerous to overgeneralize or stereotype a group of people. Athletic coaches are victims of stereotyping even though much of the conventional wisdom about coaching styles is outdated. In order to be successful in today's world, the majority of coaches have had to adapt their behavior to the coaching job that they accept and align their coaching methods both with the goals of the sponsoring organization and with the expectations of the athletes entrusted to their care (Lin, Jui-Chia, and Esposito 2005; Lombardo 1999).

Coaches at other levels of competition—including nonrevenue college sport, most high school sport, youth sport, and sport for older athletes and those with disabilities—are more likely to develop a humanistic or invitational style of coaching. They need to focus more on the total development of the people they coach than on competition results. In addition, coaches in sports that require independent thinking by athletes, such as tennis, golf, swimming, and track, need to encourage and help players to think for themselves. Those who subscribe to this invitational style of coaching need to ensure that every aspect of their program and coaching behavior is warm and welcoming to athletes. Sport participation for these athletes is an opportunity to test their limits and realize their potential as human beings.

Many successful coaches have written an autobiography or had someone write a biography of their life and coaching career. For aspiring coaches, these accounts can be inspiring and instructive. In many cases, however, one must sort through the lessons learned by another coach who lived in a different era and pick out those that stand the test of time. No matter how successful Vince Lombardi was all those years ago, the days of authoritarian, no-nonsense coaching are gone. Still, some coaches whose careers have stood the test of time used methods that are worth investigating. In considering such accounts, aspiring coaches should assess their own personality and values with an eye toward adapting them to the level and age of the athletes they expect to coach.

This introspection is typically required in the process of developing a personal coaching philosophy, which is something that all prospective coaches should do before accepting a coaching position. With experience over time, they may adapt their initial philosophy to individual situations and athletes, but it forms the foundation that guides an inexperienced coach along a path to successful coaching.

Challenges for the Future of Coaching

Coaching is difficult to describe and evaluate because it differs greatly from one situation to the next. The common identifiable theme is that coaches take part in sport in order to help athletes achieve their best performance and enjoy the experience. In other words, coaches are leaders of people engaged in sport participation.

The United States is different from other countries in that it has no generally accepted body of knowledge that coaches are expected to possess. In contrast, most developed countries, particularly those in Europe, have established a coaching education plan that is approved by the government agency responsible for sport and typically administered by the governing body of each sport. Such efforts have also been made in Canada and Australia, whose nationwide programs include five levels of coaching certification; to reach level 3, for example, a coach must complete about 100 hours of training in theoretical, technical, and practical areas.

In the United States, however, there is no official process for coaches to gain certification from a neutral agency that verifies their knowledge and skill. Therefore, it is up to sport consumers to demand at least a minimal level of expertise from their coaches and to insist on change when coaches do not measure up to these expectations.

The first step in rectifying this situation was to develop a national consensus on the NASPE (now SHAPE America) national coaching standards that differentiate between the types of coaching knowledge necessary for working with various athletes according to skill, age, and level of performance. As discussed earlier, these standards have now been endorsed by well over 100 sport organizations (SHAPE America 2006), and they form part of the essential framework for certification, along with sport-specific knowledge and competence in the strategy and skills of one's chosen sport (NASPE 2008). Now that this groundbreaking step has been taken, the next move is for each organization that has adopted the standards to develop a delivery system that is affordable and accessible to all prospective and continuing coaches.

Enforcement of coaching certification has always been a puzzle in the United States, but groups that adopt at least a minimal certification requirement have taken a necessary step. Coaches who are employed by organizations, schools, and colleges should certainly be required to meet a level of certification that is appropriate for their position. In addition, we need to better educate members of the general public about the importance of coaching certification so that they too demand it. Toward this end, coaching organizations should spend time and money educating the public so that people can make enlightened choices about coaches for their athletic experiences and those of their kids.

Enforcement of such standards leads to a certification process that is national in scope but delivered locally and that enables coaches to verify their understanding and ability to apply knowledge in practical situations. At most levels, the certification process could be made available through an interactive online system to ensure the widest possible accessibility. Higher levels of certification may require additional face-to-face learning with an emphasis on applying the principles of sport science. Finally, once coaches have achieved certification, there must be a system of continuing education to keep them up to date in their knowledge and to allow more in-depth exploration of coaching skills and competencies.

A second challenge involves recruiting, training, and supporting the army of volunteer coaches who are the backbone of most youth sport programs. Because of the high turnover rate among volunteer coaches, recruiting and training processes must be streamlined and made easily accessible and inexpensive. Efforts should also be made to reduce resignations by volunteer coaches who quit as soon as their own kids graduate to another level. Perhaps experienced coaches could be encouraged to continue by implementing a model that divides coaching responsibilities and decreases the necessary time investment.

In a related issue, coaching education and certification programs need to be made clearly relevant enough to convince sport program administrators, parents, and prospective coaches that they are worth the time they require. In contrast, unrealistic expectations doom attempts to educate and certify volunteer coaches, who may simply turn down a coaching position; the effect would be a crisis of too few coaches available to staff youth sport programs.

A third challenge is to develop strategies for recruiting females into coaching at every level. Despite the explosion of girls' sport in the last 30 years, only one-third of women's teams are coached by women coaches. For many women, family responsibilities take priority; however, in these days of shared parenting, men should accept more family responsibilities in order to help put prospective female coaches on the field.

Indeed, many women could make significant contributions to coaching young people. We accept a similar role for women as teachers in schools, so why not invite them to ball fields and gymnasiums? As part of that effort, when working to recruit and retain female coaches, we need to make their compensation equal to that of male coaches. We also need to encourage the media to promote successful female coaches as role models for aspiring coaches.

A fourth challenge is to ensure that athletes are protected from negative behavior and exploitation by athletic coaches. To this end, sport programs that employ coaches should require background checks, credential reviews, and consistent monitoring with comprehensive performance reviews. Abuse of athletes by coaches must be defined, acknowledged, and eliminated so that all athletes at all levels can have a healthy experience.

A fifth challenge is to develop a recognition system based on criteria other than just wins and losses. Though athletic performance is one measure of coaches' success, other measures should also be considered in the context of a program's goals. If teaching fundamental skills is critical for young athletes, then coaches who are masters of helping athletes develop skills should be widely recognized and rewarded. Volunteer coaches who invest much discretionary time must also be rewarded through public recognition and

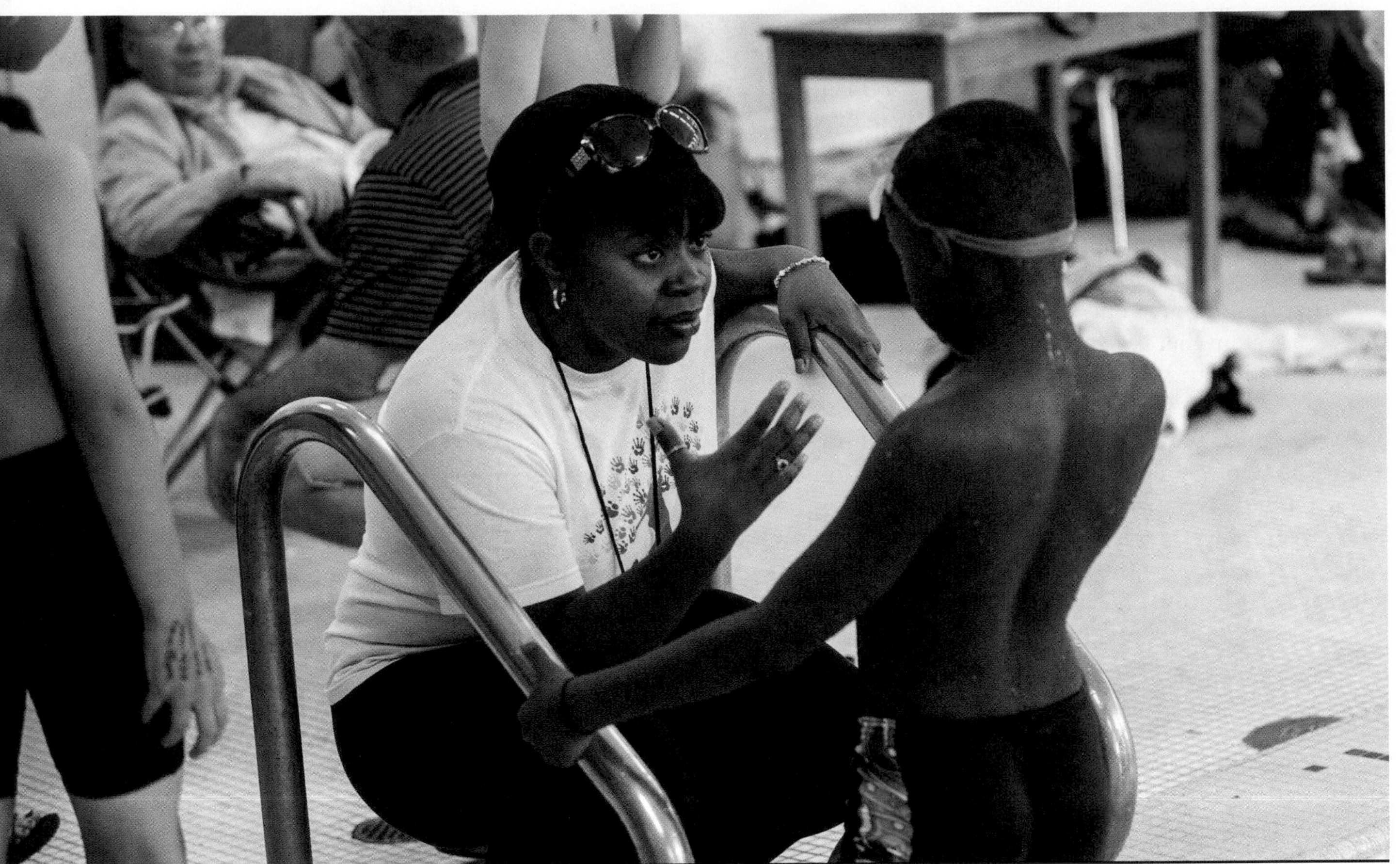

What steps are needed to increase the number of women coaches at all levels of sport?

perhaps given incentives, such as a trip to the highest championship in their sport or expense-paid educational experiences.

A sixth challenge is to recruit and promote coaches from minority groups to provide role models for both athletes and younger coaches. Lapchick's Racial and Gender Report Cards (2012, 2013) suggest that with the exception of professional basketball, very few sports have a representation of minority coaches that mirrors their presence in the population.

Chapter Summary

The influence of coaches on young people is enormous. Testimonials from former athletes abound with praise for their coaches as mentors, advisers, and heroes. Coaching athletes through the stress of sport links coaches with athletes in a bond unlike that of any other adult–child relationship.

Regrettably, coaches can also have a negative impact on young people. For example, unrealistic demands from a coach may turn children away from sport and activity, provoke resentment of authoritarian discipline, damage their self-confidence, and confirm their worst suspicions about adults wanting to use them for their own self-interests.

The chapter also explores the current status of coaching in the United States, where standards for coaching have only recently been developed, though they have now been accepted by more than 100 sport organizations. In spite of this landmark accomplishment, implementation of those standards is just beginning, and few general certification programs are widely available or mandated by organizations that sponsor sport programs.

Youth sport in the United States is unique in that its hundreds of thousands of coaches typically have little if any background in coaching. Perhaps more distressing is the fact that after they learn coaching skills on the job, they often resign from coaching as soon as their own child leaves the team or sport.

The chapter also examines the skills and competencies that are useful for coaches at different levels of sport. Each coach's philosophy should match the level of coaching required and the expectations of athletes at that particular level.

Though it is difficult to generalize about such a diverse population, coaches typically exhibit fairly conservative personalities, particularly in team sports and at the professional level. Coaches working with athletes who are more oriented toward participation than toward high performance are more likely to employ a democratic model than an autocratic model of coaching. Most aspiring coaches base their coaching behavior on that of their own former coaches and on their own experience as an athlete. The majority of coaches value hard work, discipline, respect for authority, and love of sport. Female coaches tend to be more committed to establishing a cooperative, caring team attitude, whereas male coaches tend to focus heavily on winning.

The chapter concludes with a look at challenges in the United States for coaching in the future. Unless dramatic steps are taken, it is possible that sport participation will decline as a result of dissatisfied athletes and families who expect more from coaches. Though coaching does not yet merit acceptance as a profession, there is no reason that we cannot work in that direction.

STUDENT OUTCOMES

After reading this chapter, you will know the following:

- The connection between sport and education at the high school and college levels
- Interscholastic sport trends and their positive and negative effects
- Intercollegiate sport trends and their positive and negative effects
- Challenges and possible changes for sport in educational settings

Interscholastic and Intercollegiate Sport

Interscholastic and Intercollegiate Sport

Friday nights are crazy in the state of Texas. That's when students, athletes, parents, and entire communities gather at high school football games in which teams compete both for pride and for their town's boasting rights. No other state has a tradition quite like it, and Texans of every age are knowledgeable and passionate about their high school sports, especially football. The high school football stadiums in Texas would be the envy of most schools around the country, yet they are often empty near the end of the season and during the playoffs because most of those games are played in college or professional stadiums to accommodate the huge crowds. Can you believe that the twenty most-attended high school football games in Texas history range from 36,000 to more than 50,000 fans? Here are the top five (Lone Star Gridiron 2014):

Rank	Attendance	Year	Game	Location
1	54,347	2013	Allen vs. Pearland	AT&T Stadium, Arlington
2	49,953	1977	Plano vs. Port Neches-Groves	Texas Stadium, Irving
3	48,379	2012	Allen vs. Houston Lamar	Cowboys Stadium, Arlington
4	46,339	2006	Southlake Carroll vs. Euless Trinity	Texas Stadium, Irving
5	45,790	1945	Highland Park vs. Waco	Cotton Bowl, Dallas

As the table shows, such crowds are not merely a recent phenomenon; to the contrary, the second-largest crowd gathered in 1977 and the fifth-largest in 1945.

Texas high school football was vividly shared with the rest of the country in the nonfiction book *Friday Night Lights* by H.G. Bissinger (1990). This account traced the 1988 football season of the Odessa Permian Panthers and the team's effect on the entire population of Odessa. The book's success led to a popular movie version released in 2004 and a television series that debuted in 2006.

Perhaps Texas is indeed a bit different from other parts of the United States, but high school sport continues to grow throughout the country. The best performers go on to big-time collegiate programs to showcase their skills in hopes of eventually earning millions of dollars in the professional ranks. But it all starts in youth leagues and continues in high schools.

In the past century, sport has become an important fixture in virtually all U.S. high schools and colleges. Conventional wisdom holds that sport helps complete the education of young people by emphasizing the development of physical talents, a healthy work ethic, a sound moral code, and attitudes that conform to the expectations of society.

College athletics had a modest start in a rowing contest between students from Harvard and Yale in 1852. In those early days, sport was run entirely by students for their own entertainment and benefit. As the years went by, however, that system was supplanted by one that seems to benefit the school, alumni, and student body at large while also providing questionable and sometimes improper benefits for some high-profile athletes.

The pattern of intercollegiate varsity sport programs was soon followed in interscholastic sport. Leaders in high school education supported sport programs as a means of raising youth fitness levels, which were judged to be alarmingly low during World War I. They also felt that sport participation would help students learn the value of hard work, citizenship, and good sporting behavior.

However, school-based sport grew so popular that athletes became the most admired students in school. One might think that in an educational setting, the most admired students would be those who perform best in academic work, but various replicated studies have found that athletes were the most popular with their peers, whereas bright students who were not athletes ranked ahead of students who were both bright and studious (Eitzen and Sage 1978; Hechinger 1980). Apparently it is acceptable to be a brilliant student, as long as you don't work at it; athletes, on the other hand, are admired for both talent and work ethic.

Perhaps the difference hinges in part on the fact that athletic success benefits the team—and indirectly the whole school—whereas academic success may seem more self-centered. In addition, major athletic events often double as important social occasions, where students congregate, flirt, discuss life, and rally around their school's team. As a result, athletic performance enhances social status, particularly for boys who play highly visible sports, such as football and basketball.

Student culture at most U.S. high schools values athletic achievement and positions successful athletes as admired members of the "in group." More generally, popular students are usually members of an exclusive clique that may be based on economic status, appearance, dress, or material possessions such as an attractive car. Academic standouts, on the other hand, are often treated as the butt of jokes and left out of the in group.

At the same time, in the last 30 years, the status of athletes has changed dramatically with the entry of girls into the athletic arena. Today, many of the most successful athletes are also top students and are still popular with their peers. These changes have affected the prescription for social success

Why do you think athletic success is often viewed as benefiting a school more than academic success does?

for girls in high school from one that emphasized femininity, cheerleading, domestic aptness, and appearance to one that supports girls as students, athletes, and all-around achievers.

Intercollegiate athletics presents a different picture from that of the typical high school. First, the number of students who qualify for athletic teams in college is dramatically smaller than the number who play on high school teams. Second, the philosophy and conduct of collegiate sport are greatly affected by school type and institutional views about athletics. Big-time athletic programs—labeled as Division I by the National Collegiate Athletic Association (NCAA)—emphasize winning, entertainment, and revenue-producing sports.

These programs make little apology for appearing to operate more as a professional sport organization than an educational one. In fact, some big-time college football programs collect so much annual revenue that they pay for all other sports at their university and have money left over to contribute to academic programs and nonathletic scholarships. In contrast, hundreds of smaller colleges' athletic teams purport to help students develop their physical skills just as other students develop their skills in drama, music, art, and other extracurricular activities.

The phenomenon of sport in the educational setting is stronger in the United States than in any other country in the world. In fact, most other countries offer sport programs that are community based and supported by sport clubs in towns and cities. These countries approach sport as a separate endeavor—not one that is intertwined with education. The U.S. model has likely produced both positive and negative consequences for society, and the ultimate assessment may depend on one's point of view.

Interscholastic Sport

For the purpose of this discussion, high school sport covers grades 9 through 12, although in many schools gifted athletes in seventh or eighth grade are eligible to play on high school teams. At the national level, the National Federation of State High School Associations (NFHS) provides coaching education; publishes sport competition rules, information, and research that leads to position statements on topics such as sexual harassment and hazing; and provides guidance to the state associations. At both public and private high schools, sport is typically governed by local leagues and by the state association to which they pay dues. The leagues and their schools adhere to the rules established by the state association and therefore are eligible for regional and state playoffs. Some states separate public and private schools at state-level competitions, especially if private schools have consistently won state titles.

The following sections examine trends in high school sport participation, reasons that high school athletes choose to participate or drop out, ways in which high school sport and community-sponsored sport interact, and some positive and negative aspects of high school athletics.

Participation Trends

According to the NFHS (2013-2014), the number of students participating in high school athletics has increased for 25 straight years (see figure 8.1). Furthermore, in 2013–2014, overall participation reached an all-time high of about 7.8 million thanks to record highs for both boys (more than 4.5 million) and girls (nearly 3.3 million). Texas has more athletes (about 0.8 million) competing in high school sports than any other state; it edged out California for the top spot in spite of the fact that California has about 12 million more citizens. The top 10 was rounded out by New York, Illinois, Ohio, Pennsylvania, Michigan, New Jersey, Florida, and Minnesota.

In 1971–1972, only about 294,000 U.S. girls participated in high school sport, as compared with nearly 3.7 million boys. However, following the passage in 1972 of Title IX, which mandates equal opportunity for members of both sexes, girls flocked to the athletic arena. Today, the balance still leans toward boys (58 percent male athletes to 42 percent female), but it also reflects tremendous growth for girls.

When measured not by the number of participants but by the number of teams, the top five sports for boys in order of popularity are basketball, track and field, baseball, cross country, and football. For girls, the top five in order are basketball, track and field, volleyball, fast-pitch softball, and cross country. Soccer ranks seventh for boys and sixth for girls, among whom it continues to gain popularity.

In terms of the number of participants, the most popular sport for boys continues to be American football, followed by track and field, basketball,

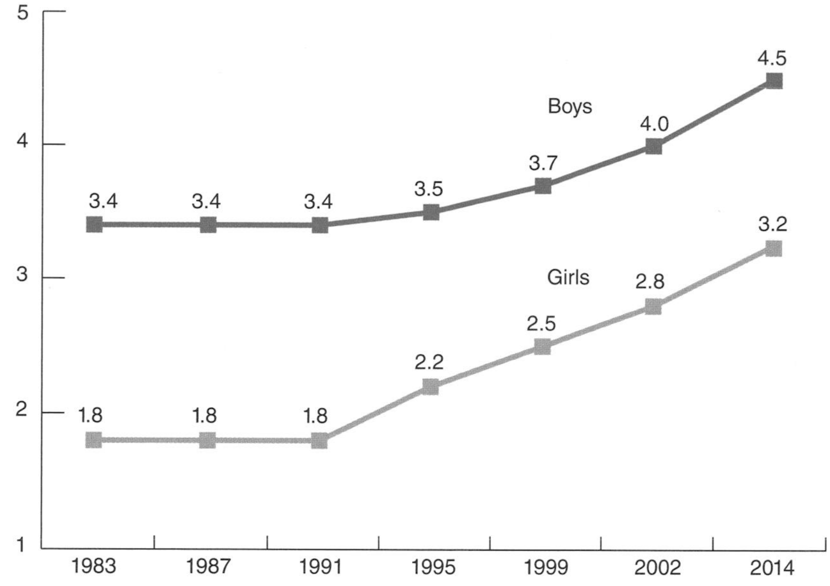

FIGURE 8.1 Boys and girls participating in high school varsity sport from 1975 through 2014 (numbers indicate millions of participants).

Data from NFHS 2013-2014.

baseball, and soccer. For proper perspective, remember that football teams typically attract and accommodate much larger numbers of participants than most other team sports. For girls, track and field took over the top spot from basketball, followed in order by volleyball, soccer, and fast-pitch softball. In addition, lacrosse has continued to grow in participation and now ranks tenth for girls and eleventh for boys. Here are some specifics about the most popular sports for high school students as measured by number of participants in 2013–2014 (National Federation of State High School Associations (2013-2014):

Girls

Track and field (outdoor)	478,885
Basketball	433,344
Volleyball	429,634
Soccer	374,564
Softball (fast-pitch)	364,297
Cross country	218,121
Tennis	184,080
Swimming and diving	165,779
Competitive spirit squads	120,593
Lacrosse	81,969

Boys

American football	1,093,234
Track and field (outdoor)	580,321
Basketball	541,054
Baseball	482,629
Soccer	417,419
Wrestling	269,514
Cross country	252,547
Tennis	160,545
Golf	152,647
Swimming and diving	138,373

Aside from the million-plus boys who play football, the overall numbers for boys and girls look nearly the same. This issue of an imbalance in participation by gender has been a consistent point of debate, in both high school and college, in terms of interpreting the intentions of Title IX. This point is revisited in chapter 13.

Evaluation of participation levels is complicated by the fact that many sports simply require fewer athletes in order to field a team. In addition, in many schools, participant numbers are limited in order to reduce the expenses associated with venues, uniforms, games, and coaches. Large squads are necessary for some sports, such as track and field, soccer, swimming, and football; in contrast, smaller squads suffice for cross country, golf, tennis, basketball, and volleyball. As a result, most schools limit the number of participants in these smaller-squad sports. However, many other athletes might be interested in participating in those sports if there were sufficient room.

The percentage of high school students who participate in sport is also affected by income level, gender, presence or absence of a disability, and geography. In areas that serve the highest percentage of kids receiving free or reduced-price lunch, only 25 percent of eighth graders participate in sport, whereas the percentage is 31 percent at middle-socioeconomic schools and 36 percent at high-socioeconomic schools. At the same time, in spite of major advances in sport participation by girls in recent years, their rates typically remain 2 percent to 5 percent lower than those for boys. In addition, children with a physical or intellectual disability are nearly five times less likely to participate in sport than those without a disability. Finally, schools located in the Northeast and Midwest generally offer more opportunities for sport participation than those in the South and West. For example, Georgia has the lowest participation rate for girls at 22 percent, and Florida has the lowest rate for boys at 30 percent (Aspen Institute 2014).

Reasons for Sport Participation and for Dropping Out

In the landmark survey *American Youth and Sports Participation* (Ewing and Seefeldt 1990), some 4,000 students in grades 7 to 12 reported their reasons for playing their best school sport. Here are the top five reasons subdivided by sex:

Boys

1. To have fun
2. To improve skills
3. For the excitement of competition
4. To do something I'm good at
5. To stay in shape

Girls

1. To have fun
2. To stay in shape
3. To get exercise
4. To improve skills
5. To do something I'm good at

It's pretty clear for both sexes that high school athletes want sport to be fun, to help them improve their skills, to get them in shape, and to challenge them in the form of competition. Although winning per se was also mentioned, it ranked only eighth among boys and twelfth among girls. Taken as a whole, this cluster of priorities doesn't exactly square with many adult definitions of sport as reflected in professional sport. Indeed, as a society, we tend to celebrate winning as the purpose of sport—otherwise, why keep score?

More recent studies (U.S. Anti-Doping Agency 2010) have found the essential reasons for sport participation to be largely unchanged, though they do reflect some refinements. Here are the top five reasons cited by youth in the general population:

1. Having fun
2. Doing my best
3. Being with friends
4. Improving my skills
5. Being healthy

The answers are somewhat different, however, among youth who choose more serious sport programs—typically, those administered by sport-specific national governing bodies. Here are their top reasons:

1. Performing well
2. Doing my best
3. Having fun (tied)
3. Improving my skills (tied)
5. Being healthy

In addition, as in the earlier study, more recent studies continue to find that responses differ somewhat by sex. For example, the Tucker Center at the University of Minnesota (Tucker Center 2007) reports that girls say they participate in sport primarily to have fun, as well as to get in shape, socialize with friends, develop skills, and experience competition.

Adolescents are in a process of developing and exploring who they are and who they can be; during this process, sport may fill a variety of needs. Most important, it provides a chance to be on a team with friends and learn to work together to achieve a common goal. It also provides an opportunity to take on a performance challenge that carries both the risk of failure and the possibility of success, along with the joy that can bring. These motivations for seeking a spot on a school team are intrinsic—that is, they come from within the person and do not depend on competitive records, trophies, or publicity.

For many young athletes, *fun* means spending time with friends, being physically active, learning new skills, and perhaps mastering them. But it also means that the stress and demands of the sport are commensurate with the athlete's abilities and commitment. If the demands are excessive, then sport ceases to be fun because of anxiety; at the same time, an activity with too little stress or challenge is also not fun because it is boring.

When young people drop out of a sport, the number one reason they give, by far, is that "it just isn't fun anymore." Lack of fun may result from not getting along well with the coach or other players on the team; it may also result simply from not being a good enough player. Other reasons often mentioned for dropping out include health problems, injury (or fear of injury), and desire to focus more on academics or other clubs (Women's Sports Foundation 2008; U.S. Anti-Doping Agency 2010).

In a sense, high school sport naturally weeds out many participants based on ability and competitive success. Athletes who warm the bench tend to lose interest and motivation to continue making an effort. At the same time, allocation of playing time is a familiar bone of contention, and competitive athletes must learn to accept the reality that these decisions are made by coaches.

Athletes can also be driven away from a team by a coach who is overly concerned with winning, autocratic in his or her coaching style, disorganized, or verbally abusive. To gain perspective on this dynamic, imagine a drama or music teacher verbally abusing a student in the midst of a play or concert in front of friends and family members. Some players are also alienated by long boring practices and a lack of empathy from coaches. In some cases, players even experience burnout due to the stress of competition or pressure to improve. Many of these complaints can be resolved by implementing better standards and education for coaches.

Parents, too, may hold unrealistic expectations for their high school athletes—especially parents who were not successful athletes themselves. They often add to the pressure, misunderstand team culture, criticize the coach unfairly, and become too involved in their child's activity. Once again, the key to developing successful team parents involves effective education and training of parents led by a coach or other expert in parental support and behavior.

Many studies have supported the theory that high school athletics are a positive force in students' lives. What benefits do you see to high school athletics?

For many high school athletes, sport conflicts with other activities they would like to try. They may also just want to spend more time "hanging out" with friends or engaging in casual sport activity. As they mature, they are naturally attracted to other interests, and if their sport or coach demands year-round dedication, they may not be willing to make the investment. Injuries from overuse or just bad luck can also put an athlete on the bench and cause her or him to lose interest (Fraser-Thomas, Cote, and Deakin 2008; Rice 2011).

Finally, it is important for parents, coaches, and school officials alike to realize that not all students have the same motivation or commitment to sport. In fact, the overall pool of thousands of high school athletes includes at least three distinct subgroups:

- *Reluctant participants.* About 25 percent of athletes feel that they *have* to participate in sport due to outside pressure. They join because of their current friends or in hopes of making new ones. They are less willing than others to play hard and practice hard, and they are likely to drop out along the way.

- *Image-conscious socializers.* This group represents about 40 percent of athletes and includes many good athletes. These individuals are motivated by the prospect of approval or other rewards. They like being perceived as good athletes, feeling important, winning trophies, being popular, staying in shape, and looking good. They may stick with school sport but are unlikely to be lifelong athletes.
- *Competence-oriented participants.* Athletes in this group love participating in sport and are likely to continue doing so after their school days are over. They work hard, practice hard, and play hard to improve their skills. Sport provides them with a means of achievement that they enjoy.

Partnerships With Community-Based Sport Clubs and Programs

Most communities whose high school varsity teams succeed can point with pride to a community program that feeds the teams. A wise coach who aspires to build a dynasty and ensure the popularity of a sport takes the time to get involved in youth sport programs and make sure that kids are introduced to the sport in their formative years. Then, as young people enter high school, the coach has the luxury of selecting athletes with sport-specific skills and strategies rather than having to teach them as beginning players.

In addition, many community summer programs hire high school varsity athletes as youth sport coaches. This approach strengthens the link between the high school and the community program. The varsity athletes act as role models for younger children and motivate them to try to achieve varsity status as they mature.

Many towns across the United States consistently produce generations of high-performing athletes in certain sports. The tradition often starts with an enthusiastic high school coach who establishes and supports a community youth sport program. Year after year, kids graduate from the youth program and fill positions at a higher level as older players are lost to graduation. The head coach looks like a genius, but the key to success rests in simply giving the time and effort to help young participants in the sport.

Club-level sports outside of the school system can also provide competition in interscholastic sport. In fact, leaders in many sports—primarily individual ones, such as tennis, swimming, gymnastics, and figure skating—encourage talented athletes to specialize in that sport at an early age and compete year round. For example, the Amateur Athletic Union's basketball and seven-on-seven football teams occupy thousands of kids in their chosen sport during the off-season. At the same time, high school soccer coaches may not appreciate national programs that entice elite soccer players to train with them instead of their high school team.

Positive and Negative Effects of Interscholastic Sport

Numerous studies have reported benefits associated with participation in high school sport. Typically, these studies have been conducted by school systems or organizations associated with schools, such as the NFHS. Relying on data collected from athletes, principals, and parents, these studies make the case for the value of athletics as an educational endeavor.

The NFHS (2004) summarized this research on its website in a document titled "The Case for High School Activities." The document cites research supporting the value of athletics in promoting a variety of positive effects: academic performance, moral development, good citizenship, high graduation rates, success in college, better attendance and graduation rates, fewer behavioral problems, higher achievement motivation, resistance to drug and alcohol abuse, development of leadership skills, good decision making, social integration, and improved self-image.

Studies cited in the NFHS (2004) summary also drew the following conclusions: More than two-thirds of parents support the value of cocurricular activities, including sport, according to the 29th annual Phi Delta Kappa–Gallup Poll of the Public's Attitudes Toward Public Schools. In addition, the Women's Sports Foundation has consistently supported the benefits of high school sport for young women, including physical fitness, social acceptance, academic success, and resistance to eating disorders. Finally, more than three-quarters of high school principals strongly support high school athletics, according to a study supported by a grant from the Lilly Endowment of Indianapolis and conducted by Indiana University in cooperation with the National Association of Secondary School Principals.

Influence of Athletics on Academic Performance

High school students who participate in athletics tend to have higher grade point averages, better attendance

APPLYING SOCIAL THEORY

Conflict Theorists and School-Sponsored Athletics

In 1961, sociologist James Coleman observed that a visitor entering a U.S. high school would likely be confronted, first of all, with a trophy case. The visitor's examination of the trophies would then reveal a curious fact: The gold and silver cups, with rare exception, symbolize victory in athletic contests—not scholastic ones. Therefore, the trophy case would suggest to the innocent visitor that he or she was entering not an educational institution but an athletic club (Ripley 2013).

Now, take the point of view of a conflict theorist who tends to see the world as dominated by economic interests. Compare the U.S. model of high school sport—in which educational institutions sponsor and promote athletic activities—with the approach used in much of the rest of the world, wherein community-based athletic clubs sponsor sport activities and schools are dedicated clearly to academic learning. Think about this comparison in the context of the educational achievement of U.S. children as compared with the achievement of their peers in other countries. In the United States, we routinely spend more tax dollars per high school athlete than per high school math student, unlike most countries worldwide. The results of an international test of critical thinking in math for 15-year-olds showed that the top results were earned by students from Shanghai, Singapore, Hong Kong, and South Korea while U.S. students finished 31st (Ripley 2013).

Do you think the United States should reconsider its approach to combining scholastic education with athletics? If we continue with our current approach, will doing so eventually affect the economic welfare of the United States?

records, and lower dropout rates than do members of the general student body. This conclusion has been reported in studies by the Women's Sports Foundation (2009a), Hartman (2008), and the NFHS (2004). In addition, interscholastic sport receives clear and strong support from virtually every segment of the U.S. population. Indeed, sport as an educational experience continues to be a critical factor in the personal development of young people, and coaches must not lose sight of that goal if they hope to retain broad support of their programs.

At the same time, a fair and comprehensive analysis of high school sport reveals both positive and negative effects of participation. One negative effect (discussed later in this chapter) is the possibility of disunity in the student body when athletes form cliques. Although cocurricular sport serves some students as a critical factor in their self-confidence, social acceptance, and physical development, this is not the case for everybody. High school athletics also exert influence on peer groups and on the overall functioning of the student body. In addition, hard choices must often be made about how to finance athletic programs.

Character Development Through Athletic Participation

Supporters of high school sport have long trumpeted its value in helping young people develop a strong work ethic, good moral behavior, healthy attitudes toward fitness, and improved academic performance. Let's see if these claims are backed up by research.

Studies have often purported to demonstrate that high school athletes are superior to nonathletes in terms of performance and attitudes in the traits just mentioned (Dworkin, Larson, and Hansen 2003; Gibbons, Ebbeck, and Weiss 1995). It is not clear from the research, however, whether the athletes developed these traits through their sport participation or already possessed them due to other influences in their lives. Simply reporting that athletes appear to have higher levels of physical, social, or moral development as compared with nonathletes does not prove a cause-and-effect relationship between athletic experience and, for example, academic performance, attitudes toward fitness, or moral behavior.

In fact, extensive research reported by Stoll and Beller (2009) suggested that participating in high school sport may *hinder* one's development of moral character. Granted, there is little dispute about sport's positive effect on social character in the form of teamwork, loyalty, and work ethic. But moral character, as defined by honesty and integrity, is not likely to be positively affected by sport unless an athlete's coach intentionally stresses it.

In traits where athletes do rate higher, it is possible that athletes have already made more progress toward a higher standard in these traits, which in turn helps them perform successfully in sport. To help assess this possibility, some studies, such as those by Fejgin (1994) and Rees and Miracle (2004), have measured student performance over time. Generally, these studies have shown that athletes are more likely to come from economically privileged backgrounds and to possess above-average cognitive skills, self-esteem, and academic ability.

Of course, it is also possible that students who are less privileged or weak in cognitive skills withdraw from sport or are excluded because of poor grades, thus affecting the results of such studies. In addition, these results do not differ greatly from research findings about *all* students who participate in extracurricular activities in school. In fact, students who choose to join a musical group, drama club, debate club, school newspaper, or other activity also show higher levels of development than does the bulk of the student body.

Adults who have gone on to success in business or in a profession often attribute their success to lessons they learned on the playing field. From their point of view, sport participation is vital for success in later life. For example, a 1987 survey of individuals at the level of executive vice president or above in Fortune 500 companies found that 95 percent had participated in high school sport, whereas 54 percent had been involved in student government, 43 percent in the National Honor Society, 37 percent in music, and 18 percent in their school's publications. It is possible that those people would have been successful regardless of their sport experience, but their personal belief and testimony can make for a powerful argument (Texas University Interscholastic League 1998).

A more recent study conducted by the accounting firm Ernst & Young (Glass 2013) showed that 90 percent of female executives around the world had participated in sport at some level. In addition, nearly 70 percent of C-level (chief) executives had competed in sport as a working adult, and 55 percent had participated in sport at the university level. More than 75 percent of these women executives said they believe that adopting behaviors and techniques from sport in the corporate environment can be an effective way of improving the performance of work teams.

Yet for all the success that former female athletes have achieved in the business world, one area of business stands out as the last barrier to overcome. In the sport business, only 2 percent of executive positions are held by women, as compared with an average of 15 percent in the business world at large. How ironic it is that although sport has been an important source of experience for many women who have risen into leadership positions, the sport business itself is an example of the need to continue campaigning for equality (Chatel 2011).

Female business executives have been particularly influenced by their sport participation. Two-thirds of them report that they exercise regularly, which is almost double the percentage of women who do so in the general population. In addition, more than four-fifths (82 percent) of female business executives participated in sport while growing up, and the vast

Indra Nooyi, the CEO of Pepsico, played cricket in college.

majority say that lessons learned on the playing field have helped them succeed in business. Here are some examples (Goudreau 2011):

Mary Schapiro—chair, Securities and Exchange Commission, lacrosse

Irene Rosenfeld—CEO, Kraft Foods, basketball

Ellen DeGeneres—television host, tennis

Mindy Grossman—CEO, Home Shopping Network, bowling

Ellen Kullman—CEO, DuPont, basketball

Weili Dai—cofounder, Marvell Technology, basketball

Sarah Palin—governor, Alaska, basketball

Beth Brooke-Marciniak—vice chair for public policy, Ernst & Young, basketball

Lynn Laverty Elsenhans—CEO, Sunoco, basketball

Most studies of high school students in sport have focused on the years of their participation. However, a comprehensive study by Carlson and Scott (2005) tracked more than 25,000 high school athletes eight years after their senior year to see if sport participation had produced any lasting effects. The results showed that high school athletes were more likely than nonathletes to participate in physical fitness activities or recreational sport, to graduate from college, to be employed full-time, and to earn a higher salary. They were also *less* likely to be smokers. Later in life, as found by another study, student-athletes were eight times more likely to be physically active than nonathletes; in addition, people who did not participate in sport as a child were 60 percent more likely to be overweight (Home Team Marketing 2013).

The most glaring negative factor associated with athletic participation was a tendency toward binge drinking. These results from the American Athletic Institute confirmed the conclusions of earlier studies (Barber, Eccles, and Stone 2001) showing higher rates of both drinking and binge drinking among athletes than among nonathletes. Many athletes seem to embrace risk-taking behavior, and alcohol abuse is one manifestation of that tendency. In addition, athletes who participate in contact sports report greater alcohol use than others, and team-sport athletes report more alcohol use than do individual-sport athletes. More specifically, in New York state, 14 percent of athletes in the seventh grade reported using alcohol in the past year. The use rate progresses to nearly 60 percent by the senior year of high school and typically continues on an upward trend through college (American Athletic Institute 2010).

Social Effects on the Student Body

In thousands of high schools, sport promotes school spirit; creates an "us versus them" mentality; and prompts social gatherings at pep rallies, ceremonies, and sport events themselves. Attending sport events and rooting for friends and acquaintances strengthens the bonds between groups of students. In addition, athletic teams often support each other by visiting each other's practices or games and cheering each other on.

In particular, the team sports of football and basketball have become an essential part of the social life of most U.S. high schools. During football season, more than 7,000 high school games are played on any given Friday night; during the winter months, basketball featuring either boys or girls is played two or three days per week, which adds up to a total of more than 18,000 games per week.

Sport events not only help unify the student body but also attract parents, siblings, and lots of supportive townspeople. In any given year, high school football and basketball attract more than 336 million spectators; in comparison, professional and college football and basketball combined attract just 133 million. In other words, high school football and basketball provide spectator entertainment for more than two and a half times as many people each year as do the professional and college sports (Home Team Marketing 2013).

Educators would point out that sport is not the only school activity that exerts such positive effects. Accordingly, the NFHS concerns itself not merely with interscholastic sport but with all cocurricular activities, and its website devotes significant space to the reasons for supporting all school-based cocurricular activities. For example, music and drama organizations often perform similar functions as sports do in after-school settings.

Altogether, according to the NFHS (2004), school activities outside of the academic curriculum cost an average of 1 percent to 3 percent of overall school budgets. However, across the United States, parents and communities have supported athletics more generously than any other school activity simply because of the number of students involved, the number of competitions staged, and the travel expenses incurred (Brady and Giler 2004b).

The social fabric of a school can also be negatively affected by division between students who participate in sport and those who do not. Because athletes spend so much time together, are admired by other students, and receive plaudits from the community and media, they tend to socialize together—sometimes to the exclusion of other students. When the "jock culture" separates itself from the student body at large, envy and mistrust often set in. Some misguided athletes interpret their social standing to mean that deviant behavior on their part is acceptable; as a result, various offenses committed by prominent athletes often fill the front pages of local newspapers with tales of poor judgment and errant behavior.

In addition, since many students, particularly males, envy athletes, emphasis on academic performance may suffer somewhat for all students. As a result, in spite of the fact that athletes generally perform above average in academics, students who excel in the classroom are often regarded as "nerds" in social circles. Fortunately, many examples can be found of students who do well in both sport and academics, particularly among female athletes.

Gender equity has transformed the scene in local high schools by enabling girls to become involved in athletic culture. Indeed, young women now have many of the opportunities for self-development, competitive training, recognition, and college athletic scholarships that were formerly restricted to young men. As a result, girls must learn to balance academics, sport, and social life in a way that didn't exist for them before the passage of Title IX in 1972.

Perhaps inevitably, in the midst of these changes, conflicts have sometimes arisen between the members of different generations in regard to societal traditions that encourage women solely toward playing a nurturing role in life. Thus girls may be faced with the challenge of acting as gutsy, tough competitors in the athletic arena even as they navigate pressure to assume a more traditional feminine role in their social environment, where they may be expected to focus on clothes, personal appearance, and boys. This challenge can be intimidating for girls, who often lack effective role models in the ranks of teachers or parents because earlier generations simply did not have the same experiences.

A student's popularity at school is also influenced by sport, especially for boys. When both members of both sexes were asked what makes a boy popular at school, 38 percent of girls said "being good looking" and 18 percent said "being good at sports." Boys essentially reversed those percentages, with 30 percent saying "being good at sports" and 15 percent saying "being good looking." For girls' popularity, however, sport was less of a factor. In fact only 4 percent of girls and 3 percent of boys thought that "being good at sports" helped make a girl popular; rather, the most often-cited factors affecting girls' popularity were "being good looking" and "having nice clothes/things" (Women's Sports Foundation 2008).

Financial Issues

In recent years, as many U.S. school districts have faced mounting budget crises, they have often viewed interscholastic sport and other extracurricular activities as possible areas to downsize, eliminate, or subsidize with user fees. For example, a *USA Today* article (Brady and Giler 2004a) recounted a dilemma in Fairfield, Ohio, where voters were asked to approve a higher tax levy to support a budget increase that would help fund extracurricular activities, including sport. After the tax levy was voted down, fees were put in place for all after-school activities.

In response, a parents' group was organized to raise money to help support the activities, but they had a tough time meeting the cost of the programs. As a result, the family of a student who participated in a sport or other cocurricular activity had to pay a participation fee ranging from $100 to more than $1,000 for some sports. In such situations, many schools do at least put a cap on the total amount that one family must pay in any given year for its kids' participation.

Fairfield's experience is not unique. In fact, a recent poll about children's health makes it clear that families of kids who want to participate in school sport now pay more than ever—and that kids from lower-income homes are being virtually shut out of the game. The poll found that a pay-for-play fee was required of 61 percent of sport participants at an average of $93 per sport; despite the cost, only 6 percent of kids received a fee waiver based on family income. When other costs of athletics such as equipment and uniforms were taken into account, the average cost of sport participation was $381 per child. In fact, among kids from households with less than $60,000 in annual income, research finds a 19 percent decrease in sport participation due to the associated costs, as compared with only a 5 percent decrease among kids from households with a higher annual income (C.S. Mott Children's Hospital 2012).

In this environment, a family with multiple children who want to play multiple sports in public schools could easily be faced with an annual cost that runs into the thousands. If this situation continued to

IN THE ARENA WITH . . .

Eagle Stadium

In 2012, the Dallas suburb of Allen, Texas, became the proud owner of what might be the most impressive and expensive high school football stadium in the country—Eagle Stadium. It started in 2009, when some Allen residents decided that the old 14,000-seat stadium (built in 1982 at a cost of $5.6 million) wasn't large enough and persuaded 63 percent of voters to approve a new stadium. Eagle Stadium boasts 18,000 seats, high-tech synthetic turf, a huge high-definition video scoreboard, a three-tiered media box, and private box seats. The stadium also features a wrestling practice facility and an indoor practice area for golf.

Impressive as it may be, Eagle Stadium was not without controversy. At the same time that the Allen school system was building the new stadium, it faced a $4.5 million budget shortfall that led it to cut 44 teaching positions and 40 support-staff positions through attrition and voluntary buyouts. The money for the new stadium came out of a different budget bucket and therefore could not be used to save teacher jobs. Therefore, residents simply had to pony up the money in the form of a property tax increase and a $119 million bond to fund the stadium, along with a performing arts center.

In addition, after all the publicity and criticism that Allen endured for its lavish spending on a football facility, the stadium had to be shut down within two years of its opening due to safety concerns. The problem involves wide cracks that emerged in the structure and allegedly resulted from faulty work by either the architects or the construction company. Both entities have assured the school district that repairs will be made at no cost to the district, but in the meantime the football team is forced to play all scheduled home games in nearby Plano (Prisbell 2014).

grow, eventually only middle- and upper-class students would be able to participate in sport. Already, in fact, many schools that charge sport participation fees have seen a drop in the number of athletes from middle- and lower-income households. This reality conflicts with the prevailing public school educational policy of providing equal opportunity for children from all income levels in the United States.

Funding for cocurricular activities typically consumes only 1 percent to 3 percent of a locality's total education budget. In some cases, that figure is even smaller. For example, in 1999, the Chicago Board of Education had a total budget of $2.6 billion, whereas activity program funding stood at $2.9 million, or about one-tenth of 1 percent (0.001) of the overall amount (National Federation of State High School Associations 2004). At the risk of seeming cynical, one might suspect that school officials and politicians often use sport as a bargaining chip in order to convince the public to vote for more money for public schools. They cut athletics first, and when the predictable public outcry materializes, the politicians respond with the solution: Vote for the increase to save school sport. Sometimes this strategy works, but when it fails, as it often does, sport programs are reduced, eliminated, or offered on a fee system.

Another effect of money on high school sport can be seen in the fact that affluent, suburban communities enjoy athletic programs that typically are more extensive, have better facilities and more qualified coaches, and contend for state championships year after year. The fact that these communities spend more on their teams and facilities is a key factor in their programs' success. Another key factor is the opportunity for most kids in these communities to grow up playing organized youth sport and taking lessons in various sports, such as tennis, golf, and sailing.

For many school districts that are struggling with budget challenges, another strategy is to simply decrease program costs. Since salaries are fixed and often negotiated, they are difficult to reduce; however, many schools have frozen coaching salaries at their current levels. In addition, some systems have carved out significant savings in transportation costs by reducing travel, using school buses instead of private buses, combining several teams on one bus, and eliminating long trips. Some states and many communities have also reduced or eliminated middle school and junior varsity sport programs and reduced the number of contests scheduled or the length of sport seasons.

Across the country, it is fair to say that most school districts have adopted several of these strategies, depending on their local situation. The reason is clear: In tough economic times, all public programs that depend on tax revenue are forced to cut back on expenses, and high school sport is no exception.

Collegiate Sport

In the past 100 years, collegiate sport has grown tremendously. The first collegiate football game was staged in 1869 between local rivals Rutgers and Princeton in New Brunswick, New Jersey. Today's behemoth of college sport, the NCAA, was officially founded in 1906 in the midst of debate over safety in college football, in which the "flying wedge" had become a popular offensive weapon. Numerous injuries and some deaths had resulted, and most observers viewed the sport as too dangerous and demanded that it be either reformed or abolished. In an effort to protect young men, rules were put in place by the NCAA to outlaw the flying wedge as a football strategy. The NCAA's first national championship was held in 1921 in the sport of track and field.

In the early days, college teams were student supported and played teams from other local colleges. Today, of course, college athletics is much larger and more diverse and offers myriad opportunities for both men and women. Here are some major changes in college sport since the 1970s:

- Gender equity in response to Title IX, which opened doors for women in sport, including athletic scholarships
- Refinement of competitive categories in the form of Divisions I, II, and III in the NCAA and similar divisions of play in the other organizations (e.g., the National Association of Intercollegiate Athletics and the National Junior College Athletic Association)
- Support for championships in more sports for both men and women at all levels
- Separation of big-time college programs from the majority of programs, which involve more modest expectations and expenses and remain more closely aligned with the original educational mission of college sport

College sport faces many challenges. To name a few, news stories abound about "football factories," abuse of athletes, coaching indiscretions, behavioral problems and deviance on the part of athletes, and racial exploitation. Most criticism is directed at and emanates from institutions with big-time sport programs; these programs tend to be where the juicy stories happen.

ACTIVITY TIME-OUT

Who Should Pay for High School Sport?

In the face of continuing economic challenges, describe how you think schools should address the daunting task of paying for high school sport. Do you favor charging user fees, reducing costs, or eliminating certain sport programs? Assume that you are a taxpayer and a parent of three children in middle school or high school who either play or would like to play high school sports. Present your case in a three- to five-minute oral report or in a written position paper limited to three pages.

Clearly, the vast majority of colleges do not run big-time athletic programs or suffer to the same degree from the associated problems. Particularly in Ivy League and Division III schools, athletic programs are more likely to maintain high academic standards, minimize expenses, compete locally rather than nationally, limit recruiting, and at least resemble the original mission of college athletics: to support and enhance the educational and academic mission of the university. However, the influence wielded by these schools is modest at the NCAA level, where larger Division I schools heavily influence much of the decision making.

Typically, college football is dominated by large state universities that were founded as land-grant institutions. Federal legislation required every state to set aside land for an educational institution; in this way, state-supported universities were founded in the late 1800s, and in the next century many of them established athletic programs. Enabling factors in this development included their sizable budgets, their facilities, and their abundance of land.

These schools also benefited from their location, which was typically in geographically isolated spots—such as Gainesville, Florida, and Lincoln, Nebraska. As a result, they offered the only big-time sport teams in their area. Indeed, with no competition from professional teams, university football teams achieved a status approaching that of religion. In contrast, university-sponsored teams in cities typically have not flourished because they just can't compete with the local professional franchise in attracting fans, media coverage, and revenue.

In the past 30 years, college sport has grown dramatically both in the number of championships staged and in the level of athlete participation. The data show that in the past 15 years alone, the number of participants has doubled. In addition, in some sports (particularly basketball and soccer), women's programs have begun to rival men's (National Collegiate Athletic Association 2013-2014).

In one striking example of growth, NCAA Division II now stages a quadrennial festival by combining its spring national championship competitions at one location in an Olympic-style setting. This approach offers multiple advantages. It capitalizes on the economy of scale, media coverage, and synergy between sports and creates a memorable experience for the athletes. The inaugural event was held in 2004 to rave reviews. After that, a festival for fall sports was held in 2006, a second spring festival was held in 2008, and the first-ever festival for winter sports was held in March 2009. The 2013 winter festival featured more than 1,200 athletes vying for five team championships and 80 individual championships in the following sports: men's and women's track and field, men's and women's swimming and diving, and wrestling (National Collegiate Athletic Association 2013b).

For the purposes of this discussion, collegiate sport includes athletic programs at four-year institutions that are members of the NCAA, which is by far the largest and most influential organization for college sport. Rules for conducting sport at these institutions are determined by the NCAA's member schools and enforced by their professional staffs. Altogether, the nearly 1,300 member institutions represent about 460,000 student-athletes who participate in 23 varsity intercollegiate sports. About 50,000 of those athletes participate in 89 national championship events (National Collegiate Athletic Association 2013-2014).

The National Association of Intercollegiate Athletics (NAIA) includes about 260 schools with smaller athletic programs, mainly in the South, that serve a total of more than 60,000 student-athletes who compete in 13 sports and vie for 23 national championships (National Association for Intercollegiate Athletics 2014). Membership in the NAIA has declined as the NCAA has offered more opportunities for small schools. In addition, more than 100 Christian colleges maintain membership in the National Christian College Athletic Association; most of them also maintain membership in the NCAA. Two-year schools are governed by the National Junior College Athletic Association, which includes 525 member institutions where a total of 60,000 student-athletes compete in 28 sports. These smaller organizations all have limited budgets, staff, and influence as compared with the NCAA, which essentially controls the majority of college athletics.

The following sections look at a variety of specific issues in college sport: participation trends, the struggle for control of women's athletic programs, distinctions between different divisions of competition, the cost of college athletics, athletic scholarships at Division I and Division II schools, positive and negative effects of intercollegiate sport, college as a training ground for professional athletes, social issues and college athletics, equity between men's and women's sport, and potential changes for the future.

Participation

For sports in which the NCAA conducts championships, participation doubled from a total of about 230,000 student-athletes in 1981–1982 to about 460,000 in 2012–2013. There are still more male participants (57 percent) than female participants. The average NCAA member institution has approximately 424 student-athletes—240 males and 184 females (National Collegiate Athletic Association Sports Sponsorship 2013-2014).

Over the past 25 years or so, the number of women's teams in NCAA championship sports has increased yearly, whereas the number of men's teams has decreased historically. Since 1988–1989, there have been 2,864 men's teams dropped and 2,038 women's teams added. Nearly every year, more men's teams than women's teams have been dropped. In 2012–2013, there was an increase in that one year of 183 women's teams and 120 men's teams compared to 48 men's teams dropped and 49 women's teams dropped in that same year. Since the 1988–1989 academic year, there has been a net gain of more than 3,000 women's teams as compared with only about 750 men's teams (National Collegiate Athletic Association Sports Sponsorship 2012–2013b).

The sports that added the most women's teams in 2012–2013 were lacrosse (40), golf (30), and indoor track (27). Since 1988–1989, the top women's sport to be added has been soccer, which accounts for 670 new programs. For men, the top sports added in 2012–2013 were lacrosse (26), indoor track (23), and cross country (17); the top-growing men's sport since 1988–1989 is indoor track, with an increase of 465 teams. These statistics show that lacrosse is the fastest-growing collegiate sport for both men and women. Even so, basketball still claims the most men's and women's teams of any sport. Here are the top sports as measured by number of teams (National Collegiate Athletic Association Sports Sponsorship 2012–2013b):

Men

1. Basketball
2. Cross country
3. Baseball
4. Golf
5. Soccer
6. Tennis
7. Track and field (outdoor)
8. Football

Women

1. Basketball
2. Volleyball
3. Cross country
4. Soccer
5. Softball
6. Tennis
7. Track and field (outdoor)
8. Track and field (indoor)

The following lists, on the other hand, show which sports serve the most individual participants. Of course, many sports are limited to smaller numbers by the required facility space.

Men

1. Football
2. Baseball
3. Track (outdoor)
4. Soccer
5. Track (indoor)
6. Basketball
7. Cross country
8. Lacrosse
9. Swimming and diving
10. Golf

Women

1. Soccer
2. Track (outdoor)
3. Track (indoor)
4. Softball
5. Basketball
6. Volleyball
7. Cross country
8. Swimming and diving
9. Tennis
10. Rowing

Research also shows trends in sport participation by athletes of various ethnic backgrounds (table 8.1). Notably, both male and female black athletes have steadily increased their percentage of participants in basketball, and male black athletes have done the same in football. However, in the past five years, the overall percentage of African Americans participating in college sport has declined by several percentage points, particularly in sports where they had previously gained steadily. The percentage of black athletes is also consistently lower in Division III schools, which tend to be private, more expensive, and of course cannot award athletic scholarships.

Control of Women's Collegiate Athletics

In the 1960s, women in college athletics were governed by the Division for Girls' and Women's Sports of the American Alliance for Health, Physical Education, Recreation and Dance, which had taken the position of supporting low-key competition for women. Wary of the abuses and negative publicity that had befallen men's programs—such as recruiting scandals, gambling on game outcomes, and paying of athletes with improper inducements—leaders in women's sport were determined to avoid them.

At the same time, as the women's movement gained steam in the early 1970s, pressure began to build to offer intercollegiate competition for women similar to that enjoyed by men. To this end, the Association for Intercollegiate Athletics for Women (AIAW) was founded in 1972, and it granted charter membership to 276 institutions. Ten years later, AIAW boasted 971 member institutions and sponsored 42 national championships in 19 sports.

The AIAW was run by female administrators and coaches who were dedicated to an education-based model of competitive athletics. Their goal was to cultivate student-athletes with an emphasis on the sport experience rather than the scoreboard. Athletic scholarships were virtually nonexistent, though a television contract was

TABLE 8.1 Student-Athlete Ethnicity Percentages for 2011–2012

	White	African American	Latino	American Indian and Alaskan Native	Asian	Other
All male sports	61.2	22.0	4.1	0.4	1.9	9.9
All female sports	69.5	12.6	4.1	0.4	2.3	11.1
Men's football	46.4	43.2	2.3	0.5	2.6	5.1
Men's basketball	29.4	57.2	2.0	0.1	0.1	11.0
Men's baseball	85.3	2.6	6.0	0.4	1.2	4.8
Women's basketball	38.2	47.9	2.0	0.6	1.1	10.2
Women's track and field	60.9	24.0	4.0	0.5	1.4	9.4
Women's softball	79.4	4.1	7.2	0.8	2.8	5.6

This table refers to Division I teams and includes only athletes receiving financial aid. It omits historically black institutions and data for responses indicating "two or more races."

Data from Lapchick 2012b.

POP CULTURE

Mighty Macs

The 2009 movie *Mighty Macs* tells the story of Cathy Rush and her team's improbable journey to the first national championship held in women's college basketball. In 1971, Rush was hired to start a basketball team at tiny Immaculata College in suburban Philadelphia. She was a recent graduate of nearby West Chester State College (now West Chester University), a perennial powerhouse in women's athletics. With no budget, no gym to practice in, and a contract that paid her just $450 for the year, Rush set out to build a team. And she did just that by convincing a number of local suburban Philly girls from Catholic high schools to join her effort. Led by six-foot center Theresa Grentz, who in those days was always the tallest player on the court, the Mighty Macs played an up-tempo style that buried their opponents.

Remember that Title IX, which mandated equal rights for girls and women in sport, was instituted only in 1972. Until then, women's college sport had none of the trappings of men's sport, such as athletic scholarships, recruiting battles, and national championships. However, by the end of the 1971–1972 season, Cathy Rush had built a team at Immaculata that won the AIAW national women's collegiate championship, beating rival West Chester in the finals in a huge upset. They went on to repeat twice, and suddenly women's college basketball was the talk of the town—and the nation.

By the early 1980s, the NCAA had taken over women's college sport with the promise that women would get the same benefits enjoyed by men. Large universities jumped in with both feet, recruiting with full scholarships and upgrading facilities and programs. In the process, Immaculata was unable to compete and faded from the national picture. However, they had started it all for women's college sport, and their story comes alive in this film.

negotiated and implemented with NBC to televise women's sport. AIAW leaders were determined to forge their own path to benefit collegiate women and avoid the potential traps of men's collegiate athletics, including commercialism, sponsorships, competitive obsession with winning, and devaluation of scholarship (Hawes 1999, 2001; Holway 2005; Katz 2005).

However, after just 10 short years, the AIAW went defunct and merged with the NCAA, yielding to pressure to embrace equal opportunities for women to compete for national championships and athletic scholarships, as men had long done. NCAA leaders recognized the potential benefits of bringing women's athletics into their fold—for example, sponsorship recruitment. Suddenly, the future of women's sport changed dramatically and moved significantly toward the male model of college sport. As this process played out, many female sport leaders lost their influential role and were replaced by male administrators, although they did fight for representation on committees, on boards, and in athletic departments.

Thus the subsumption of the AIAW into the NCAA heralded progress for women—but at a cost. Opportunities for female athletes expanded, but the philosophy of women's sport was sacrificed and replaced by one similar to that of men's sport. To put it more pointedly, women lost the power to set their own philosophy, rules, and agenda as they were absorbed into the powerful male-dominated NCAA. Yet as a social movement, the merger was a crucial step to help create a better collegiate athletic environment for all athletes regardless of gender.

With the adoption of Title IX and the eventual takeover of women's collegiate sport by the NCAA, athletic programs for members of both sexes embarked on a path of equality. As new leadership—which now included some males—took over women's sport, female athletes demanded equal rights, playing opportunities, and equal pay for coaches. At the same time, many men jumped at opportunities to coach women's sport and thus helped lead the charge toward equality.

Initially, women who had been in charge of women's athletics at their institution typically lost their power and were forced to serve under male athletic directors. However, though it took several decades, women gradually began to fill influential positions in the athletics department at many institutions. Eventually, pioneering women at some institutions took full control of both men's and women's sports as directors of athletics for all sports.

Divisions of Collegiate Athletic Programs

Fifty years ago, the NCAA divided its member colleges into just two divisions—university and college—and conducted championships at each of those levels. In 1973, its membership was redivided into three categories, and in recent years those divisions have been refined to include five (see table 8.2). The current categories include three in Division I: the Football Bowl Subdivision (FBS), which includes schools with big-time football programs; the Football Championship Subdivision (FCS), which includes schools with smaller football programs based on stadium size and average game attendance; and other Division I programs, which include schools without football teams. On average, Division I programs support nine men's sports and ten women's sports.

Each college determines the level at which it competes, provided that it meets NCAA requirements for that level. For example, a school that chooses to compete in Division I FBS must schedule opponents in the same category and support at least seven sports for men and seven for women (or six for men and eight for women). More specifically, in order to participate in Division I FBS football, an institution must garner an average attendance of at least 15,000 per home game in a stadium with permanent seating for at least 30,000.

Members of Divisions II and III operate less ambitious athletic programs, and Division III schools do not offer athletic scholarships, though they do permit grants based on financial need. Both divisions offer championships in which teams face others in the same division, but in some smaller sports the divisions are combined (National Collegiate Athletic Association 2013a).

Cost of Collegiate Athletic Programs

The enormous salaries paid to football and basketball coaches at big-time college programs—along with the economic challenges faced by higher education in general—have recently sparked more study and analysis of college sport expenses than ever before. This research has made clear that, with few exceptions, sport programs at every level are likely to cost a school a lot of money. Perhaps even more alarming, expenses seem to be accelerating faster than revenues each year.

In an effort to present a clearer and more realistic picture of its members' athletic programs, the NCAA began an effort in 2006 to improve the transparency of college sport finances. The first

TABLE 8.2 Number of NCAA Colleges and Universities by Division, 2013–2014

Division	Private	Public	Total
I (FBS)	17	103	120
I (FCS)	45	74	119
I (no football)	52	48	100
I (total)	114	225	339
II	141	154	295
III	355	88	443

Data from National Collegiate Athletic Association 2013a.

step was to require that each institution undergo an independent third-party review of its athletic program using a standardized procedure and submit the results to the NCAA for publication. Second, revenues were separated into two categories: generated revenues (for example, ticket sales and television proceeds) and allocated revenues (for example, direct institutional aid, student athletic fees, payment of utilities and other indirect institutional support, maintenance and support salaries, and direct governmental support designated for athletics). In the past, many universities that claimed their athletic programs made money simply ignored the extent of university subsidies for sport, including construction of stadiums and other first-rate sport venues (National Collegiate Athletic Association 20013f).

Here are some highlights from the NCAA Revenues and Expenses report for Division I that covers the time period from 2004 through 2012 (National Collegiate Athletic Association 2013f). The report shows that athletic programs increasingly rely on institutional subsidies to balance their budget. In 2012, the average proportion of revenue derived from the institution as a whole (that is, not from athletic department revenues) was 28 percent for FBS schools and 83 percent both for FCS schools and for Division I schools without football.

In addition, you may be surprised to learn that only 22 of the 120 FBS institutions generated enough revenues to exceed their athletic expenses in both 2011 and 2012. In other words, the bottom line is that the average Division I athletic departments are being subsidized by their institution at a level of approximately 71 percent of expenses. In addition, there appears to be a widening gap between the haves and the have-nots in big-time college football. Table 8.3 also reveals the dramatic differences between FBS schools and other Division I institutions in the categories of median total revenue and median generated revenue (National Collegiate Athletic Association 2013f).

Equally disturbing, overall athletic expenses from 2011 to 2012 grew by about 11 percent while revenues rose by only about 5 percent. That imbalance means that colleges had to subsidize athletic programs even more in order to make up the difference. If that trend continues, as indeed it appears likely to do, then either athletic programs will have to meet the difficult challenge of balancing their budget or more universities will simply have to absorb more of the expense.

The revenue that athletic programs do generate derives mainly from just three sports: football, men's basketball, and women's basketball. Here are some salient facts:

- The largest amount of revenue earned by an FBS school in 2012 was $163,295,000, whereas the smallest was $40,581,000—thus making clear the disparity that characterizes the FBS category of Division I (National Collegiate Athletic Association 2013f).
- Between 50 percent and 60 percent of FBS football and men's basketball programs reported a net income against expenses (National Collegiate Athletic Association 2013f).
- In the FCS category, only 4 percent of football programs and 8 percent of men's basketball programs reported net revenue, and even that was minimal (National Collegiate Athletic Association 2013f).

TABLE 8.3 Revenue and Expenditures by Division I Subdivision in 2012

	Median total revenue	Median generated revenue	Median total expense	Median negative net revenue
FBS	$55,976,000	$40,581,000	$56,265,000	–$12,272,000
FCS	$13,761,000	$3,750,000	$14,115,000	–$10,219,000
No football	$12,756,000	$2,206,000	$12,983,000	–$2,206,000

Note: The use of "median" figures rather than "averages" means the numbers are not additive. Also, the term "negative net revenue" results when the university paid (or guaranteed) expenses exceeding generated revenues.

Data from National Collegiate Athletic Association 2013f.

- For Division I programs without football, about 10 percent of men's basketball programs generated net revenue (National Collegiate Athletic Association 2013f).
- In Divisions II and III, virtually no institutions generate revenue that exceeds expenses (National Collegiate Athletic Association 2012a, 2012b).
- As often highlighted in the media, high-profile coaches' salaries in the revenue sports of football, men's basketball, and women's basketball have skyrocketed in recent years. As of 2013, salaries for football coaches of major programs had increased more than 90 percent since 2006 to an average of $1.8 million per year. In addition, 17 football coaches earned more than $3 million per year, led by University of Alabama coach Nick Saban, who was earning $5.5 million per year. As many people have pointed out, these coaches' salaries typically exceed even those of the college presidents they serve and of other distinguished faculty members (*USA Today* 2012).

You might think the rising costs of college sport would prompt lawmakers to pass legislation limiting coaches' salaries. However, a court has already ruled that idea illegal according to section one of the Sherman Antitrust Act, which prohibits such restraint of trade. The specific case was Law vs. NCAA, in which, in 1998, several college basketball coaches challenged an NCAA rule requiring member institutions to make one basketball coach a "restricted earnings" coach at a set salary of $16,000 per year (Edelman 2012). The fact is that college athletic departments spend almost two-thirds of their revenue on salaries and benefits, grants-in-aid (scholarships), and rental or maintenance of athletic facilities. Like all expenses at universities, all of these items are fixed costs that are affected by the prevailing market and economy.

Scholarships for Division I and Division II Schools

Many parents dream that their children will earn an athletic scholarship to pay for part or all of their college education. The hard reality is that a very small percentage of all children who start out in youth sport end up with a college athletic scholarship. Even so, such scholarships are not always out of reach, especially if the child is in the right sport, is a good student, and is open to any school that

ACTIVITY TIME-OUT

Is Collegiate Athletics Worth the Cost?

Now that you know something about the increasing financial crisis involving collegiate athletic programs, would you propose changes in the programs? If so, what changes would you suggest? Keep in mind that financial situations differ considerably across the five NCAA categories. Be specific about any changes you suggest to limit the escalating costs associated with college sport. For example, one might suggest that all athletic scholarships be eliminated. What financial effects would this change have for universities? For athletes?

You might also refer to the example of the Ivy League institutions that used to field teams at the highest level but made a courageous decision to eliminate athletic scholarships. Of course, many other schools did not follow their lead, and the result is that they generally can no longer compete for the finest athletes. It would be quite a different story if athletic scholarships were banned at all schools.

As mentioned earlier, the costs of high school athletics account for 1 percent to 3 percent of a school's overall budget, whereas that figure is about 5.5 percent at collegiate institutions. At the same time, high school sport boasts nearly eight million participants, whereas collegiate sport involves fewer than 500,000. How, if at all, do these differences affect your argument?

offers financial aid. Many athletic scholarships go unclaimed each year, primarily for women and at colleges that are not so well known.

From 1992 to 2012, the number of athletic grants-in-aid rose from about 58,000 to about 150,000 full or partial scholarships. The total amount of money granted by Division I and II schools was $2.4 billion. In Division I, grants-in-aid accounted for 15 percent of total athletic department expenditures at I FBS institutions, 26 percent at FCS institutions, and 27 percent at institutions with no football programs (National Collegiate Athletic Association 2012a). Division III institutions do not award athletic scholarships. The largest change from 1992 to 2012 occurred in the proportion of grants-in-aid awarded to women. In 1992, only 33 percent of grants-in-aid were awarded to women; by 2005–2006, however, 45 percent of grants-in-aid were allocated to women, thus mirroring their proportion of total athletes in Division I overall (National Collegiate Athletic Association 2013f).

Scholarship limits are set by the NCAA for each sport in order to level the playing field. The number of scholarships is determined as a ratio of the number of starting players needed to field a team. Of course, the limits for football are by far the largest, in part because schools claim that the violent nature of the game requires more athletes ready to serve in a backup role. When a school awards 85 scholarships for men in football, you can see how many spots for women's scholarships (85) in other sports are necessary to match that number. In many sports, the scholarship limit is much lower; for example, tennis, golf, and archery teams may be allowed only eight scholarships each. Thus the battle for equal distribution of scholarships for women and men is affected in a major way by football.

Another particularly thorny issue in some sports—such as tennis, swimming, soccer, track and field, and even basketball—involves the recruitment of international athletes, who may be awarded full athletic scholarships. In collegiate tennis, for example, this practice has resulted in almost compete domination of the individual rankings by players from other countries. As a result, U.S. families who have spent thousands of dollars on their child's tennis development may feel betrayed by a system that awards scholarships—often using public funds—to support foreign athletes rather than their own children. Legal challenges to this practice have not held up in court, but the issue persists.

EXPERT'S VIEW

Mind, Body, and Sport

When Dr. Brian Hainline assumed the role of chief medical officer for the NCAA, his first task was to consult with NCAA constituents and stakeholders in order to hear their concerns about health and safety. Overwhelmingly, the responses he received were centered on student-athletes' mental health and wellness. He then convened a task force—including several dozen scientists, clinicians, physicians, administrators, coaches, and student-athletes—that produced a 120-page NCAA publication. The report is designed to inform, educate, and stimulate both discussion and action in order to address myriad concerns about the mental health and well-being of competitive athletes—at the collegiate level, of course, but also in youth sport and even in the professional ranks.

The report sets the stage with several riveting first-person accounts provided by NCAA athletes and coaches. Next, it examines typical ailments—for example, eating, anxiety, mood, and depression disorders; substance abuse; gambling; sleep disorders; and suicidal tendencies. The report then expands on ways in which athletes are affected by social and environmental factors in the sport world. Timely topics explored here include harassment, discrimination, sexuality, and sexual violence. Finally, the report summarizes action options to help leaders in athletic departments provide for the prevention, identification, and treatment of mental health disorders among student-athletes (National Collegiate Athletic Association 2014d).

POP CULTURE

Insider's View of College Football

If you want an insider's view of big-time college football, two titles should be on your nightstand or in your e-book reader: *Fourth and Long: The Fight for the Soul of College Football* (2013) by John Bacon and *The System: The Glory and Scandal of Big-Time College Football* by Jeff Benedict and Armen Keteyian (2013). Both books provide a current look at the truths and fallacies surrounding the most popular U.S. sport. John Bacon spent untold hours with access to four celebrated Big Ten powers: Penn State, Ohio State, Michigan, and Northwestern. This quartet of schools has been challenged by scandal, NCAA sanctions, fading rivalries, and questionable leadership from athletic directors and head coaches. Yet Bacon also reveals the enduring attraction of college football as expressed by fans, marching band members, and avid tailgaters.

In contrast, Benedict and Keteyian spend more time looking at the "darker side" of college football. They shine a spotlight on the injustice faced by players who earn millions for their coaches and schools but don't have a nickel in their pocket. They also describe how so-called "hostesses" on campus are assigned to show prospective recruits a good time and urge them to commit to the school. In addition, alumni and athletic supporters of questionable background are ubiquitous around big-time sport and put schools at risk. When all is said and done, you may feel that nothing is likely to change in big-time sport because—let's face it—it really is all about the money.

You might ask why international athletes are chosen over their U.S. counterparts. Most of the answer lies in the fact that other countries have no such thing as an amateur player. In fact, many tennis players accept money, play professional events, and have racket and clothing sponsors at a young age. Indeed, their experience, training, and financial support are limited only by their performance. Typically, international players are more experienced match competitors than their American counterparts and have competed at a higher level of play. In contrast, U.S. children are not allowed to accept prize money or endorsements if they want to maintain their amateur status in order to be eligible for college athletics. The phenomenon of international athletes in U.S. colleges is complex, and no solution appears to be in sight.

Positive and Negative Effects of Intercollegiate Sport

As we've seen, it is impossible to lump all college athletic programs together since they vary so widely. For the purpose of this section, we divide our analysis into two primary groups: the roughly 800 athletic programs that are modest in expense and intensity and the roughly 300 highly competitive programs at schools where athletics follows a corporate structure (in other words, those classified as NCAA Division I FBS or Division I FCS).

Pressure to Generate Income for the University

Major college sport programs are run as corporate businesses that pay no taxes. Typically, the university expects them to be at least revenue neutral—that is, to break even. For many schools, that means securing an invitation to postseason play in order to earn the money guaranteed from a bowl game or basketball tournament appearance. Whether the athletic budget is actually balanced is a topic of discussion at many schools. It is often difficult to calculate the total expense of an athletic program because administrators assign various costs to other units of the institution. For example, facilities are often charged to the state or other building funds, fitness and weight rooms are supported by student activity fees, and stadiums are built or renovated using other development funds.

Whatever the cost, the expectation at many notable universities is to field outstanding athletic teams, particularly in the major sports. You need only check the last few years of football bowl games and NCAA basketball tournaments to compose a list of the top 50 schools that traditionally vie for national recognition.

Schools that support Division I athletic programs at either the FBS or the FCS level often justify their expenditures by pointing out that successful high-profile programs generate volumes of publicity for the university, contribute to school spirit among students, and increase donations from alumni and other prominent supporters. Taking it one step further, some schools claim that the success of their athletic teams leads to more applications for admission, thus allowing the school to select the very best of prospective students. In other words, as the claim goes, successful sport teams also improve the school academically. However, several studies reviewed by Frank (2004) suggest that such results are not likely (for more about this study, see the next section, on athlete recruitment).

At the same time, most of us know that people are generally drawn to winning programs. We can also point to examples such as the University of Connecticut (UConn). In the mid-1990s, UConn was a modest regional institution that sought to be the finest public state-supported university in New England. Not content with that relatively modest goal, a few visionaries aimed to raise UConn's profile to that of a nationally recognized university.

Toward that end, the state legislature provided more than $1 billion for new construction, thus transforming a utilitarian state university into an attractive modern campus. Next came success in men's and women's basketball, culminating in a national championship for both teams in 2004. Thus UConn was put on the map, and everyone in the country knew where it was. In addition, the football team had upgraded to NCAA Division I BCS (now FBS) and, in 2004, received its first postseason bowl bid—to the Motor City Bowl in Detroit, where it defeated the University of Toledo to finish with a record of 8-4.

You might wonder if there is a correlation between all of this campus improvement, publicity, and sport success. In fact, SAT scores for admission at UConn have increased steadily in recent years, and what used to be a safety school for state residents suddenly became the place to go. Can you think of other schools where a similar change has occurred? A few examples come to mind of schools that were virtually unknown before the exploits of one of their athletic teams thrust them into the public spotlight, if only briefly: Boise State University, Gonzaga University, the University of South Florida, and the University of Nevada at Las Vegas. For such schools, an upset win on the football field or in the NCAA basketball tournament can suddenly push them onto the national stage.

Athlete Recruitment

In *Reclaiming the Game* (2003), William Bowen, former president of Princeton University, and Sarah Levin document the realities of athletic recruitment and college outcomes of athletes as compared with nonathletes at 33 highly selective academic institutions. Relying on data from Ivy League schools, Seven Sisters colleges, and other prestigious universities, Bowen and Levin exposed the negative side of college sport at schools that do not even offer athletic scholarships.

Negative findings included the fact that athletes were four times as likely to gain admission to college as other students with comparable academic credentials. The data also showed that athletes were substantially more likely than other students to rank in the bottom third of their college class. Recruited athletes also tended to underperform academically in college as compared with predictions based on their test scores and high school grades. Of course, these are not the schools we think of when we think of big-time college sport. Indeed, it is rare for a team from the likes of Princeton, Harvard, or Yale to contend at the national level.

In 2004, Robert Frank of Cornell presented a report to the prestigious Knight Commission on Intercollegiate Athletics that assessed the effect of winning teams on applications and alumni donations. Citing a review of six studies conducted between 1987 and 2003, Frank reported that although there appeared to be several instances of small gains in admissions as measured by higher SAT scores, the increases were minor and in fact not statistically significant. He also mentioned the popular anecdote of Boston College reporting a 12 percent gain in applicants after football quarterback Doug Flutie chucked a miracle pass to defeat the University of Ohio in the Miami Orange Bowl stadium in 1984.

Frank also reviewed more than a dozen studies that measured the effect of athletic success on alumni donations. Although most studies showed little effect at statistically significant levels, one study did show that appearances in football bowl games and basketball tournaments do positively affect donations. Frank concluded, however, that little empirical evidence supports the contention that it takes a winning team or program to secure alumni donations.

Intercollegiate Athletics Reform

The Carnegie Commission for the Advancement of Teaching warned of abuses in college athletics as far back as 1929. The commission cited corrupt recruiting practices, professionalization of athletes, commercialism, and neglect of education. Sadly, these same issues are being debated today in spite of numerous efforts to reform college sport.

One of the most comprehensive analyses of intercollegiate sport was conducted by the Knight Commission (2001) beginning in the early 1990s. The analysis was initiated because the foundation's board of trustees felt that college athletics was threatening the integrity of higher education. The following problems were cited by the commission as justification for its research:

- In the 1980s, 109 colleges were censured or put on probation by the NCAA. That group included more than half (57 of 106) of the Division I FBS schools.
- Nearly one-third of present and former professional football players said they had accepted illicit payments while in college, and more than half said they saw nothing wrong with doing so.
- Of the 106 institutions included in Division I FBS, 48 had graduation rates under 30 percent for male basketball players, and 19 had the same low rate for football players.

These days, it seems that a new scandal erupts in a big-time sport program nearly every month. Football and men's basketball are the magnets for most of the scrutiny—and deservedly so. They are the big-money sports, and temptations loom large for the athletes, coaches, and administrators involved in them.

The work of the Knight Commission—an independent group of college presidents, university trustees, and former collegiate athletes—has continued, and the effect of that work is ongoing. Various reports on their continuing studies have been widely circulated in the media and pressed into the hands of college presidents and boards of trustees. Essentially, the Knight Commission advocated a one-plus-three model for reform that requires presidential control directed toward academic integrity, financial integrity, and independent certification that universities are meeting the standards set for athletic programs. The commission's view was that reform of college sport will never be achieved to everyone's satisfaction; rather, it is an ongoing process that needs continuous work.

Although the Knight Commission has no formal authority, by 2003 the NCAA had adopted almost two-thirds of its initial recommendations. Most notable was the overhaul of the governance structure of the NCAA, which put college presidents rather than athletic directors in charge. That way, if reform initiatives failed, it would be patently clear who should shoulder the blame.

However, in spite of the rule changes, the NCAA's enforcement efforts, and the leadership of college presidents, the Knight Commission concluded that the threat of college athletics operating without supervision or accountability to university leaders has increased rather than diminished. The commission calls on all members of the higher education community to unite in addressing the problems and cleaning up college athletics. The commission continues to monitor the troubling issues in collegiate sports and advocate for policies that are consistent with the universities' educational missions.

One reformist group that has taken up the gauntlet is the Drake Group (TDG). Based at Drake University in Iowa, TDG is an alliance of college faculty members at various institutions who propose seven reforms (Drake Group 2009):

1. Require that athletes maintain a cumulative 2.0 grade point average each semester.
2. Institute a one-year residency requirement before an athlete can participate in college athletics (in other words, no first-year eligibility).
3. Replace one-year renewable scholarships with need-based financial aid or multiyear athletic scholarships that extend to graduation (five years maximum).
4. Establish university policies that emphasize the importance of class attendance for all students and ensure that the scheduling of athletic contests does not conflict with class attendance.

5. Retire the term "student-athlete."
6. Make the location and control of academic counseling and support services for athletes the same as for all students.
7. Ensure that universities provide accountability of trustees, administrators, and faculty by public disclosure of such things as a student's academic major, academic adviser, courses listed by academic major, general education requirements, electives, grade point average, and instructor.

TDG has spent relatively little time working on college campuses to mobilize faculty members; instead, it has spent much of its time and resources lobbying members of Congress, pursuing court cases in support of whistleblowers, and trying to affect the general public's perception of college athletics.

A different organization, the Coalition on Intercollegiate Athletics (COIA), pursues aims similar to those of TDG but takes a much different approach. COIA is an alliance of 52 Division I FBS university faculty senates dedicated to reforming collegiate sport. Unlike TDG, COIA has worked closely with the NCAA and other college establishment groups to promote reform from *within* the college athletics family.

As a result of continual pressure from faculty groups, legislators, and the public, the NCAA (2014c) has adopted some reforms to raise academic eligibility standards for athletes. Beginning in 2016, prospective athletes must graduate from high school, complete 16 core courses, earn at least a 2.3 grade-point average, and earn a combined SAT or ACT score that matches their core-course GPA on the sliding scale. The scale allows high SAT or ACT scores to offset a lower GPA and vice versa.

The substantial media coverage of issues related to college sport in recent years has brought cries for college sport reform *now*. Indeed, sometimes it seems that the bad news just keeps coming—for example, the child-abuse scandal at Penn State University; similar allegations at Syracuse; recruiting violations and impermissible benefits to players at Ohio State University and the University of Miami; recruiting violations and academic fraud at the University of North Carolina at Chapel Hill; and illegal payments at the University of Southern California. Some critics assert that only a major overhaul of the current system can solve the problem, and even current NCAA president Mark Emmert concedes that significant changes are likely.

Typically, those clamoring for change have come from outside the system. But in 2013, players inside the system began to raise their own voices in favor of reform. Their beef with the current system can be boiled down to issues of self-interest. First, they believe that they deserve a share of the money they earn for their coaches and universities, which often treat them as unskilled workers who deserve no compensation beyond their scholarships. You might argue that scholarships ought to be enough, since the NCAA (2013f) calculates that each scholarship athlete represents an investment by the university of $105,000 per year in Division I FBS. However, for players from low-economic backgrounds, a mere stipend for spending money would represent a large step forward in recognizing their role in filling university coffers.

Second, the issue of traumatic brain injury that has cast a pall over the National Football League has spilled over to college football. Public attention is increasingly focused on the possible risk to long-term health that players face every time they strap on a helmet. Players themselves believe there is a need for immediate reforms, including guaranteed scholarships for athletes permanently injured while participating in college sport (Bishop 2013).

Longtime observers of college sport think change is inevitable, but the question is whether it will involve fundamental reform or just window dressing? Radical change would call for college sport to eschew the gobs of money it currently brings in and return to the ideal of amateur sport. That is unlikely to happen, simply because there is too much money at stake for universities and for the television networks that depend on the programming.

But what if the courts ruled that the use of athletes' likeness to advertise the college sport product makes college players professionals rather than amateurs? Furthermore, it could be ruled that athletes must be paid a reasonable wage and benefits. Or perhaps a court will rule that the NCAA has consistently violated both the spirit and letter of Title IX, which mandates equal treatment of men and women. Each of these possible scenarios might force meaningful change, but unless pressure comes from outside of the college sport establishment, the more likely outcome is a set of minor adjustments that enable the continuation of business as usual (Lederman 2012).

College as a Training Ground for Professional Athletes

Undoubtedly, one of the major factors affecting the academic performance and graduation rates of athletes in Division I FBS and FCS universities is the simple fact that some athletes have little or no interest or ability in school. Their motivation for going to college is to continue their training in order to become a professional athlete, and colleges offer the next step of training at no charge.

Indeed, Division I FBS college teams function like a minor league or developmental league for professional sport in both football and men's basketball—the two biggest revenue-producing sports. Neither the National Basketball Association nor the NFL has a player development system of its own. Instead, virtually all of their player development occurs at the collegiate level, at no expense to them; neither professional league contributes a penny to college basketball or football. In this way, these two sports are unlike baseball, which has had its own minor league system for development of young players for many years (though the number of minor league teams has declined in recent years).

Unfortunately, the odds are very long for an athlete trying to make it from high school to a top-level college and then to the professional ranks (see table 8.4).

For example, of the roughly 500,000 boys and 500,000 girls who play high school basketball, only about 5,000 boys and 5,000 girls will play at a Division I institution. Those 5,000 boys will vie for 350 roster spots in NBA professional basketball, and the 5,000 girls will duke it out for only 168 professional spots in the WNBA. Of course, the competition also includes seasoned veterans who are already there.

The sad fact is, many young people, particularly from lower socioeconomic backgrounds, pin their hopes on a successful career as a professional athlete. When that dream doesn't materialize, their absence of preparation for life through academics catches up with them. If they have only limited skills and no college degree, their options are severely limited. We look more closely at this issue in chapter 14.

Social Issues and College Athletics

College athletic programs face constant scrutiny regarding numerous social issues, including the following (Splitt 2004):

- Many schools use different admission standards for athletes than for other applicants. Although athletes must meet certain minimum requirements, coaches at all types of institution (including Ivy League schools) can often recommend admission for a limited number of athletes who meet minimum standards but fall below the average of other students who are offered admission. In fact, it has become clear in recent years that more than one university has accepted prospective athletes in spite of reading levels below those of a fifth grader (Ganim and Sayers 2014).

TABLE 8.4 Professional Career Probability

	Men's basketball	Women's basketball	Football	Baseball	Men's soccer	Men's ice hockey
High school to NCAA	3.3	3.7	6.5	6.8	5.7	11.3
NCAA to professional	1.2	0.9	1.6	9.4	1.9	0.8
High school to professional	0.03	0.03	0.08	0.5	0.09	0.07

Numbers indicate estimated percentage of athletes moving from one level to the next.

Data from National Collegiate Athletic Association 2013e.

- The recruiting practices used to attract athletes to big-time programs include lavish entertainment, parties, escorts, cash payments, and other questionable activities. According to recent information from the NCAA Division I Committee on Infractions, more than 44 percent of FBS universities (53 of 120) were sanctioned for recruiting violations between 2001 and 2011. The top violators were Arizona State and Southern Methodist, with nine and eight violations respectively. Nine schools tied with seven violations each: Auburn, UC Berkeley, Florida State, Memphis, Minnesota, Oklahoma, Texas A&M, Wichita State, and Wisconsin (Football Educator 2014).
- Once student-athletes are on campus, some schools continue to provide them with improper benefits. For example, the University of Miami is still recovering from revelations of years of impermissible benefits given to athletes by athletic booster Nevin Shapiro, who is currently in prison for masterminding a $930 million Ponzi scheme unrelated to his involvement with Miami athletes. Shapiro admitted that he gave money, cars, yacht trips, jewelry, televisions, and other gifts to more than 72 athletes between 2002 and 2010. He also claimed that he paid for nightclub outings, sex parties, lavish restaurant meals, and an abortion for a woman impregnated by a player (Fox Sports 2014).
- Perhaps the biggest recent scandal in college sport was revealed by the University of North Carolina, a large state school with an enviable academic reputation. For 18 years, advisors funneled thousands of students into fake "paper classes" to improve their grade point averages and keep them eligible. According to a scathing independent report released in October 2014 after an eight-month investigation, at least 3,100 students (and likely many more) took the classes, which were primarily housed in the department of African American studies (Ganim and Sayers 2014).
- Athletes are separated from the social fabric of campus life by living together in designated dormitories, eating together, attending required study sessions as a group, and working out in the weightroom—all to the exclusion of normal college life. As a result, the sense of entitlement that many athletes enjoy is only heightened in college, which may lead young men and women to act in socially unacceptable ways and even break laws.
- Coaches and others may encourage athletes to take minimum academic loads or less rigorous courses in order to ensure their eligibility.
- There are too few female administrators and coaches in women's college sport.
- There are too few coaches from minority groups, except at historically black colleges.
- Athletes' class attendance is often spotty due to frequent or sustained travel for competition.
- Athletic programs face a constant battle to meet Title IX requirements and thus ensure equal opportunity for sport participation among both men and women.
- Sport events are often used by students as opportunities for binge drinking, wild parties, and other rowdy behavior. When a team plays in a big game—win or lose—it is not uncommon for students to get out of control on the field or in the community.

All of these issues have been engaged by the NCAA, by various athletic conferences, and by individual schools. Some progress has been made, but vigilance must be continued in order to prevent abuses.

Equity Between Men's and Women's Sport

The rise in women's opportunities since the passage of Title IX in 1972 has still not resulted in equality between men and women. Fewer women than men participate in college sport, and advocates for women contend that the imbalance does not result from women simply choosing not to play. Despite the fact that female participation in sport keeps rising—and now stands at an all-time high in both high school and college—men gained 5,526 more intercollegiate sport opportunities over the ten-year period between 2002 to 2012 (A. Wilson 2012).

At the same time, one unintended consequence of Title IX enforcement is that many colleges have dropped men's sports that don't produce revenue in order to beef up their offerings for women.

These cancellations—which, for example, have affected men's programs in wrestling, swimming, and tennis—have raised the hackles of athletes, alumni, coaches, and sport-specific governing bodies. Moreover, in some Olympic sports, colleges provided the coaching and training for top athletes; therefore, the loss of these programs hurts U.S. prospects in international competition.

As of 2010–2011, females accounted for an average of 54 percent of the student body across all NCAA divisions and males for 46 percent. Thus, there is an 11 percent gap between the average percentage of women college students and their percentage of college athletes. In Division I schools, the percentage of *athletes* still favored men; in fact, among athletes, the numbers were exactly reversed (54 percent male and 46 percent female)—a difference of 8 percentage points between women's proportion of the Division I athletes. In Divisions II and III, the difference was even more pronounced: 20 percentage points in Division II and 18 percentage points in Division III.

In 2010–2011, women enjoyed a net gain of 113 college teams as compared with 112 for men. However, more women's teams were dropped (69) than men's (59), which seems odd considering that women are significantly underrepresented in college sport. Perhaps even more striking, in Division I, a comparison of median expenses found that FBS institutions spent two and a half times more money on their men's programs than on their women's programs. This difference is primarily due to the overall costs of football for FBS schools. When all Division I schools compared overall spending on men's and women's sport, male sports showed an advantage of 20 percent in spending. The difference in the other two divisions still favored male sports by 14 percent in Division II, and 16 percent in Division III (A. Wilson 2012).

The crux of the matter is football, which requires a huge number of scholarships and also involves other sizable expenses. These costs make football difficult to offset in women's sport programs. Division I FBS institutions are allowed 85 full scholarships for football, and coaches say they need every one of them due to potential injuries during the season. But those 85 scholarships must be offset in other sports for women, and that has proven to be a major challenge. Many colleges claim that they offer sport teams for women but cannot fill them. Some athletic leaders contend that if football were simply left out of the equation in enforcing Title IX, the sport opportunities would be quite comparable. Of course, only about 100 of the roughly 1,200 colleges sponsor big-time football, and only half of those make money for the institution.

The process of integrating equal opportunity for women into college athletics is long and slow, and no easy solution is in sight. However, as society as a whole changes, gradual changes may also be forced in sport due to public pressure, legal battles, and changing expectations for girls—starting in youth sport and continuing through high school and college sport.

Issues for Discussion and Possible Changes in College Sport

Changes in college athletics have been called for since 1929 when the Carnegie Report on Big Ten athletics was published in the *Chicago Tribune* (Splitt 2004). In fact, many changes have been made over the years. Enforcement by the NCAA has been strengthened, and college coaches are now required to understand and abide by prescribed rules when they are hired. However, faced with intense pressure to succeed, some coaches ignore the rules or bend them, especially when they are encouraged to do so by alumni or athletic boosters.

The infractions and other failures of athletic programs and of individual athletes make headlines in the sport pages and elicit appropriate hand-wringing by college officials, coaches, and sportswriters. Yet the abuses continue. Perhaps the solution lies not in setting more rules or stepping up enforcement but in reevaluating the role of college athletics, redefining the role of sport in an educational setting, and modifying policies to reflect that refocused role. Of course, the money at stake is enormous; as we have seen, big-time college sport—particularly in football and basketball—is big business. Imagine the pressure that will be exerted on those who suggest changes that might affect the status quo.

Here are some of the most compelling issues now faced by college sport. Consider them yourself and then discuss with your classmates the possible changes that could be made. If you were to prioritize the possible changes, which ones would rank highest on your list? Would you start with the most difficult problems, or with smaller issues that hold promise for change in the shorter term?

How do collegiate athletic programs ensure that female athletes receive equality in athletic opportunities, funding, and resources without hindering opportunities for male athletes?

- *Money.* Supporting college athletic teams is expensive, and it seems that many institutions are operating their athletic department as a corporate business rather than as an educational endeavor. Decisions are often made with the bottom line in mind rather than the welfare of athletes.
- *Gender equity.* Although females outnumber males on college campuses (54 percent to 46 percent), male athletes outnumber female athletes (54 percent to 46 percent). In terms of dollar allocation, the scales tip more heavily toward males; for example, at Division I schools, females receive only 41 percent of money spent on head coaches, 36 percent of money spent on recruiting, and 40 percent of overall athletic funding. Most of the disparity can be attributed to the financial demands of men's football, though at the higher levels that program also generates the bulk of the revenue (Dusenbery and Lee 2012). Overall, 40 years after the adoption of Title IX, equality has yet to be achieved in providing college sport opportunity for males and females.
- *Negative effect on academics.* Particularly in big-time programs, athletes are expected to put athletic performance first. The school dropout and graduation rates in men's football and basketball programs are well above (dropout) and below (graduation) the general student rates.
- *Racial bias.* Black athletes are often recruited for their ability to earn money and fame for the institution. However, they may be unprepared academically for college, and little effort is made to remedy that problem. Some critics accuse college athletic programs of simply using black athletes and then discarding them before graduation.
- *Athletes' rights.* Most athletic departments keep a close rein on athletes by limiting their free time and expecting them to per-

form for the university almost as professionals—but without the usual financial rewards.

- *Conflict with educational goals.* Although athletic departments extol the virtues of sport for building character, independence, good decision making, and mental toughness, their practices and policies often stunt the development of these traits in athletes.

Athletes are expected to follow arbitrary rules and sacrifice their individual growth for the welfare of the team. While these practices may build character in some sense, perhaps the military is a more appropriate place than a college campus to learn these life lessons.

You may want to add issues to this list based on your own research and experience. In any case, the question raised for all of us is this: What can we do about these problems? Take some time to discuss possible solutions with your classmates and with athletes, coaches, and administrators.

Chapter Summary

This chapter addresses sport programs sponsored by high schools and universities. The major question considered at both levels is whether athletics is compatible with the educational goals of the sponsoring institutions.

Evidence from research shows both positive and negative influences of athletics on schools as a whole, on school social structure, and on athletes themselves. Key issues are presented in the chapter in the hope that solutions can be found to preserve the best aspects of school-sponsored sport and mitigate the negative ones.

Over the past 25 years, participation has increased in both high school and college athletics, primarily due to a dramatic rise in participation by female athletes as a result of Title IX. Although opportunities for males and females are not yet equitable, they have moved significantly in that direction. As a result of new opportunities for girls, new problems have arisen, mostly centered on funding women's sport without paring back men's sport.

The chapter also examines the issue of financial support for school-based sport from a number of angles. In high school, even though the proportion of the total budget allocated to sport is modest, sport is often one of the first activities to be cut when schools face a budget crisis. The trend toward increasing revenue by charging user fees for sport participation threatens to put the sport experience out of reach for many students who come from a modest economic background.

College sport is considered in the chapter according to level of competition. The problems and publicity that make the sport pages typically involve abuses, cheating, and behavioral problems among athletes in Division I programs that are operated essentially as businesses. Most collegiate athletic programs operate at a more modest level, suffer fewer problems of abuse, and more closely approximate the educational experience that they purport to provide. However, those same schools wrestle with budget issues, gender equity, and racial imbalances.

At both the high school and college levels, the myth of the dumb jock has been discredited, though there are warning signs that some institutions encourage some athletes to emphasize athletic participation while allowing their academic efforts to lag behind. Socially, athletes are much admired by their peers, and their egos are sometimes inflated by adulation and praise from peers, coaches, and administrators. At some schools, the jock culture has become exclusionary and causes splits within the student body.

On balance, athletics in the educational setting are worth saving if educators and the public set clear goals, establish limits, and enforce standards for operation of sport programs within an agreed-upon framework and philosophy. Changes are likely to occur gradually and to reflect societal trends, including higher expectations from the educational system to provide more rigorous learning measured by higher standards for performance, elimination of racial and gender bias, and escalation of the costs of sponsoring athletic teams through university budgets.

STUDENT OUTCOMES

After reading this chapter, you will know the following:

- How and why sport has expanded globally
- How U.S. sport, the Olympic Games, and nationalism affect worldwide sport
- How the media affect global sport expansion
- The roles of athletes and coaches as migrant workers in the sport world
- How sport affects the world at large

International Sport

International Sport

The interplay between sport and society is magnified when we look at it globally rather than restrict our view to the United States. Does sport help shape societies around the world, or does it simply reflect the societies that have evolved? Consider that in the past 100 years, the modern Olympic Games have become the most significant worldwide athletic competition, embraced by virtually every nation in terms of popular interest, financial investment, and the fielding of a team of athletes. At the same time, soccer (or football, as it is called worldwide) dominates the world as the most popular game, both for participants and for spectators. Sports invented in the United States—such as baseball and football—have also grown into multibillion-dollar businesses at home but have yet to make a significant worldwide impact in either participation or spectatorship. Our American game of basketball has a strong foothold worldwide at all levels of competition, especially in China and Eastern Europe.

Functionalist theorists would point out the unifying trends that sport can bring to all cultures by promoting the "modern" ideals of industrialism and capitalism, thus improving the status of less developed nations. One example of this process would be the inclusion of opportunities for women and girls to play and watch sport in cultures where they have traditionally been excluded because of religious or cultural tradition. On the other hand, those who lean toward critical theories of sport would resist the movement toward one restrictive view of the value of sport in affecting culture. They would argue that citizens in developing countries need to integrate sport into their culture in a way that enhances the quality of life for their citizens as people, rather than exploit them as pawns in a capitalistic society.

Thus far, this book has focused mostly on sport in North America, particularly in the United States, but it would be a mistake not to consider the international role of sport. For one thing, competition between athletes from different countries has pushed every athlete to improve his or her performance. In addition, the media revolution allows us to follow sport around the world and promotes specific sports in countries where they were once unknown. More generally, sport-related international travel by athletes, coaches, and others helps us learn about and appreciate diverse cultures and forge ways of working together toward common goals.

As our world changes, it seems to shrink through technological connections and economic and political interdependence. As part of the world, sport reflects and often stimulates our increasing globalization. Here are some reasons for this trend in sport:

- The media explosion that connects countries through the Internet, television, film, satellite transmission, newspapers, and magazines
- The marketing and retailing of sport equipment, clothing, shoes, and casual wear across international boundaries
- The migration from country to country of athletes, coaches, officials, and sport administrators
- The exchange of values reflecting various cultures, attitudes toward competition, personal achievement, and socialization

Globalization of Modern Sport

Many athletic traditions practiced today originated with the ancient Greeks. In fact, most of the terms that we use to refer to sport come from Greek words—for example *athlos*, from which *athletics* is derived. Other words rooted in Greek include *gymnasium*, *stadium*, and *pentathlon*. But perhaps the most important contribution of ancient Greece to modern sport was the sheer fact of incorporating sport into its culture—a culture that has shaped much of Western thought (Spears and Swanson 1978).

Although modern sport is commonly traced back to the Greeks, Great Britain also had a huge hand in increasing the global popularity of sport. Great Britain established colonies in Africa, India, Singapore, Hong Kong, Australia, Canada, and the United States. As the saying goes, during the height of Great Britain's influence in the nineteenth and early twentieth centuries, the sun never set on the British Empire; indeed, the countries of the Empire accounted for a quarter of the world's population. British exports to these colonies included British language, customs, education systems, and law. As a result, each country belonging to the British Commonwealth was introduced to traditional English sports, and its citizens were encouraged to participate in sport as part of the preferred way of life. Competitions held within the British colonies rewarded skilled athletes to further their ambition in athletic competition under the British flag (Maguire et al. 2002).

During the seventeenth and eighteenth centuries, the British developed the popular pastimes of the privileged few—such as cricket, fox hunting, horse racing, and boxing—into sports and spread them to their colonies. During the nineteenth century, soccer, rugby, tennis, and track and field emerged as the next wave of popular sports. In the twentieth century, the sport system of the British Empire emerged as the dominant structure in worldwide sport competition. This system was founded on certain key elements: sport and games, highly skilled performers, and popularity among both participants and spectators (Elias and Dunning 1986).

In addition, **nationalism** helped develop sport in countries whose popular sports were strongly rooted in their culture; it also stoked the competitive fires between nations seeking to demonstrate the athletic superiority of their citizens. Nations established sport competitions to promote their national spirit and pride. Geography influenced the national sports adopted by various countries, as colder-climate countries naturally gravitated

The power of the Norwegian 30K cross-country team can be attributed partially to the geography of its home country.

toward winter sports and moderate-climate countries embraced warm-weather sports. Indoor sport arenas were constructed in more developed countries with a wider economic base and thus encouraged the growth of sports that are typically contested indoors.

Other countries also exerted some international influence. For example, the Germans, Swedes, and Danish influenced gymnastics, and Norway helped develop winter sports, such as skating and skiing. However, no country influenced modern sport as much as Great Britain did through its worldwide network of colonies and territories. Wherever the British went, they brought their sports and games, which took root along with their government, law, and culture (Maguire 1999).

When the United States emerged as a world power, U.S. sports also began creeping onto the world stage. Football, baseball, basketball, volleyball, and lacrosse were uniquely American, and professional ice hockey flourished in Canada and then spread to the United States. Interchange between athletes, coaches, and officials of these sports and of the traditional English sports promoted the globalization of both U.S. and English sports.

Moreover, the influence of Western culture on world sport mirrored the political and economic dominance of the West. Similarly, as the Communist world grew in importance, so did its influence on worldwide sport. During the Cold War years, Communist countries poured resources into developing high-performance athletes who captured global attention. Their governments claimed that their athletes' success was rooted in their culture and political philosophy. Of course, Western countries fought back to prove the superiority of their way of life.

Worldwide sport has been influenced the least by Islamic and African countries, generally because sport has been incompatible with either their culture, economic resources, religion, or attitudes toward gender roles. Still, efforts by international sport bodies to introduce sport in these countries have seen slow growth and isolated pockets of success. For instance, track stars from Kenya and Ethiopia provide examples of a changing view of sport in Africa. In another example, Saudi Arabia shocked the world in 2012 by entering a female track star in Olympic competition—the first appearance for any woman representing Saudi Arabia. In addition, soccer has grown significantly in some African countries, and only Europe and South America have had more teams contending for the World Cup in recent years. In 2014, however, Algeria was the only African nation ranked in the top 20 by the International Federation of Association Football (2014c).

In the last 25 years, the balance of power in worldwide sport has begun to shift. For one thing, England had faded from contention on the international stage until it served as host country for the 2012 Olympics and finished fourth in overall medal count by earning 65 medals. The return of the Summer Games to London marked the third time that Great Britain had hosted the games—the most of any country. It first hosted the Games in 1908, when it won three times as many medals as the United States, which finished second in the medal count. After the Games were cancelled in 1944 due to World War II, Britain hosted again in 1948.

Nowadays, however, African, Asian, and South American countries have begun to dominate their former British mentors in sports including soccer, cricket, table tennis, and track and field. In 2016, Rio de Janeiro, Brazil, will host the Summer Olympic Games, thus becoming the first South American (and the first Portuguese-speaking) city to host the Olympics. Pacific Rim countries have also emerged as a formidable force—and a fertile ground for sport development—due to their population size, economic influence, and rising political power.

In one striking example of this development, the selection of Beijing, China, as host of the 2008 Olympic Games was a remarkable departure from the norm. The selection was controversial, both because of China's history of Communism and because many people question China's record on human rights. Those concerns were balanced by recognition that China is now a world power—home to nearly 20 percent of the world's population—and a huge engine in the world economy. In addition, the television broadcast rights were attractive, and advertisers and sponsors eagerly entered what was a relatively new market for them.

By almost any yardstick, the Beijing Olympics were a spectacular success. In spite of the immense pressure of a worldwide audience, the local organizing authorities dealt with every contingency in an efficient and effective manner. Security was airtight, events were staged in modernistic venues, arrangements for athletes and attendees were top rate, and even the feared smog and pollution was controlled during the Games.

Perhaps the major impact of these Games will be the growing reputation of China as a sporting nation. China's athletes won 51 gold medals, the highest total of any nation in history and well ahead of the 36 golds won by the second-place finisher, the United States. When all medals were counted, the United States edged out China by a margin of 110 to 100. The message was clear: China takes sport seriously and promises to contend on the world stage for years to come.

Global Consumption of Sport

The worldwide emergence of companies such as Nike, Adidas, Puma, and Reebok has modified attitudes toward world sport consumers. For one thing, the manufacturing of sport equipment—such as soccer shoes, balls, tennis rackets, and uniforms—has become an international endeavor. Nike pushed the envelope by paying workers in developing countries only 20 to 30 cents an hour in order to produce sport clothing (Kidd and Donnelly 2000).

At the same time, China, Indonesia, Thailand, and South Korea virtually cornered the market on manufacturing by supplying cheap labor that enabled production at a fraction of the cost in other countries. Multinational companies rushed to have their products made in these factories, added their cost markups, and sold their goods in developed countries at premium prices (Kidd and Donnelly 2000). As information leaked about the exploitation of these workers—especially children—Nike and other companies modified their practices to mitigate the resulting international outrage.

From athletic shoes to casual wear, sport clothing has become a wardrobe staple in many societies. Starting with the young, people have taken to wearing athletic clothing on almost any occasion. Now it's not uncommon to see retirees wearing tracksuits in airports, malls, or anywhere else in public. The casual-dress industry has captured the clothing market by focusing on comfort and encouraging a lifestyle that is relaxed yet active.

In particular, the effect of sport shoes on the business of sport makes for a fascinating story. It began with two brothers, Adi and Rudi Dassler, who started their shoe business in their mother's laundry room in the little town of Herzogenaurach, Germany, in the 1920s. Who could have predicted that their efforts would set off a chain of events leading eventually to an explosion in the marketing and sale of sport shoes? That, however, is exactly what happened over the next 50 years, thus changing the face of the sporting world forever.

The coming-out party for the Dassler brothers took place at the 1936 Olympic Games held in Berlin just after Adolf Hitler had risen to power. The sport explosion in Germany was driven by Hitler's belief in the power of sport to mold young German men into a dominating army. The Dassler boys capitalized by putting their shoes on the feet of German athletes—and on the feet of the Games' ultimate hero, U.S. track and field athlete Jesse Owens, who won four gold medals.

ACTIVITY TIME-OUT

What About Winter Sports?

Lest we forgot the popularity of winter sports, consider that the Winter Olympic Games is hugely popular worldwide and draws formidable television audiences. The 2014 Games, hosted in Sochi, Russia, attracted an average prime-time television audience in the United States of 21.4 million over the course of 17 nights (Best 2014). Can you name the top five medal-winning countries for the Sochi Games? Take an informal survey of five friends and see if they do better than you did. Once you have the results, consider the differences between the countries that dominate the Summer Games and those that dominate the Winter Games.

Jesse Owens was one of the first athletes to wear the new Adidas apparel at the 1936 Olympic Games.

The honeymoon was short-lived, as the Dassler brothers soon began a bitter feud and parted ways just as their sport shoe business was exploding. Adi Dassler soon christened his shoes under the brand name Adidas, and Rudi moved across the river to establish his Puma brand. Originally focused on producing "soccer boots," the Adidas and Puma brands soon branched out into track and field. In the years following the fall of the Nazi empire, the two shoe brands battled it out on the soccer pitches of Europe. In 1954, a stunning victory by the German team over the favored Hungarian squad was marked by the use of new all-weather soccer shoes equipped with adjustable cleats—and the Adidas logo.

The next generation of the Dassler family, Adi's son Horst Dassler, made his mark as a 20-year-old at the Olympic Games in Australia in 1954. He masterminded a scheme to have Adidas shoes given out free to Olympic athletes and at the same time blocked the entrance of Puma shoes into the country. Ever since, the practice of giving shoes to world-class athletes as free advertisement has produced a scramble to secure the finest athletes, and the resulting boasting rights, for each brand. Although it was a questionable practice that just skirted the rules for amateur athletes at the time, it has become the custom in the sport world (Smit 2008).

By the time the Olympic Games were staged in Mexico City in 1968, the competition for top athletes to wear certain brands led to under-the-table cash payments to supposedly amateur athletes. Within a few years, actual contracts were forged with top soccer players, led by Puma's landing of the famous Brazilian soccer player Pelé for US$25,000 for the 1970 World Cup in Mexico, another $100,000 for the next four years, and royalties of 10 percent of all Puma shoes sold with his name on them. Before long, famous athletes—including Joe Namath in American football, Walt Frazier and Kareem Abdul-Jabbar in basketball, and Stan Smith in tennis—signed with either Adidas or Puma and thus shattered the dominance of Converse athletic shoes in the United States.

As the sport-shoe battle heated up, both Puma and Adidas suffered setbacks but still grew in both reputation and dominance. Then, in the 1970s, a small-time operation called Blue Ribbon Sports, based in Oregon, began to edge into the American market. Its product was the Nike shoe, a running shoe designed by former coach Bill Bowerman in his kitchen just as the jogging boom swept the United States. The Olympic Games in Los Angeles in 1984 marked the showcasing of the Nike brand, and a few years later Nike signed a young basketball phenom named Michael Jordan for a fee of about $2.5 million to endorse shoes and garments with his name on them. Adidas retaliated by bestowing a similar deal on Patrick Ewing of the New York Knicks, but Ewing's career, though a great one, never matched the influence of Air Jordan's (Smit 2008).

In the late 1970s, while Nike was dominating Adidas and Puma in the United States, yet another fledgling company entered the scene. A small-time entrepreneur in Boston, Paul Fireman, gained the

U.S. rights for Reebok, a British company that had existed since the early 1900s but fallen on hard times. In a prescient move, Fireman looked to the hottest sport market at the time: aerobics. As a result, Reebok exploded from global sales of just US$300,000 in 1980 to $12.8 million by 1983—an unprecedented burst of growth.

The sport shoe industry was changed forever. In response, Adidas purchased Reebok, and Nike absorbed Converse. The four top brands—Nike, Adidas, Puma, and, more recently, Asics—are now set to compete for world dominance. Since 2000, Nike and Adidas have been the top footwear companies, and they currently combine to control 49 percent of the international market and 80 percent of the U.S. market. In the United States, Nike boasts a 60 percent share if one includes its Jordan and Converse brands. Puma accounts for just 7 percent of the world market and 6 percent of the U.S. market (Forbes 2014a).

In some instances, economics may even replace nationalism as the basis for choosing which teams and athletes to support, especially among people who profit from the success of sport clothing companies. For example, Phil Knight, cofounder and longtime president of Nike, admitted after stepping down in December 2004 that he had rooted for sport teams that wore Nike. In fact, rather than cheering for the U.S. team in the 1999 soccer World Cup, Knight had picked his favorite teams by the uniforms they wore. For instance, rather than looking at one match as the United States versus Brazil, he saw it as Adidas versus Nike (Coakley 2004).

The United States Olympic Committee (USOC) accepts money from corporate sponsors to support the training and competition of U.S. athletes. In return, U.S. athletes must wear the logo and warm-up apparel of the chosen USOC sponsor when competing in the Games. This arrangement can lead to sharp conflicts of interest. Imagine the outrage when Nike, which had paid millions to sponsor tennis star Andre Agassi, found out that during the Olympics Agassi would have to shed his Nike attire in favor of the USOC brand.

Corporate sponsors also partially control the televised exposure of international sport. If the sponsors can promote their products by supporting the televising of a sport, then the sport gains terrific exposure in countries where the sponsor wants to advertise its products. On the other hand, if televising a sport does not benefit major sponsors financially, then spectators may have to find other media sources for following an international sport.

Popularity of Various Sports Worldwide

According to IPSOS World Monitor (2002), a French sport research firm, soccer was the most popular sport worldwide in 2002 in both participation and spectatorship. This comes as no surprise to anyone who has traveled the world and seen kids practicing their soccer skills, fields covered with players of all ages, and newspaper and televisions filled with coverage of soccer games. World Cup soccer is the most-watched international sporting event in the world. For the 2010 World Cup finals, held in South Africa, the tournament drew an estimated 111.6 million U.S. viewers—an increase of 22 percent over the 2006 World Cup. In particular, the U.S. loss to Ghana was seen by a total of 19.4 million viewers in a Saturday afternoon time slot.

Total television audience worldwide is difficult to estimate because of the necessary reliance on viewer reports that are less accurate than the standard procedures used in the United States (*New York Post* 2010; Sandomir 2010). Still, it is revealing to compare the worldwide television audience of the 2010 World Cup finals with that of the 2010 Super Bowl in American football. The Super Bowl drew a large audience indeed: 106 million. However, the World Cup championship game, which pitted the Netherlands against Spain, drew an estimated global audience of more than 700 million, thus exceeding the previous largest television audience of 600 million for the opening ceremonies of the 2008 Summer Olympics in Beijing. In addition, soccer's world governing body, the International Federation of Association Football (FIFA), reported that more than 250 million people visited its website during the 31 days of the event—another record shattered.

People living in the United States may find the soccer frenzy puzzling because they are used to American sports. Only in the last 25 years has soccer taken the United States by storm, particularly in the youth market, and it now ranks second only to basketball among U.S. youth (see chapter 6). In Latin America, soccer is an integral part of the culture and boasts huge numbers of participants and spectators, who embrace it with a passion.

The rest of the top 10 most popular sports in the world might surprise you (see table 9.1). The sheer number of people who play or watch a given sport in any country is hugely influenced by the country's population size, sport tradition, climate, and economic status. Bear in mind also that there is no precise way to arrive at these numbers; rather, researchers are forced to rely on samplings of various populations and self-reported estimates provided by sport organizations.

Were you surprised to see that after soccer, cricket and field hockey are the most popular sports in the world? Their high rankings result largely from their status as the unofficial national sports in India, which is home to a population of nearly 1.3 billion people. Both games were brought to India during the British occupation and, along with soccer, have dominated popular sport there. In the United States, field hockey is played mostly by women and girls, and mostly on the two coasts, but in the rest of the world it's a game for both sexes. For years, India dominated the Olympic Games in field hockey, winning eight gold medals, but in the 1970s other nations began to catch up in both training and competitiveness.

Cricket is also a popular sport in former British colonies around the world, but nowhere is it more popular than in India, where it is regarded almost as an unofficial religion. Cricket is played by all social classes and both genders and is hugely popular, both within the country and in international competition. In fact, the Board of Control for Cricket in India (BCCI) is acknowledged as the richest sporting body in the world. More generally, India's influence on worldwide sport popularity is likely to continue, since most analysts predict that by 2050 its population will overtake China to become the world's largest.

One U.S. sport that is growing internationally is basketball, which is now played in professional leagues in Europe, Russia, China, and South America. In addition, an increasing number of players from various countries are now starring in the National Basketball Association (NBA). For example, during the 2013–2014 NBA season, team rosters included 92 international players from 39 countries, led by stars such as Tony Parker and Joakim Noah of France; Pau Gasol, Marc Gasol, and Ricky Rubio of Spain; Dirk Nowitzki of Germany; Manu Ginobili of Argentina;

TABLE 9.1 Most Popular Sports Worldwide

Sport	Spectators and players	Regions
1. Soccer	3.5 billion	Europe, Africa, Asia, United States
2. Cricket	2.5 billion	Asia, Australia, United Kingdom
3. Field hockey	2 billion	Europe, Africa, Asia, Australia
4. Tennis	1 billion	Europe, Asia, United States
5. Volleyball	900 million	United States, Europe, Australia, Asia
6. Table tennis	850 million	Asia, Africa, Europe, United States
7. Baseball	500 million	United States, Japan
8. Golf	450 million	Europe, Asia, United States, Canada
9. Basketball	400 million	United States, Europe
10. American football	400 million	United States, Europe, Asia

These are the most popular sports around the world in terms of playing and watching combined based on several sources.

Reprinted from Topendsports, 2013. Available: www.topendsports.com/world/lists/popular-sport/fans.htm

APPLYING SOCIAL THEORY

Interactionist Theorists and Racism in Soccer

Racism has sparked an alarming number of incidents among soccer spectators, and these incidents threaten to derail the sport's popularity, especially in Europe. In what is often referred to by players and fans alike as "the beautiful game," the ugly underbelly of sport has been revealed by racist chants and displays of Nazi banners in the stands and bananas thrown at black players on the field. In some cases, players have simply exited the field rather than tolerate a racist display (Quijano 2014).

In response to these problems, soccer's world governing body, FIFA, has appointed an anti-racism task force and passed resolutions to deduct points from or issue fines to teams whose fans behave offensively. Yet even those measures seem inadequate to quell the threat of racist demonstrations. Other possible steps include taking away home games or forcing teams to play in empty stadiums, thus foregoing any profit from the sale of tickets for those games.

Take the perspective of an interactionist theorist who upholds the primacy of the worth and rights of individuals—in this case, the athletes on the field. Imagine how these athletes feel when spectators are free to taunt, insult, and intimidate players who are there to entertain the fans and play their best. Given that the sport's administrators and leaders have been unable to solve the problem and reverse the troubling trends at games, what actions could be taken by athletes themselves? Suggest possible solutions from an interactionist point of view.

Al Horford of the Dominican Republic; and Luol Deng of South Sudan.

At the same time, critics of U.S. players point to the playground origin of many players' style of play, a preoccupation with individual play, and a lack of fundamental skills and teamwork. In international competition, U.S. dominance has receded in recent years, and even when so-called American "dream teams" compete internationally, the outcome is still in doubt.

Another U.S. sport that has made international inroads is baseball. In Japan, nine of ten sport spectators watch baseball, and in South Korea that figure is seven of ten. In addition, Central American countries send a steady stream of baseball players to Major League Baseball (MLB), and 30 percent of current MLB players are international athletes.

Most U.S. residents are shocked that American football barely cracks the top 10 in worldwide popularity because the sport so dominates U.S. culture at both the college and professional levels, especially as a spectator sport. Furthermore, we know that the Super Bowl is beamed around the world to huge audiences; however, for most of the world, it is only a curiosity and a once-a-year event. In addition, the fact that few females participate in football cuts the potential participation numbers in half.

Tennis is played in more countries than any other sport except soccer, and it continues to grow in undeveloped nations due to sustained support from the International Tennis Federation. For years, in fact, the Grand Slam tournaments—Wimbledon and the Australian, French, and U.S. Opens—have supported tennis in developing nations. Ironically, athletes from some of those nations emerge to defeat players from the countries that have provided this support.

Because golf, baseball, and tennis appeal to higher economic groups worldwide, they make prime targets for corporate advertisers hoping to reach an audience with discretionary income to spend. Golf attracts older participants and, along with tennis and track and field, relies on an older viewing audience as well. In contrast, soccer and basketball attract a younger population.

U.S. Influence on World Sport

Even as soccer has gained a huge foothold in the United States among youth and students at the high school and college levels, U.S. sports have had their own effect on the rest of the world. Professional leagues thrive in the United States in the sports of American football, baseball, basketball, and ice hockey, and the best players in these sports from around the world come to the United States to compete and test their skills against homegrown U.S. players. At this point, international athletes have significantly affected every U.S. sport except football.

For example, ice hockey in the United States has been dominated for years by Canadians, as well as a few great players from other countries. Similarly, some of Japan's finest baseball athletes have migrated to the United States to share in the wealth generated by MLB. Even though Japanese baseball has lost some of its superstars to MLB, Japanese interest in American baseball skyrockets when one of Japan's players competes in the postseason.

Latin Americans have loved American baseball for years, and the proof of their talent is found in the high percentage of MLB players emerging from Latin America. In 2013, Latinos made up nearly 30 percent of MLB's players, even though they accounted for just 14 percent of the U.S. population (Lapchick 2014). Thus, while Latinos have long made their mark in baseball, their influence on the game has been solidified in recent years by a plethora of Latino talent, including all-star players.

In Little League Baseball, international teams are so successful that organizers divide the competition into two divisions to ensure that U.S. players have a place in the final rounds. Without the divisional approach, U.S. teams would likely be eliminated early in the tournament, which would also greatly reduce potential interest and TV revenue in the United States.

Sports such as tennis that are no longer typical U.S. powerhouses struggle to produce U.S. players who can compete on the world stage. Yet the United States still offers some of the most prestigious tournaments and some of the biggest prize money. Although U.S. tennis has grown significantly in participation over the past 10 years, television viewership in the United States for the U.S. Open championships has steadily fallen. In 1999, when Serena Williams and Andre Agassi claimed the singles titles, the television audience totaled 4.4 million viewers. In 2008, when the

EXPERT'S VIEW

"Grobalization" of U.S. Sport in Latin America

George Ritzer (2004) coined the term *grobalization* by combining *growth* and *globalization* to convey the increasing profit-driven, capitalist development—or "Americanization" or "McDonaldsization"—of sport in other countries. In this process, the indigenous sports of a local culture are replaced by modern corporate and commercialized sport. For example, Major League Baseball has to some extent Americanized baseball in various countries, such as the Dominican Republic, in order to mine inexpensive new talent.

Alan Klein (1991) has written about resistance mounted in the Dominican Republic to MLB's practice of actively developing and recruiting young baseball prospects to play in the United States. Many Dominican people resent MLB's interference with Dominican winter leagues and its luring of their best players to a foreign country. The same conflict is faced by other Latin American nations, including Venezuela, Cuba, and Nicaragua, who feel pride in their homegrown talent only to see top players leave to seek fame and riches in another land. Given MLB's success in developing talent overseas, other major American sport organizations have implemented similar practices. For example, many of the finest basketball players in the world now play in the NBA, while other countries' professional teams are effectively relegated to the minor leagues.

winners were Williams and Roger Federer, the tournament drew only 2.2 million viewers.

The number of U.S. television viewers of tennis has been sorely affected by the fact that only one U.S. male—Andy Roddick in 2003—has won the U.S. Open in recent years. In fact, at one point, Roger Federer of Switzerland won five consecutive men's finals. In 2013, Serena Williams' defeat of Victoria Azarenka in the finals of the U.S. Open was watched by 4.9 million people in the United States, whereas only 2.8 million watched Rafael Nadal defeat Novak Djokovic in the men's final. As in most countries, fans tune in to watch their homegrown heroes.

In golf, the phenomenon of Tiger Woods carried the sport for a number of years even as participation slumped badly. For example, CBS enjoyed an average of 11.9 million viewers in each of Woods' four wins at the Masters Tournament in Augusta, Georgia. When Tiger didn't win, the television audience fell 20 percent to 9.5 million viewers (Weekley 2009). Another analysis showed that from 1996 to 2010, when Woods trailed the leader by five or more shots on the final weekend of a tournament, televisions ratings fell by an average of 10 percent, or 1.2 million viewers (Levenson 2014).

When Woods fell from grace and lost popularity due to behavioral and marital difficulties, golf's popularity took a dramatic downturn, only to recover in 2012–2013 as Woods returned to the tour. Of course, television ratings are also affected by other factors, such as holiday weekends, the popularity of other contenders, the closeness of the leaders' scores in the final round, and the lure of a potential playoff. But as Woods ages and inevitably fades, observers will be curious to see whether another golfer can assume the mantle of "top draw" at major golf events.

Olympic Games

Perhaps no event has promoted sport around the world more than the Olympic Games. The Winter and Summer Games are huge international events that attract enormous audiences from virtually every country. Based on the original Olympic Games born in Athens, Greece, the modern Olympic Games were championed by Baron Pierre de Coubertin in 1896 (Henry and Yeomans 1984). Along with other organizers, Coubertin hoped that athletes competing on a world stage would open up communication between people of all nations, show that friendly competition could be exhilarating, promote understanding of different cultures and traditions, and serve as a model for nations working together. Those lofty goals remain a challenge, though it cannot be disputed that Olympic competition has promoted sport around the world.

The Olympic Games also helped standardize rules for sport competition. For each Olympic sport, a designated international organization determines rules of play, stages world championships, records competitive records, sets drug-testing protocols, and helps conduct Olympic events. National governing bodies in each sport take their cues from the international groups, so that all countries play by the same rules of competition—for example, standards for the field of play, equipment limitations, and even scoring procedures. For more on the Olympic Games, see chapter 10.

Media Effects on the Globalization of Sport

We cannot ignore the media's role in expanding sport worldwide. Indeed, perhaps no other factor has been more influential in spreading sporting events around the world and reducing former geographical and time constraints. As discussed in chapter 5, sport and the media exist in a symbiotic relationship: Sporting events are a staple of the media; on the other hand, the media generate millions of dollars in free publicity for sport products, teams, and athletes. As a result, sport is in the enviable position of being able to count on extensive media coverage without paying advertising fees.

Technological advances have opened up sport on television through satellite broadcasting. The top two U.S. satellite networks, DirecTV and Dish Network, allow viewers to watch sport events from any U.S. city and an increasing number of international sites. For example, people who wish to watch soccer matches played in other countries have immediate real-time access. Pay-per-view options open up a wide world of sporting events for viewers.

The Internet allows us to visit favorite team websites, learn about games and players, and listen to interviews. We can also listen to or watch

IN THE ARENA WITH . . .

China's Remarkable Olympic Journey

Historians around the world were astounded in 2008 when China not only successfully hosted the Olympic Games but also won more gold medals than any other country. For centuries, China has followed its own path and had rarely responded to the outside world. However, as globalization increased around the world—and a renewed spirit of Chinese nationalism arose—China looked to the world of sport as a symbol of its emergence. More generally, as economic revival began to create optimism at home, leaders of China began to peer outward for opportunities to enter the outside world in trade, business, and sport.

In 1932, China sent just one participant to the Los Angeles Olympics, but by 1936 it sponsored a team of 69 athletes. Still, Chinese athletes were no match for the best in the world, and they arrived home with no medals in 1932, 1936, and 1948 (the Olympic Games were cancelled in 1940 and 1944 due to World War II). As a result, China was often referred to as "the sick man of East Asia" in reference to its athletes' relative lack of physical strength and skill. In the 1950s, China reached out to its friends in the Soviet Union and adopted much of that country's model of elite sport training and competition. In this model, the government provided much in the way of financial resources, human resources, and effort; however, the training was brutal, overtraining was common, and the endeavor was only modestly successful.

As the Cold War developed, China was perceived as an enemy of the Western world, and its messy separation from Taiwan caused mainland China to withdraw from the Olympic Games and eventually drop out of the International Olympic Committee (IOC). The effect on developing athletes in China was immediate and widespread. In fact, China did not return to the world stage of sport until an unlikely hero, table tennis player Rong Guotuan, won a world championship in Germany. Rong became a national hero, and within another decade so-called "ping-pong" diplomacy led by Henry Kissinger and Richard Nixon led to exchanges with the United States and China's reentry onto the world's sporting stage.

In 1984, after an absence of more than 20 years, China entered the Olympic Games in Los Angeles and sent a team of 255 athletes who earned 15 gold, 8 silver, and 9 bronze medals. Those results renewed the Chinese spirit to compete in worldwide sport, and, less than 20 years later, China has become a world power in Olympic sport, hosted a successful Olympics, and finished second only to the United States in total number of medals won in both 2008 and 2012 (Jiang 2012).

a game in progress that may not be accessible on television and check the latest scores of games played anywhere in the world. In addition, we can read about sport events within a few hours of their completion in order to see what sportswriters think of the results. We can also share immediate reactions with friends through social networking services (see chapter 5 for more on social networking and sport).

In addition to freely covering sport, the media pay huge amounts for broadcasting rights to events such as the Olympics and National Football League (NFL) games—both of which have worldwide appeal. In fact, worldwide television rights serve as the major source of funding for the Olympic Games, and about half of the total comes from U.S. television rights alone. NBC paid US$820 million to broadcast the Vancouver Winter Games and $1.18 billion for the London Summer Games.

To retain its broadcast rights to the Games, NBC bid on four Olympic Games as a package that included the following elements: $775 million for the 2014 Winter Games in Sochi; $1.22 billion for the 2016 Summer Games in Rio de Janeiro; $963 million for the 2018 Winter Games in PyeongChang, South Korea; and $1.41 billion for the 2020 Summer Games in Tokyo (Hersh 2011). The revenue goes to the International Olympic Committee and the National Olympic Committees that help train and support athletes.

In 2008, the Beijing Games grabbed four of the top ten spots for the year in U.S. television and claimed a 20 percent share of U.S. homes on Tuesday night in prime time. Only American football drew a larger U.S. television audience. In 2010, the Vancouver Olympics amazingly ended *American Idol*'s string of six unbeaten years in audience share on a Wednesday night, when the Games drew 30.1 million U.S. viewers, as compared with only 18.4 million for *Idol* in the same time slot (*Vancouver Sun* 2010). And the 2012 London Games became the most-watched television event in U.S. history by attracting a total audience of 219 million viewers, surpassing the 215 million for the 2008 Beijing Olympics. NBC's Olympic prime-time programming averaged 31.1 million viewers, thus topping the 2008 Beijing Games by 12 percent and the 2004 Athens Games by 26 percent (Kondolojy 2012).

Even so, the NFL may be the most successful sport at attracting U.S. television sponsorship. In 1998, the league secured a $17.6 billion contract with several TV networks to televise its games. As a result, every NFL team received more than $70 million, or what amounts to nearly 65 percent on average of its total revenue (Miller and Associates 2005). By 2014, the NFL earned

The IOC makes huge amounts of money by selling the broadcast rights to televise the Olympic Games. Televising the Games enables sport to reach a global audience.

nearly $7 billion annually from its TV contracts, thus ensuring that each NFL team would receive more than $200 million before the first ticket was sold (Badenhausen 2011). In turn, the television networks sell sponsorship time during their NFL broadcasts to recoup their expenditures on rights fees. With Super Bowl advertising spots going for $3 million to $4 million per 30 seconds, you can see how networks generate their revenue from corporate sponsors.

Events such as the NFL Super Bowl are routinely broadcast around the world to more than 200 countries. That publicity helps spread the popularity of the sport, promotes football players, and increases the sale of NFL merchandise. Due to technological advances such as delayed broadcasting, satellite transmission, and improved product delivery, fans across the globe can share in the drama and excitement of a U.S. sporting event. In 10 countries surveyed by IPSOS World Monitor in 2002, American football ranked third in percentage of viewers, trailing only soccer and baseball, even though it is not even played in 8 of those 10 countries.

On closer inspection, the relationship between television and sport is even more intertwined than it seems at first. Consider the fact that if a sport organization expects to command big bucks for television rights, it must be sensitive to the needs of the broadcasters. As a result, starting times are set to attract the largest audience; rules are modified to create drama; and coaches and athletes are required to make themselves available for interviews before, during, and after the competition.

Naturally, the sports that command the most attention receive the widest TV distribution worldwide. Once networks choose their events, they do everything they can to advertise them and thereby increase their audience. Sharing international competition by networks to other countries ensures viewership from athletes' home countries, and the Olympic Games capitalize on the natural rivalries between fans from opposing nations.

The broadcast of the World Cup has helped popularize soccer in the United States, particularly among women. The success of the U.S. women's team in the 1990s provided role models for girls and encouraged them to explore their own athletic prowess. Similarly, the 2010 World Cup for men seemed to awaken the U.S. public to the importance of soccer worldwide as viewers watched the U.S. team advance into the elimination round of the final 16 countries. Without the media to televise games, the selling of soccer to the U.S. public had progressed slowly and seemed destined to fail.

As the host country for soccer's 2014 World Cup and the 2016 Summer Olympics, Brazil is positioned as the center of sport on the world stage in this decade. Furthermore, as the first South American nation to host the Olympics, Brazil is blazing the trail for other nations that have never successfully won the bidding wars to host the Games.

Television continues to be the most dominant medium for following sport around the world. But wide differences exist between countries, depending on each country's traditions and passion for various events. For example, the proportion of fans who consume televised sport is as high as 90 percent in China but a more modest 70 percent in the United States and 65 percent in France. Fans in Europe and the United States spend an average of four to eight hours per week consuming primarily televised sport, whereas Brazilians watch more than ten hours and Chinese upwards of eleven hours per week (Global Sports Media 2012).

As you might suspect, the most popular sport to watch on television worldwide is soccer, which garners the following percentages of total sports TV viewing time (Nielsen Co 2013b):

Indonesia	74
Russia	73
Malaysia	65
Italy	53
South Africa	52
Spain	51
United Kingdom	38
Germany	35
France	23
Japan	13

You may notice the absence of countries from Latin America in this group because they simply were not included in this particular study. However, earlier studies have shown that at least six countries in Latin America can boast of a high percentage of the population who watch televised soccer regularly. Those countries were led by Brazil (85 percent); the others, all of whom stood at 72 percent or higher, were Costa Rica, Guatemala, El Salvador, Honduras, and Argentina (Zona Latina 1998).

In some other countries, favorite sports may attract nearly 75 percent of the population to watch on television—for example, World Cup cross-country skiing in Norway, World Cup ice hockey in Sweden. In fact, in Denmark, 80 percent watched the men's handball 2013 championships when Denmark defeated Croatia in the semifinals, and in Finland 83 percent of the population in 2012 tuned in to World Cup ice hockey to watch the Finns compete in the bronze medal game, which they lost to the Czechs 3-2. In Great Britain, which is passionate about soccer, the Wimbledon tennis championships drew 71 percent to cheer on countryman Andy Murray, who defeated Novak Djokovic for the title in 2013 (Nielsen 2013b).

As countries such as China, Japan, and Mexico increase their participation in the global economy, their increase in sport involvement seems to indicate greater emphasis on personal lifestyle and leisure. In contrast, the growth potential appears smaller in developed countries, such as the United Kingdom and the United States, because the general population is already more satisfied with its sport involvement, which may in fact have reached its peak. This contrast is why the marketing of sport to emerging new markets is so critical to continued growth in sport popularity and revenue.

Sports that are truly international at the professional level—such as golf and tennis—rely on television coverage because their events are staged in different parts of the world every week. In addition, the top competitors represent many nationalities, and interest varies around the world depending on the performance of favorite players. For example, the four major world championships in professional tennis—referred to as the Grand Slam tournaments—are played yearly in Australia, France, England, and the United States. Worldwide coverage is critical to their success, and the television contracts involve complicated multinational agreements.

The 1936 Olympics in Germany were used by Adolf Hitler to promote his vision of nationalism.

Nationalism Versus Economics

During the middle of the 20th century, international sport competition was buoyed by strong feelings of nationalism. At least since Adolf Hitler's tragic effort to create a super race in Germany—and the resulting nationalistic tenor of the 1936 Olympic Games staged in Berlin—countries around the world have used sport as a rallying cry for patriotism. Perhaps more than any other event, the Olympic Games have thrived on the inherent nationalism built into its structure, publicity, and team medal counts.

During the rise of Communism and the Cold War between the West and the Soviet Union, athletic competition was about more than who had the best athletes. Fueled by rhetoric from sport leaders and politicians, many people began to see sport victories as validation of their society, whether democratic or Communist. In this atmosphere, when high-profile athletes won medals at the Olympic Games, their country burst with pride at the confirmation of their political ideology. The medals won by each country were totaled, and a winning nation was declared. That tradition faded significantly with the change in government in the Soviet Union, but country-specific medal counts still grab some attention. Of course, winning gold medals in worldwide competition depends on many factors, including national sport traditions, economics, and support for athlete development.

As the Cold War faded and tensions eased between the West and the former Communist countries in Eastern Europe, sport attitudes also changed. The nationalistic model began to be replaced by an **economic model** in the Olympics and in most other international sport events. Nowadays, the key factor in selecting a site for the Olympics is the financial package offered to support the Games, including the construction of multimillion-dollar athletic venues and transportation infrastructure. As a result, the process of choosing a site takes years; for example, the 2020 Summer Olympics were awarded to Tokyo in September 2013 after the IOC vetted bids from around the world. The process takes about 10 years from the beginning of a proposal to the start of the Games.

Other key factors include a city's potential attractiveness to corporate sponsors and the proposed television package for broadcasting the Games. Consider, for example, the staging of the 1996 Olympic Games in Atlanta, the home of Coca-Cola. Corporate sponsors such as Coca-Cola routinely seize the opportunity to sell their products around the world by advertising through the Olympic Games. In recent years, McDonald's has provided food in the Olympic Village for athletes; another major sponsor is Mars, whose goal is to sell snacks and candy bars to the sporting public.

The economic model for international sport can also be illustrated by the fact that Roots, a Canadian clothing company, outfitted the 2004 U.S. Olympic team with warm-ups through a corporate sponsorship. Most sponsors of sporting events are large multinational corporations dedicated to growing their business in as many markets as possible. Rather than be seen as provincial, these corporations seek to portray a global image. Because their sponsorship dollars have fueled the rapid economic expansion in sport, the sporting world depends on them to survive as a business.

Athletes and Coaches as Migrant Workers

People who make their living from sport include athletes, coaches, officials, agents, and organization officials and staff. Depending on the sport, they may travel around the globe as a natural part of their employment. Most often, they are employed by specific sport organizations that rely on international exposure and operation. Of course, sports that are indigenous to one country or region of the world do not rely on international operation.

Athletes tend to seek the highest level of competition and coaching in order to maximize their talent and earning power. Of course, they are likely to begin sport instruction near their home, but as they progress they often travel in order to secure specialized coaching and train with other elite athletes. If their country offers a national program in their sport, they may attend a special school that combines training with academic education. Athletes who live in a place where their sport is not popular or available may seek training in another country.

Athletes who train in the United States often become comfortable living here and eventually make it their home base. This is also true for their coaches, who travel with them. In some sports, such as tennis and golf, world tours offer the only

POP CULTURE

Ronaldo: The World's Most Marketable Athlete

Cristiano Ronaldo, soccer player for Real Madrid, is one of the most expensive athletes in the world. In addition to his contract with the Spanish club, Ronaldo is eminently marketable as a popular athlete in the prime of his career. His earnings in 2012 surpassed US$42 million, including his salary and endorsements, thus putting him among the top sport earners in the world (Badenhausen 2012a).

Ronaldo is so marketable in part because he plays the world's most popular sport, which appeals to consumers in Asia, Europe, and the Americas. He has also been one of the two or three best players in his sport during the past few years, and he plays for a team that is consistently among the world's best. In addition, he is blessed with a physique that allows him to model Armani underwear and a compelling personality that inspires loyalty (and at times attracts criticism). His personal life is a gossip magnet, and his romantic interests fuel constant media speculation. He also has the most Facebook fans of any athlete (more than 45 million) and more than 11 million Twitter followers (Badenhausen 2012a).

way to make a living, and both athletes and coaches spend a great deal of time on the road. They move from city to city almost every week and live in hotels and out of suitcases. The cultural experience is unparalleled, and the excitement of visiting great cities on every continent is exhilarating.

However, the endless travel and lack of contact with family and friends can lead to loneliness. Such conditions make it difficult to maintain friendships outside of the sport, and developing romantic relationships can pose a perplexing problem. In addition, if athletes indulge in sightseeing to the detriment of their competitive performance, their earning power and career may be threatened. Coaches in individual sports must also be flexible and frequent travelers, and they often switch athletes as fortunes wane or players retire. Coaching on the road makes family life difficult, and solitary nights spent in hotel rooms challenge most people, who tend to crave relationships.

Coaches of international sport teams also find opportunities in various countries. Many undeveloped countries hire coaches from more developed nations to build their systems in sports such as soccer, basketball, swimming, and track and field. Even among developed countries, coaches often move from one nation to another. In 1999, for example, England hired Patrice Hagelauer of France to head the performance development program for tennis; since then, it has hired, at various times, Peter Lundgren of Sweden, Louis Cayer of Canada, and Americans Brad Gilbert and Paul Annacone.

In spite of spending huge sums of money to recruit coaches from other countries, British tennis is still mired at the lowest level of performance, even though it boasts the most famous tournament of all in Wimbledon. Many of the leading tennis coaches in the United States also originate from other countries. People are often intrigued by different coaching approaches and reach out to international coaches who offer alternative methods and perspectives.

Officials and administrators of world sporting events also travel and often reside in foreign countries. They typically follow the world competition from venue to venue, although they may enjoy more time at home than athletes do. World championships, the Olympic Games, and similar events are not as frequent as a sport's regular season or tour events, and they are separated by weeks or months. Agents, on the other hand, usually travel constantly in order to attend events in which their athletes compete. Since they typically handle more than one athlete, they can spend endless weeks on the road serving their clients and scouting for new talent to sign.

As a result of this global travel, athletes, coaches, and officials become ambassadors for their home nation, learn about other cultures, and tend to develop a broad worldview. They probably do little to directly influence the countries where they travel, but as they develop followings, they may create strong links. For example, particular athletes may adopt or become fascinated with cultures other than their own; similarly, language barriers are reduced as people use foreign phrases and expressions just to survive.

As professional athletes and coaches mature and start families, they often arrange for their loved ones to travel with them. Imagine the experience of such a family. The educational experience for kids is priceless.

On the other hand, countries of origin are not always happy when their athletes leave home to play professionally somewhere else. As already mentioned, U.S. baseball has increasingly attracted players from Latin American countries, as well as some of the best-known Japanese players. The countries that lose athletes lose some of their most charismatic and exciting competitors and may also suffer reduced interest in local baseball.

Over the past two or three decades in many European countries, sport leagues in soccer, ice hockey, and basketball have increasingly recruited players from other countries. The motivation is to find the best available players in the world to play for local clubs. Some observers say that this recruiting hinders the development of young athletes in the home country, who see spots taken by athletes from other nations. In this way, leagues deny jobs to home-country athletes in the hope of producing a winning team (Maguire et al. 2002).

A parallel situation exists in many U.S. colleges and universities. Once the top U.S. athletes are signed to scholarships, the schools that didn't sign them recruit the best overseas athletes in hopes of competing. This growing trend has affected some sports more than others; those most affected include swimming, track and field, soccer, and tennis. Efforts to limit the number of international players have been struck down in the courts, and U.S. families may cry foul when their kids are denied athletic scholarships in favor of international players.

International competition in sport can provide a terrific opportunity for athletes, coaches, and others. On the other hand, it can also lead to complications in personal and family life, as well as culture shock and burnout. Surviving this unusual life experience boils down to how grounded people are in their fundamental values and relationships.

Using Sport for Better World Understanding

In an ideal world, international competition would be an opportunity for the people involved to learn about each other and connect on a personal level. Once someone understands and appreciates the society and culture of another, the stage is set for people to live and work together. This valued outcome does happen in world competition, but not without dedication and effort on the part of all parties.

Athletes of all ages may compete internationally if they earn a top ranking in their own country. Specific world competitions are staged in various sports for athletes aged 12 years and under, and athletes in their 50s and 60s also have their own competitions. College athletes in many sports have also benefited from traveling abroad in order to compete. For many athletes, these experiences are eye-opening cultural excursions to countries they would not normally visit. Meeting athletes from around the world helps them appreciate the humanity of all cultures and may also urge them to train harder in order to compete with the best in the world.

Some international competitions balance sport and travel. For example, high school students can sign up for tours of other countries during which they also compete at arranged sites along the way. Young people who take advantage of these tours may be sponsored by sport organizations, groups promoting international understanding, or their families. Countries often establish exchange programs for young athletes, and it is exhilarating for participants who struggle to communicate with each other to find a common bond in the language of sport. The United States is a popular destination, and most people who qualify to visit for a sport event seize the opportunity. In virtually every sport, young athletes from other countries visit and compete against U.S. kids while sightseeing and learning about American life.

Athletic coaches also have numerous opportunities to travel internationally. Most sports hold worldwide coaching conferences, and each participating nation may designate several coaches as representatives. The concept of sharing coaching philosophies is not new, and coaches from countries that lead the world in competition are in high demand as speakers and teachers. Along the way, coaches from different societies interact and broaden their outlook on the world.

Despite these potential benefits, the value of international sport competition may be narrowed if coaches and leaders focus entirely on athletic performance, thus losing the opportunity to learn about other cultures and its people. Coaches personally benefiting from international travel may view the competitive activity as more than what happens on the playing field. People who schedule such trips often find however that sightseeing is best left to the end of the trip, when competition is completed and they can relax their single-minded focus on sport.

Sport offers the potential for developing better understanding of the larger world, but this opportunity may be lost unless we structure the experience with that goal in mind. If we do not promote international appreciation through competition, we make a mockery of one of the values that we often trumpet in support of sport participation.

Chapter Summary

The British system of sport and games had the most dominant effect on the development of modern international sport. For centuries, Great Britain influenced countless countries to adopt its sport practices. In the last 50 years, this influence has been joined by other Western countries, including the United States. The configuration is likely to shift again as the world population changes and sport is embraced concertedly by additional countries, such as China.

Sport has become a global enterprise by standardizing rules, staging world competitions for athletes of all ages and abilities, and getting those contests covered by the media. Technological advancements have made sport events immediately available to fans worldwide.

Participation in a particular sport is historically popular in its nation of origin. By far the most popular sport worldwide is soccer, which is followed by cricket, field hockey, tennis, and volleyball to round out the top five. American football barely makes the top ten.

The modern Olympic Games have helped to develop sport worldwide. Most nations support the training and coaching of their athletes in order to maximize success in international competition. Extending the length and pageantry of the Games has attracted television viewers worldwide and generated millions of dollars for organizers and sponsors.

As multinational corporations realized the possibilities of advertising through international sport, they reached out to new audiences. For example, sport equipment and clothing companies discovered cheap labor in undeveloped countries and millions of consumers in developed countries.

During the Cold War, the nationalism that had been the hallmark of competition began to be replaced by an economic model of international sport. Olympic venues are now chosen on the basis of the potential revenue that can be generated. As a result, athletes from competing countries are in a sense on the same team as they ply their trade with the backing of sport apparel companies such as Nike, Adidas, and Puma.

For both athletes and coaches, sport has expanded opportunities for world travel, cultural study, and personal relationships with people from other countries. However, if the use of sport to promote cultural understanding and harmony is to progress, we must actively treat it as a valued goal. Focusing exclusively on competition may improve performance, but it shortchanges the cultural experience for athletes.

10

STUDENT OUTCOMES

After reading this chapter, you will know the following:

- A brief history of the Olympic Games
- The role of the modern Olympics in global society
- How nationalism, economics, and politics influence the Olympics
- The role of the United States Olympic Committee
- How the Olympic movement has affected athlete development and coaching and training methods in the United States

Olympic Movement

Olympic Movement

Here is the Olympic creed: "The most important thing in the Olympic Games is not to win but to take part, just as the most important thing in life is not the triumph, but the struggle. The essential thing is not to have conquered but to have fought well." The Olympic creed is attributed to Baron Pierre de Coubertin, the founder of the modern Olympic Games. Athletes are reminded of the creed by their coaches, organizers, and fellow competitors because it expresses the philosophy upon which the modern Games were founded and have been conducted since 1896.

Another important element of the Olympics is its logo, designed by Pierre de Coubertin in 1912, which consists of five interlocked rings representing the union of the five original major continents at that time (Africa, America, Asia, Australia, and Europe) and the meeting of athletes from around the world at the Games. The five colors of the rings, from left to right, are blue, black, and red across the top and yellow and green across the bottom. These colors were chosen because at least one of them can be found in the flag of every nation. The Olympic rings are a carefully guarded logo property of the International Olympic Committee (IOC) and the National Olympic Committees of each country, and they can be used only with permission. Corporate sponsors are given permission to use the Olympic logo in their advertising in return for the millions of dollars of financial support that they provide.

No other sporting event in the last 100 years has matched the widespread effects of the Olympic Games. In addition to providing a venue for the finest athletes in a variety of sports, the Games provide opportunities for spectators to enjoy international competition in virtually every nation via television or the Internet.

Over the years, nationalism developed in the Olympics as each nation took pride in its athletes and created heroes for its youth to emulate. In the recent past, fierce nationalism has been pushed aside by the economic effects of the Olympic Games on national Olympic organizations, corporate sponsors, and host cities. What was once an amateur competition has morphed unabashedly into a competition for the world's best professional athletes, many of whom capitalize financially on their Olympic success.

By now, most nations have established Olympic organizations, often under a governmental agency, such as a ministry of sport. Relying on government funds and private donations, national Olympic organizations support the development of each country's Olympic candidates in hopes of boosting their performance as they compete in the Games every four years. In many countries, sport has grown and flourished simply because of Olympic development programs that encourage young athletes.

History of the Olympics

The ancient Olympics were founded as a festival to honor Zeus, the king of the Greek gods. The Games were held every four years for more than a thousand years, from 776 BC to AD 393. Only Greeks were allowed to compete, though the event was given an international flavor by athletes from Greek colonies in what are now the countries of Spain, Italy, Libya, Egypt, Ukraine, and Turkey (Henry and Yeomans 1984).

The origin of the ancient Olympics is debated because of the plethora of unsubstantiated accounts, but some general facts are known. At the height of their popularity, the Games represented the culture that made Greece the undisputed leader of the Mediterranean. Emerging from a religious festival that lasted one day, the Games developed into a seven-day extravaganza that riveted the attention of the people of Greece and its colonies. Common men competed against soldiers and royalty for the glory of winning the coveted olive wreath symbolizing victory.

The original Games featured just one event—a footrace of about 200 yards (183 meters) down the length of the stadium. At the behest of the city-state of Sparta, more events were added, and the eighteenth Olympic Games featured a pentathlon consisting of a long jump, spear throw, sprint, discus throw, and wrestling match. In succeeding years, other events were added, including boxing, chariot racing, footraces of varying lengths, and *pankration* (a combination of boxing and wrestling) (Henry and Yeomans 1984; Leonard 1980; Rice, Hutchinson, and Lee 1958).

Even as the Games expanded their physical contests and gained popularity, religious ceremonies were not forgotten. In fact, they were always

Ruins of the temple of Zeus in Olympia, Greece, where the original Olympic Games were held in 776 BC.

critical to the celebrations in order to honor the gods. Another vital role was played by the arts, including poetry recitations, singing, and dramatic productions. In this way, every four years, the Games turned a mosaic of religion, athletics, and the arts into a national festival (Scheiber 2004).

Over time, traditional Greek religion faded, and the Games lost their significance. The decline of the Games has been blamed on the corruption of politicians and the wealthy. Athletes focused more on prize money than on the honor of competing for the olive wreath, thus losing the rich history of morality and the love of competition that had marked the Games in earlier years. The ancient Games were last held in AD 393, after which the Christian emperor of Rome, Theodosius I, banned pagan worship.

Even so, the tradition of the Olympic Games is one of the enduring contributions of Greek civilization. In addition to fostering strong belief in the value of athletics, the Games celebrated individual achievement and produced notable works of art, music, and culture. Those same characteristics sparked the rebirth of the Olympics more than a thousand years later, in 1896. When the Games began again in Athens, just 14 countries competed in nine sports: track and field, cycling, fencing, gymnastics, wrestling, swimming, weightlifting, tennis, and shooting. As of today, the modern Olympic Games have endured political conflicts, world wars, and the passing of generations (Henry and Yeomans 1984).

The modern Games were revived by Baron Pierre de Coubertin, a French educator. His vision was to replicate worldwide the positive effects of the original Greek Olympics. According to the modern Olympic charter, "Olympism is a philosophy of life, exalting and combining in a balanced whole the qualities of body, will, and mind. Blending sport with culture and education, Olympism seeks to create a way of life based on the joy found in effort, the educational value of good example and respect for universal fundamental ethical principles" (Olympic Charter 2004, 9).

Drawing from the holistic Athenian philosophy of a sound mind in a sound body, the modern Olympic movement was initiated to help people understand and appreciate their differences through competition in sport. The hope was that by establishing a community of athletes, coaches, and organizers from every country in the world, the Games would promote international understanding and goodwill (Henry and Yeomans 1984).

Effect of the Olympic Games

The Games profoundly affect their host city, the media that cover the contests, and the athletes who compete. These effects are felt in the years leading up to the competition, during the staging of the competition itself, and, in many cases, for years afterward. Most Olympic competitors devote their early years to development and training in the hope of someday qualifying for the Olympics. Once they finally realize their dream, it becomes the defining factor in their life and sets the path for the years ahead. Many trade on their Olympic success as they move on to other professions.

Host City

Cities from around the world compete to host the Olympic Games in search of prestige, media attention, and financial benefits. Olympic legacies can

The 2016 Olympic Games in Rio de Janeiro required the city to invest in massive infrastructure projects and environmental clean-up, including removing pollution from Guanabara Bay, the site of sailing competitions.

be grouped into three categories: the creation of world-class facilities; national and international recognition of the city through extensive media exposure; and community benefits, such as local volunteerism, job creation and training, youth programs, and funding for community development projects. Host cities create or refurbish sport venues in the hope that once the Olympics end, they will be used by athletes from the host country.

Up-to-date stadiums and athletic facilities are required for every staging of the Olympic Games. The host city begins by assessing its current facilities and then makes plans for constructing additional facilities as needed—for example, arenas and pools. The funding becomes complicated as various groups pitch in money in return for use or ownership of the facility long after the Games end. For example, the 1996 Games in Atlanta, Georgia, affected the long-term economy of both the city and the state.

The cost of hosting the Games can be daunting. For example, the 2004 Athens Games cost an estimated $14.6 billion, whereas the Greek government had originally budgeted $5.9 billion based on previous stagings (for example, $1.5 billion for the 2000 Sydney Games and $1.7 billion for the 1996 Atlanta Games). The 2008 Beijing Olympics are reported to have cost more than $43 billion—three times more than any other Olympic Games in history.

In contrast, the 2012 London Summer Olympics cost much less—$13.4 billion—but still more than triple the cost that had been projected when London made its bid to host the Games. Most of the cost of the venues and parks used to stage the Games were financed with public funds, and the Games themselves were essentially financed by private funds. At the same time, the economic benefits to the city of London during the Games was estimated by the government at more than $15 billion, thus basically covering the expenses, though of course that money did not go to the government directly but rather into the overall economy.

The organizers for the 2014 Winter Games in Sochi, Russia, astounded all observers by claiming that their costs exceeded $50 billion—more than China spent in 2008 to host the Summer Games, which are much larger in scope than the winter edition. If we can believe that figure (which is somewhat dubious), the cost may have been driven to such heights in part by security concerns and alleged corruption. In addition, Sochi is more of a beach resort than a winter paradise, thus necessitating massive construction of roads and facilities to host winter events (Taylor 2014; Farhl 2014). The total cost for the previous Winter Games (in Vancouver in 2010) was just $7.1 billion, and when Russia was awarded the 2014 Games its projected budget was a relatively modest $12 billion.

The 2016 Summer Games in Rio de Janeiro were projected to cost $5.6 billion when the bid was accepted in 2009 but rose to more than $15 billion by 2014 and will likely only get higher. The fact is that cost overruns at the Olympic Games are normal, as evidenced by the fact that the last 17 Summer and Winter Games involved overspending that averaged 179 percent over budget (Panja and Biller 2014).

To understand how Olympic costs reach once-unimagined heights, let's consider three general categories of spending (Cummings 2009): direct operating expenses, general infrastructure improvements, and the cost of building state-of-the-art facilities that are used only during the Games. The first category—direct operating expenses—pays for such things as the athlete village, transportation, security, and the staging of ceremonies. The average budget for this category is about $3 billion, and it is usually covered by television, tourism, and ticket revenues.

The second category involves general infrastructure improvements in the city, which, even if expensive, typically bring lasting benefits. These costs often include removing decaying housing or slums and relocating the former residents, planting vegetation, building roads, and constructing new high-rise structures. Some host cities slide these costs for redevelopment and infrastructure improvement into the Olympic budget when in fact they have little to do with the two-week event and should have been paid for with local tax dollars.

The third category is the most troublesome one after the Games are done—the expenses involved in building state-of-the-art sport facilities that are used only during the Games. These facilities include extravagant stadiums (which may seat 100,000 spectators), natatoriums, and other similar projects. After the Games, most cities are stuck paying off the debt for these venues, and in most cases the facilities are no longer of practical use.

At the 2012 London Olympics, for example, organizers chose not to use the venerable Wembley

Stadium but instead to construct a new facility at a cost of $700 million. Four years earlier, for the Beijing Summer Olympics, the Beijing National Stadium cost $423 million, but it now sits virtually idle even though it costs the government nearly $9 million per year to keep it in usable condition. The anticipated cost of the 2020 Olympic stadium for the Summer Games in Tokyo currently stands at $1.7 billion, but that figure will rise as the event draws nearer.

As you might guess from the preceding discussion, about 95 percent of the cost of hosting the Olympic Games is spent not on sport itself or on athletes but on steel, concrete, asphalt, bricks, and mortar. Cities see an opportunity to improve their infrastructure, and architects and construction companies bask in the glow of profits. However, the athletic facilities constructed for the event often sit idle afterward. Faced with this reality, many citizens wonder how their country can afford world-class athletic facilities but not first-rate affordable housing, schools, or hospitals (Panja and Biller 2014).

As the cost has skyrocketed, more countries have become hesitant to make a bid to host the Games. For example, four of the original six cities bidding for the 2022 Winter Games dropped out due to fears about cost and the difficulty of rallying public support for the bid. Soon afterward Oslo, Norway and Lviv, Ukraine also withdrew their bids resulting in the fact that the countries of Poland, Germany, Sweden, Switzerland, Norway, and Ukraine all withdrew from the bidding, thus leaving only Beijing and Almaty (Kazakhstan) as contenders—both less than ideal candidates (Abend 2014). The United States has chosen Boston for bidding to host the 2024 Summer Olympics and will likely vie against Paris (France), Hamburg (Germany), and Rome (Italy). The United States failed in its last two bids for the Summer Games, losing out to London and Rio, respectively.

For its part, the IOC has vowed to streamline the bidding process in order to make it more cost effective, more flexible, and open to some variation with an eye toward reducing the cost incurred by the eventual host city. Still, the IOC itself has come under increased scrutiny in recent years for its extravagant spending and lack of transparency. As a private organization, it is not required to make its financial practices public, and members of the IOC board of directors are appointed rather than democratically elected. Until its philosophies and practices are adjusted to conform to modern realities—particularly in the financial realm—the Olympic Games are at risk of becoming an anachronism in today's world (Abend 2014).

Sponsorship of the Games

It would simply not be possible to stage the Olympic Games today without the financial support of corporate sponsors who, along with media rights fees, essentially provide the financial underpinnings of the Games. For the London Games, the IOC solicited commitments from a dozen corporate sponsors, who paid an average of $80 million to $90 million each for the quadrennium. At the same time, the host country of Great Britain recruited its own domestic sponsors; its top-tier supporters kicked in between $50 million to $80 million, and its second- and third-tier sponsors contributed between $10 million to $20 million, including in-kind support (Murray 2012).

The Olympic Partner (TOP) program is the worldwide sponsorship program managed by the IOC since 1985. It was created to develop an exclusive and diversified revenue base for the Games and establish long-term corporate partnerships. The program offers each worldwide Olympic partner exclusive global marketing rights and opportunities within a designated product or service category. The funds derived from TOP sponsors are distributed in roughly the following proportions: 50 percent to the organizing committees for the Winter and Summer Games, 40 percent to the various National Olympic Committees, and 10 percent to the International Olympic Committee itself. Revenue from the TOP program totaled $950 million for the quadrennium that included the 2010 Vancouver and 2012 London Games.

Here are a few examples of IOC sponsorship deals. One TOP sponsorship agreement involves McDonald's, which is estimated to be paying up to $200 million for an eight-year period ending in 2020 (Murray 2012). The longest continuous Olympic sponsor is Coca-Cola, which began as the first sponsor at the 1928 Games held in Amsterdam (International Olympic Committee 2013c). TOP sponsors of the London Games are presented in the following list (Murray 2012):

Sponsor	Category
Acer	Computer technology
Atos Origin	Information technology

Dow Chemical	Chemical manufacturing
General Electric	Varied conglomerate
McDonald's	Retail food service
Panasonic	Audio, TV, and radio equipment
Procter & Gamble	Personal care and household products
Samsung	Electronics
Visa	Consumer payment systems

Media Effects

The first broadcast of the Summer Olympics was made in London in 1948. Today, the Summer and Winter Games are both broadcast to 220 countries, and the 2012 London Games reached a global audience of more than 3.6 billion people. As you might expect, the revenue derived from selling media rights to broadcast the Olympic Games constitutes a sizable source of income, and it has expanded dramatically.

The IOC negotiates broadcast deals individually for major world markets, and in the United States NBC was awarded the rights for the 2010/2012 cycle at a price of $2 billion. In fact, NBC has won the broadcast rights for every Olympic Games since Tokyo in 1964 and is committed at least through 2032—thus covering a total of 23 editions of the Games (Meylan 2014). The network's rationale is that the Olympics, unlike any other event, can attract whole families to TV watching; as a result, the Games create a unique audience for sponsors to sell to. In addition, unlike the Super Bowl, which lasts only a few hours, the Olympic Games extend over 17 days, providing multiple time slots for advertising.

As shown in table 10.1, the revenue impact of the Olympic Games has steadily increased since 1992. In addition, the media rights have already been bought for the U.S. market for the period from 2021 through 2032 at a price of $7.65 billion.

You may wonder how television networks can pay such large fees to televise the Games. The secret is that while NBC paid $894 million to broadcast the 2008 Beijing Games, it also attracted more than $1 billion in advertising revenue to offset the cost. In 2012, it paid $1.18 billion to broadcast the London Games while attracting $1.2 billion in advertising revenue. The price for a 30-second spot in 2012 was $725,000 during prime-time viewing hours (Greyser and Kogan 2013). Why would advertisers pay that much? The 2012 Summer Games set a record for the

TABLE 10.1 U.S. Television Rights Fees for the Olympics, 1992–2020

SUMMER GAMES			WINTER GAMES		
Year	Host city	Fee ($ millions)	Year	Host city	Fee ($ millions)
1992	Barcelona	401	1992	Albertville	234
1996	Atlanta	456	1994	Lillehammer	300
2000	Sydney	705	1998	Nagano	375
2004	Athens	793	2002	Salt Lake City	545
2008	Beijing	894	2006	Torino	613
2012	London	1,100	2010	Vancouver	820
2016	Rio de Janeiro	1,220	2014	Sochi	775
2020	Tokyo	1,410	2018	PyeongChang	963

Data from Huffington Post 2012.

ACTIVITY TIME-OUT

Ambush Marketing at the Olympics

Paddy Power was a hot topic leading up to the 2012 London Olympic Games. The Irish bookmaker took a low-budget but effective approach by setting up billboards near the Olympic venue claiming that "Paddy Power is the official sponsor of the largest athletics event in London this year! There you go, we said it." In reality, they were referring to an egg-and-spoon race in the French village of London, Burgundy. The London Olympics organizers were not amused and demanded the removal of the ads but eventually withdrew their objections after Paddy Power threatened legal action.

Paddy Power wasn't the only organization to pull an "ambush marketing" stunt. Not to be outdone, Nike launched a global TV campaign tied to the opening ceremonies in which amateur athletes competed in places around the world called London. They included runners in London, Ontario; cyclists in London, Nigeria; and shots from London, Ohio, and Little London in Jamaica (Roxborough 2012). Despite efforts by the IOC and the British Parliament to impose restrictions—including threatened fines in excess of $30,000—ambush marketers claimed 27 of the top 50 spots in Global Language Monitor's (2012) brand affiliation index done specifically for the London Games, which measures effective brand impact.

Other notable comparisons by Global Language Monitor showed the following:

- IOC partner McDonald's ranked behind ambushers Subway and Pizza Hut but ahead of KFC.
- Ambusher Nike led IOC partner Adidas by a wide margin.
- IOC partner British Airways trailed ambushers Lufthansa, United, and Air France.
- Ambusher Royal Philips edged IOC partner GE.
- IOC partner Procter & Gamble crushed all ambush competitors.

Without the revenue provided by global sponsors, the IOC would struggle to put on the Games. Therefore, it needs to protect companies that have invested millions of dollars in Olympic sponsorships. On the opposing side are the ambush marketers, who claim that the Olympic Games belong to everyone and that they have a right to benefit as well (Global Language Monitor 2012).

What do you think about the legality of ambush marketing and the moral questions regarding the practice? If you think ambush marketing is wrong, how would you suggest that it be controlled, and by whom? Finally, what about the increasing use of social media for ambush media? Is that simply a lost cause in terms of regulation? Why or why not?

most-watched Olympics ever, drawing a cumulative TV audience of 4.8 billion—almost two-thirds of the world's population! The U.S. audience totaled 219 million viewers and averaged 31 million per night during the 17 nights of broadcast coverage.

The Winter Games are smaller than the Summer Games in both size and scope and therefore draw a relatively smaller television audience. Table 10.2 provides a size comparison of the 2010 Vancouver Winter Games with the 2008 Beijing Summer Games.

The 2014 Winter Games in Sochi, Russia, drew a record number of television viewers worldwide for a Winter Olympics, exceeding the previous high (for the Vancouver Games) by 8 percent. However, in the United States, the average prime-time viewership for the Games was 21.4 million, which fell short of the 24.4 million average set by the Vancouver Games. Marking a significant change from Vancouver was the fact that nearly 62 million unique users consumed digital content from NBC, led by the men's hockey semifinal between

TABLE 10.2 Events in the 2008 and 2010 Olympics

	Participating countries	Events	Sports	Number of athletes
2008 Beijing Summer Games	204	302	28	10,942
2010 Vancouver Winter Games	82	86	15	2,566

the United States and Canada (Zamyatina 2014; Best 2014).

Competing networks get into the action by inviting Olympic athletes onto talk shows, showing clips of their performances, and promoting Olympic sponsors. Magazines and daily newspapers devote pages to stories about Olympic athletes and coaches, as well as the surrounding subplots involving drug testing, romance, athletes' earnings, and judging controversies.

Overall, then, it seems that every two years—when either the Winter or Summer Games takes the stage—the world steps back from other events to focus on the Olympic competition. That was the original idea of the Olympic Games, and it endures today.

Elite Performance Athletes

The motto of the Olympic Games is *Citius, Altius, Fortius*—Latin for "Faster, Higher, Braver" but universally accepted as "Faster, Higher, Stronger." These are worthy goals for every aspiring Olympian who measures success by the winning of a gold, silver, or bronze medal. Of course, few come away with a medal, but most treasure the experience of competing with the world's best in their sport. With this vision in mind, hundreds of thousands of aspiring youth around the world train and test their abilities in hopes of someday becoming an Olympian.

World championships are held in many sports under the aegis of each sport's international governing body. The Olympic Games, however, are the event where nearly all sports come together at once to stage a unique celebration of athletic competition that is the most comprehensive and lavish yet conceived. The world attends to the Games, and audiences are glued to their screens for more than two weeks. The media have latched onto the Olympics as a significant world event that can attract huge audiences and therefore hundreds of millions of dollars in corporate sponsorship. In short, the Olympics have become the largest and most successful economic engine in the sport world.

The excitement of the Olympic Games focuses the world's gaze on the best performances of elite athletes in every Olympic sport. Winning a medal at the Olympics has achieved an almost mystical status among athletes, each of whom dreams of rising to the occasion and winning a medal or even setting a world record. By comparison, succeeding at a world championship, while certainly notable, does not generate nearly the same media attention or sponsorship opportunities as winning an Olympic medal. The intense focus of world sport fans on the Olympic Games both adds pressure and confers instant fame on athletes who offer up the performance of a lifetime.

Even famous athletes in their sport jockey for opportunities to rub elbows with athletes from other sports whom they admire. Olympic athletes are clearly not inured to the celebrity factor. They are also sport fans who enjoy watching performers in other sports rise to greatness.

The emphasis on winning at the Games has become a double-edged sword. Medal winners are treated as heroes, and those who come up short are labeled as failures. In some countries, including the United States, debate rages over whether athletes who qualify for the Games but are unlikely to challenge for a medal should even be supported financially by their home country. Indeed, it is clear that the goal of the United States Olympic Committee (USOC) is to accumulate the most medals possible in a particular event. As a result, athletes who qualify but are unlikely to win a medal become something of a second-class citizen,

IN THE ARENA WITH . . .

The Greatest Olympian of All Time

For Michael Phelps, three Olympic Games produced 22 medals, including 18 golds. Never has another athlete even approached such a dominating performance over a period of 12 years on the biggest stage in sport. Usually, when we debate "the greatest ever," we look at two factors: dominance and longevity. In both of these areas, Phelps rates a perfect 10. Clearly he has been the most dominant athlete in his sport, and he has produced his best performances when it counted most. Could there be any doubters?

Winning medals at the Olympics depends in part on the number available in one's sport. Team sports offer only one gold, and even many individual sports—such as tennis, boxing, table tennis, triathlon, wrestling, and weightlifting—provide only one chance, or perhaps two, for an individual to win a medal. In contrast, in swimming and track and field, athletes often compete in multiple events, depending on their skill, their fitness, and the scheduling of the events.

Here are some other athletes whose names come up in discussions of the greatest Olympian ever:

- Jesse Owens' track-and-field performance at the 1936 Olympics in Berlin dramatically repudiated Adolf Hitler's proclamation of Aryan superiority. Owens' participation in the Games may be the most celebrated and culturally important performance by any American athlete.
- Jackie Joyner-Kersee was named by *Sports Illustrated* as the best female athlete of the twentieth century. She won a total of six medals in long jump and heptathlon over the course of four Olympics.
- Carl Lewis is the only man to successfully defend the 100-meter and long-jump titles. He won nine gold medals and one silver medal in four Summer Games and was chosen as the world athlete of the century by the International Association of Athletics Federations.
- Clara Hughes, a Canadian, won two bronze medals as a cyclist in the Summer Games and a gold, silver, and two bronze medals as a speed skater in three Winter Olympics. She stands alone as a winner of multiple medals in both the Winter and Summer Games.

Charmingly, Michael Phelps claims that he is a terrible overall athlete, based on failed attempts at a menu of other sports. Even so, it is clear that his mark on the Olympic Games will endure at least in our lifetime.

and many people believe that USOC resources are wasted on them. Others believe that just competing in the Olympic Games is a right that they have earned. Isn't competing the point of it all?

The fascination with winning medals has produced incentive plans for athletes, backed by governments and National Olympic Committees, in which they receive cash awards for each medal won. Proponents of this approach believe that cash encourages athletes to work harder; and in smaller countries where athletes have fewer opportunities to capitalize on their success as an athlete, the awards sometimes exceed $100,000. In more-developed countries, such as the United States, the opportunities for athletes are more plentiful; therefore, those countries typically award lower bonuses. In high-profile sports, the relatively modest reward for medaling ($25,000 to $50,000) is insignificant to professional athletes when compared with their annual earnings, and most donate the proceeds to a charitable organization.

Public acceptance of winning as the primary goal of Olympic athletes has fueled concentration on elite athletic competition. Kids are steered into elite development programs and encouraged to focus on preparing for a run at an Olympic medal. Though some sport leaders believe it is healthy for kids to aspire to greatness, this approach can take a toll on sport participation aimed at simply having fun, perhaps contributing to the high dropout rate in youth sport (see chapter 6). In this competitive atmosphere, once kids realize that high performance is not within their reach, they often give up on sport and turn to other activities.

Another by-product of the emphasis on winning is the increasing use of performance-enhancing drugs, which has resulted in stepped-up testing of victorious athletes, both in and out of competition. Indeed, heading into every Olympic Games, the media spend nearly as much time on speculation about which athletes are using illegal substances as they do on predictions of athletic accomplishments. Performance enhancement through drugs is discussed further in chapter 20.

The demand to produce elite athletes who might someday compete for Olympic medals has spawned ambitious talent scouting in many countries. Children younger than age six have been tested for athletic potential and offered government-funded training opportunities in a sport that seems to suit their body type, athletic skill, and temperament. During the Cold War, such government-sponsored schools produced many champion athletes in East Germany and Russia, which dedicated state money to training athletes in an attempt to prove the superiority of their culture.

In addition, the recent success of Olympic athletes from China can be traced directly to a national system of training in sport schools. At the 1988 Seoul Olympics, China earned just five gold medals and twelve medals overall. However, at the 2008 Beijing Games, Chinese athletes earned 51 gold medals and 100 overall. And at the 2012 London Games, China claimed 38 gold medals and 88 overall to finish second only to the United States. They must surely be doing something right.

In the Russian model of a tight-knit system of sport training schools adopted by China, children train hard for up to five hours per day even at young ages. They also spend time in academics, though that is clearly a secondary occupation. For these kids, the driving motivation is the dream of becoming a champion, which offers the promise of a better economic life. In particular, children from modest-income homes envision athletic success if they work hard at sport. Unlike children in Western countries, Chinese youngsters don't have to pay for—or search for—top coaches, trainers, or facilities; nor do they have to obtain sponsors, equipment, food, or lodging. All of that and more is provided by the government, as long as they demonstrate their athletic prowess and follow the rules.

Some sport observers question these methods and criticize China for exploiting children and separating them from their families. In addition, some claim that the children are abused if their performances do not measure up. But if we step back for a bit, we might ask who can criticize a government that provides opportunity for those with talent to chase their dreams (MacLeod 2007).

Shift From Amateurs to Professionals

During the last 50 years, the Olympics have shifted away from the idealistic notion that world-class athletes could compete solely for the love of the game and thus be dubbed "amateurs." Juan Antonio Samaranch, IOC president from 1980 to 2001, made clear that his mission for the Olympic Games was to attract the best athletes in the world. Their standing as amateur or professional was irrelevant to him.

During the first half of the twentieth century, sport was still supposed to be played for enjoyment, with no thought of financial reward. Only the financially well-off could afford the time and expense of playing, so sport was limited to the privileged class. However, as interest in watching sport grew, spectators became willing to pay admission fees, and money therefore became available to athletes. The available financial resources were increased by commercial sponsors and television rights fees. Yet the athletes who performed often received a relatively small portion of the revenue.

U.S. fans loved the idea of amateur athletes struggling to train and then succeeding on the world stage. But the amateur status was a front. College athletes received scholarships, and others appeared in advertisements or were hired as spokespeople or consultants. Americans pointed to other countries, particularly Eastern European Communist countries, who ignored the rules of amateurism as the IOC allowed each nation to determine what constituted amateur status.

The only athletes clearly excluded from the Olympic Games were professional athletes in basketball, tennis, ice hockey, and baseball, who earned their living by playing their sport. Rather than sending professionals, the United States sent

EXPERT'S VIEW

The World Anti-Doping Agency

The World Anti-Doping Agency (WADA) was established in 1999 to set standards for anti-doping work and coordinate the efforts of sport organizations and public authorities. The International Olympic Committee provided the impetus by convening the First World Conference on Doping in Sport in Lausanne, Switzerland. At the 2004 Summer Olympics in Athens, some 3,000 drug tests were administered; four years later, in Beijing, that number jumped by 50 percent to 4,500 tests. During the London Olympics in 2012, more than 6,000 blood and urine tests were administered to approximately 30 percent of the participants, and nine violators were caught. Another 117 had been caught during the months leading up the Games.

At the 2014 Winter Games in Sochi, two-thirds of competitors were tested, including the top five finishers in all medal events. A total of 2,812 drug tests were administered, and more emphasis was put on precompetition testing than ever; indeed, 52 percent of the tests were done before athletes competed. Of the tests given, 2,186 were urine tests, and 626 were blood tests. The samples will be kept for 10 years for possible retesting as technology advances. The record number of positive tests for the Winter Games—eight overall—included three for men's ice hockey players. The previous Winter Games in Vancouver had yielded just one positive test (Sky Sports 2014).

Historically, the sports that produced the highest numbers of positive drug tests at the Olympics from 1968 through 2012 are the following:

Weightlifting	36
Track and field	28
Cross-country skiing	12
Equestrianism	8
Ice hockey (tie)	6
Wrestling (tie)	6
Cycling	5

During that same period, Austria had the most doping cases with ten, followed by Greece and Russia with nine each, and the United States with eight (ProCon 2011).

Of course, the number of positive tests does not tell the whole story. Athletes and coaches who are determined to cheat will continue to look for doping methods that are beyond the reach of current testing protocols. As a result, an increasing number of athletes are testing positive at other events held before or after the Olympic Games. In particular, track and field has come under much scrutiny in recent years after a series of positive tests by some of the world's best sprinters from Jamaica, including former world-record holders and Olympic medalists.

college kids to compete in the Olympic Games. For some years, that approach worked, and the United States dominated world competition anyway. However, as other nations began challenging U.S. dominance, something had to give: Either the United States had to change its definition of amateurism, or the IOC had to change its rules and open up competition to anyone—amateur or professional.

Over the last 30 years, all pretense of sending amateur athletes to the Olympics has been set aside. Now Olympic athletes include primarily professional athletes, and in fact Olympic stars are *expected* to promote the Games and their sport for compensation. As a result, stars from professional teams, leagues, and tours are now welcomed into the Games.

The remaining stumbling block in the United States is the stance taken by the National Collegiate Athletic Association (NCAA) toward professionalism. The NCAA continues to define college athletes as amateurs, even though they receive athletic scholarships and other benefits. It requires young athletes hoping to qualify for athletic scholarships to remain amateurs before attending college. This rule exists only in the United States, and it severely limits the ability of athletes in expensive Olympic sports to secure financial backers when they are young.

The NCAA has on its hands the impossible task of regulating corporate sponsorship and organizational support of young athletes because they have no control over athletes before college and can only enforce rules well after the fact. Uncovering evidence of a history of accepting funds by youth athletes is difficult to track or prove. Yet supposed amateur athletes in youth sport cannot afford to compete unless their family has significant resources or secures sponsorship of some kind. Fortunately, high school sports such as basketball and American football provide development opportunities for younger athletes. But those in skating, equestrianism, tennis, golf, gymnastics, and other Olympic sports have no such viable opportunity through the school system.

Nationalism and the Olympic Movement

Within the International Olympic Committee, there are 202 National Olympic Committees (NOCs) spread over five continents (the Americas are treated as one continent). These national committees promote the principles of Olympism within their country, support their athletes, and send athletes to participate in the Games. Modern Olympic Games since 1896 developed an increasingly nationalistic flavor, no doubt partly due to the fact that only NOCs are allowed to select and send athletes to the Olympic Games. Thus athletes rightly feel that they are representing their country.

Team sports heighten the sense of nationalism. At the Olympics, the German team competes against the British team and so on. When athletes or teams win a medal, they receive it while their country's flag waves and their national anthem plays. The media show these ceremonies and note the tears of successful athletes who provide living testimony of their country's success. In addition, the opening ceremonies of the Games include a huge procession, in which every athlete and coach marches into the Olympic stadium as part of a team representing the homeland. Their clothing usually highlights their country's traditional garb or colors. Athletes from the same country march together regardless of their competitive standing, medal chances, or financial status.

Martin (1996) suggests that nationalism was catapulted into prominence by Adolf Hitler, who used the Olympic Games in Berlin as a propaganda show for Nazi Germany. Hitler's constant references to the supposed "super race" of white athletes were laid bare by the heroic achievements of U.S. sprinter Jesse Owens, a black athlete who won four medals and dominated the competition in track and field.

After World War II and the Korean War, the world settled into 35 years of what was dubbed the Cold War—essentially, a clash of cultures and governance paradigms between the Union of Soviet Socialist Republics (USSR) and the United States. Although war was never declared between these two superpowers, it was always a threat, and the tension was great. It was during the Cold War that nationalism peaked in the Olympic Games. In fact, the United States and the USSR (now the Russian Federation) have dominated the Olympic Games from 1948 through the present day (see table 10.3). No other nation has finished as the top medal winner in all that time. Since the breakup of the Soviet Union in 1991, the United States has won the total medal race in every Summer Olympic Games through London 2012.

However, Asian countries are beginning to assert themselves. China won 32 gold medals in the 2004 Athens Games and trailed the United States in the race for gold by just 3 medals. In addition, Japan, Korea, Thailand, and Indonesia became significant factors in the medal race for the first time. In the 2008 Beijing Olympics, China finally surpassed the United States in number of gold medals (51 to 36), though the United States still came out on top in terms of overall medals (110 to 100). In 2012, the United States reasserted itself by earning 46 gold to China's 38 and 104 total medals to 88 for China (see tables 10.3, 10.4, and 10.5). Clearly, however, there has been a changing of the guard in the scramble to earn the most Olympic medals.

There is some disagreement regarding how to view—and report on—medals won when comparing the performances of competing countries. The

TABLE 10.3 Top Ten Countries All-Time in Olympic Medals

Rank	Country	Gold	Silver	Bronze	Total
1	United States	1,073	860	751	2,684
2	USSR	473	376	355	1,204
3	Great Britain	247	276	283	806
4	Germany	251	260	270	781
5	France	232	254	292	778
6	Italy	235	200	228	663
7	Sweden	193	203	231	627
8	Russia	182	167	179	528
9	China	213	166	147	526
10	East Germany	192	165	162	519

Includes all Olympic Games from 1896 through 2014.

 Available: www.olympic.it/english/medal/id–winter.htm

TABLE 10.4 Top 10 Medal-Winning Countries in the 2012 Summer Olympics

Country	Gold	Silver	Bronze	Total
United States	46	29	29	104
China	38	27	23	88
Russia	24	26	32	82
Great Britain	29	17	19	65
Germany	11	19	14	44
Japan	7	14	17	38
Australia	7	16	12	35
France	11	11	12	34
Italy	8	9	11	28
South Korea	13	8	7	28

Data from ESPN 2014a.

TABLE 10.5 Top 10 Medal-Winning Countries in the 2014 Winter Olympics

Country	Gold	Silver	Bronze	Total
Russia	13	11	9	33
United States	9	7	12	28
Norway	11	5	10	26
Canada	10	10	5	25
Netherlands	8	7	9	24
Germany	8	6	5	19
Austria	4	8	5	17
France	4	4	7	15
Sweden	2	7	6	15
Switzerland	6	3	2	11

Data from ESPN 2014a.

U.S. media generally report all medals won—gold, silver, and bronze—whereas the IOC and most other countries around the world report and emphasize only gold medals. Their argument is that only one athlete wins; therefore, by definition, the silver and bronze medalists have lost the competition. In contrast, most of us in the United States view any athlete who medals as a winner.

Nationalism in the Olympics peaked with politicians' use of Olympic success as an endorsement of a country's society and system of government. When the Russians topped the standings, they crowed about the superiority of the Communist system. When U.S. fortunes rose, the United States trumpeted the ideals of democracy. Most of the hype was not about developing athletes but was merely boasting, which in reality conflicted with good sporting behavior.

As you might suspect, the Olympic Games have seen their share of politics. Here are some instances in which the Olympics were used for political purposes:

- World War II interrupted the Olympics from 1940 to 1948.
- In 1948, Israel was excluded after the threat of an Arab boycott.
- In 1954, the IOC invited both China and Taiwan to enter the Games, but both nations claimed to represent China. In response, China boycotted the Games.
- In 1960, the IOC told North and South Korea to compete as one team; North Korea refused. In addition, Nationalist China was forced to compete under the name of Taiwan.
- In 1964, South Africa was banned due to its practice of apartheid.
- In 1968, South Africa was banned again. In addition, U.S. sprinters Tommie Smith and John Carlos raised a Black Power salute during the U.S. anthem and were banned for life from the Olympics.
- In 1972, members of Black September, a terrorist faction of the Palestinian Liberation Organization, kidnapped and eventually murdered 11 Israeli athletes during the Games when their demands to release Palestinian prisoners were not met.
- In 1980, some 60 nations boycotted the Games in protest of the Soviet Union's invasion of Afghanistan.

People all over the world decry the exercise of politics in the Olympic Games, but sport cannot be separated from the world at large. In order for countries to come together peacefully, there must be at least some political cooperation between nations. Still, when countries withdraw from the Games, they cause athletes to suffer by eliminating a lifelong dream for which they have trained for years.

On some occasions, nationalism has been transcended by exceptional athletes who achieved historic results and became part of Olympic folklore. Examples include Jesse Owens' four gold medals in Berlin in 1936; Emil Zátopek's triple victory in the 5,000-meter run, the 10,000-meter run, and the marathon in Helsinki in 1952; Bob Beamon's leap of 29 feet, 2 1/2 inches (8.9 meters) in Mexico in 1968; swimmer Mark Spitz's seven gold medals in Munich in 1972; gymnast Nadia Comaneci's seven perfect 10s in Montreal in 1976; and Michael Phelps' historic winning of a total of 18 gold medals and 22 overall medals during the Athens, Beijing, and London Games.

Observers of the Olympic Games have written for years about the negative influence of nationalism on the spirit and purpose of the Games. If the competition is about athletes, they say, then one's country of origin should not matter. Critics have even suggested eliminating team sports in order to reduce the natural nationalistic fervor. They also suggest removing the flags, the anthems, and the nation-based opening ceremony march, which would be replaced by a procession featuring an international body of selected athletes.

Over the past few Olympic Games, however, the debate over nationalism has been replaced by the debate over money. The cost of staging these massive events necessitates corporate sponsors and the selling of television rights in order to bring in cash. As a result, the Games have become large and lavish, and viewers have come to expect as much. Decisions are made to accommodate television broadcasting in recognition of the importance of a large viewership, which in turn can translate into lucrative sponsorships.

IN THE ARENA WITH . . .

Women Take Their Place at the Olympic Games

Pierre de Coubertin, the founder of the modern Olympic Games, is famously quoted as saying in 1896 that "women's sports were impractical, uninteresting, unaesthetic and incorrect." Today he might change his tune; about 45 percent of the 10,800 athletes at the London Olympics were women, and two countries, the United States and Canada, sent more female than male athletes to the Games (Whitley 2012).

And women weren't just competing, they were dominating. Women on the U.S. Olympic team won 58 medals overall (compared with 45 for the men) and 29 gold medals (compared with 15 for the men). Gabby Douglas and the women's gymnastics team won gold, Missy Franklin won four swimming medals, and the women's soccer team won gold before more than 70,000 spectators at Wembley Stadium. The Williams sisters dominated in tennis, the women's basketball team won its fifth straight gold medal, and Misty-May Treanor and Kerri Walsh won their third straight gold medal in beach volleyball. For the host country, the superstar was Jessica Ennis-Hill, who shrugged off the pressure of her country's expectations and won the gold in the heptathlon. Perhaps the most historic marker was the inclusion of women's boxing for the first time, despite reservations from the primarily male Olympic administrators.

There were still marks of past inequalities. The Australian and Japanese women's soccer teams were required to fly coach to the Games while their male counterparts enjoyed business class. Controversy arose from comments in the media over the state of African-American Gabby Douglas' hair rather than her remarkable athletic achievements. Badminton and boxing organizers had to be talked out of requiring female competitors to wear skirts. Keep in mind, though, that in 1984 women were still barred from the Olympic marathon, and at the 1996 Atlanta Games 26 nations sent no women to compete. Clearly, progress is being made, and women have taken their rightful place in the Olympic Games.

United States Olympic Committee

In 1978, the U.S. Congress passed the Amateur Sports Act as federal law. The act established the United States Olympic Committee as the coordinating body for all Olympics-related athletic activity in the United States. The vision of the USOC (2010) as stated on its website is "to assist in finding opportunities for every American to participate in sport, regardless of gender, race, age, geography, or physical ability." The Amateur Sports Act also designated the national governing body (NGB) for each sport in the United States. Each NGB supports its athletes, sets the rules for competition, stages competitions, and selects athletes to compete in world championships and the Olympic Games.

The USOC is headquartered in Colorado Springs, Colorado, on land donated by the U.S. government from a former military base. Over the years, state-of-the-art training facilities have been constructed, along with new offices for staff and housing for athletes. The weather and altitude, however, have forced the USOC to develop other training venues as well—Lake Placid, New York, for winter sports and Chula Vista, California, for summer sports.

USOC Funding

Unlike many other governments, the U.S. government does not help fund the Olympic movement or Olympic athletes. Instead, honoring its tradition of private enterprise, the United States has designated the USOC as its keeper of the Olympic flame. The USOC relies wholly on private donations from Americans and sponsorship from corporations. Its annual budget has hovered around $100 million for some time—a modest amount in relation to its mission. Part of those funds support the NGBs that develop athletes in specific sports. The formula for how much funding each NGB receives is complicated and always a bone of contention. National governing bodies that do well financially on their own—such as the United States Tennis Association, whose annual budget surpasses the total USOC budget—still claim their share of USOC funds.

The USOC has realized the value of the five-ring Olympic logo as a trademark that can be loaned to corporations in return for financial support. Likewise, the sale of goods labeled with the Olympic logo provides the USOC with consistent income.

USOC Membership

USOC members include organizations from the following categories:

- National governing bodies, such as USA Baseball, USA Gymnastics, and USA Swimming
- Paralympic sport organizations (PSOs), a new category with membership still to be determined, for organizations representing athletes who are hearing impaired, visually impaired, or intellectually impaired or who use a wheelchair
- Affiliated sport organizations, such as the U.S. Squash Racquets Association, Orienteering USA, the U.S. Trampoline and Tumbling Association, and USA Triathlon. Community-based multisport organizations, such as the Amateur Athletic Union, SHAPE America, the Boys & Girls Clubs of America, the YMCA and YWCA, and the Native American Sports Council

Governance

Over the last 20 years, the USOC drew criticism from many quarters in the wake of staff turnover, a series of volunteer and staff conflicts, and conflicts of interest among board members. Critics pointed out that the USOC had morphed into an unwieldy bureaucracy that served no one, including the athletes. Indeed, until 2004, the USOC was governed by a board of directors that included more than 100 members representing the various member organizations. Another significant group within the board, the Athletes' Advisory Council, was charged with protecting the interests of all Olympic athletes. An elected executive committee of approximately a dozen board members monitored the professional staff's activity, oversaw the budget, and acted on behalf of the board between meetings. All of these representatives were volunteers, leaders in their sport, who were either appointed or elected to serve on the USOC board.

In response to the criticisms, pressure from the U.S. Congress in 2003 led to a serious USOC self-evaluation, which in turn led the USOC to streamline its committees, policies, and board of directors. Essentially, the reforms reduced

APPLYING SOCIAL THEORY

Conflict Theorists and Funding Olympic Training

Take the perspective of a conflict theorist to evaluate the role of the U.S. government or the United States Olympic Committee in developing athletes to represent the nation in worldwide competition. At present, nearly all of the financial burden falls onto families of young, prospective athletes, and the U.S. mentality holds that it is up to them to make it work, regardless of household income. In reality, the costs of training for elite athletes has put the Olympic dream out of reach for the vast majority of the U.S. population. In virtually all other countries, government funds are set aside specifically to support the training of potential Olympic athletes. Generally, conflict theorists reject the status quo of our capitalistic society in favor of a model that is more sensitive to the needs of athletes and their families.

Although the United States does have strong athletic programs associated with high schools and colleges—which are unique in the world—they often do not exist for Olympic sports. For example, the glamorous and medal-rich Olympic sports of swimming, gymnastics, and track and field get only modest attention in school-related settings. Similarly, very few schools sponsor teams in the sports that are contested in the Winter Olympics.

In order to make pursuit of the Olympic dream more accessible, should the U.S. government provide a significant amount of training funds for qualified athletes? If your answer is yes, should the funds be awarded on the basis of financial need, athletic merit, or a combination of the two?

the board to a size similar to that of the former executive committee and established four standing committees, as well as annual reporting requirements, regular self-reviews, and whistleblower mechanisms (Borzilleri 2003; *SportingNews* 2003).

The conflict experienced by the USOC between professional staff and volunteer board members or committee chairs has also been an issue for many NGBs. Arising from a clash of goals and operating styles, these staff–volunteer confrontations occur in many not-for-profit organizations. Lines of reporting are blurred, personalities clash, and frequent changes in volunteer leadership and organizational direction frustrate staff professionals, who believe that their careers are being affected by people consumed with the privileges and perks of their position. To address these pitfalls, the recent changes in USOC governance place staff supervision with the chief operating officer, thus separating it from volunteer leaders.

The role of the professional staff, which numbers approximately 375 employees, is to provide athletes with access to elite training programs, assist with training programs for potential Olympic athletes, and support athletes at Olympic events. Often, the staff works closely with NGBs—for example, providing the latest training methods, advances in sports medicine, and equipment research at Olympic training centers for use by NGB athletes. It also makes available the results of research conducted with elite athletes. NGBs also need advice on hosting competitions, training coaches, identifying talented athletes, and preparing athletes for world competition. The USOC acts as a clearinghouse for information on all of these topics, identifies experts for consultation, and produces educational materials that can be applied to multiple sports.

Pursuit of Medals

It may seem that the United States is in good shape to maintain its dominance in Olympic competition. However, in-depth analysis reveals that challenges lie ahead. Since the breakup of the Soviet Union, dozens of medals have gone to smaller nations once counted with Russia. In spite of that loss, Russia continues to snap at the heels of the United States. If the countries that previously competed for the Soviet Union were reunited, they would have amassed more medals in the 2012 London Olympics than the United States did.

Additional teams to watch now include those from China, Japan, Korea, and other Asian countries. China is the most populous nation on the planet and made exceptional showings at the Games in 2008 and 2012. It has more than tripled its gold medal production since returning to the Games in 1984. More generally, Asian governments are pouring resources into athletic training as they never have before, and they are likely to see the results for years to come.

In the 2012 London Olympics, most of the medal production for both China and the United States came from their women. U.S. women earned 58 medals overall (compared with 45 for the men) and 29 gold medals (compared with 15 for the men). Indeed, it is probably fair to say that current U.S. dominance of the Olympics hinges primarily on the performance of the U.S. women. In London, U.S. women won gold medals in gymnastics, tennis, beach volleyball, basketball, soccer, water polo, rowing, swimming, and track and field. U.S. men dominated basketball and earned gold medals in track and field and swimming, led by Michael Phelps, who accounted for 4 golds and 2 silvers by himself. Otherwise, the U.S. men produced rather modest results.

It is a bit of a puzzle to figure out how much emphasis to put on racking up a high medal count in the Olympics. If that is the singular goal, then it makes sense to put the nation's effort and money into sports where its athletes have the best chance of earning a lot of medals. That means swimming and track and field, since they award so many individual event medals. But what about the team sports—traditionally strong for the United States—where only one medal is awarded? Should we focus on sports that are traditionally strong in our culture and ignore sports that are more

EXPERT'S VIEW

Worth of Olympic Medals

It is astounding to consider the blood, sweat, and tears shed by prospective and selected Olympians whose early life is consumed by the dream of winning an Olympic medal. One might think that the ultimate prize is worth a fortune, and sometimes it is, but the value of the medal itself is more symbolic than material. For the London Olympics and Paralympic Games, each gold medal was made of 92.5 percent silver, 1.3 percent gold, and the rest copper. The silver medal contained only silver and copper, and the bronze medal was made of copper, zinc, and tin. The value of each medal was about $644 for gold, $330 for silver, and $4.71 for bronze. The bronze medal is actually made up of copper (97 percent), zinc (2.5 percent), and tin (0.5 percent), much like a U.S. penny (CBS News 2012).

Another way to look at the value of an Olympic medal is offered by Harvard Business School professor Stephen Greyser, who considers how much money an advertiser might offer a medal winner to endorse a product. The decision is likely to be based on four factors:

- How extraordinary was the athlete's performance? Did the athlete win a gold medal? Multiple medals? Did he or she set a world record?
- What is the athlete's sport? Top dollar is commanded by medal winners in track and field, gymnastics, and swimming. Medals in some sports—for example, archery, rowing, and shooting—are too low profile.
- Personality: it's okay to be a bit edgy, but a great smile and open personality go a long way.
- No baggage: a squeaky clean record and image are required.

Olympic champions who have parlayed their medals into significant sponsorships include Jamaican sprinter Usain Bolt ($20 million), South Korean figure skater Kim Yuna ($9 million), and U.S. swimmer Michael Phelps ($7 million) (Farnham 2012; Financial Underdog 2014).

popular in other countries? Our closest competitor, China, fares very well in gymnastics, diving, table tennis, badminton, and weightlifting where their naturally smaller stature is not a handicap and in fact often provides an advantage.

Athlete Development

To succeed in the Olympics, a country must develop its athletes, and to do that it must spend resources. But how best to allot them? In answering this question, the USOC must consider many factors. Let's look at a few.

Talent Identification

National governing bodies must take responsibility for recruiting large numbers of kids into their sport, offering strong competitive events for every age group, and assisting with training. By casting a wide net to find potential elite athletes, NGBs increase the odds that talented athletes will emerge.

No single system of identifying future star athletes has been accepted in the sporting world. Certain athletic attributes have been identified as critical in particular sports, but the many exceptions confound the experts. For one thing, maturation produces performance gains that simply cannot be predicted. For example, Michael Jordan was cut from his high school basketball team, yet went on to become the finest basketball player in the world.

The key to talent identification as it stands today is to gather young athletes who exhibit the best potential in their sport; encourage them; and provide them with competition opportunities (including international competition), expert coaching, and financial support. As the children develop, experts assess their natural talent and their sport progress and predict their future success.

What will it take to turn this young athlete into an Olympian?

Training

Training young athletes in the United States involves a crazy patchwork quilt of tradition, expediency, and entrepreneurship. Public schools offer sophisticated athletic programs in some sports that are affordable and geographically accessible to any potential athlete. Other sports do not have interscholastic teams or are conducted more as recreational activities.

Community-based programs in many sports get kids started and provide excellent early training. However, by the time some athletes reach the critical age of 12 or so, they may have outgrown the local competition and coaching expertise and therefore may need to travel or move in order to continue their athletic development. Here is where a family's income level can become a limitation.

The USOC has experimented with the idea of establishing mini-centers to offer training in several Olympic sports in major metropolitan areas. The jury is still out on the viability of this approach, and funding the centers continues to be an issue. Competition between athletes from different regions is made expensive by the geographical size of the United States.

As athletes advance to within a few years of potential Olympic competition, they need to gather with the best athletes in their sport in order to train, compete, and focus on their goal. Yet many NGBs do not provide this opportunity because they lack the facilities, the money, or even the commitment to do so. In some sports, private training academies provide this service, but money can still be a limiting factor. In other sports, such programs are conducted at the Olympic Training Centers in California, New York, and Colorado. Through economy of scale, these multisport facilities can offer more affordable operations, and athletes can interact with peers in other sports who may be easier to befriend than the athletes they compete with every day.

Coaching

Coaching is covered in detail in chapter 7, but it is worth reviewing briefly here because it is essential to athlete development. Indeed, coaching is typically the key to the optimal development of any athlete.

More specifically, most successful athletes are affected along the way by several coaches with different strengths. Coaches of introductory programs must understand youth, make sport fun, teach the fundamentals, and be willing to let go. Coaches of young athletes who are growing more dedicated to their sport must guide their development of competitive and physical skill, help them adjust to a changing physical body, offer a comprehensive training program, and recommend a coach for the next phase. Coaches of elite athletes aiming for world competition must understand the competitive world, capitalize on the athlete's strengths while minimizing weaknesses, tap into resources (such as specialists in sport science or advanced coaching) as needed, and be sensitive to the total makeup of the athlete as it relates to athletic performance.

While serving on the USOC Coaching Committee for two quadrenniums, I helped study the challenges faced by the U.S. coaching profession. During the eight years I served, from 1992 to 2000, we set the following goals, which were then transferred to the NGBs to implement in their respective sports:

- Improve the status and recognition of the coaching profession.
- Ensure the competence of coaches at every level by encouraging each sport to develop desired coaching competencies and help its coaches acquire them.
- Help coaches who seek to research and apply sport science in formulating training and development programs.

Spurred by those Olympic efforts, a broader coalition of organizations invested in high-quality coaching developed the National Standards for Athletic Coaches in 1995; the standards were revised in 2009 and have now been adopted by more than 140 sport organizations. Progress has since been made in translating these standards and competencies into coaching education and certification programs, particularly for high school coaches and in some Olympic governing bodies.

Chapter Summary

The modern Olympic Games have been a wildly successful international sporting tradition over the past 100 years. No other worldwide sporting event captures the same public interest, with the possible exception of the World Cup in soccer, which involves only one sport and sees interest fade in any given year in each country whose team is eliminated. At the Olympic Games, people from every country watch multiple athletes perform in multiple events as part of a festival lasting for more than a fortnight.

The Olympics have sparked athlete development programs in virtually all of the 204 nations that participate. Training elite athletes has become big business and is often supported by government funding. Athletes no longer need to be amateurs who compete merely for the love of the sport. In fact, success in the Olympic Games often provides an athlete with a financial bonanza, particularly if corporate sponsors choose him or her as a spokesperson.

During the Cold War, a nationalistic spirit dominated the Games, as countries vied for athletic supremacy to symbolically validate the superiority of their way of life. Gradually, the nationalistic fervor has faded and been replaced by an economic focus. Olympic organizers have sought to enlist the financial support of major worldwide corporations to offset the cost of staging the Games, opened the Games to professionals, and striven to exceed previous Games in breadth and quality.

Politics intertwine with the Olympic Games, and over the years multiple countries have used the Games for political purposes. Although many people are dismayed at the use of the Olympics for political reasons, others view such action as a natural way to draw world attention to injustices, such as apartheid, that are simply incompatible with the lofty ideals of Olympism.

In the United States, the USOC faces the daunting task of developing Olympic athletes. Whereas the governments of many other nations devote funding to developing their Olympic athletes, the USOC must raise money from private donations and corporate supporters.

The organization of the USOC has been under discussion and review in recent years. In 2004, several bills were put forth in the U.S. Congress to streamline USOC governance, reduce bureaucratic overlap, and simplify the daily operations of this nonprofit organization with an annual budget of about $100 million. Based on self-analysis and study, the USOC did simplify its governance by reducing the size of its board of directors from 125 to 11, reducing the number of committees from 23 to 4, and clarifying the role of management in serving the organization.

Athletes and coaches have benefited from efforts of the Olympic movement to provide better sport systems, talent scouting, support for potential Olympic athletes, and information and training for coaches. Through national governing bodies, information is filtered and adapted to each sport.

PART IV

Sport and Culture

Part IV begins in chapter 11 with a look at how moral attitudes both affect sporting behavior and are developed through sport. Most people believe that moral behavior can be taught through sport, and that is indeed the case—if the sport program or team and the coach espouse a clear philosophy, provide effective leadership, and consistently enforce rules. However, research over the past 25 years has also shown that the longer an athlete participates in sport, the less he or she tends to develop mature traits of moral decision making.

Chapters 12 through 15 address social classifications of people by race, gender, class, age, and disability. Each of these categories can exert a powerful effect on sport participation. For example, until the past 50 years, the exclusion of African Americans from the sport world mirrored the general policies of segregation implemented in the United States. Similarly, sport opportunities for women and girls in the country were severely limited until the federal Title IX legislation was enacted in the 1970s. In recent years, the inclusion of females and minorities has changed the U.S. sport landscape; specifically, participation among females and minorities has steadily increased, media coverage has expanded, and more money has been spent. Although equal opportunity has yet to be fully achieved, the effort is light years ahead of where it was just a generation ago.

Social class affects sport participation because people are drawn to particular sports that fit their interests, available time, and ability to pay. For example, affluent athletes can join private clubs, pay for coaching, and participate in expensive sports such as equestrianism, skiing, and golf. In contrast, working- and middle-class families rely primarily on public or community programs and school athletic programs, all of which are relatively affordable. Poor people and members of the working class are often drawn to sports that include violence—for example, auto racing, boxing, wrestling, and sport hybrids such as roller derby.

As baby boomers have reached retirement age, the number of people in the United States over age 50 has exceeded 100 million—nearly one-third of the total U.S. population. For most older adults, physical activity for health and lifestyle benefits replaces interest in competitive sport, though as spectators they may retain a commitment to competition. Another special population in sport is that of people with a physical or mental disability. Sport opportunities for these individuals have expanded dramatically since the passage of the Americans with Disabilities Act in 1990. In addition, both the Special Olympics and the Paralympics have become major worldwide events involving thousands of athletes who were previously left out of sport.

Chapters 16 and 17, respectively, address the intersection of sport with religion and with politics. No culture has ever functioned without some form of religious and political institutions, both of which influence people's attitudes toward physical activity and sport. Early religion in North America tended to favor development of the spirit rather than the body; in the twentieth century, however, organized religion began to embrace sport as both a worthwhile use of time and a powerful socializing agent. For their part, politicians have long recognized the psychosocial power of sport and used it to entertain the masses, socialize them toward particular ways of life, and inculcate feelings of nationalism.

As explored in chapter 18, many people have come to understand that sport offers not just competition for its own sake but also a multitude of benefits that can make a wider social impact. In fact, in the past several decades, a multitude of programs designed to benefit kids have used sport to attract participants with the enticement of physical activity and competition while placing equal emphasis on other social values such as teamwork and good sporting behavior that can be learned through sport participation. In fact, kids' programs—especially those serving disadvantaged kids—that feature sport are successfully helping to reduce crime and enable academic enhancement outside of school. At the international level, sport is used increasingly to promote peace and understanding, both among citizens of a single country and between citizens from different countries.

Chapters 19 and 20 are devoted to issues of deviance in the sport world. Chapter 19 explores the phenomenon of rule breaking in sport, why it happens, and possible strategies to reduce it. For example, the chapter examines the role of emotion and its effect on aggression, both in sport performers and in spectators. Although some types of aggression can be a positive factor in sport, athletes and coaches are not always clear about the difference between good and bad aggression. This chapter also tackles the troublesome issue of violence in sport, particularly among people with a history or culture that promotes violent behavior. Some people assume that violent sport provides an acceptable outlet for violent tendencies, but certain athletes have become notorious for their violent acts committed outside of competition.

Chapter 20 addresses performance enhancement and doping through the use of illegal substances. This recurrent problem has finally attracted the attention of both the U.S. government and key sport organizations, thus spurring better research and more stringent rules and enforcement in every sport. Sport-related gambling also continues to be a thorny issue but has gained public support during difficult economic times due to the allure of potential revenues for state coffers. This chapter also explores hazing in sport, eating disorders, and other aberrant behaviors—including some that may be life threatening—with a view toward how their troubling effects on the sporting world and individual athletes might be eliminated.

Finally, chapter 21 explores critical issues facing sport in view of larger social trends. For example, two realities of modern U.S. society are the aging population and the lengthening average life span. Many people look to enhance their later years through sport participation and spectatorship. At the same time, the population in general is facing a health crisis spurred by increases in overweight and obesity, both of which can be mitigated by appropriate physical activity.

Attitudes have changed considerably toward sport participation by people in categories based on race, gender, social class, age, and disability. Still, power struggles are likely to continue between those who favor high-performance sport and those who prefer sport participation for recreation by large numbers of people.

Advances in science and technology will push the frontiers of sport performance ever higher and continue to cause records to fall. Sport will change as societies change, and, depending on which social theory you consult, the changes will be initiated either within the sporting community or outside of it—for example, based on larger social changes reflected in laws and governmental policies and programs. What is certain is that sport *will* change to reflect society and sport can also help drive societal change.

11

STUDENT OUTCOMES

After reading this chapter, you will know the following:

- What constitutes good sporting behavior
- The relationship between sport and learned moral values
- Conflicting evidence regarding positive and negative effects of sport on moral behavior
- How parents, coaches, and others affect children's sporting behavior

Sporting Behavior

Sporting Behavior

In 2010, New York Yankees shortstop and future Hall of Famer Derek Jeter showed off his acting talents in a critical game with playoff implications against the Tampa Bay Rays. Jeter became the center of controversy when he was awarded first base by the umpire, who thought that a pitch had hit Jeter's hand, even though video replay (which was not used in Major League Baseball for such decisions at that time) clearly showed the ball hitting the knob of the bat before it rolled into fair territory. The Rays wisely threw to first base and claimed that Jeter should have been called out, but the umpire didn't agree. Jeter held his hand as if it hurt, drawing manager Joe Girardi and an athletic trainer to his side to evaluate the "injury." Later, Jeter admitted to acting and claimed that his job was to get on base: "The umpire told me to go to first, and I'm not going to tell him I'm not going" (Smith 2010).

The next batter hit a home run to put the Yankees ahead, but the Rays ended up winning the game. Still, the question heard 'round the league was whether Jeter's acting was just smart baseball or cheating. Naturally, Jeter's teammates and coaches came to his defense, claiming that his actions were justified, but many fans expressed their dismay that such a respected and revered player as Jeter would resort to cheating. After all, he could have just said it was up to the umpire to make the call, and he would have been perfectly justified in doing so.

Similarly, we often see soccer and basketball players "flopping" as if they have been fouled and wonder what has become of good sporting behavior. Is professional sport's preoccupation with winning at all costs infecting the ranks of college, high school, and youth sport?

Grantland Rice, one of the preeminent sportswriters of the early 20th century, was born in Tennessee in 1880 and became a pioneer in sport journalism—first in his home state and later in New York City, where he covered the exploits of Babe Ruth and Jack Dempsey. He completed a column about Willie Mays just before his death in 1954. As a Phi Beta Kappa graduate of prestigious Vanderbilt University—where he played football, basketball, and baseball—Rice sprinkled his columns liberally with poems and verses. One of the enduring quotes in the tradition of sport comes from the poem "Alumnus Football" in his book *Only the Brave and Other Poems* (Rice 1941):

> For when the One Great Scorer comes
> To write against your name,
> He marks—not that you won or lost—
> But how you played the game.

The term **sporting behavior** is often used to replace the traditional term *sportsmanship* in order to remove gender bias in describing human behavior in sport. For example, the Colorado High School Activities Association's (2014) mission statement includes the following bullet point: "Provide an environment that enhances personal development through sporting behavior, character education, teamwork, leadership, and citizenship while increasing values that partner the educational standards of the State of Colorado."

Throughout this chapter, the terms *sporting behavior* and *sportsmanship* are used interchangeably, depending on the source in question. The term **sportsmanship** has been defined as referring to "the ethical behavior exhibited by a sportsman [or sportswoman] or athlete . . . generally considered to involve participation for the pleasure gained from a fair and hard-fought contest, refusal to take unfair advantage of a situation or of an opponent, courtesy toward one's opponent, and graciousness in both winning and losing" (*Webster's Sports Dictionary* 1976).

High ideals notwithstanding, acceptable standards of behavior have been extolled, ignored, and given lip service by many coaches and sport participants. This chapter takes a fresh look at what good sporting behavior actually is, whether it can be taught and practiced in sport, and the attitude of U.S. society toward its importance. The chapter also considers how good sporting behavior is practiced at different levels of play; how moral development influences good sporting behavior; and how the examples provided by coaches, parents, and other athletes influence good sporting behavior.

Sporting Behavior at Different Levels of Sport

Performance sport, in which competition and winning are paramount, has dramatically influenced sporting behavior in recent years. As performance expectations increase, pressure to succeed rises as well. The value of winning can become such a seductive goal that all thoughts of moral behavior are temporarily put aside.

Professional athletes in all sports serve as role models for youthful competitors—whether they want to or not. Kids note their taunting, trash talk, disrespect, cheating, and bending or ignoring of the rules. The more successful professional athletes are, the more media attention they receive, in spite of boorish behavior or illegal acts.

Basketball Hall of Famer and sport commentator Charles Barkley once said, "I'm not a role model," by which he meant that the responsibility for moral upbringing lies not with professional athletes but with parents (Brennan 2001). Others may agree with Barkley, but the weight of evidence shows that young folks look to people whom they admire for clues about life. As a result, successful athletes who are put on display by the media impress young people who do not have caring and capable parents and coaches to help them differentiate between the positive and unacceptable traits of famous athletes.

Alex Rodriguez was suspended by MLB for one year for breaking the rules on the use of performance enhancing drugs.

At the same time, research shows that when children are systematically taught about fair play and moral development, character can be enhanced through sport (Gibbons, Ebbeck, and Weiss 1995). Still, professional athletes may exert a disconcerting influence when kids mistakenly believe that their questionable behavior contributes to their success. Young athletes may emulate that behavior to test its effectiveness, often with sad results that affect their life.

The media can contribute to such misunderstandings among youth by emphasizing winning above all else. Winners almost always get more photographs, more footage, and more lines of print. The next most popular media themes are money, ownership, coaching, and the skills needed to win. In contrast, media coverage of fairness, honesty, and consideration for other athletes is almost nonexistent, which gives the impression that these traits are unimportant (Fullerton 2003).

In contrast to performance sport, participation sport tends to take a more balanced approach to winning. In this approach, playing hard and fair wins admirers regardless of the outcome of the contest. As athletes age, they naturally tend to shift their emphasis from high performance toward participation. As discussed in chapter 3, people who choose participation or recreational sport focus mainly on enjoying the game, socializing with friends and opponents, and exercising. For millions of people who choose participation sport, even in their youth, the focus shifts away from winning, and healthy sporting behavior is viewed as a natural part of the social expectations of sport.

Young athletes have a lot to absorb just to learn the game, and this learning includes proper behavior toward others in the sport. These athletes may be too young to fully understand good sporting behavior, but they can certainly learn to follow coaches and officials in modeling acceptable behavior. As they mature intellectually, they become increasingly capable of understanding moral reasoning and controlling their feelings.

Since young people in performance sport are particularly malleable in attitude and behavior, they are the focus of most programs promoting good sporting behavior. These kids deal with the greatest pressure to perform at elite levels of sport; they also face the challenge of reconciling the conflicting behaviors they observe in various role models. To succeed in this environment, they need patience, clear guidelines, and consistent consequences for unacceptable actions. The following sample guidelines for kids were developed by clinical psychologist Darrell Burnett (2005):

- I abide by the rules of the game.
- I try to avoid arguments.
- I share in the responsibilities of the team.
- I give everyone a chance to play according to the rules.
- I always play fair.
- I follow the directions of the coach.
- I respect the other team's effort.
- I encourage my teammates.

As athletes age into their senior years, they grow in their capacity to place sport competition in a larger framework of life. The physical limitations that come with aging help older adults focus on the benefits of participation (Payne and Isaacs 2008). As they revise their goals to a realistic level of expectation, the pressure to win drops. At the same time, their reasoning ability and social experience allow them to form a code of behavior that reflects their personal value system. In most cases, people behave in a way that is acceptable to their social group—if they want to continue in that group.

Youth Attitudes

According to Michael Josephson, president of the Josephson Institute of Ethics, "The values of youth athletes are dramatically impacted by their sport experience, often for the worse." In fact, based on his research, it appears that "many coaches, especially in football, basketball, and baseball are teaching kids to cheat and cut corners" (Josephson 2007, 1).

A survey of 4,200 high school athletes revealed the following realities (Josephson 2004):

> *Coaches and parents simply aren't doing enough to assure that the experience (in sports) is a positive one. Too many youngsters are confused about the meaning of fair play and sportsmanship and they have no concept of honorable competition. As a result they engage in illegal conduct and employ doubtful gamesmanship techniques to gain a competitive advantage. It appears that today's playing fields are the breeding grounds for the next generation of corporate pirates and political scoundrels.*

These athletes are demonstrating good sporting behavior. Have you witnessed examples of *poor* sporting behavior?

To go in-depth on this issue, we can turn to a report titled "What Are Your Children Learning? The Impact of High School Sports on the Values and Ethics of High School Athletes." The researchers reported findings from a written survey of 5,275 high school athletes administered in 2005 and 2006 (for more information, visit www.charactercounts.org). The good news from the survey is that the majority of high school athletes trust and admire their coaches and learn positive life skills and good values from them. The bad news is that many coaches—particularly in the high-profile sports of boys' basketball, baseball, and football—are teaching kids how to cheat and cut corners. Here are some other findings (Josephson 2007, 2008):

- Girls practice better sporting behavior than do boys. On virtually every question, girls expressed deeper commitment to honesty and fair play. In contrast, boys were far more likely to exhibit cynical attitudes and engage in illegal or unsporting conduct.
- Behavior is worse in some sports than in others. Boys in baseball, football, and basketball were more likely to cheat, to take actions intended to deliberately injure an opponent, to intimidate, and to engage in trash talk. Such behavior was markedly less common among boys in swimming, track, cross country, gymnastics, and tennis.
- Among girls, the most negative behavior was shown by basketball and softball players.
- Coaches don't always set a good example. Most players felt that their coaches generally exhibited good sporting behavior; however, when players were questioned about

specific coaching actions, one-quarter to one-third of their answers revealed violations by coaches.

- Many high school athletes break rules and engage in unsporting conduct. Many think it is proper to deliberately inflict pain in football in order to intimidate an opponent (60 percent of males, 27 percent of females), trash-talk a defender after every score (42 percent of males, 18 percent of females), soak a football field to slow down an opponent (27 percent of males, 12 percent of females), or throw at a batter who homered in his or her last at bat (30 percent of males, 16 percent of females).
- Winning was more important than sporting behavior. More than 37 percent of males agreed that it's more important to win than to be considered a good sport. More specifically, 31 percent of males and 25 percent of females said they believed their coach was more concerned with winning than with building character and life skills.
- Cheating and theft seemed acceptable to many high school athletes. When asked about their behavior in the past year, 68 percent of both males and females admitted to cheating on a test in school, 26 percent of males and 19 percent of females said they had stolen an item from a store, and 43 percent of males and 31 percent of females said they had cheated or bent the rules in order to win.
- Hazing and bullying seemed acceptable to many high school athletes. Specifically, 69 percent of males and 50 percent of females admitted that they had bullied, teased, or taunted someone in the past year; moreover, 52 percent of males and 29 percent of females said they had used racial slurs or insults.

In spite of these grim statistics, the tide may be turning. A recent follow-up study by the Josephson Institute (2012b) revealed that—for the first time in a decade—lying, stealing, and cheating had declined among U.S. students. In the survey of more than 23,000 students, the percentage who admitted they had cheated in the past year dropped from 59 percent in 2010 to 51 percent in 2012. Similarly, the percentage who said they had lied to a teacher in the past year dropped from 61 percent in 2010 to 55 percent in 2012. In addition, the number who admitted stealing from a store dropped from 27 percent in 2010 to 20 percent in 2012. Although the percentages indicating infractions still stand well above what we might like to see, the trend of increasing misbehavior has clearly been interrupted and possibly even reversed.

Perhaps even more encouraging, 99 percent of students agreed that "it is important for me to be a person with good character," 93 percent said they were satisfied with their own character, and 81 percent believed that they are better than most people they know at doing what is right. In addition, 93 percent of students said their parents urge them to do the right things no matter the cost, and 85 percent said that most adults consistently set a good example in terms of ethics and character (Josephson Institute 2012b).

In spite of this good news, another troubling trend has also emerged. The continuous reporting in recent years of teen suicides, school shootings, and homicides committed against youthful victims should have alerted us as a society to some disturbing tendencies toward violence in our U.S. society. Specifically, one in three students say that violence is a big problem in their school, one in five report that they do not feel safe in school, and half of boys and more than one-third of girls admit hitting a person in the past year because they were angry. Furthermore, many of these violent actions are associated with prejudice, discrimination, and bullying (Josephson Institute 2012a).

One note of caution about the study: The respondents included high school athletes in a variety of sports in certain geographical locations, and it is difficult to generalize the results to all athletes due to wide variation in sport, location, coach, level of competition, and social class.

Now that we've looked at sporting behavior at different levels of sport, we can examine how good sporting behavior develops, beginning with moral development. We can also consider how moral development and moral values affect sport.

Development of Moral Values

Our behavior in sport is founded on our level of moral reasoning. Many researchers have studied the development of moral values in society, and they have advanced various theories that differ in some ways but that all link moral capacity to intellectual development. Jean Piaget, a famous Swiss

Meghan Vogel, High School Track Star

At an Ohio track meet in 2012, Meghan Vogel finished first by finishing last. After winning the state title in the 1,600-meter race, Vogel competed later the same day in the 3,200-meter race. Unsurprisingly, she didn't have much left for the second race, but she competed gamely until the stretch run, when she realized that an opponent, Arden McMath, had fallen several meters from the finish line. Without hesitating, Vogel helped McMath to her feet and virtually carried her across the finish line in front of her.

For her efforts, Vogel earned a 15th-place finish, but she also helped an opposing runner complete the race. When asked about her action, Vogel replied that "if you work to get to the state meet, you deserve to finish no matter who you are, and I was just determined to make that happen for her" (Llorens 2012).

psychologist, is renowned for his pioneering work in explaining the stages of mental development and later moral development. One of his devotees was Lawrence Kohlberg, who as a professor at Harvard University publicized his own theory of moral development beginning in the 1970s. Like Piaget, Kohlberg believed that children move through a series of stages before arriving at their capacity for moral maturity. Kohlberg's theory serves as a model of moral development for our discussion of good sporting behavior (Crain 1985; Smart and Smart 1982).

Kohlberg demonstrated through studies that people progress in their moral reasoning through a series of stages that are age-related, though not determined by age. Kohlberg asserted that moral reasoning could proceed only with intellectual development and exposure to socialization. He classified the stages into three levels, placing two stages in each level:

Preconventional

1. Punishment and obedience
2. Pleasure or pain

Conventional

3. Good boy or girl
4. Law and order

Postconventional

5. Social contract
6. Principled conscience

Let's take a closer look at each of these stages and how they influence good sporting behavior (see table 11.1 for some basics).

TABLE 11.1 Kohlberg's Stages of Moral Development

Approximate age range	Level	Stage	Focus
Birth to 9 years	Preconventional	1. Avoiding punishment 2. Gaining reward	What is best for self Exchange of favors
9 to 20 years	Conventional	3. Gaining approval; avoiding disapproval 4. Duty and guilt	Pleasing others Respecting society's rules
Older than 20 years (or never)	Postconventional	5. Agreed-upon rights; rules flexible 6. Universal ethical principles	Society bound to respect everyone's rights Respecting human dignity and justice for everyone

Preconventional Level

The **preconventional level** provides the base for moral reasoning. This level's first stage, focused on punishment and obedience, describes the moral thinking typically found in elementary school. Young students and athletes in this stage behave according to socially acceptable norms because they are told to do so by parents, teachers, and coaches. Therefore, being right simply means obeying an authority, and disobeying the authority's dictates results in punishment. This concept lies within the intellectual grasp of children; they can understand it. Whether they obey depends both on the timing and manner of delivery of the directions and on the punishment for disobedience.

The second stage involves thinking that the reason for behavior is to get pleasure for oneself. This hedonistic approach to moral choices is self-centered rather than focused on respecting the values of a group or society. Children at this stage realize that there is not always one right answer as decided by an adult authority; therefore, they test their own conclusions. They still expect punishment if their actions are wrong, but, unlike in stage one, they now view punishment as simply a risk that one takes for acting in a certain way. In other words, punishment does not *necessarily* follow wrong behavior.

Youth athletes in stage two may take certain actions because they have learned that doing so is in their self-interest. They reason as an individual engaged in egocentric behavior rather than as a member of a group or community.

Kohlberg believed that younger children typically use the preconventional level of morality because they can process it intellectually. As children mature and begin to understand how the world works, they adopt a more relativistic approach that views rules not as absolute but as changeable if the group agrees to change them. Children tend to change in moral capacity around age 10 or 11—the very time when many kids are heavily involved in youth sport. Wise coaches anticipate this development and assist it rather than limiting players to simply following coaching dictates.

For example, a good coach may enlist the help of her or his athletes in deciding appropriate punishment for players who break rules or behave inappropriately. When athletes participate in the process, they must examine the seriousness of the offense, the number of occurrences, any previous warnings, and possible sanctions or punishments. As they review the facts and consider alternatives, they establish a sense of moral decision making that helps them mature in their thinking abilities.

Unfortunately, some children get stuck in the preconventional level of moral development. As a result, they often deviate from social norms, and they may end up in a correctional institution. Some adults also exhibit this lower level of moral reasoning when justifying their actions, thus further confusing the young people who hear their opinions.

Conventional Level

The **conventional level** of moral reasoning is the level attained by most adults. In fact, the first stage of this level—the third overall stage of moral development—is the one typically found in society. In this way of being, one's behavior is guided by whatever is generally acceptable to friends, family, and community. Youth usually reach this stage in high school, and high school students often value good behavior that emphasizes love, caring, empathy, trust, and concern for others. They also try on various behaviors to see how people around them respond and then typically either modify the actions that do not conform to group standards or willingly pay the price for deviating from group standards.

The fourth stage is dubbed "law and order" because it emphasizes the importance of following laws, respecting authority, and performing accepted duties so that society can function. Without smooth societal functioning, anarchy would reign. In this stage, people see the need to follow the rules of society or work to change those with which they disagree.

The majority of any population falls into the two conventional stages because *conventional* means just that—established by general usage. Most of us stay in stage three or four for most of our lives.

Postconventional Level

Most of us do not reach the **postconventional level**. Its first stage—the fifth stage overall—is referred to as a "social contract" because people in this stage have an interest in the welfare of others. This is an autonomous, principled stage of thinking in which people adopt certain moral principles and hold to certain behaviors regardless of social punishment

ACTIVITY TIME-OUT

Moral Reasoning and Sport

What does Kohlberg's theory have to do with sport? Consider how you would answer the following questions about moral decision making in sport. For each question, list your answer, your justification, and the level of moral reasoning you used.

1. As a high school tennis player, you play varsity matches without officials. It is up to both players to honestly call whether balls land in or out. Balls on the line must be called "good," and players are expected to give the opponent the benefit of any doubt. However, your opponent seems to consistently call your shots out when they land close to the line. Should you confront him about his calls, make a few questionable calls of your own to even things out, tell your coach, or simply ignore his calls and play the match?
2. During a softball game, the opposing team's best hitter comes to the plate having hit a home run in her last at bat. Your coach orders you to "brush her back" with a high inside pitch to push her away from the plate. Should you follow your coach's direction or ignore it?
3. During basketball practice, your coach has the team work on illegal holding techniques in order to prevent the opponent from rebounding missed shots. The coach shows you the best way to avoid being caught by the officials. Even though holding is against the rules, would you follow the coach's orders and work on holding without being caught?

or reward. In fact, this is where the concept of inalienable human rights comes into play. So too does the idea of treating all people with dignity and respect regardless of their ethnic or racial background, economic class, or actions.

Kohlberg also postulated a sixth stage that relied heavily on humanistic principles of valuing human life and feeling right with oneself. In this stage, the principles of justice, fairness, and human dignity require compassion and ask us to treat all humans as individuals who deserve impartial love and concern. People in this stage are guided toward appropriate actions by certain universal laws accepted by all religions. Eventually, however, having found so few humans that seemed to have reached this sixth stage, Kohlberg basically ignored it. Indeed, apart from great moral leaders—such as Mahatma Gandhi, Martin Luther King Jr., and Nelson Mandela—few people reach this stage of moral development.

Barriers to Good Sporting Behavior

Because of the heavy emphasis on winning in sport competition, some athletes struggle with the choice between winning by any means and exhibiting good sporting behavior. For young children, it takes time to develop the necessary intellectual understanding to move beyond simply playing by the rules and begin competing in the spirit of the game as well. For older youth and adults in the conventional stage, barriers to good behavior may include customs in their sport of choice, as well as the influence of coaches and spectators. Even coaches and parents who understand good sporting behavior sometimes forgive athletes who offend because they want their team to win. The media's glorification of winners helps reinforce the importance of winning and gives the impression that our culture admires winners—not necessarily good sports.

It may be difficult to pinpoint one specific cause of the disturbing patterns of poor sporting behavior in U.S. sport, but we can at least identify the possible suspects. Clearly the preoccupation with winning at every level of sport has helped tilt the emphasis away from cultivating good sporting behavior and toward simply focusing on the outcome. In fact, most athletes admit that as they move into higher levels of competition in college or professional sport, the emphasis on winning increases dramatically. Thus we see the very best athletes exhibiting behavior that at much younger ages we would brand as unacceptable. "For evidence we need only look at the escalating problem of illegal drugs in sports which the United States Anti-Doping Agency has tabbed as the most serious problem in sports today, an ethics issue stemming from an overemphasis on winning" (U.S. Anti-Doping Agency 2010, 7).

When younger athletes are asked which athletes have the most positive effect on them as role models, they tend to name Olympic athletes first and collegiate and professional athletes last. In fact, the negative effect exerted by professional athletes as role models is likely to be one of primary contributing factors in the decline of good sporting behavior. Indeed, athletes in certain sports consistently exhibit poor patterns of behavior, particularly football, ice hockey, baseball, and wrestling (U.S. Anti-Doping Agency 2010, 7–8).

The sport media also share in the blame because they have access to every young impressionable athlete. They often focus on professional athletes behaving badly and fill the airwaves with photos and replays of poor sporting behavior. In fact, a quick review of ESPN's *SportsCenter* offers innumerable reports about bad acts and bad actors but allocates very little air time to positive behavior by athletes. If the objective is to teach and reward good behavior, then perhaps we should expect and demand better behavior by the athletes who serve as role models. Moreover, when they disappoint us by their behavior, perhaps we should either ignore them or punish them as we would a wayward child.

Moral Values Applied to Sport

Now that we've covered the stages of moral development, let's look at how they affect sport, which can play a vital role in helping young people become socialized in their environment. **Socialization** is the process of interacting with other people and learning social customs, morals, and values. As we interact with others, we form beliefs that affect how we think we should act. Others do the same through their interactions with us. Thus socialization is a dynamic process, and our understanding of our social world changes as we accumulate experiences.

Some of the theories discussed in chapter 2—including the functionalist, conflict, and interactionist theories—describe how socialization occurs in society. Let's look at how each of these theories has influenced current understanding of the ways in which athletes become socialized in sport.

Functionalist theorists view socialization as a process through which we develop social characteristics that allow us to fit into our world. Therefore, we can use this approach to study the athletes being socialized, their likely guides (such as parents and coaches), and the outcomes of the process. For example, studies by Shields (2005) and Josephson (2004) elicit information from athletes about why they participate in sport and what changes as a result of their participation. Most of these studies have presented inconclusive or even contradictory evidence, and it is difficult to generalize findings from a restricted sample size due to the wide variation of possible athletic experiences.

Conflict theory offers another approach to socialization. Advocates of this theory assume that people with economic influence use it to maintain their status in privileged positions in society. As described by Coakley and Dunning (2004), most research using this approach has focused on how highly organized sport programs with authoritarian leaders and coaches have helped develop athletes who conform to the system in order to be accepted within the group. Such systems may exploit athletes who come from lower socioeconomic classes. In spite of poor academic skills, athletes may be pushed through college as long as they have eligibility remaining, but they may never actually graduate.

One example of interactionist research into athlete participation can be found in the work of Fine (1987). As the name suggests, interactionist models emphasize interaction between athletes and their environment as the athletes form traits through the process of socialization. Typically, interactionist research has been relatively clinical and based on qualitative, in-depth interviews with athletes. The goal is to accumulate information in a natural field setting in order to understand what happens to an athlete during socialization through sport. Thus this method departs from the model of research that uses large samples of people who are questioned objectively and asked to report on their experiences.

Whatever theory one applies, the fundamental question explored in this chapter is whether sport participation builds character or negatively influences character. Or perhaps it exerts little influence at all. For years, we have accepted the premise that sport builds character with little evidence to support it. Let's look at the data that have been collected so far.

Sport as Character Builder

> *Watch your thoughts, for they become words. Watch your words, for they become actions. Watch your actions, for they become habits. Watch your habits, for they become character. Watch your character, for it becomes your destiny.*
>
> Author unknown

Does sport participation build character? This question is much more difficult to answer than it appears. In fact, experts cannot even agree on what character is; moreover, even if they did, it would still be difficult to measure. Some studies (Beller and Stoll 1994) have compared people who play sport with people who do not and have concluded that the positive traits exhibited by athletes prove that sport is beneficial. However, it could also be the case that people who play sport already possess those positive traits. Likewise, people who do not play sport can certainly develop positive character traits through other experiences. For these reasons, it has been very difficult to confirm a clear cause-and-effect relationship.

Another confounding variable is the fact that not all sport experiences are inherently similar. For example, they may vary depending on whether one emphasizes participation or competitive excellence. Sport experiences also depend on an athlete's age, ability to make moral decisions, and opportunities to make such decisions. Thus coaches may greatly influence moral decision making, depending on their philosophy of coaching and their openness (or lack thereof) to athlete-centered activity versus coach-centered activity.

Consider the different feelings about moral behavior that could arise from teammates who play very different positions. For example, contrast the likely attitude of a defensive end in American football who relies on aggressiveness—and may be urged to injure the opposing quarterback—with that of a placekicker who rarely engages in physical contact but deals with constant mental pressure to deliver successful kicks in critical situations.

Likewise, athletes who compete in big-time sport at universities adopt a moral code of behavior that fits with their ultimate objective

This athlete's ability to make sound moral decisions may differ from that of his peers.

of competing at the highest levels of their sport. Therefore, although they are relatively mature intellectually, these athletes tend to embrace a simple, practical approach of playing within the rules to avoid punishment and progress to the next level of competition. In contrast, athletes who compete for a Division III college that offers no scholarships must determine the role played by sport in their life and balance their sport activity with their pursuit of other life goals related to their studies and career. For these athletes, sport may be more of a social activity, a physical outlet, or a chance to test their skills. In this setting, moral behavior is more about comfortably fitting in with their teammates and coaches (Lyons 2013).

Table 11.2 shows the results of a survey that questioned high school athletes about their attitudes toward sporting behavior. Although the majority of high school athletes viewed negative behaviors as unacceptable, one-quarter to one-half of the respondents thought the negative behaviors were okay. Apparently, these athletes were simply reflecting moral values that they had been taught—and that may have been reinforced through sport. If we asked professional athletes the same questions, do you think the results would be similar? If not, how would they differ, and why?

Character Development in Sport

As we have discussed, performance sport emphasizes winning, pursuit of excellence, and attaining the highest possible level of performance. In this approach, opponents are often seen as enemies to be dominated, demoralized, and defeated. This

TABLE 11.2 High Schoolers' Attitudes Toward Sporting Behavior

	BOYS (% GIVING EACH ANSWER)			GIRLS (% GIVING EACH ANSWER)		
Question	**Proper**	**Improper**	**Not sure**	**Proper**	**Improper**	**Not sure**
1. A soccer coach orders a player to attack an injured body part of the other team's top scorer.	29	50	22	13	66	22
2. A key baseball player for team X is hit by a pitch. In retaliation, team X's coach orders his pitcher to throw at an opposing hitter.	25	52	24	9	71	20
3. A football lineman deliberately seeks to inflict pain on an opposing player in order to intimidate him.	60	19	21	27	40	34
4. A football coach's team is out of time-outs in a crucial game. He instructs a player to fake an injury in order to stop the clock.	37	34	29	20	49	31
5. A basketball coach teaches players how to illegally hold and push in ways that are difficult to detect.	43	31	27	22	52	26
6. A softball pitcher deliberately throws at a batter who homered in her last at bat.	30	43	28	16	59	25
7. A player trash-talks a defender after every score by demeaning the defender's skill.	42	32	26	18	56	27
8. A baseball coach instructs the groundskeeper to build up the third base foul line slightly in order to keep bunts in fair territory.	26	47	27	20	49	31

Based on Josephson 2004.

approach also accepts—and in fact expects—hard work, dedication, sacrifices, and physical risks. In contrast, participation sport emphasizes game play; the enjoyment of physical movement; and connections between mind and body, between athlete and nature, and between one athlete and another. In this approach, decisions are typically made democratically, and all players—regardless of ability—get to participate in the action.

As this comparison makes clear, performance sport puts a great deal more pressure on both athletes and coaches. In turn, when people are stretched to their limits, their moral decisions may be affected, and they may come to see winning and performance as more important than anything else. Many youth sports are conducted more in the mode of performance sport than participation sport, even though, in the long run, the athletes may not be suited to performance sport.

In contrast, neighborhood "pickup games" have been played by many generations. In playing these games, kids learn to function as a group in order to agree on what game to play, what rules to follow, who plays what position, and how to handle disputes. The outcome of the game is less important than simply getting to play. If the group doesn't agree, the game doesn't happen. As a result, players learn to call their own fouls or risk social isolation; similarly, players who hog the ball are chosen last for future games. In these ways, the group establishes and enforces moral codes of behavior, and kids work out disputes without coaches, umpires, or league organizers.

Defining Character in Sport

The concept of character varies over time and across societies. In the United States, conceptions of good character tend to be based on the ideals espoused by the nation's founders, as well as the Puritan work ethic. In colonial days, individuals were admired for working hard simply to survive in conditions that demanded nothing less. People expected others to conform to societal customs, obey parents and leaders, exhibit self-discipline and loyalty toward family and friends, and respect external rewards. These same virtues constitute good sporting behavior.

Young people should be able to transfer the life lessons they learn in sport to the workplace as they enter the adult world. Thus a major achievement of youth sport is to teach young people to act in socially acceptable ways and to instill those lessons so that they carry over into the adult years. Most resources (such as Ariss 2000) that address good sporting behavior list the following attributes as essential:

- Knowing and following the rules of the game
- Respecting teammates, opponents, officials, and coaches
- Never using or threatening physical violence
- Abstaining from taunting, bragging, or excessive celebration
- Avoiding profanity and other hurtful language
- Demonstrating honesty and resisting the temptation to cheat
- Accepting responsibility for one's actions
- Treating others as one would like to be treated

Despite the good intentions expressed in these ideals, some evidence (Stoll and Beller 2009) indicates that participating in high school sport may *hinder* the development of moral character. After compiling research covering a 20-year period and involving more than 72,000 athletes in at least 45 published and unpublished sport studies, Beller and Stoll offered the following conclusions:

- Higher levels of moral reasoning are not typically applied in the competitive athletic environment.
- Athletes scored *lower* than nonathletes on moral development.
- Female athletes scored higher than male athletes.
- Female team athletes' scores on moral reasoning declined about every three years.
- Athletes appear to get morally calloused by the competitive sport environment.
- Male athletes in revenue-producing sports score lower than athletes in nonrevenue sports.
- The longer an athlete participates in competitive sport, the lower his or her level of moral reasoning tends to be.
- Intervention programs can make a positive difference in moral reasoning and can affect that ability over the long term with support and leadership by coaches.

At the end of the day, the evidence conflicts on the question of whether sport builds character. The concept of character itself is vague, and the effect of sport participation is variable and depends on the athlete's age and situation and on the social dynamics in his or her chosen sport. Social psychologists Miracle and Rees (1994, 96) conclude that "research does not support either position in the debate over sport building character."

It may be helpful to consider two different types of character: social and moral. Social character involves teamwork, loyalty, work ethic, and perseverance. Athletes who participate in team sport exhibited high levels of social character; individual-sport athletes ranked second, and nonathletes came in third. Moral character, on the other hand, involves honesty, fairness, integrity, and responsibility. On these traits, nonathletes scored highest, followed by individual-sport athletes and then team-sport athletes (Beller and Stoll 2009).

Powerful Influence of Coaches

At this point, you may be convinced that it is overly optimistic to expect sport to automatically build good character in athletes. On the other hand, you should also be clear that sport offers dynamic and powerful social experiences that may—under the right circumstances—provide benefits. The key, according to Bredemeier and Shields (2006), lies in the behavior and leadership provided by the coach. These authors recommend that coaches use the following strategies:

- Emphasize effort and mastery of athletic tasks rather than innate ability and competitive outcome. Athletes cannot control their genetic athleticism, but they can control their effort and increase their skill through diligent work.
- Emphasize team cooperation rather than rivalry. Encourage team members to help each other and appreciate each athlete as a uniquely valuable individual.
- Help athletes appreciate the important role of mistakes as they learn and develop. Keep the atmosphere positive, focus on what athletes do right, and help them accept errors as part of the learning process.

In sum, Bredemeier and Shields hold that sport can build character—but only if coaches deliberately seek to make it happen and possess the necessary skills and training to structure the situation appropriately. The researchers indicate that emphasizing skill mastery serves as a healthier and more powerful motivator for athletes than emphasizing ego satisfaction with a primary focus on winning games.

Here are some additional key actions that coaches should take in order to teach and reinforce good sporting behavior (U.S. Anti-Doping Agency 2012):

- Model the type of behavior they are encouraging for their athletes—in other words, not only "talk the talk" but also "walk the talk."
- At every level of sport, actively teach athletes both the rules of the game and the unwritten rules. For example, practice time should include discussion of fair play, respect for others, and a healthy perspective on winning and losing.

APPLYING SOCIAL THEORY

Functionalist Theorists and Sporting Behavior

Take the perspective of a traditional functionalist theorist who holds that the institution of sport reinforces societal values and who generally supports the status quo. Apply this stance to the topic of sporting behavior. Given the research presented in this chapter by Beller and Stoll (2009) and Josephson (2007), can you still make the case that sport helps young people develop their moral reasoning ability and moral character? Focus on specific qualities of moral character, such as honesty, integrity, and fairness. Consider holding an in-class debate or group discussion or organize your answer into a two-page written position.

- Reward and reinforce players who exhibit good sporting behavior and fair play. Do so in specific and tangible ways that are clearly visible to their teammates.
- When players fail to exhibit good behavior, clearly explain the infraction, suggest a better course of action, and punish habitual offenders through loss of practice or playing time or, in serious cases, suspension from the team.
- With the support of the athletic director, educate parents and fans so that athletes receive a consistent message about good sporting behavior from significant people in their life.

Sport Ethic

A dominant sport ethic is not a new concept in sport, but it is one that constantly changes to reflect a system of values for coaches and athletes. It consists of the behavioral norms accepted and praised in the sporting culture. For example, in team sport, one generally accepted rule is that a player should not publicly criticize a teammate. Athletes who eagerly endorse the prevailing sport ethic are warmly embraced by sport owners, the media, coaches, and teammates. In contrast, those who rebel against the norms find it difficult to exist in that same world.

Case in point: Kobe Bryant is arguably one of the greatest basketball players in the history of the National Basketball Association (NBA), yet he has never been beloved by his coaches or his teammates. When paired with fellow NBA great Shaquille O'Neal and led by coaching legend Phil Jackson, Bryant wanted to dominate, and he resented O'Neal's presence and the media attention he drew. In addition, during time-outs, Bryant often shared with teammates his frequently critical thoughts about their play (Gargill and Penn 2006).

High-performance sport tends to set more clearly defined expectations for athletes. For example, dedication and sacrifice are expected and required, and there is little room for athletes to question the prevailing norms if they want to be respected by teammates and competitors. Coakley (2004) analyzed the culture of high-performance sport and identified the following dominant themes:

- The hallmark of performance athletes is their striving for excellence. They are expected to compete to win, train to exhaustion, sacrifice to meet their athletic goals, and put other areas of life aside in single-minded pursuit of sport excellence.
- Love of the game is expected, and athletes must demonstrate it. Indeed, without genuine love of the game, many athletes could not endure the sacrifices, the hours of training, or the exclusion of other areas of life.
- Commitment—to one's team, teammates, and coaches—is preached by both coaches and athletes, who accept that philosophy and are held up as role models.
- Playing in the midst of pain or other adversity serves as a badge of courage for an athlete. As soldiers are admired for their bravery in battle and their courage in facing death, so athletes are expected to deal with physical and psychological pain as the price they pay for respect.

An athlete must decide whether to embrace the current sport ethic or struggle against the system. Young athletes in particular are susceptible to the exhortations of coaches and respected teammates as they search for behavior that will earn them acceptance, praise, and respect in a world they admire. In such an atmosphere, athletes who lack a strong sense of personal identity eagerly adopt the athletic code simply because of their age and inexperience.

The people who benefit most from the current U.S. sport ethic are those who gain money or reputation when their affiliated athletes succeed. Team owners, the media, and coaches all have a stake in team performance and tend to reward those who readily accept the prevailing value system. However, this approach is not always beneficial for athletes. For example, athletes who play through pain are labeled as courageous even if they risk permanent injury. Similarly, physical courage is expected, particularly for males as supposed proof of their manhood. Admiration follows athletes who take risks without regard for the consequences. In contrast, players who shy away from physical danger are labeled unworthy of the fraternity of male athletes.

Likewise, those who overtrain may be admired for their dedication—until their overtraining interferes with their performance. In addition, eating disorders, particularly among female athletes, are prevalent in certain sports in which body weight is a factor, even though these disorders may lead to death.

As these potential pitfalls suggest, unquestioned acceptance of the prevailing sport ethic sometimes constitutes a form of deviant overconformity. Athletes may adopt behaviors that are outside the norms of society because their insulated world of sport has its own ethic. Moreover, that sport ethic may be reinforced by fans and the media, who encourage athletes to pursue athletic excellence at any cost.

In addition, when the sport ethic builds special bonds between teammates to the exclusion of bonds with others, the athlete's interpersonal relationships outside of sport may suffer. The special circle excludes even one's spouse, family, and friends. In such an atmosphere, athletes may become so cocky that they believe themselves to be special and above the rules of behavior that others are expected to follow. Indeed, the sport media are rife with examples of athletes who expect special privileges and preferential treatment and display

ACTIVITY TIME-OUT

Is Trash Talk Good or Bad?

Trash talk involves using insulting or boastful speech intended to demoralize, intimidate, or humiliate an opponent in an athletic contest. It is a common occurrence, particularly in the professional sports of American football and basketball. Opinions differ about whether it is simply a fun part of the game or a form of inappropriate behavior that degrades the competition and in some cases violates the rules of the game.

Athletes say that they use trash talk to motivate themselves and to psych out or intimidate their opponents and thus impair their performance. In spite of its widespread use, particularly in certain sports, trash talk clearly violates the rules of both high school and collegiate sport. For example, the National Federation of State High School Associations makes clear in all sport-specific rulebooks that "taunting opponents" violates the rules and that players or coaches who engage in it should be disqualified. Similarly, in the football rulebook of the National Collegiate Athletic Association (NCAA), the first rule in section 2 (Unsportsmanlike Conduct Fouls) states, "No player, substitute or coach shall use abusive, threatening or obscene language or gestures, or engage in such acts that provoke ill will or are demeaning to an opponent, game officials or to the image of the game including but not limited to:

a. Pointing the finger(s), hand(s), arm(s) or ball at an opponent, or imitating the slashing of the throat.

b. Taunting, baiting or ridiculing an opponent verbally."

The first offense draws a 15-yard penalty, and a subsequent (or flagrant) violation results in ejection from the game (NCAA 2014b).

Another name for trash talk is "insult talk," which is often used among males and often involves sexist or homophobic references. Historically, this practice has been popular in manufacturing plants, on shop floors, in fraternities, and in male-dominated offices. It has also been adopted as part of the culture in certain sports, including basketball, football, ice hockey, and soccer. It is uncommon in many other sports—for example, swimming, golf, and tennis. In the African American community, such talk is sometimes referred to as "signifying," which manifests itself in the form of boastful, humorous, insulting, and provocative comments made in an atmosphere of friendly competition. It is not uncommon to hear such talk on the street or on city playgrounds, regardless of whether sport is involved (Rainey and Granito 2010).

In the final analysis, the intent behind trash talk may help determine how offensive it is and whether it should be ignored or punished. What do you think?

a sense of entitlement. Fans who idolize these athletes encourage this antisocial behavior and then wonder what went wrong when the athletes disappoint them.

Linking Good Sporting Behavior to Mental Toughness

In recent years, an important connection has been made between good sporting behavior and emotional control. In the heat of battle, athletes often lose control of their emotions and then behave poorly. In addition, when they are highly aroused with negative emotion, they are also likely to perform poorly in athletic terms.

Fortunately, sport psychologists and coaches have also found that teaching athletes how to control their emotions can help them compete in an ideal state of emotional arousal. In that state, the athlete clearly focuses on the task at hand, blocks out distractions, relaxes tense muscles, and effectively regulates breathing. Other keys to achieving this state include rituals, positive self-talk, and visual imagery.

Since all athletes want to maximize their success, they are very receptive to learning skills to improve their mental toughness. Happily, mental toughness may also produce a strong by-product in the form of good sporting behavior. Athletes are much more likely to ignore opponents' poor behavior, as well as the vagaries of bad luck, if they have their emotions under control and are focused on their performance.

Knowledge of the rules of competition still provides the foundation for good sporting behavior. However, to develop further, athletes must also understand the *spirit* of the rules—a commitment to fair play and socially acceptable behavior from all athletes, coaches, and fans.

A related insight comes from sport psychology researchers Shields and Bredemeier (2009), who suggest that instead of blaming poor sporting behavior on competition, we should embrace the positives to be gained from a highly competitive contest. Each athlete or team pushes the other to her or his limits, and together they maximize each other's performance. In fact, opponents must cooperate with each other in order to produce their best efforts and reach excellence in performance.

Competition can also create stress for the competitors, especially if they focus on defeating others rather than on their own performance. Shields and Bredemeier (2009) have labeled that negative aspect "decompetition," which is the exact opposite of competition. In an atmosphere of decompetition, opponents see each other as enemies who must be defeated at all costs. As a result, rules of play are respected only as long as it is convenient, meaning that they are often ignored, and competition is typified by cheating, intimidation, and lack of respect. A healthy view of positive competition will enhance the ability of athletes to perform at their highest level and demonstrate mental toughness in response to the stress typically produced by decompetition.

Moral Values Taught Through Sport

In spite of the lack of convincing evidence, most people still assume that there is value in linking good sporting behavior with competition in sport. Certainly, it allows contests to take place within a common framework of rules and customs, without which chaos would reign. It is also true that young people learn moral behavior as they mature, and sport can serve as one source of experience that informs them about acceptable and unacceptable attitudes and behavior.

As young people gain intellectual maturity, their ability to process this information grows, and a personal moral code emerges. In the critical teenage years, most kids rely on their peers for guidance as to acceptable behavior. Originally, they got that information from their parents, teachers, and other adults; however, as they begin the struggle into adulthood, it becomes paramount to be accepted by their peers. In this part of their development, they exhibit the conventional level of moral reasoning typical of the "good boy or girl" and "law and order" stages.

Recognizing the powerful influence that sport can exert on youth, many organizations have begun aggressive campaigns to promote good sporting behavior. Since 1992, the Institute for International Sport has sponsored National Sportsmanship Day on the first Tuesday in March. The celebration involves youth sport organizations, schools (elementary, middle, and high), and colleges around the world totaling more than 14,000 schools in more than 100 countries. It promotes awareness of good sporting behavior by stimulating dialogue among people involved in sport (International Sport 2010).

Participating schools and organizations receive posters, role-playing scenarios, games, sport quotes, discussion questions, and other ideas for involving students, parents, teachers, and administrators. Some schools proudly display their banners and include good sporting behavior as a goal of their athletic teams. In addition, outstanding high-profile athletes are carefully screened to serve as role models and make appearances on behalf of the organization. For example, one spokesperson for the celebration has been Grant Hill, the only three-time winner of the NBA's sportsmanship award as voted by his peers. For the 2013–2014 year, the annual campaign focused on the theme of "developing a culture of nonviolence through sport" (International Sport 2010).

In Colorado, the sporting behavior program for high school athletes takes the position that sport participants are placed in a unique context of competition that can help them develop the values of self-respect and respect for others. The Colorado High School Activities Association (CHSAA) lists the following key values (2014):

Respect for self	Tolerance
Respect for others	Integrity and honesty
Self-esteem	Courtesy
Teamwork	Ethics
Discipline	Fairness
Loyalty	Pride
Courage	Integrity
Compassion	Poise
Responsibility	Humility

CHSAA has developed a guide for coaches, players, parents, and officials, titled "Game Management and Sportsmanship Expectation Guide" (2014), that lays out expectations for managing behavior during all after-school activities, including sport events.

One of CHSAA's initiatives focuses on eliminating tacit approval of taunting and other demeaning behaviors. This is a challenging goal to pursue given that the sport environment is generally one place where some people think it is acceptable to taunt, ridicule, heckle, or otherwise disrespect another human being. For example, consider some common chants directed by students and other fans at opposing teams: "We can't hear you," "We've got spirit, how 'bout you," "Where's your crowd," "You got swatted," "Start the bus," and "Hey, hey good-bye." Though traditional in sport and perhaps innocuous, these chants only reinforce an attitude that is confrontational and disrespectful (CHSAA 2014).

The Catholic Youth Apostolate of St. Louis, Missouri has joined in the effort to reward and recognize good sporting behavior by regularly reporting "random acts of sportsmanship" in its newsletter, which includes stories from various high school and middle school athletic programs. One report described a sixth-grade boys soccer game, in which one team scored an apparent goal on a header after a cross. The referee was screened on the play and didn't see it clearly, but the young player who was credited with the goal admitted to the referee that in fact the ball had struck his arm rather than his head and should be disallowed. The

ACTIVITY TIME-OUT

Running up the Score

It has become the practice in some parts of the country for high school basketball teams to "run up" the score in order to set records and gain notoriety for their school. In one such case, local fans were outraged when Bloomington High South in Indiana defeated Arlington High School 107-2 in girls basketball. In another example, in just one season, the boys basketball team at Yates High School in Houston, Texas, beat opponents by margins of 135 points, 115 points, and 99 points (twice). Some called for the coach's suspension or resignation, but their complaints fell on deaf ears. After all, the team was ranked number one in the nation by *USA Today*! What do these cases suggest about good sporting behavior? Should coaches be fired for such behavior?

POP CULTURE

The Courage to Hold Back, by Myles Campbell, Grade 4, Englewood Cliffs, New Jersey

When I first saw the movie *The Jackie Robinson Story* and heard his discussion with the Dodgers' owner Branch Rickey about "not fighting back no matter what they do to you," I thought that Robinson was a "pussycat." I knew I wasn't like that since when my brothers start something with me, I'm very quick to return the favor.

When Sharon Robinson, Jackie's daughter, came to our school I learned that Jackie Robinson was anything but a "pussycat." Like me, he was a fierce competitor who never looked to back down from a good fight. In spite of all the terrible things that were said about him and done to him, he had the courage to control his anger. He was strong enough not to fight back because his larger goal of breaking the color barrier in baseball was more satisfying than short-term revenge.

I have to wear thick glasses when I play baseball, and it gets me mad when some of my classmates call me "Four Eyes." At times I have felt like getting revenge and teaching them a few moves I have recently learned in wrestling. Although I am very tempted, I have tried to channel my anger into my game. I get back at them by playing harder. I try to concentrate better, to swing a little quicker, to throw a little faster, and to run a little swifter. By doing this, I keep getting better, and our team now wins by more runs. I have noticed less name calling. Who knows, if I continue to have the courage to hold back, like Jackie Robinson, my classmates may someday ask to borrow my glasses.

Reprinted, by permission, from Myles Campbell, 2010, "A day to promote good sportsmanship across the USA," *USA Today* Available: www.usatoday.com/sports/2010-02-27-sportsmanship-day_N.htm?loc=interstitialskip

referee agreed and disallowed the goal. Even so, the boy's team won in a close game (Archdiocese of St. Louis 2011).

Strategies for Good Sporting Behavior

Clearly, sport can provide an opportunity for young people to learn the precepts of good sporting behavior. Due to the dynamics of play and the nature of competition, athletes may be tested hundreds of times in a season and therefore develop their sense of a moral code in sport. Many of their attitudes derive from early life experiences, but the ones they learn in sport are just as likely to transfer off the field and become part of their moral behavior.

National organizations should take a lead role in promoting and supporting good sporting behavior by athletes, particularly those who compete at the high school or college level. To this end, the National Federation of State High School Associations (O'Day 2007) has published the following statement about sporting behavior to be used by high schools in promoting good behavior by fans toward opponents and officials:

> *There are high school athletes who are performing here tonight. They are friendly rivals as members of opposing teams. They are not enemies. This is the theme of interscholastic athletics . . . the idea of friendly competition. The visiting team is a guest of the home team. They are expected to be so regarded and treated.*

One school went a step further and developed a system of yellow and red cards like those used in soccer to convey a warning or penalty for improper behavior—in this case, by fans. When instances of poor fan behavior are noticed, the offending fan can be handed a card. The yellow card bears the following message: "Please model poise and confidence—our athletes need this." The red card simply says, "Your behavior continues to be inappropriate; please leave the game now" (Green 2013).

If we hope to positively influence sporting behavior, we must adopt it as a key goal of youth sport. All major youth sporting organizations have done so, but in some cases their good intentions are simply not fully implemented. Colorado appears to have a model program that is comprehensive in concept, clear in purpose, and practical to apply. Schools in Colorado are asked to adopt and promote the program; recognize athletes who are good models; and educate players, coaches, and parents.

Parents are usually the first to teach their children fair play. From their parents, young athletes learn to share, take turns, accept agreed-upon rules of the game, and accept winning or losing. As they join youth teams and leagues, they learn to either follow directions from coaches and officials or suffer the consequences, which usually involve being excluded from play. Parents continue to model good behavior during games by admiring the performance of both teams, controlling their emotions, and respecting decisions made by coaches and officials. After the game, parents need to help athletes focus on the good aspects of their performance rather than being consumed with the outcome.

Coaching behavior powerfully influences a team of young players. Along with teaching the rules, coaches must model good sporting behavior at all times. Doing so means treating everyone with respect, making fair decisions, and positively reinforcing good behavior. If instead coaches exhibit poor sporting behavior—for example, verbally abusing an official—they send a clear message to their players that such behavior is acceptable.

Coaches also need to help players modify their behavior when it does not meet acceptable standards. Sometimes good kids are bad sports. Kids may become frustrated, lose patience, get overly emotional, react to poor behavior from an opponent, or allow other issues in their life to affect their decisions. A wise coach can identify the possible cause for a poor decision through insightful questioning and suggest alternative methods of dealing with the situation.

EXPERT'S VIEW

Teachers and Coaches as Leaders Demonstrating Character and Competence

Angela Lumpkin, professor at Texas Tech University, quotes the United States Army leadership framework—"Be-Know-Do"—to emphasize the importance of character and competence. The word *be* refers to character, *know* refers to competence, and *do* refers to action taken based on character and competence. Lumpkin also notes that cadets at the United States Military Academy at West Point "are taught that leaders choose the harder right, rather than the easier wrong." She encourages the use of a similar framework for coaches to guide their modeling and teaching efforts toward good sporting behavior.

Lumpkin suggests that coaches be guided by the following approach in their actions as role models: First, if the thought of taking a certain action in an ethical dilemma causes you to have a negative, gut-level reaction, you do not take that action. Second, if you would feel uncomfortable having an action reported by the media, you do not take that action. And third, if you feel that an action would violate the moral values of someone you care about, you do not take that action. As many have said, the challenge is to act in an ethical manner even when no one is looking (Lumpkin 2010).

At some levels of play, fans can also influence the atmosphere through unacceptable behavior. In such cases, small groups of fans, such as parents, can be cautioned that their behavior is becoming a negative influence. Larger crowds require organized crowd control to ensure safety, and disruptive fans should be removed, forcibly if necessary, from the scene. Sometimes, of course, alcohol is involved, and there is no shortage of information about the effects of consuming too much alcohol before or during an athletic event. Alcohol limits must be publicized and enforced in order to prevent alcohol from turning a fan into a disruptive, rude, or dangerous instigator.

The power of role models in sport cannot be overlooked. Young athletes often model their behavior on that of their heroes in college and professional sport. If they see National Football League players taunting each other and celebrating excessively after a good play, you can bet that they'll imitate those actions during their Pop Warner football game. For this reason, the leaders of professional sport need to be pressured to eliminate poor sporting behavior from their games. Effective actions—such as rule enforcement, fines, and suspensions—can gain attention and help athletes change their behavior. Most sport organizations generally do act to address bad behavior, but often not until a public outcry inspires them to do so.

We can also do much by rewarding athletes who do exhibit good sporting behavior. Most organizations and leagues seasonally recognize certain athletes for their exemplary behavior. Even in fiercely competitive professional sports, numerous players deserve admiration for their good sporting behavior. For example, no young girl who has watched the last 10 years of U.S. women's soccer could come away with anything less than a healthy respect for exemplary sporting behavior.

Chapter Summary

Good sporting behavior has been defined as ethical behavior exhibited by an athlete. Some studies have shown that many of today's athletes are confused about the meaning of fair play and sporting behavior and have no concept of honorable competition. On the other hand, evidence also indicates that sport offers fertile ground for developing good sporting behavior, provided that such behavior is established as an agreed-upon outcome that is sought by coaches and players. In such an atmosphere, the active occasions provided by sport for moral decision making mean that sport is an ideal venue for learning moral behavior.

Highly competitive sport is more likely than participation sport to produce poor behavior, and males are more likely than females to exhibit poor behavior. Violent and contact sports have a strong history of poor sporting behavior. Various research projects with youth and high school athletes have revealed an alarming misunderstanding of acceptable kinds of moral decision making.

The stages of moral development as outlined by Kohlberg give us insight into how sporting behavior develops. To this end, the chapter examines the relationship between moral behavior and intellectual development. Young people in particular can be socialized into groups through their experience in sport and thereby learn acceptable moral behavior.

Because athletic situations vary widely, there is no definitive way to declare that sport teaches either positive or negative sporting behavior. However, an increasing number of youth sport programs, state athletic associations, and school districts are adopting clear statements of intent to promote good sporting behavior. Some are also following up with concrete programs, which include publicity, education, enforcement, rewards, and recognition of exemplary behavior in sport.

12

STUDENT OUTCOMES

After reading this chapter, you will know the following:

- How race and ethnicity are defined
- Sport participation trends among various ethnic populations
- Positives and negatives of sport in relation to racial and ethnic equality in society
- Strategies for combating challenges to racial diversity at all levels of sport

Race, Ethnicity, and Sport

Race, Ethnicity, and Sport

Arthur Ashe Jr. was a good friend of mine. I watched a young Ashe enter the world of professional tennis, win the U.S. Open and Wimbledon, and later on captain the U.S. Davis Cup team. Some years later, fate brought us together in the family of the United States Tennis Association (USTA), where we worked together to establish the first player development program to help develop top U.S. players who would be successful on the world stage. At that time, John McEnroe and Jimmy Connors had retired, and Chris Evert and Martina Navratilova would soon follow. Our task was to replace them and develop a plan to maximize the chances for young U.S. players. Our working relationship turned into a friendship of mutual respect, shared vision, and shared commitment to working toward a better world for people of all races.

You see, Arthur loved playing tennis, but he knew there were much more important matters for him to address. A student of history, he penned the unique three-volume work that has become the definitive history of black athletes in the United States: *A Hard Road to Glory* (1988). Lest the heroic exploits of innumerable black athletes be lost forever because their performances were ignored or repressed throughout history, Arthur ensured that future generations would be able to trace their past. It took years of detailed, painstaking research, but I was there to share the satisfaction of an author who contributed something of value through his own insight and effort. Later, he published an autobiography, *Days of Grace* (1993), in which he chronicled his infection with AIDS through a blood transfusion during a heart bypass operation. It wasn't long before his health deteriorated; he suffered through brain surgery and died at the age of 49 (Carter 2005).

We were the same age and grew up in the same era, but we clearly lived in different worlds of white and black. Arthur graduated from college, became a writer, and became a leader in the black community who spoke out and acted to combat racial prejudice, South Africa's apartheid, and U.S. policy toward Haitians seeking asylum here. Yet he also moved easily in the white world of tennis and the USTA. He was grateful for his own success in sport, but he hoped for so much more for the next generation of young African Americans, and he dedicated his life to making that happen. I am grateful for having shared a friendship with Arthur Ashe, from whom I learned some priceless life lessons.

The face of professional sport in the United States has changed dramatically in the last 60 years through the inclusion of African American, Latino, and Asian American athletes and their subsequent record-setting performances and domination of certain sports and sport positions. Where white males once dominated sport, the balance in some major team sports, including basketball and football, has now shifted toward black athletes. In addition, the percentage of African Americans has declined in recent years while Latinos have increased their representation in Major League Baseball, and many have achieved superstar status.

Despite the integration of athletes of diverse races and ethnicities into sport, challenges remain. Here are a few of them:

- Opening opportunities in all sports to people of all races and ethnic backgrounds, especially among youth
- Integrating athletes from all races and ethnic groups into the social fabric of the sport world and capitalizing on the diversity of participants
- Recruiting and training sport leaders—such as coaches, managers, and owners—of all races and ethnic backgrounds

This chapter examines sport participation among various racial and ethnic groups. It also considers sport participation as both a positive and a negative factor in social change, and it explores strategies for increasing participation by minority groups at all levels of sport. First, however, let's consider what we mean by *race* and *ethnicity*, then review some relevant census numbers.

Classifications of Race and Ethnicity

The terms race and ethnicity are often used interchangeably in references to various groups of people. However, it is more accurate to use *race* when referring to attributes that are passed along genetically from generation to generation and to use *ethnicity* when referring to the cultural heritage of a group of people. In the United States, all groups except whites are referred to as **minorities** since they constitute a smaller percentage of the population than the majority group (white Americans). Although these definitions may differ slightly depending on the discussion, they provide a good starting point for this chapter.

Race is not as easy to define as you might think. Due to the mixing of many generations of different races, more Americans have a mixed racial background than an unmixed one. Historically, many people have used the so-called "one-drop rule" when describing racial origins—meaning, for example, that a person who had even one drop of blood from an African American ancestor was considered African American. Of course, in popular culture, membership in a minority group might be attributed based on skin color, facial features, or type of hair. Adding to the confusion is the classification by the U.S. Census Bureau of Hispanics and Latinos as a single group with a footnote that they may be of any race (U.S. Bureau of Labor Statistics 2012e).

The term **racism** refers to the belief that race determines human traits and characteristics and that racial differences result in the superiority of a particular race. Groups that have been victims of discrimination due to racism have typically been minorities. The dominance of white males of European origin in the early days of the United States resulted in the belief by many whites that they were superior to people of other racial backgrounds.

The U.S. census of the population conducted in 1930 showed that about 89 percent of respondents identified themselves as "white," and about 10 percent identified themselves as "Negro." There was no Hispanic or Latino category at that time, but there was a category labeled "Mexican," which was used to account for just over 1 percent of the population. Take a look at table 12.1, which shows the percentages of racial groups in the United States as of 2013—a markedly different picture from that of 75 years ago.

The U.S. Census Bureau forecasts that by 2060, the number of Latino and Hispanic Americans and the number of Asian Americans will nearly double. As of 2011, in seven of the ten states with the largest Hispanic population, the largest subgroup was Mexican; the exceptions were New York and New Jersey (Puerto Rican) and Florida (Cuban) (Pew Research Center 2013b). At the same time, the white population will drop to just 43 percent of the total by 2060—the lowest percentage in the nation's history. The decline in the white percentage appears to hinge on declining birth rates among whites and on immigration by members of minority groups. These changes mean that groups who have been minorities in the United States will, when combined, become the majority (U.S. Census Bureau 2012e).

Another striking pattern is emerging in terms of where members of minority groups choose to live in the United States. According to William Frey, demographer at the Brookings Institution, "Blacks are returning to the South while Hispanics are dispersing throughout the country where there are jobs" (Frey 2010, 54). In the 1990s, most

TABLE 12.1 United States Population by Racial Group

Racial group	2013 actual %	2060 projected %
White	62.6	43.0
Hispanic or Latino	17.1	31.0
African American	13.2	15.0
Asian American	5.3	8.2
Native American and Alaskan Natives	1.6	1.5

Based on Passel and Cohn 2012e; U.S. Bureau of Labor Statistic 2013e.

Hispanic immigrants entered the country through five gateways: California, Texas, Illinois, New York, and Florida. Today, Hispanics make up at least 5 percent of the population in 30 states—up from 16 states in 1990—and they are continuing to disperse to various cities. From 2000 through 2008, Riverside, California, ranked first in total Hispanic gains, and metro Dallas and Houston followed close behind. Other gainers included Washington, DC; Atlanta; and the Florida cities of Tampa, Orlando, Cape Coral, Lakeland, and Jacksonville. Hispanic expansion slowed somewhat near the end of the decade due to the scarcity of available jobs in many areas (Frey 2010).

For blacks in the United States, the pattern is different. Almost half (more than 17 million people) live in the 11 states that were in the Confederacy—an increase of one million since 1990. The continuing southward shift has seen blacks move primarily to New South growth centers such as Texas, North Carolina, Georgia, and Florida rather than Old South states such as Louisiana, Mississippi, and Alabama. In fact, Atlanta has more than doubled its black population to surpass Chicago with the second-largest African American population in the United States.

Asian Americans tend to concentrate more heavily than Hispanics in traditional immigrant-magnet areas. In fact, more than one-third of all Asian Americans nationwide live in the top three magnet areas: New York, Los Angeles, and San Francisco. However, like the Hispanic population, Asian Americans are steadily dispersing across the country.

In another trend, four states—Hawaii, New Mexico, Texas, and California—now have minority populations that when combined exceed 50 percent of their total population. More generally, of the nation's roughly 3,000 counties, about 350 (11 percent) now have this type of "minority majority." Similarly, 13 states, as well as the District of Columbia, now have a minority majority in their population under the age of five years—up from just 5 such states in 2000. In addition, in 25 states and the District of Columbia, minorities now make up more than 40 percent of the under-five age group (Kayne 2013).

The concentration of various minority groups in particular areas of the country will likely affect the popularity of various sports in those regions. In terms of both participation and in spectatorship, certain racial groups tend to favor certain sports and ignore others. For example, consider the heavy recruiting of football players by major colleges in the southeastern United States. Football recruiters know that a higher percentage of blacks live in the Southeast and that it therefore makes sense to recruit there.

Both the size and the location of minority groups are significant when we consider the numbers of minority athletes in particular sports. When compared with their percentage of the general population, minorities are heavily represented in certain sports at elite levels and are virtually absent in others. One question to consider is whether these imbalances result from race itself or simply from issues of opportunity and culture. The following sections look closely at who participates in which sports and what factors influence that participation.

Sport Participation Among Racial and Ethnic Minorities

This section considers each major racial group and its sport participation. As a result of the Civil Rights Movement and the reduction or elimination of many racial barriers, African American athletes have assumed a dominant place in certain sports at the college and professional levels. Yet overall, blacks remain underrepresented in the vast majority of collegiate sports. (The data in this section often point to the challenges and triumphs of black athletes in the last 50 years simply because their struggle has been studied and debated widely.) To a lesser extent, Hispanics, Asians, and Native Americans have also affected sport; each of these groups has always included key contributors to sport and is continuing to battle its own set of barriers.

Because developing as an athlete requires resources—time, access, and money—the opportunities are limited for millions of U.S. kids in low-income families, many of whom also happen to be Hispanic or African American. In addition, boys in all age groups continue to have much greater access to sport opportunities than girls do. Overall, white children are much more likely to have access to—and participate in—sport activities than do African American, Hispanic, Asian, or Native American children. Of course, for decades, African Americans were systematically excluded from white-controlled sport events, programs, and organizations. Beyond such direct discriminatory practices, access to sport also varies by race based on cultural expectations and the availability of discretionary family income (Sagas and Cunningham 2014).

Among adults, the percentage of people who do not participate in leisure-time physical activity differs across racial groups, though the percentages have improved recently. Here are the 2011 percentages of inactive adults by racial group:

Hispanic and Latino	42
African American	41
Asian	33
White	30

These percentages affect not only the adults but also the children who live with them; that is, adults' participation in sport and physical activity (or lack thereof) likely influences the aspirations and choices of their children (Sagas and Cunningham 2014).

As you read this chapter, it will be helpful to refer periodically to tables 12.2 and 12.3, which show detailed information about participation in collegiate and professional sport among particular racial groups. The tables show some stark differences in the percentages of participation by different racial groups at the various levels of collegiate and professional competition. It is also instructive to compare the percentage of racial groups in sport to their percentage of the U.S. population; doing so points up significant cases of overrepresentation and underrepresentation in various sports.

African American Athletes

A quick look at the history of sport reveals that African Americans have not only moved into prominent roles in the major U.S. sports but have also reached a point of domination. In Arthur Ashe's (1988) definitive history of black athletes, he divided that history into three volumes. The first volume dealt with black athletes from the 1600s up to the time of World War I. As sport entered its golden age in the United States in the 1920s and 1930s, a few black athletes made their mark, including Jesse Owens in track and field and Joe Louis in boxing. But it was not until after World War II that integration became a reality in most U.S. sports and black athletes began to achieve a level of prominence. Most historians would agree that one of the major events in this period was the breaking of the color barrier in Major League Baseball (MLB) by Jackie Robinson.

Black athletes in U.S. sport have been studied, written about, admired, scorned, and persecuted. Through it all, black athletes have achieved notable success, and a great deal of attention has been given to the reasons for this success. Conventional wisdom, often shallow at best, has sometimes taken the form of statements such as "white men can't jump" and "blacks have brawn but not brains."

If you were to ask John or Jane Q. Public about black athletes, chances are that he or she would say that they dominate U.S. sport. However, of the roughly 35 million African Americans in the United States, nowhere near the expected percentage is involved in sport. In most sports, in fact, blacks are woefully underrepresented or completely missing. Consider, for example, sailing, ice hockey, tennis, golf, swimming, diving, soccer, cycling, figure skating, softball, volleyball, water polo, and almost all winter sports. However, in the major U.S. sports of basketball and football, as well as track and field, African Americans tend to participate in large numbers. Because those sports gobble up a huge proportion of attention, money, media, and television, many people assume that black athletes dominate sport.

African Americans in Professional Sport

From the early 1940s until the conclusion of World War II, no black athletes participated in MLB, professional football, or the National Basketball Association (NBA). Outstanding black athletes were relegated to playing in the Negro Leagues of baseball and other competitions organized for African Americans. In the latter part of the decade, each major team sport made the move to sign a black athlete, thus marking a change in U.S. sport that was to have far-reaching implications for the next 50 years. For black athletes, the five years following the end of World War II were the most memorable in their sport history (Ashe 1988).

By the end of the 1950s, African Americans had moved to a percentage of participation in the major U.S. sports equal to their percentage of the national population, which was about 11 percent or 12 percent. No doubt the Civil Rights Movement—which addressed segregation in schools, other public places, and the workplace—had a major effect on the phenomenal rise of black athletes. If we fast-forward to 2013, more than 50

TABLE 12.2 Sport Participation by Racial Group Percentage

MALES					
Racial group	**All NCAA divisions**	**Division I overall**	**Division I football**	**Division I basketball**	**Division I baseball**
White	69.4	61.2	46.4	29.4	85.3
African American	16.2	22.0	43.2	57.2	2.6
Latino	4.5	4.1	2.3	2.0	6.0
American Indian or Alaskan Native	0.4	0.4	0.5	0.1	0.4
Asian American	1.7	1.9	2.6	0.1	1.2
Two or more races	1.6	2.0	2.0	2.5	1.6
Nonresident alien	3.1	4.6	0.4	5.9	0.6
Other	3.1	3.3	2.7	2.6	2.4
FEMALES					
Racial group	**All NCAA divisions**	**Division I overall**	**Division I basketball**	**Division I outdoor track**	**Division I softball**
White	76.2	69.5	38.2	60.9	79.4
African American	8.6	12.6	47.9	24.0	4.1
Latino	4.2	4.1	2.0	4.0	7.2
American Indian or Alaskan Native	0.4	0.4	0.6	0.5	0.8
Asian American	2.2	2.3	1.1	1.4	2.8
Two or more races	1.8	2.2	3.1	2.3	2.5
Nonresident alien	3.2	5.4	4.1	3.6	1.0
Other	3.2	3.5	3.0	3.3	2.1

NCAA denotes National Collegiate Athletic Association.

Adapted, by permission, from R. Lapchick, 2013, *Racial and gender report card: College sport.* (Orlando, FL: The Institute for Diversity and Ethics in Sport). Available: www.tidesport.org/RGRC/2012/2012_College_RGRC.pdf

TABLE 12.3 Professional Players by Racial Group Percentage

Racial group	NFL	NBA	WNBA	MLB	MLS
White	30.1	19.0	20.0	61.2	47.7
African American	66.3	76.3	73.0	8.3	10.6
Latino	0.7	4.4	0	28.2	24.1
Asian American	1.1	0.2	0	2.1	1.3
Other	1.8	0.2	7.0	0.1	16.3
People of color (total)	69.9	81.0	73.0	38.0	52.3
International	42.8	18.7	9.0	28.2	42.8
Total # of players	2,721	459	153	745	547

NFL denotes National Football League, NBA denotes National Basketball Association, WNBA denotes Women's National Basketball Association, MLB denotes Major League Baseball, and MLS denotes Major League Soccer.

Adapted from Lapchick 2013c-2013g.

years later, the percentage of African Americans in professional sport is quite different (Lapchick 2013c, 2013e, 2013f, 2013g):

Football	66
Men's basketball	76
Women's basketball	73
Baseball	8

Even sports that traditionally have not included black athletes have begun to show some signs of inclusiveness. Tennis saw its first black champion in the 1950s in the person of Althea Gibson, who won Wimbledon. She was followed by Arthur Ashe on the men's side in the 1970s, but black tennis players won few other championships in the next couple of decades.

In the 1990s, however, the arrival of the Williams sisters, Venus and Serena, touched off an explosion of interest in tennis in the African American community. Suddenly, a sport that was traditionally associated with privileged white people had a pair of role models who came from modest means. They burst onto the tennis scene without traveling the hard and expensive road of junior tennis, choosing instead to vault right into professional play and making it work. Serena's accomplishment of winning a career grand slam (Wimbledon plus the Australian, French, and U.S. Opens) is often mentioned as one of the all-time top sport achievements by any black athlete.

African Americans in Collegiate Sport

In collegiate sport, African Americans now dominate National Collegiate Athletic Association (NCAA) Division I basketball for both men and women, and black men also dominate NCAA football. The next most popular college sport among both male and female African Americans is track and field. A quick look back at table 12.2 reveals stark differences between Division I athletes when compared with athletes in all NCAA divisions considered together. Specifically, the percentage of African American athletes, both male and female, is about 6 (for men) and 4 (for women) percentage points lower in the overall category than in Division I alone, primarily due to the lack of African Americans represented in Division III programs. These programs are typically housed at smaller, private schools and cannot offer athletic scholarships.

In Division I football, basketball, and track and field, African Americans far surpass their percentage of expected participation based on their share

POP CULTURE

42: The Jackie Robinson Story

In 1947, the United States was still marked by racial segregation. Separate schools, swimming pools, drinking fountains, hotels, and restaurants were the order of the day. And sport was no different. The Negro Leagues were the only option for baseball players of African American descent. Jackie Robinson changed all that when he signed a contract offered by Branch Rickey, owner of the Brooklyn Dodgers.

The popular movie *42* portrays the young Robinson as an immensely talented ballplayer who wants to focus on winning and burns with passion to become a great player. But his contemporaries were not so eager to welcome him. Some lobbied to keep him off of their team, and others threw at his head or insulted him in public or in private. Fans mocked him with mops on their head and made death threats. There was never any doubt about his baseball talent, but Robinson's personal challenge was to ignore the insults and threats and turn the other cheek.

Robinson lived up to his promise by winning the Rookie of the Year award. Two years later, he was named Most Valuable Player after batting .342 and stealing 37 bases. His lifetime batting average was .311, and he was voted into the Baseball Hall of Fame in his first year of eligibility. In his personal life, Robinson fought diabetes and was nearly blind by middle age. He died in 1972 of a heart attack at age 53, but he left a lasting legacy—not just in baseball but in all of professional sport in the United States.

of the U.S. population, which is about 13 percent. However, in all other sports at all levels of NCAA competition, African Americans account for less than 5 percent of collegiate athletes—far below what might be expected based on their proportion of the overall U.S. population.

Change did not come quickly in collegiate sport, but black athletes gradually made their presence felt. The Southeastern Conference was the last major athletic conference to integrate, in 1966. In the late 1960s, there were still no black athletes at several schools in the conference, including Alabama, Auburn, Florida, Mississippi, Mississippi State, Louisiana State, and Georgia. By 1972, however, more than 100 black athletes were playing football in the conference, and by 1975 the University of Alabama started five black athletes in basketball. That fact is somewhat remarkable when you consider the attitude of former Alabama governor George Wallace, who used physical restraint to block African Americans from attending the university in 1963. Fewer than 10 years later, in 1972, several teams in the Southeastern Conference even had black starting quarterbacks—an anomaly in those days.

Although African American athletes certainly have a large presence nowadays in the revenue-producing sports of football and basketball, the overall progress made toward racial diversity in collegiate sport is modest. The Institute for Racial and Gender Diversity assigned a grade of B to college sport for diversity in hiring, noting particular improvements in the hiring of head football coaches and head women's basketball coaches. Yet the overall picture shows that white people hold 85 percent of all head coaching positions in the NCAA's three divisions and 92 percent in Division III. White males also dominate the position of athletic director, with percentages of 89, 91, and 96 at the three divisions, respectively. It is also revealing that all college conference commissioners in every division are white males (Lapchick 2012b).

Race and Athletic Dominance

Do black athletes dominate certain sports because of race? Numerous studies, such as those cited by Entine (2000, 2004), have been conducted to examine this issue from every perspective. For example, the proportion of fast-twitch and slow-twitch muscle fibers has been cited to explain black athletes' jumping ability. Explosiveness on the track has also been attributed to the muscular makeup and a high proportion of fast-twitch fibers in black athletes. However, Ethiopian and Kenyan black athletes have dominated distance running for the last generation, and Kenyans and other East Africans are born with a high number of slow-twitch fibers. They also tend to be ectomorphs, short and slender, with a large natural lung capacity.

In contrast to East Africans, athletes of West African ancestry—including most North American, British, and Caribbean blacks—are generally poor distance runners. Rather, they tend to excel in sprinting and other sports ruled by explosiveness, speed, and power. Thus, if we simply define race according to skin color—in this case, that of black athletes—we find significant variation between different groups of blacks (Entine 2000).

Price, writing in *Sports Illustrated* in 1997, asserted the following: "Generally accepted research has shown that African American children tend to have denser bones, narrower hips, bigger thighs, lower percentages of body fat and tests also show that they run faster and jump higher." However, these are generalized observations that have not included extensive study of all types of black athletes at the world-class level. And there are certainly exceptions, such as basketball Hall of Famers Charles Barkley and Karl Malone and football Hall of Famer Warren Sapp, who do not have the characteristics listed by Price but were eminently successful in professional sport.

Some people believe that black athletes have longer arms or reach than their white counterparts. Others believe that black athletes are mentally tougher and more relaxed under pressure. However, no matter how thorough the testing is, it is difficult to isolate factors and ascribe them exclusively to race. In fact, if you were to take a random sampling of youth athletes of all racial groups, it is unlikely that you would find significant differences.

The issue is further complicated by the fact that within any prescribed definition of race, huge differences exist because race is not a precise factor. Even the basic question of who is a black athlete is not a simple one when you realize all the possible ancestral origins of blacks and variations in skin color. For example, the best-known golfer in the world today is Tiger Woods, whom many classify as a black athlete. Woods, however, refers to himself as "Cablinasian," denoting his white (Caucasian), black, American Indian, and Asian heritage. Therefore, although many observers have heralded Woods' ascension to the top of golf as a landmark moment in which a black athlete has once again proved superiority, it seems that Woods would not attribute his success to his genetic makeup.

Another possible explanation for the dominance of black athletes in certain sports is the environment in which they grow up. Since blacks are a minority group, their choices in life may be more limited because they have fewer economic resources and less hope of landing a well-paying job as an adult. As a result, many young blacks see successful athletes and envision following that path. A survey of 4,500 African American male youths by Assibey-Mensah (1997) found the following:

- When asked about their role models, 85 percent of 10-year-olds and 98 percent of 18-year-olds picked athletes or sport figures.
- Of those who picked athletes, 63 percent of 10-year-olds and 90 percent of 18-year-olds picked basketball players.
- No child picked an educator.

Young black males are also at risk of lacking an effective male role model due to the absence of a father or to the presence of a father who is unemployed. In 2013, 72 percent of births by black women involved women who were not married (U.S. Census Bureau 2013d). The significance of this statistic enlarges when paired with the fact that the median income for single mothers is $26,000, as compared with $84,000 for married couples (U.S. Census 2013d). In addition, black kids who live in inner cities may be particularly hard-pressed to find alternative role models, because successful local businesses are scarce and many potential role models have fled to the suburbs in search of a better life. Add to these complications the fact that African Americans constitute the racial group with the highest percentage of families below the poverty line, and you can see why young blacks might yearn for high-profile, high-paying careers in sport—whether or not this goal is realistic.

Football, basketball, and track are relatively affordable and are usually offered by schools, which provide athletes with coaching, uniforms, and equipment. Minority athletes are naturally

The Cowtown Riders, the polo team of the Work to Ride nonprofit program for inner city youth in Philadelphia, made history in 2011 when it became the only African American high school team to hold a national title in polo.

drawn to these sports at school because they are accessible and affordable. On the opposite end of the spectrum, expensive sports such as skiing, water polo, and equestrianism—as well as those offered primarily through private clubs, such as golf and tennis—are often out of reach for minority athletes.

In addition, African American culture, particularly in urban settings, has drawn young blacks to the basketball court, and the attraction is reinforced by friends and heroes. Television offers plenty of opportunities to watch professional role models compete in basketball, football, and, at the Olympics, in track and field. In addition, basketball courts are plentiful, relatively inexpensive to build, and able to accommodate lots of players at a low cost. As a result, playground basketball and recreational leagues that are free or low cost have served as training ground for thousands of city kids.

Stacking in Sport

The phenomenon of **stacking** was identified by activist Harry Edwards, who is widely recognized as a leading authority on issues of race and sport. Edwards is a longtime professor of sociology at the University of California at Berkeley and a consultant for MLB, the Golden State Warriors, and the San Francisco 49ers on issues of racial diversity in sport. The term *stacking* refers to an unusual distribution of whites and blacks in certain sport positions that cannot be explained by a random distribution.

For example, in football, the position of quarterback has typically been dominated by whites, whereas running backs and wide receivers have been predominantly black (see table 12.4). In baseball, pitchers and catchers have been predominantly white, whereas outfielders have more often been black. In basketball, centers and guards have been more likely to be white and forwards more likely to be black. Many of these percentages have changed in recent years as the overall percentage of black athletes has risen dramatically, but there remains the historical aberration that gave rise to the suspicion that black athletes were excluded from certain positions.

Various explanations have been offered for the apparent existence of stacking. One is the centrality theory, which holds that white athletes get placed in the center of the lineup or the middle of the team. In baseball, this means that whites are pitchers, catchers, shortstops, and second basemen; in football, it means that whites are quarterbacks, centers, middle linebackers, and offensive guards. The idea is advanced that the so-called white positions require more thinking and decision making, which were central to the outcome of the game, whereas blacks were drawn to positions requiring more raw physical talent.

Another theory is that blacks and whites tend to be attracted to certain positions and that children follow the lead of their role models and seek out similar positions in youth sport. A similar theory holds that coaches move players into certain positions based on race where they think the athletes would be most successful. Those positions are ones that require a relatively higher level of physical talent and speed and a lesser amount of cognitive ability.

As black athletes have moved into professional sport in large numbers, the concept of stacking has received less attention and sparked fewer debates.

TABLE 12.4 Stacking in the NFL (Percentage of Black Athletes by Position)

Position	1998	2003	2007	2012
Offense				
Quarterback	8	22	19	21
Running back	87	86	89	92
Wide receiver	92	86	89	87
Tight end	42	42	43	38
Offensive tackle	55	55	49	57
Offensive guard	29	41	35	46
Center	17	12	18	18
Defense				
Cornerback	99	98	97	97
Safety	91	81	84	83
Linebacker	75	80	71	70
Defensive end	79	77	73	80
Defensive tackle	63	77	76	79

Note: The overall proportion of African American players in the NFL is 69 percent.

Adapted, by permission, from R. Lapchick, 2013, *Racial and gender report card: National Football League.* (Orlando, FL: The Institute for Diversity and Ethics in Sport). Available: www.tidesport.org/RGRC/2013/2013_NFL_RGRC.pdf

Black quarterbacks have now led teams to the Super Bowl, and blacks have succeeded in the positions of pitcher and catcher. In fact, the Institute for Racial and Gender Diversity reported that as of 2007, stacking in the NFL was no longer a major concern, based primarily on the near doubling of the percentage of black quarterbacks during the previous 10 years (Lapchick 2013f).

In MLB, the concern is not so much stacking as the declining overall percentage of African American players in recent years. At the same time, it is also true that the black athletes who do perform in MLB are overrepresented among outfielders and still underrepresented among pitchers and catchers (Lapchick 2013c). If black athletes are restricted from playing certain positions, then a case can be made that racism exists in professional sport. Such racism may result in the loss of individual earnings, because players in certain positions (for example, quarterback and pitcher) tend to command greater compensation due to their high value to their team.

POP CULTURE

Is a New Day Dawning for Black Quarterbacks?

The popular belief that the quarterback position in football is a thinking position for which African Americans are unsuited has long been an example of institutional racism in the National Football League. Racism involves prejudice or discrimination against a person or group of persons based solely on race. To be clear, if a coach or owner precludes black athletes from playing certain positions, such as quarterback, that is racism. The history of positional demographics in the NFL shows clearly that, for many years, black athletes had little chance to compete for the role of quarterback.

In *Third and a Mile: From Fritz Pollard to Michael Vick—an Oral History of the Trials, Tears, and Triumphs of the Black Quarterback* (2007), the eminent *New York Times* columnist William Rhoden obtained testimony from numerous black NFL quarterbacks, such as Warren Moon, Doug Williams, Vince Evans, James Harris, Donovan McNabb, Daunte Culpepper, and Michael Vick. Rhoden chronicles the heroic struggles of black quarterbacks to overcome one of the sport's most confounding racial barriers. For decades, talented black athletes were told that their athleticism made them better suited to playing wide receiver or defensive back. Usually left unspoken was the notion that in spite of a record of success at lower levels of competition, these athletes were viewed as incapable of handling the rigors of serving as the field general of an NFL team—simply because of their skin color.

At the beginning of the 2013 NFL season, 9 of the league's 32 teams had a black starting quarterback, and 7 of them had been drafted during the previous three years. Those are the highest numbers in NFL history, and they may signal the start of a new era. Moreover, during the preceding season, three of the top four passers in the NFL in yards-per-attempt were black: Robert Griffin III (first), Cam Newton (third), and Russell Wilson (fourth). In addition, the 2014 NFL draft included more black quarterback prospects, including Teddy Bridgewater of Louisville, Tajh Boyd of Clemson, and Stephen Morris of Miami; a year later, Jameis Winston of Florida State was added to the mix. Thus it is possible that half of the NFL teams could have a black starting quarterback in the near future.

You may wonder what has changed to improve the chances that a black player will quarterback an NFL team. Most football people simply point to the fact that young black athletes are now getting opportunities they never had to throw the ball, from the youth level on through high school and college. Coaches have figured out that putting the ball in the hands of their best athlete on every play makes good sense, and the wide open offenses that now dominate every level of football provide ample opportunity to throw rather than just hand the ball off to a running back.

Another factor is the fact that the positions dominated by black players tend to require greater strength, speed, and explosiveness. Since those attributes are often the first to decline with age, black players may have shorter careers and thus less sustained earning power. In fact, the NFL positions most filled by blacks—running back, cornerback, and wide receiver—tend to have the shortest careers. Overall, it was concluded by researcher Clayton Best that "experience and career length in professional football [are] the effects of positional segregation" (Best 1987, 410). Consider that players who occupy positions typically held by blacks have a career expectancy of about three years in the NFL compared with four years for positions typically held by white players. That difference may seem inconsequential, but it means that black players have careers that are, on average, 25 percent shorter than the careers of white players, thus affecting their earning power.

Of course, limiting black athletes to certain positions also affects their long-term prospects for coaching or managing teams. Athletes who play in the central positions that require decision making and greater overall game understanding obviously have a leg up on others. The dearth of black coaches, especially in football, has been a long-standing issue.

Exploitation of Black Athletes

An unfortunate outcome of opening sport participation to black athletes has been the shameful way in which some schools, coaches, and universities exploit them for their athletic talent. Leaders in the black community speak out against exploitive practices, use the media to publicize infractions, and warn athletes to watch their backs. In spite of these efforts, the potential for black athletes to be exploited often exists even when they are quite young.

As early as middle school, when the adolescent growth spurt is in full flower, teachers, coaches, and administrators notice the gifted athletes who exhibit exceptional talent, size, or strength. These athletes may be given the benefit of the doubt in the classroom in spite of lackluster academic performance because of their athletic potential or their importance to the school team. At the end of the year, they may be promoted to the next grade in spite of substandard academic performance. A few minority athletes have made it through college without ever learning to read—for example, James Brooks, a star running back at Auburn University, whose case was one of the most dramatic to be publicized by the media (Muse 2000).

When colleges recruit top athletes and offer them scholarships, they believe that they are entitled to protect their investment. Therefore, it is normal practice at Division I institutions competing at the national level to encourage athletes to choose relatively easy majors and courses, take a lighter academic load during the season, attend mandatory study halls, use a tutor when necessary, and delay their academic progress to gain another year of athletic eligibility. All of these practices are susceptible to abuse, and coaches who are caught may lose their job and reputation. However, many are not caught, and the results include low graduation rates among minority athletes. Even those who do graduate may learn little and possess no employable skills; as a result, if they don't make it as a professional athlete, their future is bleak.

On the other hand, the professional leagues have conspired to keep college-age athletes from playing in the pros. While most athletes are not ready physically or mentally to compete at a young age, some, such as LeBron James in basketball, are ready not only to play but also to be a star. Of course, colleges don't want to lose athletes in whom they have invested time and money to a professional team before their collegiate eligibility is used up. Therefore, professional leagues and colleges work together to keep players in school even if the athletes have no interest in it and want to turn professional. Basketball finally succumbed and now requires only that a young man who enters college play one year before becoming eligible for the NBA draft. The NFL requires college players to wait three seasons. Baseball, on the other hand, has always signed young players and often encourages them to join minor league teams rather than go on to college.

An athlete's decision to turn professional rather than play one more year of college usually has to do with the potential for a lucrative contract. An athlete who is offered millions of dollars takes a terrible risk by rejecting it to return to college. If he sustains a serious injury, it may be the end of his career—and of his chance to achieve long-term financial security for his family. In the end, if the deal is good enough, most athletes leave for the pros. Even if another year in college would have been good for their athletic development or academic career—as compared with perhaps sitting on the bench for a professional team—the temptation and the security of a contract are often too great to resist.

Of course, athletes of all racial backgrounds are susceptible to exploitation in professional sport. However, because black athletes make up a large percentage of players in the major American sports, they are disproportionately at risk.

Double Jeopardy for African American Female Athletes

Despite being in the overall majority in schools and colleges, females represent only 35 percent of all high school athletes and a bit less than 34 percent of all college athletes. Although enormous progress has been made in the last 25 years, due primarily to the passage of the Title IX legislation, women still have not achieved parity in either participation or resources at any level of sport.

The case of black women is doubly discouraging. They are discriminated against twice—because of race and because of gender. Fewer than two-thirds of African American females participate in sport, whereas more than three-quarters of white girls do (National Women's Law Center 2012). At the collegiate level, black females account for 9 percent of all female varsity athletes, 6 percent of coaches of women's teams, and 3 percent of athletic administrators (Lapchick 2012b).

More detailed data show that the percentage of black female athletes has risen to 48 percent in college basketball, 24 percent in track and field, and 13 percent overall in total Division I sports (Lapchick 2012b). At the same time, however, the percentage of female black athletes has dropped 3 percent in the past four years both in the NCAA overall (all divisions) and in Division I sports as a group. These are not encouraging signs.

As one observer put it, "The African American female is a victim of sport discrimination and positional stacking within sports. She is generally restricted to basketball, track and field and the least expensive sports. (Unlike for boys, football is not an option.) Within the sports she does play, she has been historically underrepresented in the skill/outcome positions of setter in volleyball or point guard in basketball" (Lopiano 2001). In one sign of progress in recent years, African American women have excelled at the point guard position at the highest levels of competition, making that concern a relic of the past.

Elite black female athletes are offered fewer speaking engagements, endorsements, and sponsorships. Moreover, unlike some athletes, they have not been at the forefront of the Civil Rights Movement or the feminist movement because sport has been seen either as trivial or as reflective of a male model that should not be emulated by females. Two notable exceptions to this pattern are Venus and Serena Williams, who have landed huge sponsorships from Reebok and Nike, respectively. If Serena meets performance-related criteria for bonuses over eight years, she could earn upwards of $55 million from her Nike deal—and that's on top of the several million a year she earns in prize money! This is an amazing achievement for a black female athlete.

Lopiano proposes a series of actions to rectify the situation of black female athletes. Using lessons learned from civil rights battles and gender equity battles that have already been fought, she proposes collecting and maintaining accurate data on the participation percentages of black females at all levels of play to be used in an annual report card. With the gathered data, she suggests using media pressure to announce and pursue a national agenda focused on specific groups, such as high school athletes and coaches. She also advocates demanding that sport organizations and associations take action to fulfill their public responsibilities with regard to equal opportunity in sport for everyone, regardless of race or gender (Sabo et al. 2004).

Latinos and Hispanics

The term *Hispanic* is used to describe all people whose ethnic heritage can be traced to a Spanish-speaking country. *Latino*, on the other hand, typically refers to people of Latin America, including Central and South America and the Caribbean. Hispanics and Latinos together are a diverse group in ancestry and language, and people in this group may have black or white skin. As noted previously, Hispanics and Latinos have recently nudged ahead of African Americans in terms of their percentage of the U.S. population, and their percentage is forecast to increase steadily over the next few decades.

The majority of Spanish-surnamed people who live in the United States were born here. The U.S. Latino population includes the following major subgroups: 65 percent of Mexican descent, 9 percent of Puerto Rican descent, and 8 percent of Central American descent. As compared with the U.S. population at large, Latinos are younger, have more children, trail other ethnic groups in high school and college graduates, and earn less per household than the average. These cultural markers have certainly affected sport participation by Latinos. In fact,

Latino girls have the lowest sport participation on high school teams of any ethnic group at just 36 percent, as compared with 56 percent for white girls and 47 percent for black girls. It remains an open question whether that trend will continue as this population segment grows in the United States (Iber et al. 2011).

When asked to think of Latino athletes, most Americans think first of baseball. In recent years, Latinos have claimed a higher percentage of MLB players than African Americans and seem to be on an upward trend. Of the 856 roster players on Opening Day of the 2013 season, 241 (28 percent) were born outside the 50 U.S. states, and they represented 15 countries and territories. The country with the most players other than the United States was the Dominican Republic (89), followed by Venezuela (63). Other countries or territories with high numbers included Canada (17), Cuba (15), Mexico (14), Puerto Rico (13), and Japan (11) (Lapchick 2013c).

As more Latino players find success in MLB, young Latinos look up to them as role models and pour their energies into honing their baseball skills. Young men from modest economic backgrounds see few opportunities for success and economic security that are more attractive than becoming a baseball star. To capitalize on such hopes, MLB has established baseball academies in many Central American countries and made top coaches and competition available to promising prospects. Although the vast majority of Latinos who have made it to the major leagues hail from Central American countries, their successes have attracted a huge following of U.S. Latinos who identify with their origins.

The Dominican Republic has a long tradition of sending players to the major leagues, as illustrated by its lock on half of the spots on MLB's all-time Latino team, which was announced during the 2005 World Series after being selected by fans. Voting was sponsored by MLB for 60 players from seven countries and territories. The final selections included 12 players, one at each infield position, three outfielders, three starting pitchers, and one relief pitcher. Here is the lineup (Sanchez 2005):

Ivan Rodriguez, Puerto Rico, catcher

Albert Pujols, Dominican Republic, first base

Rod Carew, Panama, second base

IN THE ARENA WITH . . .

Fernando Valenzuela

Armed with an amazing screwball, "El Torito" (the little bull) was an instant success with the Los Angeles Dodgers in 1981, when he won both the National League Rookie of the Year award and the National League Cy Young Award for top pitcher. He also was the first rookie to lead the league in strikeouts. Not a bad start for a pudgy guy from a working-class background and the youngest of 12 children.

Valenzuela's success was well timed with the influx of people of Mexican heritage and the rise of Spanish influence in the United States. In fact, he became an almost instant media icon in the Los Angeles Latino community and was the focus of a wave of attention from baseball fans that sportswriters dubbed "Fernandomania." Valenzuela even won the Silver Slugger award in 1981 as the best-hitting pitcher, and at the end of the season he helped the Dodgers defeat the New York Yankees in the World Series.

Valenzuela won plenty more games after that. In 1986, he won 21 games for the Dodgers, and in 1990 he pitched a no-hitter. After his release by the Dodgers in 1991, he pitched for multiple other MLB teams—including the Angels, Orioles, Phillies, Padres, and Cardinals—though never again at the level of his early years. After his major league career ended in 1997, he continued to pitch through the 2005–2006 Mexican winter league season at the age of 44. In 2005, Valenzuela was named one of three starting pitchers on Major League Baseball's Latino Legends Team, and in 2010 he was featured in an ESPN documentary titled "Fernando Nation" as part of its *30 for 30* series.

Edgar Martinez, Puerto Rico, third base

Alex Rodriguez, Dominican Republic, shortstop

Roberto Clemente, Puerto Rico, outfielder

Manny Ramirez, Dominican Republic, outfielder

Vladimir Guerrero, Dominican Republic, outfielder

Pedro Martinez, Dominican Republic, starting pitcher

Juan Marichal, Dominican Republic, starting pitcher

Fernando Valenzuela, Mexico, starting pitcher

Mariano Rivera, Panama, relief pitcher

Latinos have also made a mark in the managerial ranks. The Chicago White Sox, World Series champions in 2005, employed a Latino as their manager, Ozzie Guillen. A three-time All-Star, Guillen spent most of his 16-year career as a shortstop for the White Sox. He is the first native of Venezuela to manage in the big leagues. Other Latino managers at the start of the 2010 season were Manny Acta (Washington Nationals), Fredi Gonzalez (Florida Marlins), and Lou Piniella (Chicago Cubs). By the opening of the 2013 season, however, only Acta remained. Still, 25 percent of coaches in MLB were Latino during the 2012 season (Lapchick 2013c).

Soccer is the most popular sport in the world, and it is clearly the king of sports among Latinos. Even so, Major League Soccer (MLS) in the United States has been a tough sell. Unlike American football, basketball, and baseball, U.S. soccer is not the best in the world. According to some estimates, MLS may be the 10th best league in the world—well behind various leagues in Europe, South America, and Latin America. A quarter of its spectators are Latino, and in 2013 nearly a quarter of its players were Latino as well (Lapchick 2013d).

The popularity of soccer among Latinos was evidenced in a miniseries titled *Raíces (Roots)*, which aired in July 2005 on the History Channel. The six-part series was hosted by Pablo Mastroeni, a member of the 2004 MLS All-Star team and a native of Argentina. The series highlighted the greats of the game from Brazil, Mexico, Argentina, Uruguay, and Colombia, including players such as Pelé, Garrincha, Romário, Ronaldo, and Alfredo Di Stéfano. As the Latino population grows in the United States, the owners and organizers of professional soccer plan to market U.S. soccer to them.

Even NASCAR is moving full throttle into the Latino market. The sport is primarily male and white, and Latinos currently make up only about 10 percent of its viewers. However, recent marketing research and initiatives have emphasized reaching out to a younger and more diverse audience in order to offset declining attendance and television ratings. As part of that strategy, NASCAR reached an agreement with Fox Deportes, a Spanish language cable channel, to broadcast 15 races in 2012 (Vega 2012).

In 2009, NASCAR launched its Drive for Diversity to train and encourage female and minority drivers and crew members. In an academy-like setting, promising professionals are mentored and sponsored as they learn their craft. The program, managed by owner Max Siegel of Rev Racing, has had limited success to date (Rev Racing 2014).

NASCAR has had a handful of Latino drivers, led by Juan Pablo Montoya of Colombia, Daniel Suárez of Mexico, and Nelson Piquet Jr. and Miguel Paludo of Brazil. In 2012, Viva La Raza Racing became the first Mexican racing team to be part of NASCAR (Vega 2012).

Latinos are also well represented in boxing, tennis, and golf. Boxing has been increasingly popular with Latinos, who have dominated the lighter weight classes (below middleweight). In tennis, two women of Latin descent, Mary Joe Fernández (Dominican) and Gigi Fernández (Puerto Rico), won Olympic Gold medals representing the United States in successive Olympic Games in 1992 and 1996. Mary Joe Fernández has gone on to become a tennis commentator on ESPN, as well as coach of the U.S. Federation Cup team. In golf, Nancy Lopez (Mexico) was named most outstanding golfer by the LPGA three times and has been voted the most influential female athlete of all time for the Latino community. Lee Trevino (Mexico) and Chi-Chi Rodriguez (Puerto Rico) were stars on the PGA Tour for many years, and Trevino won the U.S. Open, along with two other majors (British and PGA) twice each.

According to NCAA statistics, Hispanics are underrepresented in virtually all sports at the college level, making up just 4.7 percent of male athletes in all divisions and 4.3 percent of all female athletes—both much lower than their 17 percent of the overall U.S. population (Lapchick 2012b).

Asian Americans

Along with Latinos, Asian Americans are the fastest-growing minority population in the United States, but their participation in sport has been slow to develop. As compared with other racial groups, famous athletes of Asian descent are relatively few, and the group's participation in sport has generally been lower than that of other groups. The one professional sport that athletes of Asian descent have dominated, at least for a time, is women's golf. Taiwan's Yani Tseng won four of eight majors in 2010 and 2011, and South Korea's Inbee Park won three of five majors in 2013. That dominance slipped briefly in 2014 as only three Asian-born players were ranked in the top 10 list; by mid-2015, the number had doubled to 6 out of the top 10, according to the LPGA ranking list (Chi 2014; LPGA 2015b).

It is difficult to generalize about the sport participation of Asian Americans due to their varied countries and backgrounds. Many come to the United States already highly educated and established in the middle or upper-middle class. Therefore, they do not reach out to sport as a means to achieve greater economic, social, or educational goals. Instead, the goal of becoming a doctor, lawyer, scientist, or other professional is instilled in their youth by both their parents and their culture, according to professor Yun-Oh Whang, a native Korean (Lapchick 2003). Recent census data support the notion that Asian Americans have a higher household income and higher graduation rate in both high school and college than any other U.S. group, including whites.

Even so, Asians and Asian Americans can boast a number of star athletes in a variety of sports. Here are some of them:

Sammy Lee, diving
Ichiro Suzuki, baseball
Michael Chang, tennis
Tiger Woods, golf
Amy Chow, gymnastics
Se Ri Pak, golf
Kristi Yamaguchi, figure skating
Apolo Anton Ohno, speed skating
Jim Paek, hockey
Michelle Kwan, figure skating
Yao Ming, basketball
Hideo Nomo, baseball
Vijay Singh, golf
Michelle Wie, golf

According to the NCAA (2012–2013a) Asian and Pacific Islander athletes make up just 1.7 percent of all college male athletes and 2.2 percent of college female athletes. However, in large population centers with significant Asian American demographics, anecdotal evidence suggests that Asian American children are becoming more interested in sport, both as spectators and as participants. In addition, as compared with the overall proportion of Asian Americans in the population (5.3 percent), Asian Americans are overrepresented in collegiate sport in Divisions I, II, and III in women's equestrianism (13.6 percent), men's and women's fencing (14.3 percent and 18.1 percent, respectively), men's rifle (7.9 percent), women's gymnastics (7.6 percent), and men's and women's squash (9.1 percent and 10 percent). Most of these sports put a premium on skill but do not require a large physique; therefore, they may be more suited to the traditional body types of Asians (National Collegiate Athletic Association 2012–2013a).

Se Ri Pak of South Korea was inducted into the World Golf Hall of Fame in 2007.

People of Asian descent also tend to be attracted to the martial arts and yoga because such sports are part of their cultural heritage. In fact, martial arts have been some of the fastest-growing activities among the general population in recent years. Yoga now boasts more than 23 million participants, including just under 10 million core participants—those who participate more than 50 times per year (Sports and Fitness Industry Association 2013a).

Native Americans

Native Americans and Alaskan Natives made up 1.6 percent of the U.S. population in 2012, accounting for just over 5 million people. With this relatively small percentage of the population, you might not expect this group to have had much of an impact on sport, but it has produced some notable athletes over the years (U.S. Census Bureau 2013e).

The Olympic Games have produced several sport heroes for Native Americans. Probably the most famous is Jim Thorpe, a Potawatomi who won two Olympic gold medals, played professional baseball and football, and became the first president of the league that would become the NFL. His Olympic medals in 1912 were earned in the pentathlon and the decathlon, and Thorpe's records in these events stood for decades. In 1950, he was named the greatest overall male athlete of the first half of the twentieth century by the Associated Press, and a few years later ABC's *Wide World of Sports* television program named him the athlete of the century.

In the Tokyo Olympic Games in 1964, Billy Mills of the Oglala Lakota tribe won the gold medal in the 10,000-meter race. A fellow Olympian at the Tokyo Games was Ben Nighthorse Campbell, who captained the U.S. judo team and had been the U.S. champion in judo three times. Campbell went on to the serve in the U.S. House of Representatives and the U.S. Senate. Altogether, since 1904, 14 Native American have participated in the Olympics (Native American Sports Council 2009).

By 2013 the number of Native American athletes had grown in both the college and the professional ranks. The National Football League included quarterback Sam Bradford (Cherokee) of the St. Louis Rams. Major League Baseball included two Native American pitchers—Kyle Lohse (Nomlaki) for the Milwaukee Brewers and Joba Chamberlain (Winnebago) for the New York Yankees—along with Native American position players Jacoby Ellsbury (Navajo) and Shane Victorino (Native Hawaiian) for the Boston Red Sox. In addition, four-time PGA winner Notah Begay III (Navajo) has been a standout on the golf tour and a leader in the fight against Type 2 diabetes in the overall Native American community.

In NCAA basketball, sisters Jude and Shoni Schimmel (Umatilla) were thrust into the national spotlight when they led their Louisville Cardinals into the 2013 Division I championship game. Older sister Shoni then moved on to the Atlanta Dream of the Women's National Basketball Association and was selected to play in the WNBA All-Star Game, in which she scored 29 points and was named Most Valuable Player—the first rookie in WNBA history to earn the honor (Bentley 2014). For more information on Native American athletes, visit www.ndnsports.com for news, features, and statistics related to standouts in running, volleyball, lacrosse, boxing, and mixed martial arts.

The Native American Sports Council (NASC) is an affiliated organization of the United States Olympic Committee. It conducts community-based sport programs for Native Americans to encourage community participation. It also provides financial assistance for Native American Olympic hopefuls.

The North American Indigenous Games are a celebration of sport and culture for aboriginal peoples of Canada and the United States. The Games are organized by a council of representatives from 13 provinces and territories in Canada and 13 regions in the United States. In 2002, more than 6,000 athletes and more than 1,200 coaches participated in the Games, which were held in Winnipeg, Canada (Native American Sports Council 2009). The 2006 Games were held in Denver, Colorado, and the 2008 Games in Duncan, British Columbia. The Denver Games attracted some 10,000 athletes representing more than 1,000 tribes. The 2011 Games were held in Milwaukee, Wisconsin.

The 2014 Games, held in Regina, Saskatchewan, featured 3,700 athletes and 900 support staff, including coaches, managers, and chaperones. Competitors ranged from 13 to 19 years old, and 80 percent of participants were from Canada. Aside from the male-only sports of baseball and lacrosse, males and females were equally represented among the participants. The team from British Columbia won the medal count by claiming 160 medals to nip runner-up Saskatchewan (159) and third-place Ontario (149). The Games included the following sports (North American Indigenous Games Council 2014):

Archery
Athletics

Badminton
Baseball
Basketball
Boxing
Canoeing/kayaking
Golf
Box lacrosse
Rifle
Soccer
Softball
Swimming
Volleyball
Wrestling

Sport participation is not easy for many Native Americans in today's world. More than one in four Native American people live in poverty, and in 2014 the unemployment rate of 11 percent was nearly double that for Americans as a whole. Education is part of the challenge. As compared with whites, almost twice as many native people have less than a high school education, and their rate of completing college is half that of whites (Peralta 2014).

Native Americans also tend to have limited time, money, and access to sport, and culture may also limit assimilation into the U.S. sport scene. Discrimination against Native Americans is widespread, and the athletic arena is often just another battle for respect and acceptance. Native Americans have been stereotyped, displaced from their land, restricted to reservations, and saddled with poor economic status.

Legacy of Lacrosse

There is no more significant Native American contribution to sport than the game of lacrosse. Considered America's first sport, lacrosse was created by North American Indians and embraced by non–Native Americans and Canadians alike. Lacrosse is a combination of basketball, soccer, and hockey that rewards skill, speed, and agility rather than brawn.

Lacrosse participation in all age groups had been growing at an average rate of more than 10 percent nationally until 2012, when the growth rate slowed to 5.5 percent. The number of boys playing youth lacrosse has risen by 81 percent since 2007, and participation by girls has increased by 69 percent. The states with the most youth lacrosse players are New York, Massachusetts, Maryland, New Jersey, and Pennsylvania.

Lacrosse was the fastest-growing sport at both the high school and collegiate levels over the five-year period between 2007 and 2012. Among high schools, the growth rate was 47 percent in the number of schools sponsoring boys' lacrosse teams and 43 percent for girls' teams. During the same period, the number of NCAA teams grew by more than 30 percent for both men and women. In 2012 alone, 30 new varsity teams were added, and an astounding 60 more began play in 2013 (United States Lacrosse Association 2012). Table 12.5 shows participation rates for lacrosse in the United States.

TABLE 12.5 U.S. Lacrosse Participation Rates in 2012

Level	Male players	Female players	Total players	% growth (1 year)
Youth	252,060	137,570	389,630	7.8
High school	166,471	115,677	282,148	2.5
College	21,080	13,887	34,967	3.1
Professional	240	0	240	33
Postcollegiate	10,997	4,223	15,220	8.2
Total	450,848	271,357	722,205	5.5

Adapted from United States Lacrosse Association 2012.

Native American Mascots

The use of Native American names for mascots has become an issue in the U.S. capital, which is home to the NFL's Washington Redskins. Media coverage of the controversy has been intense as supporters on both sides have laid out their arguments. Team owner Daniel Snyder has vowed never to change the team name despite strong media pressure. He claims that the term "Redskins" honors the tradition and fighting spirit of Native Americans. Others view it as a demeaning, insensitive, and racist reference to people who have been badly mistreated in their ancestral home. Some media have chosen to stop using the team nickname, instead using phrases such as "the professional football team in Washington." The NFL has taken a neutral stance, trying to appear sympathetic and sensitive while not encouraging any change.

Similar controversies have arisen at all levels, from high school through the professional ranks, and in many cases team nicknames and mascots have been changed—sometimes subtly and sometimes dramatically. The complaint is that the use of stereotypical team names, mascots, and logos perpetuates an ideology that dehumanizes and demeans the cultures of Native Americans. Students of American history will recall that Native American tribes settled in North America long before Europeans "discovered" the continent. As more Europeans came to the "new world," Native American tribes had their land taken and their lives changed irreparably by these new settlers. Many Native Americans paid with their lives to defend their land, civilization, and culture.

Years later, European Americans often promoted their athletic teams at schools, at universities, and in professional sport with Native American logos, names, cheers, and mascots. Defenders of such practices claim that they were and are meant to honor the legacy of Native Americans and perpetuate memories of brave and heroic warriors. However, those who object argue that these practices blatantly stereotype Native Americans, ignore racist attitudes and displacement of populations of Native Americans, and encourage white European Americans to arbitrarily define Native American culture and experience—and in some cases even claim to be part of that heritage (King 2004).

In 2001, the U.S. Commission on Civil Rights, an independent bipartisan federal unit, called for an end to the use of Native American images and team names by non-Native schools. By 2006, the NCAA issued a policy advising schools to specifically forbid the displaying of hostile or abusive racial, ethnic, or national-origin mascots, nicknames, or imagery. Moreover, some 19 schools with team nicknames such as Braves, Redskins, Indians, Tribe, and Savages were put on notice to make changes.

The changes these schools make will be the result of self-study to ensure their use of mascots does not violate the hostile or abusive standard as judged by the NCAA. For example, schools that use the generic term Warriors without referring to Native American culture have been deemed as meeting the compliance standard. The NCAA has clarified that schools that violate the policy cannot host NCAA championships; in addition, they cannot participate in championships if their uniforms violate the policy (NCAA 2007a).

More than 1,400 professional, collegiate, and high school teams have changed their offensive names, and 20 colleges have changed their mascots—for example, the University of North Dakota in 2012 (National Coalition Against Racism in Sports and Media 2014). Four universities included on the "hostile and abusive" list in 2006 by the NCAA have been granted a waiver to retain their nickname after proving that they had support from the relevant tribe: Central Michigan (Chippewa), Florida State (Seminole), Mississippi College (Choctaw), and University of Utah (Ute) (*USA Today* 2013).

In making its recommendation to eliminate nicknames that may be considered abusive or hostile, the NCAA relied on its core principles regarding diversity and inclusion. It may take time and courage for other athletic bodies to follow the NCAA's lead, but the trend is growing. Publicity and pressure from a variety of sources have focused attention on this issue, and the battle has been joined by scholars, journalists, and leaders who oppose discrimination in any form. Progress is being made slowly but surely.

Sport and Promoting Equality

We have considered various aspects of minority participation in sport, but the more important question may be whether sport participation is a negative or positive force for those groups in achieving racial equality. Let's look at both sides of the issue.

Negative: Sport as an Unrealistic Dream in the Black Community

In spite of the relatively high percentage of black athletes in the professional sports of basketball and football the odds of making it to the professional level are exceedingly small. (See chapter 8 and table 8.4 for the odds of transitioning from youth sport to the pros.) Even so, many young black athletes still dream of making it to the pro level.

In the words of William Ellerbee, basketball coach at powerhouse Simon Gratz High School in Philadelphia, "Suburban kids tend to play for the fun of it. Inner city kids look at basketball as a matter of life and death" (Price 1997). To these kids, professional sport seems like a way out of a life marked by economic struggle, educational challenges, and poor prospects for a successful career. In addition, sport is something that young people can understand, relate to, and almost taste. The problem is that there are just not enough spots to fulfill all the dreams.

In 1990, blacks made up about 9 percent of all professional athletes, and there were nearly three times more black physicians than athletes. A decade later, the percentage of black professional athletes had jumped to approximately 20 percent, but the number of black doctors had also risen and stood at double the number of black athletes. In addition, that's just one profession, and there are many other possible choices, but many black youngsters are just not as tuned in to those possibilities.

Leaders in the black community—such as U.S. Open and Wimbledon champion Arthur Ashe—have spoken out about the need to keep black children interested in school and committed to attending college. However, a survey by Indiana University researchers of more than 1,000 black teens found that the majority of athletes chose their university not for academics but to increase their chances of being drafted by the pros. They admitted that they would do only the minimum required to stay eligible in school and if drafted would leave before graduating (Hutchinson 2004).

The NCAA began tracking graduation success rate (GSR) with the class of students entering college in 1995. Since then, the overall rate for student-athletes has increased steadily. During

EXPERT'S VIEW

"Blacks Are Retreating From Athletics"

The surprising claim in this section's header was made by Shaun Powell, author of the provocative book *Souled Out* (2008). He points out that in the early 1980s, many children of the Civil Rights era became adults who were blessed with college degrees and helped by affirmative action and a more tolerant white society. Rather than repeat the vicious poverty cycle of their parents and grandparents, they aspired to become typical middle-class Americans who could provide their children with lives previously thought impossible—filled with education, professional success, and appreciation for art, culture, and a wide variety of sport experiences. Indeed, their children are more likely to succeed in school, join the debate team, play a musical instrument, do social work, or learn the family business. Yet this "suburbanization" of black kids has not increased black participation in sport; in fact, it has decreased the pool of young black athletes.

Powell goes on to point out that the apparent domination of football and basketball by blacks is not due to natural athleticism but simply to what is available in their environment. Since many young black men have not previously been lucky enough to have role models in the ranks of dentists, doctors, administrators, TV producers, computer analysts, and university professors, they tend to gravitate toward what they do see. Poor black kids turn to basketball because it is available in every park, playground, and school in the United States. Similarly, football teams attract huge numbers of kids and reward those who work hardest to excel at the sport (Powell 2008).

this period, the NCAA has put in place stricter standards for initial eligibility and progress toward a degree; it has also created a statistic called the academic progress rate to track student-athletes' academic success. The results show that from 1984 to the 2007 entering class, the overall graduation rate for athletes improved from 52 percent to 66 percent. During that time, the rate for African American male athletes increased from 33 percent to 52 percent and the rate for female African American athletes increased from 45 percent to 63 percent (NCAA 2014c). If we narrow the analysis to athletes who played in 2013 football bowl games, the GSR was 80 percent overall, 62 percent for African American football players, and 82 percent for white football players (Lapchick 2013b).

In fact, African American college athletes graduate at a higher rate than African American students in the general student body. Specifically, African American male athletes graduated at a rate of 52 percent versus 41 percent for all male African Americans, and African American female athletes posted a 63 percent graduation rate as compared with 50 percent for all female African Americans. National rates in NCAA Division I men's basketball and NCAA Division I FBS football do lag behind the rate for all men in the general student body, but African American men in those two sports complete their degrees at a higher rate than African American men who are not student-athletes (NCAA 2014c). Table 12.6 shows the graduation success rates for 2006, 2009, and 2013 for African American athletes as compared with rates for the overall athlete population.

In spite of a general trend of improved graduation rates in the high-profile sports of football and basketball, some troubling patterns remain. For example, white female basketball players in the Division I tournament graduate at a rate of 94 percent as compared with a rate of 88 percent for African Americans—a gap of 6 percentage points. However, on the men's side, white players graduate at a rate of 90 percent as compared with a rate of just 65 percent for African American players—a gap of 25 percentage points.

Similarly, of teams in the women's tournament, 92 percent (55 teams) graduated more than 70 percent of their white players, whereas 83 percent (49 teams) graduated more than 70 percent of their black players—a gap of 9 percentage points. On the male side, however, the gap between white and black players was a whopping 40 percentage points (89 percent for whites but only 49 percent for blacks) (Lapchick 2013b, 2013c).

Universities needn't shoulder all the blame. For example, when Arthur Ashe toured predominantly black high schools in the late 1980s and early 1990s, he reported being "thunderstruck" by the emphasis they placed on sport. As he went to on to report (referring to then-current statistics), "Black families are eight times more likely to push youngsters into athletics than are white families.

TABLE 12.6 Graduation Success Rates for African American NCAA Student-Athletes (by Percentage)

	2006	2009	2013
Male	54	57	52
Female	73	76	63
Football (FBS schools)	54	58	62
Men's basketball (all Division I tournament teams)	49	54	65
Women's basketball (all Division I tournament teams)	71	76	88
NCAA student-athletes (all races)	59	62	66

Data from Lapchick 2013b; Lapchick 2013c.

The disparity is glaring, if you think of the Black parents' involvement at a sporting event compared to participation in a PTA meeting. We need to turn that around" (*Houston Chronicle* 2004).

Similarly, basketball Hall of Famer Charles Barkley has said, "Sports are a detriment to Blacks . . . not a positive. You have a society now where every Black kid in the country thinks the only way he can be successful is through athletics. People look at athletes and entertainers as the sum total of Black America. That is a terrible, terrible thing, because that ain't even one-tenth of what we are" (Shields 2002).

Barkley has used his platform as a former basketball star to get the attention of the black community. His message has been echoed by Gary Sailes, a sport sociologist at Indiana University who provides life skills training to high school and college athletes. He states, "About 95 percent of NBA players need to find a job after their careers end, and about 81 percent of those players are bankrupt when they retire from the sport." In spite of the millions of dollars commanded by superstars, not all professional players make that kind of money, and the temptation to spend lavishly is often hard to resist (Sleek 2004).

Positive: Sport as a Force for Racial Equality

Sport at every level of competition can have a positive effect on the quest for racial equality in society. The helpful outcomes of sport participation should be considered in order to take appropriate perspective on the negative effects, which are often sensationalized in the media.

Harry Edwards, an activist for more than 30 years, brings a unique perspective on the value of sport for black youth. In his opinion, the next 30 years will see a decline in black sport participation. Edwards expects the black youth community to split into two groups—middle class and poor—each of which will shy away from sport. Middle-class kids will go on to become professionals—doctors, lawyers, and businesspeople. Meanwhile, he says that black youngsters from poorer communities are dropping out of society and landing in gangs, on the street, or in jail (Leonard 2000).

Still, Edwards believes that sport offers hope for a way out of poverty, crime, and disillusionment. In his mind, sport may be the last chance to reach out to disaffected black youth (Leonard 2000). Indeed, success in sport can have a dramatic effect on the self-image and self-confidence of young people from minority populations. Athletic exploits can earn them respect and admiration from peers and the community and reassure them of their worthiness as individuals. Achievement in sport can also earn players respect and admiration from peers outside of their minority group. Minority athletes can integrate into the mainstream of their contemporaries who are members of the majority group through team membership, team leadership, and other critical roles they play in sport.

Many communities have instituted after-school sport programs to care for youths who have no parental supervision at home when school is dismissed. Kids look forward to physical activity and playing with friends after a day of inactivity in school. Adding an academic component to after-school sport programs in minority communities has encouraged kids to complete homework, learn about computers, and explore other academic interests in addition to the time allocated to participating in sport. The message conveyed to these young children is that school and sport do mix and that both can help them learn skills for future application.

A number of sports have begun outreach programs to attract minority youngsters. Among them, tennis and golf have probably initiated the most ambitious programs. Traditionally, both sports have been played mostly by affluent white families, and marketing efforts have typically been directed toward that audience and toward corporations that seek to reach consumers with household incomes well above the average. However, in an effort to reach larger audiences and open these sports to a more diverse population, programs for a broader base of young people have now been established and subsidized to introduce them to tennis and golf.

Arthur Ashe and businessman Sheridan Snyder founded the National Junior Tennis League (NJTL) in the 1970s with a unique philosophy for tennis development. The concept, called *instant competition*, got urban youth playing tennis from their first day on the courts. As they tried to play and realized it took certain skills to be successful, the kids asked for help with key techniques, such as serves and ground strokes. This was a radical departure from the traditional tennis instruction found in country clubs at the time.

Twenty-five years later, an approach called game-based teaching became all the rage among tennis coaches—a philosophy not far from the pioneering concept of the NJTL. Perhaps the most notable characteristic of NJTL programs was the requirement that they had to be free or inexpensive so that all kids had access to tennis. The necessary resources came from public parks, foundations, and fundraising projects. In 2009, the program's name was changed to the National Junior Tennis and Learning network (which has more than 600 nonprofit chapters nationwide) in order to more accurately reflect its emphasis not only on tennis development but also on education through tutoring and academic enrichment.

Interscholastic sport, supported by public tax dollars, offers sport opportunities for youngsters of all racial backgrounds at little or no charge. As a result, youth from all backgrounds can play on a team and receive coaching with all expenses paid. For those drawn to football and basketball, for example, school programs have been helpful for minority families who have modest discretionary income or none at all. Other sports that require training or competition outside of school continue to require huge financial investments from families and thus are out of reach for many minority households.

School physical education classes provide great opportunities for students to be exposed to sports that they might not otherwise have a chance to play.

Integration of young people from all racial and ethnic backgrounds occurs naturally in sports where teammates must work together for success. Even when athletes of different races compete *against* each other, they learn to respect and admire competent athletic performance exhibited by opposing players. In this way, young athletes may learn that success is based on achievement, regardless of heritage or skin color.

As a tennis coach at a predominantly white college in Pennsylvania, I consistently scheduled at least one match each spring with a historically black college during our annual trip through Virginia or the Carolinas. When our team of white players set foot on a campus of African Americans, they were curious and a bit uneasy; when they entered the college dining room to eat, all eyes were on them. As a result, they gained a bit more empathy for the minority students back home who dared to enter a mostly white university. Thus these tennis matches enhanced their appreciation for the skill and competitive spirit of athletes from a different background. The visit was often a highlight of an educational experience that offered more than simply a tennis competition.

In somewhat similar fashion, exceptionally talented minority athletes have opportunities for travel, educational scholarships, and experiences outside of their home community. These experiences open them to new possibilities and to attitudes characterized by hope and possibility rather than bitterness and discontent.

Kids who participate in sport are more likely to stay out of trouble with law enforcement and less likely to become dependent on drugs or alcohol. Granted, binge drinking by college athletes generally exceeds that by nonathletes (29 percent to 22 percent), but African American athletes, particularly women, have the lowest prevalence of binge drinking (Wechsler 2005). Although athletes as a group are not immune to temptations or antisocial behavior, the time and dedication required in order to achieve excellence in sport often take precedence over other activities that typically result in unacceptable behavior. In addition, athletes run the risk of losing their chance to play the sport they so enjoy if they violate rules for conduct and behavior.

Black athletes who do beat the odds and forge successful careers in professional sport have the opportunity to better themselves financially—sometimes in amazing ways. When their athletic career ends, they may find other opportunities as spokespersons or employees in businesses or sport organizations. In this way, upward mobility through sport has been demonstrated repeatedly by a generation of black athletes.

In addition, once they reach the peak of athletic performance, many black athletes have used their prominence to speak out for causes in which they believe. For example, improved race relations was a theme of a proposed Olympic boycott in Mexico City in 1968. When the boycott fell through, African American sprinters Tommie Smith and John Carlos instead used the award ceremony to call attention to the plight of African Americans in the United States. Although they were criticized heavily for using sport to promote their personal point of view, their actions were no different from those of many other influential people who do the same.

Michael Jordan, perhaps the greatest basketball player of all time, demonstrated the global reach of sport success through his role as a spokesperson for Nike. Kids in many countries adopted the mantra "Be like Mike" and consumed Nike products ranging from shoes to clothing in hopes of emulating Jordan's performances. He also showed how fame in one field can be transferred to the business world through ownership of a professional basketball franchise (the Charlotte Hornets) and other business ventures.

Minority athletes become role models for the next generation of athletes, and their fame is not limited to children from a single racial background. Indeed, children often choose their heroes based not on race but on performance, flair, and personality. Although some athletes reject their role as models for youth and simply want to be accepted as an athlete, the dynamics of the media, fans, and kids simply won't allow it. Prominent athletes' actions, lifestyle, and values are scrutinized and either embraced or rejected simply because they are in the public spotlight. They can choose to serve as a positive force for improving society or a negative example of behavior that should be abhorred. As the struggle for racial integration continues, sport offers fertile ground for exposing the futility of erecting artificial barriers to integration, for embracing athletes from all backgrounds based on talent and conduct, and for promoting understanding and appreciation of people from different backgrounds.

Minorities as Sport Leaders

Virtually anyone who has studied the situation of minority athletes has come away believing that leadership in sport must change in order for progress to occur. The lack of minority leadership in key positions in sport is sobering and shows few signs of improving in the near future. However, change can happen. The following sections look at some ways to increase the presence of minority groups at all levels of sport. Most of the examples involve African Americans, since their role as athletes in certain sports has been so dominant. Increasingly, though, people are also becoming more sensitive to the need for leaders from other minority groups as well.

Minorities in Leadership Positions in Collegiate Sport

Given the statistics showing the dominance of African American athletes in the collegiate and professional sports of football, men's and women's basketball, and track and field, you might expect to see similar gains in the coaching ranks and other leadership positions. However, the proportion of African American coaches sits well below the proportion of African Americans in the population at large and is much lower than the proportion of African American athletes playing the major revenue sports.

In one study, college sport received an overall grade of B in 2012 for its hiring practices in relation to race—the same grade as in the previous year. One notable area of concern involves the position of head men's basketball coach in Division I; the number of black coaches declined in number four straight years, falling from 21 percent in 2008 to 19 percent in 2012—well off the high mark of 25 percent set in 2006. Other categories were given a grade of B for hiring practices, including

TABLE 12.7 Percentages of White and Black Head Coaches (All College Sports)

	MEN			WOMEN		
Division	**I**	**II**	**III**	**I**	**II**	**III**
White	86	88	92	85	88	92
Black	8	5	4	8	5	4

Adapted, by permission, from R. Lapchick, 2013, *Racial and gender report card: College sport*. (Orlando FL: The Institute for Diversity and Ethics in Sport). Available: www.tidesport.org/RGRC/2012/2012_College_RGRC.pdf

NCAA Division I FBS head football coach, Division I women's and men's basketball head coach, and various athletic administrator positions. Division I athletic directors were graded C and conference commissioners F. Table 12.7 shows the percentage of African American coaches in all sports combined by division and gender for 2012 (Lapchick 2012b).

In 2012, in the highly visible sport of football at the NCAA Division I FBS level, 15 head coaches were African American; there were also 3 other coaches of color. The only Latino FBS head coach was Mario Cristobal at Florida International University, and the only FBS coaches of Asian descent were Norm Chow of Hawaii and Ken Niumatalolo of the Naval Academy. While these percentages of minority coaches have continued to improve in recent years, they still lag behind the percentage of minorities found in the population at large and fall significantly below the proportion of black athletes in Division I football, which in 2012 stood at 43.2 percent (Lapchick 2012b).

One popular explanation for the dearth of black coaches is the fact that only a small percentage

APPLYING SOCIAL THEORY

Conflict Theorists and Promoting Diversity

Does sport play a positive role in promoting diversity and equal opportunity? Conflict theories typically look at social class, economic power, and the struggle for control over sport—particularly popular professional spectator sports. Now that you have reviewed key statistics showing the percentages of minorities in college and professional sport at every level, do you agree or disagree with the following statements? (Keep in mind the differences in minority involvement at the ownership and administrative levels as compared with participation in the coaching and player ranks.)

- Minorities overall appear to be limited in sport leadership positions as compared with their proportion of the general U.S. population.
- Minorities appear to account for a lower percentage of sport leaders at both the college and professional level as compared with the percentage of minority participants, particularly in higher-profile sports.

TABLE 12.8 African Americans in College Athletic Administrative Leadership Positions

	MEN (%)			WOMEN (%)		
NCAA division	**I**	**II**	**III**	**I**	**II**	**III**
Athletic director	6.3	3.9	2.5	0	1.1	0.5
Senior associate or assistant	6.0	3.5	2.2	3.2	1.4	1.8
Senior female administrator	0	0	0.2	9.3	4.3	2.8

Adapted, by permission, from R. Lapchick, 2013, *Racial and gender report card: College sport.* (Orlando FL: The Institute for Diversity and Ethics in Sport). Available: www.tidesport.org/RGRC/2012/2012_College_RGRC.pdf

of athletic directors and other administrators in universities are black. For instance, the percentage of black athletic directors at Division I colleges is a modest 6.3 percent (see table 12.8). It has been theorized that white administrators know fewer black coaches, are less comfortable with them, and thus resist placing key programs in their hands.

Minorities in Leadership Positions in Professional Sport

In professional sport, the percentage of black athletes is even higher than it is in college (see tables 12.2 and 12.3). Those responsible for recruiting and hiring black coaches are the owners of professional sport franchises, along with their administrative staff members. Table 12.9 summarizes the percentage of African American coaches in professional sport.

In the National Football League in 2013, two-thirds of players were racial minorities—primarily black—whereas 26 percent of management positions were occupied by people of color. Though there were no African American owners, there were six black general managers. In addition, as of 2013, eight of the last 12 Super Bowl participants

TABLE 12.9 African American Coaches in Professional Sports by Percentage

Position	NBA	NFL	MLB	MLS	WNBA
2013					
Head coach	43	9	10	0	25
Assistant coach	44	31	13	1.6	38
2014					
Head coach	40	13	10	0	33
Assistant coach	46	29	10	8.3	52

Data from Lapchick 2013c, 2013d, 2013e, 2013f, and 2013g.

had either a black coach or a black general manager (Lapchick 2013f).

In the NBA, three-quarters of players are African American, whereas only six African Americans hold the position of general manager (of 30 teams). People of color hold 35 percent of jobs in the league office. Michael Jordan remains the only team owner of color to hold a majority stake in his team, though 23 other minorities are involved in ownership. Minorities held four CEO or president positions and 35 vice president positions (Lapchick 2013e).

Since 2004, the WNBA has regularly been the industry leader in diversity and inclusion, earning at least an overall grade of A for race and gender. In 2013, the league earned an overall grade of A+ for the second consecutive year. It earned an A for every category except general manager and vice president (Lapchick 2013g).

In Major League Baseball, more than a quarter of players are of Latino origin, whereas the number of black players continues to decline. MLB's office lists its employee roster as 9.7 percent black, 14.7 percent Latino, and 3.4 percent Asian. The ranks of general managers include three people of color—two Latino and one African American. Baseball also has the only Hispanic majority owner in the major U.S. sport leagues in Arturo Moreno of the Los Angeles Angels (Lapchick 2013c).

Major League Soccer is a bit different in that it is owned by a board of governors who invest in the league as a whole rather than in one specific franchise. In 2013, 14.7 percent of board members were minorities—8.8 percent Latino and 5.9 percent Asian (Lapchick 2013d).

Strategies to Promote Racial Diversity in Sport

As the discussion makes clear, one key strategy for promoting racial diversity in sport is to improve the hiring and retention of minority coaches and administrators in both college and professional sport. Institutions must follow guidelines for affirmative action that include strategies for recruiting minority candidates, including minorities in the hiring process, and making a good-faith effort to evaluate minority candidates objectively and fairly. Other possible strategies include the following:

- Agree on the need to improve the percentages of minorities in all sports and all sport leadership positions. Targets should be set based on percentages in the population at large and within the sport community.
- Leaders in sport must help collect data, such as those currently provided by Dr. Richard Lapchick of the University of Central Florida, that detail the participation and presence of minorities at all levels of sport. Without a baseline number to work with, efforts to improve diversity are impossible to evaluate. The process should be unbiased, objective, and transparent, and the results should be disseminated widely.
- Leaders in minority communities and heads of sport organizations should confront any instance of discrimination or racism when they become aware of it and take steps to rectify the situation.
- Major sport organizations, both amateur and professional, should adopt statements of inclusion of minorities for their players, coaches, and administrative staff.
- Major media outlets—including television, radio, magazine, and newspaper outlets—should actively recruit minorities for their staff and aggressively endorse the need for change in sport.
- All sport organizations should develop standing policies of inclusion in pictures, graphics, and media representations.
- Politicians should adopt laws to ensure that public money is used for projects and organizations committed to providing opportunity for all and improving minority representation.
- Prominent minority athletes must assume the responsibility of pointing out inconsistencies and inequities and using their popularity to help improve the future for other minority athletes.
- Local communities and youth sport organizations should adopt strong policies on nondiscrimination and actively recruit minorities to participate in sport as players, coaches, leaders, and organizers.
- Minority-owned businesses should expect appropriate action by the organizations that they support financially through sponsorship and marketing.

ACTIVITY TIME-OUT

Racial Quotas in Sport

Sport in South Africa has always been a lightning rod for racism. After all, the entire country was banned from Olympic competition and other worldwide sport competition for more than 20 years due to its apartheid policies. In spite of efforts to integrate sport countrywide, many sports continue to be bound by outdated traditions and a lack of black participants, coaches, and administrators.

At the root of this problem lies the fact that the sport culture doesn't get black kids participating in sport at a young age; therefore, it excludes them from the development pipeline. In 2014, in recognition of the lack of progress, the South African Rugby Union announced new racial quotas for the Vodacom Cup, a developmental rugby competition. Teams are now required to field 7 black players as part of their 22-man squad; in addition, at least 5 of the 7 must be starters, and at least 2 must be forwards.

Given the history and attitude toward racial quotas in schools and colleges in the United States, do you think imposing racial quotas in certain sports should be considered? Why or why not?

Chapter Summary

This chapter reviews the significance of racial and ethnic background in sport. It examines supposed differences in physical prowess between races and considers whether they might derive from genetics or environment. At present, no clear evidence exists either way, though research is ongoing. It is likely that both factors will prove to be relevant in most sports.

The chapter also compares participation by minority groups at various levels of sport with the number of minorities in the general U.S. population. Generally, the data show that black athletes dominate certain major U.S. sports, including basketball and football, at both the college and professional levels. Baseball, which led professional sport in integration efforts and formerly had a significant number of African Americans, has fallen back to less than 10 percent even as Latino players have advanced to 28 percent of MLB. In all other sports, whites overwhelmingly dominate in terms of participation at every level of play.

The chapter briefly reviews the history of minority athletes and notes the exceptional influence of outstanding black athletes. Most gains in participation by minorities have occurred since World War II, after which college and professional sport was opened up to black athletes. Latino athletes are exceedingly well represented in professional baseball, easily surpassing black athletes by percentage. In other sports, however, Latinos are generally poorly represented, as are Asian Americans and Native Americans.

The chapter presents both the positive and negative effects of sport on the cause of racial and ethnic equality. Although progress has not always been smooth, sport has shown the potential to be a positive force for racial integration. On the other hand, sport also has negative aspects, including minority preoccupation with sport at the expense of schooling and alternative career choices.

Even as black athletes dominate some college and professional sports, black athletes in general continue to face struggles. Their participation tends to be limited to just a few sports, and their access to the majority of sports is still limited. In addition, powerful sport institutions tend to exploit the physical abilities of black athletes at the expense of their potential to lead a fulfilling life. Moreover, leadership positions in sport at all levels continue to be dominated by whites, thus affecting efforts to open opportunities for African Americans as coaches or other leaders in the sport world.

The chapter presents strategies for reducing the present inequities in sport and invites readers to offer creative strategies of their own. For the progress of the last 50 years to continue at the same pace, we must muster a collective commitment to racial diversity in sport at every level of play.

13

STUDENT OUTCOMES

After reading this chapter, you will know the following:

- The historical roles of women in and out of sport
- How Title IX has affected women's sport participation
- How increased sport participation by females has affected society
- Current challenges in women's sport

Women and Sport

Women and Sport

Child participation in exercise and athletics is generally seen as an asset for American families—both dual- and single-parent. Sport not only provides kids with social support but also often brings them into closer contact and communication with their parents. And while research reveals that mothers and fathers provide similar levels of encouragement and support for both their daughters and their sons, evidence also indicates that girls are often short-changed by fathers who spend more time in sport with their sons.

Most fathers today would probably say that they support the athletic exploits of both their sons and their daughters. The fact is, however, that boys tend to identify their father as the mentor who taught them the most about sport, whereas girls tend to rank their father in the number three spot, behind their coach and physical education teacher. Girls rank their mother in fifth place, and boys rank her in sixth place. If parents, particularly fathers, don't encourage girls to enter sport when they are young, it may not happen at all, especially given the elimination of so many physical education programs in recent years (Women's Sports Foundation 2008).

One of the most consistent forms of discrimination has been the forcing of certain social roles upon women throughout history. From the time of the ancient Greeks to the present day, societies have relegated females to subservient roles revolving around childrearing, family, and sex. Changes in U.S. society in the last 40 years have dramatically altered the roles available to women, but the quest for equalizing women's opportunities in society remains short of its goal.

A majority of women in the United States now take part in the workforce. According to the U.S. Bureau of Labor Statistics, 58 percent of all women are in the workplace, and 76 percent of mothers with children between the ages of 6 and 17 years worked in 2012. In contrast, in 1960, the percentage of working women was just 36 percent; it peaked at a high of 60 percent in 2000. The decline since then has resulted in part from economic factors that have also affected male workers.

The educational attainment of women in the labor force has risen, and 38 percent of working women now hold a college degree, as compared with just 11 percent in 1970. Moreover, in 2012, women accounted for 52 percent of all workers employed in management, professional, and related occupations, which is more than their 47 percent share of overall employment (U.S. Bureau of Labor Statistics 2014b) Even so, women overall in the workforce hold more part-time jobs than men, work fewer hours, and earn only 82 percent of what males earn for comparable work and hours worked. In addition, men still dominate the higher-paying executive jobs. These shifts in the workforce mean that women now shoulder a large burden in seeking and keeping their jobs, helping ensure access to health care for their families, and still serving as the primary caregiver in most families.

When women enter the workforce, the largest household expense is that of child care in most regions of the country. This cost is one reason that the number of stay-at-home moms rose to 29 percent of mothers in 2012, as compared with an all-time low of 23 percent in 1999—still well below the 49 percent of four decades ago (Fottrell 2014).

Along with decades of fighting for equality in employment opportunities, women have campaigned for and significantly progressed in gaining admission to institutions of higher education, rights in marriage, roles in the armed forces, and opportunities for sport participation. The sporting world changed greatly with the passage in 1972 of the federal Title IX legislation, which granted females equal opportunity for sport participation. Even so, their foray into the sporting world also meant that they faced new forms of discrimination. This chapter explores the factors that have affected women's sport participation, the sweeping changes that have occurred in sport over the past 40 years, and the challenges that women in sport still confront.

Historical Role of Women

To fully understand the magnitude of the first female breakthroughs in sport, we first have to appreciate the context in which these pioneering women lived. Since the time of the ancient Greeks and Romans, the family was based on a patriarchal model wherein the male was the absolute ruler. He alone could own property and enter into business contracts, and if his wife violated social customs or his wishes, he could punish her. In many societies, if a husband determined that his wife was guilty of infidelity, he could have her put to death.

The subjugated role of women was reinforced by societal institutions. Even the church made it clear that the male was the head of the family, and it often portrayed the female as an agent of the devil whose role was to tempt the male. Women could not act as clergy and were expected to adhere to the teachings of men.

The prescribed role for women remained the same for centuries. The male was always the leader, the family provider, and the center of power. The female was the child bearer and nurturer and keeper of the home. Females were not even allowed to engage in physical exercise other than that required by their domestic roles. They were expected to look attractive to men, dress prettily, and be well mannered. They were expected to depend on men.

Women and Sport Before Title IX

For centuries, sport participated in assigning a limited role to women by excluding them from participation and resisting efforts to include them. Girls have been ignored, ridiculed, and even disciplined for their efforts to compete in sport (Rice, Hutchinson, and Lee 1958; Spears and Swanson 1978). It wasn't until the mid-1800s that women even ventured into physical activity programs founded at colleges such as Mount Holyoke and Vassar. These early programs of physical education were typically led by medical doctors who were dedicated to improving the health and fitness of students. Exercise for girls was carefully controlled and emphasized graceful, ladylike movements. Competitive sport was ruled out as simply inappropriate for women.

Even so, a few women dared to participate in individual sports, such as tennis and golf. Gradually, women were generally accepted into other

Jackie Joyner-Kersee, one of the top female athletes of the second half of the 20th century, was an Olympic gold medalist in the heptathlon, which is comprised of seven track events: 100-meter run, high jump, shot put, 200-meter run, long jump, javelin throw, and 800-meter run.

sports that were considered relatively feminine because they involve grace, beauty, and coordination—for example, figure skating, gymnastics, and swimming. Power and strength sports were still deemed inappropriate for women, and even the Olympic Games banned women from most track and field events. To put it simply, running, jumping, and throwing heavy objects were not consistent with the prevailing social view of women. In 1920, the Olympics invited only 64 women but more than 2,500 men. At the Berlin Games in 1936, the number of female participants grew to 328, and male participation rose to nearly 4,000 (Fanbay 2005).

A few female athletes gained fame during the 1920s and 1930s. Glenna Collett-Vare was a remarkable amateur golfer who won the U.S. Women's Amateur Golf Championship six times between 1922 and 1935. Helen Wills Moody dominated women's tennis in the 1920s and 1930s by winning eight Wimbledon titles, eight U.S. national titles, and every set she played in competition between 1927 and 1932. The most famous and perhaps best athlete was Mildred "Babe" Didrikson Zaharias, whose accomplishments included two gold medals and one silver medal in track and field at the 1932 Olympics. As a golfer, she dominated both the amateur and professional fields, and she was also a tennis player who could compete with the best players in the United States.

In 1950, in view of these accomplishments, the Associated Press named Zaharias the greatest female athlete of the first half of the century. (In the second half of the 20th century, the top female athlete, according to *Sports Illustrated for Women* in 2000, was track-and-field Olympian Jackie Joyner-Kersee, followed closely by tennis legends Billie Jean King, Chris Evert, and Martina Navratilova.) Other women also made their historical mark in professional sport. For example, the popular movie *A League of Their Own* chronicles the trials of the All-American Girls Professional Baseball League during World War II. Taking a broader view, the documentary *Dare to Compete: The Struggle of Women in Sports* traces the history of women in sport as a whole.

These outstanding female athletes blazed the trail for women to enter the sport world. But their successes would not open up sport opportunities for the majority of women until society changed its general view of a woman's role. Here are some of the reasons that people gave for excluding women from sport.

Females Aren't Interested

In hindsight, lack of interest was a particularly irrational justification for excluding girls from sport. Given that girls had little access to sport, few sport role models, and no encouragement to play sport from social institutions such as families, schools, and churches—of course they appeared uninterested! Instead, they were expected to become cheerleaders, pompon girls, and majorettes; play in the band; and fill the stands to cheer on the boys.

Physical Activity Harms the Female Body

In the last century, led by physicians and physical educators at universities across the United States, people gradually awakened to the positive benefits of physical activity for girls. Though at first limited to certain physical activities deemed "ladylike," girls were at least encouraged to become aware of their bodies for reasons of health and appearance. Eventually, research began to show that girls could train their bodies to become stronger and faster and endure longer without damaging their physique.

Still, it wasn't until the late 1970s that experts began to concertedly affirm the positive values of sport participation for females. For example, in 1978, Klafs and Lyon said, "Let it be stated here, unequivocally, that there is no reason, either psychological, physiological, or sociological, to preclude normal, healthy females from participating in strenuous physical activities, nor does such participation accentuate or develop male characteristics. Strenuous activity for the well-trained and well-conditioned female athlete results in good health and accentuates the very qualities that make her a woman" (Klafs and Lyon 1978, 10).

Although female leaders in sport forged a brave path toward physical activity for girls, they also held girls back. Up through the 1950s, leaders of women's sport limited the types of acceptable sport and encouraged girls not to become "too" competitive. The norm in the 1950s for college women in sport was the "play day" or "sport day," in which women from several colleges gathered at one campus and were assigned to teams for the day. The events were largely informal and encouraged mass participation. Several sports were typically played, and competition was low key and usually conducted in a round-robin format. The closing event was a tea or social hour during which the "girls" could talk with each other (Spears and Swanson 1978).

When the National Collegiate Athletic Association (NCAA) threatened to take over women's sport, leading female coaches and administrators fought against it. They preferred the more ladylike approach to sport, in which female athletes were tempered by good manners, winning was deemphasized, and femininity was maintained. Remnants of this approach can be seen in some current team names, such as the Lady Lions, Lady Vols, or Lady Tigers. Imagine if men's teams were called names such as the Gentlemen Bears, Gentlemen Gators, or Gentlemen Warriors!

Early physical education classes touted the benefits of exercise for young women.

Women Cannot Compete With Men in Sport, So They Don't Deserve Equal Opportunity to Play

Once a few girls dared to compete against boys, it was perhaps inevitable that objections would arise about the relative skill and physical prowess of girls versus boys. For instance, my high school boys' tennis team competed against a young girl named Tory Fretz, who played first-position singles on the boys' team for Harrisburg High School and went on to a professional career. She defeated every boy in the conference, usually by a lopsided score. Her performance was an eye-opener for adolescent boys and was experienced as humiliating for her victims, who endured teasing and taunting.

Unlike Tory Fretz, however, most girls are at a disadvantage when competing against boys once puberty sets in. Before puberty, girls can compete equally with boys in any sport. But once the relative size, strength, and body proportions change during puberty, an individual's comparative athletic ability also changes. Therefore, to achieve equal opportunity in sport, women needed a whole new structure for girls' sports, and it would have to be built starting from little history, equipment, or tradition.

Girls With Natural Talent in Sport Are Probably Lesbians

Girls who gravitated toward sport were often suspected of lesbian tendencies long before the term *lesbian* was even used in polite society. Women who liked sport and seemed to have more testosterone were looked at askance by males and females alike. The average person had little notion of the balance of testosterone and progesterone that exists in both male and female bodies. Therefore, when women who were stronger and faster or could hit harder excelled in women's sport, some observers suspected that they were really men disguised in women's bodies.

In the Olympic Games, gender testing was an issue for years due to the seemingly masculine appearance of many great female athletes. **Gender verification** was required for nearly 30 years—until the 1996 Atlanta Games—after which all Olympic gender verification was discontinued at the urging of virtually all professional medical associations, including the American Medical Association. The extensive procedures used for verification were too complex, uncertain, and expensive. Furthermore, very few athletes ever failed the tests. In addition, with the advent of doping control policies that included urine tests conducted under direct supervision, it became virtually impossible for a male athlete to escape detection even if he did try to pose as a woman (Genel 2000).

Even so, the issue of gender testing made headlines once again in 2009, when the International Association of Athletics Federations (IAAF)—the world governing body for track and field—performed gender tests on 18-year-old South African star Caster Semenya. Partly motivated by her relatively masculine appearance, the IAAF requested that she be tested for gender verification after she delivered amazing performances in the 800-meter run at the world championships. It had also been reported that Semenya has no ovaries but rather internal male testes that have not descended.

The controversy dragged on for 11 months, until July 2010, when the IAAF cleared her to resume competition. The IAAF refused to reveal the medical details in dispute or make any comment, so it is likely that we will never know exactly why a doctor questioned her gender or why it took so long to adjudicate the issue (*Daily Mail* 2010). Semenya was chosen to carry the South African flag during the opening ceremonies of the 2012 London Olympic Games, where she went on to win the silver medal in the 800-meter run.

Returning to a historical perspective, oppressive social attitudes toward women and lesbians continued for years to be heavily weighted against women's equal participation in sport. To get a flavor of such attitudes, consider this quote from Woody Hayes, a famed football coach at Ohio State University (Vare 1974, 38):

IN THE ARENA WITH . . .

The Women's Sports Foundation

The Women's Sports Foundation came to life in 1974 shortly after the historic Title IX legislation was passed. It was founded by tennis legend Billie Jean King, along with strong support from notable Olympians such as swimmer Donna de Varona and skier Suzy Chaffee. The organization's mission is "to advance the lives of girls and women through sports and physical activity" (Women's Sports Foundation 2014).

Since its establishment, the foundation has been nurtured by more than 225 trustees—strong advocates and role models for girls and women—to become a viable, essential, and trailblazing voice for using sport to promote healthy living for girls and women. The foundation has advocated for the rights of females in sport; addressed legal issues; supported funding equality in sport programs; and fought against discrimination due to gender, race, ethnicity, or sexual orientation.

The foundation's major programs include fundraising events, athletic scholarship awards, the annual National Girls and Women in Sports Day, operating an information resource center, and compiling research relevant to females in sport and physical activity. In 2010, the foundation formed a strategic partnership with the University of Michigan School of Kinesiology to form SHARP—a sport, health, and activity research and policy center for women and girls.

Foundation founder Billie Jean King is the first U.S. female to have a sport stadium bear her name—the USTA Billie Jean King National Tennis Center, which is home to the U.S. Open tennis championships in Flushing Meadows, New York. This honor resulted from King's pioneering leadership in establishing the Women's Tennis Association (WTA), which operates the women's professional tennis tour. Her vision, energy, and devotion to the cause of the Women's Sports Foundation have brought even wider recognition and honors, culminating in her being awarded the Presidential Medal of Freedom in 2009.

To learn more about the Women's Sports Foundation, visit its website at www.womenssportsfoundation.org.

ACTIVITY TIME-OUT

Public Information About Equity in Athletics

Check out your university to see how it stacks up in terms of equity between male and female sport teams, participants, coaches, and budgets. Visit http://ope.ed.gov/athletics/ and type in the required information for your school: the undergraduate enrollment, the school name, the state in which it is located, and its NCAA division. Once you have studied your school's data, write a one-page summary of what you found. Include your own observations and conclusions and any questions you have about the data.

I hear they're even letting w-o-m-e-n in their sports program now [referring to Oberlin College]. That's your Women's Liberation, boy—bunch of goddamn lesbians. . . . You can bet your ass that if you have women around—and I've talked to psychiatrists about this—you aren't gonna be worth a damn. No sir! Man has to dominate . . . . [T]he best way to treat a woman . . . is to knock her up and hide her shoes.

Title IX

Social change throughout the 1950s and 1960s helped change women's sport. The women's movement of the 1960s—including organizations such as the National Organization for Women and the Women's Action Group—helped further the movement for equality of women and men. In the sport world, however, it was the passage of **Title IX** that ultimately gave women an even playing field with men. (For a comprehensive work on the substance, effects, and challenges of Title IX, consult *Title IX* by Carpenter and Acosta [2005].) Passed in 1972 by the U.S. Congress, Title IX stated the following:

No person in the United States shall, on the basis of sex, be excluded from participation in, be denied the benefits of, or be subjected to discrimination under any education program or activity receiving federal financial assistance.

When Title IX was passed, there was little immediate outcry, because the United States was in the throes of ensuring equal protection for all students, regardless of race or gender, in public education. Most parents agreed that their daughters should have the same right to a fine education that their sons had. It wasn't for some time that people understood that sport was included in the decree and that big changes would have to be made.

The imbalance in sport participation between boys and girls was dramatic until the 1970s. At that time, nearly 3.7 million boys played varsity high school sport, but only 295,000 girls did so. Even more unbalanced, boys received 99 cents of every dollar spent on sport. At the college level, about 180,000 men played varsity sport, but just 32,000 women did so (Women's Sports Foundation 2009b).

Once Title IX was passed, many questions were raised about what it really meant and what specific changes had to be made. Did it mean that girls had to have as many teams as boys had? Did girls get half the money spent on sport, thereby reducing funding for boys unless more money was allocated to sport overall? Though many people thought girls should have an equal chance to participate in sport, few wanted to see cuts in programs for boys. What a dilemma!

After much debate and foot dragging, the Office for Civil Rights published guidelines in 1975 to clarify what it meant to comply with Title IX. To be eligible for federal funding, schools and colleges had to meet any of three tests:

1. Proportionality test: If a school is 50 percent female, then no less than 45 percent of its athletes should be female. The 5 percent deviation was deemed the allowable margin.
2. History-of-progress test: A school demonstrates progress toward expanding women's programs, particularly over the three most recent years.
3. Accommodation-of-interest test: A school shows that it has fully accommodated the interests and needs of the underrepresented (generally, female) sex. Any remaining inequality exists due to lack of interest by female students or to the inability to field additional teams for athletic competition.

As these clarifications were issued, female athletes and their advocates began filing legal suits. In one of the lawsuits, the U.S. Supreme Court surprisingly ruled that Title IX did not apply to sport since sport was not supported by federal funds. Three years later, the U.S. Congress responded to this decision by passing the Civil Rights Restoration Act, clarifying that it did indeed intend Title IX to apply to sport. President Ronald Reagan vetoed the law, but his veto was overridden by Congress.

Shortly after the passage of Title IX, massive changes began to be made in high school and college sport. Most schools and colleges were slow to respond, but the process had begun. Supporters of male athletics initiated numerous lawsuits to delay the inevitable, but women gradually began to assert their rights and demand sport opportunities at every level.

Women and Sport After Title IX

In the 40 years following the passage of the Title IX legislation, the numbers of girls and women playing sport has changed dramatically. Here are some details:

- Participation in sport and physical activity by females of all ages has continued to increase overall and among those who exercise daily, the proportion of women improved from 15.6 percent in 2010 to 17 percent in 2013, whereas males posted a smaller increase from 21.5 percent to 21.7 percent during the same time period (Statistics Portal 2013).
- Females predominate in certain activities, such as aerobic exercising (70 percent), exercise walking (61 percent), exercise with equipment (53 percent), and swimming (53 percent) (S. Hoffman 2013, 203). Women are also more likely than men to join exercise classes at gyms, a fact that is evidenced by their dominance in yoga (74 percent) and Pilates (84 percent) (Sports Marketing Surveys 2013).
- Women have made remarkable participation gains in high school and college sport and in the Olympic Games. For details, see tables 13.1 through 13.4. In the past 40 years, women's participation on U.S. teams has nearly equaled that of men.
- Olympic performances by women improved dramatically as training intensified and the pool of competing athletes enlarged. Joan Benoit Samuelson's time for the marathon in Los Angeles in 1984 was faster than all men's times before 1956. In Olympic swimming, the women's record in the 100-meter freestyle, set in 1992, was faster than all men's times before 1964. In cross-country skiing, the Olympic record for women in the 15-kilometer race, set in 1994, was faster than all men's records before 1992.

The following subsections examine several outcomes of the increased presence of females in sport and physical activity.

Women as Sport Fans

As women's participation in sport exploded, females also became avid sport fans. Moreover, many females began watching sport to track the performances of their favorite athletes and appreciate the competition—not just as spectators but now as fellow participants.

- You may be surprised to learn that 62 percent of women say they watch sport on television either regularly or occasionally. In comparison, only 42 percent watch soap operas regularly or occasionally (Gumpel 2009).

TABLE 13.1 High School Sport Participation by Gender

Year	Boys	Girls
1971–1972	3,666,917	294,015
2013–2014	4,527,994	3,267,664

Data from National Federation of State High School Associations 2012-2013.

TABLE 13.2 College Sport Participation by Gender

Year	Men	Women
1981–1982	167,055	64,390
2008–2009	240,822	180,347
2013–2014	271,055	207,814

Data from NCAA Participation Study 1981-1982 to 2013-2014.

TABLE 13.3 Women in the Summer Olympic Games

Year	Female participants (% of total)
1900	1.6
1960	11.5
1984	23
1996	34
2000	38
2004	41
2008	42
2012	44

Data from International Olympic Committee 2014a.

TABLE 13.4 American Women in the Olympic Games

Olympic year	Total number of U.S. athletes	Number of U.S. female athletes	Female percentage of U.S. athletes
1972	428	90	21
1992	619	203	33
2008	596	286	48
2012	530	269	51

Data from Smith and Wynn 2013.

- Female viewers outnumber male viewers for three major sporting events: the Kentucky Derby, the Winter Olympics, and the Summer Olympics. Coverage of the Olympic Games has traditionally catered to a female audience, and much of the airtime is devoted to women's gymnastics, figure skating, and beach volleyball (Owens 2010).
- Games played in the National Football League (NFL) are by far the most popular sport on U.S. television, drawing 64 percent of all Americans (73 percent of men and 55 percent of women). The Super Bowl now draws an audience that is 46 percent female, and in 2011 the third-ranked television show among women aged 18 to 49 was *Sunday Night Football*, which trailed only *Dancing with the Stars* and *Grey's Anatomy* (Braverman 2011; McBride 2011a).
- Women have changed the NFL's television audience from 2009 to 2013 by increasing their viewership by 26 percent versus an 18 percent increase for men. Similarly, Sunday night football viewing has increased by 25 percent among women versus only 10 percent among men. NFL ratings from 2012 to 2013 were flat overall because the male audience dropped by 2 percent while the female audience grew by 3 percent (Chemi 2014).
- After NFL football, NASCAR is the second most-watched sport on television, and 37 percent of its viewers are female (Thompson 2014).
- Women make up 32 percent of Major League Soccer (MLS) fans, 30 percent of Major League Baseball (MLB) fans, 32 percent of National Hockey League (NHL) fans, and 30 percent of National Basketball Association (NBA) fans (Thompson 2014).

Popularity of Women's Sport

Women's sport at every level of competition has begun to attract large numbers of spectators. Here are some landmark attendance figures:

- In 1973, at the height of the women's movement, Billie Jean King defeated Bobby Riggs to win the "Battle of the Sexes" in front of 30,472 fans—then a record for the largest crowd to attend any tennis match, and one that stood until 2010 (Women's Sports Foundation 2009a). The match that broke the record was an exhibition between Serena Williams and Kim Clijsters in the tiny country of Belgium. That match, staged in Brussels, set the new attendance record of 35,681.
- In December 2013, the University of Kentucky drew a record crowd of 23,706 spectators for its women's basketball game against Duke University. That is the highest attendance at a women's college basketball game not involving one or both of the sport's two historical powers: the University of Connecticut and the University of Tennessee (Waldron 2013).
- In 2012, eight NCAA women's basketball programs outdrew their men's programs for the year. The schools included familiar names, such as Baylor, Notre Dame, Delaware, and Louisiana Tech (Bowman 2012).
- The 2013 U.S. Open women's final scored higher television ratings than the men's final. The match, which featured Serena Williams and Victoria Azarenka, drew the highest overnight rating for the U.S. Open in 11 years—a 4.9 rating versus the 2.8 rating drawn by the men's match between Rafael Nadal and Novak Djokovic (Cronin 2013).
- The University of Utah women's gymnastics team set an attendance record in a 2011 dual meet with the University of Florida by drawing 15,558 fans. In 2014, its average attendance for home meets was 14,376—the highest in the nation for the 30th time (University of Utah 2014).

The top 10 attendance leaders in NCAA women's sport in 2012–2013 were as follows (rank given in parentheses): the gymnastics teams at Utah (1), Alabama (2), and Georgia (9) and the basketball teams at Tennessee (3), Iowa State (4), Louisville (5), Baylor (6), Notre Dame (7), Connecticut (8), and Purdue (10) (University of Utah 2014).

Not everything is rosy in women's sport. In 2013, when UConn defeated Louisville for the NCAA women's basketball championship, the teams played before a half-empty arena in New Orleans. Basketball is still the most popular women's sport, but attendance has dropped, television ratings have flattened, and, perhaps not unrelated, shooting percentages and scoring have reached all-time lows. Only one team, Tennessee, averaged more than 10,000 fans in 2013, and a majority of Division I women's basketball teams struggled to average 1,000 per game (Longman 2013).

On the bright side, in 2014, interest seemed to pick up again in women's basketball for UConn's historic ninth national championship victory, in which it routed unbeaten Notre Dame 79-58. The game drew a 2.8 television rating—the highest for any ESPN women's college game in a decade—and reached 3.2 million households and 4.3 million viewers. Not to be outdone, the 2014 Women's National Basketball Association (WNBA) finals delivered its best overnight TV ratings (0.6) since 2007 for game two between eventual champion Phoenix Mercury and the Chicago Sky.

Given the huge popularity of women's soccer since the 1980s, you may not be surprised by the sport's attendance numbers. More than 650,000 tickets were sold to the 1999 women's World Cup, and the final match drew a women's sport record of 90,185 to the Rose Bowl in California. That final, which pitted the United States against China, earned an 11.4 Nielsen rating and a 31 percent market share, thus reaching more than 11 million households. This was the most-watched soccer game (male or female) in U.S. television history, and more than 40 million viewers tuned in (Women's Sports Foundation (2009b, 45).

Following those glory days for U.S. women's soccer, the national team finished 2011 as runner-up to Japan and captured the gold medal in 2012 at the Olympic Games, drawing a television audience of 4.3 million fans on a Thursday afternoon. National team stalwart Kristine Lilly retired in 2010 at age 39 after representing the United States in five World Cups and three Olympic Games

POP CULTURE

Serena Williams: Iconic Superstar

From her childhood as an African American female living in a rough neighborhood of Compton, California, tennis player Serena Williams has blazed a trail of athletic excellence that has resulted in career earnings of more than $54 million in prize money—the most in history for any female athlete. Playing a sport traditionally unwelcoming to African Americans has posed a career challenge for Serena, who burst on the scene alongside her older sister Venus by exhibiting a brand of tennis that featured power and athleticism rarely seen from women on the court.

Serena Williams was ranked number one in the world for the first time in July 2002, regained the top spot for the sixth time in February 2013, and ended 2014 on top once again at the age of 33—a time when most tennis careers are winding down. Along the way, she has won more singles, doubles, and mixed-doubles titles at the sport's major tournaments than all other active players, whether male or female. She is also the most recent player to have held all four major titles simultaneously (in 2002 and 2003) and has won four Olympic gold medals—one in singles and three with sister Venus in doubles.

Serena Williams' influence has reached far beyond the tennis court. Her matches have drawn record-setting television audiences, and her image has graced the cover of the "Body Issue" of *ESPN The Magazine*, *New York Times Magazine*, *Essence* magazine, and *Fitness* magazine. As a muscular athlete, she has had to overcome traditional standards of beauty and femininity and embrace her skin color, competitive passion, and aggressiveness. Harry Edwards, author of *The Revolt of the Black Athlete* (1985), considers her "one of the three most transcendent athletes of his lifetime alongside NBA champion Bill Russell and NFL great Jim Brown." She is recognized by 91 percent of the U.S. public and has inspired a new generation of black female players, as evidenced by the presence of four African American women under age 21 playing in the 2013 U.S. Open—an unmatched record (Novy-Williams 2013).

across part or all of four decades. Teammate Abby Wambach holds the all-time world goal-scoring record among both women and men with 182 goals to her credit (U.S. Soccer 2014).

Men as Fans of Women's Sport

Men deserve some credit for contributing to spectatorship in women's sport. Although the opportunity to watch women's sport on television has been limited as compared with men's sport, the women's events that are shown almost always draw more men than women in their viewership. More men watch WNBA games and women's college softball (McBride 2011a). For the 1999 women's soccer World Cup, men accounted for 49 percent of the audience, women for 36 percent, and children for 15 percent (Women's Sports Foundation 2009b). In 2011, the women's soccer World Cup final pitting the United States against Japan drew 8.3 million men and 5.2 women. Similarly, the 2011 women's U.S. Open tennis final drew 2.7 million men and 2.4 million women. In fact the only women's sport that consistently draws more female than male viewers is figure skating, for which 70 percent of the audience is female (Van Riper 2011).

Men enjoy watching women compete for a variety of reasons. Some like the relative novelty of seeing women competing. Some like to root for the underdog—for example, professional golfers Annika Sorenstam and Michelle Wie, who, albeit without success, dared to compete against male golfers. Others enjoy watching talented and skilled athletes compete, regardless of whether they are male or female—just as they might enjoy watching performers of either sex in music, drama, and dance. In addition, some men, particularly as they age, relate better to the level of athleticism exhibited by women—for example, in basketball—whereas men's play is dominated by athletes who seem like giants to most of us.

Male viewers may also be attracted to a certain style of play. For example, women's basketball tends to feature more passing and teamwork than does its male counterpart. This style appeals to basketball purists, who prefer a game built on teamwork over the modern male version that emphasizes individual play and slam dunks. Women's tennis also has its own style of play, which is much different from that of the men, yet female players still exude power and athleticism along with agility and grace.

There is also no substitute for results. The U.S. women's soccer team has garnered a large audience, both male and female, largely due to its excellence of play in the recent 15 years. The team's Olympic gold medals and World Cup championship thrilled us and inspired patriotic pride. We loved watching star players such as Mia Hamm, Brandi Chastain, Kristine Lilly, Michelle Akers, and Abby Wambach. Men's soccer may be more popular worldwide, but in the United States no other soccer team has ever captured the attention of the nation as these women did.

By the 2012 London Olympics, 44 percent of the participants were female, and the U.S. fielded a team with more females than males for the first time in its history. The 2012 Olympics also marked the first time that every sport included women's competition; the last barriers were overcome with the addition of women's boxing and taekwondo. In addition, every participating country included at least one female athlete in its delegation. Even so, controversies arose, including the fact that fewer events were offered to females in various sports and the decision by Australia and Japan to fly their women's basketball and soccer teams, respectively, in economy class while their male counterparts flew first-class.

The Battle for Equity Continues

In spite of the remarkable progress made by girls and women in sport, equity remains a pressing challenge. Athletic opportunities for girls and women remain clearly unequal, and the urge to congratulate ourselves for the progress made in the past 40 years should not cause us to slack off now.

Girls, particularly those of color, have far fewer opportunities than boys to participate in sport; moreover, when they do play, they typically must tolerate inferior facilities, equipment, coaching, and publicity. Although high school sport for girls has experienced many consecutive years of increased participation, girls still trail boys in high school sport by 1.2 million participants. In addition, fewer than two-thirds of African American and Hispanic girls participate in sport, whereas more than three-fourths of white girls do (National Women's Law Center 2012).

At the college level, females receive 63,000 fewer sport participation opportunities than males do (193,000 for females versus 256,000 for males). Female college athletes also receive $183 million less in NCAA athletic scholarships than male athletes do ($965 million for females versus

$1.15 billion for males). Significant inequities also exist across the board in terms of overall budgets, recruiting budgets, transportation, facilities, and uniforms (Lapchick 2012b).

Marked differences also continue to exist between females and males in the opportunities available to them for continuing their athletic career in the professional ranks. Even if they do manage to pursue a professional career, they face inequities in earning power and in being represented in the ranks of coaches, administrators, and athletic officials. In addition, television and media coverage is still predominantly fixated on male sport, and media executives claim that they are simply acceding to the wishes of the potential audiences (Messner and Cooky 2010).

Advocates for the rights of girls and women in sport have continued to press their case, and their efforts include resorting to the courts when faced with intransigence by athletic organizations or educational institutions. One recent case involved Quinnipiac University of Connecticut, which was sued under Title IX for gender inequities in its athletic programs.

At first, the case focused on the unequal treatment of the Quinnipiac women's volleyball team and its coach. It soon became clear, however, that the university was relying on various deceptive practices to appear to be in compliance with Title IX—for example, counting female track athletes three times (as members of the cross country, indoor track, and outdoor track teams). The case was eventually settled out of court, and the university agreed to make sweeping changes that included offering more athletic scholarships for women; equalizing staffing and staff pay for women's teams; equalizing the quality of facilities; and improving the treatment of female athletes in terms of equipment, travel budgets, scheduling, housing and dining, and other support services (Women's Sports Foundation 2013).

Social Issues in Women's Sport

As sport opportunities and fitness activities for women have increased, new social issues have arisen. For example, prior to women's participation in sport and physical activity, little or no attention was paid to issues such as women's fitness and the design of exercise clothing specifically for a woman's body. This section explores several social issues that have emerged as women have entered the playing field.

Women's Health

In 1994, Donna Lopiano of the Women's Sports Foundation summarized the benefits of women's participation in sport and physical activity. Specifically, benefits have been identified and substantiated in the psychosocial, physical, behavioral, and emotional realms. In addition, research has shown that introducing girls to sport and physical activity at an early age is essential in helping them make exercise a lifelong habit. In fact, Linda Bunker (1988) of the University of Virginia has concluded that if a girl does not participate in sport by the time she is 10, there is only a 10 percent chance that she will participate when she is 25 (Women's Sports Foundation 2009b).

The amount of physical activity that a young girl gets relates multiple factors, including her race and culture and the influence of people around her. White girls (56 percent) are more likely to participate in sport than are black girls (47 percent) or Hispanic girls (36 percent) (Iber et al. 2011). Girls from middle- and upper-middle-class homes are more likely than girls from less affluent homes to participate in vigorous physical activity.

In addition, girls who grow up in a culture that ascribes relatively narrow female roles oriented toward childbearing and families value the sport experience differently than girls who grow up with access to a wider range of possible roles. Moreover, families who struggle economically are more likely to encourage girls to spend time helping in the home and caring for younger siblings. Indeed, girls who grow up in poor urban settings may face daunting barriers to sport participation (see chapter 14 for more about these challenges).

The health benefits of exercise extend beyond fitness. Research has shown that teenage female athletes are less likely than nonathletes to use illicit drugs (marijuana, cocaine, and others), to be suicidal, or to smoke. They are also more likely than nonathletes to have a positive body image (Women's Sports Foundation 2009a). These benefits mirror those found for male athletes and speak to the value of encouraging young people of both sexes to take better care of their body and develop a strong self-concept that helps them resist peer pressure.

Teenage female athletes are also less likely than nonathletes to get pregnant, more likely to abstain from sexual intercourse, and more likely to experience sexual intercourse at a later age (Women's Sports Foundation 1998). In this light, one might wonder if the relative lack of sport participation among economically disadvantaged girls correlates with their significantly higher rate of teenage pregnancy.

More generally, ample evidence shows that moderate and consistent levels of sport and other physical activity are essential to overall good health and well-being for both girls and women. For example, physical activity helps prevent obesity, heart disease, cancer, osteoporosis, and Alzheimer's disease and related forms of dementia. Females who are physically active also achieve higher academic performance and attend college at a higher rate than peers who are inactive. In addition, female sport participants typically develop a healthier body image and overall self-image, as well as feelings of self-confidence. For more detailed information, consult *Her Life Depends on It* (Women's Sports Foundation 2009a).

The risk for many health issues—such as osteoporosis, breast cancer, and heart disease—can be lowered by engaging in physical activity. What must society do to encourage young women to become—and stay—physically active?

As our culture continues to encourage women to join the workforce and contend for leadership roles, the lessons of the playing field appear to be just as helpful to females as they are to males. Various sport experiences help women develop critical skills needed for building a successful career—for example, leading, handling pressure, taking pride in accomplishment, and working as part of a team.

In a 2014 study conducted by espnW and the Ernst and Young Women Athletes Business Network, three of four female executives say that a candidate's background in sport influences their hiring decision. The survey respondents were high-ranking executives, and 52 percent of them had participated in sport at the university level, whereas that figure was just 39 percent for women at lower levels of management. Only 3 percent of women in executive roles said that they had never played a sport. One conclusion drawn from the study is that elite female athletes may be "an untapped leadership pipeline for business" (Otani 2014).

Broadly speaking, the evidence overwhelmingly shows that exercise and sport participation are good for women and girls. You wonder why it took so long for society to realize this fact and encourage healthy activity among the female half of the population. To learn more and get the latest facts and figures about women in sport, visit the website of the Women's Sports Foundation.

Lesbian Athletes

The stereotype that strong, female athletes must be lesbian is false. It is true, however, that athletes who are lesbian still face misunderstanding and discrimination in the sporting world. Some famous female athletes, such as tennis players Billie Jean King and (later) Amelie Mauresmo, have been frank with the media about their sexual orientation. King's bisexuality notwithstanding, she is an icon for women's liberation and a role model for many people; at the same time, though she is popular among women, her fan base among men is much smaller. More recently, some fans were stunned when Sheryl Swoopes, three-time WNBA Most Valuable Player, revealed her lesbianism. Although she was previously married and has a son, Swoopes told the world that she currently has a female life partner.

Pat Griffin was a pioneer in exposing and clarifying issues related to lesbian athletes. Griffin has been a top athlete, coach, and spokesperson against homophobia and other prejudice in sport. In her book *Strong Women, Deep Closets* (1998), she analyzed lesbian experience in the sport world. In it, she admitted to once dating a male wrestling coach in order to cover up her lesbianism and save her coaching job. Strong leaders like Pat Griffin have given voice to the lesbian athletes who fear that showing their sexuality will damage their career.

Not all discrimination against lesbian athletes comes from outside of women's sport. This fact was highlighted at Penn State University in the early 1990s, when women's basketball coach Rene Portland created a furor by stating in the press that she did not recruit or allow lesbians on her team. The controversy escalated in 2005, when a former player, Jennifer Harris, filed a federal discrimination lawsuit against coach Portland alleging discrimination because of the player's sexual orientation.

Attempts to mediate the situation were unsuccessful, and an internal investigation led the university to fine Portland $10,000 and order her to take professional development courses devoted to diversity and inclusiveness. She was also warned that she would be dismissed for any future violations (Associated Press 2006b, 2006c). Portland resigned her position in 2007 after 27 years as the women's basketball coach. In spite of growing acceptance in society at large, this situation illustrates the fact that lesbian athletes are still at risk for harassment, exclusion, or perhaps even expulsion if their coaches or teammates disapprove of their sexual orientation.

The pace of acceptance of LGBT (lesbian, gay, bisexual, and transgender) persons in our U.S. society has accelerated rapidly in recent years. Many student-athletes who identify themselves as LGBT are now speaking out, and people under 30 years of age are routinely more accepting than those of any previous generation. At colleges around the country, and in athletic departments, there is clearly a generation gap with respect to sexual orientation. In addition, as has been well documented, some coaches and players fear having their team or school labeled as a haven for lesbian athletes. This fear, of course, creates an intimidating environment for athletes who would like to be more open and honest.

One recent example involves the falling-out between Baylor women's basketball coach Kim Mulkey and her star player, Brittney Griner. When Griner came out publicly as a gay athlete during her last year in college, Mulkey feared that Griner's openness would affect the Baylor program's recruiting. In addition, Griner's statement conflicted with the university's policy, which did *not* include sexual preference in its nondiscrimination statement. However, since Griner had brought fame and plenty of revenue to the women's basketball program—twice being selected as national player of the year—campus leaders were forced to take a more tolerant view regarding sexual preference.

As society has changed, it has become clear that educational institutions have a responsibility to ensure that homophobia is eliminated from their campus, both overall and in their athletic programs. Indeed, ignorance, fear, and bigotry are the very antithesis of the values that an educational institution should stand for and promulgate. Perhaps we have begun to realize what we have done—not only to LGBT athletes but also to those who have not learned to accept them. Unless the needed changes are made, sport for girls and women will continue to struggle for wide acceptance and equal opportunities for generations to come.

Sportswear

As girls and women have moved into sport, they have sparked changes in sport clothing by demanding attire that fits their unique needs. In response, apparel companies have raced to design sport clothing for women and implemented marketing campaigns to attract buyers of athletic gear designed specifically for women. These developments have affected both the economy of sport business and cultural attitudes about females in sport. Let's look at two significant developments in sport clothing: the sport bra and athletic footwear.

Sport Bra

The sport bra was invented in 1977 to give women participating in sport the same kind of physical support that men had enjoyed for years. Hinda Miller and Lisa Lindahl created a prototype for the sport bra by imitating the male athletic supporter that "pulled the body parts closer to the body" (Sharp 1994). Eventually, their creation was called the Jogbra, and females quickly adopted it for comfort and safety and as a way to limit embarrassment and perform uninhibitedly during vigorous activity.

It wasn't long before clothing companies began marketing versions of the sport bra that not only facilitated physical activity but also looked attractive. Women began wearing sport bras under their jerseys, but soon they shed their jerseys in gyms, on courts, and on fields. Female athletes found the comfort and freedom exhilarating.

When Brandi Chastain ripped off her jersey to celebrate the 1999 U.S. women's victory in the World Cup soccer championship, it was a landmark moment in sport. Her action was captured on film, and her image was viewed round the world. Chastain's sport bra somehow symbolized to different people all that was either right or wrong with women in sport.

Many accepted it as an expression of pure joy at victory. After all, the gesture had been made previously by male soccer players and tennis players—notably Andre Agassi and Andy Roddick of the United States. Others saw it as a celebration of a strong, muscular woman who was proud of her body.

Yet Chastain's action also ignited a storm of criticism. Some saw it as a striptease, as if she were offering her body to male viewers. Others thought it was calculated to draw attention. Whatever one's opinion, her act stimulated debate and exposed the conflict in both male and female opinions about women's bodies and their acceptability in public view.

Athletic Shoes

As girls and women flocked to sport participation, improper athletic footwear posed a recurrent issue. Forced to wear sneakers designed for male feet, female athletes suffered in silence. In particular, female basketball players, who are typically well above average in size, were forced to wear men's basketball sneakers, and they complained about the bulk, weight, and width of the male shoes. Things changed in the 1990s, when athletic shoe companies began designing and marketing shoes specifically for female feet (Brown 2001). In 1996, at the Atlanta Olympics, basketball player Sheryl Swoopes became the first woman to endorse a shoe—the "Air Swoopes." In 2001, the inaugural WNBA All-Star Game became a celebration of how far women in sport had come: Five of the All-Stars wore basketball shoes designed specifically for them.

On average, a female foot is narrower and thinner than a male foot. In addition, although foot shape

Is the amount of skin shown by women wearing sport bras any different from the amount of skin shown by cheerleaders? Why is one act more socially acceptable than the other?

varies from one female to another, a woman's foot generally has a wider forefoot and a narrower heel than a male's foot. It is no surprise, then, that orthopedists named poorly fitting shoes as a major cause of the high incidence of sport injuries in women and girls, particularly in the knee, ankle, and lower leg (Sports Doctor 2000).

Modern athletic shoe development—led by Nike, Reebok, and Adidas—has introduced the public to terms such as *pronation*, *stability*, and *motion control*. New concepts in design have helped absorb shock, stabilize the foot, and reduce injuries among both high-performance athletes and casual recreational athletes (Pribut and Richie 2002). In addition, shoes are now made to accommodate the typical differences between male feet and female feet.

The athletic shoe industry has benefited considerably from the increase in female participation in fitness and sport activities. Indeed, women now spend 80 percent of all sport apparel dollars and control 60 percent of all money spent on men's athletic clothing (Holland 2014). Kevin Plank, CEO of Under Armour, expects that his sales of women's sport gear will come to equal or surpass his sales for men's gear. His company currently earns about one-third of its revenue from women's sportswear, and both his company and market leader Nike report a 25 percent to 30 percent growth on the women's side in 2013. In 2014, Under Armour announced its biggest-ever ad campaign ($15 million) aimed at women. To promote the effort, the company signed Brazilian supermodel Gisele Bündchen, ballerina Misty Copeland, and skier Lindsey Vonn (Mirabella 2014; Harwell 2014b).

How does Ronda Rousey and her participation in mixed martial arts alter your perception of female athletes?

Objectification of Female Athletes

As strong, independent women move into the sport world, they attract multiple types of attention. A female athlete's strong and agile body, with its defined musculature, can be a magnet for millions of viewers. In addition, as clothing trends have changed, women have shifted from dowdy dresses, boxy pinnies, and kilted skirts to form-fitting swimsuits, gymnastics leotards, and skimpy outfits on the tennis court. Moreover, though the sport bra was a technical improvement for women and serves a utilitarian purpose—allowing them to move freely—it also symbolizes the duplicity in society's view of women both as strong athletes and as sex objects for men (Schultz 2004).

Female athletes may be looked at as sex objects regardless of whether they want to be seen that way. In fact, successful female athletes are often judged more by their appearance than by their athletic success. For example, Jan Stephenson was more famous for her physical attractiveness than for her golf game, even though she was a fine golfer. Similarly, Anna Kournikova long held the title of sexiest female tennis player but was roundly criticized for her popularity because she never won a singles tournament. She was in fact ranked among the top 10 players, but that did not mollify critics who believed that she capitalized on her looks rather than her talent.

At the same time, are female athletes sometimes partly responsible for this objectification? At every Olympic Games, there is a rush to promote the Games in part by focusing on attractive female athletes. While the men get most of their attention for their athletic success and their odds of winning a medal, a whole different culture is built around women who are both athletically gifted and sexy. In fact, *Playboy* magazine's "Women of the Olympics" issue rivals the annual *Sports Illustrated* "Swimsuit Edition" as eye candy aimed primarily at male readers.

This attention makes it possible for female athletes—for example, Lindsey Vonn (skiing), Danica Patrick (auto racing), Sloane Stephens (tennis), Alex Morgan (soccer), Skylar Diggins (basketball), Leryn Franco (pole vault), and Ronda Rousey (martial arts)—to have almost a second career highlighting their physical attractiveness. No doubt these and other women know that publicity shots and features can only help their career and indirectly promote their sport. And who is to say what is appropriate for an attractive athlete who is blessed with natural beauty that she chooses to enhance through physical training?

Many female athletes are conflicted about posing to show off their bodies. Some favor it, either because it helps promote their sport or because they think it dispels the notion that you can't be sexy if you're an athlete (Topkin 2004). When female athletes do intentionally display their bodies, some people may question whether such images are appropriate for public viewing, especially by younger children. Suggestive images of both male and female athletes can be controlled and standards of decorum can be established—but only if the market demands it—and a cutting-edge advertising agency will do whatever attracts attention and gains publicity, as it was hired to do.

Consider this advice from the Women's Sports Foundation in its publication titled "Media—Images and Words in Women's Sports: The Foundation Position" (1995). This document was reviewed by more than 50 of the nation's most highly visible champion female athletes.

> *Women are no different from men athletes in the skill, dedication, and courage they bring to their sports. Sports commentary and reporting, like the use of the English language in general, should reflect the fundamental equality of women and men, both on and off the field. There is nothing wrong with women wanting to look feminine/attractive from a traditional perspective. However, female athletes deserve the same respect for their athletic abilities as is afforded male athletes. When a female athlete appears in a sport publication or advertisement to promote her sport or fitness product, she should be portrayed respectfully as is her male counterpart . . . as a skilled athlete.*

Here are some suggested guidelines for media images of female athletes (Women's Sports Foundation 1995):

- Female athletes should look like athletes; they should be shown doing a skill they do well.
- A female athlete's clothing should be authentic for her sport.
- A female athlete should have all of her appropriate clothes on and should not be in the process of dressing or undressing.
- Certain body parts (breasts or buttocks) should not be the focus, nor should the image be a sexual one.
- The athlete's pose or movements should be authentic, not appear dainty, shy, or seductive. Nor should she be gazing adoringly at men in the photo or at consumers viewing the ad.
- Photos and captions should go together; the caption should not undermine the image.
- Young female athletes should not be portrayed as being older than they are.
- The final image should be something that any woman could feel proud of as a current or future athlete.
- What if the woman or girl in the photo was your daughter, your mom, or a female friend?

Global Status of Women in Sport

While the numbers of women in sport continue to rise in the United States, that trend is not typical around the world. The social system in many nations, particularly Arab ones, discourages women from sport participation. In these places, adherence to a traditional view of women as subservient to men and focused on the home prevents girls from exploring their physical side through sport and activity.

As shown in table 13.3, the percentage of women participating in the Summer Olympics has increased steadily—for example, from 34 percent in 1996 to 44 percent in 2012. Similarly, at the 2000 Olympic Games, 36 countries—almost 30 percent of the 123 participating nations—sent no female athletes, but that too has changed. In 2008, only five countries entered an all-male team, and none did so in 2012. Even so, female participation rates have not grown in all countries, especially those where women's overall rights lag behind those of men. Moreover, in countries dominated by poverty, famine, political instability, and religion, females are virtually excluded from sport participation. Some countries—for example, Ethiopia, Saudi Arabia, Algeria, Kenya, and Nigeria—are beset with wider social problems than women's sport participation.

Female followers of Islam are blocked from participation because of a decree that women should be covered in public, thus making it difficult if not impossible to participate in sport. Moreover, in such cultures, women who seek to participate in sport are seen as threats to the social, moral, and religious codes of their societies and even as repudiating their culture in favor of Western influence. Saudi Arabia, for example, had been one of the last countries in the world that completely barred women from sport participation. Yet even Saudi Arabia allowed two women to enter the 2012 Olympic Games in London.

Hope for sport participation among Muslim women was given a boost by the recent success of Sania Mirza of India in women's professional tennis. In 2005, her first year on the professional tour, she skyrocketed from a virtual unknown to a world ranking of 31st. In 2007, she earned her highest world ranking at number 27; then, in 2009, she became the first Indian female tennis player to capture a Grand Slam title by winning the mixed doubles at the Australian Open.

While wearing traditional tennis clothing that exposes her arms and legs, Mirza retains her spiritual values by praying up to five times a day. She sets an example of a modern Indian woman who stands for progressive thinking while respecting her religious background. In 2010, she married Shoaib Malik, a Pakistani citizen, which brought critical headlines in her home country. Her success is the antithesis of the strait-laced image of a conservative Muslim woman hidden behind a veil (Bahri 2005).

Similarly, at the 2004 Olympic Games in Athens, Rubab Raza, then 13 years old, became the first Pakistani female swimmer to represent her country in the Games.

In the 2000 Sydney Olympics, more than 110,000 people saw Nouria Merah-Benida win the 1,500-meter run, thus following up on the 1992 Olympic championship performance of her Algerian countrywoman Hassiba Boulmerka. These two runners have sparked debate about whether women might break out of the mold of Arab tradition and enjoy athletic success. Indeed, at the 2008 Beijing Olympics, 60 of the 958 medals awarded went to citizens of Muslim-majority countries—44 to men, 15 to women, and 1 to a female in an open/mixed competition (Amr 2008).

In the 2012 London Olympics, Sarah Attar (representing Saudi Arabia) ran a heat in the 800 meters qualifying race. She finished dead last but earned a standing ovation from the audience, who appreciated her groundbreaking entry by competing fully clothed—covered from head to toe.

"You've Come a Long Way, Baby"

Incredible as it may seem today, the slogan shown in this sidebar's header was used by the Phillip Morris Company to promote its Virginia Slims cigarettes to a target audience of teenage girls and young women under the age of 35. The marketing ploy sought to link smoking to the increase in women's freedom and empowerment during the 1970s and early 1980s. In a canny marketing twist, Virginia Slims became the key sponsor of the fledgling women's professional tennis tour; as a result, many people "credit" women's tennis for popularizing smoking by young women. Thankfully, the phrase has now been separated from its association with smoking and is often used to salute the progress made over the last 40 years by girls and women in sport.

Worldwide, the story in developed nations mirrors that in the United States. White women from middle-class backgrounds are most likely to be supported by their families and communities to participate in sport, strive for excellence, and embrace physical activity. The benefits include enhanced self-image, better health, and greater resistance to disease. These benefits should be available to all women, but the reality is that some must still fight against repressive customs in order to experience them.

Barriers for Women in Sport

Learning about the gains made by women in sport during the last few decades may lead you to think that there is not much more for women to accomplish. But a closer look reveals that additional changes are necessary in order to create full equality of opportunity in sport for females. Perhaps progress will be initiated outside of the sport world as women continue to gain power and influence in business and to affect more of what is portrayed in the media. As society changes, so does women's sport. Yet sport can also serve as a catalyst for change that is led by confident, determined females with a public stage on which to share their beliefs and dreams.

Title IX Challenges

The most perplexing question facing Title IX enforcement on college campuses focuses on American football and the 85 athletic scholarships awarded for football at most Division I schools. These schools must provide 85 women's scholarships just to match the football total. Once these 85 men's and 85 women's scholarships have been awarded, a university then decides how many other scholarships it can afford for other sports.

In response, many athletic directors have completely dropped less popular, non-revenue-producing men's sports, such as wrestling, tennis, golf, gymnastics, and swimming. As a result, programs rich in tradition—some of which had earned national championships—have suddenly disappeared. Governing bodies for these sports—for example, wrestling and tennis—have mounted campaigns to reinstate them. Although they are careful not to criticize Title IX, the underlying mumbling blames women. Dropped sports are referred to as "unintended consequences" in recognition of the fact that the authors of Title IX never intended to harm men's sport by opening up women's sport (National Women's Law Center 2012).

"Where is the money going to come from?" That's the plea of every athletic director and college president faced with Title IX compliance. In essence, we've taken their athletic budget, which was largely devoted to men's sport, and asked them to split it down the middle for men and women. On top of that, they are unwilling to reduce support for football—the main revenue sport at 131 Division I institutions and a source of publicity, pride, recruiting, and alumni donations. For them, it would simply be unthinkable to reduce the number of football scholarships, though others might ask why, if it takes only 22 men to play football—11 on offense and 11 on defense—85 scholarships are needed.

ACTIVITY TIME-OUT

Football and Title IX

Some people have proposed that colleges leave football out of Title IX compliance. In other words, equalize the number of scholarships for men and women, but do not include the 85 football scholarships in the mix. Is this a fair solution to the issue of equal opportunity for females? Proponents of this view contend that football is a different animal and that there is no comparable activity for girls. Moreover, at large Division I institutions where the football team *makes* money, that revenue can help support other sports.

Is leaving football out of Title IX an equitable solution? If not, what other ideas would you offer an athletic director who faces increasing costs without an increasing budget?

The football picture at the high school level is very similar, though athletic scholarships are not a factor. Instead, the focus is on budgets for uniforms, equipment, fields, coaching salaries, and publicity. In every category, football is still a huge expense.

Physical Activity Participation and Dropouts

If we compare statistics for physical activity among women with those for men, we find some striking differences. Specifically, inactivity is higher among women (33 percent) than among men (29 percent), and it increases with age, standing at 26 percent for ages 18 to 44, 33 percent for ages 45 to 64, 40 percent for ages 65 to 74, and 52 percent for age 75 and above. Women are also more likely than men to fail to meet national guidelines for both aerobic exercise and muscle strengthening activity (American Heart Association 2013).

Females over the age of seven reported their favorite physical activities as exercise walking (56.1 million), swimming (28.4 million), and exercising with equipment (27 million). According to the Sporting Goods Manufacturers Association's 2007 Annual Fitness Survey, females account for at least 50 percent of total participants in 15 of the leading fitness activities (Women's Sports Foundation 2009b, 36). These activities include walking for fitness, aerobics, running, treadmill running, Pilates, yoga, tai chi, stair climbing, and elliptical-machine training.

The Women's Sports Foundation has found that interest in sport is similar among younger boys and girls but that some key differences do exist. Girls tend to start sport participation a year or two later than boys do, which often means that they have less experience, skill, and practice than boys of the same age. By age 14, girls drop out of sport at a rate six times higher than that of boys. In short, girls tend to start participating in sport later and drop out of it sooner than boys (U.S. Anti-Doping Agency 2012).

Differences also appear with the overall category of females. For instance, girls of color and those from low-income families typically end their participation in organized sport sooner than peers who are white or from middle- or higher-income families. In addition, girls who live in urban and rural areas enter sport later and drop out earlier than those who live in suburban communities. Reasons for these differences include household chore responsibilities, the need to care for younger siblings, lack of funds, transportation issues, and unsafe neighborhoods.

To address the question of why girls drop out of sport, one study (Boxill, Glanville, and Murray 2011) collected data from teachers and from girls aged 14 to 17. The results are shown in figure 13.1. The

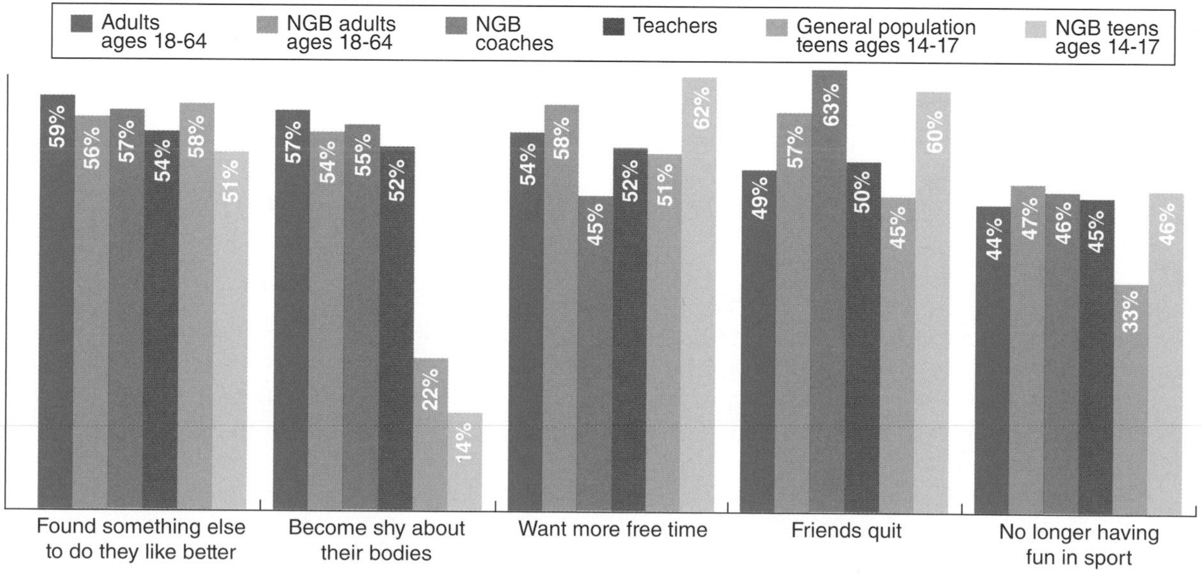

FIGURE 13.1 Top reasons that girls become less active in sport.

Reprinted, by permission, from J. Boxill, D. Glanville, and T. Murray, 2011, "What sport means in America; A study of sport's role in society," *International Sport Coaching Journal* 4: 2-45.

major factors identified by girls who represented national sport governing bodies included wanting more free time and having friends who dropped out. Adults cited girls becoming shy about their bodies, though girls that age did not agree with this assessment. Both adults and girls felt that girls often found something else they liked to do better, and in fact girls do seem to be attracted to a wider range of social activities than boys are.

Women as Leaders in Sport

Women still occupy a small percentage of leadership roles as compared with their proportion of either the sport population or the at-large population. Perhaps the most disappointing percentage is that for female coaches in collegiate women's sport. The 2014 percentage of 43 percent is nearly the lowest percentage in history; indeed, in 1972, when Title IX was enacted, the percentage was 90 percent. Here are some other percentages for women in significant leadership roles in high school, college, and Olympic sport (Acosta and Carpenter 2014):

Collegiate head coaches	43
Collegiate athletic directors	22
Collegiate sport information directors	12
Collegiate head athletic trainers	32
Heads of state high school athletic associations	6
International Olympic Committee members	21
United States Olympic Committee members	37

Additional information, including percentages for professional sport, can be viewed in the Racial and Gender Report Card updated annually by Richard Lapchick at the University of Central Florida.

Equal Pay for Equal Play

Opportunities for women in professional sport have expanded significantly in tennis, golf, basketball, and soccer; in fact, in these sports, building a professional career is a realistic goal for an athlete who is good enough. Some other sports—including gymnastics, track and field, figure skating, and swimming—offer prize money and endorsement possibilities now that the Olympics allow professional athletes. In fact, after the 2012 Summer Olympics in London, female athletes collected two to three times more money in endorsement contracts than did male athletes. Overall, however, as compared with men, women still struggle to make a career in professional sport, and in many cases the financial compensation barely covers their expenses.

APPLYING SOCIAL THEORY

Feminist Theorists and Increasing the Number of Female Coaches

Take the perspective of a feminist theorist to suggest strategies for increasing the number of female coaches at every level of play. As background, recall that in women's college sport before the existence of Title IX, 95 percent of women's teams were coached by females. Today, in contrast, just 43 percent of women's teams have a female head coach (and only 2 percent of men's teams). The statistics are similar in youth sport and high school sport.

Begin your consideration by examining the value to girls and women of having female coaches as role models, mentors, and confidants. You might also consider what values women bring to the coaching role as compared with men. Next, propose several practical strategies for adjusting the proportions of male and female coaches to create greater equality of opportunity.

In tennis, for example, the prize money for men at the four Grand Slam events (Wimbledon and the Australian, French, and U.S. Opens) traditionally exceeded the prize money for women. Though all four Grand Slam events now offer equal prize money for men and women, some have pressured them to reverse that decision. In addition, at other tennis events, men and women still receive significantly different levels of compensation. The argument against paying women the same amount as men usually goes something like this:

- Women don't play the same level of tennis that men play. In a head-to-head match, a good collegiate men's player would defeat most women on the professional tour. (This is probably true.)
- Women are not as strong, don't hit the ball as hard, and play mostly a baseline game featuring rallies rather than an exciting power game. (It is true that women play more of a baseline game, but the men's short points dominated by powerful serves can be boring to watch. Many fans like the rallies in women's tennis.)
- Women play a best-of-three format in championship matches, whereas men play best-of-five and therefore work harder. (Men do play five sets, but who wants to watch a match that takes five hours between exhausted competitors? Two out of three creates more excitement because every point has more effect on the match's outcome.)
- Fans come to see the men, and ticket revenue should be the basis of the prize money. (The men argued this point for years—until the women's game and superstar personalities started to grab the headlines. Suddenly, the men backed off of this stance.)

Here are some other notable facts about pay for female athletes versus pay for male athletes (all amounts are given in U.S. dollars):

- In basketball, the average salary for WNBA players for 2012 was $72,000, whereas the NBA average was $5.5 million. The team salary cap was $878,000 in the WNBA and $58 million in the NBA. The highest possible salary that could be paid to a WNBA player was $105,000, whereas the NBA's highest salary was $30 million (for Kobe Bryant of the Los Angeles Lakers). Top WNBA players have found that the only way to make more money is to spend the WNBA's off-season playing in Israel, Turkey, or Russia, where they can earn an additional $750,000 playing for seven months. Of course, that means playing year round, which takes its toll on one's body (Steele 2012).
- In soccer, players earn $6,000 to $30,000 per year in the National Women's Soccer League, which was launched in 2013 after two earlier women's pro leagues folded. Player salaries may be supplemented by their national federations of Canada, Mexico, and the United States (Kassouf 2013). In contrast, male players in Major League Soccer made an average salary of $148,693 for 2013 with wide variation depending on the player (Finch 2013).
- Women's golf has struggled in recent years with the loss of sponsors and tournaments, which lowered the total prize money to about $41 million during 2010 and again during 2011. The total rebounded to $48.9 million in 2013 and rose again in 2014 to a total of $56.3 million—an average of $1.76 million for each of 32 events (Ladies Professional Golf Association 2013). The top female earners were Stacey Lewis at $2.5 million and Inbee Park at $2.2 million. At the same time, the male PGA tour offered more than $250 million overall with an average purse of $5 million for each of 45 events. Its top earners in 2014 were Rory McIlroy at $8.2 million and Bubba Watson at $6.3 million (ESPN 2014e, Golf Today 2014, Ladies Professional Golf Association 2015a).
- Although huge endorsement deals are scarce for women, tennis star Venus Williams signed a five-year, $40 million deal with Reebok. A year later, her sister Serena topped her with a Nike contract that, if she earns the performance-related bonuses, could make her the richest woman in sport, with a possible net income of $55 million to $60 million. Of course, this income doesn't even include her prize money for playing tennis (Badenhausen 2014a).

- In women's sport, the big money is found in tennis and golf. Although several female golfers have earned money in the seven figures, the top female athletes overall are still tennis players, as well as figure skater Kim Yuna and race car driver Danica Patrick. For 2014, the five highest-paid female athletes, including both earnings and endorsements, were Maria Sharapova ($24.4 million), Li Na ($23.6 million), Serena Williams ($22 million), Yuna ($16.3 million), and Patrick ($15 million) (Badenhausen 2014a).
- In 2014, the top 50 highest-paid athletes were all male with the lone exception of Maria Sharapova, who ranked 34th. The next highest ranking for a woman went to Serena Williams, who was 55th (Badenhausen 2014a).
- Although the endorsement deals available to some top female athletes may stun the average fan, the amounts commanded by women and men still differ considerably. Based on endorsements only—that is, without counting prize money—the top women earners in 2014 were Sharapova ($22 million), Na ($18 million), and Yuna ($16 million). Among male athletes, the top three were Tiger Woods ($55 million), LeBron James ($53 million), and Roger Federer ($52 million) (Badenhausen 2014a).

Inequities still exist in college sport as well. Unlike professional sport, which determines earnings based on what the market will bear, collegiate sports are governed by Title IX restrictions, which by law promise equality for women and girls in terms of dollars spent. However, in spite of significant progress made toward that goal, glaring inequities remain.

For example, at NCAA Division I FBS schools in 2012, men's athletics accounted for 74 percent of overall expenses. Of course, the major difference in expenditures involves the amount spent to support football teams, which are by far the most expensive collegiate teams. More specifically, comparisons of median expenditures have shown men at $2.3 million and women at $1.2 million for team travel, men at $569,000 and women at $268,000 for recruiting, and men at $742,000 and women at $270,000 for uniforms and equipment (NCAA 2013f).

Comparing money spent on athletic scholarships at Division I FBS schools, the total allocated in 2012 was $4.4 million for men's sport per school and $3.3 million for women's sport. Total coaching salaries stood at a median of $8.6 million for men's sport and $2.7 million for women's sport. In basketball, the median head coach salary was $1.2 million for men's teams and $376,000 for women's teams (many of which are coached by men). Football coaches earned the highest median salary at $1.6 million (NCAA 2013f).

EXPERT'S VIEW

Media Coverage and Female Athletes

This groundbreaking 56-minute video presentation features scholars, award-winning coaches, and athletes who discuss and share their perspectives on the status of women's sport in the media. They confront myths about past media coverage—such as the notion that "sex sells" women's sport and the belief that no one cares about girls participating in sport. The video was produced and made available, free of charge, by the Tucker Center for Research on Girls and Women in Sport at the University of Minnesota in partnership with Twin Cities Public Television. It has received an Upper Midwest Emmy Award in the sport documentary category for confronting the hard fact that although more than 40 percent of all sport participants are female, women's sport gets only 4 percent of media sport coverage. You can check out the video at www.cehd.umn.edu/tuckercenter/multimedia/mediacoverage.html.

Media Coverage of Women's Sport

More media coverage of women's sport would likely boost its popularity and would certainly increase the opportunities for girls and women to see female role models in action. In the past 20 years, however, viewers are receiving *less* coverage of women's sport (table 13.5), and sport news is still being delivered almost exclusively by men (Messner and Cooky 2010). Happily, there have been some bright spots, some of which are mentioned earlier in this chapter. Women's sport broadcasts that have periodically earned strong ratings include professional tennis, college and professional basketball, World Cup and Olympic soccer, and various Olympic events in the Winter and Summer Games.

Still, according to Sarah Laskow, "the U.S. sports media spends—if we're being generous—less than 5 percent of its time covering women in sports." Even at the Winter Olympics—where female sport tends to get a relatively large amount of coverage—the gap between coverage of male and female sports in 2010 exceeded 20 percent. Four years later, however, NBC's coverage of the 2014 Winter Olympics set a new standard by nearly equalizing the prime-time broadcast hours of men's sport and women's sport. Male athletes were featured 45 percent of the time, women 41 percent of the time, and mixed-gender events in the remainder (Laskow 2014).

ESPN, the self-proclaimed leader in sport television, founded espnW in 2010 to promote women's sport in television, in film, at live events, and on digital and social platforms. Though its progress has been modest, in the summer of 2013 ESPN reached an average of 10 million women per month and more than 4 million through espnW in particular.

The sport viewing characteristics of the two genders differ in significant ways. The average male aged 35 to 49 spends 227 hours per year watching sport, whereas the average woman spends just 92 hours. When women do watch sport, they often choose men's sport. They also prefer sport narratives and human interest stories, whereas men typically just want statistics, performance history, and live action. Nearly half of men see themselves as super sport fans, but just one in five women do (McBride 2011a).

These numbers suggest that although many viewers clamor for more women's sport to be broadcast, it is not clear that others would tune in. Meanwhile, the business realities of television demand that networks try to attract large audiences and please their commercial sponsors. Therefore, if women's sport proves that it can attract a big audience, then the business model will be adjusted. So far, audiences have demonstrated their preferences for women's sports that are perceived as more "feminine," such as figure skating, tennis, gymnastics, swimming, and volleyball. If power and strength are required in a sport—for example, judo, shot put, weightlifting, softball, and boxing—chances are that they will not be given large blocks of screen time (Laskow 2014).

Figure 13.2 shows the disappointing percentage of television coverage devoted to women's sport in 2009. Not only is this figure low, but also it represents a decline since 1989. In some years, coverage for women reached the 8 percent to 10 percent mark, only to fall back to a level of 1.6 percent in the Los Angeles area and 1.4 percent of ESPN's

TABLE 13.5 Percentage of Sport Network News by Gender, 1989–2014

Year	1989	1993	1999	2004	2009	2014
Both genders	3.0	1.1	3.1	2.4	2.1	2.4
Male	92.0	93.8	88.2	91.4	96.3	94.4
Female	5.0	5.1	8.7	6.3	1.6	3.2

Adapted, by permission, from C. Cooky, M. Messner, and M. Musto, 2015, "It's Dude Time!" A quarter century of excluding women's sports in televised news and highlights shows. In *Communication and sport* (Thousand Oaks, CA: Sage Publishing), 6.

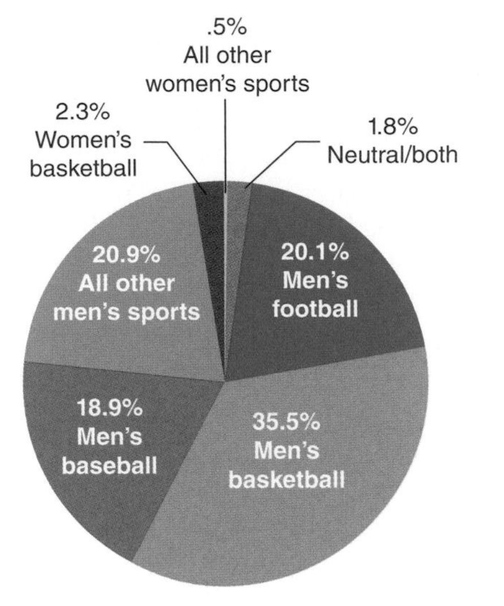

FIGURE 13.2 Sports covered in combined coverage on TV news and *SportsCenter* in 2014.

Adapted, by permission, from C. Cooky, M. Messner, and M. Musto, 2015, "It's Dude Time!" A quarter century of excluding women's sports in televised news and highlights shows. In *Communication and sport* (Thousand Oaks, CA), 10.

SportsCenter airtime. As you can see in figure 13.2, the vast majority of sport television is devoted to the "Big Three" male sports: football, basketball, and baseball (Messner and Cooky 2010).

Golden Age of Sport Reborn

Perhaps in this new century we'll recreate the excitement of another "golden age of sport"—and this time around, it will include women and girls. To reach that goal, significant changes are still needed in the world of sport. However, they will never fully occur without concomitant changes in society. The following discussion addresses some changes that will promote equality.

The percentage of women in the workplace is nearing that of men, but salaries for females still lag behind those of their male counterparts for doing same work. The proverbial glass ceiling also still prevents many women from reaching upper management. Indeed, workplaces, government agencies, and the courts are all still dominated by men, yet they can also be used to help eliminate discriminatory practices. The effort requires us to challenge the rigid sex roles that have historically guided society, expand our definitions of sexuality, and accept those who are lesbian and gay. Doing so will help us all find equal places in society.

We also need to collect data to show inequities in all forms, particularly in women's sport activities, to show us where we still need to work in order to reach equality. This effort has been undertaken by people like Billie Jean King, founder of the Women's Sports Foundation and the professional women's tennis tour; Dr. Richard Lapchick, author of the Racial and Gender Report Card; and Donna Lopiano, former executive director of the Women's Sports Foundation. These people and others have taken it upon themselves to inform the public of salient issues and statistics about racism, sexism, and other related topics. They have been supported by a growing cadre of female sport leaders who are determined to enhance the legacy of opportunities for physical activity and competitive sport for future generations of girls and women.

In addition, women's sport leaders and sympathetic corporate sponsors need to challenge each other to press ahead. Advocates for women's sport must aggressively recruit, train, and mentor young girls and women into key positions of influence in coaching, officiating, administration, athletic training, marketing, and the media. By taking their place in these positions, women can become a more powerful influence in the sport world.

Indeed, women must aggressively pursue leadership positions in sport organizations at every level. In 1994, Kathy Woods became the first female president of the United States Professional Tennis Association, a trade group with a membership of more than 13,000 tennis teaching professionals. A few years later, Judy Levering ascended to the presidency of the United States Tennis Association (USTA)—again, the first woman to do so. Within a few more years, two other women—Jane Brown and Lucy Garvin—followed their lead to the top job. In 2015, former professional player Katrina Adams, who is an African American, became USTA president, breaking yet another barrier. In addition, Anita DeFrantz of the United States became the first female elected to the International Olympic Committee. These trailblazers deserve appreciation—and a new succession of women to follow their lead.

Leaders in women's sport must take the initiative to look for ways to make their sports produce revenue so that men become their allies rather than remaining their competitors. A few colleges have figured out how to earn money from women's basketball and gymnastics, but other sports and schools lag behind. Leaders of specific professional women's sports need to build on the attractiveness of their product of athletes who are strong, independent women.

Parents of girls must also help by encouraging them to take the first step into exercise and sport at a young age. Even more critically, parents must support girls through their early teen years, when they are most likely to drop out of sport. Fathers in particular need to step up to the plate and become advocates, role models, and mentors for their daughters, just as they are for their sons.

In addition, recreational community-sponsored sport teams, high school teams, and collegiate teams must help lead the way to ensure equal access and encouragement for girls and women in sport. College sport needs to get over its preoccupation with football and men's basketball if it is to truly serve its university mission rather than focusing merely on revenue production, opulent athletic arenas, and mining alumni for donations earmarked for athletics rather than the overall institutional mission.

Finally, we must continue to educate people about the value of sport for women. Never underestimate the power of the mind in convincing people of the need to combat sexism in sport. In the early 1980s, as a college professor at a midsize state university, I was invited to join a semester course called "How to Combat Sexism in the Classroom." The class was taught on Saturdays by five women who knew their stuff and could argue their case. Although few men attended, all of us—women and men—learned strategies to combat sexism, applied them in our own classes, and received feedback from students and colleagues. Our lives have never been the same. Many of the lessons I learned all those years ago are still a vital part of my thinking and working character.

Chapter Summary

This chapter examines women in sport, beginning with ancient Greece and Rome, when women were virtually excluded from all sport activity, including the Olympic Games. That exclusion lasted until the 1850s, when U.S. women gradually began to play selected games.

During the first half of the 20th century, physical educators encouraged women's sport and physical activity in colleges as a route to good health. However, athletics were deemed too violent, competitive, and aggressive for young women. It wasn't until the late 1960s, when the women's movement took hold, that women realized that competitive athletics were another restriction for them to conquer.

In 1972, the U.S. Congress passed Title IX, which states that no person can be excluded from participation in sport on the basis of sex in any educational program receiving federal assistance. Title IX set the stage for years of lobbying by those in control of men's programs who did not want to give up any of their funding or perks to women. Numerous lawsuits were filed, and the law was challenged, but in the end it was reaffirmed.

The next 40 years have been exciting for girls and women, as opportunities have opened up in the world of sport. The proportion of female athletes has risen rapidly, proving that girls want to participate in sport, though some men had suggested otherwise. Women and girls have become consumers of sport, buying sport equipment and clothing, watching sport on television, signing up for youth sport programs, and making their presence felt in high school and collegiate sport. Research has overwhelmingly attested to the benefits of physical activity for girls and women. Numerous studies have shown improved academic performance, self-image, confidence, and physical health—all benefits similar to those enjoyed by boys for years.

Ideological conceptions of women have had to be modified in order to fit their newly aggressive attitudes toward equal opportunity, equal pay, and equal representation as coaches, administrators, and leaders. The marketplace has confirmed the popularity of female athletes as role models and awarded them multimillion-dollar endorsement deals, particularly in tennis. The ideal woman is now strong, lean, and attractive. As women have gained confidence, their expectations have changed to include equal opportunities to develop and fulfill their individual potential.

Despite all the positive changes for women in sport in the second half of the twentieth century, women are still underrepresented in sport leadership, in sport business, and in the sport media. Continued progress cannot be made without persistent effort and determination on the part of women and the men that they can recruit to assist them.

14

Social Class and Sport

STUDENT OUTCOMES

After reading this chapter, you will know the following:

- The importance of social, economic, and cultural capital
- The social classes and the typical characteristics of each
- Sport access and sport barriers due to social class
- Who controls amateur and professional sport
- The opportunity for social mobility through sport

Social Class and Sport

Youth sport costs are simply getting out of control; in fact, if the trend continues, the average family will be priced right out of sport. Maybe you've always loved sport and hope that someday your kids will get the chance to become successful athletes. If so, you'd better have your eyes wide open about the financial commitments required for participation in many sports. Parents who are savvy consumers need to explore the costs of youth sport and find opportunities that fit their family budget. Certain sports just don't make sense for kids from all economic levels. Perhaps we wish it weren't so, but you'll see the reality very quickly.

It is no secret that many individual sports—such as golf, tennis, skiing, gymnastics, and swimming—are pricy, from beginning youth clubs to high-performance training programs. Indeed, it is not unheard of in these sports for parents to spend upwards of $25,000 per year for one child with stars in his or her eyes. But even team sports, which have traditionally been a bargain, are beginning to stretch family budgets.

For example, baseball, which used to be regarded as "America's pastime," can now cost parents $4,000 or $5,000 per season. Even for a 10-year-old, fees can rise as high as $1,500. Then there is the cost of uniforms (not just one, but several combinations) and equipment, including shoes, bats, and gloves. Add to that the cost of game tickets for the parents and the cost of parking. In addition, it's now typical to have at least one or two multiday away trips, which of course add the costs of hotel rooms, transportation, and meals on the road. On top of all this, there's also the pressure to pay for your kid to work with a specialized position coach in order to keep up with his or her peers (Butler 2011).

Given these costs, it's little wonder that Little League Baseball participation has been declining, especially in inner cities where fields are scarce, costs are higher, and kids seem to have lost interest in the sport. What was once the national game has moved to the suburbs with families who are able and willing to foot the bill.

"We hold these truths to be self-evident, that all men are created equal." In 1776, Thomas Jefferson penned these words as the opening of the United States Declaration of Independence. He meant to convey that all people are born with equal rights. A natural assumption that follows is that everyone has the freedom to get an education, find work, vote for leaders, and perhaps even become a leader. U.S. society has traveled far in trying to live up to those ideals, yet the evidence suggests that equal opportunity still does not exist for a large portion of the population. Instead, opportunity is limited for many by social class, race or ethnicity, gender, or disability.

Indeed, Americans are divided according to economic class, and each class tends to possess different material goods, income levels, inheritances, education levels, work descriptions, and influence on others. Regardless of how we define or divide these classes, members of each one experience real differences in opportunity. This chapter defines a **social class** as a category of people who share similar positions in society based on their economic level, education, occupation, and social interaction. Although we pride ourselves in the United States on being a supposedly classless society, our form of capitalism naturally allows for different possible levels of economic success.

Capitalism is an economic system based on the accumulation and investment of capital by individuals who then use it to produce goods or services (Sage 1998). We tend to downplay the idea of social class in this country because it conflicts with our ideal of an equalitarian society. But we need to recognize that there are in fact different economic classes and that they expand to include our social system. Inequities in U.S. society are obvious: power, prestige, and wealth. When we assign classes according to levels of power, prestige, and wealth, we refer to **social stratification**. Other forms of stratification include race, gender, age, and disability, which are covered in other chapters.

Turning to the sport world, we can readily see how social class influences a family of four that decides to attend a professional football game. In 2013, the average ticket price to see a National Football League (NFL) game rose to $81.54, and the average premium ticket cost $247.85. But ticket prices are not even the whole story. For a family of four to attend a game in Dallas, which has the highest costs in the league, the total cost would come to $634.78. That figure includes tickets, two beers, four soft drinks, four hot dogs, and an amazing $75 for parking. In an area where the median annual family income is $56,954, the football outing costs the family about 58 percent of its weekly income. Perhaps it is no surprise, then, that in-person attendance at NFL games has been dropping consistently ever since it posted a high in 2007 (Victor 2014).

If this family belonged to the economic upper class, they would likely contact friends who have a skybox, inquire about availability, and end up with seats that included complimentary refreshments and possibly a parking pass. In contrast, a middle-class family would likely save for a once-a-year excursion, perhaps buy cheaper seats, and treat the game as a special occasion. A working-class family would likely wait for a special promotion or a discounted group ticket—or opt to attend a preseason game or scrimmage instead.

Both social capital and economic capital help people access different levels of society. Let's define the different kinds of capital. **Economic capital** refers to the financial resources that a person has or controls; people inherit, earn, invest, and spend money depending on their background and occupational status. **Social capital** depends on family, friends, and associates and includes resources based on group memberships, relationships, and both social and business networks. **Cultural capital** comprises the skills and abilities that people gain from education and life experiences; it may include attitudes, expectations, and self-confidence (Bowles and Jenson 2001).

Some reciprocity is at work here. Cultural capital affects how we see the world of sport; conversely, sport participation offers an opportunity to develop cultural capital. For example, a young girl from the middle class may view sport as a way to be accepted into a social group. Her parents may encourage her interest in sport in order to promote her fitness, help her gain self-confidence, and perhaps help her earn a college scholarship. Her athletics coach helps her learn to set goals, employ self-discipline, and perform under the pressure of competition. Sport also helps her form a self-concept as a skilled, fit competitor. All of these influences help her during the confusing years of early adolescence by enhancing her cultural capital.

In the United States, we like to think that sport transcends social class. We want to believe that hard work and dedication ensure success and that failure results simply from a lack of perseverance. In the land of the free, we are all free to participate in and watch sport. However, our economic, social, and cultural capital largely defines what sports we watch and participate in; it also affects our chances at success in sport.

Social Class

Most people gain their economic capital through their annual earnings. In the United States, the median family income for 2012 was $51,373 for a family of four (figure 14.1). Asian families had the highest average income, and black families had the lowest (figure 14.2).

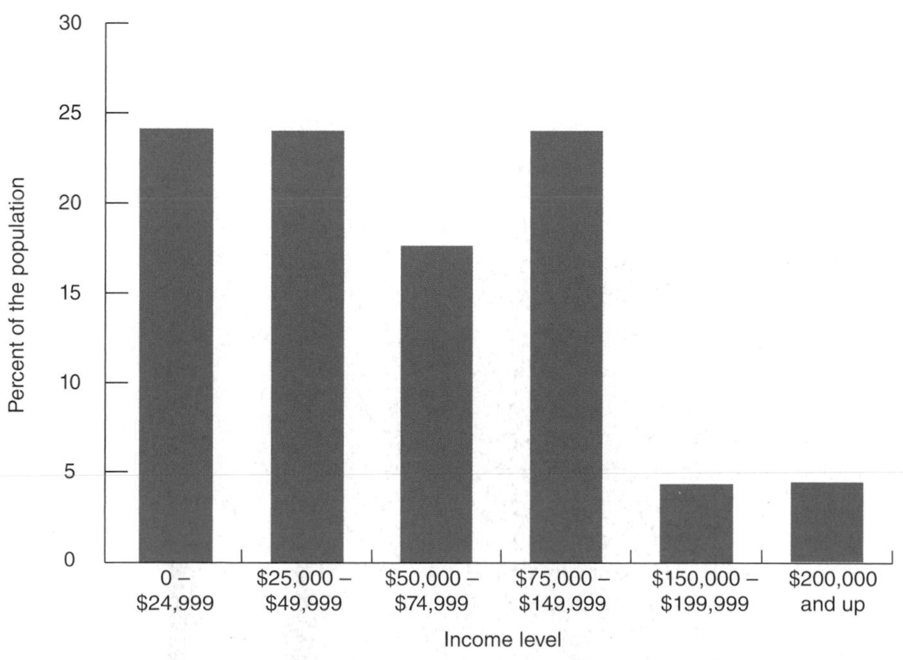

FIGURE 14.1 U.S. percent distribution of household income in 2012.

From U.S. Census Bureau 2012b.

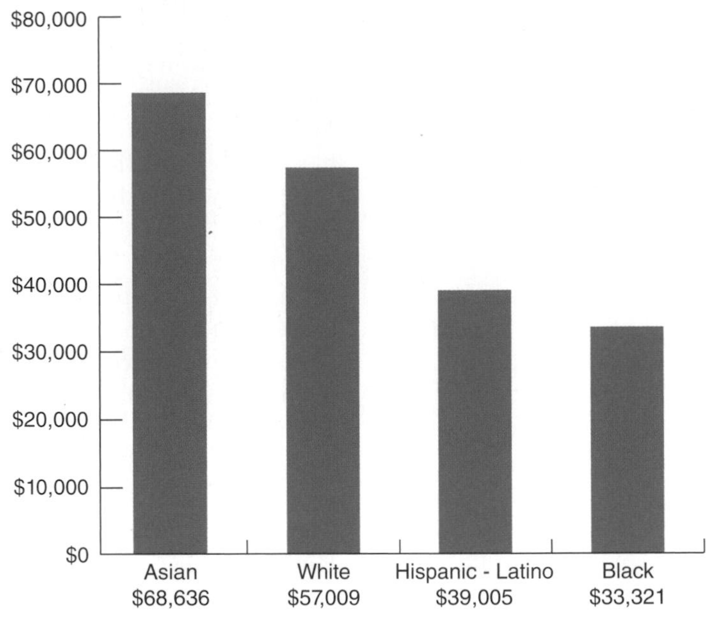

FIGURE 14.2 Median household income in 2012 by race.

From U.S. Census Bureau 2012b.

Of the multitude of ways to divide people into economic classes, this chapter uses the following categories: upper, upper-middle, middle, and lower. The **upper class** makes up the top 1 percent of U.S. households, and members of this class control about 35 percent of the nation's wealth. In fact, the top 10 percent of U.S. households control about 71 percent of individual and family wealth. Members of this class have plenty of disposable income and many choices as consumers. Their children often attend the best private schools, their families often belong to exclusive clubs, and their children are often expected to mature in a way that meets the expectations of their parents. People in this economic class essentially control much of the financial world and seek to maintain their position in society.

The **upper-middle class** is composed of professionals such as physicians, attorneys, business leaders, and managers. Typically, members of this class have considerable discretionary income and join private clubs for social experiences. While most do not have the economic resources to exist without their earned income, they do tend to be white-collar professionals and therefore supervise and influence others in the workplace. People in the upper-middle class often value education and strive for advanced degrees. They establish a network of contacts that serves them throughout life. They also often become leaders in government and can affect laws to maintain their position.

The **middle class** is the largest economic group in the United States. They must carefully choose their expenses for daily living and leisure spending. They often work as skilled laborers, as teachers, and in service industry positions. Their earned income provides their economic base, and many middle-class families rely on two wage earners.

The **lower class** is composed of unskilled laborers who essentially do work that is assigned and supervised by others. Their income often barely meets the minimum wage standards set by the government, and they have few chances to improve their economic level. In 2012, the official poverty rate for all U.S. citizens was 15.9 percent—more than 48.8 million people (U.S. Bureau of Labor Statistics 2012b). To be considered below the poverty line, annual family income must be below $23,492 for a family of four (figure 14.3).

Social Class and Sport Activity

Families in different economic classes differ widely in their general access to sport and in the particu-

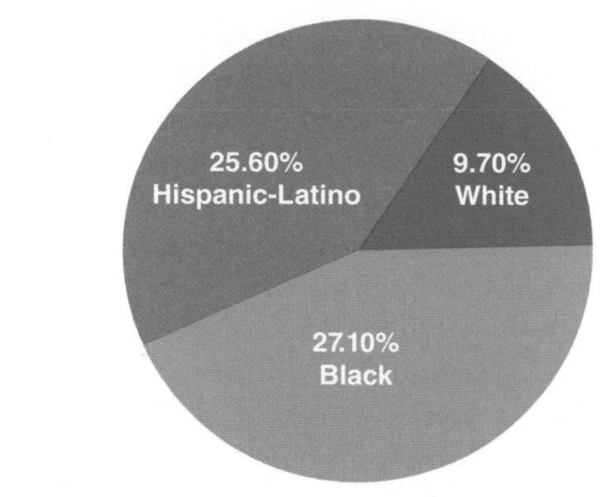

FIGURE 14.3 U.S. families below the poverty line by race.

From U.S. Census Bureau 2012b.

lar sports that they are likely to choose. Let's look now at how social class affects both sport participation and sport spectatorship.

Social Class and Choice of Sport

Sport participation has always been more popular among, and accessible to, members of the upper class due to their abundance of leisure time and money. Historically, in fact, people of wealth have used sport both as entertainment and as a way to demonstrate their wealth. They have also often used sport to build social capital through networks and contacts in business. Many of today's sports—such as tennis, golf, equestrianism, and sailing—were traditionally pastimes of the wealthy, and many business deals have been consummated after a round of golf or a set of tennis. Current U.S. society is similar in that people with the highest income levels typically have the highest rates of sport participation. They also are more likely to attend sporting events, and they even watch more sport on television (Booth and Loy 1999).

Both the upper and the upper-middle classes have favored sports—such as those just listed, as well as polo and skiing—that are typically performed at private clubs. Other typical choices of the upper-middle class include Olympic sports such as gymnastics, figure skating, swimming, riflery, and archery. As most of these sports are individual, they are often expensive to participate in. In team sports, the most popular choices of upper-middle class families in certain geographic areas are ice hockey and lacrosse, both of which often involve club teams rather than school teams and typically cost considerably more than other team sports. The facilities for all of these sports are often costly, and the individual or family bears the sizable expenses of training and traveling to competitions.

Members of the working class (that is, the lower-middle class) are more likely to choose community sports that are readily accessible and inexpensive. Community youth sport programs get kids started in sport, and many kids go on to play on interscholastic teams that are subsidized by schools and taxpayers. Coaching and facilities are typically free, and athletes with talent can enhance their performance at a modest expense to their family. Team sports dominate this class, since they are cheaper to stage, accommodate more players on a field or court, and provide a social environment as well. Popular examples include basketball, football, soccer, baseball, softball, and volleyball. Parents often serve as volunteer coaches or officials in order to stay involved with their children and keep expenses within reason.

Members of the poor and working classes devote so much time to earning a living and taking care of basic needs that they have little time or money left to spend on sport. However, as the U.S. standard of living improved over the years, blue-collar families have been able to participate in or watch certain sports that appeal to them and are readily accessible to the public, inexpensive to play, and available in public recreational facilities (Sage 1998).

Those who have higher levels of income and education and work in professional or managerial roles are the most ardent and frequent consumers of health and fitness activities and sport. They value physical fitness and enjoy leisure activity. In contrast, those who labor physically are less likely to feel the need or inclination to exercise or participate in sport. They are more likely to spend leisure time resting for the next day of work (Gruneau 1999).

Members of the lower economic classes typically choose sports characterized by violence and uncertainty based on physical strength and daring. Examples include boxing, wrestling, weightlifting, auto racing, and motorcycle racing These sports are often available at low cost and in urban areas and are accessible to all. They lean toward the masculine ideal of toughness—a trait that kids from modest backgrounds may find necessary for survival (Coakley 2004). At the same time, many people with lower incomes live in rural areas, and they may favor sports that are readily accessible, such as hunting and fishing. Two skill sports that lack vigorous physical activity that are popular with this social group are bowling and pool.

French sociologist Loïc Wacquant (2004) joined a gym on the south side of Chicago in a predominantly black neighborhood. There he learned the importance of boxing for boys from the lower socioeconomic class who are looking for a legitimate way to establish self-respect and a sense of masculinity. The alternative to boxing for many kids in that neighborhood was "to end up in jail or dead in the streets." Boxing has traditionally appealed to the lower economic classes and to recent immigrants to the United States. Many boys in the cities have turned to boxing to try to escape lives marked by a lack of employment prospects. They have preferred the controlled violence of the boxing ring to the random violence of the streets. Over the past century, boxing in the United States has been dominated by Irish, Italians, Jews, African Americans, and, more recently, Latinos.

IN THE ARENA WITH . . .

Roller Derby

Roller derby gained popularity first in the 1930s and then again on television in the 1980s and 1990s, but it had never been much more than a curiosity. In 2009, however, the film *Whip It*, directed by Drew Barrymore, introduced audiences to the revival of roller derby for girls. The film follows the character Bliss Cavender as she negotiates the unfamiliar world of girl power in sport. Described as hip, innocent, and klutzy all at once, the story is a somewhat trite tale of a young girl coming of age in a venue that is unfamiliar to most of America.

Recently dubbed the "fastest growing sport in America," roller derby is one of the few sports that feature live combat, collisions, and contact for girls. It now boasts a unique punk aesthetic or third-wave feminist ethic. According to the Women's Flat Track Derby Association (WFTDA), which oversees and promotes the sport internationally, roller derby was revived in Austin, Texas, in 2003, when there were about 50 teams worldwide. By 2014, there were more than 1,550 leagues, plus another hundred or so apprentice (labeled "fresh meat") leagues for players new to the sport. All-female amateur leagues are run by women and feature five-on-five competition between teams of women (Women's Flat Track Derby Association 2014), although some local leagues for men have sprung up along with a few coed leagues.

Roller derby participants skate around a circular track to earn points by leading the pack and blocking out opponents who seek to take their place. The sport is rough, violent, fast, and exciting for players and spectators alike. The culture has been described as "tough, edgy, creative, slutty, low-class, bawdy and like being in a blender." The game highlights are speed, combat, and collisions. All hits are legal from the mid-thigh to the shoulders except those to the back.

The WFTDA describes its sport as "real, strong, athletic, revolutionary." Participants often adopt a "bad-ass" image, including plenty of body tattoos, and adopt nicknames such as Anna Mosity, Michelle O'Bamya, Pain Fonda, Habeas KarcAss, Sandra Da O'Clobber, and Thea Nihilator (Roller Derby Worldwide 2014). The vast majority of leagues are made up of women over age 18 who hold down regular jobs by day as artists, designers, nurses, engineers, waitresses, and college professors; some are also stay-at-home mothers. It's hard to classify them by social strata but easy to describe their passion for the sport. In addition, being gay, straight, bisexual, or transsexual is no big deal as long as you can skate, says E. Smackulotta from Durham, North Carolina (Dixon 2014).

For more information about Roller Derby in the United States, check out USA Roller Sports, which is the national governing body for roller sports of the United States Olympic Committee (USOC).

ACTIVITY TIME-OUT

Popularity of Squash

Squash is played in a four-walled court by either two or four players who hit a small hollow rubber ball with a racket similar to a tennis racket but smaller. The object is to force the opponent to either miss or be unable to return your shot in the air or on one bounce. There are more than 50,000 squash courts worldwide, and 8,500 of them are in Great Britain. The game has no time-outs and typically features longer rallies than its American cousin—racquetball—thus producing an intense physical workout. A typical player burns 600 to 1,000 calories in one hour of squash. As a result, *Forbes* magazine has rated it as the healthiest sport to play (World Squash Federation 2014).

In 2013, there were more than 1.4 million squash players in the United States, and over the past five years participation has increased by an impressive average of 17 percent per year (Sports and Fitness Industry Association 2014). Do you know anyone who plays squash? Is it offered at your college or university? Which social class do you think favors playing squash?

Basketball is unique in that it appeals to all classes and is popular in the suburbs, rural areas, and the city. At its heart, however, it is a city game with its own history, hierarchy, and heroes. A driveway, an asphalt playground, or a parking lot with a hoop can provide the court. Anyone can play, and winners typically stay on the court to challenge all comers. The dream of escaping the ghetto through basketball has been the subject of articles, books, and motion pictures, such as *White Men Can't Jump* and *Hoop Dreams*. A few players do make it to the professional level, but the odds are minuscule for the millions of kids who dream of doing so.

Social Class and High-Performance Sport

Young athletes who aspire to high-performance sport must invest large amounts of time and money in training and competition. If their family doesn't have the resources to support their dream, their chances of success are severely curtailed. The choice of sport is critical, since the opportunities to develop in some sports depend heavily on economic investment, whereas others can be pursued at a more modest expense.

Young people from the upper and upper-middle classes typically do not develop strong motivation to succeed in highly competitive sport. Their exposure to a family that makes a living in business or a profession influences their interests from their earliest days. Sport tends to be seen as a diversion—something done for fun. Family and friends encourage these children in selected sports—such as golf, tennis, sailing, and skiing—so that they can acquit themselves admirably on social occasions. Many friendships are developed and business deals arranged on the golf course or tennis court. These sports are also often included in family vacations. A certain level of skill and understanding of such sports is expected, just like good table manners and other social graces.

Young men from the middle class often see sport as a way to establish their masculinity and to gain social capital by acceptance in their peer group. Since this motivation often combines with the cultural capital instilled by their parents of self-discipline, hard work, and focus on achievement, middle-class youth often become high achievers in sport. Moreover, coaches of youth sport tend to reward the work ethic and reinforce the behavior of high-achieving athletes.

Middle-class families tend to support their kids' quest for excellence and often sacrifice financially to cover training costs. Indeed, it is not unheard of for a family to move to another part of the country so that a child can train with a better coach or experience better competition. In tennis and golf, families with exceptionally talented kids often move to warm climates where the competition is strongest and the private academies are typically located. At the extreme, families even split apart, with one parent moving with the talented athlete and the other staying behind because of a job or other children.

Male athletes from lower classes also link sport to masculinity because sport provides a chance to exhibit fearlessness and aggressiveness. Since these individuals often can't compete with young men from higher classes in school or in material possessions, their sport success becomes the badge of courage that defines them (Messner 2002).

Olympic Sport

Olympic sports were historically dominated by the upper classes, and many sports in the modern Olympic Games (both Summer and Winter) reflect that pattern. The leaders of the Olympic movement were typically males from well-to-do backgrounds. They promoted the sports indigenous to their social class and for years limited participation to amateurs. By excluding professionals, they restricted participation to athletes from their social class, since athletes with limited resources couldn't afford to train as amateurs. In fact, early definitions of *amateur* were based on social class, and athletes from lower economic classes were categorized as non-amateurs.

If nothing else, the problem with limiting the Olympics to amateurs was simply that doing so excluded some of the best athletes. Furthermore, extensive reports indicated that some athletes violated the rules and secretly accepted money to cover training expenses. Some countries established free training schools that prepared their young athletes for the Olympics, in effect turning their athletes into professionals. Discussion about these Olympic restrictions came to a head in the 1980s, and after the 1988 Games, the International Olympic Committee voted to allow professional athletes in each sport to compete in future Games pending approval of that sport's international sport federation (Amateur Athletic Foundation Olympic Primer 2005). (Only a handful of federations did not approve professional athletes in their sport.)

In the wake of these changes, most of the recent Olympic athletes in the United States have come from working-class or middle-class families who sacrificed to support their child's Olympic quest. Olympian David Hemery (1986) studied 63 of the recent top performers, including athletes from 22

APPLYING SOCIAL THEORY

Conflict Theorists and Penalizing the Lower Economic Classes

In a capitalistic society such as the United States, economic power and influence is determined by personal wealth and income. Those who are in the upper economic classes have primary influence and control over our society including sports at virtually every level of competition. The result is that people in the lower economic classes are often disenfranchised from sports participation even at a recreational level. If they dare to dream of achieving a high performance level of competition, they are faced with almost insurmountable odds of succeeding.

Take the point of view of a conflict theorist and identify the most daunting barriers a youngster from the lowest economic classes might face and discuss the effects of those barriers. You might consider potential barriers such as lack of adult role models, costs, transportation, parental involvement and emotional support, safety, hunger, drugs, and child care for siblings. Once you have identified at least four barriers, suggest potential solutions for each one. Be realistic but creative in designing solutions and identify the following:

- Who should take the lead in implementation of your strategies?
- What is the source for the financial resources needed?

sports and 12 countries. His sample, which was relatively small and focused on the best of the best, fell into the following class distribution:

Poor	22%
Working class	26%
Lower-middle class	3%
Middle class	44%
Upper-middle class	3%
Upper class	0%

Athletes who aspire to compete in certain sports at the Olympic Games run into special problems. Many Olympic sports are not emphasized or even offered at high schools or colleges. High-performance athletes must pursue their athletic dreams through private academies and competitions that are expensive and time-consuming. Olympic sports that require specialized training include gymnastics, swimming, judo, weightlifting, boxing, and almost all winter sports (though a limited number of schools and colleges offer varsity programs in winter sports). Families must often move to allow their kids to train with a top coach living in another part of the country. Athletes of modest means may seek employment to help them afford competition, travel, and coaching. Some corporate sponsors help provide jobs for prospective Olympians.

Another option for prospective Olympians is to train at one of the U.S. Olympic training centers. Of course, athletes have to qualify for these programs, but if they do, the costs of training are generally borne by the U.S. Olympic Committee or the national governing body of the given sport. In many countries, the expense of training future Olympians is borne by the government and administered by the minister of sports. In the United States, government funding for training has been debated for many years.

Cost of High-Performance Sport

Many people are unaware of the financial investment it takes to compete at the highest levels, whether in the Olympics or in professional sport. This is where parents of talented kids can put whatever social and cultural capital they possess to good use in order to cushion the financial impact of elite training. Perhaps the most expensive sports are the equestrian events. Owning and caring for a competition horse can cost upwards of $100,000 per year. In addition, unlike other athletes who travel, equestrians must also ship their horses in order to compete nationally and internationally at the highest levels (United States Equestrian Team Foundation 2010).

For another example, let's look now at the yearly expenses of a tennis player. If the player attends 12 national tournaments a year at a cost of $1,500 to travel to and compete in each, then he or she must budget $18,000 just for starters. If a parent or coach travels with the player, then the expenses increase, especially if the athlete pays the coach for his or her time. In addition, weekly lessons (some group based and some individual) cost an average of $250 each, and athletes living in a cold climate pay more so they can practice on an indoor court. The player must also cover the expense of tennis rackets, shoes, clothing, and other incidental equipment, which can easily total up to more than $2,500 per year unless the player gets an endorsement deal with a clothing or racket company.

Many young athletes also use the services of a fitness gym or physical trainer and perhaps a sport nutritionist or sport psychologist. These fees can easily add several thousand dollars per year in expenses. All in all, the cost will probably exceed $25,000 a year for frugal athletes and may reach $50,000 if money is not a concern.

Families with no financial worries may send their sport prodigy to a live-in academy in a warm climate where they can play tennis (or soccer, golf, or basketball) half the day and attend a private school the other half. Expenses at such a facility are likely to exceed $60,000 for the school year alone, which means there will be additional costs if the athlete continues to train or compete during the summer months. (For more information about private sport academies, see chapter 6.)

You can see how children of most families face limited opportunities in certain sports. As noted earlier, the median income for all U.S. households in 2012 was just over $50,000. In contrast, families whose combined annual income exceeds $100,000 rank in the top 5 percent to 10 percent of all U.S. families. The average family, with that total income of $50,000, can't begin to afford sports like high-performance competitive tennis. Indeed, even wage earners making a six-figure salary can't afford to spend a quarter or half of the family's income on sport training for one child.

This prohibitive expense is why team sports are the most popular options for most kids. The costs are reasonable, and most families can finance sport participation if they are creative and frugal. Of course, many families have figured out that team sports are more affordable, so the competition is keen. As a result, children whose families are well off financially might find it better to develop their skills in a more exclusive sport and compete for a national championship against fewer opponents.

Social Class and High School Sport

Children from lower-class families usually do not have much family support in playing sports since their families are struggling to make ends meet. Girls are often expected to help out with household chores and care for younger siblings. The sport dropout rate for girls over age 14 is much higher than that for boys, particularly among girls of color and those from low-income families (U.S. Anti-Doping Agency 2012).

In addition, research discussed in a *USA Today* article shows that "the most affluent high schools—those in the top quarter of the state of New Jersey—have won athletic championships at more than twice the rate of those in the bottom quarter." The categories were based on the median household income in the school neighborhood and the percentage of students receiving federal free or reduced lunch (Brady and Sylwester 2004). Here are the specific percentages of schools in each category that have won state athletic championships:

Top quarter	40%
Upper middle	22%
Lower middle	22%
Bottom	16%

The expense of sailing limits this sport to financial elites.

Schools in wealthier neighborhoods tend to have better sport facilities, better coaches (because the pay is better), more money for equipment, better weight rooms, and booster clubs to pay for extras. These athletes also have team jackets, shirts, uniforms, banquets, rings, and other goodies that are out of reach for kids at other schools.

The training in youth sport in affluent communities also tends to be better organized. Families typically start their kids early and encourage them to attend specialized coaching camps to refine their skills. These kids might go to a summer camp for tennis, soccer, golf, swimming, or a more traditional team sport such as basketball, soccer, or volleyball. At such camps, they are exposed to top coaching and rub elbows with other talented kids from outside their neighborhood.

The *USA Today* article (Brady and Sylwester 2004) also specifically addressed the high school in Glen Rock, New Jersey, which won 13 state titles over the course of five years in the 10 core sports analyzed in the article: four in football, four in girls' track, three in girls' soccer, one in baseball, and one in boys' track. The median income in the Glen Rock neighborhood was $120,000—more than double the statewide median. Similar sport statistics abound for suburban school districts in southern Connecticut, such as those in Greenwich, New Canaan, and Westport—all of which are within easy commuting distance of New York City and have high per-capita incomes. This pattern in high school sport statistics is replicated around the country in affluent, typically suburban communities.

One glaring omission in the study involves the fact that it included only basketball, soccer, outdoor track, football, girls' volleyball, girls' softball, and baseball. What do you think the study would have shown if tennis and golf had been included? How often have you heard of an inner-city high school winning a state championship in tennis or golf?

The scarcity of golfers and tennis players in urban environments is not due solely to a lack of affluent families. Accessibility to golf courses and tennis courts is also limited in urban settings simply due to space limitations and building and rental costs. Renting an indoor tennis court in New York City can cost $100 an hour because they are so expensive to build and maintain. Similarly, aside from the few public golf courses in city parks, golf facilities are few and far between.

There are some exceptions to the general trends in high school sport statistics. Small rural communities sometimes excel at sport because their kids have few choices for entertainment and therefore tend to participate in sport at high rates. In another example, some inner-city high schools have a strong tradition of excellence in basketball, both because playgrounds abound and because kids follow history.

Some boys may learn that their role model who makes millions in professional sport came from a similar socioeconomic background. In this way, sport gives them a sense of hope and a road map for fulfilling their dreams of upward mobility. They typically choose team sport, since training can often be found close by at modest expense. As they mature, they can continue to improve their skills through high school varsity programs and eventually hope to win an athletic scholarship to college. Sport programs at all levels set aside funds to provide scholarships for youth from poorer families and are eager to assist deserving and talented kids.

Solutions to Financial Barriers in Sport

Access to sport has been opened up to some degree in the United States through community sport programs available to all kids in a community. Many programs are staged at public school facilities or parks that are supported by taxpayer funds. Although programs usually charge a modest user fee, lower-class families who qualify for scholarships based on income can often still send their kids to the programs. Usually recreation departments—again, supported by taxpayer funds—provide facilities and some equipment and pay for coaching. Most communities typically offer team sports that can accommodate large numbers of players at modest expense. Some communities also offer swimming or tennis as after-school or summer programs.

Some activities are promoted by nonprofit community organizations established to fund and organize programs in a given sport. These nonprofit groups are often assisted by their national governing body and supported financially by local donors, government grants, fundraisers (such as auctions and dinner dances), and business donors who want to support their local community. Typically, these nonprofit organizations provide programs at very modest fees and welcome every child regardless of ability to pay.

Other strong sources of youth sport programs include private organizations such as the YMCA and YWCA, the Boys & Girls Clubs of America, Catholic youth organizations, Jewish community centers, police athletic leagues, church leagues, Girl Scouts and Boy Scouts, and Big Brothers Big Sisters. All are dedicated to providing healthy recreational experiences for kids, and many concentrate on serving disadvantaged neighborhoods. Although their goal is not to produce high-performance athletes, if a talented child is spotted in the program they often have ways to provide additional support for extended training or scholarships for specialized programs.

Control of Amateur and Professional Sport

People who hold power in the sport world can either bring about change or prevent it. The power in sport differs by level of competition. In local, high school, and recreational sport programs, a board of directors usually hires staff members to administer the programs. Parents, politicians, and others in the community may join the board or exert their influence from outside of the organization. Even at the local level, those who make program decisions typically have their own biases and ideas about how a sport should be presented and run.

At the national level, the people who control the money make decisions about how to run the sport programs. Their economic capital is based on the organizations they head rather than on their personal wealth. However, most of the people who have a say at the national level of sport belong to the upper or upper-middle class by virtue of their income, background, and robust social and cultural capital.

In 2013, *Sports Illustrated* listed its 50 Most Powerful People in Sport for the year. Generally, the group includes businessmen who are personally well-off and hold the power to determine what sports we watch, when, and what it costs us to do so. The top 50 includes no athletes and only two females—Sharon Byers of Coca-Cola North America at number 41 and Cindy Davis of Nike Golf at number 46. Here are the top 10 (Rushin 2013):

1. Roger Goodell, NFL commissioner
2. David Stern, NBA commissioner
3. Philip Anschutz, AEG owner
4. John Skipper, ESPN president
5. Bud Selig, MLB commissioner
6. Stan Kroenke, Kroenke Sports Enterprises owner
7. Mark Lazarus, NBC Sports chairman
8. Jacques Rogge, IOC president
9. Phil Knight, Nike chairman
10. Mark Walter, Guggenheim Partners CEO and Los Angeles Dodgers owner

This group represents a new kind of leadership in the sport world that is replacing the previous generations of "gentleman owners," such as Busch, Hess, Wrigley, and even Steinbrenner. Today's leaders are business executives trained to make money through sport using every available tactic. The importance of the close ties between sport and the media is obvious; they have collaborated to push the sport world into leading broadcast properties. Of course, the sport commissioners are hired and fired by the owners of the franchises; therefore, though they do wield significant influence and power, they are also limited by their employers who evaluate their performance.

At the United States Olympic Committee, the board of directors and the officers were traditionally white and male. In recent years, however, women and blacks have gradually been included in the controlling group of the USOC. LeRoy Walker, a distinguished track-and-field coach, was the first African American to serve as president; Sandra Baldwin, a leader in the world of elite swimming, became the first female president.

The people who control sport in the United States often base their decisions on the welfare of the organizations or businesses that they head. They decide which sports receive high visibility, what image is portrayed of each sport, and what accompanying messages are sent to sport consumers. Of course, they need to please the customer, and for the most part that means taking a conservative, mainstream position on all issues. They can be conscious of public sentiment and media criticism, but they also have the means to influence or deflect much of that.

One of the most powerful people in sports is John Skipper, president of ESPN and cochairman of Disney Media Networks. Since 2012, Skipper has strengthened the position of ESPN as the leader in sport news and increased the value of the company to more than US$50 billion, far exceeding any other competitor (Badehausen 2014b).

The key to the future for ESPN is forging long-term, multiplatform agreements with major rights

ACTIVITY TIME-OUT

Power at Your University

Investigate your university to assess how sport decisions are made. Who gets involved in the big decisions—the college president, the board of trustees, politicians (if yours is a state university), big donors, coaching icons, student leaders, athletes, the media, fans? Interview at least three people in different positions who influence the decisions and ask them to list the five most powerful people in sport at your school. (Remember to define power as the ability to bring about or prevent change.) To help make your interviews fruitful, you might ask who wields the most influence at your university in areas such as adding or dropping a particular sport, building a new sport facility, increasing student fees to support sport activities, accepting a major new sport sponsor, allocating scholarships by sport, or accepting a bowl bid for the football team. Feel free to use your own examples.

EXPERT'S VIEW

Why Millionaire Athletes Go Broke

Roy Hadley, an attorney who counsels clients in legal matters associated with professional sport, shares some sobering statistics. A young National Basketball Association (NBA) or NFL athlete who signs a contract worth millions of dollars may think he is suddenly rich, but within a few years his life could be in tatters. In fact, 78 percent of NFL players eventually face bankruptcy or other financial distress soon after they retire; similarly, within five years of retirement, 60 percent of NBA players are broke (Torre 2009; Holmes 2012; Pagliarini 2013). How could this be possible? To understand, let's consider a hypothetical first-round draft pick who signs with a team for a $10 million bonus. Here's how it may very well be spent:

- First, he has to pay federal, state, and local taxes. With good legal advice, he may limit his taxes to 45 percent. He's now down to $5.5 million.
- Second, he's got to pay his agent a percentage of the gross figure—not the after-tax amount. At the going rate, that's probably going to cost him $300,000. Now he's down to $5.2 million.
- Third, he needs somewhere to live, and since he has lots of cash he decides that a $4 million mansion is just about right as compared with his teammates' digs. He's now down to $1.2 million.
- Fourth, everyone needs a car, and a super-luxury vehicle might cost him $250,000. Now we're looking at a remaining $950,000.
- Finally, he needs clothes, jewelry, electronic gadgetry, gifts for family and friends, household expenses, and travel expenses that are compatible with his new lifestyle. In addition, he'll soon have a slew of former friends and new acquaintances asking him for loans or investments in their business schemes that "can't miss," and he may also want to buy a new house for his mom.

Whew! Where did all that "guaranteed money" go? And now what does he do? The fact is that young men who claim these exorbitant bonuses and salaries may also have a short professional career with no backup plan for the rest of their lives. In addition, if the player gets divorced, his ex-wife will claim that she and any children are entitled to be supported in the lifestyle she envisioned when he struck it rich. However, while superstars temporarily have a huge income, they may also have had little real education and no training in finance, and therefore they are often at the mercy of business advisors (Hadley 2010).

holders and distributors. For example, current long-term contracts are in place with Major League Baseball, College Football Playoff, NBA, ACC, Big 12, U.S. Open tennis, WNBA, American Athletic Conference, Mountain West Conference, and Rose, Sugar, and Orange Bowls. A new agreement is in place with the SEC Network and digital platforms. Agreements are also solid with Cablevision, Cox Communications, Charter Communications, AT&T U-Verse, National Rural Telecommunications Cooperative (NTRC), and Dish network.

As an example of his creative leadership to push the company into the future, Skipper led a drive to conceive and build a new 195,000 square-foot facility, Digital Center 2, at the Connecticut headquarters. Completed in 2014, this new space boasts numerous technical innovations and is designed to support future mobile offerings.

At the same time, Skipper has led the charge to enlarge ESPN's female sports audience by creating espnW as an initiative designed to serve, attract, and inspire female fans. In view of the media exposure of women's sports covered in chapters 5 and 13, it will be interesting to follow the growth of espnW. If successful, it could have a major effect on one of the most frustrating inequities between males and females in the world of sport.

Class Mobility in Sport

Part of the American dream has always been the ability to enhance one's social or economic status in life through hard work and discipline. A popular corollary holds that those who do not improve their status must not have the motivation or discipline to do so. Sport provides an opportunity, however challenging it may be, to improve one's social and economic status through success on the playing field. Once again, the conventional wisdom holds that hard work is even more important than talent in reaching the ultimate prize in a given sport.

The typical example illustrating social mobility through sport is that of a football or basketball player, or perhaps a boxer, who comes from a low-income family and makes his way to the professional ranks, where he commands a huge contract. By earning millions of dollars, the athlete automatically joins the upper class—a society he may find it difficult to fit into.

There are multiple possible dimensions to rising in class status through sport. The most obvious is the education that comes along with continuing a career in sport—even if a professional sport career is not realistic. Most lower-class kids who passionately latch onto sport realize that maintaining their academic eligibility allows them to pursue their sport. If they keep up their grades, they may also earn an athletic scholarship that opens up the possibility for higher education that their parents never had. The knowledge and friends gained through their college education then sets them up for employment opportunities beyond their social and economic class even if they never make it as a professional athlete.

Athletes who participate in college sport seem to have more opportunities than nonathletes do. The reason for their success may be the sport experience, which teaches discipline, teamwork, and leadership. Of course, they may also possess innate capabilities that allow them to succeed in sport, and athletic participation may enhance those abilities. Sport participation may also help them build their own social and cultural capital. Surely, their education, personal expectations, and social networks help them in the business world. In fact, numerous research studies have documented both male and female business leaders who participated

POP CULTURE

Warrior

The film *Warrior* is an American sport drama that tells the story of two estranged brothers who end up competing against each other in a mixed martial arts (MMA) tournament. Actor Nick Nolte plays the father of the two boys and was nominated for an Academy Award for best supporting actor. The film was released in 2011 and has won critical acclaim as one of the best of the fight films that have flooded the market since the 1990s.

Mixed martial arts has gained in popularity in recent years and has even begun to replace boxing as the primary fighting sport. Drawing much of its appeal from its roots in Brazilian jiu-jitsu, MMA now boasts more than 977,000 competitors in the United States. Perhaps even more impressive are the 2.2 million people who train in MMA not for competition fighting but as a fitness activity (Sports and Fitness Industry Association 2014).

The appeal of sport movies such as *Warrior* often lies in their adulation of the Everyman who, despite societal oppression, rises above his station in life by battling courageously against impossible odds. The appeal of violence also exerts a strong pull for those who feel cheated by society and wish that they could fight their way out of poverty.

in sport and attribute their business success at least in part to the lessons they learned in sport (Acosta and Carpenter 2014; Carlson and Scott 2005).

In every sport, certain athletes stand out because they appear hungry to succeed. When these athletes come from lower-socioeconomic families, people usually conclude that they are striving to escape a life of poverty. Indeed, a number of elite athletes on the world stage have emerged from poor countries to become international celebrities who are wealthy as compared with their countrymen.

French sociologist Loïc Wacquant, who authored *Body and Soul: Notebooks of an Apprentice Boxer* (2004) based on his three years of study at a boxing gym in Chicago, quotes from some of the men he encountered there who express the love–hate feelings they have for their sport and profession. Here is what one boxer said: "I wish I had been born taller, to a rich family. I wish I was smart and had the brains to go to school an' really become somebody important. For me, I can't stand the sport, I hate the sport, but it's carved inside of me so I can't let it go." More than 80 percent of the boxers Wacquant interviewed said they didn't want their son to become a boxer. Said one, "No, no fighter wants his son to box. . . . [T]hat's the reason you fight. . . . [I]t's too hard, jus' too damn hard" (Coakley 2004, 341).

How likely are young athletes to make it to the professional level? Evidence from the National Collegiate Athletic Association (2013e) indicates that only a small percentage of athletes make it from high school to college to professional sport. The odds of a high school athlete making a collegiate team are only about 5 percent, which means that 95 percent of athletes have no chance of a career in sport beyond their high school years. Furthermore, only 3 percent of college athletes make it to the pros. So, of all high school athletes, roughly 0.15 percent make it to a professional career. These are small odds indeed. In spite of many inspiring biographies of athletes who moved from poverty to the professional ranks, the percentages are stacked very high against such mobility.

When we track athletic success, the results may be affected by the sports involved. We have already seen that many sports—including golf, tennis, swimming, and gymnastics—tend to attract athletes from upper-middle-class families. Their records are often lumped in with large-scale research studies on class mobility, but their chances of achieving upward mobility are limited since they're starting from a relatively high level. Similarly, female athletes have fewer sports through which to gain upward mobility due to the dearth of professional sports for women.

In another example, players in the Women's National Basketball Association (WNBA) earned an average salary of $72,000 in 2012 versus an average of $5.5 million for men in the NBA. However,

The minimum salary for WNBA players is around $35,000 while the minimum salary for NBA players is around $450,000. How do these numbers affect social class?

it is hardly fair to compare the men's and women's leagues, since the NBA has a history of 66 years and the WNBA only 16 years. The leagues also differ in that the men play 82 regular season games, whereas the women play only 34, thus limiting the revenue that the women's game can generate. At this point, the two leagues use different business models based not on gender discrimination but on potential earnings.

Understanding the limited chances for women to make it in professional sport reinforces the amazing success of Serena and Venus Williams. Coming from Compton, California—an economically depressed area rife with crime and poverty—they have risen to the top of the sporting world in a sport usually reserved for members of the upper classes. The result has been Grand Slam championships for both women and record-setting endorsements, which in Serena's case are worth more than $50 million!

Similarly, LeBron James is likely the best basketball player in the world, but his early life involved frequent moves from one apartment to another with his 16-year-old mother. He's now one of the richest athletes in the world (he earned $53 million in 2013) and has acquired the nickname "King James." In December 2014 he met some real royalty when Prince William and Duchess Kate visited with him after the Cavaliers–Nets game in Brooklyn. LeBron was thrilled as he tweeted his good fortune to followers and paid tribute to what basketball has done for him (Rosenthal 2014).

The losers in the quest for upward mobility through sport are the thousands of children who hold an unrealistic view of their potential and misjudge the odds of realizing their dreams. Leaders in the African American community decry the tendency of young black males to put all their hopes into a possible professional contract. Those goals are unrealistic for all but a special few, and when lower-class families emphasize sport over academics, most are setting their kids up for failure.

Arthur Ashe Jr. (featured in chapter 12) shared his views on the importance of education in a *New York Times* op-ed titled "Open Letter to Black Parents" (Ashe 1977). Although the statistics cited by Ashe have changed, the sentiments he expressed remain poignant and relevant:

> *Unfortunately, our most widely recognized role models are athletes and entertainers—"runnin'" and "jumpin'" and "singin'" and "dancin'." While we are 60 percent of the NBA, we are less than 4 percent of the doctors and lawyers. While we are about 35 percent of Major League Baseball, we are less than 2 percent of the engineers. While we are about 40 percent of the NFL, we are less than 11 percent of construction workers, such as carpenters and bricklayers. Our greatest heroes have been athletes such as Jack Johnson, Joe Louis, and Muhammad Ali. These were the ways out of the ghetto. We have been on the same road—sports and entertainment—too long. We need to pull over, fill up at the library, and speed away to Congress, the Supreme Court, the unions, and the business world.*

Yet the lessons learned through sport participation are also valuable for young athletes, even if a pro career is not in the cards. Hard work, determination, sacrifice, and teamwork can certainly be valuable assets in their future careers. Perhaps the optimistic view of social mobility through sport makes sense when considered in this light.

Chapter Summary

Although Americans prefer not to emphasize social classes, the economic differences between families in our society are clear. Of course, people in the upper socioeconomic classes prefer to maintain the status quo, since they are comfortable with their position. In addition to economic capital, social and cultural capital affect which sports people choose to watch and play; at the same time, through sport, people in lower classes may improve their social standing.

Strong relationships exist between social class and the types of sport that people tend to choose, both for participation and for watching. People from the upper classes tend to choose individual sports and sports that are often played at private clubs not open to the public. They also choose sports that are more expensive to pursue, whether for recreation or high-performance training.

Most people in the middle and working classes gravitate toward team sports that are more affordable. In most communities, children can take advantage of free or low-cost programs at the community level in order to begin playing a traditional team sport and then continue their career in the public schools at no cost. Team sports emphasize the traditional American values of hard work, discipline, determination, and teamwork. Athletes who do well are admired for their all-American values, whereas those who fail are criticized for supposed laziness or lack of effort.

Sport is controlled largely by people in charge of large media conglomerates; heads of professional sport leagues; heads of the Olympic Games; and owners of professional sport franchises, stadiums, and facilities. Almost without exception, these leaders in sport have been white males who tend to perpetuate the status quo, which has clearly favored them. They hold the power to make or prevent change in sport.

The odds are stacked against achieving rags-to-riches social mobility through success in sport. In spite of a few poster boys and girls who have risen from poverty to great riches, the majority of athletes never play professionally. However, using sport to build academic motivation or obtain funding for higher education may be an individual's best ticket to improving his or her social and economic class.

15

STUDENT OUTCOMES

After reading this chapter, you will know the following:

- Special populations in sport and the challenges they face in sport participation
- How the Americans with Disabilities Act has affected special populations
- The role of the American Association of People with Disabilities
- Sport opportunities for older adults and for people who are physically or mentally challenged
- Issues facing older athletes and those with a physical or mental disability

Special Populations and Sport

Special Populations and Sport

There is little question that American Trischa Zorn is the greatest Paralympian of all time. Blind since birth, she competed in seven consecutive Paralympic Games, from Arnhem in 1980 to Athens in 2004. Along the way, she captured an amazing 55 medals—41 gold, 9 silver, and 5 bronze—more than anyone else. She was inducted into the Paralympic Hall of Fame in 2012 in London and was included in an honorary list of the top dozen Paralympians of all time.

Zorn was recruited to the University of Nebraska in spite of being legally blind after missing the U.S. Olympic team by hundredths of a second as a 16-year-old backstroker. She went on to become a four-time All-American and three-time academic All-Big Eight honoree before graduating in 1987 with a degree in elementary and special education. After teaching for 10 years in the Indianapolis public schools, she decided at age 38 to go to law school. She completed her law degree with honors from Indiana University School of Law in 2005 and currently works for the United States Department of Veteran Affairs.

Born without irises in her eyes, Zorn was the first person with a congenital disability to receive artificial iris implants. Since birth she had only been able to see objects closer than three feet (about a meter) from her, but after her landmark surgery her vision has improved to 20/150. Zorn is just one of hundreds of exceptional athletes with a physical disability who display their prowess in worldwide competition at the Paralympic Games.

This chapter covers three unique populations in sport: people who are physically challenged, people who are mentally challenged, and older adults. Each group faces unique circumstances and has traveled a different path toward acceptance and accommodation in our society. Their widespread participation in sport and recreational activities is relatively recent, and it is now supported by the law at every level of government.

Nearly 57 million people in the United States have at least one physical or mental disability, and this number will increase as the average age of the population increases. According to the U.S. Census Bureau (U.S. Bureau of Labor Statistics 2012c), nearly 20 percent of U.S. residents have a disability. Yet historically, people with a disability have had few chances to pursue their American dream of equality of opportunity.

Things began to change dramatically when the federal government started enacting legislation—such as Title V of the Rehabilitation Act of 1973—addressing various issues of discrimination, including discrimination against those with a disability. Then in 1990, President George H.W. Bush signed the Americans with Disabilities Act (ADA), a landmark law that effectively limited long-standing discriminatory practices. These legislative acts brought about various changes, such as requiring that government buildings be accessible to people with a disability.

Older adults (age 50 or more) are often included as people with a disability as they begin to combat both physical and mental problems of aging. However, even for relatively fully functioning adults older than age 50, opportunities for sport participation are limited.

Life expectancy has steadily increased, and the maturing of the baby boomers has resulted in an explosion of older adults. The number of U.S. residents of age 50 or over reached 108 million in 2014, which means that they make up one-third of the total U.S. population (Gillian 2014). Furthermore, people over 50 account for more than 40 percent of consumer spending, and those over 55 own 77 percent of all financial assets in the United States (Ness 2012).

As the population ages and seeks a good quality of life, their focus lands on physical health and fulfilling social relationships. Sport and physical activity can contribute to a healthier lifestyle, help fight disease, and prolong life. To serve this burgeoning population, sport programs and physical exercise facilities are critically adjusting their marketing and programming strategies.

Americans with Disabilities Act

After a long and tedious battle to ensure the rights of all people with a disability, President George H.W. Bush signed the **Americans with Disabilities**

Act (ADA) into law in 1990. Before this legislation, living with a disability was often characterized by discrimination and segregation. The situation was not unlike that suffered for centuries by minorities and women. Since its passage, the ADA has been amended several times, and it will continue to be refined as court decisions clarify and interpret the law.

Unfortunately, some recent Supreme Court decisions have eroded ADA protections for people with a disability by placing severe restrictions on the class of people who are protected, narrowing the remedies available to complainants, and expanding the defenses available to employers. However, in the 2004 decision *Tennessee v. Lane*, the court ruled that the state of Tennessee must allow plaintiffs to sue for financial damages over inaccessible courthouses (United Cerebral Palsy 2004).

Let's review the history of laws preceding the ADA that removed barriers for various groups and laid the groundwork for a society that affirms the equality of people with a disability. In the late 1960s, major civil rights legislation changed the face of America. Led by Dr. Martin Luther King Jr., who envisioned a society that was just and inclusive for all as expressed in his famous "I Have a Dream" speech, the Civil Rights Movement created major changes in schools, businesses, public buildings, federal funding, transportation, and virtually every other area of life.

Many young people today have a hard time believing that until the 1960s African Americans were excluded from playing intercollegiate sport in most parts of the country and that no blacks appeared in the major professional sport leagues until the late 1940s. Baseball player Jackie

The ADA requires that adequate seating be provided for spectators with a disability.

Robinson was the first player to break the color barrier in 1947, and within 30 years black athletes were dominating U.S. professional basketball and football.

In the 1970s, women's rights took the stage. Although women had the right to vote, their rights in the workplace were abysmal, and their earning power was a fraction of that of males. Women began to claim an equal place in society and agitated for fairer opportunities. Title IX legislation established the equal rights of females in sport participation; in response, colleges, high schools, the media, and the public slowly adjusted to a world in which women, like men, could be fit and competitive and become champions.

In the late 1960s, the last of the major antidiscrimination statutes of the Civil Rights Movement was passed with the enactment of the Fair Housing Act. However, that act did not include people with a disability in its protected classes. Likewise, Title VII of the Civil Rights Act prohibited discrimination on the basis of race, religion, national origin, and sex in the sale and rental of housing—but again offered no protection for those with a disability.

Finally, in 1988, the Fair Housing Act was amended to add two new protected classes of people: those with a disability and families with children. Two years later, President H.W. Bush declared at the signing of the Americans with Disabilities Act, "This Act is powerful in its simplicity. It will ensure that people with disabilities are given the basic guarantees . . . of freedom of choice, control of their lives, [and] the opportunity to blend fully into the mosaic of the American mainstream" (Americans Disability Technical Assistance Centers 2004, 9).

The ADA addressed discrimination against those with a disability in general employment, state and local government, public accommodations, telecommunications, and transportation. The purpose of the law was to provide a clear and comprehensive national mandate to eliminate discrimination against individuals with a disability and to establish standards that are clear, strong, and enforceable. Over the past 15 years, many advances have been made as courts have upheld the law and interpreted its application and as organizations have adopted similar statements of inclusion for people with a disability.

In reading this brief historical review, you may have noticed how recently the developments occurred for creating fairness for people with a disability. Fortunately, businesses, schools, churches, public programs, organizations, and of course governments have all adjusted their practices to conform to the law. Current opportunities in sport participation emanate from this shift in societal attitude. Why shouldn't people with a disability have the same opportunities to enjoy sport and fitness activities that others enjoy? The challenge is to welcome their participation and accommodate their needs in the sporting world.

Although the last decade has seen quantum leaps in improving the quality of life for people with a disability, they still face significant inequalities in key areas of living (U.S. Bureau of Labor Statistics 2012c). Here are some key facts:

- Only 41 percent of people with a disability are employed, whereas 79 percent of those without a disability are employed.
- As compared with people who do not have a disability, three times as many people with a disability live in poverty, with an annual household income below $15,000 (this figure is adjusted yearly).
- Adults aged 21 to 64 with a disability had median monthly earnings of $1,961 versus $2,724 for those with no disability.
- People in the oldest age group (80 and older) were about eight times more likely (71 percent versus 8 percent) to have a disability than those in the youngest group (age 15 to 24).
- People with a disability are twice as likely to have transportation problems, and many go without needed health care.
- People with a disability are less likely than those with no disability to socialize, eat out, and attend religious services.
- Only 34 percent of people with a disability say they are very satisfied with life, whereas 61 percent of people with no disability say so.

Sport and recreation opportunities are less important than issues of fair housing, access to buildings, access to schooling, fair employment opportunities, and access to health care. At the same time, sport participation—whether at the competitive level or the participation level—enriches life for all of us.

EXPERT'S VIEW

Marc Sickel: Fitness for Health Founder

In 1986, inspired by his personal struggles with physical limitations as a child, Marc Sickel founded Fitness for Health, a fitness center that works exclusively with people who have a disability. He started the business to help children overcome physical, emotional, and neurological disabilities and has since expanded his services to accommodate all ages, including seniors who are concerned about overall wellness, bone and joint health, and fitness for daily activities.

Fitness for Health is on the cutting edge of the emerging "inclusive fitness" movement that is tailored to individuals with special needs. The U.S. Center for Disease Control and Prevention reports that half of the country's 21 million disabled adults either don't exercise regularly or don't exercise at all. In response, prestigious organizations that educate and certify physical trainers—such as the American College of Sports Medicine—began offering a specialty certification in 2008 in concert with the National Center on Health, Physical Activity, and Disability. At the same time, a growing number of universities are adding inclusive fitness to their curriculums as a field of study.

Fitness for Health works with people with a wide range of special needs and disabilities, including autism, cerebral palsy, attention-deficit/hyperactivity disorder (ADHD), Down Syndrome, and poor gross-motor skills. The professional staff is constantly adapting fitness equipment to accommodate visual perception training and sensory and motor integration feedback and to ensure that clients enjoy physical movement (Prince 2014).

American Association of People with Disabilities

The **American Association of People with Disabilities (AAPD)** was founded in 1995 as a nonprofit organization to represent all Americans with a disability. Family members and friends are welcome to join AAPD and are encouraged but not requited to contribute a tax deductible donation. AAPD was conceived and is advised and managed *by* people with a disability *for* people with a disability. It is not a government program. Although AAPD's mission is much broader than fairness in sport, it does provide leadership and engage in lobbying to ensure that recreational opportunities exist for its constituency.

According to AAPD (2015), more than one in five Americans—over 50 million people—have a disability. Nearly half of these people are of employable age, yet only one-third are employed. Government program plans that support working people with a disability cost U.S. taxpayers more than $357 billion each year, and a similar amount is lost in earnings and taxes because of this group's high rate of unemployment. People with a disability also constitute a significant consumer group, wielding more than $200 billion annually in discretionary spending and spurring technological innovation and entrepreneurship within business by sensitizing all employees to design products that can accommodate people with disabilities (Brault 2012).

Since the passage of the ADA, many sport-specific governing bodies have expanded their programs for people with a disability. As a result, you may notice pictures of physically disabled athletes in their literature, videos, and materials for coaching courses. Whenever possible, athletes with a disability are mainstreamed into regular sport programs, but athletes with a severe disability require specialized coaching and rules for competition.

Sport Participation for Athletes With a Physical Disability

According to the Americans with Disabilities Act, the term **disability** applies to any individual who has a physical or mental impairment that

POP CULTURE

Ice Warriors

If you're a sucker for gritty action, team and personal drama, and real-life heroism, then you won't want to miss *Ice Warriors.* This 2014 film is based on the quest of the U.S. Paralympic sledge hockey team to win a gold medal in Sochi, Russia. The team was made up of athletes whose disabilities derived from various causes—some congenital, others due to accident or illness, and some due to war injuries sustained in Iraq or Afghanistan. Two of the team's youngest players were best friends in high school who suffered together through the nightmare of a car accident, amputation, and then rehab.

The drama builds as Team USA loses early to Russia but rallies to defeat Canada in the semifinals, thereby earning another shot at the hometown Russians. Ignoring an enthusiastic crowd more than 7,000 strong—who screamed for the home team at the top of their lungs—the plucky Americans pulled out a breathtaking 1-0 victory for their second consecutive gold medal. If you loved the movie *Murderball* about wheelchair rugby players, then you won't want to miss *Ice Warriors.* It aired on PBS in November 2014, but you can access it online for a terrific hour and a half of entertainment (Mandell 2014; T. Porter 2014).

substantially limits one or more of the person's major life activities. For example, a physical disability might involve the loss of a limb, the loss of a sense such as hearing or sight, or other physical impairment due to disease or accident. In the conduct of sport, the degree of disability is taken into account in order to ensure fair competition.

The Paralympic Games are the second-largest sporting event in the world, trailing only the Olympics. The inaugural Paralympics were staged in 1960 in Rome and included about 400 athletes from 23 countries. In 2012 the Summer Paralympic Games in London attracted more than 4,000 athletes representing 164 countries and competing in 20 sports. The total in-person audience was 2.7 million, and it took the support and assistance of more than 70,000 volunteers to stage the event. In 2014, the Winter Paralympic Games in Sochi included 547 athletes from 45 countries competing in five sports—the newest of which was snowboarding. A record 316,000 spectators (86,000 more than in Vancouver in 2010) viewed the events, which were staged with the assistance of more than 4,000 volunteers (International Paralympic Committee 2014). The following sports are included in Paralympic competition:

Winter Games

- Alpine skiing, including snowboarding
- Biathlon
- Cross-country skiing
- Wheelchair curling
- Ice sledge hockey

Summer Games

- Archery
- Rugby
- Basketball
- Sailing
- Shooting
- Bocce
- Soccer
- Cycling
- Swimming
- Equestrianism
- Table tennis
- Fencing
- Tennis
- Men's goalball

Track and field
Judo
Volleyball
Powerlifting
Canoe
Rowing
Triathlon
Dance

Many of these sports are played using a wheelchair—for example, fencing, volleyball, basketball, rugby, dance, and tennis.

The mission of U.S. Paralympics is "to be the world leader in the Paralympic movement by developing comprehensive and sustainable elite programs for our athletes [and] . . . to utilize our Olympic and Paralympic platform to promote excellence in the lives of persons with disabilities." Founded in 2001, U.S. Paralympics is the division of the United States Olympic Committee (USOC) that focuses on enhancing programs, funding, and opportunities for persons with a physical disability to participate in sport (U.S. Paralympics 2015).

This is a clear statement of commitment to producing excellence in competitive sport by athletes with a physical disability. Because the Paralympic movement operates under the aegis of the USOC, it generally follows the Olympic model for the development of athletes and applies a similar philosophy and purpose. The Paralympic division oversees 5 winter sports and 22 summer Paralympic sports and serves as the national governing body for 6 of those sports.

In order to participate in the Paralympic Games, an athlete must meet eligibility standards established by the International Paralympic Committee. Eligible athletes include, for example, those with amputation, blindness or visual impairment, cerebral palsy, spinal cord injury, multiple sclerosis, or dwarfism. Eligible athletes who have qualified through competitive performance are selected for financial support, coaching assistance, and training for the next Paralympic Games. They are required to comply with the policies of the U.S. Anti-Doping Agency, including unannounced out-of-competition testing.

In 2000, the USOC put a comprehensive development plan in place to ensure that U.S. athletes with a disability have every chance of performing to their highest potential. Funds in excess of $23 million were committed between 2000 and 2004

IN THE ARENA WITH . . .

Esther Vergeer

How is it possible that a tennis player could win 470 matches in a row? You'd have to ask wheelchair champion Esther Vergeer from the Netherlands. She went undefeated from January 2003 until her final event before retiring at the Paralympics in London in 2012. And before that streak, she had won 89 straight matches to accumulate a record of 559 wins in 560 matches. Vergeer became a paraplegic after spinal surgery at age 8 but didn't pick up wheelchair tennis until age 12. She ended up dominating the sport by spending more than 13 years ranked number one in the world and winning 21 Grand Slam singles championships and four Paralympic gold medals.

Wheelchair tennis allows players to play the ball after the second bounce even outside of the boundaries of the court, which allows them to reach the ball despite having to maneuver their wheelchair into position. In fact, wheelchair players can compete against able-bodied players—and do so in both high school and college—with the only adjustment being that they are allowed the two bounces. Newly designed lightweight wheelchairs offer excellent mobility to allow players to move quickly around the court. Other than using the chair, they play the game in just the same way that is played by people without a disability.

TABLE 15.1 Paralympic Games—Total Medal Count by Country

2012 (London)		2014 (Sochi)	
China	231	Russia	33
Great Britain	120	United States	28
Russia	102	Norway	26
United States	98	Canada	25
Australia	85	Netherlands	24

to soliciting sponsors for support, educate the media, and provide coaches with training and support. Thanks to this effort, U.S. Paralympic athletes finished the 2012 Summer Games in London ranked fourth in the world after earning 98 medals. In the 2014 Winter Games in Sochi, the U.S. team finished second and earned 28 medals (see table 15.1).

Elite athletes don't just pop up. They develop over many years and require nurturing through expert coaching, organizational support, competitive events, and financial assistance. Grassroots programs that provide opportunities for athletes with a disability are scattered throughout the United States. They depend heavily on local leaders and dedicated coaches in each community.

The Paralympic Academy is an annual USOC-supported event that is held in each state. The various academies last one or two days each and are designed to introduce sport to potential Paralympic athletes aged 12 to 18. They also provide training for coaches, program administrators, families, and community leaders involved in local Paralympic sport programs. In addition, by attracting media attention, state academies help garner public attention and support for the mission.

The real work of ensuring equal opportunity for disabled athletes occurs at the community level. When practicable, programs should include all young athletes and make adaptations as required for athletes with a disability. This practice provides economy of operation and viable competition for athletes who may not find local events to participate in or other athletes to train with. A national competition is relatively easy to put in place because of the limited number of athletes involved, whereas aggressive efforts are needed if local programs are to flourish in every community in the country (U.S. Paralympics 2015).

Sport Participation for Athletes With a Mental Disability

According to the Special Olympics, people with a mental disability include those identified by an agency or professional as having intellectual disability, cognitive delay, or significant learning or vocational challenges due to cognitive factors that require specially designed instruction. Special Olympics is an international organization that involves 185 countries and serves more than 4.4 million people who have an intellectual disability. Founded in 1968 by Eunice Kennedy Shriver, the organization gives people with intellectual disability opportunities to develop their full potential, build their physical fitness, demonstrate courage, and experience joy and friendship through sport. It provides year-round sport training and competition.

Since its inception, Special Olympics has helped its athletes improve fitness, develop motor skills, increase self-confidence, and enhance self-image. The benefits—which make sport attractive to all athletes—have helped Special Olympians develop physically, socially, and spiritually. People with a profound disability can participate in Special

ACTIVITY TIME-OUT

Learn About Sport Wheelchairs

You might think that athletes who participate in wheelchair sport use a regular wheelchair both for daily use and for their sport. However, you really can't compete at your best unless you've got a custom-fitted sport chair, and it may even be designed for your favorite sport. Wheelchair sport has grown exponentially in recent years, and manufacturers continue to tinker with design, materials, balance, and weight to deliver high performance under challenging manipulation by competitive athletes.

Do some research and then summarize your findings in either a two-page paper or an oral report to your classmates. You might seek information about the cost of sport wheelchairs, critical design elements, materials, durability, and sport-specific customization. Can sport chairs work for daily use as well, or are they limited to sport activity? What about handcycles? How are they different, and what are they used for? Are chairs made just for kids or women, or does one chair fit all?

Olympics through the Motor Activity Training Program, which was developed by specialists and emphasizes training and participation rather than competition.

The worldwide reach of Special Olympics takes dramatic form in the Special Olympics World Games, which are held every four years for both summer and winter events. Previous editions have been held in Nagano, Japan (the first Games held in Asia, in which more than 1,800 athletes participated); Shanghai, China; and Athens, Greece (Special Olympics 2014). In 2015, the World Games returned to the United States after an absence of 16 years. Hosted in Los Angeles, the summer event drew 7,000 athletes who were supported by 3,000 coaches and 30,000 volunteers from 117 countries. The summer sports are aquatics, athletics, badminton, basketball, beach volleyball, bocce, bowling, cycling, equestrian, soccer, golf, gymnastics (artistic), gymnastics (rhythmic) handball, judo, half marathon, kayaking, open-water swimming, powerlifting, roller skating, sailing, softball, table tennis, tennis, triathlon, and volleyball. The winter sports are alpine skiing, cross-country skiing, snowshoeing, figure skating, floor hockey, snowboarding, and speed skating.

Special Olympics divides its operations into seven world regions: Africa, Asia Pacific, East Asia, Europe and Eurasia, Latin America, Middle East and North Africa, and North America. In the North American region, most U.S. states are home to a Special Olympics office that offers and coordinates Special Olympics activities in all 33 sports. Funding is provided by the international organization, along with local financial support.

The first Special Olympics were held in Chicago in 1968 and attracted 1,000 athletes from the United States and Canada. The inaugural Winter Games were held in 1977 in Colorado and involved 500 athletes. By 1987, the Summer Games had grown to include more than 4,700 athletes from 70 countries. A year later, the International Olympic Committee officially recognized Special Olympics. The Games continued to expand, and more than 7,000 athletes from 150 countries competed in the Special Olympics World Summer Games in 2003 in Dublin, Ireland—the first Special Olympics Summer Games ever held outside of the United States (Special Olympics 2014).

Coaches, family members, and other volunteers are essential to the Special Olympics sport programs. Most donate their time to the athletes and are rewarded with smiles, hugs, and satisfaction. These dedicated volunteers are the lifeblood of the organization, and they allow it to offer programs and competition at no charge to participants. To train coaches and officials for the Special Olympics, state organizations cooperate with various

IN THE ARENA WITH . . .

Eunice Kennedy Shriver, 1921–2009

Born into wealth and privilege—the fifth of nine children in what some have called the U.S. version of a royal family, the Kennedys—Eunice Kennedy Shriver chose to lobby for those who are powerless. Her older sister Rosemary had a "mild form of retardation," as it was called in her day. Rosemary was lobotomized in 1941 and spent most of her life in an institution; she died in 2005. While Eunice's brothers John and Robert went on to careers in politics and suffered untimely deaths, Eunice raised her own family of five children.

At the same time, she was keenly aware of larger realities. Worldwide, more than 200 million people in the world have an intellectual disability—about 6.5 million in the United States. More than 80 percent of people with an intellectual disability live in low-income countries.

Special Olympics defines intellectual disability as a condition involving an IQ below 75 that manifests before age 18. The disability may occur before or during childbirth or result from disease, injury, or another problem in the brain (Special Olympics 2014). Individuals with an intellectual disability are at greater risk than others for virtually every medical malady, including vision problems, tooth decay, and obesity. They were once locked away in institutions, and they are still bullied, sexually abused, ignored, and unemployed at far greater rates than the rest of the population.

Shriver's vision of athletic competition for people with an intellectual disability helped release an entire population from a prison of ignorance and misunderstanding. She often recited the Special Olympics oath: "Let me win. But if I cannot win, let me be brave in the attempt." Shriver's indomitable spirit carried her through the early days when the Special Olympics movement was called Camp Shriver and took place in her backyard. From there, it spread nationally and eventually internationally, and it has helped change laws and attitudes in every country regarding people with an intellectual disability.

In recognition of Shriver's contributions around the world, she received many honors and awards, including the Presidential Medal of Freedom, the highest civilian award given in the United States; the French Legion of Honor; induction into the National Women's Hall of Fame; the NCAA Theodore Roosevelt Award; and the International Olympic Committee Award. In addition, she received 14 honorary doctorates from prestigious universities, including Yale, Princeton, and Georgetown (Special Olympics 2014).

sport governing bodies. Since many athletes require personal support and supervision, the demands of coaching and officiating are extremely people intensive and require proper training.

Participation in Special Olympics is valued regardless of the participant's skill. To accommodate all, Special Olympics offers both performance and participation tracks; that is, events are held both for highly skilled athletes and for those whose athletic accomplishments are more modest (Special Olympics 2014).

Sport Participation for Older Athletes

No doubt you've heard about the aging population in the United States and its effect on health care and social security. The first "boomers" turned 65 in 2011, and that age group will be growing faster than the U.S. population in general. As of 2014, 108 million U.S. adults were over the age of 50—roughly one-third of the total population (Gillian 2014). Adults over age 55 control 77 percent of the

ACTIVITY TIME-OUT

Hook Up With Special Olympics in Your Area

If you would like to experience the thrill of volunteering with or coaching Special Olympians, you can locate programs in your area by visiting the organization's website to find contact information for your state office. The contact will be able to refer you to a program or competition in your area. The experience will be one that you never forget!

net worth of U.S. households, totaling $7 trillion, and account for twice the discretionary spending of younger market segments.

Many industries, including sport and fitness, are just beginning to recognize the potential of the aging adult marketplace (Ness 2012). The fitness industry is seeing the effects of the older population as those in the 55-plus and 65-plus age groups show a significant drop in inactivity, outpacing all other age groups. Older adults tend to prefer fitness activities over the team, outdoor, and individual sports that tend to attract younger participants (Sports and Fitness Industry Association 2014). As a result, the older group continues to drive the fitness industry by swelling membership rolls at health clubs, where they currently make up 25 percent of members (IBISWorld 2013). In fact, one chain of fitness centers—Welcyon, Fitness After 50—began in Minnesota and has spread through the Midwest in hopes of replicating what the Curves chain did for women (*Franchise Times* 2014).

As mentioned earlier, adults older than 50 years are often included among people with a disability due to disabilities associated with age. They also have organizations that advocate for their equal treatment. The largest and most powerful is AARP, which boasts a membership of more than 40 million people. AARP asserts a strong voice on issues such as taxation, insurance, health care, and social security—all of which older adults often deal with as they leave the workforce. Due to the wide diversity of physical needs faced by AARP members, the group encourages Americans to engage in at least the minimum amount of physical activity recommended by the U.S. Surgeon General. This can be achieved by walking several times per week or participating in other forms of moderate physical activity.

The International Council on Active Aging (ICAA) is a relatively new group that promotes quality of life, physical activity, and sport participation by older adults. It publishes a newsletter and a bimonthly magazine, *Journal on Active Aging*. ICAA also hosts conferences to share research information and educate people about creative approaches to innovative programming, staff training, and product selection to assist in the aging process. Its more than 5,000 members include many commercial organizations and health clubs seeking to accommodate older adults in their programs and facilities (ICAA 2010).

Performance Sport for Older Adults

In most sport organizations, senior divisions for competition have existed for years, though historically most of them began at age 35 or 40. Today, thanks to increases in life expectancy, being 35 or 40 hardly makes one a senior athlete. Senior divisions are now called **masters** divisions and usually begin at age 50. By that age, most athletes are unable to compete physically with younger people who are in their physical prime, so they seek competition within their own age group for both social and competitive reasons.

A few remarkable older athletes do continue to compete with younger athletes. One example is Martina Navratilova, who was still competing in the main women's professional tennis tour when she turned 50 in 2006. For most athletes, however, masters competitions such as the Senior Olympics and the Senior PGA tour provide an opportunity to continue testing their skills and satisfying their competitive drive.

In 2015, for instance, more than 12,000 athletes competed in 19 sports at the National Summer Senior Games (aka Senior Olympics) held in Bloomington-Minneapolis-St. Paul, Minnesota. The minimum age for entry is 50, and athletes are divided into age groups at five-year increments. The Games began in 1987, and now more than 35 percent of the competitors are female.

The Senior Olympics negotiated with the USOC to obtain usage rights to the Olympic name, though the senior organization as a whole is now referred to as the National Senior Games Association. Its Summer Games include archery, bowling, badminton, basketball, cycling, golf, horseshoes, race walking, racquetball, road racing, shuffleboard, swimming, table tennis, tennis, softball, track and field, triathlon, volleyball, and (its newest sport) pickleball.

Competitors qualify for the national events through state events held annually in the various age divisions. Most of these athletes have been competing all their life and have slowed down the aging process by improving their diet, working on their fitness, and keeping up with the latest advances in sport science and sports medicine (National Senior Games Association 2010).

Clearly, however, older adults suffer in performance capacity as compared with younger competitors; specifically, research has shown that after age 50 physical ability declines by about 1 percent per year up to age 80, when it begins to decline more rapidly (World of Sports Science 2009). One of the constant struggles for most senior athletic competitions involves the question of whether to admit only the best athletes or to encourage virtually all senior athletes to compete as part of the quest for a healthier lifestyle. To resolve this dilemma, most senior competitions set up a logical

EXPERT'S VIEW

The International Council on Active Aging

Colin Milner is chief executive officer of the International Council on Active Aging (ICAA), a coalition of more than 8,200 organizations that manage, own, or operate more than 40,000 locations (such as retirement communities, senior centers, rehabilitation centers, and workplace wellness and fitness centers) in 37 countries around the world. Milner founded the organization in 2001 to "change the way we age" by embracing the aging process through promotion of good health, disease prevention, and living life to the fullest. He is recognized by the World Economic Forum as one of "the most innovative and influential minds" in the world on aging-related topics (ICAA 2015).

Among a host of strategic actions, the two initiatives of the organization that stand out most are the ICAA conference and the *Journal on Active Aging*. The annual conference brings together professionals from around the world who spend a week networking and learning from each other, as well as listening to outstanding speakers and authors in the field of aging. By sharing creative program approaches, practical philosophies, and innovative new products and equipment, attendees stay on the cutting edge of active aging. The *Journal on Active Aging* is published six times per year and filled with articles that help professionals stay current in the field, challenge their creativity, and inspire them to push forward against the inevitable obstacles they face.

ICAA's active aging philosophy aims to change the way people age by helping them stay active in all areas of life: physical, spiritual, emotional, intellectual, professional, and social. The philosophy embraces a concept of being "engaged in life" that encourages older adults to participate fully in life regardless of socioeconomic status or health conditions. For more information about ICAA, visit its website at www.icaa.cc.

qualifying process for progressively higher levels of competition.

Participation Sport for Older Adults

As the U.S. population continues to tilt toward older adults, all trends point toward an explosion in physical activity among people over age 50 in the next few decades. Indeed, many people now consider 50 to be middle age and expect to live another 25 years or more. They want those years to be fun, vital, and active. In this quest, of course, their health is a major concern, and slowing the aging process is a top priority.

Recreational sport offers the best opportunity for older people to have fun, enjoy activity, test their skills, socialize with age peers, and stay fit. In addition, every community offers free or low-cost programs for its citizens, and now more of these programs are beginning to target adults who are 50 or older.

Older adults are turning to activities and sports in which they can participate for a lifetime—for example, swimming, walking, tennis, golf, dance, biking, skiing, bowling, yoga, and weight training. In addition, some team sports—such as softball, basketball, and volleyball—are also thriving with the use of rule adjustments and age-specific groupings to ensure competitive parity. In contrast, as people age, they are less likely to choose sports that require maximum strength, quick bursts of energy, and body contact—all of which increase the risk of injury.

Most people who are 50 or older still crave the excitement of participating in sport, want to stay fit, and enjoy the intellectual challenge of trying to outsmart an opponent. They also still gain confidence and get a "high" from competing or moving vigorously. In short, they value the experience of youthfulness, and sport helps them attain it. Indeed, though they may reduce the frequency, duration, or intensity of their sport participation, they may enjoy it even more. Rules, rankings, and awards are less important to many people who have enjoyed achievements earlier in their life, and now the simple fact of getting to play offers its own reward.

In St. Petersburg, Florida, the legendary Kids and Kubs softball league has been around for nearly 85 years. The club's 56 members gather at 10:30 a.m. in North Shore Park to play a doubleheader every Tuesday, Thursday, and Saturday. They divide into two teams and go at it. The minimum age is 75! One player, Paul Good, who was 95 at the time, said, "It adds years to your life and life to your years!" Some years ago, the club reached a landmark when George Bakewell took the field at age 101 along with his son Elton, who was 75. Ethel Lehmann broke the gender barrier in 2005 by joining the group at age 75 along with her husband (*St. Petersburg Times* 2005).

The Kids and Kubs pay about $100 per year to play, and they must purchase a team uniform, two pairs of white pants, and a Kid and Kubs T-shirt. Team members look forward to exhibition games against local politicians, kids, and other older players. They also travel to other states to test themselves. The annual road trip in 2008 featured a much-anticipated sojourn in Hawaii, where they competed with a Japanese team. All of the players were old enough to have potent memories of the military combat galvanized by the Japanese bombing of Pearl Harbor. Kids and Kubs has also sent teams to senior world championships around the country, winning the over-80 division in 1998 and finishing third in the 1999 Senior World Softball Championships. Their next step is to establish feeder leagues in nearby communities such as Tampa, Sarasota, and Bradenton to start training "youngsters" who can eventually move up to their league.

Not to be outdone, the Freedom Spirit senior women's softball team (age 70 and older) in Clearwater, Florida, has competed in national tournaments since 1995. The team has been quite successful at the World Senior Games, winning three straight gold medals between 2001 and 2005 and then adding five silver medals and two bronze. Their leader and co-founder, Ethel Lehman, is now 85 and also plays for the Kids and Kubs. She has been featured in the Personal Best Athlete Profile by the National Senior Games Association (2014).

In tennis, the United States Tennis Association holds national championships for men 90 and over and for women 85 and over. Though some seniors still play singles, most opt for doubles play, and matches are typically just two sets long with a 10-point tiebreak instead of a third set if necessary. Similarly, in golf, tournaments are held based on age groups, and a senior professional tour showcases some excellent golf. One concession to age for many senior players is to seek out golf courses that are considerably shorter to compensate for their diminishing power.

Many older people who value being physically active are also heading to the gym. In fact, this age group has swelled the membership rolls of fitness clubs in recent years, participating in activities such as yoga, strength training, treadmill running, and various other group exercise programs. Even among those who are not currently physically active but aspire to be, the activities that are highest on their list after age 55 are swimming for fitness, fitness classes, hiking, working out with free weights, and working out with machines (Sports and Fitness Industry Association 2014).

Issues for Special Populations in Sport

Although many sport opportunities have opened up for special populations, we must further expand the opportunities for older athletes and athletes with a disability in order to meet the needs of this rapidly growing group. As the demographics shift to an older population, the proportion of people in these categories will increase, as will demand for the following:

- Widespread acceptance of the need for sport for special populations
- Funding support from public and private sources
- Organizational support by all sport bodies, including national sport governing bodies
- Programs offered at the community level through parks and recreation departments
- Training for coaches, officials, and sport administrators who understand and want to work with the target populations
- Equipment and rule modifications that allow special populations to participate in sport
- Sport opportunities that include all athlete populations when appropriate
- Media support for publicity and information

All people should have access to participation in recreational sport regardless of age or disability. While most people acknowledge this fact, conflict arises when programs do not exist or budgets do not permit expanded activities. In some sport activities, it works well to include special populations with the general population, but combining all populations is not always possible. Similarly, aging can prevent players from competing with younger players in a meaningful way; in those cases, senior or masters categories usually spaced in five-year intervals is the typical solution. Public programs in schools and recreation departments should be required to provide access for older adults and athletes with a disability.

Pickleball

Pickleball was invented in 1965 in Bainbridge Island, Washington, and it has recently undergone a rebirth due to its popularity in active-living adult communities. It's a combination of tennis, table tennis, and badminton played on a court the size of a badminton court. It uses rules similar to tennis, a wooden paddle, and a perforated plastic ball (think Wiffle ball). It is also easy to learn yet attracts skilled athletes as well. The hottest spot in the country for pickleball is The Villages, an active-living adult community in central Florida with more than 80,000 residents, 150 outdoor pickleball courts, and more than 2,000 regular players.

The USA Pickleball Association sets the rules, provides information, and even stages a national championship divided by age groups. What makes it so appealing? Well, it appeals to the baby boomers who want to be physically active and socially involved but are looking for a sport that isn't too hard on their bodies. The game requires less running than tennis or badminton but calls for similar skills. For more information, visit USA Pickleball's website at www.usapa.org.

Advances in equipment, such as this four-wheeled mountain bike, have made it possible for athletes with disabilities to enjoy many sports that were once unavailable to them.

Sport organizations at every level should seek ways to accommodate special populations. High school and collegiate sport have barely scratched the surface of possible inclusion. For example, numerous tennis players using wheelchairs have competed on their high school varsity teams and gone on to compete in college. In 2003, a wheelchair user from Oakville High School in St. Louis, Missouri, received his varsity letter after compiling a 15-3 win–loss record during his senior year. The only concession to wheelchair players in such competition is that they may play the ball after two bounces rather than the customary one bounce. This simple change has allowed nondisabled and physically disabled players to compete with each other—a perfect example of a policy of inclusion (Woods 2004).

Community sport programs typically cannot accommodate special populations because there are not enough participant to form a functional group in a given age group or ability level. As a result, they need to explore creative methods of including these populations in existing programs. However, as the older population groups continue to increase, more programs for older adults are springing up due to the demand and the availability of so many older players.

Educational conferences and programs of study need to be sponsored by organizations that serve people who are elderly or disabled and by sport governing bodies and colleges and universities. Training is sorely needed in order to help coaches, officials, and sport administrators work effectively with special populations. People with sport experience are good candidates to fill these roles, but more people are needed who have a particular interest in serving these populations. Family members and friends should be recruited, trained, and put to work.

Equipment advances have made sport participation possible for many older or physically disabled athletes. For example, lightweight sport wheelchairs permit athletes to play a variety of sports, including basketball, tennis, fencing, volleyball, and rugby. Similarly, lighter bats, golf clubs, and rackets allow easy manipulation by athletes. In addition, artificial prostheses allow athletes without limbs to run, jump, and play sports in ways never imagined in the past. Likewise, aids for people with visual or hearing impairment allow them to track balls, run on their own, and play multiple sports.

Finally, the media must help educate the public about the needs of special populations. Television features about older athletes and those with a disability serve as powerful tools in garnering public support for sport access for all athletes. Movies can also affect the general population's understanding of, and empathy for, the experiences of special populations. For example, the award-winning 2005 documentary *Murderball* was rated as the number one sport movie of all time by the popular movie-review website Rotten Tomatoes. The film examines the sport of wheelchair rugby, which is a combination of wheelchair basketball, ice hockey, handball, and rugby union. Competitors must have at least some loss of function in at least three limbs and are typically quadriplegic. The sport is played in 25 countries and is a summer Paralympic sport.

Many other films also feature people triumphing over disability; examples include *Ray*, *My Left Foot*, *The Miracle Worker*, *Johnny Belinda*, *Children of a Lesser God*, *Rain Man*, *Elephant Man*, and *A Beautiful Mind*. Through these films, people became and continue to become enlightened and inspired by the challenges and successes of populations that many know little about.

Chapter Summary

This chapter identifies special populations as athletes who are older adults or who have a physical or mental disability. Members of these groups face challenges that affect their chances for sport participation.

In recent years, national laws have been passed to protect these three populations in the United States. For example, the Americans with Disabilities Act, passed in 1990, has spurred greater understanding of the need to accommodate people with special needs.

Physically disabled athletes may compete nationally and internationally under the supervision of the Paralympic Games. Much like the Olympic Games, the Paralympics are contested every four years in both winter and summer events. Medals are awarded in 25 sports, and more than 5,000 athletes compete at each Para-

APPLYING SOCIAL THEORY

Social Theory and Special Populations

You now have some idea of the challenges involved in providing sport and physical activity opportunities for older people and people with a physical or mental disability. Such opportunities may take the form of competitive sport organized by age groups, modified sport that accommodates disabilities, or simply opportunities to participate in vigorous physical activity as a healthy form of recreation. Challenges in delivering such programs include issues of funding, equipment modification, programming, coaching, and publicity.

Consider the social theories you studied in chapter 2. Which of those theories would be most likely to address the needs of these populations? Choose the theory that would likely carry the banner and explain your choice.

lympic Games. (The London summer Games had more than 4,000 athletes and the Sochi winter Games attracted nearly 550 athlete.)

Athletes with an intellectual disability may compete in the Special Olympics, which hosts state, national, and international competition. More than 4.4 million athletes are involved in the Special Olympics movement, and that number is expected to continue to grow worldwide.

Older athletes, often referred to as masters athletes, also compete worldwide. Age-based categories (up to and including 90 years of age) ensure equitable competition in various sports staged in the United States by the National Senior Games Association. The achievements of these older athletes are becoming increasingly inspirational to an aging population looking for healthy challenges in their later years.

Participation sport for older athletes and athletes with a disability is not as well organized as performance sport but is offered throughout the United States. Typically, these activities are sponsored by schools, recreation departments, and other local sport organizations. They emphasize healthy physical activity to enhance quality of life. Efforts to include people with special needs in mainstream sport programs are growing and gaining acceptance.

To ensure continued progress in sport for special populations, we must address some key issues. Among them are consistent funding; education of coaches, officials, and sport administrators; effective publicity; and support from sport organizations at every level.

STUDENT OUTCOMES

After reading this chapter, you will know the following:

- How religion has affected sport throughout history
- The interrelationship of sport and religion
- How athletes use religion in sport
- How institutions and organizations use both religion and sport
- How coaches and sport organizers use religion
- Conflicts involving religion and sport

Religion and Sport

Religion and Sport

In 2014, North Carolina Mooresville High School football coach Hal Capps was ordered by his school to stop leading his players in prayer before and after games and to stop participating in baptisms of his players. More generally, U.S. courts have made it clear that coaches should not organize, lead, or participate in prayer or other religious proselytizing before, during, or after a game or practice. Yet in many school systems, particularly in the southern United States, many people believe that team prayers can be a positive thing.

For example, one recent poll showed that 40 percent of Americans take a favorable view of athletes' public expressions of faith, whereas 32 percent don't care and only 19 percent take a negative view (Grey Matter Research 2012). Expressions of faith by athletes may take the form of speaking about it in interviews, making religious signs such as crossing oneself, or pointing heavenward or kneeling down to face Mecca after making a good play. Will people endorse the rights of athletes to express their religious beliefs in ways that are unfamiliar? A sidebar later in this chapter featuring Husain Abdullah, a devout Muslim playing in the NFL, explores this question.

Religion is belief in a god or supernatural force that influences human life. Humans in every society on record have created belief systems about the supernatural. Such beliefs are often essential to the core structure of a society, and they help humans understand their purpose for living and how they should spend their days, treat others, and deal with death and the question of an afterlife. Indeed, religion plays a central role in helping people find purpose and meaning in life, in allaying fears of the unknown, and in providing guidelines for interacting with others. It can also provide a basis for moral codes that keep society functioning and respectful of all persons. Shared religious customs can bind people together through common acts and unite them in spirit.

More than a quarter of people in the United States say that God influences the outcome of sporting events. According to a survey by the Public Religion Research Institute, more than half of U.S. residents also believe that "God rewards athletes who have faith with good health and success." When asked if God plays a role in who wins, 27 percent said yes, though the results varied across regions and religions: 36 percent in the South, 28 percent in the Midwest, 20 percent in the Northeast, and 15 percent in the West. Other proportions of those saying yes included the following: 40 percent of nonwhite Christians, 38 percent of white evangelicals, 29 percent of Catholics, and 19 percent of white mainline Protestants (Public Religion Research Institute 2013).

Religion and sport share a common trait in that both have been labeled as an "opiate of the masses" (Hoffman 1992). In the 1800s, Karl Marx wrote in *The Communist Manifesto* that religion was used as an opiate by governments to distract people from their miserable life and instead focus them on an afterlife. Similarly, people have accused political leaders of encouraging sport participation and spectatorship in order to distract citizens from economic or political concerns (see chapter 17).

At first glance, sport and religion may seem unrelated. Throughout history, however, people have often linked the two and blended them into their belief system. At times, organized religion has been at odds with sport and has viewed games as not worthy of humankind. The belief was that people live on earth to develop their spiritual side and that pursuing leisure through sport simply detracts from that mission.

One of the main reasons that the Americas were explored and settled was the possibility of religious freedom. Still, though many athletes in many sports have followed religions other than Christianity, no religion has dominated U.S. sport as the Christian faith has. Thus, much of the discussion in this chapter focuses on Christianity, but certain sections deal specifically with the Jewish and Muslim faiths. In 2012, people of the Jewish faith made up 1.7 percent of the total U.S. population, and Muslims accounted for 0.6 percent.

U.S. trends in religious affiliation are shown in figure 16.1 and table 16.1. The research, conducted by the Pew Research Center (2012a), revealed that the U.S. population self-identifies primarily as Christian. It is also continuing to become less Christian, due primarily to an increase in people who classify themselves as unaffiliated—that is, who

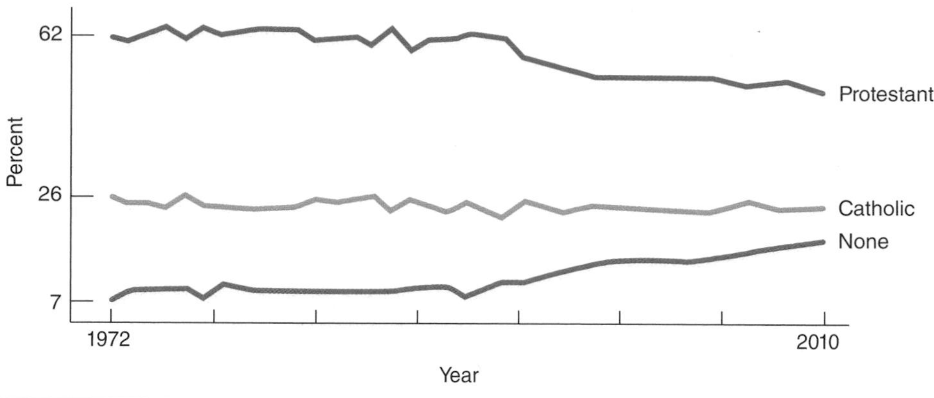

FIGURE 16.1 Long-term trends in religious affiliation in the United States.
Adapted from Pew Research Center 2013.

have no stated religious preference or identify as atheists or agnostics. This group increased from 16 percent in 2008 to 20 percent in 2012.

In 1990, 86 percent of U.S. residents identified themselves as Christian, but by 2008 that percentage had fallen to 77 percent and by 2012 to 73 percent. The 2012 results also marked the first time in Pew Research Center surveys that the percentage of Protestants dipped below 50 percent.

The historic mainline churches and denominations have suffered the steepest declines, whereas nondenominational Christian churches have trended upward. The number of white "born-again" (evangelical) Protestants held steady at 19 percent, whereas the proportion of those who identified as white mainline Protestants declined from 18 percent in 2008 to 15 percent in 2012 (Pew Research Center 2012a).

TABLE 16.1 U.S. Trends in Religious Affiliation, 2008–2012

Religious affiliation	2008 %	2010 %	2012 %
Christian (total)	77	76	73
Protestant	52	51	48
Catholic	22	23	22
Mormon	2	2	2
Orthodox	1	1	1
Other, including Jewish and Muslim	5	5	6
Unaffiliated	16	17	20
Don't know	2	2	2

Some totals don't add to 100 due to rounding.
Adapted from Pew Research Center 2012a.

ACTIVITY TIME-OUT

Effect of Muslim Religion on Sport

After Christianity, Islam ranks second in world popularity. Investigate how sport or sport participation is affected in countries with a Muslim majority. For example, look into how it affects youth sport, school sport, elite competition in world events (including the Olympics), participation by women and girls, or the popularity of professional sport. You might also explore whether sport in Muslim-majority countries tends to be conducted independently of the predominant religion—or are sport and religion closely intertwined?

In today's sport world, we may see athletes praying together before or after a contest, making the sign of the cross before attempting a foul shot in basketball, crediting God for a victory, or quoting scripture to justify their pursuit of excellence in sport. In the last century, organized religious leaders have gradually embraced sport as another avenue by which to reach the masses and influence their behavior toward what they envision as a worthy, godly existence. This change in philosophy has given rise to the particular interrelationship of religion and sport that exists today. In that context, this chapter examines the interplay between religion and sport, the use of sport within religion, and the use of religion within sport.

Religion and Sport in History

The ancient Greeks mingled religion with athletics; in fact, demonstrations of athletic prowess formed a major part of their religious festivals. The Greeks portrayed their gods as perfect physical specimens who took pleasure in the pursuit of physical excellence. They held the Olympic Games and their athletic contests to honor Zeus, the king of their gods.

The Olympic Games were suspended, however, by the Roman emperor Theodosius I, who as a Christian wanted to stamp out paganism. In those days, the Games were a series of pagan rituals that featured many footraces along with some "sports" that were violent and life threatening. Favorites included chariot races in which horses and drivers risked life and limb. Also popular was *pankration*, a no-holds-barred combat sport that melded elements of boxing, wrestling, and street fighting (Gertz 2004). Often, the festivals also included animal sacrifices.

Early Christians did not think that sport was evil, and the apostle Paul wrote approvingly of physical activity. But the history of paganism surrounding sport events caused the early church to separate itself from the sports engaged in by the pagan masses. In addition, some church leaders felt that the body was inherently evil and should be subordinated to the spirit. Therefore, they viewed time spent in exercising the body as detracting from time that should be devoted to the spirit.

The church's negative attitude toward sport might have declined with the advent of the Protestant Reformation in the early 16th century. However, the Puritanical interpretation of religion that was eventually transported to America embraced a new asceticism that pushed the physical side even further into the background. The Puritans believed that the body's only purpose was to perform the physical labor necessary for survival. They thought that no time should be spent in leisure pursuits, and they saw evil in pursuits that involved gambling, harmed animals (as in cockfighting), or pleased the participants (Eitzen and Sage 2002).

By the mid-1850s, however, people in the United States began to change their attitude toward sport. As the population shifted from rural to urban—and production shifted from manual labor to the industrial age—physical well-being became a concern. Under the leadership of physicians and, surprisingly, ministers, the notion of a sound body achieved through physical activity once again gained favor. Leading universities hired medical doctors to promote the health of their students, and those doctors founded departments of physical education. Influential Christian men, labeled "muscular Christians," extolled physical fitness as a virtue that fit well with godly behavior as a means to glorify God. Near the end of the century, this emerging acceptance of a positive link between body and spirit led to the founding of the Young Men's Christian Association (YMCA, now known as the Y).

Although churches still battled to set aside the Sabbath (Sunday) as a holy day of rest, church leaders began to accept and even promote sport, as long as it did not interfere with developing the people's spiritual side. The lone holdout to this trend was the Congregational Church in New England, which in 1957 became the United Church of Christ; this church viewed sport and games as inconsistent with developing the soul.

In the 20th century, the bond between sport and religion expanded in the United States in ways never envisioned by the founding fathers. In fact, sport and religion became established as two institutions that often cooperate to promote a better life for their constituencies. Churches sponsor sport, and many sport figures promote churches. Some people have even declared that sport is a religion, though that view is difficult to substantiate.

Christian Influence on Sport

Eventually, churches realized that they could attract people to their doors by offering social occasions that involved sport. As a result, they constructed gymnasiums, sponsored basketball and softball teams, provided playing fields, and encouraged people to come for the sport and stay for the Sunday services. For example, the Catholic Church founded the Catholic Youth Organization to organize sport leagues for young people, and Protestant groups supported the YMCA and the Young Women's Christian Association.

Housed in gymnasiums around the country, the Ys became a powerful force in providing organized sport for youth while espousing a broader purpose of developing their minds and spirits. Accordingly, the hallmark of the Y movement was the famous triangle representing mind, body, and spirit. The YMCA even established what is now Springfield College in Massachusetts to train its instructors. In fact, for many years, Springfield College was the preeminent institution for studying physical education and sport.

Another major contribution to U.S. sport emanated from Springfield and the YMCA in 1891, when Canadian James Naismith invented basketball—a game that became the most-played sport in the United States and is now taking off

POP CULTURE

Holy Goals for Body and Soul

Bishop Thomas John Paprocki is a native of Chicago's south side who has been playing ice hockey since the 1960s. Today, he still plays goalie in a masters hockey league, and in his spare time he runs marathons. He draws lessons from his experiences in competitive sport and applies them to daily life. He also finds purpose in helping young adults connect sport with God in their lives, and that is the focus of his book *Holy Goals for Body and Soul: Eight Steps to Connect Sports With God and Faith* (2013). In Paprocki's view, everyone is called to a life of holiness, which can be encountered and strengthened during a workout at a health club or in training for a marathon. In drawing parallels between sport and life, he explores eight "F words": fear, frustration, failure, fortitude, faith, friendship, family, and fun. "Who better than a Catholic bishop who plays goalie to make the connections between sports and the challenges of daily living?" says Tony Esposito, Hall of Fame goalie for the Chicago Black Hawks.

worldwide. A few years later and just a few miles from Springfield, William Morgan invented volleyball at the YMCA in Holyoke, Massachusetts. Thus, two popular team sports indigenous to the United States were produced by the YMCA.

The sport world welcomed the backing of religion since it promised to spread access to sport for the average citizen. Athletes also seized upon religion as a way of addressing their fears in the face of competition. Whereas some athletes are simply superstitious, others use their religious beliefs as part of their effort to stay safe, find good luck, and calm their nerves. Many athletes acknowledge praying before important contests and attest to achieving focus through prayer.

Athletes also use religion to ascribe a deeper sense of purpose to their sport participation. Powerful motivation can be obtained from the belief that God's will calls them to develop their talent in order to glorify God. Some athletes believe that God has a plan for their life that involves their becoming a top athlete. Others justify their consuming passion for sport by using their sport success to gain the attention of fans and testify about their faith in God.

Christian athletes often quote Scripture to justify their complete dedication to sport and hard work as a way of glorifying God. In this vein, one favorite verse for some athletes is I Corinthians 9:24: "Surely you know that in a race all the runners take part in it, but only one of them wins the prize. Run, then, in such a way as to win the prize." Another favorite is found in I Timothy 4:7–8: "I have fought a good fight, I have finished my course, I have kept the faith" (Deford 1976, 92–99).

Coaches and owners of sport teams often promote the link between sport and religion because it reinforces a code of conduct that they prefer for their athletes. At the same time, the sport pages are full of tales of professional athletes involved in violence, drugs, cheating, promiscuity, and alcohol abuse. In many cases, the athletes in these stories lack a personal religious belief or other strong moral code that might have prevented dubious choices. Their stories of rehabilitation often involve acceptance of a new moral code based on religious belief and reinforced by teammates and friends who are fellow believers (Coakley 2004).

Protestantism has always preached absolute belief in the value of hard work, self-discipline, and striving for success. Indeed, in the United States, those characteristics are widely considered to be all-American and to provide the very foundation of the nation. These values are endorsed beyond all others by athletic coaches in this country, and even the most talented athletes cannot reach their full potential unless they have at least a nodding acquaintance with hard work and self-discipline. The lessons learned on the playing field and extolled in the sanctuaries of churches are often identical: Work hard, play hard, and do your best to win every day!

According to Overman (1997), traditional Catholic doctrine emphasized that the body was a "temple of the Holy Spirit" and therefore should be kept pure rather than developed through physical activity. Protestants, on the other hand, trumpeted competition as an opportunity for people to prove their value through achievement and become the best they could be. In more recent times, both Catholicism and Protestantism have fully embraced sport as a special way of glorifying God by developing physical and competitive skill.

Because the belief systems of Protestantism, sport, and to some extent Catholicism are so closely intertwined, they have developed considerable synergy. They each reinforce the value system of the others and together help young people organize their lives according to the code of both church and sport. Religion and sport share a tendency to resist social change and to maintain the status quo that benefits both institutions.

Sport and Religions Other Than Christianity

Religions directly affect their believers' attitudes toward physical activity, sport, and competition; in many cases, they also set different standards for males and females. The result is that sport in a given culture may be either promoted or severely restricted according to the culture's religious teachings. Table 16.2 indicates the global strength of major world religions. Here, we focus on Judaism and Islam, both of which have significantly influenced North America and other parts of the world.

Judaism

Although Jews make up just 0.2 percent of the world's population, Judaism has played a prominent role in the United States because its religious beliefs are part of the general Judeo-Christian heritage. The Old Testament recounts the history

TABLE 16.2 Size of Major Religious Groups Worldwide, 2012

Religious Group	Worldwide %
Christianity	31.5
Islam	23.2
Unaffiliated	16.3
Hindu	15
Folk (includes African traditional, Chinese folk, Native American religions, and Australian aboriginal)	6
Buddhism	7.1
Other (Bahai, Sikhism, Shintoisam, Taoism, Wicca, Zoroastrianism)	0.8
Judaism	0.2

Data from Pew Research Center 2012b.

of the Hebrew people, and Jesus Christ of the New Testament was a Jew. Thus the early Christians were essentially Jews, and the Christian religion that developed and expanded around the world had its roots in Judaism.

Jews have played a somewhat obscure role in sport, probably because they make up a relatively small proportion of the U.S. population. Yet they have affected American sport through enviable success in boxing. Many Jewish athletes have also been celebrated for their achievements in the Maccabiah Games, a unique event similar to the Olympics but open only to participants from a Jewish background.

Perhaps the best-known Jewish athletes in U.S. sport have been Hank Greenberg, a slugger for the Detroit Tigers in the 1940s, and Sandy Koufax, a Hall of Fame pitcher for the Brooklyn and Los Angeles Dodgers. The most prominent Jewish baseball player since Koufax has been Shawn Green of the Los Angeles Dodgers, who at one point ranked number two in salary behind superstar Alex Rodriguez of the New York Yankees. All of these athletes were challenged by fans and the media for their decisions not to play baseball on Yom Kippur, the holiest day of the year for Jews and a day when they atone for their sins. In spite of the pressure to play in the World Series or playoffs, these principled men chose to put their beliefs before their livelihood.

Other notable Jewish athletes have included Sid Luckman, quarterback for the Chicago Bears, and Red Auerbach, a coaching legend who led the Boston Celtics when they dominated the National Basketball Association (NBA). Perhaps the most amazing achievement by any Olympic athlete was the 1972 performance by Mark Spitz, who won seven gold medals in swimming. Other Olympic champions who were Jewish include Kerri Strug, a gymnast who won a gold medal at the 1996 Summer Games, and Sarah Hughes, a gold medalist in figure skating at the 2002 Winter Games. Professional tennis players who left their mark include Brad Gilbert and Aaron Krickstein, as well as Eddie Dibbs and Harold Solomon, who were dubbed the "Bagel Twins" (Slater 2003).

The first half of the 20th century was blessed with the golden age of sport, particularly in the 1920s and 1930s. During that time, Jewish men dominated American boxing in virtually every weight class except heavyweight and won some 30 world boxing titles. The most famous of these boxers were Benny Leonard and Barney Ross, who stood out in the 1930s. Jewish men pursued boxing because, like other poor immigrants to the United States, they viewed it as an avenue of hope. Other ethnic groups who have dominated boxing at one time or another include the Irish, the Polish, Puerto Ricans, African Americans, and, more recently, Latinos and Hispanics.

Jewish basketball players also flourished in inner-city basketball long before African Americans began to dominate the sport. During the 1940s, Jewish boys who were the sons of immigrants played street basketball in cities such as New York and Chicago and laid the groundwork for the NBA. In fact, in 1946, the first basket scored in the Basketball Association of America, the forerunner of the NBA, was scored by Ossie Schectman, a Jewish member of the New York Knickerbockers. Schectman and others—including Sonny Hertzberg, David Stern, and Red Auerbach—were covered in *The First Basket* (2008), a documentary film exploring the origin of inner-city basketball, the role of basketball in the lives of young immigrants seeking to become Americans, and the gradual decline of Jews in professional basketball through the early 1950s.

Young Jewish men in the 1940s honed their skills in synagogues, in Young Men's Hebrew Associations (YMHAs), and throughout the Borscht Belt in upstate New York. Colleges in the cities were stocked with Jewish players, and at one time St. John's University in New York had a team starting five Jews. Other notable Jews who made their mark in basketball include coach Larry Brown, Washington Wizards owner Abe Pollin, and announcers Howard Cosell and Marv Albert (*First Basket* 2008). After the 1950s, as more Jewish families stabilized their economic base by establishing businesses and working in crafts, they encouraged their children—both male and female—to pursue their education in order to prepare for careers that were longer lasting and more socially acceptable than professional sport.

Islam

Islam ranks second only to Christianity in world popularity and has been growing rapidly in the United States as more immigrants arrive from Muslim-majority countries and more African Americans join Islam. Muslims believe that every action they take must glorify Allah (God). Male Muslims have participated in sport for centuries and built a history of success, particularly in soccer and basketball. Females in Muslim cultures have largely been excluded from sport participation, primarily due to restrictions on their attire.

One of the best-known Muslim athletes is Muhammad Ali, who was recognized as the world's greatest boxer after compiling a professional career record of 56 wins (37 by knockout) and only 5 losses. Ali is also renowned throughout the world for his religious practice and political activism. Born as Cassius Marcellus Clay Jr., he carried that name as he won an Olympic gold medal in Rome in 1960 but soon converted to the Nation of Islam and adopted his new name.

Ali fought against racism, the military draft, and war by speaking eloquently and passionately about social injustices that were incompatible with his religious beliefs. During the Vietnam War, Ali refused the draft and suffered the wrath of the public for supposedly being cowardly and un-American. He was stripped of his boxing championship and sentenced to five years in prison—a sentence that was overturned three years later by the U.S. Supreme Court. Eventually, Ali rejected the teaching of the Nation of Islam and converted to Sunni Islam. Later in life, Ali developed Parkinson's disease; however, despite living with obvious tremors in his limbs, he has become a symbol of courage and political activism for many U.S. sport fans and has been honored for both his sport success and his fidelity to his personal religious beliefs (Gale Group 2010).

Islam makes no prohibition against sport participation; historically, in fact, sport and games were part of the expected teachings given by parents to their children. Muslims have always encouraged youth to run, jump, and engage in basic physical activities, and Islamic tradition has long included swimming and weaponry practice. However, in conservative Muslim countries, sport for women has largely been very limited or ignored. Even so, a few Muslim women have made their mark on the Olympic Games. At the 1992 Barcelona Games, Algerian Hassiba Boulmerka won the gold medal in the 1,500-meter run. At the 2012 London Games, female athletes were sent to the Olympics for the first time by Brunei, Qatar, and Saudi Arabia. The London Games were also the first in which women competed in all 26 sports; at the same time, clothing rules were relaxed in various sports so that Muslim women could compete.

Saudi Arabia's decision to send two women to the 2012 Games was made under international pressure. Although neither athlete met the qualifying standards, they participated under the IOC's universality clause, which allows athletes to compete when their participation is important for

IN THE ARENA WITH . . .

Husain Abdullah

In a National Football League (NFL) game against the New England Patriots, Kansas City Chiefs safety Husain Abdullah was hit with a 15-yard penalty for unsportsmanlike conduct after falling to his knees after returning an interception for a touchdown. The refs saw him as a player who was celebrating in a way that was prohibited by league rules, when in reality he was practicing sajdah, a religious prayer. The penalty stood during the game, but the next day an NFL official admitted that it should not have been flagged. After all, how was Abdullah's action any different from the iconic pose of Tim Tebow, whose characteristic one-knee position of thanksgiving—known as "Tebowing"—was never seen as an issue by the NFL.

Husain Abdullah is a devout Muslim, which he demonstrated in deciding to forgo the entire 2012 football season in order to make a spiritual pilgrimage to Mecca with his brother, who was a fellow NFL player. Neither player knew if he would be able to reclaim a spot in the league after the year off, but Husain was snapped up by the Chiefs and has been an outstanding player for them. His brother did not catch on with another team and is now out of the league (Strauss 2014).

"reasons of equality." The two women—Wujdan Shahrkhani in judo and Sarah Attar in track and field—were required by their delegation to be accompanied by a male guardian and wear certain clothing during the competition.

Two years later, Saudi Arabia sent no women to the Asian Games because, according to the Saudi Olympic Committee, none had yet reached the level of international competition. The committee did assert its intention of including women on its 2016 Olympic team in Rio de Janeiro "on a good scale" (Human Rights Watch 2014). According to Mohammed al-Mishal, secretary-general of the Saudi Olympic Committee, the kingdom is focused on training women to compete in four sports—equestrianism, fencing, shooting, and archery—which he says are "accepted culturally and religiously in Saudi Arabia." He also indicated that his country's education ministry was directed in 2014 to study the possibility of introducing physical education for girls in Saudi public schools (Human Rights Watch 2014).

Another example of Muslim sport participation is found in Aya Medany of Egypt, who at age 23 competed as a pentathlete in the London Olympics, her third Olympic Games. Her sport requires that she fence, swim, ride a horse, run, and shoot—but her Muslim religion demands that she do it all with her body covered. She has adjusted to running with the hijab, even though it puts her at a disadvantage.

However, swimming in an outfit that covers her body became illegal when the governing bodies of swimming outlawed full-body suits because they proved to be "super-fast." Thus Medany finds herself caught between loyalty to her religious beliefs, attention from Egyptian media, and Olympic rules for sport clothing. She's fearful that she'll be forced to retire at the peak of her physical skill for reasons that are hard to understand (Williams 2012). Although she did not medal at the London Games, she was honored in 2014 with the International Olympic Committee's Women in Sport trophy for the continent of Africa in recognition of her trailblazing career as a pentathlete.

Due in part to restrictive dress codes, Muslim women have been few and far between in the sport world. Indeed, it is estimated that more than 500 million Muslim women around the globe are essentially banned from sport participation. People attempting to change the culture and practices in conservative Islamic countries have been careful, realizing that by winning a few battles for women's rights they may lose the larger war. For example, as of 2014, women in Saudi Arabia could not go anywhere without a male chaperone, nor could they drive a car or vote in elections, though that last ban is expected to be lifted for local elections in 2015 (*Week* 2014).

Still, change may slowly come, as courageous women and men in Muslim cultures agree to allow more choices for women in all areas of society. As an example, sport hijabs are available that address concerns for athlete safety and comfort while still providing coverage and modesty. Sport hijabs are made of various materials, including moisture-wicking fabrics, stretchable polyester, stretchable cotton, and fleece. They let Muslim females participate in sport and physical activity without worrying that their hijab will shift or tear. Sport-specific hijabs are also available—for example, in soccer and other team sports, in the martial arts, in winter and water sports, for general fitness, for running, for outdoor sports, and for helmet sports (*Guardian* 2014).

Use of Religion in Sport by Athletes

Now that we've examined the major religions that influence sport in North America, we can take a closer look at how athletes balance religion and sport. Athletes in competitive sport use religion in many ways. Here are a few:

- To justify their commitment to high-performance competitive sport
- To handle pressure and uncertainty
- To enhance bonds with teammates
- To guide moral decisions

In recent centuries, Judeo-Christian teachings have emphasized the obligation of individuals to fully develop their talent in order to glorify God. In addition, a number of religious principles apply well to sport competition, including discipline, sacrifice, intense training, and commitment to rigorous performance. Personal achievement is viewed as something to be valued and encouraged, and intense dedication to winning is viewed as honorable and pleasing to God. This view bears some similarity to the capitalistic belief that individual achievement is a mark of success and hard work and therefore is looked upon favorably by God.

Athletes often use their religious beliefs to reduce the pressure that they feel in competition. Some adopt the point of view that the outcome is in God's hands, which leaves them free to relax and focus on their own execution. Others pray before or during a contest to ask for divine guidance during play. Some also might ask specifically for a favorable outcome (Eitzen and Sage 2002). Many soccer players use religious rituals, such as touching a crucifix or making the sign of the cross, before attempting a penalty kick. Players in American football sometimes point to the sky to acknowledge their gratitude to God when they score a touchdown; others kneel in humble appreciation.

Prayer is a powerful practice in which believers communicate with their god. The three major religions in the United States—Christianity, Judaism, and Islam—endorse prayer as a central practice of their faith. In recent years, sport psychologists have explored the implications of working with

APPLYING SOCIAL THEORY

Feminist Theory and Female Muslim Athletes

Take the perspective of a feminist theorist and consider the frustration felt by girls and women in countries where Islam is the dominant religion. Young girls are typically banned or greatly restricted from participating in sport and physical activity, but no such restrictions are placed on boys or men. How would you propose to change the culture in countries where traditions and religion combine to restrict sport opportunities for females? Who or what organizations could be enlisted to support such changes? Is it worth the effort, or should we simply allow other cultures to evolve on their own?

athletes who believe in prayer. Evidence suggests that athletes who practice prayer should be encouraged to use it in order to help them deal with the pressure, uncertainty, and depression that can be part of competitive sport. Traditionally, prayer has been used to confess sins, express adoration, petition for needs, intercede for others, and offer thanksgiving. In sport, athletes tend to use prayer for three purposes (Watson and Czech 2005):

- To cope with uncertainty and anxiety
- To put life and sport into perspective
- To invest sport participation with meaning

Many athletes also use religious beliefs to strengthen their bonds with their teammates. When people share their personal beliefs and discuss weighty matters such as the meaning of life, they take certain risks with each other and often develop strong trust and loyalty. Members of a team who share common religious beliefs may attend study groups and religious services together, pray together, and work together to support youth organizations or charities with a similar religious affiliation. These activities enhance athletes' relationships with each other and help them hold one another accountable for their actions both off and on the field.

As human beings, of course, all athletes face moral decisions in life, and they encounter many of these situations in sport. When young, people are taught to follow the rules, and they often do so unquestioningly. As they grow, however, they examine the meaning behind moral decisions, assess what is generally acceptable in society, and often use religious teachings as their guide. Religious teachings can be used to address questions about cheating, lawbreaking, drug abuse, intentional harming of an opponent, and proper behavior after winning or losing. Many Christian athletes use the popular phrase "What would Jesus do?" for guidance in everyday decisions made on or off the athletic field.

Use of Sport by Athletes to Promote Religious Beliefs

One popular religious justification for striving so hard to win is that achieving fame through sport performance enlarges an athlete's sphere of influence. Athletes then have the opportunity to share their religious beliefs and influence people to follow their religious path. In this way, they view winning as a way to glorify God and spread God's message. Famous athletes command large audiences filled with people who are influenced by hearing how the athletes live. Athletes who become role models can powerfully influence the behavior of young athletes as they struggle with growing up and making their own decisions in sport and life.

Athletes who come from a fundamental or evangelical Christian orientation often use phrases such as "witnessing for Christ" to describe one of their primary responsibilities as a "born-again" Christian. They do not hesitate to share the specifics of their personal commitment to Christ, what that commitment means in their lives, and how important they think that commitment should be in others' lives. They can serve as powerful recruiters for Christian organizations, schools, and churches where youth can join with others committed to following the same faith.

Many athletes do much more than use words to promote their beliefs. Professional athletes who want to give back to their sport, community, or society often donate money to charitable causes or establish a charity in their name. Some choose charities that helped them or a loved one in a time of trouble. Others choose charities that help impoverished neighborhoods where they grew up. Of course, charitable organizations that promote certain religious beliefs are attractive to athletes who subscribe to the principles of a given organization.

Some athletes are also generous with their time, especially during the off-season. They talk to fans, sign autographs, and make personal appearances to promote causes they believe in, often for no remuneration. For example, summer camps staged by Christian organizations such as the Fellowship of Christian Athletes (FCA) provide opportunities for Christian athletes to contribute to the overall development of young athletes and share their faith. Specialized sport camps can also teach skills and strategy, but the most enduring lessons often come from famous athletes who share their beliefs with aspiring youngsters.

Celebrity athletes may also use their religious beliefs to guide their choices of commercial products to endorse. For example, many religiously conservative athletes choose not to endorse alcoholic beverage products or appear in commercials that use sexual innuendo or other content that might be deemed offensive.

The Tim Tebow Foundation, founded by the well-known Christian athlete, includes Timmy's Playrooms in children's hospitals, the W15H program that grants wishes to sick teens, and a five-story hospital in the Philippines.

Use of Religion by Coaches, Organizations, and Owners

Some coaches use religion as a social construct to unify their team. As pointed out in the previous section, when athletes share a belief system, this common ground can pull a team together, and the athletes involved will work very hard to avoid letting down their teammates. Like soldiers in warfare who count on each other for support, athletes have to know that they can count on each other as they enter the athletic arena.

Over the years, some coaches have invited informal team chaplains to lead their team in prayer before and after games. Typically, the chaplain prays for God to bless the contest by preventing serious injuries and allowing athletes to perform at the high level that reflects their athletic talents. These prayers are emotionally powerful for team members who are religious and consider prayer an important part of their life. These athletes do not find prayer unusual, because they pray regularly in their own lives. For example, more than likely they have also prayed more than once as a student, asking God to help them perform well on an exam. Athletes are much more likely to use prayer in sport if they also use prayer in their daily lives.

For their part, coaches are much more likely to use prayer at private church-sponsored schools than at public schools, where the courts have clearly ruled that coach-led prayer is illegal. Some teams get around that ban by sharing a moment of silence, during which athletes can engage in silent prayer or choose not to participate. Students enrolled at a secondary school or college that is church related expect prayer to be part of the school culture, whereas students in public school do not.

Coaches also know that young athletes are susceptible to temptations in their lives. With this in mind, some coaches establish priorities for their athletes that place God first, family second, academics third, and commitment to teammates fourth. This guideline helps the coach influence the decisions of young athletes to keep them out of trouble. Romantic attachments and partying fall farther down the priority list, and their lower priority reduces the chances that an athlete will make a poor choice.

Most coaches consider themselves role models and molders of talent in the persons they coach. They believe that if their athletes adopt a system of values centered on spirituality, work ethic, respect for family, and academic learning, then they as coaches will have performed a terrific service for these young people. In this way, many coaches view teaching sport skills and strategies as their least important role.

There are, however, pitfalls. When a coach advances a particular brand of religion with players, he or she excludes those who follow a different path. Religion may promote cliques of players who rally around a set of beliefs, thus isolating nonbelievers and damaging a team's social fabric and unity. In fact, just such a situation prompted a religious discrimination lawsuit filed in New Mexico in 2006 against a football coach who labeled two Muslim players as "troublemakers" and kicked them off the team. The case was settled out of court, and the players eventually transferred to another school (American Civil Liberties Union 2007).

The Freedom From Religion Foundation is a national nonprofit educational charity based in Madison, Wisconsin, that claims to be the nation's largest association of atheists and agnostics dedicated to keeping religion and government separate. In one case, the foundation filed a complaint with Clemson University in South Carolina asking the university to separate religion from its football program. While acknowledging that student-athletes can pray, conduct Bible studies, and engage in other religious activities on their own, the suit asserted that coaching staff members, who are public employees (Clemson is a public university), should not require such activities or participate in them with their athletes (Watson 2014).

More specifically, the lawsuit included assertions that coach Dabo Swinney "shows a preference for religion over nonreligion, alienates players who don't believe as he does, and creates a culture of religious coercion with the football program." It also alleged that the football team was required to attend a Fellowship of Christian Athletes breakfast where players would "testify" and attend a local church as a team. During one year, the suit alleged, 87 devotionals were organized under the guidance of the team chaplain. According to the foundation, it filed a similar complaint against Appalachian State University in 2012, after which the university rectified the situation by creating a stronger separation between its football program and religious activity (Watson 2014).

There are also positive examples of coaches recognizing religious differences among their players. Doc Rivers, now coach of the NBA Los Angeles Clippers, has been named Coach of the Year (with the Orlando Magic in 2000) and won an NBA championship (with the Boston Celtics in 2008). In his first season as Magic coach, he observed the team's traditional pregame prayer and noticed that one of his players, Tariq Abdul-Wahad, had his arms folded and looked very uncomfortable. Before the next game, Rivers told his team, "Hey, we're no longer praying before a game. But let's take a minute, close your eyes, and since we all have different religions, different Gods, just take a minute to compose. If you want to pray individually, you can do that." After that game, Abdul-Wahad walked up to Rivers, hugged him with tears in his eyes, and said, "Thank you. That is so important to me. No one has ever respected my Muslim religion. I'm going to give you everything I've got" (Amick 2014).

Organizers of professional sport leagues have also encouraged prayer breakfasts and Bible studies shared by opponents in the off-season and before or after a game. It can be both thrilling and confusing to see a couple of dozen NFL players kneeling in prayer on the field after a football game during which they tried to annihilate each other. The players point out that in the larger game of life, they are all brothers striving to do God's will and that by praying together they show respect for God, the game, and their opponents.

Organizers of the Olympic Games have also provided opportunities for athletes to gather and share their beliefs as they prepare for competition. Young men and women from a variety of backgrounds and sports find that they share a common spiritual experience and realize that they face similar temptations, trials, and uncertainties. Though it is not endorsed by the Olympic organizers themselves, many religious organizations capitalize on the Games by hosting their own events, such as prayer breakfasts featuring well-known speakers and former athletes; scripture studies; and prayer groups for interested athletes, spectators, and local citizens.

ACTIVITY TIME-OUT

Should We Mix Sport With Religion?

By now, you understand that sport and religion have a fairly tight relationship at almost every level of competition, from high school on to the Olympics and the professional ranks. On balance, do you think this is a healthy thing for sport? Encouraging athletes with identical or similar religious views may build team cohesiveness, but it can also drive a wedge between players who have different views. Would it be appropriate for a Muslim, Jew, or Mormon to also express his or her faith publicly on the public stage provided by sport? Make a case for your position that sport either should or should not be closely intertwined with religious practice.

In one example of religious outreach at the Olympic Games, the London Olympics accommodated religious athletes by providing the services of 193 chaplains, a prayer room in every venue, and a multifaith center in the Olympic Village. The multifaith center included all nine faiths that have a presence in Great Britain: Christian, Muslim, Hindu, Sikh, Jewish, Baha'i, Jain, Buddhist, and Zoroastrian. In addition, faith leaders helped launch a "Faith" pin badge—the fifth badge created to celebrate the diversity and inclusion represented by the Games. Other events during the games included prayer breakfasts hosted by such groups as the Salvation Army and a series of eleven interfaith walks throughout South London, during which participants could visit temples, churches, and mosques in the lead-up to the Games (Regional Interfaith Network 2012; Hirst 2012).

Since 1984, a strong religious presence at the Games has also been established by the Christian outreach ministry Lay Witnesses for Christ International (LWFCI). The group offered Christian Olympians 10 days of events, inspiration, and prayer under the theme "Bridging the Gap: UK Outreach 2012." Its "Evening With the Stars" event was led by former Olympian Carl Lewis. The group also partnered with the local 15,000-member Kingsway International Christian Centre—located in the middle of London's Olympic zone—to draw congregations as large as 25,000 (Kingsway International Christian Centre 2012).

Many athletic contests begin with a ceremony to mark the significance of the occasion. In the United States, the two most common elements in opening ceremonies are the national anthem and an invocation. In recent years, praying at public events sponsored by schools has been questioned in regard to its fairness to people who do not practice Christianity. Some who offer the prayers speak to the wide range of beliefs of the audience, whereas others offend some listeners with phrases referring to "Our savior Jesus Christ" or similar language.

In June 2000, the U.S. Supreme Court ruled that public schools cannot constitutionally organize school prayers at regular sporting events. At the same time, the court reaffirmed the right of players and fans to pray by themselves at such events and the right of students to pray together of their own accord. In other words, separation of church and state prohibits only school officials from organizing prayer at regular school functions. For many Americans, this stance by the court marks a departure from a long-standing tradition of public prayer offered at official public functions of all kinds, including sport events (*Santa Fe* 2000).

In baseball, both minor and major league teams (especially those in the Bible Belt) sometimes use "faith nights" to attract spectators to their games. Local churches encourage their members to attend the games, which may feature Christian singers, players who share their testimonies, and faith trivia quizzes for prizes. These promotions have been a marketing success for minor league teams struggling to entice fans. Game attendance is also promoted by religious organizations, such as Athletes in Action and the Fellowship of Christian

Athletes, and is often heartily endorsed by parents and community leaders (Cherner 2005).

To avoid offending spectators who do not care to participate in faith nights, the religious events are scheduled before the game, perhaps in the parking lot. Cities involved include Hagerstown, Maryland; Johnson City, Tennessee; Columbus, Georgia; Birmingham, Alabama; Nashville, Tennessee; Mobile, Alabama; Tulsa, Oklahoma; and Portland, Oregon (Cherner 2005).

Organizations Using Sport to Promote Religion

Numerous Christian organizations have flourished in the United States over the past 60 years by combining religious teaching and sport. Perhaps the oldest and largest of these organizations is the Fellowship of Christian Athletes, which was established in 1954 by Don McClanen, Paul Benedum, Branch Rickey, and other Pittsburgh businessmen. It is still the largest interdenominational, college- and school-based Christian sport organization in the world. From its modest beginnings, FCA has grown into an organization that now includes more than 450,000 people on more than 10,000 campuses and has reached nearly 2 million coaches and athletes (Fellowship of Christian Athletes 2015).

The FCA was originally aimed at the major sports, and the charter members included football great Otto Graham and baseball pitcher Carl Erskine. The FCA publishes a monthly magazine and offers study guides, videos, and materials for Bible study and meetings. The organization has a commercial sponsor in Chick-fil-A and more than 74,000 individual donors, all of which contribute to its total annual revenue of more than $88 million. The mission of FCA (2015) is "to present to athletes and coaches and all whom they influence the challenge and adventure of receiving Jesus Christ as Savior and Lord, serving Him in their relationships and in the fellowship of the church."

The basic organizational unit of FCA is the local huddle, which can be established at a high school, at a college, or in a community. Team members meet regularly in the huddle to study the Bible, follow devotional guides, and discuss their lives in Christian faith and sport. Most often, the huddle advisers are coaches who assist student leaders. Local huddles distribute information about FCA opportunities, such as widely held summer camps. At these camps, famous athletes dedicate their time to teach sport skills, talk about their faith, and encourage young athletes to follow the precepts of FCA: integrity, service, teamwork, and excellence.

Key figures in the FCA (and other organizations promoting sport and religion) have included Tom Landry, famous coach of the NFL's Dallas Cowboys, and one of his quarterbacks, Roger Staubach. They carried impeccable sport credentials as "winners" and used that platform to testify to the importance of their faith in the "game of life." The personal dedication of these men and hundreds of others through the years has influenced hundreds of thousands of young people. No young person can help but be impressed by a famous athlete whom she or he looks upon as a hero.

Another Christian sport organization is Athletes in Action (AIA), a branch of Cru, which was previously known as Campus Crusade for Christ. AIA is a group of former college athletes who travel the country playing exhibition games against amateur teams, including collegiate teams, especially early in the season. AIA has secured approval from the NCAA to compete against NCAA members, and its players typically take advantage of the halftime and postgame period to talk about their faith.

Sport missionaries like those from AIA generally try to convince young people to "follow the right path." They typically present a fundamental view of religion and rarely speak out on social issues such as discrimination against women or minorities, drug abuse, cheating, and violence in sport. They've been labeled with phrases including "jocks for Jesus" and "the God squad" and tend to present God as desiring to become the master coach for all people who seek Him. No matter the audience, their talks tend to focus on positive stories about good things happening to Christian athletes, finding faith, and receiving a higher reward (Athletes in Action 2014).

Similarly, Pro Athletes Outreach sends professional athletes to meetings, camps, and events held by other organizations. These athletes talk about sport, their faith, and what their faith means in their everyday life. Once limited to white, middle-class boys, such organizations have gradually come to include girls and some racial minorities. They tend to thrive in working-class communities among athletes who play traditional team sports. Perhaps not surprisingly, most of these religious sport organizations are strongest in the U.S. Bible Belt.

One other organization of note is the National Christian College Athletic Association (NCCAA), which was founded in 1968 and now includes more than 100 colleges. It represents more than 13,000 collegiate athletes and 700 collegiate coaches; it sponsors championships in 20 sports. The NCCAA divides itself into two divisions: Division I encompasses liberal arts colleges, and Division II comprises Bible colleges. Programs at NCCAA schools are dedicated to students and serve a larger purpose than simply winning athletic contests. Christian teachings are part of the total learning experience on these campuses and throughout these sport programs.

Using Sport to Promote Christian Colleges and Secondary Schools

Perhaps the best-known university in the United States is Notre Dame, a Roman Catholic school famous for the exploits of its football team. Notre Dame has such a large fan base throughout the United States that it independently negotiates multimillion-dollar agreements for the rights to televise its football games rather than operating as part of an athletic conference like most colleges do. Many kids grow up knowing that Notre Dame is

EXPERT'S VIEW

Mixed Martial Arts and Christianity

Professors Nick Watson of York St John University in Great Britain and Brian Bolt of Calvin College in Michigan are both experts in kinesiology, sport, and religion. In an article for the *Conversation*, they explore the apparent conflict between participation in mixed martial arts (MMA) and the Christian faith. To focus their discussion, they report a question posed by U.S. MMA champion Scott "Bam Bam" Sullivan in an interview for the *Times* of London: "Can you love your neighbor as yourself, and at the same time knee him in the face as hard as you can?"

MMA is a combination of kickboxing, Brazilian jiu-jitsu, Greco-Roman wrestling, and Thai boxing that features punching, kicking, kneeing, grappling, and elbowing your opponent until he or she concedes. Participation in this violent sport and others, such as football and boxing, has been justified by some Christian leaders as a form of "muscular Christianity," which is embraced by men who imagine Jesus as a fighter. One pastor and MMA enthusiast has even expressed the view that men are made for combat, conflict, and dominion.

Many Christians and theologians have expressed theological objections to MMA. In addition, a growing body of research on MMA and boxing highlights the risk of traumatic brain injury, psychiatric conditions, physical disability, and perhaps even death. At its heart, the rap against MMA is that its goal is to intentionally beat your opponent into submission. How can one reconcile faith with the inevitable brain bleeds, concussions, and emotional trauma?

Since many athletes who participate in violent sports (especially American football) have been outspoken about their Christian faith, wouldn't it be fascinating to hear how they view the apparent contradictions between their beliefs and their chosen sport? That is one of many fascinating questions that experts like Watson and Bolt will continue to explore and pose to their students (Watson and Bolt 2015).

the place to go for football, and the university has been fortunate to parlay its reputation into both sport and academic excellence (it enjoys a high graduation rate among its athletes).

Notre Dame's allure was burnished during the tenure of Knute Rockne, a football coaching legend during the 1920s. Rockne stood up to the anti-Catholicism that prevailed in the United States at the time and to criticism from the Ku Klux Klan. In fact, the "more Rockne was exposed to prejudice around him, the more he was attracted to the religiosity around him at Notre Dame" (R. Robinson 1999).

Religion and sport are also intertwined at Brigham Young University (BYU), which was founded by the Church of Jesus Christ of Latter-Day Saints (the Mormons). In fact, the interrelationship is made explicit in the athletic department's statement of purpose: "Build a distinctive, exceptional athletic program that is fully aligned with the mission and values of Brigham Young University and The Church of Jesus Christ of Latter-day Saint" (Brigham Young University 2015). More recently, Oral Roberts University (Tulsa, Oklahoma) and Liberty University (Lynchburg, Virginia) have used sport promotion to gain early notice for their schools. Founded by evangelists Oral Roberts and Jerry Falwell, respectively, these schools find no conflict between their Christian values and the quest to win games. In fact, winning draws more attention to their programs and allows them to spread the word of God. Other well-known universities that have made their mark in sport include Texas Christian University, Baylor University, and Southern Methodist University.

Many other private schools have also used sport to gain publicity, swell their pool of applicants, and attract an academically better-qualified student body. Smaller schools typically put their money into basketball since it is less expensive than football. As a result, many small Catholic schools are well known in the basketball world—for example, St. Joseph's, La Salle, Villanova, and Immaculata in Philadelphia; St. John's in New York; Marquette in Milwaukee; Gonzaga in Spokane, Washington; Loyola in Chicago; and Georgetown in Washington, DC.

Many private secondary schools founded as Christian schools have also dedicated themselves to excellence in sport in order to help attract students. Since their funding relies on donations and private tuition payments, they need to show value delivered for the money not only in academics but in all programs. They realize that top performance in sport attracts fans, builds school cohesion, and encourages boosters and donors. Indeed, it is no accident that many top professional athletes have graduated from these schools over the years. Top high school athletes are recruited and often offered scholarships based on need or academic performance in order to gain their contribution on the field or in the gym.

Among the most well-known Catholic secondary schools are Christ the King in Queens, New York; DeMatha in Hyattsville, Maryland; and St. Anthony in Newark, New Jersey. These schools have been perennial basketball powers (Huff 2005). In football, Bishop Gorman High School in Las Vegas finished 2014 as the top-ranked high school team in the country according to USA Today Sports. In fact, the school has been so dominant—winning six straight state championships—that Nevada lawmaker Harvey Munford proposed a draft bill to ban it from the state playoffs (Hagar 2014).

Conflict Between Sport and Religion

Conflicts sometimes arise between sport and religious belief—for example, as mentioned earlier, the inherent violence of MMA and the Christian principle of loving one's neighbor as oneself. Similarly, how is it an act of love for one's fellow human to put a bone-crushing tackle on an opponent, throw at a baseball batter's head, slide hard into second base to break up a double play, or humiliate an overwhelmed opponent by running up the score? These actions are not unusual in most sport settings.

When confronted with such contradictions, athletes who have well-defined religious values often draw the line at certain behaviors that they deem inappropriate. However, they may still overlook actions taken by coaches or teammates over whom they have little or no control. Their attitude is that they are responsible only for their own behavior and for living according to their principles.

Researchers have studied the beliefs of high-level athletes in various sports who must reconcile their Christian faith and moral attitudes with the realities of competitive sport. More specifically, research by Kretschmann and Benz (2012) revealed that athletes typically adopt one of the following four coping strategies to allow themselves to compete while maintaining their religious beliefs:

- God gives you talent and expects you to develop and use it to glorify God. Others are given talents in academics, the arts, music, or business; your gift clearly consists of athletic talent that begs to be nurtured.
- God loves you whether you win or not, so the pressure to focus only on winning is foolish and contradictory.
- God is the greatest motivator, and you need to give full effort in everything you do, including your athletic training and performance.
- God has a plan—this is the key coping strategy—and knows what is good for you

Dmitriy Salita (right) is a Ukraine-born Orthodox Jewish boxer from Brooklyn. Do you see a conflict between religious beliefs and the act of boxing, which requires the athlete to repeatedly, and forcefully, hit an opponent?

and is guiding you along a path. In fact, God may be using you to influence nonbelievers through your sport participation.

Jeremy Lin is an unusual man. He is one the few people—and one of the even fewer Harvard graduates—who can make a living as a professional basketball player. He is also one of the few Asian Americans in professional sport. But even more anomalous, he is a religious person at the highest level of professional sport. When the game is on the line, Lin is proud, assertive, and often the center of attention. These traits help make him a great ballplayer, but they also conflict with the Christian ethos. In Lin's view, he "does not work hard, practice endlessly so that he can please others. . . . [R]ather he says his audience is God and he has submitted himself to God and given up his game to [God]" (Brooks 2012).

Some other athletes simply put their spiritual beliefs aside while participating in sport. They follow the customs of their sport on the field and reengage their spiritual beliefs off of the field. Although this approach is common, however, it can provoke criticism if an athlete's on-field behavior does not square with his or her off-field spiritual pronouncements. Indeed, some actions in sport may be legal but not ethical. These actions are often difficult to evaluate because they involve intent, which can be hard to determine. For example, did a defensive end maliciously slam into an opposing quarterback with a preexisting injury? Or was it just happenstance during a routine pass rush? Moreover, in some sports, such as boxing, the intent is more straightforward—for example, to win the fight by punching the opponent into submission.

Conflict between sport and religion can also take the form of competing for the attention of their adherents. Many pastors have found that they must compete with sport events and children's sport activities on Sundays when members of their flock choose whether to prioritize church attendance, family time, or sport time. Some churches have responded strategically by offering services at alternative times on Saturday or Sunday evenings to avoid the competition. Others sponsor athletic teams and leagues in order to control scheduling and even increase their church attendance through sport (Briggs 2013).

Chapter Summary

Historically, religion and sport have interacted in both negative and positive ways. Among the ancient Greeks, religious festivals featured athletic contests. Over time, many religions came to view sport and games as mundane diversions that detracted from people's spiritual development. In the last 100 years, however, religion and sport have often forged mutually beneficial links through which each promotes the other.

For example, church leaders have used sport and athletes to attract people, especially youth, to their facilities and to recruit believers into their religious family. At the same time, sport leaders have used religion to justify competition as a worthy pursuit and to control the conduct of athletes. In addition, coaches have promoted prayer to enhance performance and foster team togetherness. They have also reinforced religious values to encourage their athletes to work hard, practice teamwork, and commit to team goals.

Although Christianity, particularly Protestantism, has been the dominant religion in the United States, other religions such as Judaism and Islam have also made their mark on the sporting world. Over the years, various organizations have developed due to the link between sport and religion. For example, the Young Men's Christian Association and Young Women's Christian Association built sport facilities across the United States and organized thousands of sport programs for all ages. The Fellowship of Christian Athletes has grown steadily over the last 60 years and now boasts more than 10,000 organized "huddles" that involve more than 450,000 athletes.

Christian secondary schools and colleges have also used sport to gain positive publicity and attract students and donors. They make no apologies for embracing the competitive ethic of striving for excellence. For example, both Liberty University and Oral Roberts University are following the path first trod by Notre Dame with its famed football teams and by Roman Catholic universities with a tradition of excellence in basketball. Athletic success has also been used to generate positive publicity by religious secondary schools, such as Bishop Gorman, DeMatha, Christ the King, and St. Anthony.

Athletes have used religion on a personal level by asking for God's help during performance, using prayer to focus in their preparation for competition, and using religion to justify their striving for athletic excellence. Many prominent athletes have also used their sport success as a platform for sharing their religious beliefs and influencing young athletes to stay on the "right path." In some cases, however, religious beliefs have interfered with an athlete's sport participation when customs or expectations of the two institutions clashed.

Religion has helped people in the United States justify their preoccupation with sport. In some cases, it has also joined in that preoccupation, urging the pursuit of excellence through sport and convincing athletes that their religious beliefs should accompany them in the athletic arena. By promoting sport and using famous athletes to deliver their message, religious leaders gain the attention of young men and women. Conversely, by applying the tenets of a worthy spiritual life to sport, participants can enjoy a powerful endorsement of what otherwise might seem a self-indulgent pastime.

STUDENT OUTCOMES

After reading this chapter, you will know the following:

- How government and sport interact locally, nationally, and internationally
- How government may interact with sport to protect the rights of all citizens
- How governments use sport to promote identity and unity among citizens
- How governments use sport to promote social values
- How sport creates nationalistic feelings that reinforce governmental policies
- How political groups within sport organizations can direct the development and delivery of sport to consumers
- Why sport personalities, athletes, and coaches may lean toward a conservative political philosophy

Politics and Sport

Politics and Sport

The Olympic Games have often been a victim of the international politics of the day. For example, the 1936 Berlin Games were used by Adolf Hitler as a vehicle for Nazi propaganda about purported Aryan racial superiority. The folly of Hitler's claims was laid bare by Olympian Jesse Owens, an African American sprinter who captured four gold medals in Berlin. In 1972, the Munich Games were shaken by the kidnapping and murder of 11 members of the Israeli Olympic team by the Palestinian group Black September. In 1980, the United States led a group of 65 nations that boycotted the Moscow Games in protest of the Soviet Union's invasion of Afghanistan. Four years later, Russia and 14 allied countries returned the favor by boycotting the Los Angeles Games.

Political concerns have continued to affect the Olympics in the current century. In 2008, the choice of Beijing, China as the host country was widely seen as an opportunity for a rising world power to assert itself in spite of concerns about its human rights violations. In 2014, human rights took the stage again as the political story of the Sochi Winter Games focused on Russia's laws restricting the rights of LGBT people, which generated protests from a variety of countries.

In 2016, Brazil will become the first South American country to host the Olympics. However, in preparing for its curtain call, the country is encountering challenges in meeting construction deadlines that have been complicated by its role as host country for World Cup soccer in 2014. Plans have also been held hostage by a lack of cooperation between national, state, and city governments throughout the process, as each unit blames the others for delays, cost overruns, and public safety concerns.

The lesson to be learned is that major sporting events are often inextricably linked with politics—from the start of the selection process, to the preparations, and on through the competition itself.

Politics is the art and science of governing, influencing governmental policy, or holding control over a government. Even though the term often carries negative connotations, politics is a dominant component of any culture. This chapter examines the interrelationship between politics and sport from four primary perspectives: (1) how governments use sport to improve people's quality of life and regulate sport to safeguard the public; (2) how sport can reinforce the prevailing political structure and status quo; (3) how nations sponsor international teams in world sporting events to promote patriotic pride and facilitate international relations; and (4) how political dynamics play out within sport institutions themselves. Let's examine each perspective more closely.

The first perspective examines how sport is used by governments to improve the quality of life of their citizens and how they regulate sport to safeguard the public and protect citizens' rights. In the United States, the government regulates the conduct of sport, particularly when public money or public land is involved. The legislative and judicial branches of government also make decisions regarding antitrust issues in sport; levy taxes on the public to finance some aspects of sport; and referee conflicts between sport performers, owners, unions, and organizations.

In a related area of interest, communities sometimes build their identity largely through local professional sport teams, community teams, or local university or high school teams. Political leaders may use sport to unify citizens around a common interest, such as attracting a professional franchise to their city. Rooting for the home team often links city residents who might otherwise feel isolated from their government or each other. Governments also use sport to facilitate social integration. For example, they may use sport to reduce juvenile delinquency, improve academic performance through after-school programs that combine academics and sports, and encourage healthy competition between disparate ethnic or racial groups.

The second perspective examines how sport can reinforce the prevailing political structure and status quo. Political leaders often use sport to promote self-interest or support for the government that they lead. Generally, sport organizations, leaders, coaches, and athletes support the establishment that serves them well.

The third perspective focuses on how nations sponsor international teams in world sporting events in order to promote patriotic pride. National teams that succeed in competition against national teams—for example, in the Olympic Games—can inspire a sense of identity and pride in a country's citizens. In addition, success in international competition is also used to justify a particular nation's government or way of life. International sport events are also used to advance political aims when certain nations boycott events or are restricted from participating by other countries whose leaders are offended by their social practices. Finally, sport offers a way of maintaining good relationships or building understanding among nations.

The fourth perspective explores the politics of sport institutions themselves. Within each sport, different interests struggle over who will set the policies and procedures and who will benefit from the decisions made—the team owners, athletes, or spectators. As with all organizations, the people who organize and govern particular sports or leagues develop political structures within their group. People in the political structure campaign to influence policy decisions, financial commitments, and competition rules. Given these realities, leaders in sport organizations must often become consummate politicians in order to convince their constituency to follow their vision for the success of the organization and the sport overall.

Government regulations help ensure that athletes are safe while on the court or field.

Government Promotion of Physical Activity and Health

Governments sometimes take on responsibility for the health and welfare of their citizens. In the United States, the Centers for Disease Control and Prevention (CDC)—a division of the federal Department of Health and Human Services—disseminates the latest information linking physical activity to better health. In its role of preventing and controlling disease, the CDC makes strong recommendations for every citizen to participate in physical activity.

The most recent recommendation from the U.S. government for physical activity calls for children to engage in one hour or more of moderate or vigorous aerobic physical activity per day. This activity should include vigorous physical activity on at least three days per week. For adults, the CDC suggests performing at least 150 minutes (two hours and 30 minutes) per week of moderate activity, or 75 minutes of vigorous activity, or an equivalent combination of the two (Centers for Disease Control and Prevention 2015).

The official position of the U.S. government holds that regular physical activity contributes to health, promotes well-being, and reduces the costs of medical care. Therefore, it is in everyone's interest to use healthy activity as a means of ensuring a higher quality of life, increasing longevity, and reducing the expense and ravages of disease. Research demonstrating the value of exercise for slowing the aging process has been a popular topic for the CDC, particularly as longevity increases and the U.S. population ages. Increasing longevity affects the U.S. government considerably, since it portends increased costs for health care and a greater need for long-term care facilities. It may even threaten the solvency of the Social Security system and Medicare.

In the 1950s, physical testing of military recruits made it clear that U.S. youth were woefully lacking in physical fitness. Then, in a test of minimum muscular fitness developed by Hans Kraus and Sonja Weber, 57 percent of U.S. schoolchildren failed one or more of the six tests. That percentage compared quite poorly with a failure rate of only 8 percent among schoolchildren in Austria, Italy, and Switzerland. The results made big news, and President Dwight D. Eisenhower eventually founded the President's Council on Youth Fitness, headed by Vice President Richard Nixon. The result was a series of publicity releases touting the virtues of physical fitness (Rice, Hutchinson, and Lee 1958).

In 1961, President John F. Kennedy established the President's Council on Physical Fitness and Sports (PCPFS) to promote physical fitness and sport participation by the U.S. citizenry. The council's first recommendation was for all schools to provide at least 15 minutes of vigorous exercise per day. At that time, 75 percent of U.S. schools had no daily class for physical education.

Perhaps the most enduring contribution of the President's Council has been to develop standards of fitness for schoolchildren. These standards have been in place in schools for more than 50 years (Hackensmith 1966). Now referred to as the President's Challenge, the program has been expanded from the original target audience of schoolchildren to include fitness tests and standards for people of all ages and for families who want to work together on living healthily. In 2010, President Barack Obama renamed the President's Council by executive order to be called the President's Council on Fitness, Sports and Nutrition. The mission of the council was redefined as follows (President's Council on Fitness, Sports, and Nutrition n.d.):

> *To engage, educate, and empower all Americans across the lifespan to adopt a healthy lifestyle that includes regular physical activity and good nutrition.*

The two most significant changes in the mission involved including people of all ages and adding nutrition to the traditional emphasis on physical exercise. At the same time, First Lady Michelle Obama launched an accompanying White House campaign dubbed "Let's Move" in partnership with the Department of Health and Human Services, the President's Council, and Major League Baseball (MLB). The specific charge of this campaign is to combat the rapid rise in childhood obesity by improving education about and access to healthy food and regular physical activity, both at school and outside of school hours (White House 2010).

Government in Sport

Many governments around the world, particularly those that have established a ministry of sport, aggressively promote sport participation, financially support high-performance athletes who represent their country in international competition, and help fund public athletic facilities. No such agency exists, however, in the United States, and though some people would welcome governmental support, most sport advocates believe that U.S. society is better served by keeping government red tape, endless discussion, and partisan bickering out of the sport world. Some citizens might even question the constitutional right of the U.S. government to interfere in sport.

As discussed in chapter 10, the U.S. Congress designated the United States Olympic Committee (USOC) to develop and conduct amateur sport and to train and support Olympic and Paralympic athletes. Although the government does not directly fund the USOC, it did donate a closed military base to provide the site for the USOC headquarters and training center. The USOC raises its own funds to conduct its business. Although the U.S. Congress does not normally interfere with the USOC, in 2003 it did step in when the USOC met with scandal involving breach of ethics and internal strife. The resulting changes began to take effect in 2005, and the hope is that the USOC will steadily progress in bringing itself under order (see chapter 10).

Safeguarding the Public

The government in the United States acts in various ways to promote the safety of citizens. Part of this work involves discouraging or outlawing sports that are dangerous or involve cruelty to animals. For example, bullfighting, cockfighting, and other so-called sports that abuse animals are punishable by fine or imprisonment. In addition,

EXPERT'S VIEW

The Institute of Medicine's Committee on Sports-Related Concussions in Youth

In spite of recent publicity about professional athletes who have suffered from traumatic brain injuries (TBIs), there appears to be a culture of resistance among young athletes in the United States wherein they are hesitant to report possible concussions or comply with treatment plans. At the same time, TBIs are increasing in frequency. Consider, for example, the recent 67 percent increase in the number of sport- and recreation-related concussions and TBIs diagnosed in hospital emergency rooms among youth (an increase from 150,000 in 2001 to nearly 250,000 in 2009) (Institute of Medicine 2013).

According to a study by the U.S. Institute of Medicine (2013), concussions are more frequent among high school athletes than among their college counterparts. They are particularly common among males in football, ice hockey, lacrosse, and wrestling and among females in soccer, lacrosse, and basketball. Concussion rates are also higher among youth who have a history of concussion. In addition, the committee found little scientific evidence to suggest that current sport helmets reduce the risk of concussion.

The committee concludes that more research is needed on youth concussions. Specifically, it advocates implementing a national surveillance system to accurately track the number of injuries and identify changes in the brain as a result of these injuries over the life span. It also recommends evaluating sport rules, playing practices, and equipment in order to reduce the incidence of concussion.

The source of this report—the Institute of Medicine—is part of the private, nonprofit U.S. National Academies, which receive no direct funding from the government. They were, however, established by the U.S. Congress and the executive branch to protect the health and welfare of the people of the United States. Do you think this prestigious group of medical and scientific experts should recommend public policies or laws to better protect youth from sport injuries? Or do you believe it is up to those in the sport world to make such changes? What are your reasons?

sports that are inherently dangerous to participants—such as boxing, bungee jumping, skydiving, and auto racing—are carefully monitored and subjected to government regulation.

Governmental agencies also regulate sports that may be reasonably safe within a controlled environment, such as boating, fishing, hunting, firearm use, water sports, and bicycling. These activities are the subject of various rules, training requirements for instructors and participants, and protective equipment requirements. The government also regulates outdoor activities that may affect the natural environment or endanger species; for example, it regulates where, when, and how fishing can be done.

The government also strives to protect the public in sports in situations where unruly fan behavior could pose a risk or a terrorist attack could threaten the staging of a large event. For many U.S. citizens in my generation, the first wake-up call to terrorism in sport came in 1972, when a Palestinian terrorist group took Israeli athletes hostage during the Summer Olympics in Munich, Germany. After a day-long standoff and a failed rescue attempt, eleven Israeli athletes, one German police officer, and five of the eight kidnappers were dead (Lowitt 1999).

Nearly 25 years later, at the Atlanta Olympics, a bomb went off in Olympic Park, killing two people and injuring more than a hundred others. Panic set in, events were suspended, and spectators feared for their safety, but the Games went on. Five years later, the main suspect, Eric Robert Rudolph, was found hiding in the mountains of North Carolina.

The Olympics have always been a potential target for those with a political axe to grind, and security costs have continued to rise. For the 2012 Summer Olympics in London, the original security force numbered 10,000, but as the games approached an additional 13,700 guards were added at a cost of more than $400 million. Once the Games concluded, the final tally for security was $1.6 billion (Weir 2011).

Of course, terrorism hit home in the United States on a new level in 2001, when terrorists attacked New York City and Washington, DC. In every sporting event since that time, security plans have been a major priority. More recently, the terrorist bombing at the 2013 Boston Marathon killed 3 people and injured 264 more. The FBI identified the culprits as a pair of brothers of Chechen descent who were motivated by extremist Islamist beliefs and the wars in Iraq and Afghanistan. One brother was killed after pursuit and the other was found guilty of 30 charges relating to homegrown terrorism, including using a weapon of mass destruction and malicious destruction of property resulting in death. Undaunted by the tragedy, the event was held again the following year, when the number of participants jumped from about 27,000 runners to more than 36,000. They ran under the watchful eye of double the previous number of police officers using enhanced security procedures and surveillance cameras.

Other possible prime targets for terrorism include the many college football stadiums—some filled with more than 100,000 fans—on any autumn Saturday throughout the United States. Similarly, the Super Bowl staged by the National Football League (NFL) draws not only a live audience but also a worldwide television audience that could potentially witness an attack. With such risks in mind, authorities routinely prohibit aircraft from flying within miles of the stadiums on game days. Other common security measures include bomb searches, undercover police, alarm systems, and video surveillance. Anyone who enters the event facility may be searched, and strict limits are placed on what people are allowed to bring into the facility. Anyone who appears suspicious is quickly moved aside for further investigation.

The financial costs of these precautions have driven insurance premiums to more than $1 million a year for a typical NFL stadium. The combined cost of security precautions and insurance protection have substantially increased the expenses borne by sport promoters, who have passed them along to fans.

Protecting the Rights of Citizens

The government can play a key role in protecting the rights of its citizens in sport. For example, in 1972, the U.S. Congress passed Title IX, which declared that women and girls must have equal access to sport (see chapter 13). Organizations that refused to meet the standards were denied federal funds of any type. Similarly, in 1990, U.S. president George H.W. Bush signed the Americans with Disabilities Act, which protected the rights of athletes with a physical or mental disability (see chapter 15). As a result, public facilities, including sport facilities, must meet certain standards to accommodate people with a physical disability.

The USOC does its part by providing sport competition and training for athletes with a physical disability. Indeed, nowadays, the Paralympic Games immediately follow the Olympic Games and are conducted in the same venue with the full support of the International Olympic Committee (IOC) and most national sport governing bodies.

Civil rights legislation has made it illegal for governmental bodies that support or regulate access to sport programs to engage in discrimination on the basis of any of various protected characteristics. Although private clubs continue to have some leeway in determining their membership, any public facility or program must provide equal access for all persons. As a result, national sport governing bodies are expected to develop policies that ensure equal access to all athletes. People who take issue with the conduct of any organization or facility in this regard can seek redress in a court of law in order to be protected from discrimination based on such factors as race, creed, national origin, religious preference, and sexual orientation (see chapters 12 through 16).

Other U.S. laws protect the rights of children (through child labor laws) and the rights of athletes to play as professionals and to represent a specific country. Other laws regulate the use of performance-enhancing drugs in sport. In 2005, the U.S. Congress held hearings on drug use in MLB and threatened to toughen the rules unless MLB significantly changed its policies on drug testing and penalties for infractions. At that point,

ACTIVITY TIME-OUT

Protecting Kids in Youth Sport From Criminal Coaches

Do you think that the government at any level should require criminal background checks before a person is allowed to serve as a coach for youth sport? Investigate the relevant issues and develop a well-reasoned argument either for or against government involvement in this aspect of youth sport. In formulating your position, consider the following issues.

The Amateur Athletic Union, which employs more than 65,000 coaches across the United States, discovered at one point that some of its coaches had committed crimes, including theft, drug delivery, incest, and murder. In Seattle, Washington, a pilot program checked the roster of 4,236 coaches and discovered 38 felons (Willmsen 2004).

In 2012, USA Swimming—the national governing body for swimming—published a list of more than 60 swim coaches whom they banned from any further association with swimming. Although many of the offenses had been widely known, the offending coaches had often been allowed to resign one position and simply move on to another location where people were unaware of their previous behavior.

The process of conducting background checks can be tricky. For instance, background checks performed at the state level often do not ferret out infractions in other states. As a result, a coach can simply change his or her name and move to a new state; for that reason, neither state nor federal name checks are sufficient. Fingerprint testing is the most accurate, but the cost may be nearly $50 per coach, which raises the question of who pays the fee. Youth sport organizations say they can't afford it, and volunteer coaches resist paying as well. Should this cost be treated as a government expense?

Some state legislatures, such as Florida's, have passed bills requiring background checks, but as of 2014 only nine states had any form of state law requiring mandated background checks for youth sport coaches who volunteer or are employed by an independent, private league or sanctioning body not affiliated with a school or other governmental agency (Little League 2015b). Most organizations are hesitant about outside (government) influence and are concerned that state mandates will require background checks that they can't afford (Basichis 2010).

After you have concluded your research and developed a position, summarize it in a two- to three-page paper and be ready to debate your conclusion in class.

both the league and the players' union realized that tougher drug enforcement was necessary and approved much more stringent policies.

Protecting the Financial Interests of the Public

Sport is a huge economic engine in the United States, and, whether directly or indirectly, the money wrapped up in sport affects every citizen. In the past, the U.S. government sometimes stepped in to direct and control the expansion of a sport as it grew in power and significance. For example, in cities where proposals were advanced to use public money to build stadiums or arenas that would benefit the owners of a professional franchise, governments have sometimes stymied such a proposal or put it to a public vote.

Historically, laws have been passed exempting U.S. professional sport leagues from antitrust laws (see chapter 4). As a result, MLB, the NFL, and the National Basketball Association (NBA) each have a virtual monopoly on their sport and therefore wield tremendous influence over their athletes, ticket prices, television rights, and revenue sharing between teams and cities. The key point here is that when government decides what is in the public interest, those who have economic power and influence are more likely to affect government decisions than those who have little power or influence. Also, owners of professional sport franchises are often able to further their business interests by claiming that their success will benefit the community, including other local businesses such as hotels and restaurants.

Indeed, local governments often give huge tax incentives to owners of professional franchises in order to convince them to locate or keep their franchise in a certain city. In addition, when an owner loses money due to mismanagement, excessive player contracts, or changes in the economy, he or she may ask the city for a better tax deal or threaten to leave town for a more attractive financial package. For example, the Oakland Raiders football team relocated to Los Angeles in 1982 only to move back to Oakland in 1995 when it could not agree on a deal for a new stadium in Los Angeles. The city of Oakland offered the team some $63 million in up-front incentives, loans, and other benefits to return (CNN Sports Illustrated 2001).

Government Promotion of Identity and Unity Among Citizens

Local and state governments have long used sport to promote pride, identity, and unity among citizens. By attracting a professional franchise, city leaders expect to capitalize on their financial investment by providing entertainment to residents and creating a bond among people of all backgrounds forged by a common interest in the home team. Indeed, on any given Monday morning during football season, the performance of the local professional team is a hot topic. Strangers use the fortunes of the local team to break the ice in conversations. If the team performs beyond expectations, fans feel a little bit prouder to be a part of their city and maybe just a bit better about life. In contrast, an entire populace can be cast into gloom due to a seemingly unimportant detail, such as a flubbed field goal in the waning seconds of a game.

Even very large metropolises such as New York, Chicago, and Los Angeles rally around their home team. In strikingly diverse racial and ethnic groups, city residents and suburban dwellers join to support their teams. Although most residents never actually see a professional game, they form strong opinions about the team's performance and learn the details through the print and electronic media. Team jerseys and hats appear throughout the city, and at every turn the team logo is displayed on billboards and auto stickers.

A particular type of fan support grows around pro teams that are cast in the image of their city and its historic ethnic groups. For example, the name of the Broad Street Bullies (as the Philadelphia Flyers were once known) reflected their rough-and-tumble approach to the game of hockey that resulted in a world championship. Over the years, the pride of the City of Brotherly Love has been invested in the Flyers in the National Hockey League (NHL), the "Iggles" (Eagles) in the NFL, and the Phillies in MLB. In this city dominated by ethnic enclaves of immigrants, fans are unique in their approach to sport, fanaticism, and impatience with their heroes. This is a city that cheered the triumph of a hero on the steps of the Philadelphia Art Museum in the classic film *Rocky* and booed Santa Claus at an Eagles game.

Likewise, Baltimore and Boston teams have been in a love affair with their fans for decades. Generations of families have shared a special sport fanaticism, and even when younger generations moved away they never lost their passion for their true home team. Teams that are relatively new to their cities, such as teams in the Sun Belt, do not have the same hard-core fans. Some games don't even sell out on a Sunday because of the fans' more modest interest in professional sport and the fact of competition from too many other leisure activities, especially outdoor activities.

Special sporting events also can help unify a city. Hosting the Super Bowl, the National Collegiate Athletic Association (NCAA) basketball tournament, baseball's All-Star Game, the Olympic Games, the Pan American Games, various collegiate championships, or even youth national championships can draw a community together by uniting businesses, media, and fans. Often, the economic benefits accrued by the host city more than compensate for the expenses of staging the event. Local volunteers may spend long hours helping operate the event in exchange for perks such as access to tickets.

A notable example of a city using sport to build an identity is Indianapolis, which labels itself the "amateur sports capital of the world." Through the entrepreneurial activities of a local sport com-

Boston has a strong tradition of fans of all ages cheering for their home team.

mission, the city aggressively bids to host every imaginable amateur sport championship and has staged more than 250 national and international sporting events. The city is also home to collegiate sport (the NCAA) and high school sport (the National Federation of State High School Associations), as well as the American College of Sports Medicine. In fact, a dozen national sport organizations have located their national headquarters in Indianapolis.

The city's business community has been steadfastly supportive, and the financial bonanza to the city's economy has enabled the government to improve the downtown and add sport and recreation facilities that are the envy of similar cities. All told, since 1979, Indianapolis has hosted more than 400 major sport events, which have had an economic impact exceeding $2 billion dollars (*American Outlook* 2011).

Even smaller cities use sport to build unity. They may focus on a particular sporting event, on a local college, or even on the local high school. State universities located away from large metropolitan areas usually garner tremendous fan support because they have no competition from professional sport events or teams. In some states, such as Texas, fans take their high school football very seriously, and the local football team is a source of town pride.

Nationalism and Sport

Sport events in the United States are typically replete with patriotic symbols that unify people by encouraging them to celebrate their shared heritage and common bonds. Games often open with the national anthem, the presentation of colors by a military team, a marching band playing rousing music, and perhaps even a military jet flyover. Organizers also stage halftime activities featuring music and dance that celebrate the culture and history of the area or of the nation.

Each year, one American football game stands out for its intertwining of nationalism and sport. As many as 100,000 people attend the classic Army–Navy game, which is usually held in Philadelphia, and the game also enjoys a national television audience. Decades ago, this game not only matched the two military academies but also boasted some of the best football players. Both teams were among the elite in college football and featured superstars such as Doc Blanchard, Pete Dawkins, and Roger Staubach.

Though recent years have seen a decline in the performance level of both teams, the Army–Navy game remains a memorable occasion. The pomp and circumstance, along with the hearty rooting sections of cadets and midshipmen, create an atmosphere unlike any other in college sport. As the U.S. Air Force Academy has improved its sport programs, it occasionally dominates football among the three academies, but the Army–Navy game still has the cachet. Soldiers, the brightest and best of the nation's youth, and an undeniable patriotic theme permeate the day and bestow significance on the game regardless of the level of play.

Nationalism is an expression of devotion to one's country. In times of war or disaster, such as the attack on the World Trade Center in New York in 2001, expressions of nationalism take on a poignancy that unites citizens. Shared tragedy helps create a strong bond among people of diverse backgrounds. Therefore, when national symbols such as the American flag are displayed at sporting events and carried on live television, millions of people collectively take pride in their country in spite of their apparent differences. In the United States, our most significant annual sporting event is arguably the Super Bowl, which draws about 100 million viewers around the world. Traditionally, it has also involved lavish displays of nationalistic pride before the game, at halftime, and even in many of the advertisements tied to the event. Recognition of U.S. troops is always deemed appropriate, and who can object to that?

As discussed in chapter 10, perhaps no sporting event has traded on nationalistic feelings as much as the Olympic Games have. Adolf Hitler staged the 1936 Olympics in an attempt to demonstrate the supposed superiority of the Nazi government and way of life. At the 1972 Games, East Germany claimed 90 medals—more than any country in the world in proportion to its size (East Germany was about the size of California). In comparison, the United States won 94 medals, and the Soviet Union won 125. Since 1972, the system of selection and training that produced those medals has been discredited because of the abuse of young athletes and the use of illegal drugs fostered by the East German government. Thus the success of East Germany's Olympic athletes served as a source of national pride that, once exposed, turned into a national embarrassment.

The expulsion of South Africa from the Olympics in 1964 and 1968 affected world opinion about South Africa's long-standing practice of apartheid. The resulting publicity helped build the pressure for major reform in a government that had repressed black citizens for centuries. Similarly, the People's Republic of China was long ostracized for its dismal record on human rights. However, in a remarkable change, Beijing was chosen to host the Olympic Games in 2008. China believed that its selection showed other nations' approval of its progress in righting the wrongs in the country. More likely, however, the choice of China as host reflected respect for and acknowledgement of its economic influence in the world rather than its performance regarding human rights.

Sport and the Promotion of Social Values

In the United States, sport is a largely conservative institution that promotes traditional values and can integrate people into the social construct. Generally, sport strives to maintain the status quo by teaching people mainstream values or perhaps by functioning as a distraction for people who are unsatisfied with society or their lives. Yet sport can also serve as a platform from which to point to the need for change.

In the United States, striving for excellence is a critical social value, and success is measured by achievement. Competition spurs people to perform to the maximum of their ability and to reach heights of excellence that they might never have thought possible. The U.S. recipe for success is to work hard, show discipline, and remain dedicated to personal goals. No shame is seen in defeating or being defeated, because in striving to win against the competitor both athletes are inspired to perform at their best.

In China, the values learned through sport can be very different. According to writers who studied Chinese attitudes toward sport in the 1970s,

POP CULTURE

A New Day for Sport and Politics?

In *Game Over: How Politics Has Turned the Sports World Upside Down* (2013a), Dave Zirin makes the case that a reborn confluence of sport and politics is upon us. For example, athletes at all levels have been seen wearing T-shirts proclaiming "I Can't Breathe" or "Black Lives Matter" or "Hands Up, Don't Shoot" in protest against overaggressive policing of black people. It may not be a new problem, but the fact that well-known athletes such as LeBron James, Magic Johnson, Kobe Bryant, and Reggie Bush have embraced the stance is a sign of the times. The college women's basketball teams at Notre Dame and the University of California joined in with their own T-shirts of protest.

During the Civil Rights Movement and the Vietnam war, athletes routinely made their political views known. In some cases, these actions isolated them from sport. In recent years, however, most athletes have been silent and followed advice from handlers, agents, and sponsors to keep their views private lest they offend anyone. For example, Michael Jordan, Tiger Woods, and Tim Tebow have all been reluctant to publicly endorse politicians in spite of pressure to do so. But things seem to be changing.

Using social media tools such as Twitter, athletes can now share their thoughts directly with fans on hot issues. Let's face it: Athletes can get the public's attention, and when they get behind a cause, they can influence people to at least consider the issue—particularly young people who are searching for answers. In the world of sport—where such discussions have often been repressed, ignored, or condemned—we just might be seeing the dawning of a new day (Zirin 2013a).

the prevailing attitude did not view winning as the ultimate goal. Rather, Chinese sport emphasized cooperation to achieve a group goal, friendship, and physical fitness. Little emphasis was placed on individual success, and athletes displayed devotion to the success of the group (Johnson 1973a, 1973b, 1973c). In the last few decades, some of those attitudes have changed, and China has become a world power in competitive sport, which culminated in Beijing's selection to host the 2008 Summer Olympics.

Adults use competitive sport to teach kids the lessons they believe necessary for later success in life. Kids learn that by trying their best to win in sport, they can develop the life skills needed in order to compete in the world. Those skills could also be developed through academic achievement, excellence in the arts, or exploration in technology and invention. Yet sport is often the first thing that comes to people's minds when they want to teach children the right habits for future success.

Sports are used throughout the world to socially integrate people from diverse backgrounds. For example, Northern Ireland has invested extensively in sport facilities in order to promote constructive interaction between Protestants and Catholics. In France, sport is often seen as a way of regenerating French youth and improving social discipline. And many countries, including England and the United States, use sport to combat urban unrest and reduce crime and juvenile delinquency (Coakley and Dunning 2004).

Sport as an Opiate of the Masses

Throughout much of history, various critics have charged that governments use sport to distract their citizens from societal inequities. These critics assert that government uses sport as an "opiate" to calm the masses, dull their senses, and distract their attention from their everyday social or economic problems. In this view, the hype given to sport puts the citizenry to sleep on matters of deeper significance. This charge has typically been leveled at authoritarian governments, especially those in countries with a large number of poor people (Eitzen 2004).

Developing countries have learned to use sport well. Powerful governments in the world's poorest nations have effectively rallied their citizens to support national teams representing their homeland. In most countries, the chosen sport is soccer or *football* as it is called in most of the world. For example, Brazil has embraced soccer as a national pastime and elevated its most famous son, Pelé, to the status of legendary hero. The exploits of the Brazilian soccer team have united rich and poor in a country beset with myriad social and economic tensions. Brazilian pride is stoked by every success achieved by the national soccer team. And around the world, Brazil is respected for its tradition of excellence in world soccer competition.

Brazil's unprecedented role in international sport was sealed when it was chosen to host both the World Cup soccer event in 2014 and the Olympic Games in 2016. As the first country in South America to be so honored, it faces the challenges of raising funds, building athletic facilities and supportive infrastructure, and meeting ambitious deadlines. IOC officials have noted their concern about the pace of the preparations and dubbed them even more troubling than those for the problematic Athens Games.

The charge of using sport as a distraction has also been made in the United States by public figures such as Bill Bradley, a star basketball player for Princeton University and later for the New York Knicks. After his basketball career, Bradley entered politics and became a U.S. senator; he was also a presidential contender in 2000. In the early days of his political career, he referred to sport as "a temporary fix, an escape from the problems of the world such as war, racism, and poverty that distracts the minds and saps the energies of people away from the problems of the lower classes" (Hoch 1972, 12).

Typically, political activists seek changes in their present government by criticizing those in power for diverting attention from critical social problems. A contemporary example can be found in Noam Chomsky, a brilliant political activist and professor of linguistics at the Massachusetts Institute of Technology. Chomsky has been acknowledged as one of the most influential voices in contemporary political discussions and is a left-wing critic of U.S. foreign policy. He certainly views sport as an opiate of the masses (Tsiokos 2005):

> *Sports keeps people from worrying about things that matter to their lives. Sports is a major factor in controlling people. Workers have minds; they have to be involved in something, and it's important to make sure they're involved in things that have absolutely no significance. So professional sport is perfect. It instills total passivity.*

Social critics may well ask, How do you explain the U.S. preoccupation with sport when the country still faces racial tensions, discrimination against women and ethnic groups, a rising national debt, concern for the long-term welfare of senior citizens living on limited incomes, the challenge of providing affordable health care, rising rates of obesity, continued assaults on the environment, and a deepening divide between the so-called red and blue states? Rather than facing a distrustful nation with so many questions, U.S. leaders may find it better to keep citizens focused on the Super Bowl, the March Madness of college basketball, the start of spring training for baseball, and the next Olympic Games (Huston 2005).

Critics also ask why cities spend millions to attract or retain professional sport franchises when that money could be used to help people living in poverty, build affordable housing, raise teacher salaries, improve school facilities, fight crime, and provide high-quality health care. It may be that people simply choose to focus their energy on more positive events. They may also feel powerless or unable to address the issues raised by social critics.

Sport and the Status Quo

Generally, in the United States, people associated with sport are politically conservative. More specifically, social theorists would classify most athletes, coaches, owners, executives, sportcasters, and sport promoters as functionalists—people who have invested their life in the sporting world and are grateful for the opportunities it has given them. Although there are notable exceptions—athletes and coaches who are politically liberal—they stand out because they are unusual. In this context, then, *conservative* refers to people who adhere to traditional methods or views and generally seek to perpetuate the status quo. On the other hand, *liberal* refers to those who are not bound by authoritarianism, orthodoxy, or tradition and are open to—and often seek—change from the status quo.

Owners of professional sport teams generally benefit from maintaining a political structure that supports them and is influenced by them. As a group, owners are typically very wealthy older white males who, of course, are products of their upbringing and experience. They may have little in common with the athletes on their teams, who often have a different racial or ethnic heritage and come from radically different economic circumstances. As for those who worked their way to the top, the leaders in most sport organizations have no desire to change the social structures and standards that they used in obtaining their current position.

Coaches at every level of competition tend to have a conservative outlook. They strongly believe in the traditional values of hard work, discipline, perseverance, and respect for authority. Regarding society, coaches often favor the status quo and resist change. In fact, coaches in the United States often play an authoritarian role (Eitzen 1992). Coaches are judged publicly on their job performance after every game. They are held responsible for their team's winning or losing, and if the percentage of losses is too great, they lose their job.

As a result, coaches tend to seek control of their own destiny by controlling the behavior of their athletes. They have strong opinions about how athletes should dress, act, wear their hair, represent their school, and interact with the media. Coaches may also have a direct interest in an athlete's academic performance, which affects athletic eligibility; in an athlete's friends, who may get the athlete into trouble; and even in an athlete's boyfriend or girlfriend, who might distract from his or her athletic performance. Athletes often follow their coaches in their political leanings; in fact, they may not question their coaches. These athletes are typically admired by their peers, fawned over by adults, and looked upon as heroes by younger people. They enjoy a high social status, especially during their teenage years, and if they continue on to a professional career, their success explodes.

Typical athletes choose to participate in sport and submit to the direction of various coaches. They learn to push themselves physically and mentally in order to succeed and perhaps to punish their body. If they are successful, the reinforcement provided by winning encourages them to continue to punish their bodies in order to continue their success. Athletes who are in the public eye are taught from an early age that they represent their parents, peers, community, and school. Coaches warn athletes against aberrant behavior that might reflect negatively on those who rely on them. Athletes learn to act in ways that

APPLYING SOCIAL THEORY

Functionalist Theory and Politics and Sport

Take the perspective of a functionalist theorist—typically, one who occupies a position of power and responsibility in sport, such as an owner, league commissioner, college president or athletic director, Olympic official, and member of a board of directors. Generally, this group of people would prefer to maintain sport as a functioning social institution that, in their view, is helpful to players, coaches, fans, and the public at large. When considering financial contributions to political causes, these individuals typically have four choices:

- Support the Republican candidate
- Support the Democratic candidate
- Support the best candidate regardless of party affiliation
- Support both candidates in order to hedge their bets

Explain in a two-page paper which of these four positions is most likely to appeal to a sport leader with a functionalist view—and why.

are socially acceptable and adhere to the standards of the existing community.

Perhaps even more important to today's athletes is the advice that they receive from their agent, who likely tells them that if their public image is controversial, then corporate sponsors are unlikely to shower them with lucrative endorsement fees. For example, throughout Michael Jordan's career, he was criticized by many people who felt that he should speak out, particularly about issues related to African Americans, and support certain political candidates. Indeed, in 1990, when black businessman and former Charlotte mayor Harvey Gantt ran as a Democrat against race-baiting civil rights opponent Jesse Helms—who even opposed making Dr. Martin Luther King Jr.'s birthday a national holiday—Jordan refused to take a stand in his home state. Instead, he pointed out that Republicans "buy Nike sneakers too" (Granderson 2012).

In deciding whether or not to share their views about social issues, athletes also consider team cohesion, which is part of the formula for success in team sport. Team members who think alike, share common goals, and sacrifice for the good of the group are popular with coaches and fellow athletes. In contrast, those who march to a different drummer are accepted only if their athletic contributions are exceptional. In this way, sport encourages conformity to behavior that is considered by society to be normal (Sage 1973).

In recent years in the United States, the Republican party has generally tended toward a more conservative platform, whereas the Democratic party has leaned toward a more liberal platform. However, it would be a mistake to classify all Republicans as simply conservative or all Democrats as simply liberal. There are, in fact, many shades of gray on both sides that depend on the specific issues being discussed.

As the 2004 U.S. presidential election loomed, the *Yale Daily News*, a student newspaper published at Yale University, featured an article titled "Many Elis Break From Norm, Lean Right" (August 2004). Yale has a long history of being a politically left campus; however, the "Elis," or members of the Delta Kappa Epsilon fraternity, broke tradition to lean right. The fraternity's membership included many football, baseball, and soccer players. One after another, these players said that they believed many varsity athletes on campus were politically conservative in contrast to the rest of the student body. In their view, athletes at Yale tended to vote Republican.

Indeed, in a poll taken early in the year by Yale's sport publicity staff, 62 football players said they planned to vote for Republican candidate George W. Bush, 27 planned to voted for Democratic candidate John Kerry, and 11 were undecided. The conservative stance of many football players might have been due to more than their sport participation. In fact, twenty of the players hailed from Texas, 35 percent came from Southern states, and about 13 percent were from the Midwest—all regions that are traditionally Republican. Only four players called a northern city home. In the end, perhaps the player's choice for president was not so surprising considering their origins.

In the 2012 U.S. presidential election, the owners of franchises in the four major leagues (MLB and the NFL, NBA, and NHL) donated a total of nearly $2 million by the end of August. Democrats collected just over $750,000 of that total, whereas Republicans, as usual, received the majority—nearly $1.25 million. The NBA was the only league where donations made to Barack Obama exceeded those made to Mitt Romney, though not by much (Reader 2012). In the 2008 presidential election, the choice had been between a former Navy boxer and war hero in John McCain and a younger pickup hoops player in Obama. The total donations from sports figures to McCain was $248,300 compared to $197,034 for Obama, or 55.8 percent for McCain and 44.2 percent for Obama.

In the previous two elections, Democratic candidates received no more than 16 percent of professional sport figures' donations. This should not come as a shock to us. For one thing, Republican presidents have tended to leave professional sport empires alone, whereas Democrats often have pushed for more regulation of sport. Sport owners and leaders also tend to support Republicans because they typically favor lower taxes for the well-to-do. As a result, elite professional athletes in football and basketball—who are predominately African American—often feel conflicted because their sympathies most often align with Democratic candidates but their very full pocketbooks cause them to lean toward Republicans and their preference for less government and lower taxes (Lavigne 2008).

These generalizations notwithstanding, it would be a mistake to lump all athletes—or others involved in sport—together as if they move in lockstep. In the NFL and NBA, for example, owners are mostly rich white men who generally hold different social and political views than many of the athletes who populate their teams. In golf, however, most of the players have grown up in country clubs, and 95 percent of them are Republicans. NASCAR drivers favor Republicans by a similar margin, but their background is generally much different from that of golfers. More often than not, they represent a white Southern mentality, often with a flavoring of conservative religious belief and support for the National Rifle Association.

As professor William Kelly pointed out when interviewed for the *Yale Daily News* article cited earlier, athletes in more individualized sports may be less conservative than team-sport players. Examples of these sports include squash, tennis, track and field, gymnastics, and skiing. Kelly also stated that female athletes are often less conservative than male athletes, perhaps because they are less satisfied with the status quo and therefore are more likely to desire change.

Using Sport to Change Society

Is it possible to change people's attitudes, feelings, and beliefs through the sport experience? Some people may respond quickly to this question with personal examples, whereas others may be more cautious. Over the years, sport has sometimes dramatized social inequities or injustices, such as racism, gender bias, and homophobia.

In 2014, for example, the media grabbed hold of the tabloid-ready story of Los Angeles Clippers owner Donald Sterling being caught on tape in a compromising conversation with his girlfriend, who was 50 years his junior. In the conversation, Sterling was heard disparaging African Americans and chastising his girlfriend for inviting them to sit with her at Clippers basketball games. Sterling's comments were insensitive, abhorrent, and explosive—all the more so in a sport where 77 percent of the athletes are African American.

Within a week, CNN host Anderson Cooper interviewed Sterling and helped illuminate the racial prejudice and warped social views of an owner who was clearly out of touch with mainstream America. The NBA's response was swift and clean—a $2.5 million fine (the maximum allowed by NBA bylaws) and a lifetime banishment for Sterling. The action removed him from control of the team, installed a temporary executive, and made plans to auction the team to a new owner.

Champion athletes have a platform from which to share their views if they so choose. For example, boxer Muhammad Ali spoke his mind about the military draft, the Vietnam War, and racial prejudice. Tennis star Arthur Ashe Jr. spoke about the same issues, though in a much different way than Ali did. Olympic athletes Tommie Smith and John Carlos used their Olympic success to raise the Black Power salute during the playing of the American national anthem in 1968 in Mexico City. Tennis player Martina Navratilova was open about her lesbianism during her professional career and is still wildly popular. Billie Jean King preceded Navratilova and in some respects gave Martina the courage to affirm her sexuality publicly. King was also a relentless pioneer for women's rights through the Women's Sports Foundation. More recently, male athletes such as NBA player Jason Collins and NFL prospect Michael Sam have come out during their active career.

In terms of economic issues, baseball player Curt Flood basically sacrificed his outstanding baseball career to stand up for a player's right to free agency and some degree of self-determination as a professional athlete. He abhorred the idea that athletes could be bought and sold by team owners with no say in the decision. You have to wonder if today's professional athletes understand the sacrifice that Flood made in order to make a statement that ended his career but eventually brought freedom and wealth to so many athletes that followed.

These examples demonstrate how some athletes have used sport to agitate for societal change. Whether or not they achieved their immediate goals is beside the point. Their efforts raised consciousness and inspired others to stop and question their own views. These outspoken athletes are all the more remarkable for having acted forcefully in an institution that generally preserves the status quo. Their actions reflect those of critical theorists who strongly believe in the power of sport to change hearts and minds and eventually society at large.

Use of Sport by Politicians

U.S. athletes who win a Super Bowl, World Series, or other major event can bet on receiving a congratulatory phone call from the president. In the last 60 years, virtually every U.S. president has used his image as a sport fan to link himself to the populace at large. Presidents have thrown out the

John Carlos and Tommie Smith

Whatever you might believe about the use of sport to promote a political agenda, some Olympic athletes through the years have seized their opportunity to make a statement to the world. John Carlos and Tommie Smith chose the medal ceremony for the 200-meter run at the 1968 Mexico City Olympic Games. During the playing of the Star-Spangled Banner, they each wore black socks and no shoes and raised a black-gloved fist upward while staring down in a salute to Black Power and a protest against African American poverty in the United States. The third medal winner, Peter Norman of Australia, joined them in protest by prominently displaying a patch representing the Olympic Project for Human Rights (OPHR).

Prior to the 1968 Olympic Games, Carlos and Smith had become founding members of OPHR, which advocated a boycott of the Games unless four conditions were met: withdrawal from the Games by South Africa and Rhodesia because of their apartheid policies; restoration of Muhammad Ali's world championship boxing title (taken because of his refusal to be drafted into the U.S. military), replacement of IOC president Avery Brundage (an avowed white supremacist who had supported Hitler's hosting of the 1936 Games), and the hiring of more African American coaches. The boycott failed once the IOC withdrew invitations for South Africa and Rhodesia, but the athletes were not swayed.

Forty-seven years later, the actions of Smith and Carlos remain relevant. In recognition of their courageous actions, these two men—Smith the son of a migrant worker and Carlos a product of Harlem—have been granted honorary doctorates from their alma mater, San Diego State University, and shared the Arthur Ashe Courage Award at the 2008 ESPYs presented by ESPN.

first ball of the baseball season, attended the U.S. Open tennis championships, and graced the opening ceremonies of the Olympic Games. President Richard Nixon even suggested certain plays that he thought the Washington football team should use in its quest for a Super Bowl title. In fact, Nixon was perhaps the first U.S. president to use sport contacts and his keen personal interest in sport to portray himself as a regular guy (Ball and Loy 1975).

More recently, President Barack Obama has appeared in the sport media offering his predictions for the NCAA men's and women's basketball tournaments. He also shared his personal opinion that the NCAA football championship should involve a playoff system rather than relying merely on polls. Even more notable was his unprecedented decision to support the bid of his hometown of Chicago to host the 2016 Olympic Games by flying to Copenhagen, Denmark, and addressing the delegates before the vote. Unfortunately for Obama and Chicago, the International Olympic Committee chose Rio de Janeiro instead.

For athletes who achieve notable success, one of the most coveted rewards is a visit to the White House following their victory. Young athletes are impressed by the experience and tend to rank it high among their personal highlights. At the same time, the president and his invited political allies use the occasion to solidify their support and demonstrate a personal admiration for winners of major competitive events.

At the local level, state governors, members of the state legislature, mayors, and other political figures are never far from view at major sporting events in their area. Mayors almost routinely make a friendly wager on the outcome of major contests involving their city's team; when they lose, they award the winner a symbolic prize indigenous to their region. The media pick up on the wager, and the politicians manufacture a media opportunity both before and after the event. Modern politicians did not invent the use of sport to enhance their image. For centuries, kings, queens, and heads of state have seized upon athletic contests as public

Politicians' involvement in sport serves many roles.

relations opportunities. Current politicians are simply following a well-worn script.

Some athletes have even used their sport fame to propel themselves to political prominence once their playing days ended. Notable examples include Jim Ryun, Olympic distance runner and U.S. representative from Kansas; Jim Bunning, Hall of Fame pitcher for the Detroit Tigers and U.S. senator from Kentucky; Jack Kemp, Buffalo Bills quarterback and U.S. representative from New York; Bill Bradley, Hall of Famer for the New York Knicks and senator from New Jersey; Jesse Ventura, professional wrestler and governor of Minnesota; and Arnold Schwarzenegger, bodybuilder and governor of California. On the local level, celebrities such as high school and college coaches parlay their name recognition into public roles as mayors, commissioners, and community leaders.

Politics Within Sport

Every major sport is controlled internationally by a governing body that sets the rules of play, defines age groups for competition, sanctions competitions, stages world championships, administers drug tests, and promotes the sport worldwide. The organization comprises representative governing bodies from every participating nation, and organizational officials are elected from within the membership. The process of electing members to the international board of directors is clearly political and not unlike what transpires in other governmental elections. Powerful nations protect their turf and self-interests by forming liaisons with other nations, dispensing favors, and using their vast resources to advance their influence. Nations with less influence form coalitions to push for a place at the decision-making table.

The picture at the international level is replicated at the national level in every country. National boards wield awesome power, and aspiring leaders campaign for years to earn a place of prestige on the board. Depending on who sits on the board, an organization's mission may tilt toward any of various possible agendas—for example, developing high-performance athletes, increasing participation by the masses, showing sensitivity to minorities, demonstrating compassion for athletes with a physical disability, attracting more spectators, or generating more revenue by marketing the sport. In an ideal world, a national governing body would have the will and means to do all of the above and more.

Some other organizations are dedicated to youth sport. Some take a multisport focus—for example, the Amateur Athletic Union—but most focus on one sport. When more than one organization emerges in a single sport, as in youth soccer, the result may include a confusing war of words and political clashes about purpose, rules, and championships.

In the United States, interscholastic sport is loosely governed by the National Federation of State High School Associations. As the word *federation* suggests, the organization has minimal control. It sanctions no national championships and allows each state to set its own rules of competition. As a result, policies differ widely from state to state and can be confusing for athletes and their families, especially those who move from one state to another.

Over the years, college athletics in the United States has endured several political battles between organizations fighting for control. At this point, the winner has been the NCAA, which claims the bulk of colleges and universities as members. The NCAA has created multiple levels of competition (Division I, II, and III) and allows each school to choose its level provided that it meets certain standards. The philosophical differences between the three levels generate controversy and political horse trading. Big schools want to be free to spend their money and conduct what amounts to a quasi-professional sport program. Smaller schools, where sport is more student centered, demand more accountability from institutions, stronger academic standards for athletes, and emphasis on participation rather than high performance.

In U.S. professional sport, various competing leagues spring up to challenge existing professional leagues. Some competing leagues enjoy success, such as the American Football League, which eventually merged with the established NFL. The two football leagues found that together they could be more efficient, powerful, and attractive to commercial sponsors and television stations than two competing leagues could be.

In contrast, professional tennis has suffered from being divided into two organizations—one for women and one for men. Although women and men often play at the same tournaments, their separate organizations compete for facilities (such as practice courts, weightrooms, training rooms, and media rooms), courts for matches, prize money, commercial sponsors, and fan loyalty. So far, politics and distrust from both sides have blocked a beneficial merger. The result is a fractured delivery of the professional game that confuses fans around the world and limits the appeal of both men's and women's tennis to potential commercial sponsors.

Chapter Summary

This chapter discusses how sport and politics interact locally, nationally, and internationally. The U.S. government is responsible for protecting the rights of its citizens; to that end, it enforces certain safeguards in sport, ensures that the rights of all citizens are respected in sport, and protects the financial interests of the public.

Governments use sport to develop local, state, or national identity and to promote unity among citizens. Governments and political leaders also use sport to promote dominant social values and encourage social integration of all citizens. Critics of government accuse politicians of using sport to distract citizens from other pressing issues or to reinforce the status quo. Politicians also often use sport to enhance their personal image.

When athletes succeed in international competition, their excellence is often attributed to the superior way of life of their home nation. The Olympic Games have been used repeatedly to validate systems of government, generate support for political leaders, and prove the superiority of various ethnic or racial groups.

Sport events are typically staged with nationalistic displays that include the national anthem, marching bands, patriotic themes, and flag presentations. Citizens who take pride in their country are more likely to reelect current governmental leaders and feel content with their society.

In the United States, when young children are exposed to sport, they experience the socialization process of learning to respect authority, work hard, persevere, rebound from failure, and cooperate with others. Sport is just one way in which these traditional American values are passed to the next generation.

At the same time, sport can sometimes be a powerful agent in promoting societal change. The sport world constantly reminds fans, participants, and the public at large that changes are occurring. For example, the emergence of African American athletes on the public stage, and later the rise of women's sport, confirm recent landmark changes in U.S. culture.

Within sport organizations, politics influences the direction of the group and determines who leads the group. Those who advocate for radical change within a sport fight to select sympathetic leaders, whereas those who do not want radical change rally around their chosen candidates. Most athletic groups have gradually begun to reserve a place at their decision-making table for females, minorities, and athletes with a disability. Through such diversity, sport can grow by reaching out to new populations of participants and fans.

Finally, the chapter examined the tendency for coaches and athletes to be politically conservative. Their political philosophy tends to be influenced by their sport training, which teaches them to respect traditional values and authority figures and to embrace the ideals of hard work, discipline, and positive attitude. Those who succeed in sport, as in other arenas, often want to conserve the environment in which they have excelled.

18

STUDENT OUTCOMES

After reading this chapter, you will know the following:

- A definition of development through sport and physical activity
- The benefits of sport that have been substantiated through research
- The distinct benefits of sport at various ages
- The four types of developmental sport program
- The nature of sport development programs in the United States and worldwide
- Potential sources of funding for sport development programs

Development Through Sport

Development Through Sport

Volley Against Violence is a partnership between the Boston Police Community Tennis Association and the Sportsmen's Tennis and Enrichment Center. It gives 125 to 150 youth from all ages in the greater Boston area free tennis sessions on Friday evenings with professional coaches and volunteer Boston police officers. Along with an introduction to tennis and skill development, the players learn strategies for addressing conflicts and challenges in ways that do not employ violence.

When the Sportsmen's Tennis and Enrichment Center was founded in 1961, it became the first indoor nonprofit tennis facility built by and for the African American community. A small group of friends believed in the transforming power of tennis as a sport that could promote the healthy development of at-risk kids with a focus on sport, academics, life skills, and good citizenship. The club has served the greater Boston community for more than 50 years and provided a model for similar programs and facilities in all major U.S. cities. Most of them have been closely affiliated with National Junior Tennis and Learning, which was founded in 1969 by Arthur Ashe and now includes more than 500 nonprofit, free or low-cost tennis and educational programs serving a total of more than 250,000 youngsters annually.

Countless cultures have used sport and physical activity to enhance the quality of life for participants. Such efforts have sometimes focused on training elite athletes, but they have also generally acknowledged the fact that all citizens can derive immediate personal benefits from participating in sport and other physical activity. In recent years, the use of sport and physical activity for developmental purposes has become more clearly focused, better organized, better funded, and more appreciated as a way to improve society for all people regardless of age, gender, disability, and income level.

This chapter examines how sport and physical activity are used for personal and societal development; specifically, it describes the types of development programming and their potential for achieving their objectives. It also considers sport development programs from a worldwide perspective and their possible effect on global health issues, cultural understanding, and peace among nations. In addition, the chapter explores the potential benefits of these programs in the United States in terms of underprivileged youth and older adults, academic performance, crime reduction, and health issues such as obesity and diabetes.

Benefits of Sport and Physical Activity

If you think back to chapter 1—which laid out the differences between sport, physical activity, and games—you may recall that in order for an activity to be classified as a sport, it must include physical activity, rules set by a governing body, competition, and, typically, specialized equipment or venues to play in. For the purposes of this chapter, we can view physical activity and sport as one overall category, much in the same way the Sports and Fitness Industry Association (2013a) does in its reports about sport participation. This combination means that when we refer to *sport* in the chapter, we are including physical activities such as strength training, running, Pilates, yoga, and walking or swimming for recreation.

The benefits of sport can be placed into the following categories:

- *Fun.* Physical movements are performed for recreation and are pleasurable for the participant.
- *Better health.* Types of physical activity that enhance the participant's physical well-being include cardiorespiratory and muscular strength exercise, endurance exercise, and flexibility activities. Regular sport participation promotes the functioning of all body systems and helps develop resistance to disease.
- *Social integration.* Sport activities promoting interpersonal interaction, cooperation, and competition affect participants' social development and help them develop teamwork and social skills.
- *Moral development.* Sport activities can provide participants with opportunities to develop an acceptable moral code and make moral choices. A positive personal moral code includes development of honesty, integrity,

EXPERT'S VIEW

John Young

John Young founded Reviving Baseball in Inner Cities (RBI) in 1989 in south central Los Angeles. As a former Major League Baseball (MLB) player and scout with the Detroit Tigers and other teams, Young was alarmed by the trend of fewer African Americans choosing to play baseball, particularly in cities. Consider the fact that in the 1940s—before Jackie Robinson joined the Dodgers in 1947—MLB included no African American players. By the mid-1980s, African Americans accounted for 18 percent of major leaguers. By 2012, however, that percentage had dropped to just 7.2 percent as a result of baseball's decline in popularity in inner cities (Cook 2013).

John Young saw the developing trend and founded the RBI program to promote the games of baseball and softball in disadvantaged areas. He partnered with the Boys & Girls Clubs of America and focused on helping kids overcome obstacles, such as street gangs, lack of academic support, and social disadvantages. By 1991, the RBI program had been absorbed by MLB as a youth outreach program now supported by all 30 Major League teams, which represents a commitment of more than $30 million worth of resources (Major League Baseball 2015).

As a result, over the past 25 years, Young has seen his vision grow into a nationwide program that has served more than a million kids and currently serves more than 120,000 boys and girls in 185 cities. MLB has drafted more than 185 players from the program, but the real achievement can be seen in the hundreds of thousands of alumni whose lives have been enhanced.

fairness, and responsibility. The key to developing moral decision making is for coaches to set the program philosophy, allow players to confront moral choices, and encourage them to adopt the best course of action.

- *Personal development of self-esteem and self-efficacy.* Sport enhances an individual's sense of self-worth, self-concept, and feelings of adequacy. In particular, youth can experience a feeling of success through sport that improves self-confidence and promotes a positive personality.
- *Cognitive development.* Sport can improve a person's thinking, help improve academic performance, and allow the brain to continue healthy growth even at advanced ages.

Benefits of Sport at Various Ages

The accepted benefits of sport apply generally to participants of all ages, but the significance of various benefits can be affected by age. For example, children are in the process of growth and maturation, and physical activity can have a powerful effect on their development. Older adults, in contrast, are fully developed and are more focused on maintaining physical health, avoiding disease, and enhancing the quality of their daily life. Let's look at some of the key differences between age groups.

Childhood

Childhood is the time from birth through the elementary school years. It is the period of the most rapid growth and development that human beings ever experience—physically, emotionally, cognitively, and socially. Children begin to learn about their world through movement, and they can develop skills for exploring their world by practicing fundamental movement skills. During their early years, children should learn to walk, run, skip, hop, balance, fall, catch, throw, and kick—to list just a few fundamental movements.

Once these basics are under control, they are capable of learning and enjoying basic sport skills, playing games, and learning to participate in sport. Children also can use sport to enhance their self-concept in its early stages of development by mastering certain physical activities and learning new ones. Children are also introduced to ideas of fair play, playing by the rules, being a good sport, and cooperating with teammates.

Team sports are particularly attractive to children because they introduce kids to working together for a common goal, accepting their role on a team, and learning to deal with winning and losing in competition. However, leaders in many individual sports—especially ones such as tennis, golf, squash, and sailing—have also developed admirable youth sport programs to include children who normally would not be exposed to their sport.

Sport also fills an important role if it is fun, invigorating, and challenging for youngsters. Their attitudes and habits about lifelong physical activity are likely to be formed at this stage of life.

Youth

This category includes youngsters in middle and high school who are in transition between childhood and the adult world. Sport and physical activity can continue to affect all dimensions of their development if they continue to be physically active. Unfortunately, the system in our culture tends to weed kids out based on their competence in sport; as a result, during adolescence, more than half of children who were physically active drop out of sport. Just over 50 percent of all youth in the United States are involved in at least one organized sport at age 12, and by high school 70 percent of those have been lost to sport (Kelley and Carchia 2013):

All youth under age 18	50 million
Youth athletes age 12 and under	27 million
High school athletes	8 million
College athletes	400,000

Those who enjoyed success as children often feel lost and betrayed by the people who encouraged them in sport. It is difficult for youth to maintain or enhance their self-concept when they are cut from a school team, which implies to them that they lack talent.

Puberty also affects youth in that they must deal with a rapidly changing body that is unfamiliar to them. Moreover, growth spurts that occur before or after similar changes in most of their peers can cause embarrassment, self-consciousness, and social withdrawal. In addition, sport participation may take a backseat to the development of sexual interest, which may consume a considerable portion of a young person's thoughts and time.

Youth is a critical time to help people stay physically active in a way that is fun, challenging, and enjoyable. New sports and physical activities should be explored that allow participants at all levels of experience and skill to join in. Youth need to realize and accept that their world of physical activity and sport need not revolve only around traditional team sports. The challenge is to expose them to a wide variety of physical activities that are enjoyable now and hold promise for future participation.

Adulthood

For many of us, the adult years are consumed with discovering who we are and want to be, forming close relationships with others, challenging ourselves intellectually, and plotting a career path. Young adults tend to experiment with various

ACTIVITY TIME-OUT

Development Activities

Pick a sport of your choice—either one that you have played or one that you would enjoy exploring. Now consider whether that sport has specific development programs or at least the foundation for reaching out to specific groups. You cannot assume that simply participating in a sport will necessarily promote development. Granted, participation is likely to enhance physical skill, but your aim in this inquiry is to determine whether your chosen sport has developed or could develop a formula and process to do more than simply produce skilled players or provide fun for participants. Report to your class about what you discover.

behaviors, try them on, and decide whether they fit. The years of young adulthood usually involve some physical activity chosen to improve fitness, appearance, and attractiveness to others. One's commitment to physical activity can be challenged by the pressures of college, work, or starting a family, and for some people the easy response is to reduce or altogether drop regular physical activity. Indeed, young adults who are healthy and busy may feel invincible and allow physical activity to slip to the bottom of their priorities.

Faced with this challenge, some people find motivation and support by joining a group or team for sport or physical activity. Doing so can help a person persist in being active while also enlarging his or her circle of friends and contacts. In contrast, those who choose a sport or activity that they can do alone often have the toughest time persisting.

Adults who have experienced sport as fun and exhilarating are the most likely ones to continue their commitment, because they seek that familiar thrill as a stress reducer and respite from work. On the other hand, people who view physical activity as "work" often dread the "workouts" they believe they should do but don't feel like doing. The key for them is to identify an activity that they would look forward to and never want to miss out on.

Older Adulthood

Older adults who continue an established pattern of physical activity are lucky in that they decided long ago that doing so was important for them; alternatively, perhaps they simply enjoyed it so much that they made time for regular physical recreation. For those who slipped away from physical activity during their adult years, health concerns may help them refocus on its importance to their fitness, health, and disease resistance. In addition, in the back of their mind, questions may loom both about length of life and about quality of life in the years they have left.

Older adults tend to gravitate toward physical activities that are group oriented, especially once they retire from the workforce. They treasure the social interaction with friends and acquaintances who share their interests. Many people are also drawn to sport-related travel, and at this stage of life they may have enough time and money to afford it.

As we age, most of us become concerned with the expected decline of our cognitive functions. Recent breakthroughs in research clearly show that physical activity can help us continue to generate new brain cells and strengthen the connections in those that we already have. Many older folks would much rather walk, swim, play golf, or play tennis than settle for a life of crossword puzzles to keep them intellectually vibrant.

Finally, though it is not a topic for this chapter on development, current research and practice in communities designed for older adults always involve programs to encourage ongoing physical activity. In fact, the lifestyle promoted in many of these communities is referred to by the term "active living." It implies that people are happier and healthier if they remain active.

Development Programs for Children and Youth

Recent history has seen myriad uses of sport and physical activity to enhance the overall development of children and youth. Each program is designed to fit local needs and to complement other programs available in the community. The emphasis of each program is determined by the founders and board of directors. Let's look at some of the most common program philosophies (American Sports Data 2005).

Stand-Alone Sport and Physical Activity Programs

Stand-alone sport and physical activity programs are typically established to teach youngsters the skills and strategies of various sports and to introduce them to competition. The expectation is that they will improve their physical capabilities, test them in competition, and build a foundation for later participation as they age and improve.

Team sports are a particularly popular means for teaching social and moral values, good sporting behavior, and teamwork. In many individual sports, more emphasis is placed on developing independence, self-reliance, self-discipline, and confidence. Examples include tennis, golf, martial arts, dance, swimming, wrestling, track and field, and a host of extreme sports.

Interest in the martial arts continues to expand throughout the United States as a competitive sport, a fitness activity, and a means of self-defense. The traditional martial arts of judo and taekwondo have been Olympic sports for some time, and both have national governing bodies housed at the U.S. Olympic Training Center in Colorado Springs. In addition, as mixed martial arts (MMA) continues to grow in popularity, its followers may choose to practice it as a personal discipline, either for fitness or as a competitive sport. Two other martial arts, tai chi and cardio kickboxing, also draw strong participation as fitness activities. Overall, martial arts participation in the United States involves nearly 18 million people—a level of popularity rivaling that of any traditional popular sport (Sports and Fitness Industry Association 2013a).

Many U.S. parents encourage their children to pursue the martial arts in order to build discipline and self-confidence as well as fitness. Young people may also participate in the martial arts as a means of self-protection due to the prevalence of bullying. In addition, many kids enjoy exploring various styles and methods of martial arts, which gives them a diverse appreciation along with a variety of skills.

At-Risk Prevention Programs

Many communities have used sport as a hook to attract children and youth who are deemed at risk of school delinquency or running afoul of the law. For example, the Police Athletic League offers activities that include sport, arts and crafts, and dance. In this program, the local police department contributes funding to youth programs, and many officers volunteer as leaders and coaches.

Another organization that is particularly popular across the southern part of the United States is the Boys & Girls Clubs of America. Among other things, it offers inner-city programs such as midnight youth basketball leagues to encourage kids to participate in sport rather than roam the streets looking for trouble.

In the northern part of the country, YMCAs and YWCAs (now referred to simply as the "Y") and Jewish Community Centers (JCC) are plentiful and offer attractive facilities along with sport programs for kids. In many cases, Y offerings include classes and programs for the whole family, thus enabling these facilities to function as family recreation centers.

Another example is Girls in the Game, founded in 1995 by a small group of women in Chicago to ensure that girls are exposed to and participate in sport and fitness activities. The target population is one identified in chapter 12 as least likely to be physically active—inner-city minority girls. The 2012 demographics for the Girls in the Game program showed the following proportions by race and ethnicity: 43 percent Hispanic or Latino, 38 percent African American, 4 percent Caucasian, 9 percent other or unknown, and 3 percent multiracial. By age, the proportions were as follows: 9 percent for ages 7 and 8, 33 percent for ages 9 and 10, 36 percent for ages 11 and 12, 16 percent for ages 13 and 14, and 6 percent for age 15 or higher. Research has shown that girls who are physically active and involved in healthy-lifestyle programs earn higher grades; are more likely to graduate; develop higher self-esteem; and are less likely to drink, use drugs, or engage in other risky behavior (Girls in the Game 2015).

Sadly, 1 in every 6 girls in the United States today is overweight—a dramatic increase from 1970, when only 1 in 21 girls was overweight. In addition, only 16 percent of urban 11th- and 12th-grade girls take a gym class, whereas 52 percent of boys do. Faced with these sobering statistics, the leaders of the Girls in the Game program realized that their girls needed more than just sport, and the program was expanded. The girls also wanted information about nutrition, health education, and leadership development, and these components have now been integrated into the program. Funding and facilities for the program have been obtained through partnerships with the city of Chicago, public schools, and public parks, as well as fundraising efforts and the largesse of private donors (Girls in the Game 2015).

A distinctly different approach is taken by Up2Us, a national coalition of sport-based youth development organizations. The coalition's flagship program is Coach for America (CFA), which recruits coaches to teach sport and nutrition to kids in under-resourced communities in the hope of preventing childhood obesity. The coaches encourage kids to stay off the streets and stay in school; they also help kids build their self-esteem and positive self-image. CFA is funded by an AmeriCorps grant from the Corporation of National and Community Service, a federal government program established by the U.S. Congress.

Academic Enrichment and Sport Programs

Academic enrichment and sport programs have spread across the country, and they are often geared especially to serve economically disadvantaged youth. These programs typically offer a safe haven after school and include sport and other physical activity as well as an academic focus. They often provide tutors and devote time to having kids complete school homework assignments.

Many federal and state grants have been made available to establish such programs because they promise to improve participants' academic performance and encourage good citizenship while also offering fun and recreation through sport. To supplement their grant money, organizations in this category often sponsor fundraising events. The organizations are typically established as nonprofits, which means that they can receive tax-deductible donations from businesses and individuals.

Nationwide programs of this type have been established in golf and tennis—the First Tee and National Junior Tennis and Learning (NJTL). The First Tee is an initiative of the World Golf Foundation. Its stated mission is "to impact the lives of young people by providing learning facilities and educational programs that promote character-development and the life-enhancing values through the game of golf." The program espouses nine core values: honesty, integrity, good sporting behavior, respect, confidence, responsibility, perseverance, courtesy, and judgment (First Tee 2010). The NJTL was founded by professional tennis players Arthur Ashe and Charles Pasarell more than 40 years ago, when it was the first program of its kind. For more detail about this program, refer back to the chapter's opening vignette.

Although these programs are sponsored by their respective national sport organizations, their purpose is not to develop elite athletes but to expose underserved populations to the sport in the hope that they become lifelong participants and spectators. Because these programs are either free or very low cost to participants, funding poses a local challenge even though the programs are national in scope. In most cases, program organizers reduce costs by recruiting volunteer coaches and obtain revenues by sponsoring an array of fundraising events.

Day camps are a great way to incorporate education into a physically active and fun-filled day.

Academic Development and Sport Programs

Programs that integrate sport and academics seek to attract the interest of youth by combining the two. For example, an after-school enrichment class in math could use sport statistics as a vehicle to interest kids and show practical applications. Similarly, kids can practice and improve their language skills by writing about sport situations, athletes, or events such as the Super Bowl and other championships. Reading about sport can also stimulate a lifelong habit of reading in youngsters who might otherwise be uninterested in it. Even history can come alive for young people who are exposed to information about sport origins, famous athletes, and world record holders.

Similarly, scuba diving courses can incorporate the rudiments of marine biology or oceanography to get kids excited about the sciences of studying bodies of water and their effects on society. Sport experiences can also provide a vehicle for teaching young people moral codes and decision making skills and enhancing their character development. Participation in team sports and other physical activities can also facilitate social development that transfers into the classroom and the workplace if the experiences are properly structured and delivered.

Other sport and physical activity programs focus on helping participants develop an appreciation of nature; examples include programs involving snow sports, hiking, camping, and wilderness survival skills. Kids who participate in such programs can learn much about nature, geography, forestry, and the environment through outdoor activities in the mountains, on the water, in the desert, or on a trip through the Everglades. When programs expose kids to nature and teach them how to interact with the environment, they also produce the positive by-product of enhanced self-confidence in facing unfamiliar or uncertain surroundings.

These various educational sport programs fill a need for after-school care that kids enjoy in a safe environment. That need derives from the fact that in modern U.S. society, families typically have both parents in the workplace (where women now outnumber men), thus often leaving kids to fend for themselves after school unless they are enrolled in an after-school program. The importance of including sport and other physical activity in such programs is crystal clear for a generation of youth who get too little physical exercise, often have a poor diet, and are bombarded by video games and other technological diversions that frequently replace physical play and exercise.

International Outreach Through Sport

Outside the United States, sport and physical activity have played significant roles in promoting better health and well-being, preventing disease, and enhancing the quality of life for people of all ages. The organizations discussed in this section

IN THE ARENA WITH . . .

Project Coach

The Project Coach after-school program embodies a different twist on using sport for academic development. The program gives economically disadvantaged minority teenagers the opportunity to serve as sport coaches for elementary-age kids. Founded in 2002 by professors Sam Intrator and Don Siegel at Smith College in Massachusetts, the program is designed to help distressed communities in nearby Mt. Holyoke and Springfield use the appeal of sport to aid in the academic and social development of youth. At the outset, the organizers determined that simply arranging sport opportunities for participants was unlikely to affect their academic performance, in spite of many claims that it would do so.

Instead, Project Coach operates on the thesis that sport coaching, by its very nature, provides a unique opportunity to develop various supercognitive skills. Indeed, successful sport coaches must be effective goal setters, communicators, and planners. They must also be able to take charge, build teamwork and camaraderie, and think strategically and deliberately. In addition, they operate in an environment that requires quick judgments, initiative, and improvisational thinking. All the while, they must also serve as motivators, role models, and confidants for their charges. In short, they need to develop a skill set that is also crucial for success in academics.

Since its inception, the program has helped solve the problem of finding youth sport coaches in underserved communities. It has also provided a laboratory for teenagers to enlarge their skills through coaching. Participants undergo intensive training that exposes them to the purposeful planning of youth sport focused on enabling the best possible development of participants. Project Coach is a brilliant idea that has evolved over the years into a youth sport program that works—both for the younger participants and for the youth coaches, who become agents of change in struggling communities (Intrator and Siegel 2008).

of the chapter promote regular physical activity for all people all over the world.

The World Health Organization (WHO) has taken the lead in the fight against noncommunicable diseases, such as cardiovascular disease, cancer, diabetes, and chronic respiratory disease. According to a WHO report (2003), "Unhealthy diets, caloric excess, physical inactivity and obesity, and associated chronic diseases are the greatest public health problem in most countries in the world."

Worldwide, more than 31 percent of adults aged 15 or over do not engage in sufficient physical activity; more specifically, the rate is 28 percent among men and 34 percent among women. This is a big problem, because insufficient activity is the culprit in more than 3 million deaths per year (World Health Organization 2014). Moreover, physical inactivity is estimated to cause about 6 percent of deaths globally and is the main cause of more than 20 percent of breast and colon cancers, more than 25 percent of diabetes cases, and about 30 percent of ischemic heart disease cases (World Health Organization 2014). The groups most affected are women, older adults, people from lower socioeconomic groups, and people with a disability.

People are becoming more sedentary the world over, and the result is an alarming increase in obesity and poor health. The WHO believes that regular physical activity, active play, and sport can directly affect major risks to good health, such as high blood pressure, high cholesterol, obesity, tobacco use, and stress (World Health Organization 2014).

Another key international sport organization is the International Olympic Committee (IOC). As a promoter of elite performance at the highest level of worldwide competition, the IOC has a different take on the value of sport for all. The IOC believes that human development through sport is based on the three core values of the Olympic movement: excellence, friendship, and respect. In this conception, excellence involves giving one's best; making progress toward personal goals; and benefiting from the healthy combination of a strong body, mind, and will. The second core value, friendship, encourages us to use sport as a way to develop understanding of people from all over the world. The third core value, respect, includes respect for self, for one's body, for others, and for the rules and regulations of sport; it also encompasses fair play and support for the battle against doping in sport.

The IOC believes that in addition to promoting physical wellness, sport can contribute to a safer, more prosperous, and more peaceful society. Specifically, it can help bridge cultural and ethnic divides, enable the creation of jobs and businesses, promote tolerance and nondiscrimination, and reinforce social integration. The Olympic Charter describes the IOC's social responsibility in this way:

> *The goal of Olympism is to place sport at the service of the harmonious development of man, with a view to promoting a peaceful society concerned with the preservation of human dignity.*

In reviving the Olympic Games near the end of the nineteenth century, founder Pierre de Coubertin, a French educator, asserted that the Olympics should serve as a strong advocate of international cooperation and emphasize the social and human values of sport. Lest you think that these descriptions of the Olympic movement are simply esoteric philosophies, consider the following IOC initiatives:

- *Bringing sport to rural and underdeveloped communities.* In cooperation with the Food and Agriculture Organization of the United Nations (U.N.), the IOC has provided basic sport equipment and facilities to encourage people toward a lifestyle of physical activity. Nations that have benefited include Burkina Faso, Cambodia, Ecuador, Tanzania, Niger, Mauritania, Guinea, Samoa, and Laos.
- *Local economic development.* In cooperation with the U.N. International Labour Organization, the IOC has implemented a major poverty alleviation and economic development program in Mozambique. Highlights of the program include providing funding to enable more than 600 primary-school children from underprivileged families to attend school. The program also provides women with training so that they can manufacture school uniforms and produce groceries to be sold at market. In addition, a sport training center has been built to serve more than 1,000 children through sport and education programs.

- *Rehabilitation of war victims.* In collaboration with the International Paralympics Committee, the IOC has established a project to provide rehabilitation through sport for people injured by war and other persons with a physical disability. This project has begun in Angola and Portugal.
- *HIV/AIDS prevention through sport.* The IOC has partnered in the fight against HIV/AIDS with the U.N., UNICEF, and the International Federation of Red Cross and Red Crescent Societies. As part of this effort, the IOC and the U.N. jointly published the first HIV/AIDS toolkit designed specifically for members of the sport community. It is available in five languages and provides guidance for athletes, program suggestions, and sources of further information. Jointly sponsored seminars by all the involved organizations are held regionally to develop strategies for dealing with the HIV/AIDS pandemic.
- *Bringing hope and joy to refugee camps.* Again in cooperation with the U.N., the IOC has worked since 1996 on sport projects for refugee camps and resettlement areas around the world. The effort is designed to foster hope and optimism among people who are bored by idleness and weighed down by the stress of a burdensome daily existence.

Peace Initiatives Through Sport

The U.N. Sport for Development and Peace International Working Group (SDP IWG) was created in 2004 to help governments develop their sport systems while also initiating programs to use sport in promoting peace between communities, ethnic groups, and countries. At its core, this group is dedicated to using sport and other physical activity to build peace throughout the world. In order to build strong civil societies, all people must be exposed to the concepts of tolerance and friendship between disparate groups. Toward this end, sport offers the opportunity to present conflict prevention measures and discourage actions that generate aggression, hatred, and fear.

While it is recognized that sport inherently promotes conflict between opposing players and teams, the sport framework offers an opportunity to engage in conflict that is constructive, healthy, and peaceful. Sport can be conducted within the bounds of certain formal rules, traditions, and unwritten rules in the spirit of competition. As a result, sport can allow highly contested athletic events to serve as a model of citizen competition and cooperation at the same time.

Of course, one strong negative outcome of conflict is violence, whether in sport or in society at large. Disagreements between groups of people

APPLYING SOCIAL THEORY

Figurational Theory and Changing the World Through Sport

Figurational theorists emphasize interconnections between people, which are referred to as figurations. The idea is that we are all connected by networks, media, business, the economy, and politics. We are also connected by sport at the local level, national level, and worldwide.

Having now read about how sport and physical activity can link us together and improve life for people worldwide, take a figurational perspective and develop your own list of the five most important areas in which you think sport can be used to positively affect the world internationally. Consider past, current, and present international concerns and pick five that you think sport could realistically affect. Rank your five choices, explain your ideas, and share them with a small group of classmates via Blackboard or another electronic system at your school.

IN THE ARENA WITH . . .

Olympic Truce

International Olympic Committee President Thomas Bach believes that "sport and politics can work together to build a better and more peaceful world" (International Olympic Committee 2013b, 1). Appearing before the General Assembly of the United Nations, he encouraged all nations to support (which they did) a resolution to observe the Olympic Truce during the Olympic and Paralympic Games in Sochi. President Bach stressed that the sport movement must remain politically neutral but not "apolitical"; to the contrary, the sport world must always consider the political, economic, and social implications of its decisions.

The concept of the Olympic Truce dates back to the eighth century BC, when warring states suspended hostilities during the Games. The practice was reintroduced during the 1992 Games, and the U.N. General Assembly has adopted a similar resolution before every edition of the Games held since then. The resolution was submitted to the U.N. on behalf of the Olympic movement by the president and CEO of the Sochi 2014 Organizing Committee. It was titled "Sport for Peace and Development: Building a Peaceful and Better World through Sport and the Olympic Ideal" (International Olympic Committee 2013b).

cause gang-related crime, ethnic and racial conflicts, and wars within and between countries. These conflicts affect entire societies and often harm innocent bystanders who become targets or victims.

Amid these realities, sport can serve as a model to communities in conflict by demonstrating a commitment to the values of human rights and democracy. Through the establishment of self-governing leagues that respect the rights of all individuals and groups, as well as the sport tradition, participants can learn firsthand how to exist in a more peaceful manner.

Sport can contribute to peace building in a variety of ways. Here are a few, based on Kvalsund (2007):

- *Security*. Sport programs can provide a safe haven for children, especially those who have grown up with war and even perhaps participated in war.
- *Rebuilding economies*. Sport facilities need to be funded, constructed, and used by everyone. They can serve as centers for socialization, cultural programs, and education and training outside of school.
- *Rebuilding traumatized populations*. Those who have lived with war, apartheid, genocide, human trafficking, or other heinous social disasters need to rebuild mental and emotional health. Sport can provide an outlet to aid in healing and repair.
- *Political structure*. Sport bodies can become models of democratic functioning, influence citizens' attitudes toward government, encourage participation, and raise citizens' expectations for leaders.
- *Communication*. Sport is easily communicated through radio, television, and the Internet and can be of interest to society at large. The demand for sport news can encourage free communication and build loyalty and pride in the performance of athletes. Sport can also provide a model of athletes from disparate backgrounds or ethnic or racial groups working as a functional team with respect for each other.
- *Reconciling torn societies*. Sports participated in by people from conflicting sides offer opportunities for athletes to respect each other as performers and come to know one another as people. Once competition has ended, competitors can spend time together discussing social problems, identifying solutions, and building trust in each other.

POP CULTURE

Invictus

The 2009 film *Invictus* tells the compelling story of Nelson Mandela of South Africa as he is elected to be that nation's first black leader after serving 27 years in prison for his efforts to wipe out apartheid. One of the tools he uses to unite the white and black populations is the remarkable success of the national rugby union team, which has always been heavily populated by white players, as they seek the World Cup. Due to tradition and culture, black athletes in South Africa play football (soccer) but not rugby. As the national leader, Mandela donned the uniform of the Springboks team and became cheerleader-in-chief for his countrymen. In spite of their relative underdog status, the team rallied to win the cup and the hearts and minds of South African citizens. Mandela shrewdly used this sport team to build national pride, unity, and spirit in a fledgling and wobbly union.

On May 7 and 8, 2009, the First International Forum on Sport, Peace, and Development was broadcast live around the world from the Olympic Museum in Lausanne, Switzerland. The discussions were wide ranging but focused primarily on using sport to promote peace and national cohesion. This international sharing of concepts, ideas, and practical solutions has begun to open up understanding of the larger role that sport can play in society beyond providing physical fitness, fun, and recreation. The Second International Forum was held in Geneva, Switzerland in May 2011 and resulted in the adoption of ten recommendations. In the eighth recommendation, the group

> *urges International Sport Federations, National Olympic Committees, and other entities of the sports movement to strengthen their activities as partners for development and social change, in close cooperation with governmental institutions, the private sector, and civil society organizations (United Nations 2011, 32).*

The crusade to use sport as a meaningful and galvanizing tool for community development, peacekeeping, and reconciliation is currently led by the International Olympic Committee in partnership with the United Nations. Even the popular media have begun to notice these efforts, as was evidenced in a landmark article in *Sports Illustrated* by Alexander Wolff titled "Sports Saves the World" (2011).Wolff recounts pioneering efforts to use soccer around the globe in disadvantaged countries such as Kenya, Lesotho, and Zimbabwe, where the specific focus is on eliminating the scourge of AIDS. In Rio de Janeiro, boxing is featured in a campaign cleverly titled "Fight for Peace," and a brave approach in the Middle East uses basketball leagues to promote peace between Israelis and Palestinians.

Potential Funding Sources for Sport Development Programs

The ambitious efforts described in this chapter must be supported financially in order to become reality, especially in poor and underdeveloped communities and countries. Who should we look to for the necessary funds to create and sustain these programs? To date, the leaders that have stepped up include the IOC; the U.N.; and the U.N. Educational, Scientific, and Cultural Organization. There must also be other international groups interested in improving life for citizens in all countries, even if their help is motivated by self-interest.

For example, international sport organizations have a vested interest in helping stabilize and assist underdeveloped countries so that their sport can thrive and become a positive contributor in combating poverty and disease. In fact, many sport organizations already sponsor multiple programs

ACTIVITY TIME-OUT

Sport Development and Peace Initiatives

To explore additional topics and current events related to sport development and peace initiatives worldwide, visit the website of the International Platform on Sport and Development at www.sportanddev.org/. There you will find links to various relevant websites, as well as the latest news and reporting on efforts to use sport in improving health, wellness, and quality of life, particularly in poor and developing nations. Pick a sport development project that interests you, take notes about the specifics, and be ready to share with your classmates during an assigned class discussion.

for coaches and athletes in Africa, especially in countries that are struggling for survival. Professional sport leagues and organizations that hope to expand their reach worldwide would also do well to financially support the establishment and growth of local programs in their chosen sports.

Multinational corporations provide another potential source of new funds as they expand their reach worldwide. These corporations cannot afford to simply exploit a country and its workforce without offering development opportunities in the locales where they operate. Although one might argue that they have a moral duty to do so, they are more likely to get on board when they see that their bottom line benefits from their support of efforts to improve the lot of the population where they function daily. Countries that operate in widespread international locations need to invest in their local communities at those sites just as they do in their home country.

Government groups must also bear responsibility for providing appropriate funding, especially in poorer communities and among people who are disadvantaged. Without erecting insurmountable roadblocks in the form of red tape, delay, and bureaucracy, governments must be creative in disbursing funds on a matching basis with other groups in order to maximize their impact.

These efforts also need help from social organizations and institutions, such as schools, community centers, recreation departments, and faith-based organizations. Repetition and separateness are not efficient; nor is duplication of effort. Instead, definitive success requires coordination and cooperation between the various groups who want sport and physical activity programs to play a broader role than merely providing sport competition. Therefore, they must work together to maximize their collective resources.

Finally, a message needs to be crafted and delivered to charitable organizations at every level and to charitable citizens who have the financial resources to contribute. People around the world who hope for world peace and reconciliation can help work toward those goals by supporting efforts to provide opportunity through sport.

Chapter Summary

This chapter takes a broad view of sport for development on the local, national, and international levels. It summarizes the documented benefits of sport and physical activity and specifically examines how those benefits can differ for people of various ages.

The chapter also explores the four types of educational and developmental sport programming and details their differences. Some programs simply offer sport; some combine sport and education; and others use sport as a tool to prevent crime, encourage staying in school, and build positive social characteristics in youth. Over the years, the growth and success of many such programs have been documented as enhancing the lives of youngsters, particularly those in underserved communities suffering from poverty, neglect, and lack of effective leadership.

Stepping out of the United States, the chapter also looks at the role that sport can play in other countries, particularly those that have been impoverished or torn apart by war, whether from within or from without. In such situations, sport can be part of the solution for rebuilding and regenerating local and national pride, hope, and conciliation. Led by such prestigious organizations as the United Nations and the IOC, this use of sport is directed toward improving the health and well-being of all citizens.

Finally, the chapter considers possible funding sources for sport development programs, both in the United States and abroad. Without sizable long-term financial backing, these programs will fail, especially in poor communities. Therefore, it is up to governments, sport organizations, and the business community to work together to ensure continuing opportunities through sport.

STUDENT OUTCOMES

After reading this chapter, you will know the following:

- Issues pertaining to rule breaking in sport
- How emotion helps create deviant behavior
- How aggression affects sport
- The problem of violence in sport, both on and off the field

Violence and Rule Breaking in Sport

Violence and Rule Breaking in Sport

Early in the 2014 baseball season, New York Yankees pitcher Michael Pineda was ejected from a game and subsequently suspended for 10 games by Major League Baseball (MLB) for the presence of a foreign substance believed to be pine tar on his neck. Here's how it came about.

In the Yankees' previous series of games against their archrival, the Boston Red Sox, various people noticed a brown substance on Pineda's hand during the game. However, the Red Sox did not bring this observation to the attention of the umpires until the middle of the game, by which time the substance had disappeared. It had been noted by members of the media, and some discussion ensued among fans and pundits, but the incident was quickly forgotten.

A week later, the same teams met again, and the Yankees again sent Pineda to the mound. This time, it was clear to everyone that he had a brown glob on his neck and appeared to be rubbing his hand over the area between pitches. The Red Sox were outraged, the umpires agreed that it was a violation of the rules, and within a day MLB suspended Pineda. Wow, what happened here? Our erstwhile national pastime of baseball sure is confusing!

Everyone agrees that a pitcher who uses a foreign substance is breaking MLB rule 8.02(b), which prohibits the use of any foreign substance by a pitcher. Yet according to the majority of players and managers interviewed about the incident, "everybody does it, and in fact has for years." If it's not pine tar, it may be petroleum jelly, slippery elm, lip balm, or sunscreen. Some claim that they use it to better protect the batter from an errant fastball but Hall of Fame pitcher Gaylord Perry scoffs at such logic and says bluntly, "These foreign substances simply help sinkers sink better and breaking balls break better; that's why pitchers use it" (Madden 2014, 1).

More instructive is the reaction of those within baseball to the rule infraction, which included statements along the lines of "it's not like he was shooting up PEDs out there on the mound" and "everyone does it, so it's no big deal" (Laird 2014). In fact, the overall response seemed to indicate that you can bend or break the rules a bit, but don't flaunt it—and don't get caught. If you do get caught, admit your infraction, and take the punishment like a man. So it seems like Major League Baseball has written rules that are sometimes overridden by "unwritten rules." But how are we supposed to know which are which and whether or not players are cheating?

This chapter explores the role of sport rules—written and unwritten—and the prevalence of rule breaking by athletes, both in competition and outside of the game. It also examines the typical norms of group and individual behavior deemed acceptable in sport and considers examples of deviation from those norms.

In addition, the chapter explores the key topic of violence in sport, both during competition and in the form of off-field incidents that affects athletes' families, friends, and reputations. The discussion also considers the role of emotion in stimulating violent behavior, which can affect teammates, opponents, and women with whom an athlete interacts. In some cases, violence is committed by fans, thus threatening to repel fellow fans and injure innocent bystanders.

Rule Breaking

In order to participate in a sport, you have to learn the rules of the game. In basketball, for example, you can't dribble with two hands, walk more than two steps while holding the ball, or hit the arm of an opponent who's shooting. In soccer, you can't intentionally touch the ball with your hand, run into an opponent without trying to play the ball, or commit a foul in the penalty box without giving up a penalty kick. And in tennis, you can't touch the ball with your body or clothing, reach over the net, serve from inside the line, or throw your racket in frustration.

No matter your age, if you participate in sport, you quickly find out that there are plenty of rules to learn, understand, and follow. Types of rule include rules of play, team rules, school rules, and league rules. Athletes who ignore the rules of play risk being hit with a penalty, suspension, or even dismissal from the sport. Professional athletes and other high-profile athletes also risk drawing the ire of the media and fans for behavior that is socially deviant.

Sometimes athletes break a rule because they are unaware of it, do not understand it, or violate it accidentally. At other times, they may intentionally break a rule, hoping not to get caught, in order to interrupt an opponent's flow. They may do so to vent frustration and anger.

Does rule breaking in the current era happen more than, less than, or about the same as in past times? Today's athletes cheat in many ways: scoring, modifying equipment illegally, committing fouls when officials aren't looking, participating in brawls, "flopping" to the ground as if they have been fouled, and calling phony injury time-outs to gain a strategic advantage. However, students of sport history remind us that these practices are nothing new; indeed, they have always been a part of game playing.

For example, baseball players have long been accused of cheating by doctoring the baseball or throwing spitballs that cause the pitch to break unpredictably. Similarly, ice hockey has always been notorious for its fights, and many fans are even disappointed if a fight doesn't break out. Although illegal, these examples of cheating have been tolerated as part of the game unless a player is caught blatantly in the act. In recent years, the most recognized form of blatant cheating has been the use of performance-enhancing drugs, but even after suspension for such offenses many players return to action without further sanction, and some are even rewarded with lucrative contracts.

In reality, there is probably less rule breaking in modern sport than there used to be, thanks to improved officiating, clearer rules, video replays, immediate media commentary, and a certain maturity that has evolved in most sports over the years of competition (Dunning 1999). For example, golfer Tiger Woods was assessed a two-stroke penalty at the 2013 Masters Tournament after golf rules expert Dave Eger—who had previously worked for the PGA Tour—happened to be watching at home and reported to tournament officials that Woods had made an illegal drop during his second round of play.

When athletes and coaches break the rules today, they often do so unintentionally or because they've concluded that doing so may advance them toward their ultimate goal. For example, an offensive lineman in American football may risk a penalty for holding to keep the opposing team from flattening and possibly injuring his quarterback. Similarly, a defensive back may intentionally hold or knock down a receiver who has outrun him in order to prevent giving up a touchdown. In these cases, a player is willfully and rationally breaking a rule, accepting the penalty because the alternative would be more harmful to his team. Most of us would agree that these are not examples of cheating but rather of rational rule breaking.

In other cases, athletes break a rule and attempt to justify their action with the defense that "everyone is doing it" or "it's a bad or confusing rule." However, if athletes disagree with a rule—perhaps because they find it unclear, unfair, or unnecessary—then they have an obligation to enlist the support of others and work to change it. Every sport organization has an established procedure for proposing rule changes, and athletes, coaches, and officials all have an obligation to follow the set process for rule changes.

Olympic competitors are generally the most admired group of athletes, but even there one finds cases of questionable moral behavior. At the 2012 London Olympics, for example, a number of competitive badminton players were dismissed from the competition because they clearly lost a match on purpose in order to set up a more favorable seeding and opponent in the next round. While not illegal, their actions offended the spectators, elicited boos, and made a mockery of the spirit of the competition. Similarly, a soccer goalkeeper was penalized after she intentionally held the ball long after a shot in an effort to let the clock run out, and a swimmer openly admitted taking illegal extra kicks in his world-record, gold-medal race (but officials did not detect his actions and so he suffered no penalty). Because such infractions rarely result in a penalty, many athletes simply assume that it is acceptable to ignore the rules.

Another reason that more people seem to be following the rules these days relates to the rapid growth of organized youth sport. A coach's primary role in youth sport is to teach young athletes the rules of the game and help them learn to abide by them. To aid in that work, organized programs such as the Citizenship Through Sports Alliance have sprung up around the United States to promote good sporting behavior. Other national programs—backed by universities, youth sport organizations, or national governing bodies—also publicize good behavior and reward players who demonstrate it.

Good sporting behavior is also the subject of books, websites, and videos. In addition, coaching clinics often feature sessions about teaching good sporting behavior. These tools help coaches, parents, and sport leaders explain to young people the differences between acceptable and unacceptable behavior and suggest constructive ways to handle frustration and control aggressiveness. Athletes who learn these lessons at a young age develop positive habits that last a lifetime.

Most sport programs have long offered awards for good sporting behavior, often as a sort of consolation prize for athletes who were not chosen as the most outstanding or most valuable player or as a team captain. Recently, however, these awards have been supplanted by awards recognizing team behavior, and many high schools have incorporated an emphasis on good sporting behavior into their athletic philosophy. Moreover, many have also promoted good sporting behavior by displaying relevant banners in the gym, developing catchy slogans, and distributing informative literature.

The NCAA suspended Syracuse men's basketball coach Jim Boeheim for nine games and imposed harsh sanctions on his program because of violations involving academic misconduct, extra benefits, and the university's drug testing policy.

By the time most athletes reach high school, they have been exposed to several years of youth sport, during which they have learned the fundamental rules of specific sports and the boundaries of acceptable behavior. As they advance to higher competitive levels, the action becomes faster, the players more skillful, and, sometimes, the rules looser. Good coaches make sure that their athletes know to abide by the rules or face disciplinary action, including lost playing time.

In addition to rules governing competition per se, myriad off-field regulations also exist to ensure fair competition and protect the rights of people involved in sport. Sport administrators and coaches must learn these rules, understand how to apply them, and make sure that athletes carefully follow them.

Major deterrents and punishments for breaking the rules have evolved over the years, particularly in college sport. The 2014–2015 NCAA Division I Manual includes 426 pages of rules, explanations of rules, and examples of decisions in response to rule breaking. Believe it or not, the manual used to be even bigger, peaking at nearly 500 pages, but officials intentionally shortened it by eliminating some rules. This still-hefty compendium is a document that school athletic officials and coaches are expected to read, understand, and live by. Similar manuals are available for NCAA Divisions II and III, and they check in at 398 and 278 pages respectively (NCAA 2013d).

The purpose of the NCAA rules is to protect the rights of honest athletes and coaches and to eliminate cheating. In the last 30 years, all collegiate athletes, coaches, boosters, and athletic administrators have been charged with the responsibility of understanding and obeying the NCAA rules. Given their complexity, however, this is no simple task, and schools now hire specialists in rule enforcement to guide their athletic personnel and monitor actions to prevent both unintentional and intentional rule breaking. A college that discovers a rule violation is advised to turn itself in for sanctions before the NCAA finds out on its own and comes to investigate.

In recent years, the NCAA has stepped up its penalties for violations. As a result, coaches have been fired, athletes have been punished by suspension from games or even from a season, and athletic programs have been severely hindered for years to come. When the media learn about a violation, the resulting publicity affects the reputation of the university and its people and affects admissions, fundraising, and recruiting of future athletes. Schools also suffer huge financial penalties when banned from postseason competition, which can be worth millions of dollars.

What should our expectations be about the moral behavior of athletes? Is it best to follow the rules to the letter? Do we even consider that beyond the written rules of sport, there may also be unwritten rules that are sometimes even more important? If unwritten rules do exist, should they be organized, codified, taught, and treated as an official part of a sport's culture? Let's look at some classic examples of such conflicts in sport.

In an infamous 1994 case, friends of figure skater Tonya Harding intentionally injured her chief rival, Nancy Kerrigan, by hitting her knees with a crowbar. Everyone agreed that the abhorrent act had no place in sport and decried the intentional injury to an opponent outside of competition. But what about athletes who are encouraged to physically injure an opposing player during competition? For example, in the National Football League (NFL), some New Orleans Saints coaches and players were suspended in 2012 for operating a bounty system that rewarded players for injuring opponents.

In an example of historic importance, when the legendary Jackie Robinson broke the color barrier in Major League Baseball in 1947, he not only had to contend with racist invective from opposing players and fans but also encountered pitchers who tried to intimidate him by throwing "high and tight" on the inside corner of the plate. Robinson responded by laying down a bunt along the first base line, forcing the offending pitcher to cover first base. At that point, given Robinson's background as an All-American running back in college football, most pitchers simply avoided making the play rather than risk a collision. Most of us today would applaud Robinson's behavior—not because it is part of baseball, but because it represents a greater moral good and takes a stand against racism.

Finally, there is the issue of athletes serving as role models for youth. In spite of the widely quoted claim of star basketball player (now TV commentator) Charles Barkley that he "ain't no role model," the facts show otherwise. The reality is that kids look up to their sport heroes and imitate their behavior. For example, when Michael Jordan ruled basketball, many kids wanted, in the words of a famous advertising slogan featuring Jordan, to be "like Mike." Perhaps we should not expect professional athletes to be heroes, but shouldn't they at least follow the rules of sport, both written and unwritten? If not, it may be time to stop claiming that sport produces citizens of good character and just accept it as a childhood diversion.

Emotion and Sport

The human emotions experienced through and within sport add flavor to our experience of the world. For the most part, we are taught to keep our emotions in check during daily life, and males in particular are often pressured to subvert strong emotions as a requirement of culturally sanctioned masculinity. In sport, however, we are free to express emotions—as long as we do so within reason.

An athletic contest that goes down to the wire generates a level of excitement that, for most of us, is unusual in daily life. While such excitement is energizing, it is also sometimes stressful. Indeed, the stress of a sporting event may cause us to experience a feeling of nervousness, perspiration, clammy palms, a headache, and clouded thoughts. The more important the event, the more exciting and stressful it may be. Once the outcome is decided, the ecstasy of victory or the agony of defeat takes over. It may be hours or even days before the strong feelings subside and full equilibrium returns.

When emotion overcomes us to the point where we stop thinking clearly, deviant behavior can result. For this reason, in the heat of the moment, an athlete may commit an egregious foul, let loose a stream of profanities, or even become violent. Later, after cooling off, the actions that he or she committed in the midst of competition may seem immature, antisocial, and even despicable.

Big-time sport exploits the emotional makeup of athletes. The stage is set before the game by the coach, who often psyches up the athletes by using music, pep talks, slogans, footage showing moments of sport glory, or visits by VIPs who exhort players to perform. Then, as the athletes enter the arena, the band fills their ears with stirring music, cannons or fireworks go off, and the crowd roars for the home team. If their state of arousal gets too high, they may not prosper. In particular, athletes who play a high-skill sport may need to lower their arousal in order to achieve best performance. Many U.S. team sport athletes, most notably football players, seem to thrive on excitement and high energy.

Anger is a normal emotion that often gets a bad rap. In and of itself, it is neither good nor bad. No one has ever gotten in trouble simply for being angry, but that may change if a person is unable to control that anger or channel it productively. In fact, anger can be a very positive emotion if it is used to fuel outrage at a social injustice or unfair treatment of someone. Athletes can also use anger to help them work and compete harder at high levels of intensity. For example, in a contact sport such as American football, an angry lineman who is rushing the passer might be very tough to block.

Yet anger can easily become a negative factor in a sport that requires clear thinking, good decision making, or fine motor skills. For instance, it is certainly not helpful for a quarterback to be angry when he has to handle the ball smoothly and carefully, choose his receiver from multiple options, and then launch a precise spiraling pass to avoid the defender. Similarly, anger is rarely an asset in highly skill-dependent sports such as golf and tennis.

Spectators are also affected by the emotional excitement. For many people, the traditional pregame cocktail party, tailgating, and consumption of alcohol have become synonymous with sport. Many students seem to view big-time college football games as an excuse for binge drinking, and by halftime some fans are barely able to function. In fact, some families are so put off by the crude behavior exhibited at college football games and many professional sport events that they do not feel comfortable bringing their children. Colleges and professional teams have experimented with limiting the number of drinks sold per customer, stopping alcohol sales after halftime, and restricting alcohol consumption to pregame tailgating. An increasing number of venues are banning alcohol outright, though of course some fans smuggle in their own supply.

The NCAA has no rules about alcohol sales that apply to sporting events hosted by universities, but it does prohibit alcohol sales at the 89 sport championships it administers in Division I. For example, alcohol sales were prohibited at the 2014 NCAA men's basketball championship at AT&T Stadium in Arlington, Texas. Times, however, are changing, as indicated by the approval of alcohol sales at the same stadium in 2015 for the inaugural Division I College Football Playoff title game between Oregon and Ohio State. Alcohol was also sold at the six bowls affiliated with the championship playoff (Tracy 2015).

Fans who have been plied with alcohol are more likely than their sober counterparts to engage in a variety of behaviors, some of which can be problematic. For example, they may perform the wave, cheer their team's good plays, and try to get in front of a television camera. They may also boo opposing players, taunt officials, and insult visiting fans. If their football team wins an important victory, they may rush the field to pull down the goalposts. Unruly fans may also let their emotions carry over to the postgame celebration. In spite of increased security, mobs of fans sometimes get out of control, brawl, destroy property, and generally embarrass their school or city. At that point, their behavior is no longer all in good fun.

Recent steps to curb student drinking at football games include a policy enacted at the University of Minnesota that is modeled on a program at the University of Wisconsin. Under the rules of the program, a student who is kicked out of a game for drunken rowdiness is barred from attending future games unless she or he passes an alcohol breath test at the gate. Students under age 21 must be completely free of alcohol to enter the stadium, whereas those 21 or older must test below a 0.08 in blood alcohol content (Associated Press 2009).

Lest you think that such behavior is limited to the United States, let's take a peek at the behavior of fans at soccer games around the world. Soccer seems to inspire passion like no other sport, and because it is played worldwide and frequently matches country against country, people sometimes make a huge emotional investment in the game. Particularly in countries where the fan base consists largely of poorer or less educated people, the behavior may be even worse than anything typically seen in the United States.

For instance, the **hooliganism** of British soccer fans has been a tradition for several hundred years. Usually, the label *hooligan* is applied to working-class men who disrupt soccer games with antisocial behavior. They may direct their aggression against referees, opposing players, team owners, or other spectators. They may drink excessively, exchange insults, destroy property, and even interrupt the game. In fact, the incidents become so pervasive—with fans running onto the field, throwing beer cans, pitching stones, and generally frightening other spectators—that the British government got involved in an effort to control the growing violence.

Even though the British media may sensationalize the stories, violence by fans at sporting events, particularly soccer, has reached genuinely alarming levels. In fact, because soccer is played worldwide and enjoys a passionate following, the incidence of violence at soccer matches likely exceeds that of any other sport (Young 2004).

While hooliganism per se has been primarily a British phenomenon that has gradually faded, a somewhat similar group of fans referred to as "ultras" has emerged in some European countries and in North Africa. Ultras are fanatical soccer supporters whose acting out may take the form of hateful chants, racist and abusive remarks intended to intimidate opposing players and fans, and in some cases violence. Ultras have been prominent in Italy, Egypt, and Turkey, and their rise has sparked similar groups in Belgium, Germany, and the Netherlands. Unlike hooligans, whose main purpose is to physically fight hooligans of opposing clubs, ultras primarily support their own team and tend to display their team colors proudly, carry signs, and sit in reserved sections of the bleachers.

Many groups of ultras are simply enthusiastic fans, but they too can go too far. In one dramatic example, the Egyptian soccer team Al-Masry was suspended from competition for two years in response to riots following a match against its Cairo rival Al-Ahly, at which 74 people were killed. News of the ban resulted in yet more violence, during which a 13-year-old boy was shot dead (Handley 2012).

Soccer hooliganism led to a 35-minute delay in this match between Slovan Bratislava and Sparta Prague as flares were thrown onto the pitch by Sparta supporters.

Aggression and Sport

Aggression is simply a form of behavior directed toward another person; it is not an emotion or attitude. By definition, it is a forceful action of attack intended to dominate or master something or someone. It is intentional, and that intent may be either good or bad, depending on one's perspective. Good aggression in sport creates high energy or initiative—for example, when a basketball player goes hard after a loose ball or a tennis player charges to the net in order to seize the point with a winning shot. Therefore, in most sports, an athlete who displays aggression is praised and rewarded for his or her behavior, especially in contrast to exhibiting behavior deemed passive and defensive (Weinberg and Gould 2015).

Good aggression is often well learned in sport, and it can be carried over into life at large and into the workplace in particular. It is often referred to as "assertiveness," and we often spend hours training workers to be more assertive in both professional and personal life. Assertiveness enables people to stand up for their beliefs and rights without injuring others.

However, there is another side of aggression that is hostile and destructive, whether physically or psychologically; indeed, in this form of aggression, one's very intent is to harm or injure another person. This negative aggression often stems from frustration or arises in response to a perceived injustice (perhaps a bad call by an official), an insult (such as trash talk), or a wrong act (for example, dirty play or cheating) (Abrams 2010b).

Among avid fans, aggressive behavior is often directed at fans of the visiting team just because they root for the other side. Consider the widely publicized case of San Francisco Giants fan Bryan Stow, who was savagely beaten by two Dodgers fans in the parking lot of Dodger Stadium after a 2011 baseball game. Stow, now 45 years old, is brain damaged and disabled and requires care 24 hours a day. His attackers have been sentenced to prison terms of eight and four years (Associated Press 2014b).

In contact and collision sports such as American football, soccer, ice hockey, lacrosse, boxing, and wrestling, a fine line exists between hostile aggression with an intent to harm or injure and the more controlled aggression that is necessary to compete in these sports. Therefore, players need to be taught at an early age how to play tough but clean. They also need to develop the ability to exercise self-control even when provoked, whether intentionally or not. Actions that fall within the rules should be reinforced, and those that do not should be eliminated or penalized immediately. Similarly, young athletes should be taught how to execute risky skills (such as tackling in American football and heading the ball in soccer) in a way that does not put the player or the opponent at undue risk for serious injury.

More generally, athletes and fans alike should be taught that reckless aggression aimed at injuring someone will ultimately ruin the performance of the aggressor. Intentionally inflicting injury detracts from the more critical performance issues of competitive play. Coaches, owners, and families who value their athletes must do their part to stamp out ruthless violent behavior by working to create a sport environment in which such behavior not only does not pay but also leads to dismissal or banishment.

Violence in Sport

Violence pervades some sports because of their nature and the athletes they attract. The violence that takes place during an athletic contest may carry over into violent behavior off the field, and then both athletes and society suffer the consequences. Young athletes may also use the athletic arena to test their masculinity and to establish acceptance by peers.

Violence is highly visible in U.S. sport because it is so prevalent in televised events. Violent plays are shown over and over in instant replays as the sport announcers exclaim over the hit, tackle, block, or body check. Athletes who deliver these violent acts are lionized by fans and teammates for their aggressive play. If a serious injury occurs, however, the tide shifts as people suspect the athlete's motives and admit that perhaps the game got out of hand.

On-Field Violence

U.S. society seems to be confused about the place of violence in sport, particularly when the sport itself promotes aggressive play and physical abuse of an opponent's body. For instance, American football is a collision sport, and a number of other sports—wrestling, boxing, ice hockey, and lacrosse—all require violence just to play the game. Even high-performance basketball and soccer involve heavy body contact and physical intimidation, and baseball can be violent when collisions occur at a base or at home plate.

More generally, many sports involve some form of tackling, blocking, sacking, body checking, or jabbing. Furthermore, the place of violence becomes even less clear when it involves acts prohibited by the rules but accepted by the competing athletes. Examples of such borderline violence include fistfights between players, hard body blocks in basketball, brushback pitches in baseball, and intentional fouls in basketball.

Of course, many sports—for example, golf, tennis, volleyball, swimming, skiing, equestrianism, dance, and track and field—involve little or no violence. These sports emphasize skill and lack body contact. They also tend to be favored by participants who have better education and financial resources and whose attitudes toward violence differ substantially from those of many working-class athletes.

Traditional masculinity is often rooted in bravery, willingness to risk bodily harm, toughness, and personal aggressiveness. These traits are often exhibited in the role models that boys grow up with, and boys are typically accepted by their peers if they mimic these traits in order to prove their worthiness as men. Failure to do so can result in labels such as "sissy," "wuss," or worse.

In addition, sport has traditionally been associated closely with warfare. Indeed, coaches who condition athletes to risk bodily harm for the good of the team often use the language and ethics of war. Think of typical sport news headlines: "Vikings destroy Patriots," "Eagles bury Giants," "76ers blow out Nets," "Duke blitzes Wake Forest," "Gators swamp Bulldogs," "Oklahoma guns down Longhorns," and so on. Perhaps it is not a surprise that players give teammates the highest compliment when they say, "He's a guy you wanna go to war with."

Even in this intense environment, some players go so far that their behavior is questioned even by other players. Two of the dirtiest current NFL players are defensive tackle Ndamukong Suh of the Miami Dolphins and guard Richie Incognito of the Buffalo Bills (*Sporting News* 2013; DeMarzo 2013). Both players have earned their reputation by repeatedly committing violent acts such as illegal hits and eye gouging with the intent of injuring opposing players. Incognito had a checkered career in college at Nebraska and then Oregon and eventually was kicked off of both squads. In the NFL, his pattern of on-field violence continued and resulted in fines and suspensions. In 2014, he was accused of bullying and harassing Miami Dolphins teammate Jonathan Martin, suspended by the NFL, and eventually released by the Dolphins.

Ndamukong Suh was named an All-Pro starter in 2014—the fifth time in six seasons he was selected as one of the best among his peers. Yet he also paid a $70,000 fine for stomping on the calf and ankle of opposing quarterback Aaron Rodgers during a playoff game in which Green Bay won 30-20 over the Lions. The NFL originally suspended Suh for one game, but an appeal officer reduced the punishment to a fine without suspension. Over the course of his career, Suh has been fined more than $200,000 by the NFL, and his 38 penalties are the second-most by a defensive lineman since 2010. Apparently, the punishment is not having its intended effect (Rothstein and Werder 2014).

Violence in American football is not always directed against opponents; it can also threaten teammates. Consider the 2006 case of Northern Colorado backup punter Mitchell Cozad, who brutally attacked starting punter Rafael Mendoza in an attempt to obtain the starting role. Cozad stabbed Mendoza in the knee of his kicking leg and was found guilty of second-degree assault and sentenced to seven years in prison.

One of the more bizarre examples of violence in sport occurred in a boxing rematch in 1997 that became known as the "the Bite Fight" when Mike Tyson bit Evander Holyfield's ear and was penalized by means of a 2-point deduction. The referee was ready to disqualify Tyson, but Holyfield wanted to continue. Tyson then bit Holyfield on the other ear, tearing off the top and spitting it into the ring. This time Tyson was disqualified.

In another biting incident, striker Luis Suarez bit Italy's Giorgio Chiellini during the 2014 World Cup in Rio de Janeiro and was suspended from the sport for a record four months and fined £66,000. Sadly, this was not Suarez's first brush with such behavior, nor is it likely his last. He has also been penalized for racially abusing a Manchester United opponent and biting a Chelsea player. With this latest penalty, Suarez has been suspended for 48 matches since 2010 (Gibson 2014).

Professional ice hockey struggled for years with its reputation for violence and could not seem to reconcile stricter rules and harsher penalties with the popularity of game fights. Indeed, many hockey supporters relish the breakout of violence and anticipate the potential fights. However, at the beginning of the 2005 season, the National Hockey League (NHL) adopted three new rules regarding violence:

- Instigation penalties: A player who instigates a fight in the final five minutes of a game receives a game misconduct and an automatic one-game suspension. The player's coach is fined $10,000. The suspension times and fines double for each additional incident.
- Officiating: Zero tolerance is allowed for interference, hooking, and hold obstruction.
- Unsporting conduct: Players who dive, embellish a fall or a reaction, or fake injury in an attempt to draw penalties are fined. Public complaints and derogatory comments toward the game also result in fines (MSNBC 2006).

Five years later, in response to a series of serious injuries to players from blows to the head, the NHL, with the full support of the players union, outlawed blindside hits to the head. The rule prohibits a "lateral, back-pressure, or blindside hit to an opponent where the head is targeted and/or the principal point of contact." The league has the option to review such hits and mete out discipline (Srakocic 2010).

Hockey is known for frequent physical altercations—so much so that a commonly told joke talks about going to a boxing match and seeing a hockey game break out. Many fans seem to love the fights, and broadcasters are happy when their ratings go up due to fights. The NHL also thrives in part on other forms of violence that generate drama and elicit emotion, including cross-checks to the throat, heads slammed into the glass, and punches thrown toward a player whose back is turned. Those who defend fighting as part of the appeal of the game generally believe some of the following:

- Fighting can intimidate opponents and get into their heads.
- Momentum can swing quickly, and the spark is often a fight.
- Players often retaliate against other players who started it.
- Fighting can be used to suck opponents into committing a penalty.
- When you have fast, vigorous physical play in a small space with multiple players trying to position themselves, the occasional fight is bound to happen.

In spite of the apparent popularity of hockey fights, the European hockey leagues and the Olympics have survived quite well in spite of the fact that they explicitly prohibit fighting and punish it more severely than the NHL does. These policies haven't seemed to affect the popularity of the game worldwide (Klein 2012).

As women's sport continue to become more competitive, and as female athletes sometimes imitate their male counterparts, violence is bound to occur among female athletes as well. In 2009, University of New Mexico women's soccer defender Elizabeth Lambert was suspended indefinitely for rough play, which included tripping, kicking, rough tackling, and delivering a forearm shiver to the back. But the coup de grace came when Lambert yanked Brigham Young forward Kassidy Shumway to the ground by yanking her ponytail, images of which quickly appeared on YouTube and led the sport news for several days (ESPN 2009).

In 2010, Baylor University basketball star Brittney Griner punched Texas Tech's Jordan Barncastle after the two jostled each other for position beneath the basket. Perhaps Griner was responding to more than just that interchange. As a player who stands 6 feet 8 inches (2 meters) tall, Griner has gotten a lot of attention throughout her college and professional career from teams who attempt to neutralize her height advantage by roughing her up—pushing, shoving, and generally annoying her—in the hope that she will either become passive or "lose it" and get removed from the game.

These two incidents may not be part of a trend toward more violence in women's sport, but they do cause us to step back and wonder if the emphasis on winning portends a change in the way females participate in sport. We know that violence is primarily a male-owned behavior and that sport is simply a microcosm of society, yet the media sensationalizes incidents like these, much to the dismay of women's sport leaders and coaches (Abrams 2010a; Moltz 2010).

No sport body sanctions unnecessary violence, but legions of fans still exult when a fight breaks out. Even though altercations rarely last long or produce any benefit, some people clearly just get excited about watching grown men tussle like schoolyard kids. And in sports that have a high incidence of physical contact, an occasional fight is probably inevitable.

For spectators who love to watch dangerous sports, the attraction derives in large part from their fascination with the physical test of courage and mental and emotional toughness (Klein 2012). The possibility of serious physical harm raises the stakes for competitors who enjoy watching others respond to the challenge, just as many people are fascinated by those who challenge nature through mountain climbing, cliff diving, ski jumping, and innumerable other risky physical tests.

Unfortunately for athletes in violent collision sports, the price of their participation may not become clear until years later. By that time, the damage is done, thanks to the repeated brutal hits and other physical punishment they endure. This wear and tear becomes clearer in middle age, and that is when we tend to see former hockey players and football players hobbling around and perhaps struggling just to participate in the activities of daily living.

Concussions and Sport

Sport at all levels, and in particular the youth level, is the scene of growing concern about the rising incidence of concussions, as well as the treatment protocols used for athletes who have suffered one. A concussion is a traumatic brain injury (TBI) that changes the way the brain works. It results from a blow to the head and involves certain symptoms that can appear either immediately or some time later. The symptoms may include blurred or double vision, seeing stars, sensitivity to noise or light, headache, dizziness or balance problems, nausea, vomiting, trouble sleeping, fatigue, confusion, difficulty remembering or concentrating, and loss of consciousness.

A concussion can occur in any athlete of any age participating in any sport or recreational activity. However, children and teens are more likely to suffer a concussion, and they take longer to recover than adults do. During the 10-year period ending in 2007, the number of youth athletes taken to emergency rooms with concussions in the United States doubled; during the same period, the number of concussions attributed to team sport participation tripled. Alarmingly, one study estimated that more than 40 percent of high school athletes who experienced a concussion returned to full participation before they were fully recovered from their injury (NFL Evolution 2013).

Taking a broader view, one study of the epidemiology of concussions among U.S. high school athletes estimated that 300,000 sport-related concussions occur each year. The study was conducted during the 2008–2009 and 2009–2010 school years and focused on a national sample of athletes participating in 20 sports. The findings showed that, as you might expect, more concussions occurred during competition than during practice. The largest number of concussions were in American football and girls' soccer. The highest rate of concussions compared to athlete exposure were in American football, boys ice hockey, and boy lacrosse followed by girl's lacrosse and soccer (Marar et al. 2012). Table 19.1 shows the top six

TABLE 19.1 Concussion Incidence and Rates Among High School Athletes in Selected Sports

	Number of concussions	Rate per 10,000 athlete exposures
Boy's sports		
Football	912	6.4
Wrestling	112	2.2
Soccer	103	1.9
Basketball	96	1.6
Lacrosse	93	4.0
Ice hockey	80	5.4
Girl's sports		
Soccer	159	3.4
Basketball	107	2.1
Lacrosse	60	3.5
Softball	58	1.6
Field hockey	51	2.2
Volleyball	31	0.6

Data from Marar et al. 2012.

boys and girls sports that showed the highest total number of concussions in both practices and games along with the rate of concussions based on the rate per 10,000 concussions.

The first law in the United States to address concussion concerns in youth sports was the Zackery Lystedt Law adopted in 2009 by the state of Washington. Since then, similar legislation has been passed by all 50 states and the District of Columbia. The laws vary somewhat by state, but they all essentially do the following:

- Call for school districts to develop concussion guidelines and educational programs.
- Require parents and guardians to sign a concussion and head injury information sheet each year before an athlete is allowed to practice or compete.
- Require immediate removal of the athlete from play if a concussion is suspected.
- Require written clearance from a health care professional before the player is permitted to return to play.
- Provide legal immunity for the school district if it complies with the law.

In 2006, Zackery Lystedt was a 13-year-old middle-school football player who collapsed from a traumatic brain injury when he was allowed back into the game just 15 minutes after suffering a concussion. He spent the next nine months in a coma and emerged severely handicapped. Five years later, he has regained his sight and his ability to speak but still struggles to walk despite years of therapy (MomsTeam 2014).

In 2014, the White House hosted a summit titled "Healthy Kids and Safe Sports Concussion Summit" that brought together young athletes, academics, medical professionals, and parents to raise awareness of head injuries among young athletes. The Obama administration has made a commitment to raise awareness, conduct research, and help sport leaders identify and treat concussions responsibly.

The topic of concussions typically centers on the game of American football for good reason. One of those who have worked to raise the alarm about traumatic brain injury in football is Dr. Gay Culverhouse, former president of the Tampa Bay Buccaneers, who shared her observations in her book *Throwaway Players: Concussion Crisis From Pee*

A League of Denial

In *League of Denial: The NFL, Concussions, and the Battle for Truth* (2013), coauthors Mark Fainaru-Wada and Steve Fainaru delivered a bruising exposé about the NFL and its refusal to admit the full extent of its problem with head injuries. Specifically, the book details how the NFL denied the damage done to its players by concussions and chronic traumatic encephalopathy (CTE), which were literally driving some players to madness. Over nearly two decades, in spite of increasingly convincing research to the contrary, the NFL attempted to cover up the connection between football and brain damage.

Fainaru-Wada and Fainaru, who worked for ESPN, featured the career of former Pittsburgh Steeler and Hall of Famer Mike Webster, who died of a heart attack at age 50 after more than a decade of physical and psychological turmoil. His life after football was marked by a marriage that ended in divorce, homelessness, going broke, endless medical ailments with no health insurance, and finally being under the care of a psychologist. Dr. Fred Krieg, a clinical psychologist, offered that Webster had "the football version of a punch drunk which doesn't get better. . . . [Y]ou just get more and more demented" (Litsky 2002). This book and the documentary film that followed have helped focus the public's attention on a critical issue—not just for the NFL but for all people involved in or affected by football.

Wee Football to the NFL (2011). She has testified before Congress about head injuries in football and worked to ensure that the NFL put an independent neurologist on the sidelines of every game. Her account of the broken lives of players whose careers had been ended—and lives changed—by repeated head injury was one of the first to publicly point the finger at the NFL for its denials and cover-ups.

The problem was addressed further in *League of Denial* (Fainaru-Wada and Fainaru 2013; see sidebar), which documented the seriousness of the issue and the extent of the NFL's efforts to downplay it. The book was an eye-opener for many fans and especially for parents of young football players. The pathologist who examined former NFL player Mike Webster's brain quoted an NFL doctor, who told him, "If only 10 percent of the mothers in this country begin to believe how dangerous a sport football is, that will be the end of football" (Brinson 2013, 3). The A.V. Club, an entertainment website, said in its review of the documentary that "football is a dead sport walking in the United States. It may look healthy, vibrant, and more profitable than ever. But in a few generations it will be a flimsy husk of itself at its height. The damning evidence is all here" (McFarland 2013).

For its part, the NFL agreed to a $765 million settlement in a lawsuit addressing brain injuries among its 18,000 retired players. The settlement includes compensation for players (with a cap for specific conditions), as well as $10 million for further research and $75 million to screen players who file claims of injury or disability. The suit involved some 4,500 players—some suffering from dementia, depression, or Alzheimer's that they blame on repeated blows to the head. They accused the league of concealing the dangers of concussions, rushing players back to action, and glorifying the jarring hits that cause concussions (Associated Press 2013).

As of the 2013–2014 NFL season, the topic of concussions remained front and center. The courts had yet to rule on the proposed $765 million settlement between the NFL and its players. In the meantime, at least 152 concussions were documented during the season, and more former players spoke out about their struggles in later life due to head trauma. Before the season began, owners approved a new rule designed to reduce hitting with the crown of the helmet, but enforcement was uneven and controversial. Twenty receivers suffered concussions during the season, and in week 12 alone fourteen players were forced to exit games because of concussions—the most in any single week (Breslow 2014).

By the conclusion of the 2014 season, the NFL reported that concussions had dropped 25 percent to a four-year low. The league claims that the decline was due to "a culture of change" in terms of coaches and players modifying their tackling techniques and better enforcement of existing rules that outlaw helmet-to-helmet hits and tackles targeting the head and neck areas. The NFL reported 111 concussions during the 2014 regular season, down from 148 in 2013 and 173 in 2012 (Mihoces 2015).

In light of concerns about football and head injury, perhaps it is not surprising that Pop Warner youth football saw participation rates drop nearly 10 percent between 2010 and 2012. That works out to a loss of nearly 25,000 players—the largest drop in the program's history (Breslow 2014).

Consequences of On-Field Violent Behavior

Violent acts within sport shorten careers, permanently disable people, and reduce the earning power of the victims. In professional football, particular attention has been focused in recent years on the practices of delivering blows to an opponent's head and spearing an opponent by leading with the helmet. In addition, quarterbacks are particularly susceptible to a blindside rush, and the concussions suffered by prominent quarterbacks have crippled some teams and forced some great athletes into premature retirement (Fainaru-Wada and Fainaru 2013).

Most professional athletes who suffer an injury either try to keep playing or return to play too soon. As a result, they often exacerbate the injury; in other cases, their body overcompensates for the previous injury and thus predisposes them to other problems. Why do they do it? Most view it as a badge of honor to play with pain and injury—as something that tough guys do. The sad result is that more and more athletes live the rest of their lives with a bad back, bad knees or shoulders, and a host of other complaints. Football players who carry the ball are literally running targets, and they have the shortest careers in the NFL—on average, just three or four years.

The NFL and its players union have a variety of programs to aid former players, including the 88 Plan, which helps pay expenses for players with dementia. A *New York Times* analysis of 73 former NFL players reports that they experience dementia at several times the national rate, although the

EXPERT'S VIEW

Robert Cantu, MD

Dr. Robert Cantu is the preeminent U.S. expert on head trauma in sport and the author of *Concussions and Our Kids* (2012)—a timely, essential guide for parents, coaches, and all people committed to keeping kids safe in sport. Cantu is a clinical professor of neurosurgery and codirector of the CTE Center at the Boston University School of Medicine. He also chairs several committees on concussions for the NFL and the NFL Players Association and consults with various teams in the NFL, NHL, and National Basketball Association (NBA). His passion is sport safety, including accident reduction, injury treatment, equipment modification, rule changes, improved on-field medical care, and coaching techniques to avoid injury.

Cantu is an avid runner and has competed numerous times in the Boston Marathon. He also plays tennis regularly. Perhaps surprisingly, he continues to be an outspoken advocate for the sport of boxing, though committed to the safety of all participants. He has authored more than 350 scientific publications, including 30 books on neurology and sports medicine. He is also a frequent guest on the major television networks, where he discusses topics related to concussions and sport.

NFL continues to discredit such studies. Fortunately, other athlete advocates have embraced the cause and begun to gather factual information that could lead to modifications in equipment, rules, and medical care, as well as limitations on playing careers when athletes are at risk (Schwarz 2009).

Professional football teams invest millions of dollars in their key players. If the starting quarterback goes down, the team's fortunes are likely to plummet. League administrators are slowly realizing that protecting players is crucial to keeping them on display and that curbing excessive violence helps the league. Similarly, in the NBA, protecting players from violent fouls is crucial to the welfare of the league.

Violent on-field acts can also rob big-time college football teams of their best players. For example, during the 2009 college football season, daily headlines across the country chronicled the progress of Florida quarterback and Heisman Trophy winner Tim Tebow after he suffered a midseason concussion. Fortunately, his team had a bye for the next week, which gave him two weeks of therapy and rest from football before he returned to action.

In addition, on-field violence presents a poor example to youth. Kids cannot withstand even the same amount of physical abuse that adults can. They have less mature bones and muscles and are more susceptible to injury, including career-threatening injury. Moreover, since younger athletes reach physical maturity at different rates, games may match athletes of vastly different size and weight. In youth and high school sport, clear rules against violence are needed in order to protect the health of all players.

Off-Field Violence

It is not clear whether on-field violent behavior leads to off-field violence. Common sense suggests that people who become accustomed to using physical intimidation and violence in sport might naturally revert to such behavior when facing conflict outside of sport. In addition, athletes who hang out at bars, restaurants, or clubs are often treated as targets for other tough guys, who bait them with insults and disrespect. In such situations, the athlete, who feels his manhood is being challenged, may struggle not to respond with physical force.

At the same time, even when athletes do respond physically, the cause is not necessarily sport. The athlete may simply be reflecting his natural disposition, his upbringing, or a cultural attitude established outside of sport. Indeed, such factors might be what led him to choose a violent sport in the first place. For example, as discussed in chapter 14, young males from lower socioeconomic classes tend to embrace sport in order to prove their masculinity. As a result, any challenge to their manhood may leave them feeling compelled to respond or lose face in front of their peers.

The problem of violence can be exacerbated by alcohol consumption, particularly binge drinking, and, as discussed in chapter 8, studies show that athletes are more likely than nonathletes to binge. Like anyone, athletes who are not in full command of their faculties are more likely to lose control and commit violent acts.

Another sensitive topic for many athletes is the apparent rise in violence against women among male athletes. Most men would be quick to say that they respect women and certainly don't intend to harm them. Yet college student athletes, particularly those in contact sports, commit sexual assault at a significantly higher rate than nonathletes, and the problem seems to be growing. Here are some statistics from the National Coalition Against Violent Athletes on its website at ncava.org:

- A three-year study showed that while male student-athletes make up 3 percent of the population on college campuses, they account for 19 percent of sexual assaults and 35 percent of domestic assaults on campuses.
- One in five college football recruits on top 25 Division I teams have a criminal record.
- On average, a college rapist will rape seven times before being caught.
- The general population has a conviction rate of 80 percent for sexual assaults, whereas the rate for athletes is only 38 percent. Even when student athletes are accused of a sexual assault, it appears that universities are reluctant to aggressively investigate or prescribe punishment to student-athletes.

The National Football League receives more negative publicity relating to players' behavior than any other professional sport. That fact is due in large part to the extreme popularity of the sport and the media attention it generates. Since Roger Goodell became NFL commissioner, he has made efforts to improve the image of the league's players, which had suffered mightily. In the years since, player run-ins with the law have continued at a similar pace to that under his predecessor Paul Tagliabue although there are signs of improvement such as a steady decline in the number of arrests from a high in 2006 to the present day (Schrotenboer 2013c).

Two areas of continuing concern in relation to NFL players' off-field behavior are arrests for possession of illegal firearms and arrests related to alcohol. Drunk driving accounts for about 27 percent of all NFL arrests, and NFL players are about twice as likely as the average male to be arrested for an infraction related to guns (Schrotenboer 2013c). Most of the legal issues occur in the off-season when players have more free time than they do during the tightly controlled and intensely focused football season.

In reviewing crime statistics for NFL players versus others in the general population, we must be careful to consider who and what we are comparing. The facts show that the arrest rate among professional athletes for assault and domestic violence is about one-third of the rate for all males in the U.S. population. Moreover, when athletes' behavior is compared with that of other young men in their general age range of 21 to 35, athletes' behavior is markedly better. Even their arrest rate for drunk driving is about half the rate for all men under age 30 (Le Batard 2013).

Black NFL players are arrested nearly 10 times as often as whites, though 66 percent of NFL players are black. Many black players say that they are unfairly singled out for nothing more than "driving while black" and accuse law enforcement officers of racial profiling. When police officers encounter a young black man in an expensive car or in an upscale neighborhood, they often become suspicious. In the general population, black drivers were arrested during a traffic stop at double the rate of white drivers, according to the documents released by the U.S. Department of Justice (Schrotenboer 2013b).

Is it difficult or nearly impossible to turn the violence off as soon as a practice session or game ends? The majority of athletes who display violent on-field behavior don't continue their aggression off the field. If they did, the court records and news media would surely let us know. We simply do not have enough research to address this question, nor do we have complete data about the incidence of domestic violence by athletes. Most victims prefer not to publicize such incidents until they become frequent or incapacitating, and most women do not wish to press charges. In fact, according to the National Coalitions Against Domestic Violence, only about 25 percent of all physical assaults and 20 percent of rapes are reported to the police. The reasons for not reporting range from embarrassment, to fear of retribution, distrust of the police, and mistrust of our system of laws (Johnson 2014).

Some athletes do develop a sense of entitlement as their fame grows (Benedict and Yaeger 1998). Whatever city they're in, elite male athletes are surrounded by female groupies. The athletes often treat

EXPERT'S VIEW

Katherine Redmond

Katherine Redmond was raped by a varsity football player while she was a student and lacrosse player at the University of Nebraska. She sued the university and vowed to dedicate her life to preventing others from having to deal with violent acts perpetrated by athletes. To that end, she founded the National Coalition Against Violent Athletes in 1998. The organization's mission is to educate the public about issues involving athletes and violent behavior and to provide support to victims—including advocacy, referrals, and research—so that they can regain their sense of value and self-worth. The organization also works to ensure that athletes are held to the same standards and laws as others in society.

Through her experiences and training, Redmond has become a national expert on athlete violence and has served as a consultant in many high-profile cases. These cases have included the Kobe Bryant sexual assault case; a University of Colorado rape scandal; an Air Force Academy sex scandal; Title IX cases at the University of Notre Dame, the University of Oklahoma, Arizona State University, and the University of Washington; and many other high-profile rape and domestic violence cases. She has also appeared on numerous television shows and in the print media and serves as a paid consultant for the NFL, where she helped develop stringent zero-tolerance policies. She has been named an American Hero by *Reader's Digest* and was nominated for the *Cosmopolitan* Fabulous Female Award.

these women with disdain and yet are still tempted by their offers of sex. Basketball Hall of Famer Wilt Chamberlain boasted in his autobiography that he had slept with more than 20,000 women, which, if true, shows a definite degree of deviance (ESPN 1999).

Two well-known cases of professional athletes being accused of sexual assault involved basketball player Kobe Bryant of the Los Angeles Lakers and football player Ben Roethlisberger of the Pittsburgh Steelers. Both players admitted to having a sexual relationship with their accuser, but they maintained that the encounter was consensual. Essentially, the cases came down to the proverbial "he said versus she said" without definitive evidence on either side.

A more recent example is that of former NFL player Darren Sharper, who was an All-Pro and then an on-air analyst for the NFL Network. He has been investigated for rape and other sexual assault charges in five states, including California, Arizona, Louisiana, Nevada, and Florida. In each case, Sharper is accused of spiking a woman's drink and then sexually assaulting her, although he claimed the sex was consensual. In 2015, he pleaded no contest in Los Angeles and guilty in New Orleans.

Rapes perpetrated by athletes on college campuses seem to be increasing at an alarming rate. One in five women on a given college campus will be raped, 85 percent will know their attackers, and 90 percent of those rapes will go unreported. In 2012, players at five major NCAA schools were charged with sex crimes. In 2013, students at 29 universities brought legal action related to sexual violence. At the University of Oregon, three varsity basketball players were dismissed from the team and eventually suspended from the school for rape charges, and five football players at Vanderbilt University were dismissed for a gang rape in 2013. In 2012, *Campus Safety* magazine published sexual assault statistics and stated the following in its summary:

> *College men who participated in aggressive sports (including football, basketball, wrestling, and soccer) in high school used more sexual coercion (along with physical and psychological aggression) in their college dating relationships than men who had not (Gray 2012).*

Similar incidents have occurred at the high school level, including the widely publicized case of two football players in Steubenville, Ohio, who were found guilty of gang rape by a juvenile court. The two young men, then 16 and 17 years old, were judged guilty of digital penetration of an intoxicated

16-year-old girl at an alcohol-fueled party and later texting pictures of the girl naked. Both teens were classified as sex offenders, and they were sentenced to juvenile detention of one year and two years, respectively. The Steubenville City School superintendent was charged with tampering with evidence and obstructing justice and was eventually forced to resign. Three other employees were also implicated in an attempted cover-up (Dooley and Effron 2014).

Another case that drew national attention happened in Maryville, Missouri, in 2013. Daisy Coleman was just 14 when she accused a prominent high school football player of raping her while a friend of his filmed the event. Even though Coleman reported the incident to the authorities and gained the support of the county sheriff, the prosecutor eventually dropped the case because he felt that it could not be proven. Meanwhile, Coleman's mother was fired without warning from her job, violent threats were made against the family via social media, and they were forced to leave town. After they left, their house was burned to the ground (Lowe and Sandreczki 2013). Nearly two years after the nightmare had begun, Daisy. Coleman was hospitalized after a suicide attempt brought on by continuing attacks via social media (Alter 2014).

Perhaps the best-known case in 2013 involved charges brought against quarterback Jameis Winston of Florida State University, who had won the prestigious Heisman Trophy for his remarkable on-field exploits. Winston's reputation was clouded by accusations of rape, which he characterized as consensual sex. To this point, due to lack of sufficient evidence, no charges have been filed, although the university is under scrutiny for its handling of the complaint (Luther 2013). Eventually the plaintiff filed a civil suit against Winston, and he countersued with no resolution so far. Once again, this case seems to have gotten stuck at the point of "he said, she said."

Campus sexual violence cases that involve athletes seem to follow a pattern: a woman admires a man for his athletic performance, becomes friendly with him, and, after consuming alcohol, finds herself in an unsafe environment where her protestations of "no" go unheeded. Too many young male athletes see women as the "spoils" of being a jock. In some cases, a group of athletes egg each other on and later claim that the victim was simply "asking for it" in the way she dressed, behaved, or consumed drugs or alcohol (Zirin 2013b).

At the U.S. military academies, a culture of bad behavior and disrespect among athletes has been identified as part of the continuing problem of sexual assaults at the schools. In 2013, scandals rocked teams at all three academies; nearly two-thirds involved the Air Force Academy. There has been a steep increase in reported assaults, from 25 cases in 2008–2009 to a high of 80 in 2011–12, and then a slight decline to 70 in 2012–2013 at all three academies combined. Charges brought against three former football players at the Naval Academy were eventually dropped, but one of the young men was dismissed from the academy for lying to investigators. The widely publicized incident drew attention to an apparent culture of binge drinking and casual sex, along with questionable procedures for handling such charges through military personnel rather than public courts (Baldor 2014).

In January 2014, President Barack Obama took the unusual step of appointing a special White House task force to examine the handling of sexual violence cases on the nation's college campuses. He charged the group with developing clear guidelines for universities to follow. He also put schools on notice that under the umbrella of Title IX funding, they would be held accountable for their handling of sexual violence cases. In addition, 55 universities were listed as being under investigation for their handling of sexual violence complaints. The task force's first report, titled *Not Alone*, was completed in April 2014 (White House 2014).

In addition to rape, other types of violence committed by athletes have also captured the attention of the news media and sport fans. Domestic abuse cases occur far too often, but few can match the shocking case of Carolina Panthers player Rae Carruth, who hired a friend to perform an execution-style murder of his girlfriend, Cherica Adams, after she refused to get an abortion. She was eight months pregnant when she was shot and killed; miraculously, the baby survived. Carruth is currently serving a 24-year sentence for his conviction in 2001 (Hausmann 2013).

Another tragic case was that of Kansas City Chiefs linebacker Jovan Belcher. In 2012, he fatally shot Kasandra Perkins, his girlfriend and the mother of his infant daughter, then drove to the team's training facility to confront Chiefs general manager Scott Pioli and head coach Romeo Crennel. Shockingly, he told the two men, "I need help and I wasn't able to get it," then shot himself in the head. His mother has filed suit against the Chiefs for causing and exacerbating Belcher's erratic thoughts and actions through their handling of football-induced brain damage (Hruby 2014).

ACTIVITY TIME-OUT

Who Should Be The Judge?

One of the ongoing criticisms of the National Football League in recent years has targeted the process used to deal with players who violate league rules regarding acceptable personal conduct. This criticism was heightened in 2014 by the case of NFL player Ray Rice, who was caught on video striking his fiancée. The case called into question whether the league had a stated policy and procedures in place or simply made things up as it went along. Up to this point, the league commissioner had taken it upon himself to function as judge, jury, and executioner—a process that seems inconsistent with the U.S. legal system.

If it were up to you, how would you structure the process for dealing with player behavior that results in violations of league rules with respect to acceptable personal conduct. Along with several classmates, discuss the options and develop your position. Use the following statements to guide your deliberations but do not feel bound by them. Develop a process that seems fair to you.

- The league should not administer any punishment until after a final legal disposition of the case.
- Investigation into player conduct should be conducted by an independent arbitrator approved jointly by the league and the NFL Players Association. Both the league and the players association may have a representative present during the hearings, which shall be recorded and transcribed.
- If either the league or the accused is dissatisfied with the final disposition by the arbitrator, they shall have the right to appeal to the league commissioner.

In 2013, tight end Aaron Hernandez of the New England Patriots was arrested and charged with the murder of an acquaintance. Hernandez came into the league after a rocky past, and, though he was judged to have first-round talent, he was not drafted until the fourth round because teams were wary of his reputation for bar fights and marijuana use. Once he became a professional, he proved his worth on the field and earned a $40 million contract extension in 2012. A year later, however, he was in jail awaiting trial for murder (Schrotenboer 2013a). He was found guilty of first degree murder by a jury trial in April 2015 and sentenced to life in prison without the possibility of parole (Fox 2015).

In 2014, two very different cases of domestic abuse involving NFL players filled the news media, eventually forcing the NFL to develop a detailed policy for handling such situations. In the much-publicized case of Ray Rice, who was caught on tape hitting his fiancée, NFL commissioner Roger Goodell initially suspended Rice for two games but later made the suspension indefinite. However, upon Rice's appeal, a judge ruled that the second penalty was "arbitrary and an abuse of discretion," essentially saying that applying a second penalty was impermissible for the same offense. During the process, Rice was released by the Baltimore Ravens, and he has yet to catch on with another team (Associated Press 2014c).

During the same time period, All-Pro running back Adrian Peterson of the Minnesota Vikings was charged with and pleaded guilty to reckless assault of his four-year-old son after whipping the boy with a tree branch. The whipping resulted in large bleeding sores on various parts of the boy's body. Peterson was suspended for the rest of the 2014 season, and though he appealed the decision, it was not lifted (Schottey 2014; Katersky 2014). By April of 2015, Peterson's suspension was lifted and he joined his teammates for preseason practices in June.

Lest you think that domestic violence is only a male problem, three recent cases involving professional female athletes make clear that both sexes can engage in violent off-field behavior. Ex-WNBA player and Olympic gold medalist Chamique Holdsclaw pleaded guilty in 2014 to aggravated assault and possession of a firearm during the commission of a felony. After a confrontation with her ex-girlfriend, Jennifer Lacy, Holdsclaw broke Lacy's car window with a bat and then fired a shot into the car. She was sentenced to three years of probation and fined $3,000 under a plea agreement (Associated Press 2014a). Soccer superstar and Team USA goalkeeper Hope Solo was charged with violent assault against her half-sister and nephew at a late-night party. Eventually, the domestic abuse charges were dropped because the alleged victims refused to cooperate with the prosecution (ESPN 2014d). Two WNBA stars who play for different teams, Brittney Griner of the Phoenix Mercury and Glory Johnson of the Tulsa Shock, were arrested in April of 2015 for assault on each other, and eventually both players were suspended for seven games by the WNBA for domestic violence. In spite of the situational drama, the basketball stars were married in May of 2015 and announced that Glory was pregnant. A month later, Brittney declared that she was not ready for the marriage commitment and announced plans to seek an annulment of the marriage (Reinhard 2015; Warren 2015).

Could reports of violent behavior by professional football and basketball players be rooted in part in racist fears among members of the U.S. public? In 2013, as shown in table 12.3 in chapter 12, African Americans accounted for 66 percent of NFL players and 77 percent of NBA players. With such dominance also comes some degree of jealousy and suspicion on the part of white people toward black men whom they see playing an aggressive and even violent game on the football field or, to a lesser extent, the basketball court. More generally, a variety of surveys have shown that a majority of white people believe that black people are more aggressive, violent, and more likely to be involved in violent crime than official statistics indicate they are (Welch 2007).

At the same time, as of 2012, just 9 percent of Associated Press sport editors were people of color (that figure did at least constitute a 6 percent increase since 2010) (Lapchick 2012a). Thus, to a large extent, the United States appears to have white sport journalists writing for a white audience that may already hold prejudiced views of black men. When a violent incident involves a football or basketball athlete, it receives exhaustive media coverage. African American men dominate those sports, and if they are involved in violent behavior it is practically guaranteed that the case will be widely publicized.

African Americans such as Satch Sanders, who helped the Boston Celtics win eight world championships, are outraged by the portrayal of African American athletes as prone to violence. Sanders and others point to the millions of dollars that famous athletes donate to schools, charities, and youth foundations. Indeed, most professional athletes are solid family men who respect their wives, mothers, sisters, and women in general. Joyce Williams-Mitchell is former executive director of the Massachusetts Coalition of Battered Women's Service Groups and an African American woman who hates the violent image of athletes. She says, "It is a myth! Most batterers are men who control women through their profession, and they include police officers, clergymen, dentists, and judges. Athletes get the headlines, though, and an unfair public rap. Men from every profession (regardless of race) have the potential to be batterers" (Lapchick 1999).

As stated earlier, we need more research before coming to any conclusions about violence and sport. Rather than rely on sensational examples from the media, we need solid data with which to compare rates of occurrence across groups. Drug and alcohol use should also be noted, since in some cases they—and not sport—may be the cause of violence. No one is helped by sensationalized reporting or hidden facts. The attention given by the White House to the issue of sexual violence on college campuses sends a clear message that there will be repercussions if such behavior does not change. Perhaps professional sport leagues need to take similar action to reduce or eliminate such behavior by their athletes. There are still too many athletes whose behavior is overlooked if they can play the game well; meanwhile, victims and family members pay the price for our failure to respond decisively to violent behavior.

Reducing Violence

Earlier in the chapter, we discussed the stringent standards that NHL has imposed since 2005 to reduce on-ice violence. Clearly, NHL officials had decided that changes were necessary in their athletes' behavior. As this effort illustrates, violence can be significantly reduced if those in charge of a sport agree that doing so is a worthy goal.

The National Football League has recently become a de facto leader in studying the data on brain trauma,

APPLYING SOCIAL THEORY

Feminist Theory and Violence by Athletes

Assume that you adhere to a feminist social theory and are deeply committed to the welfare of females who suffer physical or sexual violence perpetrated by athletes at your university. Regardless of whether you are male or female, you—or a friend, sister, or cousin—could be involved in such an incident.

Investigate what cases have happened on your campus and how they were handled by the athletic department and the student affairs division. Also evaluate your campus's openness about such crimes, its efforts to educate people about how to prevent them, and the clarity of its policies and procedures for reporting them if they do occur. Are the local police involved, or are charges handled internally by the school? If possible, determine also whether the athletic department trains its coaching staff to educate and advise athletes about these issues and whether penalties for infractions are clearly spelled out.

Compare what you learn with your classmates' results and discuss whether you think more can and should be done to reduce the frequency of sexual violence or the methods for handling complaints or charges.

modifying rules to reduce the incidence of such injuries, defining and teaching safer methods of play, and exploring equipment modifications to increase safety. Team owners have an investment in their athletes and can't afford to lose star players. Families don't want to see their kids injured or sentenced to a life of physical disability. League officials need to protect their superstars so they can continue to market them to potential spectators. Almost everyone in sport has a financial investment not only in the productivity of athletes but also in their health and well-being; therefore, everyone stands to gain by protecting them.

What can be done? Once unacceptable in-game acts of violence are clearly defined in the minds of officials and coaches, penalties can be assessed immediately when the acts occur. Offenders can be immediately suspended from that game and future games. Players can also be fined, but forced inactivity carries more weight with most athletes. Coaches and teams who condone violent play can also be punished until they find the risks too great to continue using such tactics (NHL rules, for example, now punish coaches when players break the rules). The NFL would do well to explore longer suspensions of athletes, especially those who foul repeatedly.

Off-field violence can be addressed in part through educational programs, such as the nationwide Mentors in Violence Prevention (MVP), founded in 1992 at Northeastern University. MVP is the largest program to use athletes to address violence against women (Lapchick 1999). Similar programs must be initiated in schools, churches, sport programs, and every other potential avenue. Professional sport leaders must see that it is in their self-interest to minimize violence, and they must become leaders in the campaign against violence rather than waiting for others to take action.

Society at large must also address the issue of violence. Violent acts in the sport world may grab headlines, but such acts also pervade businesses, professions, and the world of education. Passionate discussions about gun violence consume U.S. society, and all agree that the results are tragic, but consensus about methods for solving the problems seem to escape us. When linked to social class and race, violence raises uncomfortable discussions that some people would rather avoid. But according to the U.S. Department of Justice, African American men have a one in three chance of spending time in prison (Chaddock 2003). Without addressing violence in light of such factors as race, ethnicity, sexual preference, and education level, U.S. society may witness antisocial actions for years to come.

Chapter Summary

Learning the rules of the game is a key aspect of sport participation. Yet at every level of play, some athletes break the rules—sometimes repeatedly—either out of ignorance or, more likely, to gain an advantage over the competition. The most blatant rule breaking in modern-day sport involves the use of performance-enhancing drugs, which is also the type of infraction that receives the most media attention.

Yet in comparison with previous generations, today's sport participants seems to engage in less rule breaking, thanks to better officiating and to well-organized youth sport programs where players learn the rules of the game. In addition, rules have been modified over the years to make them clearer and easier to interpret consistently. Moreover, video replay technology allows everyone to observe infractions (in slow motion), which makes it difficult to argue with an official who has the clear evidence at his or her fingertips. Finally, the immediacy of the electronic media allows observers to critique athletes' behavior on the field so that rule breakers are publicly chastised and embarrassed.

This chapter also explores the role of emotion and its influence on both players and spectators. While our emotions provide the spice of life and feed our passions, they also need to be reasonably well controlled and channeled in positive ways. Anger often arises in competitive sport, and it can be used either positively or negatively. Among spectators, the combination of anger and alcohol consumption often results in abusive behavior that is unpleasant and even dangerous to other fans or players.

Aggression is generally viewed as a positive trait in sport; in fact, players who hustle after loose balls or aggressively defend their goal are typically admired. But when aggression takes on the characteristic of inflicting intentional physical harm to an opponent, then the meaning of true sport is lost.

Contact or collision sports—such as football, ice hockey, wrestling, lacrosse, and boxing—have long been among the most popular sporting events. Fights on the court, on the field, or at the rink seem to attract some fans, yet the consequences are suffered by the players. Violent hits have been outlawed by the rules, and players are generally better protected from senseless violence than ever before. In the NFL, players have finally revealed the indignities that they live with after their career is done due to the violent hits they absorb over the years. As a result, the reality of the risk of permanent disability or even death due to brain trauma has finally gotten some attention from the league.

Off-field violence continues to be a concern and is often linked to athletes who play violent sports. Rape and other violent acts against women appear to have increased, and the problem is being addressed by organized countermeasures led by the White House. College campuses seem to be particularly risky sites for women who associate with fraternity men or male athletes in settings where alcohol is present. Perhaps even more concerning is the often-dubious manner in which universities and professional sport organizations handle complaints of sexual or physical violence.

STUDENT OUTCOMES

After reading this chapter, you will know the following:

- Issues relating to doping and performance-enhancing drugs
- The problems of eating disorders
- Issues involved in hazing in sport
- The debate about sport gambling

Deviance and Sport

Deviance and Sport

For most people in the United States, even those who were not fans of cycling, Lance Armstrong was a true American hero. We marveled at his athletic exploits, his toughness and courage as a cancer survivor, and his efforts to serve as an inspiration to all. As a result, when he denied accusations of doping, many of us took him at his word and defended him against his accusers, who seemed to be obsessed with dethroning him after a decade of dominance. He fooled us all.

Armstrong was eventually revealed as a pathological cheater, a narcissistic playboy, and a ruthless destroyer of the reputations and careers of his teammates and co-conspirators. Not only did he ruin his own reputation, but also the sport of cycling has been so damaged that it may not recover. How can we trust the results of any race?

Several books have chronicled the rise of Armstrong and fellow cyclists Tyler Hamilton and Floyd Landis through the late 1990s and 2000s. Their ascent was followed by a gradually growing cloud of suspicion and doubt—and eventually resulted in lives ruined by cheating and dishonesty. The story has also been addressed in numerous articles and several television interviews with the principal players.

In addition, now that some time has elapsed, a good place to start learning about this dramatic sequence of events is the U.S. Anti-Doping Agency's (2012) detailed 200-page report on cheating at the U.S. Postal Service Pro Cycling Team, for which Armstrong raced. Next, read Hamilton's book *The Secret Race* (2012), written with Dan Coyle, and then *Wheelmen* (2013) by Wall Street Journal reporters Reed Albergotti and Vanessa O'Connell. The most recent book is *Cycle of Lies: The Fall of Lance Armstrong* (2014) by Juliet Macur of the *New York Times*.

As founder of the Livestrong Foundation, which provides support for cancer patients, Lance Armstrong was admired as a philanthropic and compassionate man who was thankful to survive the scourge of cancer and dedicated his reputation and life to helping others do the same. Instead, we now have a discredited athlete stripped of all seven of his Tour de France titles, stripped of France's most coveted Legion of Honor award, exposed as a drug cheat, and having brought countless co-conspirators down with him. His story is a fascinating tale of a hero who turned out to be someone altogether different from who we thought he was.

People in a society are expected to conform to the rules and norms of the group. Those who do not conform are labeled as deviant. The word **deviant** means departing from something, especially from an accepted norm. Deviating can be positive or negative; however, in U.S. vernacular, *deviant* is often equated with *devious*, which carries a decidedly negative connotation. It is in this negative sense of the term that this chapter explores deviance in sport.

The label *deviant* might also be applied to the behaviors covered in chapter 19: violation of the rules of play, unrestrained aggression during competition, and the apparent rise in violence both on and off the field. This chapter focuses on four additional forms of deviant behavior: the use of performance-enhancing substances, eating disorders, the hazing of athletes, and gambling in sport. Each of these topics has been addressed prominently in the news media in recent years, and sport organizations have made concerted efforts to control and regulate their impact on sport. Despite those efforts, these issues continue to plague organized sport competition; indeed, they threaten the very essence of sport as a fair and equitable contest that celebrates athletic prowess without harming the athletes or the sport itself.

The abundance of attention paid to the misconduct of college and professional athletes in the United States may suggest that athletes generally lack good moral values and are out of step with mainstream America. This chapter explores whether that impression is justified by comparing the incidence of deviant behavior among athletes with the incidence among others in U.S. society. It also addresses the related question of whether sport promotes, encourages, or rewards deviant behavior—or, conversely, whether people who are attracted to sport may be predisposed to deviant behavior.

Typically, when we study deviant behavior, we are dealing with behavior by a person who is either unaware of the norm or simply rejects it. The term **underconformity** refers to behavior that does not conform to the generally accepted rules of sport. Such behavior may involve breaking team rules, school rules, or rules of competition. For example, many athletes use profanity, haze teammates, drink alcohol, argue with others, or bet on the outcome of a sport event; however, such behavior is labeled as deviant only if it goes beyond accepted limits.

Another form of deviance involves **overconformity** to the expectations of high-performance sport. Examples of overconformity include drastically altering food intake to gain or lose weight and using supplements to improve strength or bulk up muscles. As with underconformity, many athletes engage in similar practices but do not carry them to the extreme that constitutes deviant behavior, in this case overconformity.

Excessive conformity may manifest itself in following the rules and customs of sport too well. Particularly in high-performance training, athletes may put such a high priority on sport that they ignore or undervalue other critical areas of life. For example, they may sacrifice friendships, ignore their family, or neglect academic studies due to single-minded dedication to sport training. In the long run, such behaviors are counterproductive.

Overconformity is often found in the United States in the growing sport of competitive cheerleading. During the 2013–2014 school year, more than 120,000 girls and nearly 3,000 boys were high school cheerleaders, and cheerleading is now recognized as a sport by the National Federation of State High School Associations. As the sport has grown, it has evolved from cheers aimed at raising school spirit to exhibits of great athleticism and gymnastic skill. Unfortunately, this evolution has also made cheering the most dangerous sport for girls; it carries the highest rate of catastrophic injury in girls' sport and accounts for two-thirds of all catastrophic injuries in female athletes.

Although the most common injuries in cheerleading are strains and sprains, concussions rank next and account for about one-third of all cheering injuries. Most injuries occur in practice, and they break down as follows: stunts (33 percent), tumbling (22 percent), tossing (18 percent), and pyramids (15 percent) (Straus 2013). In 2012, the American Academy of Pediatrics Council on Sports Medicine and Fitness put forth a set of simple safety measures designed to reduce the injury rate during cheerleading stunts, and rules to that effect have since been adopted by the American Association of Cheerleading Coaches and Administrators. Some observers also pointed out the fact that in spite of the risks inherent in cheerleading, the overall injury rate in cheerleading is just 0.57 injuries per 1,000 exposures, which ranks it seventeenth highest out of twenty sports tracked (Marar et al. 2012).

Performance Enhancement Through Drugs

Perhaps no sport-related issue has received more attention in recent years than the use of drugs and other performance-enhancing substances. This is not a new topic, nor is there convincing evidence that drug use is more prevalent today than in the past. The difference lies in the media's reporting, the increasingly aggressive drug-testing programs, and the sophisticated methods that abusers use to mask their actions.

One of the earliest mentions of performance-enhancing substances was made by Galen, a Greek physician who was born in AD 129 and practiced sports medicine. Reports from the early Olympic Games indicate that athletes used herbs, animal proteins, and mushrooms in their efforts to improve performance. In the 19th century, French athletes reportedly drank a concoction of wine and cocoa leaves in an attempt to reduce sensations of fatigue and hunger.

In the modern era, the 1952 Oslo Olympics were marred by heavy use of stimulants. The use of anabolic steroids was reported first at the 1960 Rome Olympics and again at the 1964 Tokyo Games. From that time until the 1980s, the illegal use of doping substances increased substantially due to lack of awareness and failure to detect. In 1983, media attention focused on illegal drug use at the Pan American Games, where 19 athletes were found in violation. The problem of doping in sport received intense international attention at the 1988 Seoul Olympics, where Canadian Ben Johnson, winner of the 100-meter run, tested positive for steroids and was disqualified (Lajis 1996).

Modern athletes use three distinct types of drug: (1) prescription and over-the-counter medications, (2) stimulants, and (3) anabolic steroids.

Prescription drugs and **over-the-counter drugs** promote healing from sickness or injury or mask pain to allow the athlete to return to competition. Although elite athletes who mask their pain to continue competing may be at risk for long-term disability, they argue that it is their personal decision whether to risk the early return. Many athletes realize that a quick return is essential if they want to keep their place on the team. Moreover, fans and the media applaud the athlete who guts it out after an injury, even though the athlete may be masking the pain with medication. Decisions to use restorative drugs should be made with honest medical advice. Young athletes should involve their parents in the decision rather than rely on their coach, trainer, or team medical staff.

In 2014, a group of eight retired players filed a lawsuit against the National Football League (NFL). Led by three prominent members of the 1985 Super Bowl champion Chicago Bears—quarterback Jim McMahon, Hall of Fame defensive end Richard Dent, and offensive lineman Keith Van Horne, the players alleged that the league had illegally provided them with risky narcotics and other painkillers that numbed their injuries and led to medical complications and drug addiction.

According to the suit, team doctors administered the drugs without using prescriptions, keeping medication records, or explaining the potential side effects. The players also say that they were not told of injuries they had suffered and were urged to return to play. Plaintiff J.D. Hill, who played for seven years in the 1970s, says that he was supplied with "uppers, downers, painkillers, you name it while in the NFL. I became addicted and turned to the streets after my career and was homeless. Never took a drug in my life, and I became a junkie in the NFL" (Nuckols 2014).

The second class of drug used in sport is that of **stimulants**, such as caffeine, cocaine, Benzedrine, Ritalin, and Methedrine. Stimulants have been used rampantly in professional sport for decades. Players use them to get hyped up before competition and to heighten their arousal level. Indeed, amphetamines (often referred to as "speed") are a fact of life in professional baseball, football, and basketball, and high-performance athletes feel pressured to use them just to stay competitive.

The third category of drugs in sport comprises **anabolic steroids** and related substances that increase muscle size, decrease fat, and produce secondary male sex characteristics. Anabolic steroids are faster and more effective than any physical training program in increasing size, strength, and speed. As a result, they have been used to help produce apparently miraculous performances by weightlifters, track-and-field athletes, football players, and baseball players. Evidence points to chronic steroid use by some athletes in virtually every high-performance sport.

Other performance-enhancing substances used and abused by aspiring athletes include vitamins, health foods, human growth hormones, amino acids, and natural herbs. Athletes may also use blood doping, in which an athlete is injected with oxygen-carrying red blood cells derived from blood previously withdrawn from the athlete. Now let's take a closer look at anabolic steroids and other performance enhancers.

Hall of Fame defensive end Richard Dent is one of eight named retired NFL players suing the NFL for illegally supplying them with risky painkillers that numbed their injuries and led to medical complications.

Steroids

Steroids increase an athlete's muscle size, speed, and power; they can also enhance masculinity, aggressiveness, sense of well-being, and sexual prowess. For decades, sport fans dismissed reports of drug use in sport. In the United States, fans preferred to accuse Eastern Communist countries, led by East Germany, as the main offenders in the Olympics. When evidence of illegal drug use became well publicized after the fall of the East German government, U.S. observers merely nodded and assumed that the bad guys had finally been caught. In reality, however, U.S. Olympians had been quietly adding performance-enhancing substances to their own training regimens.

In 2004, at the Athens Olympic Games, the world finally insisted on tougher drug testing. As part of this process, popular U.S. athletes, particularly in track and field, were finally caught and labeled as drug cheats. Others were cast under a heavy cloud of suspicion—for example, premier sprinter Marion Jones, whose partner, sprinter Tim Montgomery, was banned from the competition. Jones, along with dozens of others, was implicated in the investigation of BALCO Laboratories in California. Although she never failed a drug test, she was found guilty and sentenced to prison on the basis of information contained in BALCO records. Montgomery was banned following testimony from BALCO founder Victor Conte, who pleaded guilty to distributing steroids and was sentenced to four months in prison. Conte has also admitted supplying Jones and other Olympic and professional athletes with illegal drugs (ABC News 2004; Layden 2004).

Drug testing now involves year-round random testing that can be conducted at any time, day or night, including when athletes least expect it. These policies are the only sure way to catch sophisticated violators who have learned how to clean out their systems prior to competition or scheduled tests. In response, the International Olympic Committee (IOC) has increased the number of tests conducted both before and during the Games; it also retains samples for eight years, thus allowing the use of new testing protocols as they are developed to test samples from previous competitions. At the Games, athletes can be tested at any time, without prior notice, and all medal winners are automatically tested immediately after their event. Here are some key results of testing in recent years (International Olympic Committee 2014d):

Summer Games

- 2000 (Sydney): 2,359 tests and 11 positives
- 2004 (Athens): 3,667 tests and 26 infringements
- 2008 (Beijing): 4,500 tests and 15 positives (including six horses in equestrian events)
- 2012 (London): 5,000 tests and 9 positives

Winter Games

- 2002 (Salt Lake City): 700 tests and 7 positives
- 2006 (Turin): 1,200 tests and 1 positive
- 2010 (Vancouver): 2,100 tests and 1 infringement (which did not result in a ban)
- 2014 (Sochi): 2,453 tests and 8 positives

The 2012 London Games were the scene of a record number of drug tests. An official count of 5,051 blood and urine tests were administered, and a few weeks later an additional 1,200 tests were conducted at the Paralympics at the same venue (International Olympic Committee 2014d). In addition, during the six months prior to the Olympic Games, 107 athletes were sanctioned for doping offenses and banned from the competition (Grohman 2012).

In December 2013, IOC president Thomas Bach announced that the IOC's executive board had approved a $10 million fund to pay for research into developing new technology for catching drug cheats. At the same time, the IOC asked national governments to contribute the same amount to the World Anti-Doping Agency for its own research projects. Authorities are particularly interested in developing methods that are more reliable and effective than the standard urine and blood tests; possibilities include testing hair and cell samples (Wilson 2013).

The small country of Jamaica has long been known as the home of the finest sprinters in the world, both male and female. As a result, the world of track and field was stunned in 2013 when it was revealed that six Jamaican athletes had tested positive for banned substances. They included Veronica Campbell-Brown, Asafa Powell, and Sherone Simpson. Subsequently the head of the Jamaican Anti-Doping Commission revealed that only one out-of-competition test had been carried out in the five months leading up to the 2012 Olympics. As a result, the commission's entire board resigned, and the commission was reconstituted by the country's prime minister (Dawes 2013).

Professional sports in the United States are also stepping up their efforts to eliminate the use of banned substances. As part of this process, players unions have finally accepted significant penalties for drug use in their contract agreements with Major League Baseball (MLB) and other leagues.

For its part, MLB seems to have moved beyond its "steroid era," which extended from the mid-1990s through the mid-2000s, when the sport finally instituted steroid testing. The steroid era changed the sport's history books. For example, Babe Ruth's record of 60 home runs in a single season stood for 34 years until Roger Maris hit 61 homers in 1961. For the next 35 years, no player hit more than 52. Then, from 1998 to 2006, players hit more than 60 homers six times. Mark McGwire set the new record at 71 in 1998, and that was topped by Barry Bonds, who hit 73 in 2001. It wasn't until 2010 that Mc Gwire finally admitted his steroid use. In November 2005, MLB and the players union agreed to tougher penalties that include a 50-game ban for the first offense, a 100-game suspension for the second, and a lifetime ban for the third.

The new approach did not come easily. After a series of negative comments from prominent members of the U.S. Congress about the apparent "steroid problem" in baseball, MLB commissioner Bud Selig appointed former U.S. senator George Mitchell to head an investigation into the use of both anabolic steroids and human growth hormone in baseball. In 2007, after a 21-month investigation, Mitchell gave Selig a 409-page report that implicated 89 major league players, including superstars Roger Clemens, Barry Bonds, Miguel Tejada, Andy Pettitte, Rafael Palmeiro, Eric Gagne, and Jason Giambi. The teams that had the most players mentioned in the report were the New York Yankees with 22, the Baltimore Orioles with 18, and the Los Angeles Angels with 16 (ESPN 2007).

Another baseball steroid scandal came to light in 2013, when more than a dozen MLB players were accused of obtaining human growth hormone from the Biogenesis health clinic in the Miami suburb of Coral Gables. The scandal was revealed by the *Miami New Times*, though it refused to release documents to MLB. The clinic's owner, Anthony Bosch, was sued by MLB in an attempt to gain information, and he eventually agreed to cooperate in exchange for having his name removed from the lawsuit (Oz 2013).

With that information in hand, MLB suspended Milwaukee Brewers player Ryan Braun for the remainder of the 2013 season for his involvement in the scandal; as a result, he lost $3.25 million in salary. MLB also suspended New York Yankees star Alex Rodriguez through the 2014 season, though he was allowed to continue playing during his appeal of the decision. After serving his suspension, Rodriguez returned to the Yankees in 2015 at the relatively advanced age of 39, and it will be interesting to see how long he can continue to play at the major league level. Twelve other players accepted 50-game suspensions with no right of appeal, including three who were All-Stars in 2013: Everth Cabrera, Nelson Cruz, and Jhonny Peralta (Oz 2013).

In 2014, MLB and the players association agreed to toughen the league's drug policy. Under the new rules, players who are suspended during a season are ineligible for that season's playoffs. This change closes a loophole that infuriated critics in 2013, when Peralta and Cruz served their suspensions in time to return for the playoffs. The new rules also increase the suspension for a first violation from 50 games to 80 and for a second violation from 100 games to a season-long 162; the penalty for a third violation remains a lifetime ban from baseball. In addition, a player serving a season-long suspension loses all his pay for that year.

The new agreement also toughens the league's testing regimen, increasing the number of in-season random urine tests from 1,400 to 3,200, including at least two for each player. Off-season tests also increase, from 250 to 350. In addition, 400 random blood collections will be conducted to detect human growth hormone in addition to the mandatory single test for each player during spring training (ESPN 2014b).

Bill Romanowski was an NFL star who won four Super Bowl rings and was twice named to the Pro Bowl. His book *Romo: My Life on the Edge—Living Dreams and Slaying Dragons* was released in 2005. According to *Publishers Weekly*, the book is about 30 percent football and 70 percent apothecary. Romanowski details his consistent drug use, which allowed him to play at a high level and return more quickly from injuries. He admits to having used ephedrine, THG, DMSO cream, prescription-strength Motrin, and Naprosyn—and he claims he would do it all over again. Romanowski might have been an aberration, but his open account of extended drug use helped draw people's attention to drug use in professional sport (*Publishers Weekly* 2005).

Bode Miller, who won the 2004 World Cup series in skiing, made some surprising comments to the media, saying that drugs such as erythropoietin (EPO) carry minimal risk and can help skiers if taken under supervision. While EPO is usually taken to boost endurance, Miller claimed that it could also make dangerous ski runs safer by improving instantaneous decision making (BBC Sport 2005). At the 2006 Turin Olympics, Miller won no medals and didn't seem to care; in fact, he vowed not to ski again for the U.S. team. Nonetheless, he returned at the 2010 Vancouver Games as a changed man, both in attitude and dedication. The controversial athlete who had once declared that "it's easy to ski drunk" had found a renewed sense of purpose and commitment. His reward was a bronze medal in the men's downhill event (Sappenfield 2010).

Although it does not necessarily enhance athletic performance, substance abuse by college athletes continues to be a concern. A 2014 report by the National Collegiate Athletic Association (NCAA) revealed several notable trends in the substance use habits of student-athletes. Contrary to public perception, excessive drinking is trending downward among student-athletes. Overall substance use is higher among athletes in Division III than among those in Divisions I and II. Use of substances other than alcohol is higher among male athletes than female athletes. Marijuana use is highest among male lacrosse players (46 percent), followed by male swimmers (33 percent) and male soccer players (31 percent). In most other male sports, the usage rate is around 20 percent; in women's sports, it averages closer to 15 percent (NCAA 2014f).

Responding to Doping

Virtually every sport organization has begun to clarify and enforce its rules about drug use. The World Anti-Doping Agency Code defines its purpose as follows:

> *To protect the athletes' fundamental right to participate in doping-free sport and thus promote health, fairness and equality for athletes worldwide and to ensure harmonized, coordinated and effective anti-doping programs at the international and national level with regard to detection deterrence and prevention of doping (World Anti-Doping Agency 2015)*

ACTIVITY TIME-OUT

Aren't Drugs the American Way?

Some people sincerely believe that it is foolish to try to ban substances. They suggest removing the rules and testing programs, which they say don't seem to work anyway, and allowing athletes to use substances with the advice of health professionals. In this view, drug testing will never keep up with those who are intent on using illegal substances, and elite athletes simply can't keep up with their peers unless they level the playing field by taking banned substances.

One justification for allowing drug use in sport is that many nonathletes rely on drugs to deal with daily life. Even some preschoolers are put on Ritalin to help them focus. Parents may take sleeping pills or use tranquilizers or alcohol to relax. Other people use drugs to prevent pregnancy, cope with menopause, enhance sexual function, lower blood pressure, counter the aging process, fight migraines, and on and on. Some college students rely on caffeine or amphetamines to study for exams, and truck drivers may take these drugs to stay awake on long hauls. With all this in mind, some people wonder why athletes should be any different.

What do you think? Would you continue down the same path of drug testing in sport, change the approach to drug testing in sport, or eliminate drug testing altogether? To help you decide, make a list of the pros and cons of allowing performance-enhancing drugs in sport and compare your list with those of your classmates. Once you've considered all of this information, make your overall decision and justify it.

That broad definition is followed by numerous descriptions of doping methods and lists of illegal substances. Meanwhile, others press ahead to discover new masking agents that hide drugs and new combinations of substances that cannot be detected by current testing. As in most cases of illegal behavior, it seems that the perpetrators are always just a step ahead of the enforcers.

Drug testing in sport is complicated by debate about cold medicines that are banned but still taken, perhaps by an athlete who simply contracts a cold just before a championship. Wouldn't the average citizen do the same if he or she caught a cold and needed to go to work? In Vancouver in 2010, Lubomir Visnovsky, a Slovakian ice hockey player, was reprimanded after testing positive for pseudoephedrine, which can be used as a stimulant at high doses. Visnovsky told officials that he had been taking Advil Cold & Sinus medication. Similarly, before the Games began, Russian ice hockey player Svetlana Terenteva tested positive for tuaminoheptane, which she attributed to using a cold remedy (Olympics Fanhouse 2010).

Controversy can even accompany athletes' use of everyday vitamins, which of course are consumed daily by many people around the country. Are such vitamins illegal for athletes? Is it illegal to use Gatorade, sold at grocery stores, to aid hydration and fight heat exhaustion? In addition, at U.S. health food stores, you can find and read the claims of thousands of agents that are not regulated by the U.S. Food and Drug Administration (FDA). Thus the questions about drug use in sport seem to be unending—and sometimes so confusing that no solution seems possible. There are signs of progress, however, both in drug testing and in educational programs that combat the use of performance enhancers by athletes at all levels. Some high schools are even drug-testing all students in cocurricular activities, although the expense to do so appears to be prohibitive in most areas.

The IOC continues to lead the world in drug testing and can be relatively nimble in adjusting its policies because it does not have to secure approval from a players union before taking action. For the same reason, NASCAR was recently able to install a relatively stringent program. Even so, of all of the U.S. professional sports, baseball has the most complete policy due to the scrutiny and negative publicity it received during its steroid era. As for other major U.S. team sports, both professional football and basketball randomly test their athletes

EXPERT'S VIEW

Don Catlin, MD, Father of Drug-Testing in Sport

Dr. Don Catlin has more than three decades of experience at the highest levels of anti-doping efforts and drug-testing in sport. In fact, at UCLA in 1982, he founded the first U.S. anti-doping lab. He has provided testing services to the IOC, the World Anti-Doping Agency, the United States Olympic Committee, MLB, the NFL, the NCAA, several Olympic Games, and the soccer World Cup. His analytical research has been instrumental in developing drug tests for performance-enhancing drugs, blood boosters, and designer steroids. Catlin is the longest-tenured member of the IOC Medical Commission and a professor emeritus of molecular and medical pharmacology at UCLA.

In 2004, Catlin cofounded the Banned Substances Control Group (BSCG) to offer a supplement-certifying program enabling manufacturers to establish that their brands and products are safe and free of drugs. Given that there is no effective oversight of supplements by the FDA in the United States, BSCG is providing a service to manufacturers and consumers alike by ensuring that products do what they are designed to do without harmful side effects (Banned Substances Control Group 2015). By shifting his emphasis from the drug testing of elite athletes to ensuring the safety of dietary supplements, Catlin also helps millions of everyday people who rely on supplements for their health and welfare.

several times a year, both during the season and in the off-season. Only ice hockey limits testing to training camp and during the season.

The most hopeful sign that has emerged recently comes from trials of a new kind of testing program. In this longitudinal testing plan, individual blood levels of various substances would be established for each athlete, and later testing conducted at irregular intervals would identify any significant changes. This procedure holds much promise for identifying athletes who insist on circumventing established rules (Quinn and Fainaru-Wada 2008).

The IOC now forces all international sport governing bodies to institute effective drug testing. Although the testing varies across sports, it conforms to the basic IOC-recommended format, which includes unannounced random testing throughout the year, mandatory testing of competition winners, and minimum standards for frequency of testing. These practices have led to an increase in disqualifications. In addition, legal actions, such as the one taken against BALCO Laboratories in California, has helped publicize doping offenses and thrown the weight of public support behind stronger enforcement.

Clearly, the standard is set by the IOC, which has established doping as a deviant behavior. In that environment, no sporting organization accepts doping as proper or within the bounds of acceptable behavior (Luschen 2000). Even so, some athletes continue to choose that path, and continued drug use in sport could lead to the following issues:

- Fans, parents, and kids might reject sport as an activity that is unhealthy and not worthwhile.
- Corporations that follow public sentiment might withdraw their financial support. If conventional wisdom lumped sport in with other negative social activities, the benefits of being a corporate sponsor would fade quickly.
- Sport officials would accept the reality that unless strong action was taken, sport could be restricted to drug users as athletes who refrain become also-rans.
- Widespread drug use would affect athletes' long-term health long after their use had been discontinued. It would become commonplace to see athletes with a shorter life span and diminished quality of life.
- Young athletes would be enticed at an early age to follow the example of their sport heroes.
- Female athletes who use drugs in their early years might risk their ability to bear children later.
- Genetic engineering might produce athletic capabilities now only dreamed of and thus relegate even performance enhancers to being a thing of the past.

Addressing these issues requires action on the part of all people invested in sport. For example, it requires sport leaders to work together to ensure the health and welfare of athletes. They must develop new attitudes and creative solutions to drug use in order for the sport world to avoid a rapid descent into competition dominated by chemicals. It is also crucial for international sport bodies to work together and address the issues effectively. Otherwise, if certain countries solve the problems in their own programs, they will be unable to compete with athletes from other countries who continue to use doping.

The media can also help by exposing doping in sport in a fair and unbiased manner. Blaming specific athletes is not useful if they are simply the victims of the situation. Coaches, sport administrators, officials, and sponsors must accept their share of the blame and face the need for change.

For their part, parents can band together to insist on consistent policies that ensure fair competition for their kids. Educational programs on doping should be made available to families and athletes should be required to participate in them.

In addition, sport scientists can volunteer to provide guidance and recommend policies that support sport organizations in this effort. People who earn their living from sport or work with athletes to enhance performance can agree to a code of ethics that considers the welfare of athletes and of sport in general.

Finally, sport participants themselves can think carefully about the value of any practice that may threaten their well-being. If athletes who love sport and value fair competition join together to restrict drug use in sport, they can catalyze powerful change in the sport world. The alternative is to withdraw from high-performance sport and move toward a society that values participation in sport regardless of the level of performance (Peretti-Watel et al. 2004).

Eating Disorders in Sport

One example of overconformity in sport involves athletes who develop eating disorders that are either caused by or related to their sport. Athletes who are highly competitive often go to extreme lengths to maximize their chance for success. In some sports, maintaining a lower body weight is clearly advantageous, whether for appearance or for performance itself.

Athletes in sports that focus on physical appearance are at high risk for developing eating disorders. These sports include gymnastics, dance, figure skating, diving, and cheerleading. Other athletes are also at high risk in sports that reward leanness or have specific weight classes for competition, such as cross country, wrestling, martial arts, horse racing, rowing, and swimming. In contrast, power sports that rely on strength or body mass are less likely to encourage eating disorders, though cases do occur in every sport.

Most high achievers in sport are also highly disciplined and determined. They set lofty goals and spend many hours each day striving to reach them. Moreover, they are rewarded for behavior that demands perfection, high motivation, attention to detail, and sometimes even obsession. These tendencies may become even more powerful if fellow athletes, coaches, and parents encourage the athlete to maintain thinness.

The three most common eating disorders found in athletes are **anorexia nervosa**, **bulimia nervosa**, and **compulsive exercise**. Anorexia is exhibited by people who starve themselves in order to achieve what they perceive as an ideal body weight; no matter how thin they are, they may still regard themselves as fat. Bulimia involves binge eating followed by purging. Compulsive exercise is characterized not by undereating but by overexercising. These disorders may become so serious that they lead to death. They may be preceded by more benign behaviors, including diuretic or laxative use, dieting, fasting, eating certain foods in rigid patterns, and consuming inadequate protein; being preoccupied with food may be another precursor.

These disorders can occur in both men and women and in any sport; athletes are more at risk than nonathletes are. Depending on the sample of athletes and the study methodology, research shows that as many as one-third of female athletes have an eating disorder. The percentage is highest among females who compete in aesthetic or judged sports, such as gymnastics and figure skating. In addition, more than one-third of college female athletes report attitudes that put them at risk for anorexia nervosa. In contrast, about 10 percent of male athletes have an eating disorder. In the U.S. population at large, including athletes and nonathletes, about one in ten cases of eating disorders involve males (National Eating Disorders Association 2014). Another study found that 59 percent of female college athletes felt that parts of their body were too fat, whereas only 20 percent of

IN THE ARENA WITH . . .

Christy Henrich

Christy Henrich was the third-ranked U.S. gymnast in 1988, when a gymnastics judge told her that if she hoped to make the U.S. Olympic team she needed to lose weight. Unfortunately, Henrich turned to anorexia and bulimia, which took her life in 1994 due to the resulting multiple organ failure. Her weight had dropped to only 47 pounds (21 kilograms). Henrich wasn't the only gymnast to feel such pressure. Consider these statistics: In 1976, the average female Olympic gymnast was 17 years old, stood 5′ 3″ (1.6 meters), and weighed 106 pounds (48 kilograms). By 1992, the average competitor was 16, stood only 4′ 9″ (1.45 meters), and weighed just 83 pounds (37 kilograms) (Pace 1994). At the 2012 London Olympics, Gabby Douglas, who won the gold medal in the all-around, stood only 4′ 11″ (1.49 meters) and weighed 90 pounds (40 kilograms) (Mooney 2012).

males felt that way (Nichols 1997; Sundgot-Borgen and Torstveit 2004).

Clearly, then, females are more likely candidates for an eating disorder. Research indicates that in the United States, 66 percent of high school girls and 17 percent of high school boys are on a diet at any given time. These figures include both athletes and nonathletes. Of course, women who have careers in the entertainment and modeling industries also have a high incidence rate due to the pressure to limit their body weight (National Eating Disorders Association 2014).

Females who develop an eating disorder are likely candidates for the **female athlete triad** (see figure 20.1), which includes disordered eating, amenorrhea (absence of menstruation), and osteoporosis (loss of bone density). Let's briefly consider each component. As we have seen, eating disorders are serious, chronic medical and psychological disorders that can be fatal. Excessive exercise and restricted eating cause an energy deficit that stresses the body and changes its hormone levels. Individuals with untreated chronic anorexia or bulimia may die prematurely from heart problems, salt disorders, suicide, or other health disorders.

The female athlete triad also affects the reproductive system, which shuts down the menstrual cycle, and can cause infertility due to a lack of hormone secretion. An eating disorder that leads to irregular or absent menstruation may produce low levels of estrogen and other hormones, which in turn can lead to low bone mass and a fragile skeleton. As a result, a young women may have a bone mass comparable to that of a 70-year-old and therefore be at high risk for fractures (American College of Sports Medicine 2011).

Before Title IX opened up athletic opportunities for women in the United States, eating disorders were relatively rare in sport. Instead, the struggle with expectations regarding low body weight and a slim figure was experienced mainly by actresses, models, and other female entertainers. Now, athletes also feel those expectations, combined with the pressure to perform in their sport. Female athletes who are goal-oriented perfectionists are at particularly high risk. Eating disorders may also be caused in part by parents and coaches who send unhealthy messages to young female athletes about their body weight.

Some research indicates that men may be especially insensitive to the feelings of their daughters, sisters, or wives and therefore contribute to the problem (Women's Sports Foundation 2001a, 2001b). Therefore, it is important to educate not just females but also males about the female athlete triad. This importance is magnified by the fact that 80 percent of coaches in girls' youth sport are male, as are 60 percent of coaches in college women's team sports.

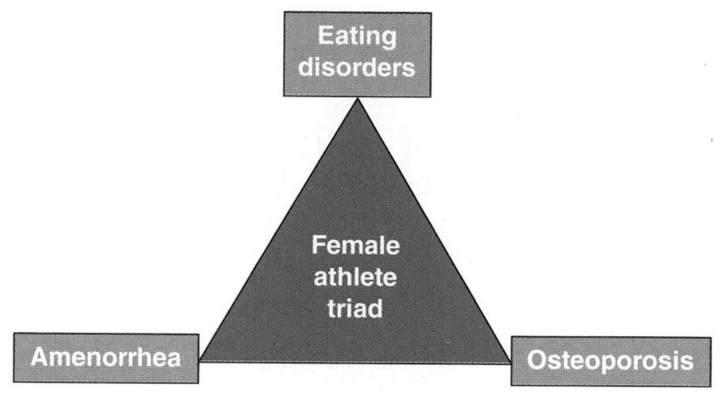

FIGURE 20.1 The female athlete triad.

The continuing problem of eating disorders has been confronted by national organizations, health professionals, coaching educators, and parent educators. These people have helped raise public awareness, and health professionals are now trained to recognize possible signs of an eating disorder. Coaches and parents also need to look for these warning signs and seek help at the first indication of a developing problem. Treatment of the triad often requires a team approach that includes a nutritionist, a physician, and a psychologist, along with strong support from family members, friends, teammates, and coaches.

Hazing in Sport

According to the National Federation of State High School Associations (NFHS), **hazing** is "any action or activity which inflicts physical or mental harm or anxiety, or which demeans, degrades or disgraces a person, regardless of location, intent or consent of participants" (2006). Hazing usually takes the form of a rite of passage that one must endure in order to gain acceptance into a particular group, such as a fraternity or athletic team. While hazing is not new, it has captured public attention as hazing practices have evolved from actions that were mostly annoying to actions that threaten physical or psychological harm. Activists who fight against hazing liken their cause to that of ending sexual harassment.

It is often a short leap from hazing to the more reprehensible and dangerous behavior of bullying. Both problems involve some degree of interpersonal

APPLYING SOCIAL THEORY

Feminist Theory and Eating Disorders

Sport has been a historically male activity from its beginnings until about 40 years ago, when significant changes began with the passage of the Title IX legislation in the United States. However, most of the sport world is still controlled by males, who hold most positions of power and leadership, and male coaches still heavily outnumber their female counterparts at every level. That fact may be a strong contributing factor to the fact that female athletes experience eating disorders at a much higher rate than male athletes do. Of course, sport is not the only arena where females are expected to be hypersensitized to their body weight and appearance.

Taking the perspective of a concerned feminist theorist, what specific guidelines would you recommend for coaches of high school or college females in order to minimize the incidence of eating disorders? List at least 10 guidelines that you think all coaches—male and female—should be expected to know and implement.

violence, an imbalance in power and status, and both short- and long-term consequences. However, bullying is always marked by aggressive behavior intended to cause harm, and it is typically repeated over time. In contrast, hazing may have some of those qualities but much less frequently or not at all.

Real-life examples of hazing and bullying abound. One recent case took place in the NFL. Amid a flurry of media reports in 2013, Stanford graduate and second-year Miami Dolphins player Jonathan Martin quit the team, debated ending his professional career, and contemplated suicide. Allegations surfaced that Martin had been bullied by teammates, and the NFL responded by commissioning a report to investigate the allegations. The 144-page report concluded that at least three teammates had "engaged in a pattern of harassment" of Martin, as well as another young lineman and an assistant trainer. It also found that verbal and physical abuse was widespread and accepted as part of the team culture; in other words, this was a classic case of bullying (Shpigel 2014).

Just a few years earlier, in 2011, the death of Robert Champion, a drum major at Florida A&M University, had brought attention to hazing in marching band culture. Champion died on a road trip with the band after enduring a hazing ritual on a bus, where he was physically brutalized by bandmates. In the aftermath, the college's famed Marching 100 was suspended for more than a year, the band director was fired, and the college president was removed. Widespread remorse and outrage sparked a dramatic change in a campus culture that had traditionally permitted hazing. Officials put in place a zero-tolerance policy and implemented educational efforts to prevent such inhumane behavior in the future (Geli 2012).

The StopHazing website (2015) clarifies several facts about the practice, asserting that it is goes far beyond fraternities and sororities. In fact, the practice affects the military, athletics, marching bands, religious groups, professional schools, and, increasingly, high schools. The StopHazing organization makes clear that hazing involves more than foolish pranks and is a form of victimization—an act of power or control by one person over another. Moreover, it is premeditated, abusive, degrading, and often life threatening.

In judging whether a given behavior constitutes hazing, we can ask the following questions:

- Is alcohol involved?
- Will current members of the group participate along with new ones?
- Does the activity risk emotional or physical abuse?
- Is there a risk of injury or a question of safety?
- Would you have any reservation describing the activity to your parents, a professor, or a university official?

- Would you object to the activity being photographed for the school newspaper or filmed by a local TV news crew?

If you answer yes to any of these questions, the activity is likely hazing.

All athletes are at risk for hazing, which can involve excessive alcohol consumption (the most common hazing behavior); excessive physical punishment; assignment as a personal servant to others; sleep or food deprivation; actual or simulated sex acts; consumption of disgusting food combinations; prank phone calls; stealing and shoplifting; and restrictions on associating with certain people. More serious, even life-threatening hazing rituals include being violent toward others, being paddled, being kidnapped, and being abandoned. Men are much more likely than women to be threatened with extreme or harmful behavior.

One comprehensive study of hazing (Allan and Madden 2008) involved undergraduate students at 53 colleges and universities. The researchers analyzed more than 11,000 individual survey responses and conducted more than 300 in-person interviews. The findings indicated that 55 percent of college students involved in clubs, teams, and other organizations had experienced hazing. The most common forms of hazing included alcohol consumption, humiliation, isolation, sleep deprivation, and sex acts. Among athletes in team sports, 74 percent of respondents had experienced hazing—the highest percentage for any group, though fraternities and sororities were close at 73 percent. The most common hazing behavior was participation in drinking games, which was reported by 47 percent of athletes (Allan and Madden 2008).

Among women, hazing tends to include more acceptable initiation rites, such as extending practice sessions, taking oaths, doing volunteer work, dressing up for team functions, or participating in other activities that build the team. However, at the University of New Mexico, the women's varsity soccer team welcomed first-year athletes to the team by forcing them to drink excessive amounts of alcohol, strip naked, and endure a spray of urine. Two young women were hospitalized, two twin players quit the team immediately and left the school, and twenty-two players were suspended for one game, which the team forfeited. The coach, a 14-year veteran, was suspended for a week, and at the end of

Bullying isn't limited to high school or collegiate sports. NFL player Jonathon Martin (right) quit the Miami Dolphins because of alleged bullying by his teammates, including Richie Incognito (left).

the season her contract was not renewed (*Santa Fe New Mexican* 2014).

Historically, many athletes and coaches viewed hazing as a benign ritual that built team unity, created camaraderie, and helped new athletes gain acceptance. However, as the seriousness of hazing escalated, teams and schools have stepped in to ban hazing practices. According to StopHazing, which monitors legal developments related to hazing, most U.S. states have banned hazing; the exceptions are Alaska, Hawaii, Montana, South Dakota, New Mexico, and Wyoming. In addition, both the NCAA and the NFHS have established written policies against hazing; they also publish literature and sponsor educational seminars to combat hazing.

Hazing incidents produce a variety of outcomes. Sometimes, the victim dies, as in the earlier example of Robert Champion and in the case of Chuck Stenzel, a student at Alfred University whose death stimulated national research on hazing. Some incidents end in lawsuits, such as one in which a California school district paid $675,000 to a Rancho Bernardo High School baseball player who was sodomized with a broom handle in the locker room after a game (Farrey 2002; Geli 2012).

The California case was hardly the only hazing incident to involve a sexual component. Perhaps even more shocking was a 2008 case in Las Vegas, New Mexico, in which six high school football players were accused of sodomizing six younger teammates with a broomstick during training camp. Moreover, coaches turned a blind eye. In the aftermath, the head football coach and all five assistants resigned, and the ringleader of the assaults pleaded guilty in juvenile court and was sentenced to 21 months in a juvenile detention center. In 2010, the seven players who were assaulted filed a civil lawsuit for unspecified damages against their offending teammates, the high school, and all officials and coaches. They claimed that the football program tolerated a culture of inappropriate sexual behavior (Leibowitz 2010).

In another case, the tight-knit community of Sayreville, New Jersey, was rocked by a scandal in 2014 that resulted in seven high school football players being criminally charged with hazing and sexually assaulting four teammates in the locker room. The veteran coach was suspended indefinitely from his tenured physical education position, and the 2014 football season was cancelled after only three games. The Sayreville community loved its football team, which had won three consecutive New Jersey sectional titles from 2010 through 2012 and had made the playoffs 18 years in a row. One year later—after much soul searching, discussion, and finger pointing—the superintendent of schools announced that football would return to Sayreville in 2015 with full community support (Tufaro 2015; Schweber, Barker, and Grant 2014).

Gambling and Sport

Gambling on sport activities is nothing new; in fact, reports of the practice go back for centuries. In early colonial days, gambling focused on horse racing, cockfighting, boxing, and bearbaiting (Leonard 1980). As baseball gained popularity in the nineteenth century, local ball clubs began to pay some players under the table, and fans began betting on games. When the National League was formed near the end of the century, baseball became an openly professional game enjoyed by the masses; as a result, under-the-table payments became a thing of the past, but betting on games continued (Stephan 1994).

The general public became keenly aware of illegal sport gambling when the infamous Black Sox scandal hit the headlines. In the 1919 World Series, the Cincinnati Reds beat the Chicago White Sox in a disputed set of games. Investigations revealed that eight White Sox players were guilty of "dumping" the series in return for a financial payoff from gamblers who bet heavily on the Reds to win. The players were frustrated by what they considered to be unfair salaries. During that time, players did not have the option to declare themselves free agents and sign with another club for better wages. Decades later, gambling came to the fore again in baseball, when Pete Rose, one of the game's all-time greats, was banned from the sport and from the Hall of Fame because he bet on baseball during his career. He steadfastly denied the charges until it became clear that he had no hope of reinstatement, at which time he admitted guilt.

College basketball suffered a betting scandal in the early 1950s, when investigations revealed that players at eight colleges had fixed some 86 games over a period of three years. Thirty-two players were involved in the point-shaving scandal.

Gambling has also touched professional basketball in the United States, where it involved not a player but an official. In this case, longtime NBA referee Tim Donaghy pleaded guilty to federal charges of conspiracy to engage in wire fraud and transmitting wagering information. He was sentenced to 15 months in federal prison in 2008 and served 11 months before his release to a halfway house. The investigation revealed that Donaghy had a gambling problem, was in debt, and tried to recoup his losses by engaging in more betting. His book *Personal Foul: A First-Person Account of the Scandal that Rocked the NBA* chronicled his dealings with organized crime and the "underworld" and described how easy it is for NBA officials to affect either the outcome of a game or whether the predicted point spread is covered (Jordan 2015).

Scandal arose in Germany in a case that involved gambling and soccer. Just one day before tickets were to be released for sale to the public for the 2006 World Cup, a number of officials and players were implicated in a series of fixed games that had occurred during the previous year. The referees had made dubious calls, awarded suspect penalty shots, and conspired to change the outcome of the game (Deutsche Welles 2005).

In another case involving soccer, Europol, the European Union's criminal intelligence division, announced in 2013 that it had uncovered 680 suspicious soccer games played during the three years ending in 2011. It has long been thought that match fixing is rampant in global soccer, but hard evidence now substantiates that match fixing is corroding the integrity of the game at every level. Indeed, it is not limited to just a few countries that we can shrug off by blaming an ineffective government or an uninterested population. Rather, gambling-related fraud has become soccer's biggest problem—bigger than flopping, doping, or hooliganism. Such corruption is made relatively easy by the fact that betting on sport is legal in most countries (Phillips 2013).

The problem with gambling on sport is that it calls into question the integrity of the performances delivered by players, officials, coaches, and others. For example, players who stand to gain sure money can be tempted to throw a game or shave points. Once the public loses confidence in the integrity of the sport, its popularity is certain to decline. How many times have people watched a boxing match and been astounded at the decision, or watched international judges at the Olympic Games show a clear prejudice toward athletes from certain countries?

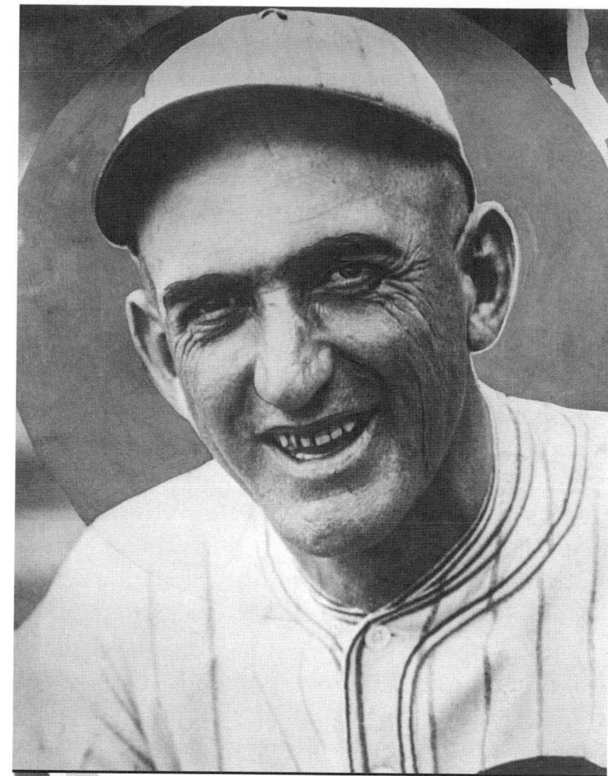

Shoeless Joe Jackson was one of eight White Sox players who were found guilty of fixing the 1919 World Series.

Nor is sport gambling limited to professional and collegiate sport. In one Florida case, nine youth football coaches were arrested after an 18-month investigation by the Broward County sheriff's office into a system of high-dollar gambling on Pee Wee football. Up to $20,000 was bet on one rivalry game, and the league championship drew more than $100,000 in bets. Coaches openly swapped cash with spectators and set the point spreads on the games. After the news broke on ESPN's *Outside the Lines* in 2011, illegal wagering was pushed underground but continued unabated. Most of the coaches involved had previous criminal records and were involved in other illegal activities related to narcotics and organized crime (Lavigne 2012).

In the United States, 48 of 50 states allow some type of legalized gambling; the exceptions are Utah and Hawaii. The American Gaming Association estimates that illegal wagers total about $380 billion annually, whereas only $3.5 billion is wagered legally in the state of Nevada. About two-thirds of all sport betting in Nevada involves professional sport, and more bets there are placed on the Super Bowl than on any other single-day event, to the tune of nearly $100 million in 2013. After paying off winning bets, the Nevada sports books earned a tidy $7.2 million. Because bettors on the Super Bowl are largely unsophisticated bettors, Nevada sports books have earned huge profits in 21 of the past 23 Super Bowls.

Another huge payoff comes from betting on March Madness, the NCAA men's basketball tournament, which involves more than 60 games played over a three-week period. The event is estimated by the FBI to attract $2.5 billion annually in illegal wagers; in contrast, about $80 to $90 million is wagered legally on the event through the Las Vegas bookmakers (American Gaming Association 2013).

The NCAA and the major U.S. professional sport leagues have taken a strong stand against legalized gambling in order to preserve the integrity of their games. Colleges are particularly sensitive to sport betting, and they mete out harsh penalties to students, athletes, coaches, and administrators who violate NCAA rules against gambling. At the heart of their concern is the fact that almost all gambling profits benefit organized crime. Those profits are funneled into other illegal activities, such as prostitution, loan shark operations, and drug trafficking (NCAA 2007b).

In 1992, the U.S. Congress passed the Professional and Amateur Sports Protection Act to declare sport betting illegal in every state except Nevada, Oregon, Montana, and Delaware, which had preexisting laws regarding sport gambling. As of 2014, Nevada is the only state to offer a full range of sport gambling; Delaware permits limited sport gambling. Both Oregon and Montana currently ban sport betting. Though gambling has recently been legalized on riverboats and reservations in various U.S. locations, sport betting continues to be off-limits in most states.

Delaware formulated plans in 2009 to expand sport gambling on individual professional games and collegiate sports. However, a three-judge panel of the U.S. Court of Appeals for the Third Circuit said that the Delaware plan violated the 1992 federal law. The Delaware plan had been challenged by the NCAA and all major U.S. professional sport leagues, who contended that it would harm their sports. The court, however, did allow the state to continue so-called "parlay" bets, in which a bettor must select the winners of at least three separate NFL games in a single wager (CBS News 2009; Frommer 2009).

In the early 2000s, involvement in gambling by college students was relatively overlooked as campus communities focused their attention on binge drinking and how it overlapped with use of other drugs. Midway through the decade, however, as legalized gambling grew throughout the United States, colleges began paying more attention to gambling behavior by students. The prevalence of gambling among college students is about three times higher than it is among the general population. The most popular forms of gambling by college students include purchasing lottery tickets; playing games, such as slot machines at casinos; and playing games of skill, such as poker and sport betting. One study showed that 72 percent of students had gambled within the past year and that 35 percent of those had bet on a sporting event (Doraiswamy 2012).

A 2008 study of gambling and problem gambling among college students in Florida showed that 77 percent of males and 60 percent of females reported gambling at least once in the previous year. They gambled primarily for entertainment, to win money, and to socialize. The study also revealed that about 25,000 college students in Florida are likely experiencing gambling and gambling-related problems. In addition, nearly 15 percent of Florida college students were deemed at risk for gambling problems, whereas that was the case for just 7 percent of Florida adults and 8 percent of Florida adolescents. Moreover, the number of college students classified as pathological gamblers more than doubled the number reported for adolescents and quadrupled the number for adults (Florida Council on Compulsive Gambling 2008).

College athletes have a higher rate of problem gambling than nonathletes. Athletes who are problem gamblers and in significant debt—especially to bookies and loan sharks—are particularly vulnerable when approached to shave points or fix games. According to the NCAA, in 2012, about 25 percent of male athletes and 5 percent of female athletes admitted wagering on sporting events within the past year. Students who were identified as problem gamblers were more likely than other students to be heavy drinkers and regular users of tobacco and marijuana. Problem gambling was also related to binge eating and greater use of weight-control measures.

Here are some additional statistics about gambling by college students (Engwall, Hunter, and

Steinberg 2004; Florida Council on Compulsive Gambling 2008):

- Two-thirds of college students report gambling at least once in the past year.
- Male college students (78 percent) are more likely to gamble than are females (60 percent).
- In one study, the most frequent type of gambling among college students was sport-related—26 percent on professional sport, 18 percent on nonprofessional sport, and 18 percent on sport pools—thus accounting for a total of 62 percent of gambling on campus. The next most popular form of gambling was the lottery at 39 percent.
- College athletes are more likely than nonathletes to bet on sport, games of skill, and card games. Nonathletes are more likely to bet at casinos, play the lottery, or use slot machines.
- College students who gamble tend to show higher than normal tendencies to engage in drug and alcohol abuse, high-risk sexual behavior, and eating disorders and to have a grade-point average below 2.0. Their debts from gambling range from $100 to more than $5,000 and are usually spread across several credit cards.

The NCAA opposes all forms of legal and illegal wagering at any level (college, professional, and amateur) on sports in which it conducts championships. This stance includes Division I Football Bowl Subdivision games and emerging sports for women. The NCAA believes that sport wagering has become a serious problem that threatens the well-being of student-athletes and the integrity of college sport. Here are some salient facts highlighted by the NCAA (2007b):

- The Internet has made it easier than ever for student-athletes to place bets in virtual anonymity and with no supervision.
- Student-athletes are viewed as easy marks by organized crime and organized gambling.
- Student-athletes who gamble are breaking the law and jeopardizing their athletic eligibility.
- When student-athletes become indebted to bookies and can't pay their debts, they are at risk of being forced to undermine the outcome of an athletic contest or shave points.
- NCAA rules prohibit athletes, athletic department staff, and all conference and national staff from engaging in any type of sport wagering.

Some progress is being made, according to a 2012 NCAA survey of student-athletes (2013c) whose results were compared with the results of similar surveys completed in 2004 and 2008. The most recent survey noted a decrease in frequent wagering by Division I men's basketball players—one of the target groups for education about the risks and consequences of gambling. It also found a decrease in the incidence of Division I men's basketball and football players sharing information (such as injury status) with outsiders. The survey found that men still greatly outnumber women as social, frequent, and heavy gamblers in all three divisions. Indeed, up to 26 percent of males compared with only 10 percent of females across all divisions reported that they gambled on sport during the past year—a violation of NCAA rules. Perhaps surprisingly, the highest incidence of gambling occurs among male athletes in Division III.

Men's golf poses a particular problem across all three divisions because 20 percent of male golfers report wagering on sport at least monthly. No other sport even shows a percentage that reaches double digits. In Division I, for example, 19 percent of male golfers reported social levels of wagering, as compared with just 6 percent of Division I male basketball players and 5 percent of football players. The NCAA is taking steps to address this anomaly in golf through aggressive education and publicity throughout the collegiate golf community (2013c).

The strongest justification for legalizing sport gambling comes from those who suggest that it can provide a bailout for local and state governments, which are searching for new revenue streams. When the government promises to channel gambling profits into education or youth sport programs, some public officials and many citizens are tempted to embrace sport wagering as a revenue stream. Proponents point out that, without legalized sport gambling, the profits generated by gambling go to illegal operations and organized crime, whereas this money could be used for worthier causes. New Jersey has been rapidly liberalizing its gambling policies in an attempt to replace lost revenue caused by the failure of most of the large casinos in Atlantic City in the wake of increased opportunities for gambling in neighboring states (Nathanson 2014).

Those opposed to sport gambling believe that it corrupts youth, allows organized crime to become directly involved in sport, and takes money from people who can't afford to lose it. They say that the benefits of legalized gambling would go to bookies, a few gamblers, and offshore Internet betting sites. Meanwhile, those who suffer would include athletes pressured to throw games or shave points, fans who lose faith in the legitimacy of games, gamblers who lose money, coaches who feel pressured to become deceitful about their team's chances of winning being affected by injuries to key players, and perhaps the U.S. system of sport, which could lose any semblance of integrity and eventually lose the fans that have made it so successful.

According to federal law, online gambling is basically illegal, and the Justice Department has taken the position that the federal Wire Act covers all forms of gambling. Some of the largest online poker sites were shut down by the U.S. government in 2011. Since then, the Justice Department has clarified its position to assert that the law only referred to sports wagering. Online gambling can be legalized by states for their residents. Nevada, New Jersey, and Delaware have officially legalized online gambling, and others such as Pennsylvania and California are working on it. Online gambling has typically focused on "skilled gaming" (for example, poker), but the future most likely involves fantasy sport. Among male college students, 51 percent participate in a fantasy sport league (just 8 percent of college women do). Along with the thrill of playing a sport online, the attraction lies in the possibility of winning money or a designated prize (Finger 2013).

Current laws, rules, and public opinion have rejected legalizing sport gambling. However, as citizens have become more tolerant of gambling at casinos, on Native American reservations, and in state lotteries, the general aversion to gambling seems to be subsiding. Stay tuned for what is likely to be a growing trend toward liberalizing gambling opportunities at both the state and federal levels.

Although certain spectator sports have long depended on gambling—for example, horse racing, auto racing, and dog racing—most sports have steered clear of it. No doubt the debate will continue.

Chapter Summary

Deviance occurs in sport when athletes do not conform to accepted standards of behavior. The chapter compares the frequency of deviance among athletes and coaches to the frequency in the general population. In spite of abundant media accounts suggesting otherwise, evidence indicates that athletes generally conform to expected stan-

ACTIVITY TIME-OUT

Should We Legalize Sport Betting?

You're now familiar with some of the arguments for and against sport wagering, as well as a description of the situation as it exists today. Throughout the United States, however, gambling has been gaining in public acceptance, in part because of the revenue it could raise to help cash-strapped states. Standing in opposition are the major professional sports and the major college sport organizations, who are fearful that legalized gambling could ruin their events and turn the public away from sport. Others figure that since sport gambling is already occurring, it would be better to legalize it, regulate it, and channel the financial rewards to worthy causes.

List the pros and cons of legalizing sport betting in your home state. Once you have compiled your list, compare it with those of your classmates to see if you have overlooked any pertinent facts. Next, develop a one-page statement explaining and justifying your position. Indicate whether your reasoning is based on social theory, moral reasoning, pragmatic business interests, or concern for preserving the integrity of sport.

dards of behavior and in fact probably exceed those standards.

Drug use to enhance athletic performance appears to be increasing in spite of strong actions to eliminate the practice. Doping has become more sophisticated, and the various responses that combine testing programs with penalties for violators seem unable to keep up with the creativity of athletes driven to excel by any means. In fact, some observers think it would be more honest and fair to athletes to simply allow the use of performance-enhancing substances and thus even the playing field because all athletes could choose to use drugs legally. They argue that the current enforcement approach—which trails the ingenuity of athletes, coaches, and trainers who choose to cheat—simply rewards the cheaters in sport.

Eating disorders affect more female athletes than male athletes. People who participate in sports that emphasize physical appearance—such as gymnastics, ice skating, dance, and cheerleading—are at greatest risk for developing an eating disorder. Others at risk include athletes in sports that favor leanness, such as wrestling, cross country, and swimming. The most common eating disorders are anorexia, bulimia, and compulsive exercise.

Hazing in sport has burst into prominence in recent years due to a number of widely publicized deaths, injuries, and humiliations suffered by athletes at the hands of their teammates. Although hazing is not limited to athletes, researchers estimate that more than 80 percent of college athletes are exposed to hazing; in high school, nearly 25 percent of hazing victims are athletes. The alarming trend of more frequent serious hazing incidents seems to have slowed, due to wide publicity, educational programs, and state laws against hazing.

Gambling on sport is illegal in almost every U.S. state, and sport organizations at the professional and collegiate levels have taken a strong stand against it. Unfortunately, illegal betting on sport—encouraged by organized crime—has tarred the image of sports affected by game fixing and point shaving. Arguments for and against legalizing sport gambling continue to this day.

21 Future Trends in Sport

STUDENT OUTCOMES

After reading this chapter, you will know the following:

- Social trends likely to affect sport
- The conflict between performance sport and participation sport (including the effects of money, sponsorship, facilities, programs, and sport popularity)
- The influence of changing attitudes toward sport participation
- How spectatorship affects sport participation
- Effects of technology on equipment, training, performance enhancers, and media support of sport
- How different social theorists would effect change in sport

Future Trends in Sport

It's pretty rare for anyone to predict the future with any accuracy, but if you study trends—and analyze the odds of those trends gaining traction, stalling, or disappearing—you might make some educated guesses. Take a moment to imagine what changes might occur by 2025 or 2050. Here are some questions to get your creative juices going:

- Would you support raising the height of the regulation basketball goal from 10 feet to 12 feet (about 3 meters to 3.7 meters) in order to decrease the dominance of extremely tall players with limited skills, thereby recapturing some of the magic of the skillful game of the past? Or lowering the hoop to 9.5 feet (about 2.9 meters) for women so that their game more nearly imitates the current male version?
- Will advances in medicine enable injured or aging athletes to replace damaged limbs so that they can still compete at a high level with a custom-fitted prosthetic device?
- Will computers replace sportswriters? Perhaps information from box scores can be gathered via the Internet, analyzed by computer, and reported as a game summary. It is already happening.
- What does the future hold for American football in light of rising concern about concussions and other forms of brain injury? Will new technology enable us to make helmets that better protect players? Or will rule changes provide an answer? If no changes are made, will the game retain its popularity, or will parents simply forbid their children to play it?
- Is it just a matter of time before parents can determine the gene mix of their offspring in order to maximize their chances of become an elite athlete?
- Can you imagine the creation and popularization of a new sport in the United States that draws participants away from the team sports that have traditionally dominated youth sport? What would that new sport look like?

Add your own predictions here—no matter how outlandish—and then consider the odds of those changes occurring.

One of my favorite college teachers, Lee "Pappy" Warren, professor of history at East Stroudsburg University, used to tell us, "There are four kinds of people in this world: Those that know, and know that they know; those that know, and don't know that they know; those that don't know, and know that they don't know; and those that don't know, and don't know that they don't know."

I've pondered those words over many years and have become convinced that Pappy was a wise man. He valued education, learning from the past, and self-study as the path toward enlightenment and a better society. With that in mind, after reading this book, noting current events in sport, working through the student activities, and discussing sport issues with others, you should be much closer to the first group identified in Pappy's saying—"those that know, and know that they know." Your understanding of sport in society should be light years ahead of where it was when you began your studies.

Even so, the picture is not complete without a peek at the trends that are likely to shape the future of sport. This chapter considers those trends and invites you to predict where they will lead. Where you find potential trends inconsistent with your personal values, you may begin to form a plan of action to influence the future of sport in a way that you believe will help society.

If you and I do nothing, it is possible that events and influences in our society will shape sport participation—or lack of it—in ways that we find unhealthy or even harmful. Those who profit financially from sport as entertainment, promote spectatorship, and ignore participation in sport by average citizens may take complete control over the sporting world. Given the potential for sport to enhance every citizen's quality of life, such a narrow focus would be a shame.

Social Trends

Social trends are difficult to predict since we have no way of knowing how societal influences will affect people's state of mind, our economy, and our values. In addition, worldwide trends, such as the rise in terrorism, may drastically affect our lives in ways that are difficult to predict. For example, the shrinking of our world into a global economy of interdependence has the potential to either bring our world closer together in cooperation or split us farther apart in conflict.

In U.S. society, certain social trends seem clear. First, the population is rapidly aging, and the proportion of the populace that is older than 50 years will continue to rise in the immediate future. As a result, a large proportion of the population will focus much attention on concerns about quality of life, health care, and the productive use of leisure time after retirement. Between 2014 and 2050, the U.S. population is expected to grow more slowly than in the recent past, and a modest decline in international migration is also forecast. By 2044, more than half of all Americans are projected to belong to a minority group. In fact, the Latino and Hispanic population is expected to triple and thus account for 30 percent of the overall U.S. population; in addition, because this group will be younger than other racial groups, it will also have a higher birth rate (U.S. Bureau of Labor Statistics 2015).

Second, the rights of all people—regardless of age, race, gender, sexual preference, or disability—will continue to be protected, and discrimination laws are likely to be strengthened in the United States. Thus the stage is set not only to protect the rights of every citizen but also to enhance quality of life by opening up avenues for new experiences and adventures even for those who may have been victims of discrimination in the past.

Third, those who have benefited most from supporting performance sport will fight to protect their investment in sport. In fact, rather than just protecting the status quo, they will bring ingenuity to strategies for expanding the influence of performance sport. This group will continue to strengthen the bonds between big-time collegiate sport, professional sport, and the Olympic Games.

In this vein, the field of sport management is growing rapidly and will continue to expand as sport organizations search for ways to enhance their bottom line by enticing and serving consumers. Education in sport management is available at more than 435 U.S. universities, and it includes training in sport-related event management, finance, human resources, law, marketing, public relations, and program management. People trained in sport management are playing an increasingly critical role in professional sport, amateur sport, nonprofit organizations (such as the YMCA and YWCA), sporting goods manufacturing, sporting event, and sport facility management (Hoffman 2013).

Fourth, the human tendency to push against barriers will result in development of new materials and processes that produce better sport equipment, facilities, and training regimens so that elite athletes can challenge the frontiers of athletic achievement. As athletes benefit from scientific advances, records will continue to be broken. Another key area of research will involve the ongoing effort to rid sport of performance-enhancing substances that provide an unfair advantage to some athletes, create mistrust on the part of fans and the media regarding great performances, and threaten the integrity of athletic competition at every level.

Fifth, attitudes toward gambling in the United States have shifted dramatically in the past 30 years, resulting in a proliferation of state lotteries, expanded casino gambling, and online betting. If we consider only revenue from gambling, Americans spent more money on gambling in 2009 ($92.3 billion) than they did on all live events, all movies in theaters, and all forms of recorded music—combined (Rose 2011). Once considered a moral issue that led to legal prohibitions, gambling now enjoys strong public support and is bolstered by states that crave a share of the profits to fill their coffers.

Sport leaders at the professional and college levels have always vehemently opposed sport wagering and still fear that it will lead to bribery, fixed outcomes of games, and a public loss of interest in sport. Even so, online sport betting is legal, and millions of dollars are bet on sport. State leaders and politicians sense a change in public opinion about gambling and are eager to tap a potential new revenue stream from legalized sport wagering (Rose 2011).

Previous chapters have discussed the changing demographics of the United States, where minorities will soon become the combined majority, led by the rapidly increasing number of Latinos and Hispanics. Their favorite sport is soccer, for both participation and spectatorship. To date, of course, youth soccer in the United States has been popularized by suburban upper-middle-class families. In the rest of the world, however, it is viewed as "the people's game" and is populated by children of the working class. Indeed, as history tells us, that is where most of our great champions come from in every sport (Didziulis 2010).

The most popular sports in the United States—football, baseball, and basketball, all of which were invented here—are effectively large-scale intramural affairs in which we compete against ourselves. Basketball shows promise of considerable worldwide growth, but baseball expansion is modest, and American football seems to be unique to this country. Soccer has come late to the party in U.S. sport but could very well become number two in popularity within a decade.

Sixth, coaches will adapt to their athletes by increasing their coaching competence and adjusting their coaching philosophy to meet athletes' needs. At the same time, athletes will pressure coaches to endorse a certification process that indicates coaching knowledge, skill, and competence at various levels of coaching. The availability of online coach training has already begun to eliminate the two most daunting barriers to continuing education of coaches: time and cost.

Conflict Between Performance Sport and Participation Sport

There has always been keen competition between performance sport and participation sport. The competition centers on publicity, funding, accessibility, cost, facilities, coaching, and recruitment of players into one track or the other. During the past century, performance sport has had the edge in just about every category. But things may change in this century as a result of our changing demographics, the shift to an older population, a potential national crisis due to rising costs in U.S. health care, and in some cases lack of interest in performance sport. It seems more likely, however, that both categories of sport will grow steadily—but perhaps for different reasons. Let's look at the potential for expansion of each.

Performance Sport

The institutions that support performance sport are strong, well funded, well established, and determined to perpetuate their roles. They include powerful businesspersons, athletic directors, college presidents, and commercial sponsors who have joined with the media to glorify the finest athletes in the world. The emphasis on superior athletes storming the barriers of performance makes for a captivating story. We love to see athletes run faster, jump higher, hit harder, and prove their power in sport, especially if their success can be attributed to hard work, dedication, and the overcoming of obstacles. Vicariously, their success becomes our success, and we rejoice in it.

Performance sport at the youth level will continue to thrive as youngsters and their families follow their dreams of achieving competitive success. Youth programs will grow as parents thrust their potential prodigies into sport training before they even enter grade school. The major barrier for many talented kids will continue to be the expense of such training and competition. Young people from modest financial backgrounds will thus continue to gravitate toward inexpensive sports, such as those offered in school-based programs. Meanwhile, skiing, tennis, golf, and many other Olympic sports will continue to lie beyond the financial reach of the working and middle classes.

High schools will continue to offer varsity programs and, particularly in affluent communities, will expect excellence from their teams. Major team sports, such as football and basketball, will continue to rely on high school programs to develop talent with the help of off-season programs, camps, and leagues that keep kids playing one sport year round. The expense of these high-performance programs will continue to rise, and many will be forced to adopt user fees to pay for them. However, in many communities, parks and recreation programs will provide summer and off-season sport activities at modest cost and provide need-based scholarships for those who qualify.

Most colleges will struggle to fund their athletic programs but invest in them as a tool for publicity and recruitment of students. College football and basketball unite the college family like no other events. As a feeder system for professional sport, major colleges will continue to fight to retain the athletes in whom they invest time, money, and effort. The question of whether athletes should be paid to play has been framed in language that now uses the term "full costs" of college attendance, which implies that some additional amount of discretionary funding will become part of athletic scholarships. Athletes who are lured by the glamour and financial rewards of leaving college early in order to turn pro will force the issue of financial compensation for what is essentially professional play.

Professional sport will continue to thrive. The investment in football, basketball, baseball, and ice hockey by broadcasters and corporate sponsors will continue to grow, and advances in the delivery of sport programming through television and the Internet will expand. Individual sports, led by tennis and golf, are also thriving at the professional level and will continue to expand worldwide.

Professional basketball for both men and women is poised for a worldwide expansion in the near future, and franchises in other countries are likely to become a reality that leads to true world championships. Baseball may also expand, though its popularity to date has been limited to a few countries. American football seems destined to remain uniquely American.

As mentioned earlier, soccer is on a steep trajectory of growth. As immigrants continue to enter the United States and the Latino and Hispanic population steadily grows, increased cultural interest in soccer will follow. As a sport that accommodates both males and females—as well as players of all sizes, shapes, and body types—it can appeal to millions of kids who lack the size or strength to compete in elite basketball or American football. As a result, a new generation of Americans who played soccer as children will become adults who are likely to encourage their own children to at least try the sport.

Owners of professional sport franchises and league officials will continue to convince cities to build more elaborate facilities to host their teams; indeed, city officials will scramble to attract professional franchises in order to enhance their economy. However, the trend toward publicly financed stadiums will slow due to recent economic woes. Public officials are reluctant to add to the daunting financial challenges their cities face by taking on long-term debt to build facilities that primarily benefit millionaire professional sport owners. Therefore, rather than having the public absorb two-thirds or three-quarters of the cost of a new facility, team owners will be expected to provide more of the financing.

As soccer continues to rise in popularity, the number of athletes competing for spots on high school, collegiate, and professional teams will increase.

The parity between teams in the National Football League (NFL) will continue to stir fan interest because any team has a chance to play in the Super Bowl if it makes good management decisions. Major League Baseball (MLB) will shift toward a similar philosophy, dooming the longtime dominance of big-market teams such as the New York Yankees. Indeed, MLB will be forced to change if it has any hope of regaining its former title as America's pastime. Otherwise, the decline in youth baseball participation, particularly in urban settings, portends a continued decline in popularity for the sport. Baseball officials and team owners must come up with a plan to ensure that every franchise has at least a possibility of being competitive through mandatory revenue sharing more like the NFL's approach.

Olympic sports will continue down the path of professionalism. The finest athletes in the world will showcase their talents in bigger and better Games staged in countries that can offer the financial package to host them. Women's sport will grow in popularity through the Olympic movement; in addition, led by soccer and basketball, professional women's leagues will grow in strength and popularity. Corporate sponsors will invest huge resources to support the Olympic Games, and the emphasis of the Games will continue to shift from nationalism to corporate dominance.

Despite these predictions, the outlook for performance sport isn't all rosy. If improvements are not made in drug testing and control of performance-enhancing substances, the public could become disenchanted with professional sport as athletes continue to use illegal substances in pursuit of exceptional performance. Led by the Olympics and, more recently, Major League Baseball, significant progress has clearly been made toward more comprehensive drug testing in all sports. Yet no drug enforcement effort will ever completely eradicate cheating, because there will always be athletes, coaches, and others who experiment and try to exceed the reach of testing programs.

Scientific advancements in equipment and sports medicine may enable athletes to perform at levels heretofore believed out of reach. If the public begins to see athlete performance as the result of technological achievement, however, people may lose interest. The humanity of sport requires a delicate balance of technology, financial interests, entertainment, and the athlete's struggle to achieve.

Youth programs will continue to struggle to provide development for superior athletes who come from modest financial circumstances. In the meantime, some parents will become frustrated with the demands made by performance-oriented programs and coaches. Families who choose to expose their children to a wider range of activities will find themselves left out of performance-oriented programs. In addition, kids who do not excel early in their sport career may become discouraged and withdraw from sport before they have a chance to blossom in it. The dropout rate for kids in performance sport will continue to be high.

Participation Sport

As Americans continue to struggle with health, people will begin to recognize how important exercise and sport are to controlling body weight, enhancing energy, resisting disease, improving physical appearance, and enjoying a better quality of life. Leaders in the medical and health professions are doing a better job than in the past of educating the public about the value of sport and physical activity, particularly in fighting the alarming trends of obesity and overweight. Even the White House, under the leadership of First Lady Michelle Obama, has joined the effort to help kids eat better and be more physically active.

As discussed in chapter 18, sport will continue to be used as a development tool in order to combat crime and encourage physical activity. Sport programs for youth that combine academic enrichment and good citizenship will grow and prosper as a way to improve quality of life for kids in the United States and all over the world. Underdeveloped countries have only begun to explore the power of sport to attract and motivate their youth toward higher achievement. In addition, all countries will continue to explore ways to use sport to promote better understanding between nations and move us toward a more peaceful and respectful attitude worldwide.

Most youth sport programs attract large numbers of children between the ages of 6 and 8; however, more than half of them drop out of sport by age 14. And when they reach high school, only a fraction of those who did continue in youth sport will make their high school varsity team. The system has a built-in rejection mechanism because of the focus on performance rather than participation that forces the majority of young people to drop out of sport. Possible solutions include expanding the number of athletic teams sponsored by schools and instituting no-cut policies, at least in certain sports.

Another possibility is to field teams with different ability levels and training intensities; this system has been used successfully for generations by private schools that require every student to devote time each day to athletics and exercise.

Another possibility is to sponsor complete intramural programs within schools to attract the masses of students who do not play varsity sport. At the college level, an increasing number of students are drawn to sport clubs, which are much less intense than varsity teams yet still offer competition against teams from nearby schools. In fact, some traditional varsity sports are good candidates for conversion to club status in order to reduce out-of-control athletic budgets. The key is to find the money and facilities to support expansion of intramural and club teams. One way to address the problem of inadequate facilities is to establish lighted athletic fields that can be used for longer hours; this model may soon be followed by high schools.

In these ways, perhaps the model of sport at many schools will shift from focusing on the school's win–loss record to taking pride in the total number of students who participate in sport at any level or engage in regular physical activity. For educational institutions, that approach certainly makes good sense.

Community programs that emphasize participation sport will also grow as young athletes search for opportunities to exercise, be with their friends, and have fun outside of school. The reduced emphasis on competition will be attractive to kids and families who have no aspirations as athletes but simply want to participate in sport and enjoy it. This approach does away with the demands for hours of practice, year-round devotion, expensive coaching, and specialization in just one sport; instead, it values the opportunity to play for the purpose of recreation.

Extreme sports will continue to grow, as will sport activities that are focused on the player, informally organized, and novel in required skills and strategy. Newer sports—such as ultimate, paintball, rock climbing, mountain biking, cardio kickboxing, and snowboarding—will take their place among more traditional recreational sports, such as biking, hiking, and other natural outdoor activities.

Co-ed teams may also encourage sport participation. Sports that adapt well to co-ed play include softball, volleyball, soccer, tennis, and golf, to name just a few. In this way, participation sport is a natural drawing card for the many teenagers interested in spending time with members of the opposite sex.

Young people aren't the only ones participating in sport. As health costs continue to climb, health insurers and employers will explore the benefits of encouraging physical activity among employees in order to minimize health risks, loss of productive work days, and financial burden

IN THE ARENA WITH . . .

Brooklyn Bridge Park

In the 1950s in New York City, piers were constructed on the East River waterfront for commercial shipping and warehousing; below the piers ran the tunnel for the number 2 and 3 subway lines. The piers have now been converted to free, public recreational space overlooking the river with a spectacular view of the Manhattan skyline. Part of that space is now Brooklyn Bridge Park—an innovatively designed public recreational facility in a high-density city. The park is built on existing pier structures that extend into the East River, and pier 2 is a five-acre roofed space that features basketball, handball, shuffleboard, and bocce courts, along with a fitness gym and children's playground. Adjacent piers hold synthetic-turf soccer fields and beach volleyball courts. The layout includes plenty of space to walk, jog, roller-skate, bicycle, and picnic—all of which is accessible from the nearby subway.

on health insurance programs. As the number of older adults approaches 100 million—of the total U.S. population of about 300 million—their influence will be felt in every facet of society. In this environment, sport provides opportunities for regular exercise, social interaction, and enhanced self-image—all important contributors to healthy living for older adults.

As with performance sport, participation sport also faces some obstacles. The first obstacle is simply lack of interest in sport on the part of those who played as children but dropped out. These adults need to be wooed back into sport with the offer of a different kind of experience. At the same time, leaders need to commit to increasing physical activity among young people, creating a change in consciousness among parents and kids through consistent marketing, and waging publicity campaigns about the value of sport programs based not on winning but on participation.

A second major obstacle is the competition for money and facilities with traditional performance sport programs. Advocates of participation sport need to overcome the ingrained bias toward performance sport by enlisting the support of the masses; after all, they certainly outnumber the relative few involved in performance sport. Ultimately, tax dollars support school programs, extracurricular programs, community programs, and parks and recreation programs. With that in mind, why shouldn't those dollars be spent to benefit more kids rather than being concentrated on a small group of elite athletes?

Part of the problem lies in the fact that most sport leaders were competitive athletes, and they tend to perpetuate similar programs. Changing the status quo will take a new breed of leaders who are dedicated to participation sport and willing to shake things up. They will also need patience, since it is not likely that change will happen quickly or without consistent pressure. And they will need to enlist the aid of powerful allies such as physicians, health insurers, corporate leaders, and politicians.

Finally, activities other than sport will continue to compete for people's time. Electronic entertainment has become a powerful competitor, but the lack of physical activity that results from spending hours in front of a screen may contribute to a national health crisis. Creative minds must work to educate people about the benefits of physical activity, and then it is up to sport organizers to make sport accessible, convenient, and fun for participants.

POP CULTURE

Team Handball

You may be unsure just what the sport of team handball is. In the United States, we tend to think of handball as a game of hitting a small rubber ball against a wall (think squash or racquetball with no racket). Team handball, however, is a new game—and an Olympic sport played by men, women, or co-ed groupings on an indoor court larger than a basketball court. It's also the number two sport in popularity in Europe.

To get the idea, picture playing soccer with your hands, water polo without water, or lacrosse without sticks and you've got it. Each team has seven players, including a goalie, who try to score more goals than their opponent. On average, teams score about 20 goals a game, so it's fairly high scoring and characterized by constant action and a bit of body contact. Team handball is played in 183 nations but is most popular in Europe, where it was invented. Hotbeds of the sport include the Scandinavian countries, Balkan countries, Russia, Germany, France, Spain, and newcomer Brazil.

Team handball is also expanding in format. Beginner kids can play mini handball, and older players also have the option of playing beach handball or street handball, which opens up the sport to virtually anybody. This new game is also catching on quickly on U.S. college campuses as a club sport. Maybe it's a new sport for you to try!

Effects of Social Changes

Social changes have affected sport over the last 60 years and will continue to do so. As discussed in chapter 12, the U.S. Civil Rights Movement of the 1960s opened up sport to minorities. Since then, African Americans have become dominant in football and basketball, and Latinos now account for one-third of MLB players. As more minorities move into the middle class, their children will begin to explore other sports, such as tennis, swimming, golf, and volleyball—all of which were once the exclusive province of affluent whites. As these sports become more inclusive, minorities will occupy positions of influence, such as those held by coaches, organizers, and members of governing boards.

As discussed in chapter 13, the women's movement that ushered in Title IX in 1972 changed sport dramatically. The explosion in female participants has changed sport forever, but equity with male participants remains an elusive goal. Steady pressure to conform to the law will be required by women's rights advocates, and female athletes must also continue to be assertive. Efforts during the next decade might seek to achieve the following outcomes:

- Educational and athletic leaders approach the philosophy and application of Title IX not as an obstacle to circumvent but as a positive step toward enfranchising 50 percent of the U.S. population of potential athletes.
- Athletic programs at high schools and colleges are evaluated on the basis of the value they deliver to athletes rather than the revenue they produce.
- Women are actively recruited and nurtured in sport leadership roles, including coaching and administration.
- Compensation for females in sport is equitable and based on performance rather than on who or what sport they coach.
- Issues of life balance are addressed in sport and sport-related professions in order to avoid burnout and dropout among talented athletes, coaches, and administrators.
- Football is no longer the primary focus of education-based sport programs, regardless of its popularity or revenue production; instead, the norm is broad-based programs that serve all potential athletes.

Girls face some unique issues in sport. For example, on average, puberty arrives two years earlier in girls than in boys, thus affecting their physical capacity and sometimes their interest in sport at an earlier age. Girls who enter puberty earlier report lower physical self-perception in terms of body fat, overall self-concept, and appearance, as well as lower scores on a physical activity enjoyment scale. In contrast, those whose maturity comes later tend to be more intrinsically motivated and derive more enjoyment from physical activity and sport (Labrozzi et al. 2013).

As a result, teenage girls often drop out of sport just when many boys, fueled by new levels of testosterone, are consumed by competitive sport. With this difference in mind, we need to establish a clear path to help young girls transition from performance sport to participation sport before they drop out for good.

As the Latino and Hispanic population expands to become approximately one-third of the population, girls and women from this culture need to be integrated into a U.S. culture that values lifelong physical activity and sport participation. Latino and Hispanic girls are introduced to sport later than other racial groups and also drop out earlier. Inducing them to become more physically active is a challenge that affects the overall health of the U.S. population, as well as the campaign to reduce overweight and obesity.

Older women, too, will continue to have a significant effect on sport. Those who love performance sport will prolong their careers with expanded professional, semiprofessional, and community leagues that offer strong competition. However, the vast majority of women who don sneakers and activewear are looking for a healthy workout to maintain their physical appearance, control body weight, socialize, have fun, and increase their energy for the demands of daily living. The influx of females in participation sport requires calls for both new sports and variations on traditional sports; examples include the recent surge of female participation in yoga, tai chi, and strength training.

As mentioned earlier, the aging of the U.S. population may be the most influential trend of all in sport. Age-group competition for older adults will continue to grow as some seniors seek the thrills of competitive sport and the challenge of testing themselves against other competitors or against the environment. Other older adults are more interested in exercise simply to maximize good health, posture, energy, social interaction, fun, and release from stress. In order to meet the needs of these older athletes, coaches and program leaders will need to continue to tinker with the formula for sport. The best approach for older adults seems to consist of more frequent but shorter workouts at less intensity. This group also looks to socialize either during or after physical activity, and opportunities to do so should be made available in a comfortable setting.

Sexual preference will continue to be an important topic in the sport world. Historically, sport has not been kind to lesbian, gay, bisexual, or transgender (LGBT) athletes, and this has been particularly true of performance sport. A few successful LGBT athletes have publicly addressed their sexuality, but most have quietly concealed it in order to avoid controversy. Perhaps for this reason, the Gay Games and various local gay athletic organizations have grown substantially around the world.

The Gay Games were founded in San Francisco in 1982, when they attracted 1,350 participants. Attendance grew steadily, and the 1994 edition in New York City registered more than 10,000 athletes. Successive games in Amsterdam, Sydney, Chicago, and Cologne have all surpassed that number. In 2010, competitors from 70 nations competed in 35 sports, and the Games drew an opening-ceremony crowd exceeding 25,000 that was entertained by music stars Agnes and Taylor Dayne. Unlike other world competitions, the Gay Games enable people from all walks of life to compete against each other regardless of skill level, age, or physical challenge. The Games define winning as achieving one's best, and competitors are matched against others of similar skill.

The success of the Gay Games does not relieve traditional sport—competitive or recreational—of its responsibility to welcome LGBT people to its facilities and programs. Like anyone, LGBT people join local teams and clubs to enjoy physical activity, meet new people, receive emotional support, and have fun—not to experience mistreatment from the historically homophobic sport world. As public acceptance of LGBT people grows, more athletes will have the courage to announce their sexual preference and insist on equal opportunity.

Indeed, in 2013, several professional athletes—led by Jason Collins of the National Basketball Association and Michael Sam of the NFL—came out to the world, thus marking a major social change in the stereotypical anti-gay cultures of professional basketball and football. At the college level, basketball star Brittney Griner came out as a lesbian during her senior year at Baylor University in spite of the university's exclusion of sexual preference in its nondiscrimination statement (see chapter 13).

In a broader societal perspective, the majority of the U.S. public now supports the rights of LGBT people to marry, build a family, and claim the legal and financial status enjoyed by heterosexual citizens. Over time, the sport world will increasingly reflect that attitude change and begin to integrate LGBT folks as athletes, coaches, and sport administrators.

Historically, sport participation has also been generally closed to people with a mental or physical disability. However, with the advent of laws prohibiting discrimination against people with a disability, their sport participation has blossomed as well. For example, the Special Olympics and the Paralympics have offered both performance and participation sport to people with a disability at the national and international levels. In addition, local communities and schools have gradually sought to add sport programs for people with a disability and, wherever possible, to include these athletes in existing programs. Some sports have been modified and others invented to enable participation by people with a disability. The keys to sustaining the growth in opportunities for these athletes are education, financial support, and effective training for coaches.

Effects of Spectatorship

Spectatorship has always been a double-edged sword for sport. Some marketing studies have shown that increases in participation are attributed to increases in the number of spectators and to the popularity of star athletes. Certainly, Michael Jordan's amazing basketball career and soaring popularity raised interest in basketball worldwide. Yet soccer grew by leaps and bounds in the United States with virtually no heroes or stars until Mia Hamm and her teammates captivated fans with their remarkable international record. Clearly, then, a sport does not necessarily need to have transcendent players in order to become popular.

Fans' access to sport will of course increase as television coverage continues to expand. Pay-per-

The Paralympics have helped bring performance sport for athletes with disabilities to the forefront of the sporting world.

view channels will carry selected sport programs, and channels exclusively devoted to specific sports, such as golf and tennis, are already available. The Internet will continue to revolutionize spectatorship, as people will be able to follow their college team, high school team, and even youth sport event, such as the Little League World Series, from anywhere in the country—or the world.

The question is this: Will increased access create more sport fans, or will it simply give current fans more choices and induce them to spend more hours in front of a screen? If we believe that participation in sport will increase in the future, will spectatorship also increase?

Consider the average person who has time commitments to work, family, and of course the general responsibilities of daily life. Carving time out of that schedule for exercise and sport participation has proven to be a perplexing challenge for most people. If they also increase the amount of time they spend *watching* sport, something else will have to suffer because ten hours of leisure time per week can be split in only so many ways.

Power brokers in sport will mount a vigorous campaign to attract spectators in order to enhance their products. For them, participation is irrelevant; their revenue comes from paying spectators, commercial sponsors, and media rights. One potential strategy for power brokers is to press for legalized sport gambling in order to get fans more actively involved in their favorite teams and players. Pressure will mount on local and state governments to legalize sport gambling as the next step following the legalization of gambling at Native American reservations and offshore locations. Taxpayers will be faced with the dilemma of weighing suspicions about gambling interests against inducements, such as allocating a percentage of gambling revenues toward education, youth sport programs, or other popular social programs. Internet gambling, now legal, will attract scrutiny as it grows and prospers.

EXPERT'S VIEW

Elite Sled Dogs and Human Performance

We've all heard or taken part in arguments about which athlete is the greatest. The discussion may involve basketball players Michael Jordan and LeBron James, Olympic sprinter Usain Bolt, or perhaps a professional boxer or marathon runner. You might not realize that the greatest athletes of all may just be the dogs who pull the sleds at the Iditarod. What can we learn from Iditarod canines about training the great athletes of the future?

These elite sled dogs are typically a mixed breed that includes a bit of Siberian husky heritage. They are specially bred for speed, desire, and resilience. When they compete in the Iditarod, they can run an average of 100 miles (about 160 kilometers) per day for eight or nine days working at 50 percent of their maximal aerobic capacity for hours at a time. As part of a team of dogs, they can run sub-four-minute miles for 60 to 70 miles (roughly 100 to 115 kilometers). No other animal—and certainly no human—can match that feat.

As the preceding description suggests, it's not the fastest dogs that win. In his book *The Sports Gene* (2013), David Epstein recounts that in the past sled dogs were bred for speed. They raced full-out between checkpoints and then rested. But four-time Iditarod champion Lance Mackey could not afford to breed fast dogs, so he bred instead for drive and desire in order to select dogs who might be a bit slower but never stopped running. He found out that he was winning races because his dogs were pulling not necessarily faster but longer without rest (Epstein 2013).

The dogs' performance attracted plenty of attention, some of it from the Pentagon's research arm, known as the Defense Advanced Research Projects Agency (DARPA), which funds and conducts research in part to further exploration of human performance. The armed forces are always interested in learning how to enhance the performance of military personnel, who may be called on to perform rigorous physical tasks for days on end with little or no rest or nutrition. DARPA research with animals is typically done by exercise physiologists to lay the groundwork for subsequent experiments with humans in order to push the boundaries of human performance.

To understand how to prepare military personnel for extreme endurance activities, exercise physiologists and veterinarians studied how the sled dogs control their body heat during long periods of vigorous activity. They also studied the composition and structure of the dogs' muscles at the cellular level, as well as the effect of diet on their performance. Remarkably, they discovered that the dogs performed best by using fats rather than glucose to mobilize energy and resist fatigue. The next step is to translate the studies to humans and perhaps push the limits of physical endurance further than before, even at elite levels of performance (Alexander 2010).

More politicians are also looking toward approving sport betting in order to combat mounting financial deficits in their states due to recent economic hardships. The first state to challenge prior bans on sport betting was Delaware, which wanted to open up sport betting in 2009. The National Collegiate Athletic Association and all leaders from the major U.S. professional sports joined together to resist the efforts, and eventually the courts ruled against Delaware. But the stage is set, and pressure to expand sport betting will continue, as will debate about the right course of action.

Effects of Technology

The relentless search for performance excellence, combined with the quest to sell new products, will continue to spur research and development of new sport facilities and equipment. For example, new technology will improve field surfaces, court surfaces, and pool construction. On a smaller scale, it will also bring improvements in tennis rackets, golf clubs, vaulting poles, baseball bats, footwear, and other sport equipment.

One positive effect of equipment advances will be the ease with which a beginning player can learn a new sport or an intermediate player can improve. For example, the larger heads of newer tennis rackets and golf clubs have added performance consistency to hundreds of thousands of weekend warriors' games. The story is much the same with adjustments in the length and design of skis.

Technological advances will also enable high-performance athletes to move faster, jump higher, hit harder, and improve their consistency. However, some advances may also carry increased risk to the athlete's body, which may not stand up to the increased forces of movement. As a result, injury monitoring is critical in order to prevent harm to elite athletes who embrace new technology. A good example can be found in the rush to install synthetic turf on football fields some 30 years ago. Athletes could run faster and jump higher on the artificial turf, but the rate of injuries exploded because human joints simply could not withstand the force. As a result, athletes and coaches forced a return to natural grass fields in order to protect athletes' careers and health.

Training methods based on scientific research will also improve as we learn how to push the human body to the limit. Improved methods of strength and endurance training will be combined with enhanced nutrition to equip athletes to perform better for longer periods of time. Improved methods will also include better systems of training to prevent overuse injuries, strengthen traditional trouble spots, and shorten the recovery time for sport injuries. For example, it will be possible to rehabilitate high ankle sprains and torn anterior cruciate ligaments in half the time it takes now (Van Riper 2009). In addition, permanent disabilities will be reduced by new procedures for joint and tissue repair and replacement. Already, synthetic knees, hips, and ankles are becoming commonplace, and other joints will follow. Indeed, sport participation and even professional careers will be prolonged by surgical interventions we cannot yet imagine.

During competition itself, coaches will have access to information about the physical state of their athletes from the sidelines. This information will include, for example, assessment of head injuries, lack of conditioning, and risk of injury. As a result, coaches will no longer have to rely on how athletes say they feel; instead, they will rely on scientific assessments, even in the midst of competition.

The prevalence of head injuries in contact sports, such as football and soccer, has recently gained widespread public attention. We've become more aware of the long-term effects of concussions and other head trauma, which have resulted in many fine former athletes suffering for a lifetime once their playing career is over. The next few years are likely to see more research, better equipment, and a more cautious protocol for treatment.

Drugs and other performance-enhancing substances will continue to be a hot topic. As drug-testing protocols become more accurate and routine, some athletes will still attempt to cheat. The question is whether sport organizers' technology can keep up with those who seek to circumvent the testing.

A final, far-reaching issue is that of genetic engineering to produce exceptional athletes. The moral, ethical, and legal issues of this possibility will be hotly debated in the coming years as science forges ahead in exploring ways to alter genetic makeup. Imagine parents choosing the genetic makeup of their child—or even adjusting it during childhood. For most of us, these questions are too complicated to comprehend, and it is likely that the debate will rage for years.

Effects of the Electronic Media

In the last 25 years, the Internet has opened up possibilities that did not even seem to exist just a few decades ago. Here are a few ideas about what may happen in the next 25 years.

As mentioned previously, fans will have a wider range of sport to watch on their phones, tablets, and computers, which will also be hooked up to larger screens. The action will be viewed on demand, so that people do not have to plan their day around watching sport but can do so when it fits their mood and schedule. It is virtually certain that fewer fans will watch the traditional big games that networks choose to feature, because fans will now have access to all games. Anyone who supports a college team will be able to see that team in action on any given day. In addition, fans of less popular sports will be able to watch their favorites rather than just whatever network television executives choose to present. Movement in these directions has already begun, and consumers will gradually demand even more choices.

The wildly popular fantasy teams and leagues that provide interactive entertainment will also continue to grow. With these options, live games that only allow you to watch passively can be replaced with exciting fantasy games in which you act as the coach. Internet games that simulate professional sport shift the role of the user from that of spectator to that of the coach who picks the players on the team, chooses the defensive or offensive strategy, and calls plays.

At the same time, athletes themselves will be more accessible to their fans through online chat rooms and discussions. Where athletes were once hidden by game uniforms and helmets and protected from contact with fans, the athlete of the future will need to learn to be more open, accessible, and personable. Some coaches at both the college and professional level encourage players to communicate with fans and supporters so as to build interest in the team while others restrict such contact because of instances of inappropriate or offending off-the-cuff comments by athletes.

For sport fans watching at home, the use of multiple high-definition cameras showing varied angles—plus instant replay capability—has generated sport viewing options that are compelling and informative and often provide a better perspective than that of a fan in the live audience. The next step is to attach body cameras to athletes so that fans see the action develop from the athlete's perspective. The technology already exists but the application has yet to be engineered or applied.

Of course, as the view from the couch keeps improving, sports arenas will work to keep up by offering experiences using advanced technology to fans who have spent money on tickets. The majority of fans already come armed with some electronic receiver in the form of a smartphone or iPad so Wi-Fi access throughout the stadium is a critical fan requirement. New apps will provide fans with new options, such as ordering food and drink from their seat, gauging the wait time at restrooms, and moving to better available seating. Of course, immediate access to instant replays—to be watched repeatedly or shared with friends—is also a critical perk.

ESPN has dominated sport coverage for the last few decades and now boasts 10 popular channels across the world, including ESPN, ESPN2, ESPN News, ESPN Classic, and ESPN College. It also attracts high traffic to ESPN.com, which delivers sport news 24 hours a day. ESPN also is the leader in sports news using social media; in 2015, it attracted 15.9 million Twitter followers to ESPN and an additional 14 million followers to SportsCenter in just the month of February (Bennett 2015).

ESPN's credibility is established; athletes trust it to get their message out, and fans trust the reporting. But social networks and other digital media may cut into its market soon. In fact, professional teams are

ACTIVITY TIME-OUT

The Change Constant

"The only thing that is constant is change." This observation, attributed to the Greek philosopher Heraclitus, has stood the test of time. What changes are likely to occur in the next five or ten years in sport? Surely we should be able to predict at least that far ahead based on the clues now within our reach.

With the help of one or two classmates, develop a list of the three most important changes that you think will occur in sport in the next five years. Then list three more that you think will occur in the next ten years. For example, do you think the popularity of American football—either in participation or spectatorship—will increase, stay the same, or decrease over the next five years? Ten years?

Consider all that you have learned this semester—the clues you've come across in your reading and class discussions—and consult with your friends at school. Then list the changes that you would bet on (if you were a betting person). Share them with your classmates and justify each choice.

now using their own digital channels to link fans to each other and connect them to the team's brand. Through these channels, as well as social media, such as Facebook and Twitter, teams can connect their sponsors to their fans, sell tickets, and generate profits. As stadium seats are priced out of the reach of middle-class families (for example, the New York Yankees' $1,000 seats), social media can connect fans with their team even if they never attend a game. If fans feel they are important to the team's success, can access inside information, and can share opinions with other fans, you may have hooked them for life (Reed 2010).

Will Sport Change?

If you have any doubt about whether sport will change in the coming years, simply look at the last 60 years. Since the 1950s, sport has expanded dramatically to become a huge corporate moneymaker. Professional football, basketball, baseball, ice hockey, tennis, and golf have made multimillionaires out of athletes and sustained the corporate organizations that regulate and control these sports. We once thought that an athlete who earned $10,000 for a single season of play was amazingly rich.

Indeed, when Joe DiMaggio agreed in 1949 to the first $100,000 contract to play center field for the New York Yankees, we thought that was the zenith of sport compensation—yet today's superstars sign contracts in excess of $30 million per year and often add an equal amount of revenue from endorsement contracts (Roberts 2004). Even taking inflation into account, athletes' salaries have risen tenfold over the last quarter century, while the median real hourly earnings of the average American worker have remained essentially flat since 1980 with the only gains going to the top 10 percent of workers (Desilver 2014).

As discussed throughout this book, social changes have opened up opportunities for people of all races and ethnic groups, for women, and for athletes with disabilities. These changes are not the end; more are yet to come.

Who Will Lead the Way?

If we apply social theories to future trends, here are some possible scenarios.

Those who follow functionalist theory would likely take the view that sport can be changed from the inside by improving the current sport culture through better marketing and promotion, presentation of athletes as role models, a fan-friendly emphasis at events, and promotion of record-setting performances. This approach applies the traditional conservative philosophy that holds to maintaining the status quo but improving it by producing more of what currently exists.

Reformists who use functionalist theory might call for changes such as finally equalizing opportunities for females, minorities, and athletes with a disability. They are also likely to fight for control of the use of performance-enhancing substances in order to ensure equal competition. Similarly, they may pressure collegiate sport to compensate athletes with modest wages in Division I programs while also limiting entry into the professional ranks until age 20 or so.

All of these proposals suggest that sport can be improved by tinkering with the current model and adjusting to trends while maintaining the essential integrity of the model.

Those who seek more radical changes in sport may use conflict theory to present their case. They may envision a new model that opens up sport as a form of healthy recreation and cooperative physical activity for all citizens. They reject the current corporate structure, the emphasis on winning, the bottom-line mentality, and the exploitation of athletes for the benefit of the power brokers who make millions from their performances. In a conflict theorist's vision, spectator sport would take a back seat to participation in physical activity and sport for all citizens. As a corollary, public funding should be spent on facilities for participation rather than huge stadiums that promote passive viewing of a few superathletes. The welfare of athletes and participants would take precedence over the financial interests of wealthy team owners and university athletic departments.

Feminist theorists push to improve the number of women in coaching, administration, media, and other key leadership positions. As women assume more strategic roles in sport, their history and experience will alter future trends, for example ensuring equal opportunity for all rather than a few privileged athletes. LGBT athletes will become more comfortable in the sport world, and fans, teammates, and competitors will embrace their presence and contribution.

Interactionist theorists see the changes in sport as coming from the bottom up. That is, athletes themselves will force change that better suits their needs. Two groups of athletes stand out as potential agents of change—youth and older adults—both of whom are poorly served by the performance model for sport. Instead, these groups emphasize participation, healthy living, cooperation rather than competition, and accommodation of all skill levels. If changes in traditional sport are not forthcoming, it seems likely both young and senior athletes will invent sport models of their own that better address their needs and interests. Extreme sports have already made a mark among young people, and perhaps similar changes will become popular with senior athletes.

Critical theorists might also affect youth and high school sport. If educators take the lead in defining the value and place of sport, programs might look very different. Intramural sports that include all students have the potential to grow in high schools, as they have done in colleges, as students increasingly demand that facilities be available for physical recreation rather than merely for a relatively few privileged athletes. Parents will have to insist on a new approach to youth sport that supports participation for every child regardless of economic level, ability, race, gender, or disability. To support such efforts, critical theorists will exert pressure to shift significant funding from performance sport to participation sport. The success of programs will be judged not by the win–loss record but by the number of young people who participate and continue playing year after year.

Another significant change will be to establish standards of coaching at every level and avoid hiring coaches who are not appropriately certified. Public opinion could lead the way to this change in order to protect athletes who are directly affected by inadequate coaching. Parents are likely to insist on a level of coaching that reflects better education, a clear philosophy of coaching that matches program goals, and a more humanistic style of relating to athletes. The use of online education has opened up accessible and cost-effective coaching education. As a result, coaches who use outdated approaches and authoritarian methods will be more likely to struggle, especially in educational settings.

In addition, critical theorists will look at the current expenditure of public funds to support professional franchises and stadiums, as well as the so-called "sweetheart deals" that entice wealthy franchise owners to move a team to a particular

Who will lead the changes in sport? Coaches? Athletes? Or you?

city. A reformist critical theorist would rather see that money spent on facilities or programs that directly benefit local citizens by offering opportunities to participate in sport rather than watch it. Compromises may be struck that allow some money to be spent on both participating and spectating if it can be shown that one approach also benefits the other.

The question of leadership still has not been answered. History shows that very few athletes become agents of change, especially during their playing days. Why risk all they have worked for unless they have suffered badly in the present system? A retiring NFL player who admits that he cannot read in spite of holding a college degree might have cause; but of those who are frustrated, few have the courage or eloquence to express it. However, recent lawsuits against the NFL by former players assert that teams have affected their long-term health by overprescribing drugs and painkillers, withholding information about injuries, and encouraging athletes to continue to play in spite of injuries.

Coaches are not likely to rebel against a system that has been their life. Similarly, owners of professional teams, leaders in major sport organizations, and athletic directors have all invested their lives in the sport establishment and generally have been well rewarded in return.

Who Will Fight for Change?

Will it be you—someone who has studied sport, thought about it, and developed some strong opinions? Will it be parents who want a better experience for their children? Maybe it will be independent sport institutes, such as the Center for the Study of Sport in Society at Northeastern University, or politicians who believe they can advance their career by taking up the mantle of sport change, or academic leaders at universities, or sportswriters and commentators.

Alternatively, will changes occur as a reflection of a society that continues to adjust its values, economics, and political philosophies? Perhaps large coalitions of citizens will find themselves on the same side of arguments and band together to bring about change. Demographic analysis makes clear that U.S. society is heading quickly toward a large population dominated by older adults. That group has money, time, and a keen interest in sport as part of a healthy lifestyle; indeed, exercise for its own sake will never be able to compete with the joy of sport or the social interaction that it encourages. The fitness gym offers physical training benefits but lacks the universal appeal of games and sport. In the near future, a large proportion of our population will look to sport for help in blazing a new trail of longer, healthier lives.

What do you think?

Chapter Summary

This chapter examines social trends that may affect the role of sport in your life. The major trends identified include a doubling of the Latino and Hispanic racial group; aging of the population; protection for all people regardless of age, race, gender, sexual preference, or disability; continued expansion of performance sport by corporate sport leaders; enhancement of coaching competence; and technological improvement that may enhance sport performance.

The chapter also considers the conflicts between the consumers and leaders of performance sport and those of participation sport. These conflicts include struggles over funding, use of facilities, public programs, and access for everyone.

In addition, the chapter discusses the effect of opening sport participation to people of all ages, racial groups, and ethnic groups, as well as both genders, LGBT people, and people with a disability. The demand for expanded programs and the related need for more financial support are concerns that are likely to create struggles between various advocacy groups.

The chapter examines sport watching from both a positive and a negative point of view. Whereas traditional performance sport will continue to try to grow its fan base and provide entertainment, we may find that a parallel growth in participation sport conflicts with these goals. Yet when spectatorship enhances participation, and vice versa, the two groups can benefit from the synergy of working cooperatively.

In other trends, technological advances will affect athletes' ability to generate exceptional performances and ease the way for beginning athletes to take up new sports. Performance-enhancing substances will continue to constitute a knotty problem for sport administrators. And time, money, and effort will be allocated to ensure equal competition opportunities for everyone. Improved methods of sports medicine will enable better treatment and recovery from injuries and will include replacement of body parts that break down from overuse.

Finally, the chapter considers *how* sport might change in the future, who will lead those changes, and what they might focus on. History teaches lessons about how changes have occurred in the past, but peering into the future is more challenging. In the final analysis, changes in sport will be dictated by changes in our society, by our needs, by our values, and perhaps by outside influences. Perhaps *you* will be a catalyst for change in your community!

GLOSSARY

abuse—Willful infliction of injury, pain, mental anguish, intimidation, or punishment.

adult-organized sport—Sport organized by parents or a governing body and involving structured activities carried out according to a fixed set of rules.

amateur—One who emphasizes participation in sport rather than outcome and engages in sport for intrinsic satisfaction, such as improving fitness, enjoying competition, refining physical skills, working as part of a team, or simply embracing the challenge and excitement of testing skills against nature or other competitors.

Amateur Sports Act of 1978—Act of the U.S. Congress that established the United States Olympic Committee (USOC) and outlined its responsibilities.

American Association of People with Disabilities (AAPD)—Largest national nonprofit cross-disability organization, which serves the 56 million Americans with a disability.

Americans with Disabilities Act (ADA)—Landmark national legislation protecting the rights of Americans with a disability.

anabolic steroid—Hormone, usually synthetic, used to temporarily increase muscle size and sometimes abused by athletes.

anorexia nervosa—Eating disorder characterized by self-starvation.

appreciation—Increase in value over time.

athlete-organized sport—Sport organized by athletes, without adult supervision, in which activities are less structured than in adult-organized sport and rules are made up as play progresses.

bed tax—Tax on hotel guests that provides revenue for a state or locality to put toward financing various projects, such as public sport stadiums.

biomechanics—Study of the structure and function of biological systems by applying principles of physics to human motion.

biophysical domain—Sport science subdiscipline including physiology, biomechanics, nutrition, and sports medicine.

bulimia nervosa—Eating disorder characterized by overeating (bingeing) followed by purging, usually through laxative use or self-induced vomiting.

burnout—Exhaustion of physical or emotional strength as a result of prolonged stress; possible cause for an athlete to stop participating in competitive sport.

capital assets—Tangible property that cannot be converted easily into cash.

capitalism—Economic system based on accumulation and investment of capital by individuals who then use it to produce goods or services.

compulsive exercise—Eating disorder characterized not by altered food intake but by too much exercise in order to purge calories.

conflict theory—Theory based on the work of Karl Marx that sees sport as being built on the foundation of money and economic power.

content research—Type of research in which data or pictures are collected from sources such as articles and video programs and assigned to thematic categories.

conventional level—Second level of moral reasoning, which includes most adults and society at large and in which behavior is guided by what is acceptable to others.

corporate sport—Another name for the business of professional sport.

critical theory—Theory that looks critically at culture and seeks to determine the source of authority wielded by one group over another.

cultural capital—Skills and abilities that people gain from education and life experiences and that may include attitudes, expectations, and self-confidence.

depreciation—Decrease in value over time, as of equipment, tools, or athletes.

deviant—Descriptor applied to behavior differing from accepted norms.

direct spectator—One who attends a live sporting event at a stadium, arena, or other such venue.

disability—Condition of mental or physical impairment that limits capacity in life.

economic capital—Financial resources possessed or controlled.

economic model—Model emphasizing the financial profit to be made from any endeavor.

electronic media—Media outlets using electronic technology such as television, radio, and web-based operations.

ethnicity—Cultural heritage arising from the social customs of a group of people.

ethnography—Study of data collected by researchers who immerse themselves in an environment and keep recorded conversations or notes.

exercise physiology—Study of human systems to enhance strength, speed, and endurance.

extrinsic reward—Motivation that comes from other people by positive or negative reinforcement in the form of verbal praise and approval or tangible rewards such as trophies, prizes, grades, or money.

female athlete triad—Combination of three conditions: disordered eating, amenorrhea, and osteoporosis.

feminist theory—Social theory investigating the effects of gender in society.

figurational theory—Theory proposing that we are all connected by networks of people, who are interdependent on one another by nature, through education, and through socialization.

focus groups—Interviews with small groups of people to elicit information and opinions.

functionalist theory—Theory approaching sport as a social institution that reinforces the current value system in a society.

game—Kind of play that shows more evidence of structure than play; is competitive; involves clear goals for participating; can be mental, physical, or both; is governed by either informal or formal rules; involves a winner determined by luck, strategy, or skill; and results in an end product such as prestige or status.

gender verification—Process used for 30 years by the International Olympic Committee to test female athletes; intended to ensure fair competition but discontinued in 1999 as demeaning, unnecessary, and unreliable.

hazing—Action that inflicts physical or mental harm or anxiety or degrades a person, regardless of location, intent, or consent.

hegemony theory—Critical theory focusing on dominance, or the power that one individual or group wields over others.

high-performance athlete—Athlete of any age who aspires to the highest levels of performance and typically becomes a professional athlete.

historical research—Research examining trends in sport over time.

hooliganism—Rowdy, violent, or destructive behavior; term often used to describe behavior of working-class men who disrupt soccer games with violence, excessive drinking, exchanges of insults, destruction of property, and interruptions of the game.

indirect spectator—One who listens to or watches sport electronically by means of radio, television, or the web or who reads about sport in print media such as newspapers and magazines.

interactionist theory—Theory that views society from the bottom up rather than from the top down and that focuses on social interactions based on the realities that people choose to accept.

interview—Face-to-face personal questioning to elicit information, attitudes, or opinions.

intrinsic reward—Reinforcement that comes from within a person such as fun, enjoyment, good health, self-satisfaction, or improved fitness.

lower class—Lowest level of the social class system, consisting of unskilled laborers who do work that is assigned and supervised by others.

masters—Classification in competitive sport for older athletes that usually starts at age 35 and is divided into subgroups at 5- or 10-year intervals.

middle class—Middle and largest level of the economic class system in the United States, including, for example, skilled laborers, teachers, and people in the service industry.

minority—Portion of the population that differs from the larger portion in terms of a given criterion, such as race.

motor learning and behavior—Field of study focused on relatively permanent changes in motor behavior that result from practice or experience.

naming rights—Legal rights purchased by a corporation to name an athletic stadium or facility (e.g., American Airlines Arena in Miami) as a means of advertising.

nationalism—Spirit of loyalty and devotion to a nation; a strong characteristic of worldwide sport competition, such as the Olympic Games.

nutrition—Field of study focused on how exercise and physical performance in sport is affected by food and drink.

overconformity—Behavior that goes beyond what is generally accepted, which in sport includes such examples as altering food intake or using supplements to meet an ideal body image.

over-the-counter drug—Nonprescription drug designed to promote healing from sickness or injury or to mask pain.

pedagogy—Study of the art and science of teaching.

personal seat license (PSL)—License that gives a fan the right to buy season tickets for specific seats in a stadium.

philosophy of sport—Study of the definition, value, and meaning of sport.

play—Free activity that involves exploring the environment, expressing oneself, dreaming, and pretending; that involves no firm rules; and in which the outcome is unimportant.

politics—Art and science of government, of influencing governmental policy, or of holding control of a government.

postconventional level—Highest level of moral reasoning; autonomous, principled level of thinking, in which a person adopts certain moral principles and holds to the behavior indicated by them regardless of social punishment or reward.

preconventional level—Basic level of moral understanding, in which being right means following authority with the understanding that punishment will be received if one doesn't follow the rules.

prescription drug—Drug prescribed by a doctor in order to promote healing from sickness or injury or to mask pain.

print media—Media that take printed form, including newspapers, magazines, and books.

private funds—Monies raised from owner contributions, league contributions, bank loans, loans from local businesses, and personal seat licenses.

professional athlete—Paid performer who works by training to hone physical skills to the highest level for competition with other elite athletes.

psychosocial domain—Sport science subdiscipline that focuses on psychology, motor learning and behavior, and pedagogy.

public funds—Money raised from public sources, such as sales taxes, proximity and beneficiary taxes, general obligation and revenue bonds, and tax increment financing.

public tax funds—Tax funds collected by local and state governments that are used to provide services to citizens.

qualitative data—Data collected through interviews or observations of individuals or groups or through analysis of societal characteristics and trends.

quantifiable data—Study producing data that can be counted and analyzed statistically.

race—Attributes passed along genetically such as height, eye or skin color.

racism—Belief that race is the primary determinant of human traits and that racial differences produce inherent superiority in a particular race.

religion—Belief in a god or supernatural force that influences human life.

revenue-producing sport—Intercollegiate sport, such as football or basketball, that typically produces more revenue than expense for the university.

revenue sharing—Sharing within a league of income from television contracts and other sources of revenue in order to protect teams in smaller markets that may yield less income.

social capital—Capital that depends on family, friends, and associates and includes resources based on group memberships, relationships, and social and business networks.

social class—Category of people who occupy similar positions in society based on economic level, education, occupation, and social interaction.

socialization—Process of interacting with other people and learning social customs, morals, and values.

social media—Internet-based communication between people through vehicles such as Facebook, MySpace, Twitter, YouTube, and blogs.

social stratification— Class assignments based on levels of power, prestige, and wealth.

social theory—Theory about society and social life that is based on systematic research and logic and that provides frameworks for evaluating a present situation and perhaps discovering a need for change.

societal analysis—Use of social theories to examine life from a social point of view.

sociocultural domain—Sport science subdiscipline that includes history, philosophy, and sociology.

sociology—Study of a society, its institutions, and its relationships that attends to social issues, social organization, and the potential for social change.

sport—Institutionalized competitive activity that involves physical skill and specialized facilities or equipment and is conducted according to an accepted set of rules in order to determine a winner.

sport announcer—Media personality who broadcasts sport events.

sport history—Study of the tradition and practices of physical activity and sport over time and in different countries, cultures, and civilizations.

sporting behavior—Behavior characterized by fair play and respect for others.

sport participation—Process of playing an active role in sport.

sport psychology—Study of human behavior in sport, including performance enhancement and treatment of disorders that affect optimal performance.

sport pyramid—Way of understanding sport that approaches human activity in terms of four elements: play, games, sport, and work.

sportsmanship—See *sporting behavior*.

sports medicine—Branch of medicine that deals with prevention, care, and rehabilitation of injuries caused by participation in physical activity and sport.

sport sociology—Study of sport and physical activity in the context of the social conditions and culture in which people live.

sport spectator—One who watches sport.

stacking—Unusual distribution of white and black athletes in certain positions in a sport that cannot be explained by random distribution.

stimulant—Kind of drug that produces a temporary increase in functional activity or efficiency.

survey research—Research conducted through questionnaires.

Title IX—Landmark U.S. legislation passed in 1972 that requires any institution receiving federal funding to provide equal opportunities for males and females.

total salary cap—Total financial commitment that a team is allowed to make to all players on the roster in combined salary and benefits.

underconformity—Behavior that does not conform to generally acceptable standards, including, in sport, such actions as rule breaking, hazing, and excessive drinking.

upper class—Highest level of the U.S. economic class system, made up of the top 1 percent of households and controlling over 35 percent of the nation's wealth.

upper-middle class—Second highest level of the social class system, made up of professionals (such as physicians, attorneys, managers) who typically have significant discretionary income.

work—Purposeful activity that may include physical or mental effort to perform a task, accomplish a goal, overcome an obstacle, or achieve a desired outcome, and which can characterize sport as it moves toward the professional level. May include high-performance youth sport programs that prepare competitors for a professional career.

youth sport—Sport engaged in by children ranging from 6 to 12 years old.

REFERENCES

AAHPERD [renamed SHAPE America]. 2013. Recommended requisites for sport coaches (position statement) www.shapeamerica.org/admin/loader.cfm?csModule=security/getfile&pageid=4574. Accessed 1/16/2014

ABC News. 2004. BALCO chief on sports doping scandal. December 3. http://abcnews.go.com/2020/story?id=297995&page=1. Accessed May 22, 2005.

Abend, L. 2014. Why nobody wants to host the 2022 Winter Olympics. http://time.com/3462070/olympics-winter-2022/. Accessed December 15, 2014.

Abrams, M. 2010a. Female violence in sport: Maybe it isn't just the testosterone. *Psychology Today.* www.psychologytoday.com/blog/sports-transgressions/201003/. Accessed January 13, 2015.

———. 2010b. Learn the difference between anger, aggression, and violence. Excerpted from *Anger Management in Sport.* Champaign, IL: Human Kinetics.

Acosta. V. and Carpenter, L. 2014. Women in intercollegiate sport: A longitudinal national study, thirty-seven year update, 1977–2014. www.acostacarpenter.org.

Alexander, B. 2010. It's the dog in you. *Outside Magazine*, March. www.outsideonline.com/fitness/endurance-training/It-s-the-Dog-in-You.html. Accessed June 6, 2014.

Alexander, D. 2013. 2013 Houston Astros: Baseball's worst team is the most profitable in history. www.forbes.com/sites/danalexander/2013/08/26/2013-houston-astros. Accessed December 23, 2013.

Alfred University. 1999a. High school hazing: How many students are hazed? www.alfred.edu/hs_hazing/howmanystudents.cfm. Accessed October 16, 2010.

———. 1999b. National survey of sports teams: Who is most at risk? Where are hot spots? www.alfred.edu/hs_hazing/mostatrisk.cfm. Accessed October 16, 2010.

Allan, E., and Madden, M. 2008. Hazing in view: College students at risk. www.stophazing.org/wp-content/uploads/2014/06/hazing_in_view_web1.pdf. Accessed January 15, 2015.

Alter, C. 2014. Maryville rape case teen attempts suicide. http://nation.time.com/2014/01/07/maryville-rape-case-teen-hospitalized. Accessed January 14, 2015.

Amateur Athletic Foundation Olympic Primer. 2005. Issues of the Olympic Games. Olympic reports. www.aafla.org./6oic/primer_frmst.htm. Accessed October 17, 2010.

American Academy of Pediatrics Council on Sports Medicine and Fitness. 2012. Cheerleading injuries, epidemiology, and recommendations for prevention (policy statement). *Pediatrics.* DOI 10.1542/peds.2012-2480. Accessed January 16, 2015.

American Association of People with Disabilities. 2015. About AAPD. www.aapd.com/what-we-do/. Accessed May 6, 2015.

American Athletic Institute. 2010. The problem: Alcohol use in adolescents. www.panhandlepreventioncoalition.org/THE%20PROBLEM.pdf. Accessed January 12, 2014.

American Civil Liberties Union. 2007. Recent ACLU cases defending the constitutional rights of non-Christian religions. www.aclusandiego.org/recent-aclu-cases-defending-the-constitutional-rights-of-non-christian-religions/. Accessed May 31, 2015.

American College of Sports Medicine. 2011. The female athlete triad (informational brochure). www.acsm.org/docs/brochures/the-female-athlete-triad.pdf. Accessed May 6, 2015.

American Gaming Association. 2013. Sports wagering fact sheet. www.americangaming.org/industry-resources/research/fact-sheets/sports-wagering. Accessed May 27, 2014.

American Heart Association. 2013. Physical inactivity: Statistical fact sheet—2013 update. www.heart.org/idc/groups/heart-public/@wcm/@sop/@smd/documents/downloadable/ucm_319589.pdf. Accessed January 5, 2015.

American Outlook. 2011. Indianapolis sports strategy. Fall. www.americanoutlook.org/q--a-indianapolis-sports-strategy.html. Accessed January 11, 2015.

Americans Disability Technical Assistance Centers. 2004. Historical context of the Americans with Disabilities Act. http://www.dol.gov/odep/topics/ADA.htm. Accessed May 6, 2015.

American Sport Education Program [now Human Kinetics Coach Education]. 2010. Overview. www.asep.com/overview.cfm. Accessed July 10, 2010.

American Sportscasters Association. 2009. ASA names "Top 15 Women Sportscasters," Visser voted no. 1. www.americansportscastersonline.com/top15womensportscasters.html. Accessed June 19, 2010.

American Sports Data. 2005. *American team sports: A status report.* Hartsdale, NY: SGMA.

Amick, S. 2014. NBA teams struggle with religion, prayer as sensitive topic may unify or divide players. Huffington Post. www.huffingtonpost.com/2014/05/06/nba-religion-prayer_n_5275096.html. Accessed May 13, 2014.

Amr, H. 2008. The Muslim Olympics? www.brookings.edu/research/opinions/2008/0828-muslim-olympics. Accessed July 16, 2010.

Anastasio, D. 2000. *The pinky ball book.* New York: Workman.

Archdiocese of St. Louis. 2011. Random acts of sportsmanship recognized www.archstl.org/node/4328727. Accessed February 14, 2014.

Ariss, J. 2000. Sportsmanship. Reprint from *Touching Base Magazine.* www.slopitch.info/library/sportsmanship.htm. Accessed May 10, 2004.

Ashe, A., Jr. 1977. An open letter to black parents: Send your children to the libraries. *New York Times*, February 6, section 5.

Ashe A, Jr., and Rampersad, A. 1994. *Days of grace.* New York, NY: Balantine.

———. 1988. *A hard road to glory.* New York: Warner Books.

Aspen Institute. 2014. Project play: Facts: Sports Activity and Children. www.aspenprojectplay.org/the-facts. Accessed May 6, 2015.

Assibey-Mensah, G. 1997. Role models and youth development: Evidence and lessons from the perceptions of African-American male youth. *Western Journal of Black Studies* 21 (4): 242.

Associated Press. 2006. Mediation unsuccessful in Penn State bias lawsuit against coach. *USA Today*, May 15. www.usatoday.com/sports/college/womensbasketball/bigten/2006-05-15-psu-mediation_x.htm. Accessed June 1, 2006.

———. 2006c. Penn State coach accuses group of trying to exploit bias case. *USA Today*, May 18. www.usatoday.com/sports/college/womensbasketball/bigten/2006-05-18-portland_x.htm. Accessed June 1, 2006.

———. 2009. Alcohol-related rowdiness spawns tests. http://sports.espn.go.com/ncf/news/story?id=4485528. Accessed October 26, 2009.

———. 2013. NFL, ex-players agree to $765M settlement in concussions suit. www.nfl.com/news/story/0ap1000000235494/printable/nfl-expla. Accessed May 22, 2014.

———. 2014a. Holdsclaw pleads guilty to charges. www.foxsports.com/wcbk/story/chamique-holdsclaw-pleads-guilty-to-charges-in-assault-case-061413?ocid=ansfox11. Accessed January 15, 2015.

———. 2014b. Judge sends "cowards" to prison for near-fatal beating of Giants fan Bryan Stow. www.nydailynews.com/sports/baseball/prison-cowards-beat-giants-fan-death-article-1.1621252. Accessed May 21, 2014.

———. 2014c. Ray Rice wins appeal, suspension vacated immediately. http://huffingtonpost.com/2014/11/28/ray-rice_n_6237962.html. Accessed January 15, 2015.

Association for Women in Sports Media. 2014. About Association for Women in Sports Media. http://awsmonlin.org/about/. Accessed April 28, 2015.

Athletes in Action. 2014. About us. www.athletesinaction.org/discover/about. Accessed January 11, 2015.

August, H. 2004. Many Elis break from norm, lean right. *Yale Daily News*, November 11. www.yaledailynews.com/ article.asp?AID=27281. Accessed January 29, 2005.

Auman, G. 2004. Muslim basketball player quits USF team. *St. Petersburg Times*. www.sptimes.com/2004/09/16/Sports/Muslim_basketball_pla.shtml. Accessed January 24, 2014.

Azanian, M. 2014. The NFL's most valuable teams. www.forbes.com/sites/mikeozanian/2014/08/20/the-nfls-most. Accessed November 20, 2014.

Bacon, J. 2013. *Fourth and long: The fight for the soul of college football.* Simon and Schuster. New York.

Badenhausen, K. 2011. The NFL signs TV deals worth $27 billion. www.forbes.com/sites/kurtbadenhausen/2011/12/14/the-nfl-signs-tv-deals-worth-26-billion. Accessed December 16, 2014.

———. 2012a. Is Cristiano Ronaldo the world's most marketable athlete? www.forbes.com/sites/kurtbadenhausen/2012/07/11/is-cristiano-ronaldo-the-worlds-most-marketable-athlete/. Accessed January 25, 2014.

———. 2012b. Why ESPN is worth $40 billion as the world's most valuable media property. www.forbes.com/sites/kurtbadenhausen/2012/11/09/why-espn-is-the-worlds-most-valuable-media-property-and-worth-40-billion. Accessed December 24, 2014.

———. 2013. Tiger is back as top-paid sports star. www.forbes.com/sites/kurtbadenhausen/2013/06/05/tiger-woods-is-back-on-top-of-the-worlds-highest-paid-athletes. Accessed June 26, 2013.

———. 2014a. The world's highest paid female athletes 2014. www.forbes.com/sites/kurtbadenhausen/2014/08/12/the-worlds-highest-paid-female-athletes-2014/. Accessed January 6, 2015.

———. 2014b. The value of ESPN surpasses $50 billion. *Forbes* www.forbes.com/sites/kurtbadenhausen/2014/04/29/the-value-of-espn-surpasses-50-billion/. Accessed May 29, 2015.

Bahri, C. 2005. Spearheading the empowerment of Muslim women. www.happynews.com/news/1172005/spearheading-the-empowerment.htm. Accessed May 24, 2006.

Baldor, L. 2014. "Culture of disrespect" fuels academy sex assaults. Associated Press. http://gazette.com/culture-of-disrespect-fuels-military-academy-sex-assaults/article/1512336. Accessed January 9, 2014.

Ball, D., and Loy, J. 1975. *Sport and social order: Contributions to the sociology of sport.* Reading, MA: Addison-Wesley.

Ballparks. 2006a. Bank of America Stadium. http://football.ballparks.com/NFL/CarolinaPanthers/index.htm. Accessed August 30, 2010.

———. 2006b. Gillette Stadium. http://football.ballparks.com/NFL/NewEnglandPatriots/newindex.htm. Accessed August 30, 2010.

Balyi, J., Way, R., Norris, S., Cardinal, C., and Higgs, C. 2005. Canadian sport for life: Long-term athlete development resource paper. Vancouver, BC: Canadian Sport Centres. http://canadiansportforlife.ca/sites/default/files/user_files/files/CS4L%202_0%20EN_Jan17_web%20FINAL.pdf. Accessed October 18, 2010.

Banned Substances Control Group (BSCG). 2015. Don Catlin, M.D. BSCG Chief Science Officer and Co-founder. www.bscg.org/don-catlin-md-cso-co-founder/. Accessed January 18, 2015.

Barber, B., Eccles, J., and Stone, M. 2001. Whatever happened to the jock, the brain, and the princess? Young adult pathways linked to adolescent activity involvement and social identity. *Journal of Adolescent Research* 16 (5): 429–55.

Barmasse, J. 2014. How much value does a postseason appearance hold for MLB franchises? http://thefieldsofgreen.com/2014/10/02/how-much-value-does-a-postseason-appearance-hold-for-mlb-franchises/. Accessed November 25, 2014.

Basichis, G. 2010. Florida youth sports coaches to require background checks. http://dailyplanet.corragroup.com/2010/04/florida-youth-sports-coaches-to-require-background-checks. Accessed July 23, 2010.

BBC Sport. 2005. Miller "surprised" EPO is illegal. http://news.bbc.co.uk/sport2/hi/other_sports/winter_sports/4334612.stm. Accessed June 1, 2006.

Bearak, B. 2012. Women finally get their chance to be contenders in Olympic boxing. *New York Times*. www.nytimes.com/2012/08/06/sports/olympics/women-participate-in-olympic-boxing-for-first-time.html. Accessed September 3, 2013.

Beaujon, A. 2013. *New York Times* passes *USA Today* in daily circulation. Poynter, April 30. www.poynter.org/news/mediawire/211994/new-york-times-passes-usa-today-in-daily-circulation. Accessed December 24, 2013.

Beller J., and Stoll, S. 2009. Hahm-Beller Values Choice Inventory (HBVCI).paragraph 1.9. www.webpages.uidaho.edu/center_for_ethics/Measurements/HBVCI/hbvci.htm. University of Idaho Center of Ethics. Moscow, ID. Accessed May 6, 2015.

Beller, J., and Stoll, S. 1994. Sport participation and its effect on moral reasoning of high school student athletes and general students. *Research Quarterly for Exercise and Sport* Supplement 65 (March). A-95.

Benedict, J., and Keteyian, A. 2013. *The system: The glory and scandal of big-time college football.* New York: Random House.

Benedict, J., and Yaeger, D. 1998. *Pros and cons: The criminals who play in the NFL.* New York: Warner Books.

Bennett, R. 2014. MLS equals MLB in popularity with kids. www.espnfc.com/story/1740529. Accessed June 4, 2014.

Bennett, S. 2015. The 20 most popular brands on #Twitter. www.adweek.com/socialtimes/top-brands-twitter-060215/614504. Accessed June 18, 2015.

Bentley, A. 2014. Native Americans in pro sports. http://blog.nrcprograms.org/native-americans-in-pro-sports. Accessed January 2, 2015.

Bentley, K. 2012. Fairness in the 2012 Olympics: Women's boxing added to maintain equality. http://voices.yahoo.com/fairness-2012-olympics-womens-boxing-added. Accessed September 3, 2013.

Best, C. 1987. Experience and career length in professional football: The effects of positional segregation. *Sociology of Sport Journal* 7 (4): 410–20.

Best, N. 2014. NBC releases Winter Olympics ratings data. www.newsday.com/sports/olympics/nbc-release-sochi-winter. Accessed December 17, 2014.

Birrell, S. 2004. Feminist theories for sport. In *Handbook of sports studies*, ed. J. Coakley and E. Dunning, 61–75. London: Sage.

Bishop, G. 2013. With simple protest, players join push for NCAA reform. *New York Times*. www.nytimes.com/2013/09/25/sports/ncaafootball/with-simple-protest-players-join-push-for-ncaa-reform.html?_r=0. Accessed January 14, 2014.

Bissinger, H. 1990. *Friday night lights*. New York: Da Capo Press.

Blodget, H. 2012. Don't mean to be alarmist, but the TV business may be starting to collapse. *Business Insider*. www.businessinsider.com/tv-business-collapse-2012. Accessed December 17, 2014.

Blumenfeld, M. 2013. Forbes: Phil Mickelson wins first British Open, incurs 61% tax rate. www.atr.org/forbes-phil-mickelson-wins-first-british-a7773. Accessed July 28, 2013.

Blumstein, A., and Benedict, J. 1999. Criminal violence of NFL players compared to the general population. *Chance* 12 (3): 12-15.

Booth, D., and Loy, J. 1999. Sport, status, and style. *Sport History Review* 30 (1): 1–26.

Borzilleri, M.J. 2003. USOC targets positions, pay raises. *The Gazette* (Colorado Springs, CO), June 11.

Bowen, W., and Levin, S. 2003. *Reclaiming the game: College sports and educational values*. Princeton, NJ: Princeton University Press.

Bowles, W., and Jenson, M. 2001. Cultural capital. www.williambowles.info/mimo/refs/tece1ef.htm. Accessed January 1, 2006.

Bowman, J. 2012. Are there women's basketball programs that outdraw men's basketball? www.swishappeal.com/2012/11/21/3659730/ncaa-womens-basketball. Accessed January 5, 2015.

Boxill, J., Glanville, D., and Murray, T. 2011. What sport means in America: A study of sport's role in society. *International Sport Coaching Journal* 4 (Spring): 2–45.

Bradford, M. 2014. Geno, a leader; Muffet, a manager: Two top coaches with very different coaching styles. www.fullcourt.com/ncaa/24805/geno-leader-muffet-manager-two-top-coaches-very-different-coaching-styles. Accessed November 30, 2014.

Bradstreet, K. 2013. New women's sports channel to feature 100% female athlete coverage. http://business.transworld.net/126524/news/new-womens-sports-channel-to-feature-100-female-athlete-coverage/. Accessed January 2, 2014.

Brady, E., and Giler, R. 2004a. In a lot of cases, they have no other choice. *USA Today*, July 3.

———. 2004b. To play sports, many U.S. students must pay. http://usatoday30.usatoday.com/sports/preps/2004-07-29-pay-to-play_x.htm#. Accessed May 7, 2015.

Brady, E., and Sylwester, M. 2004. Trends in girls' sports. *USA Today*, June 17.

Brault, M. 2012. Americans with disabilities: 2010. Household economic studies. Current population reports. www.census.gov/prod/2012pubs/p70-131.pdf. Accessed May 29, 2015.

Braverman, S. 2011. No surprise: 64% of Americans watch NFL football; 73% of men and 55% of women. Harris Poll #108. October 14. vbythenumbers.zap2it.com/2011/10/14/no-surprise-64-americans-watch-nfl-football-73-of-men-55-of-women/107308/k. Accessed May 7, 2015.

Bredemeier, B., and Shields, D. 2006. Sports and character development. President's Council on Physical Fitness and Sports. *Research Digest*, March, series 7, number 1.

Brennan, D. 2001. Sanctity of sport. www.tothenextlevel.org. Accessed October 30, 2004.

Breslow, J. 2014. The NFL's concussion problem still has not gone away. *Frontline*. www.pbs.org/wgbh/pages/frontline/sports/concussion-watch/the-nfls-concussion-problem-still-has-not-gone-away/. Accessed May 7, 2015.

Briggs, D. 2013. The Final Four, travel teams, and empty pews: Who is winning the competition between sports and religion? www.huffingtonpost.com/david-briggs/final-four-travel-teams-and-empty-pews-who-is-winning-the-competition-between-sports-and-religion_b_3006988.html. Accessed January 11, 2015.

Brigham Young University. 2015. Mission statement. The official site of BYU athletics. http://byucougars.com/athletics/mission-statement. Accessed June 1, 2015.

Brinson, W. 2013. Frontline PBS doc "League of Denial" examines NFL concussion problem. www.cbssports.com/nfl/eye-on-football/24051122/frontline-pbs-doc-league-of-denial-examines-nfl-concussion-problem. Accessed January 13, 2015.

Brooks, D. 2012. The Jeremy Lin problem. www.nytimes.com/2012/02/12/opinion/brooks-the-jeremy-lin-problem. Accessed January 22, 2015.

Brown, M. 2001. The shoe's on the other foot. http://healthlibrary.epnet.com/GetContent.aspx?token=af362d974f80-4453-a175-02cc6220. Accessed June 8, 2006.

Bruce, T. 2000. Never let the bastards see you cry. *Sociology of Sports Journal* 17 (1): 69–74.

Bunker, L. 1988. Lifelong benefits of youth sport participation for girls and women. Speech presented at the Sport Psychology Conference, University of Virginia, Charlottesville.

Burnett, D. 2005. Sportsmanship checklists and information for kids. www.printablechecklists.com/checklist38.shtml. Accessed October 18, 2010.

Butler, J., and Lopiano, D. 2003. The Women's Sports Foundation report: Title IX and race in intercollegiate sport. New York: Women's Sports Foundation.

Butler, S. 2011. $4,000 for youth baseball: Kids' sports costs are out of control. www.cbsnews.com/news/4000-for-youth-baseball-kids-sports-costs-are-out-of-control/. Accessed April 26, 2014.

Cantu, Robert. 2012. *Concussions and our kids*. New York: Houghton Mifflin Harcourt.

Carlson, D., and Scott, L. 2005. What is the status of high school athletes 8 years after their senior year? *Statistics in brief: National Center for Education Statistics*, 1–19. Washington, DC: U.S. Department of Education.

Carpenter, L., and Acosta, R. 2005. *Title IX*. Champaign, IL: Human Kinetics.

Carter, R. 2005. Ashe's impact reached far beyond the court. SportsCentury biography. http://espn.go.com/classic/biography/s/Ashe_Arthur.html. Accessed August 15, 2010.

Cary, P. 2004. Fixing kids' sports: Rescuing children's games from crazed coaches and parents. *U.S. News and World Report*, June 7.

Cauchon, D. 2005. Childhood pastimes are increasingly moving indoors. *USA Today*, August 12.

———. 2009. Women gain as men lose jobs. *USA Today*, September 2.

Caulfield, B. 2011. 1.2 million fewer American households own a television. www.forbes.com/sites/briancaulfield/2011/05/03/1.2-million-americans-households-just-killed-their-television/. Accessed December 23, 2014.

CBS News. 2009. Delaware sports betting dealt legal blow. August 31. www.cbsnews.com/stories/2009/08/31/sportsline/main5277188.shtml. Accessed November 13, 2009.

CBS News. 2012. How much are Olympic medals actually worth? www.cbsnews.com/news/how-much-are-olympic-medals-actually. Accessed May 3, 2015.

Centers for Disease Control and Prevention. 2014. Childhood obesity facts. www.cdc.gov/healthyyouth/obesity/facts.htm. Accessed November 26, 2014.

———. 2015. How much physical activity do adults need? www.cdc.gov/physicalactivity/basics/adults/index.htm. Accessed July 5, 2015.

Chaddock, G. 2003. U.S. notches world's highest incarceration rate. *Christian Science Monitor*, August 18.

Chatel, A. 2011. There's no crying in baseball: The sports world needs more women executives. www.thegrindstone.com/2011/05/14/career/theres-no-crying-in-baseball/. Accessed February 12, 2014.

Chemi, E. 2014. The NFL is growing only because of women. *Business Week*. www.bloomberg.com/bw/articles/2014-09-26/the-nfl-is-growing-only-because-of-female-fans. Accessed May 7, 2015.

Cheredar, T. 2014. Following HBO & CBS, Starz may launch a standalone online TV service. http://venturebeat.com/2014/10/30/following-hbo-cbs-starz-may-launch. Accessed December 25, 2014.

Cherner, R. 2005. If you billed it around faith, they will certainly come. *USA Today*, July 22.

Chi, S. 2014. Asian grip on women's golf slips. http://thediplomat.com/2014/06/asian-grip-on-womens-golf-slips/. Accessed January 1, 2015.

Citizenship Through Sports Alliance. 2005. 2005 youth sports national report card. www.shapeamerica.org/publications/resources/teachingtools/coachtoolbox/upload/TACE_NationalGrades05.pdf. Accessed May 7, 2015.

CNN Sports Illustrated. 2001. Jury rules for NFL. http://sportsillustrated.cnn.com/. Accessed May 22, 2001.

Coakley, J. 2004. *Sports in society*. 8th ed. New York: McGraw-Hill.

———. 2010. The "logic" of specialization. *Journal of Physical Education Recreation* 81 (8): 16–25. http://dx.doi.org/10.1080/07303084.2010.10598520. Accessed January 4, 2014.

Coakley, J., and Donnelly, P., eds. 1999. *Inside sports*. London: Routledge.

Coakley, J., and Dunning, E., eds. 2004. *Handbook of sports studies*. London: Sage.

College Sports Information Directors of America (CoSIDA). 2001. Over 200 women sign up as members of Female Athletic Media Relations Executives (FAME). *CoSIDA Digest*, April.

Colorado High School Activities Association (CHSAA). 2014. Game management and sportsmanship expectation guide. www2.chsaa.org/activities/sportsmanship/pdf/Sportsmanship_Manual.pdf. Accessed December 20, 2014.

Condor, R. 2004. Living well: When coaches and parents put too much emphasis on winning, kids drop out. *Post-Intelligencer* (Seattle, WA), September 30.

Cook, B. 2013. Baseball's lack of black players reflects flawed U.S. youth development system. www.forbes.com/sites/bobcook/2013/04/10/baseballs-lack-of-black-players-reflects-flawed-u-s-youth-development-system. Accessed November 27, 2014.

Cooky, C., Messner, M., and Hextrum, R. 2013. Women play sport, but not on TV: A longitudinal study of televised news media. *Communication and Sport*. http://connection.sagepub.com/blog/2013/08/14/women's-sport-covering. Accessed January 1, 2014.

Crain, W. 1985. *Theories of development*, 118-136. Englewood Cliffs, NJ: Prentice Hall.

Cronin, M. 2013. Open women's final scores higher TV ratings than men's final. www.tennis.com/pro-game/2013/09/us-open-womens-final-score-better-tv-ratings-men/49130/#.VQo3CmctH6U. Accessed January 4, 2015.

Crosset, T. 1999. What do we know and what can we do about male athletes' violence against women: A critical assessment of the athletic affiliation and violence against women debate. *Quest*, August.

Crosset, T., Benedict, J., and McDonald, M. 1995. Male student-athletes reported for sexual assault: Survey of campus police departments and judicial affairs offices. *Journal of Sport and Social Issues* 19 (2): 126–40.

C.S. Mott Children's Hospital. 2012. Pay-to-play sports keeping lower-income kids out of the game. *National Poll on Children's Health* 15 (3), May 14.

Culverhouse, G. 2011. *Throwaway players: Concussion crisis from Pee Wee football to the NFL*. Behler Pub: Burlington, Iowa.

Cummings, D. 2009. Beijing's empty venues reveal heavy cost of Olympics. www.findingdulcinea.com/news/sports/2009/feb/Beijing-s-Empty-Venues-Reveal-Heavy-Cost-of-Olympics.html. Accessed October 18, 2010.

Curnutte, M. 2007. Financial gap widening between NFL's haves and have-nots. http://usatoday30.usatoday.com/sports/football/nfl/2007-02-25-financial-gap_x.htm. Accessed May 7, 2015.

Daily Mail. 2010. Caster Semenya finally proves she's woman enough to run after 11-month gender row. www.dailymail.co.uk/sport/othersports/article-1292473/Caster-Semenya-set-athletics-return-following-gender-row.html. Accessed August 10, 2010.

Davies, A. 2013. Why has coverage of women's sport stopped post Olympics? www.cnn.com/2013/08/07/sport/olympics-women-equality-attar. Accessed February 1, 2014.

Dawes, M. 2013. Entire board of Jamaican anti-doping body RESIGN amid sprinters drug scandal. *Mail Online*. www.dailymail.co.uk/sport/othersports/article-2512204/Jamaican-anti-doping-body-board-resign-amid-drug-furore.html. Accessed May 26, 2014.

Deans, J. 2010. Super Bowl ends MASH finale's 27-year reign as most-watched US TV show. www.theguardian.com/media/2010/fe/08/super-bowl-most-watched-show. Accessed December 23, 2014.

Deford, F. 1976. Religion in sport. *Sports Illustrated*, April 19, 92-99.

DeMarzo, J. 2013. How Richie Incognito became the NFL's No. 1 villain. www.nypost.com/2013/11/05/how-richie-incognito-became-nfls-no-1-villain/. Accessed May 21, 2014.

Desilver, D. 2014. For most workers, real wages have barely budged for decades. www.pewresearch.org/fact-tank/2014/10/09/for-most-workers-real-wages-have-barely-budged-for-decades/. Accessed June 18, 2015.

Deutsche Welles. 2005. Referee scandal threatens Germany's World Cup. January 24. www.dw-world.de/dw/article/0,1564,1467560,00.html. Accessed January 31, 2005.

Didziulis, V. 2010. What does the future hold for U.S. soccer? www.poder360.com/article_detail.php?id_article=4439. Accessed August 1, 2010.

Dixon, A. 2014. Roller derby rolls on. *Herald-Sun* (Durham, NC). www.heraldsun.com/news/localnews/x143265713/Roller-derby-rolls-on. Accessed January 6, 2015.

Dixon, N. 2010. A critique of violent retaliation in sport. *Journal of the Philosophy of Sport* 37 (1): 1–10.

Dodds, T. 2000. Opening minds no harder than opening doors. *American Editor*, January–February.

Donnelly, P. 2004. Interpretive approaches to the sociology of sport. In *Handbook of sports studies*, ed. J. Coakley and E. Dunning, 77–91. London: Sage.

Dooley, S., and Effron, L. 2014. Steubenville, Ohio high school student convicted of rape released. http://abcnews.go.com/US/steubenville-ohio-high-school-student-convicted-rape-released/story?id=21435713. Accessed January 14, 2015.

Doraiswamy, S. 2012. Gambling addiction: A lesser-known college health issue. www.mindthesciencegap.org/2012/11/12/gambling-addictions-a-lesser-known-college-health-issue/. Accessed January 17, 2015.

Drake Group. 2009. Proposals. www.thedrakegroup.org/proposals.html. Accessed August 15, 2010.

Dubner, S. 2007. NFL vs. MLB as a labor market: A freakonomics quorum. http://freakonomics.blogs.nytimes.com/2007/11/28/nfl-vs-mlb-as-a-labor-market-a-freakonomics-quorum/. Accessed June 14, 2010.

Duncan, M., and Messner, M. 2005. Gender in televised sports: News and highlights shows, 1989–2004. Amateur Athletic Foundation of Los Angeles. www.aafla.org/9arr/ResearchReports/tv2004.pdf. Accessed June 1, 2006.

Dunning, E. 1999. *Sport matters: Sociological studies of sport, violence, and civilization*. London: Routledge.

Dusenbery, M., and Lee, J. 2012. Charts: The state of women's athletics, 40 years after Title IX. *Mother Jones*. www.motherjones.com/politics/2012/06/charts-womens-athletics-title-nine-ncaa. Accessed February 13, 2014.

Dworkin, J., Larson, R., and Hansen, D. 2003. Adolescents' accounts of growth experiences in youth activities. *Journal of Youth and Adolescence* 32 (1): 17–36.

Edelman, M. 2012. Why an NCAA cap on college coaches' salaries would be illegal. www.forbes.com/sites/marcedelman/2012/12/19/why-a-salary-cap-on-ncaa-coaches-is-illegal/. Accessed October 25, 2013.

Edwards, H. 1973. *Sociology of sports*, 63–69, appendix A. Homewood, IL: Dorsey Press.

Edwards, J. 2013. TV is dying, and here are the stats that prove it. *Business Insider*. www.businessinsider.com/cord-cutters-and-the death-of-tv-2013-11-24. Accessed December 23, 2014.

Eitzen, S. 1992, December. Sports and ideological contradictions: Learning from the cultural framing of soviet values. *Journal of Sport and Social Issues* 16, 144-149.

Eitzen, S. 2003. *Fair or foul: Beyond the myths and paradoxes of sport*. 2nd ed. Lanham, MD: Rowman & Littlefield.

———. 2004. Social control in sport. In *Handbook of sports studies*, ed. J. Coakley and E. Dunning, 370–81. London: Sage.

Eitzen, S., and Sage, G. 1978. *Sociology of American sport*. Dubuque, IA: William C. Brown.

———. 2002. *Sociology of North American sport*. 7th ed. Boston: McGraw-Hill.

Elias, N., and Dunning, E. 1986. *Quest for excitement: Sport and leisure in the civilising process*. Oxford: Blackwell.

Engwall, D., Hunter, R., and Steinberg, M. 2004, May-June. Gambling and other risky behaviors on university campuses. *Journal of American College Health* 52 (6), 245-255.

Entine, J. 2000. *Taboo: Why black athletes dominate sports and why we're afraid to talk about it*. New York: Public Affairs.

———. 2004. Sport and Ethnicity 2. Is your sporting talent predetermined by your ancestry? *Peak Performance*. www.pponline.co.uk/encyc/0657b.htm. Accessed May 7, 2015.

Epstein, D. 2013. *The sports gene: Inside the science of extraordinary athletic performance*. New York: Penguin.

Ericsson, K.A. 2012. Training history, deliberate practice, and elite sports performance: An analysis in response to Tucker and Collins review—What makes champions? *British Journal of Sports Medicine* 47: 533–35.

ESPN. 1999. Wilt spoke of regrets, women and meadowlark. ESPN.com, October 13. http://espn.go.com/nba/news/1999/1012/110905.html. Accessed May 10, 2005.

ESPN. 2007. Mitchell report: Baseball slow to react to players' steroid use. http://sports.espn.go.com/mlb/news/story?id=3153509. Accessed May 26, 2014.

———. 2009. New Mexico player banned, apologizes. http://sports.espn.go.com/ncaa/news/story?id=4629837. Accessed July 26, 2010.

———. 2010. 46 coaches on banned list. http://sports.espn.go.com/oly/swimming/news/story?id=5220940. Accessed October 19, 2010.

———. 2013a. David Stern: NBA revenue up to $5B. http://espn.go.com/nba/story/_/id/8629046/david-stern-estimates-nba. Accessed June 25, 2013.

———. 2013b. Player salaries and team payroll. http://espn.go.com/mlb/team/salaries/_/name/nyy/. Accessed November 23, 2013.

———. 2013c. Yankees hit with $28M luxury tax. http://espn.go.com/espn/print?id=10154043&type-HeadlineNew&ima. Accessed November 20, 2014.

———. 2014a. London 2012 Olympics: Medal tracker—Overall. http://espn.go.com/olympics/summer/2012/medals. Accessed December 20, 2014.

———. 2014b. MLB ups length of drug-use bans. March 28. http://espn.go.com/espn/print?id=10690127&type=HeadlineNews&image. Accessed May 27, 2014.

———. 2014c. Sochi 2014 Olympics: Medal tracker—Overall. http://espn.go.com/olympics/winter/2014/medals. Accessed December 20, 2014.

———. 2014d. Solo domestic abuse charges dropped. http://espn.go.com/espnw/news-commentary/article/12162480/hope-solo. Accessed January 15, 2015.

———. 2014e. Tour money leaders (PGA and LPGA). http:espn.go.com/golf/moneylist/_/year/2014. Accessed January 1, 2015.

ESPN MediaZone. 2013. Hannah Storm. http://espnmediazone.com/us/storm_hannah/. Accessed January 2, 2014.

Ewing, M., and Seefeldt, V. 1990. *American youth and sports participation*. Lansing: Institute for the Study of Youth Sports at Michigan State University.

Fainaru, S., and Fainaru-Wada, M. 2013. Youth football participation drops. http://espn.go.com/espn/print?id=9970532&typc=story. Accessed November 14, 2013.

Fainaru-Wada, M., and Fainaru, S. 2013. *League of denial: The NFL, concussions, and the battle for truth.* New York: Random House.

Fanbay. 2005. Women at the Olympics. www.fanbay.net/olympics/women.htm. Accessed September 25, 2005.

Fantasy Sports Trade Association (FSTA). 2013. Industry demographics. www.fsta.org/?page=Demographics. Accessed May 7, 2015.

Farhl, P. 2014. Did the Winter Olympics in Sochi really cost $50 billion? A closer look at that figure. www.washingtonpost.com/lifestyle/style/did-the-winter-olympics-in-sochi-really-cost-50-billion-a-closer-look-at-that-figure/2014/02/10/a29e37b4-9260-11e3-b46a-5a3d0d2130da_story.html. Accessed December 18, 2014.

Farnham, A. 2012. What's Phelps' medal worth? *ABC News*, August 1. http://abcnews.go.com/Sports/olympics/phelps-olympic-medal-worth/story?id=16898929. Accessed December 20, 2014.

Farrey, T. 2002. Sports hazing incidents. https://espn.go.com/otl/hazing/list.html. Accessed June 16, 2015.

Feigen, J. 2008. Artest: I'm excited about joining Rockets—If Yao wants me. *Houston Chronicle.* July 31, 2008. www.chron.com/sports/rockets/article/Artest-I-m-excited-about-joining-Rockets-if-1765069.php. Accessed December 31, 2013.

Fejgin, N. 1994. Participation in high school competitive sports: A subversion of school mission or contribution to academic goals? *Sociology of Sport Journal* 11 (3): 211–30.

Fellowship of Christian Athletes. 2015. About FCA. www.fca.org/about-fellowship-of-christian-athletes/mission-and-vision/. Accessed May 7, 2015.

Financial Underdog. 2014. How much money do Olympic athletes earn by competing? http://moneyramblings.com/money-olympic-athletes-earn/. Accessed December 20, 2014.

Finch, C. 2013. What is the average amount of money a professional soccer player makes in a year? http://everydaylife.globalpost.com/average-amount-money-professional-soccer-player-per-year-35008.html. Accessed January 5, 2015.

Fine, G. 1987. *With the boys: Little League baseball and preadolescent culture.* Chicago: University of Chicago Press.

Finger, R. 2013. Online gambling: A pastime whose time has come. www.forbes.com/site/richardfinger/2013/06/30/online-gambling. Accessed December 14, 2014.

First basket, The: A Jewish basketball documentary. 2008. www.thefirstbasket.com. Accessed October 2, 2010.

First Tee, The. 2010. The First Tee life skills experience. www.thefirsttee.org/club/scripts/view/view_insert.asp?IID=158931&NS=PUBLIC&APP=106. Accessed May 7, 2015.

Fischer-Baum, R. 2012. Watch as America's stadiums pile up on the backs of taxpayers through the years. http://deadspin.com/5964116/animated-infographic-watch-as-americas-stadiums-pile-up-on-the-backs-of-taxpayers. December 4. Accessed November 21, 2014.

Fish, M. 2009. Donaghy accused of probation violation. ESPN NBA. http:/sports.espn.go.com/nba/news/story?id=4420908. Accessed November 13, 2009.

Florida Council on Compulsive Gambling. 2008. Gambling and problem gambling prevalence among college students in Florida. www.gamblinghelp.org/assets/research_pdfs/Gambling_and_Problem_Gambling_Prevalence_Among_College_Students_in_Florida.pdf. Accessed January 13, 2015.

Football Educator. 2014. College football recruiting violations—Collegiate sports' skeletons in the closet revealed. www.thefootballeducator.com/college-football-recruiting-violations. Accessed December 11, 2014.

Forbes. 2013. How the National Football League can reach $25 billion in annual revenues. www.forbes.com/sites/monteburke/2013/08/17/how-the-national-football-league-can reach-25-billion. Accessed November 20, 2014.

———. 2014a. Footwear offers opportunity for brand consolidation for Under Armour. www.forbes.com/sites/greatspeculations/2014/06/13/footwear-offers-opportunity-for-brand-consolidation-for-under-armour/. Accessed December 16, 2014.

———. 2014b. The world's highest paid athletes. www.forbes.com/athletes/list/tab:overall. Accessed January 5, 2015.

Fottrell, Q. 2014. More women are quitting the workforce. MarketWatch, October 3. www.marketwatch.com/story/more-women-are-quitting-the-workforce-2014-10-03. Accessed January 3, 2015.

Fox. 2015. Timeline: The murder investigation surrounding Aaron Hernandez. www.myfoxboston.com/story/22698193/timeline-the-murder-investigation-surrounding-aaron-hernandez. Accessed June 10, 2015.

Fox News Latino. 2014. U.S. goalie Tim Howard delivers World Cup performance for ages, becomes national hero. http://latino.foxnews.com/latino/sports/2014/07/02/goalie-tim-howard-turns-in-world-cup-performance-for-ages-but-cant-save-us/. Accessed November 26, 2014.

Fox Sports. 2014. Ex-Miami booster alleges extra benefits. June 6. www.foxsports.com/collegefootball/story/Report-Former-Miami-booster-Nevin-Shapiro-gave-impermissible-benefits-to-Miami-athletes-081611. Accessed December 11, 2014.

Franchise Times. 2014. Book of brands. Welcyon, Fitness after 50. www.franchisetimes.com/Franchise-Opportunities/index.php/name/Welcyon-Fitness-After-50/listing/63696/. Accessed May 7, 2015.

Frank, R. 2004. Challenging the myth: A review of the links among college athletic success, student quality, and donations. Report to the Knight Commission on Intercollegiate Athletics. www.knightcommission.org/index.php?option=com_content&view=article&id=73&Itemid=4. Accessed October 19, 2010.

Fraser-Thomas, J., and Cote, J. 2006. Youth sports: Implementing findings and moving forward with research. *Athletic Insight: The Online Journal of Sport Psychology.* www.athleticinsight.com/Vol8Iss3/YouthSports.htm. Accessed January 3, 2014.

Fraser-Thomas, J., Cote, J., and Deakin, J. 2008. Examining adolescent sport dropout and prolonged engagement from a developmental perspective. *Journal of Applied Sport Psychology* 20: 318–22.

Frey, W. 2010. Race and ethnicity. *State of metropolitan America: On the front lines of demographic transformation*, 50–63. Washington, DC: Brookings Metropolitan Policy Program. www.brookings.edu/metro/MetroAmericaChapters/race.aspx. Accessed October 18, 2010.

Friedman, D. 2012. Social media in sports: Can professional sports league commissioners punish "twackle dummies"? *Pace Intellectual Property, Sports, and Entertainment Law Forum* 4 (2). http://digitalcommons.pace.edu/pipself/vol2/iss1/3/. Accessed December 24, 2014.

Friedman, H. 2013a. Do your kids need more competitive capital? https://hbr.org/2013/09/do-your-kids-need-more-competi/. Accessed January 3, 2014.

———. 2013b. When did competitive sports take over American childhood? *Atlantic* www.theatlantic.com/education/archive/2013/09/when-did-competitive-sports-take-over-american-childhood/279868/. Accessed January 3, 2014.

Frommer, F. 2009. Delaware sports betting dealt legal blow. Associated Press. www.cbsnews.com/stories/2009/08/31/sportsline/main5277188.shtml. Accessed November 13, 2009.

Fullerton, R. 2003. Watching the pros vs. playing the game: How sports coverage affects community-level athletes. www.cces.ca/pdfs/CCES-PAPERSum-Smith-Fullerton-E.pdf. Accessed June 1, 2006.

Gaines, C. 2013. Chart: The average University of Texas football player worth $578,000. September 23. www.businessinsider.com/chart-the-average-university-of-texas-football-player-is-worth-578000-2013-9. Accessed December 21, 2013.

———. 2014. The NFL makes $6 billion annually just from national television contracts. www.businessinsider.com/chart-national-tv-contracts-nfl-mlb-nba-nhl-2014-9. Accessed December 23, 2014.

Gale Group. 2010. Muhammad Ali. http://ic.galegroup.com/ic/bic1/ReferenceDetailsPage/ReferenceDetailsWindow?displayGroupName=K12-Reference&prodId=BIC1&action=2&catId=&documentId=GALE%7CK1607000293&userGroupName=tlc049072579&jsid=9e070d4d8525eac5019fe019367ed670. Accessed May 7, 2015.

Gallup. 2005. Six in 10 Americans are pro football fans. www.gallup.com/poll/14812/Six-Americans-Pro-Football-Fans.aspx. Accessed June 13, 2009.

Gallup Poll. 2013. Sports/Gallup historical trends. www.gallup.com/poll/4735/sports.aspx. Accessed April 23, 2015.

Ganim, S., and Sayers, D. 2014. UNC report finds 18 years of academic fraud to keep athletes playing. www.cnn.com/2014/10/22/us/unc-report-academic-fraud. Accessed December 11, 2014.

Garcia, C. 1994. Gender differences in young children's interactions when learning fundamental motor skills. *Research Quarterly for Exercise and Sport* 66 (3): 247–55.

Gargill, S., and Penn, N. 2006. The ten most hated athletes. *GQ*. www.gq.com/sports/profiles/200601/most-hates-athletes?printable=true. Accessed January 20, 2014.

Gasgreen, A. 2013. "The rise of women." www.insidehighered.com/news/2013/02/21/new-book-explains-why-women-outpace-men-education. Accessed January 13, 2014.

Geli, E. 2012. How to stop hazing. *Halftime*, January/February. http://halftimemag.com/articles/01-2012/01-2012-features/how-to-stop-hazing.html. Accessed May 28, 2015.

Genel, M. 2000. Gender verification no more? *Medscape Women's Health Journal*. http://ai.eecs.umich.edu/people/conway/TS/OlympicGenderTesting.html. Accessed October 19, 2010.

Gertz, S. 2004. Revisiting the pagan Olympic Games. *Christianity Today*, August 16. www.christianitytoday.com/ch/news/2004/aug19.html. Accessed October 19, 2010.

Gibbons, S., Ebbeck, V., and Weiss, M. 1995. Fair play for kids: Effects on the moral development of children in physical education. *Research Quarterly for Exercise and Sport* 66: 247–55.

Gibson, O. 2014. Luis Suarez banned for four months for biting in World Cup games. *Guardian*. www.theguardian.com/football/2014/jun/26/world-cup-luis-suarez-ban-biting-uruguay. Accessed January 13, 2015.

Gillian, B. 2014. Top 10 demographics and interests facts about Americans age 50+. AARP Notebook. htpp://blog.aarp.org/2014/05/14/top-10-demographics-interests-facts. Accessed January 8, 2015.

Girls in the Game. 2015. About us. www.girlsinthegame.org/content/index.asp?s=475&t=About-Us. Accessed June 4, 2015.

Gladwell, M. 2008. *Outliers: The story of success*. New York: Little, Brown.

Glass, A. 2013. Ernst and Young studies the connection between female executives and sports. www.forbes.com/sites/alanaglass/2013/06/24/ernst-young-studies-the-connection-between-female-executives-and-sports/. Accessed February 12, 2014.

Global Language Monitor. 2012. Olympic ambush marketers continue to dominate London 2012. www.languagemonitor.com/olympics/olympic-ambush-marketers-continue-to-dominate-london-2012/. Accessed December 20, 2014.

Global Sports Media. 2012. Consumption report 2012: A study of sports media consumption and performance in 10 international markets. www.iabuk.net/sites/default/files/research-docs/Great_Britain_EMAIL.pdf. Accessed December 17, 2014.

Global Sports Media. 2013. Consumption report 2014, U.S. overview. http://sportsvideo.org/main/files/2014/06/2014-Know-the-Fan-Study_US.pdf. Accessed February 23, 2015.

Golf Today. 2014. Big purses hurting PGA tour says golf agent. www.golftoday.com.uk/news/yeartodate/news04/pgatour2.html. Accessed January 6, 2015.

Goudreau, J. 2011. The secret to being a power woman: Play team sports. www.forbes.com/sites/jennagoudreau/2011/10/12/secret-power-woman-play-team-sports-sarah-palin-meg-whitman-indra-nooyi/. Accessed December 2, 2014.

Gould, D. 1993. Intensive sport participation and the prepubescent athlete: Competitive stress and burnout. In *Intensive participation in children's sports*, ed. B.R. Cahill and A. Pearl, 19–38. Champaign, IL: Human Kinetics.

Granderson, LZ. 2012. The political Michael Jordan. http://espn.go.com/nba/story/_/id/8264956/michael-jordan-obama-fundraiser-22-years-harvey-gantt. Accessed May 16, 2014.

Gray, R. 2012. Sexual assault statistics. *Campus Safety Magazine*. www.campussafetymagazine.com/article/Sexual-Assault-Statistics-and-Myths. Accessed January 14, 2015.

Green, L. 2013. The impact of professional and collegiate sports at the interscholastic level. www.linkedin.com/pub/lane-green/b5/b47/94a. Accessed May 22, 2015.

Gretz, A. 2012. Gary Bettman talks revenue, "modest drop" in concussions. www.cbssports.com/nhl/blog/eye-on-hockey/19206827/gary-bettman-talks-revenue. Accessed October 12, 2013.

Grey Matter Research and Consulting. 2012. Most Americans are comfortable with the intersection of religion and professional sports. www.greymatterresearch.com/index_files/Sports_and_Religion.htm. Accessed January 10, 2015.

Greyser, S., and Kogan, V. 2013. NBC and the 2012 London Olympics: Unexpected success. www.hbs.edu/faculty/Publication%20Files/14-028_99a0100c-7dcc-4fc4-bf29-6c0bd2f5561d.pdf. Accessed December 20, 2014.

Griffin, P. 1998. *Strong women, deep closets: Lesbians and homophobia in sports*. Champaign, IL: Human Kinetics.

Grohman, K. 2012. Testers nab more than 100 athletes—WADA. Reuters. http://ca.reuters.com/article/idCABRE86N1B520120724. Accessed May 20, 2014.

Gruneau, R. 1999. *Class, sports, and social development*. Champaign, IL: Human Kinetics.

Guardian. 2014. Olympics 2012: Sports hijabs help Muslim women to Olympic success. www.theguardian.com/sport/the-womens-blog-with-jane-martinson/2012/jul/23/sports-hijabs-muslim-women-olympics. Accessed May 13, 2014.

Gumpel, E. 2009. Two women make video game history. *Entrepreneur*. www.entrepreneur.com/article/217924. Accessed August 30, 2010.

Hackensmith, C. 1966. *History of physical education*. New York: Harper & Row.

Hadley, R. 2010. Another flock of NFL lambs could be headed to financial disaster in long term. www.standard.net/topics/sports/2010/04/28/another-flock-nfl-lambs-could-be-headed. Accessed April 20, 2010.

Hagar, R. 2014. Nevada legislator wants Bishop Gorman banned from football playoffs. http://usatodayhss.com/2014/nevada-legistlator-wants-bishop-gorman-banned-from-football-playoffs. Accessed January 11, 2015.

Handley, M. 2012. When it's right to punish football clubs for their fans' behaviour. www.huffingtonpost.co.uk/matthew-handley/egypt-football-riots-when-its-right-to-punish-clubs_b_1376918.html. Accessed June 13, 2015.

Hargreaves, J., and McDonald, I. 2004. Cultural studies and the sociology of sport. In *Handbook of sports studies*, ed. J. Coakley and E. Dunning, 48–60. London: Sage.

Harrell, E. 2009. South Africa slams Semenya's gender test. *Time*. www.time.com/time/printout/0,8816,1921847,00.html. Accessed September 24, 2009.

Harris Interactive. 2004. Trends and tudes. Vol. 3, Issue 9, September. www.harrisinteractive.com/news/newsletters_k12.asp. Accessed June 1, 2006.

Harris, K. 2004. Pro athletes get in the political game. Sun Sentinel (Fort Lauderdale, FL), October 29.

Harris Polls. 2015. Football's still doing the touchdown dance all over baseball's home plate. www.harrisinteractive.com/NewsRoom/HarrisPolls/tabid/447/mid/1508/articleId/1546/ctl/ReadCustom%20Default/Default.aspx. Accessed April 23, 2015.

Hartman, D. 2008. High school sports participation and educational attainment: Report to the LA84 Foundation. http://library.la84.org/3ce/HighSchoolSportsParticipation.pdf. Accessed February 12, 2014.

Harwell, D. 2014a. An empire built with hugs. *Tampa Bay Times*, January 4.

———. 2014b. Women are one of the sporting-goods industry's biggest-growing markets—and one of its most ignored. www.washingtonpost.com/news/business/wp/2014/10/14/a-12-y. Accessed January 4, 2015.

Hausmann, J. 2013. 10 NFL stars charged in awful crimes. http://heavy.com/news/2013/06/nfl-players-arrested-crimes-aaron. Accessed May 23, 2014.

Hawes, K. 1999. Women's sports enter NCAA arena. *NCAA News*, December 6. http://web1.ncaa.org/web_files/NCAANewsArchive/1999/19991206/active/3625n32.html. Accessed August 15, 2010.

———. 2001. Grant carried on the "idea" long after AIAW fell. *NCAA News*, May 21. http://web1.ncaa.org/web_files/NCAANewsArchive/2001/Association-wide/grant%2Bcarried%2Bon%2Bthe%2B_idea_%2Blong%2Bafter%2Baiaw%2Bfell%2B-%2B5-21-01.html. Accessed August 15, 2010.

Hechinger, F. 1980. About education. *New York Times*. February 19, 1980.

Hemery, D. 1986. *Sporting excellence, a study of sport's highest achievers*. London: Collins Sons.

Hersh, P. 2011. NBC will remain the Olympic network in the United States. http://articles.chicagotribune.com/2011-06-07/news/chi-nbc-will-remain-the-olympic-network-in-the-united-states-20110607_1_olympic-network-nbc-s-olympics-usoc-and-ioc. Accessed February 7, 2014.

Hershberger, M. 2014. 4 Theories on why Americans haven't adopted soccer like the rest of the world. http://matadornetwork.com/sports/4-theories-americans-havent-adopted-soccer-like-rest-world/. Accessed December 24, 2014.

Hirst, M. 2012. London 2012: How do the Olympics handle religion? www.bbc.com/news/uk-17515410. Accessed January 11, 2015.

Hoch, P. 1972. The world of playtime, USA. *Daily World*, April 27, 12.

Hoffman, P. 2013. A win for suffering greyhounds in Florida. www.care2.com/causes/a-win-for-suffering-greyhounds-in-florida.html. Accessed January 8, 2015.

Hoffman, S. 2013. *Introduction to kinesiology*. 4th ed. Champaign, IL: Human Kinetics.

Hoffman, S.J. 1992. *Sport and religion*. Champaign, IL: Human Kinetics.

Holbrook. J.E., and Barr, J. 1997. Contemporary coaching: Trends and Issues. Carmel, IN: Cooper.

Holland, S. 2014. Marketing to women quick facts. http://she-conomy.com/facts-on-women. Accessed January 4, 2014.

Holmes, L. 2012. ESPN's "Broke" looks at the many ways athletes lose their money. www.npr.org.blogs/monkeysee/2012/10/02/162162226/espns-broke. Accessed January 8, 2015.

Holway, L. 2005. A fight to the death: NCAA vs. AIAW. Unpublished manuscript. Bryn Mawr, PA: Bryn Mawr College.

Home Team Marketing. 2013. Why high school sports? High school: A better audience. www.hometeammarketing.com/wp-content/uploads/2013/07/high_school_sports_infographic.pdf. Accessed January 12, 2014.

Houston Chronicle. 2004. Marvelous messenger. www.chron.com/content/chronicle/sports/special/barriers/ashe.html. Accessed October 10, 2004.

Hruby, P. 2014. A search for answers. *Sports on Earth*. www.sportsonearth.com/article/66304992/. Accessed May 23, 2014.

Huff, D. 2005. Best by state: The top high school athletic programs in America. http://sportsillustrated.cnn.com/2005/magazine/05/11/top.high.map0516/. Accessed January 15, 2006.

Huffington Post. 2012. What NBC paid for US Olympic rights over the years. www.huffingtonpost.com/2012/08/01/nbc-paid-us-olympics-rights_n_1729726.html. Accessed December 20, 2014.

———. 2014. Bruno Mars breaks Super Bowl halftime show ratings with 115.3 million viewers. February 4. www.huffingtonpost.com/2014/02/04/bruno-mars-halftime-show-ratings_n_4722666.html. Accessed December 23, 2014.

Human Rights Watch. 2014. Saudi Arabia: No women on Asian Games team. www.hrw.org/news/2014/09/17/saudi-arabia-no-women-asian-games-team. Accessed January 10, 2015.

Huston, W. 2005. Sports is the opiate of the masses. *American Daily*, January 18. www.americandaily.com/2951. Accessed January 18, 2005.

Huizinga, J. 1950. *Homo ludens: A study of the play element in culture*. Boston: Beacon Press.

Hutchinson, E. 2004. Hornung was honest about Black athletes, many universities aren't. AlterNet, April 7. www.alternet.org/columnists/story/18358/. Accessed December 16, 2004.

Iber, J., Regaldo, S., Alamillo, J., and De Leon, A. 2011. *Latinos in U.S. sport.* Champaign, IL: Human Kinetics.

IBISWorld. 2013. Baby boomers: A burgeoning customer market. www.ibisworld.com/media/2013/04/08/baby-boomers-a-burgeoning. Accessed January 9, 2015.

IMG Academy. 2015. Full-time tuition rates. Athletic and personal development. www.imgacademy.com/sites/default/files/academics/050614_Performance_Academy_Rate_Card.pdf. Accessed April 29, 2015.

Imray, G. 2013. South African rugby to return to racial quotas. NBC Sports. www.nbcsports.com/other-s0ports/south-african-rugby-return-racial-quotas. Accessed February 24, 2014.

Institute of Medicine. 2013. Committee on sports-related concussions in youth. www.iom.edu/Reports/2013/Sports-Related-Concussions-in-Youth-Improving-the-Science-Changing-the-Culture/Report-Brief103013.aspx. Accessed May 15, 2014.

International Council for Coaching Excellence, Association of Summer Olympic International Federations, and Leeds Beckett University. 2013. International sport coaching framework, version 1.2. Champaign, IL: Human Kinetics.

International Council on Active Aging. 2010. www.icaa.cc/. Accessed July 20, 2010.

———. 2015. About us. www.icaa.cc/. Accessed May 30, 2015.

International Federation of Association Football (FIFA). 2010. World Cup South Africa. Television audience report. www.fifa.com/mm/document/affederation/tv/01/47/32/73/2010fifaworldcupsouthafricatvaudiencereport.pdf. Accessed December 24, 2014.

———. 2014a. Big count. www.fifa.com/worldfootball/bigcount/index.html. Accessed December 15, 2014.

———. 2014b. World Cup Brazil results and players. www.fifa.com/worldcup/players/index.html. Accessed December 24, 2014.

———. 2014c. The FIFA/Coca-Cola world ranking – Ranking table. www.fifa.com/fifa-world-ranking/ranking-table/men/index.html?i. Accessed December 15, 2014.

International Health, Racquet, and Sportsclub Association (IHRSA). 2014. IHRSA health club consumer report: 2014 health club activity, usage, trends and analysis (press release). www.ihrsa.org/blog/2014/9/4/2014-ihrsa-health-club-consumer-report-is-available.html. Accessed October 15, 2014.

International Olympic Committee. 2013a. 15th World Conference on Sport for All—Lima. www.olympic.org/news/15th-world-conference-on-sport-for-all-lima/209983. Accessed April 20, 2014.

———. 2013b. IOC president outlines his vision for the partnership between the worlds of sport and politics at the UN General Assembly. www.olympic.org/news/ioc-president-outlines-his-vision-for-the-partnership-between-the-worlds-of-sport-and-politics-at-the-un-general-assembly/216674. Accessed May 17, 2014.

______, 2013c. London 2012 Olympic Games Official Report. Vol. 3. www.olympic.org/Documents/Reports/Official%20Past%20Games%20Reports/Summer/ENG/2012-RO-S-London_V3_eng.pdf. Accessed May 3, 2015.

———. 2014a. Factsheet: Women in the Olympic Movement. Update—May 2014. www.olympic.org/Documents/Reference_documents_Factsheets/Women_in_Olympic_Movement.pdf. Accessed January 4, 2014.

———. 2014b. Marketing report: London 2012, chapter 3 (Broadcasting), 113–21. www.olympic.org/Documents/IOC_Marketing/London_2012/LR_IOC_MarketingReport_medium_res1.pdf. Accessed December 19, 2014.

———. 2014c. Factsheet: Sochi 2014 facts and figures: Update – February 2015. www.olympic.org/Documents/Games_Sochi_2014/Sochi_2014_Facts_and_Figures.pdf. Accessed January 9, 2015.

———. 2014d. Factsheet: The fight against doping and promotion of athletes' health. www.olympic.org/Documents/Reference_documents_Facthseets/Fight_against_doping.pdf. Accessed June 11, 2015.

International Paralympic Committee. 2014. Sochi 2013 Paralympic Winter Games. About Us. www.paralympic.org/sochi-2014/about-us. Accessed January 9, 2014.

International Sport. 2010. National Sportsmanship Day. www.internationalsport.com/nsd/. Accessed July 9, 2010.

Intrator, S., and Siegel, D. 2008. Project Coach: Youth development and academic achievement through sport. *Journal of Physical Education, Recreation and Dance* 70 (7): 17–23.

IPSOS World Monitor. 2002. Trend profiler II: Couch and field: Eight sports' global draw. First quarter, 2002. www.ipsos.ca/prod/wm/. Accessed October 21, 2004.

Isadore, C. 2014. Buffalo Bills sell for more than $1 billion. money.cnn.com/2014/09/09/news/companies/buffalo-bills-sale/index.html. Accessed April 24, 2015.

Jacobson, D. 2007. The revenue model: Why baseball is booming. www.bnet.com/article/the-revenue-model-why-baseball-is-booming/210671. Accessed October 19, 2010.

Jenkins, S. 2010. On television, highlights of women's sports are running low. *Washington Post*, June 4. http://pqasb.pqarchiver.com/washingtonpost/access/2049347001.html?FMT=ABS&FMTS=ABS:FT&date=Jun+4%2C+2010&author=Sally+Jenkins&pub=The+Washington+Post&edition=&startpage=D.1&desc=On+television%2C+women%27s+sports+highlights+are+running+low. Accessed October 19, 2010.

Jiang, X. 2012. Through turbulence to influence: China's Olympic journey in the context of globalisation and nationalism. *The International Journal of Sport and Society* 2 (4).

Johnson, J. 2014. #FreeMarissa: Why prosecution for domestic violence goes wrong and why Marissa shouldn't bear the brunt of it. http://feminist.org/blog/index.php/2014/07/31/freemarissa-why-prosecution-for-domestic-violence-so-often-goes-wrong-and-why-marissa-shouldnt-bear-the-brunt-of-it/. Accessed June 9, 2015.

Johnson, W. 1973a. And smile, smile, smile. *Sports Illustrated*, June 4, 76–78.

———. 1973b. Courting time in Peking. *Sports Illustrated*, July 2, 12–15.

———. 1973c. Sport in China. *Sports Illustrated*, September 24, 82–100.

Josephson Institute. 2008. The ethics of American youth—2008 summary. https://charactercounts.org/programs/reportcard/2008/index.html. Accessed May 13, 2015.

———. 2012a. The ethics of American youth: 2012. https://charactercounts.org/programs/reportcard/2012/installment_report-card_bullying-youth-violence.html. Accessed February 13, 2014.

———. 2012b. The ethics of American youth: 2012. https://charactercounts.org/programs/reportcard/2012/installment_report-card_honesty-integrity.html. Accessed February 13, 2014.

Josephson, M. 2004. Character counts: Sportsmanship survey. Josephson Institute. https://charactercounts.org/programs/reportcard/2004/index.html. Accessed May 13, 2015.

———. 2007. Report reveals propensity of high school athletes to lie and cheat when the stakes are high. Josephson Institute. www.charactercounts.org. Accessed September 1, 2009.

Joyner, J. 2012. Public financing of private sports stadiums. www.outsidethebeltway.com/public-financing-of-private-sports. Accessed July 20, 2014.

Juliano, W. 2013. Flaw in the Yankees' budget plan? Breaking down MLB's revenue sharing system. www.captainsblog.info/2013/01/23/flaw-in-the-yankees-budget-plan-breaking-down-mlbs-revenue-sharing-system/18956/. Accessed November 21, 2014.

Kaiser Family Foundation. 2010. Generation M2, media in the lives of 8- to 18-year-olds. http://kaiserfamilyfoundation.files.wordpress.com/2013/01/8010.pdf. Accessed January 5, 2014.

Kamboj, P. 2013. The world's most popular sports. http://ezinearticles.com/?The-Worlds-Most-Popular-Sports&id=6259531. Accessed July 23, 2014.

Kaplan, D. 2014. Grand plan for tennis. *SportsBusiness Journal*, August 25. http://sportsbusinessdaily.com/Journal/Issues/2014/08/25/In-Depth/Main.aspx. Accessed November 21, 2014.

Kassouf, J. 2013. A quick look at NWSL salaries. http://womens.soccerly.com/2013/04/11/nwsl-salaries-national-women. Accessed January 5, 2015.

Katersky, A. 2014. Adrian Peterson's appeal denied. http://abcnews.go.com/Sports/adrian-petersons-appeal-denied/story?id=27569302. Accessed January 15, 2015.

Katz, S. 2005. Sub-mergent power: Struggles for equality under the AIAW/NCAA merger. Unpublished manuscript. Bryn Mawr, PA: Bryn Mawr College.

Kayne, E. 2013. Census: White majority in U.S. gone by 2043. http://usnews.nbcnews.com/_news/2013/06/13/18934111-census-white-majority-in-us-gone-by-2043?lite. Accessed December 29, 2014.

Kelley, B., and Carchia, C. 2013. "Hey, data data—swing!" *ESPN The Magazine*, July 16. http://espn.go.com/espn/story/_/id/9469252/hidden-demographics-youth-sports-espn-magazine. Accessed January 3, 2014.

Khatchaturian, A. 2012. Power ranking the 10 greatest sporting events worldwide. http://bleacherreport.com/articles/1053090-power-ranking-the-super-bowl-and-the-10-greatest-sporting-events-in-the-world. Accessed December 29, 2013. Kidd, B., and Donnelly, P. 2000. Human rights in sports. *International Review for the Sociology of Sport* 35 (2): 131–48.

Kidd, B., and Donnelly, P. 2000. Human rights in sports. *International Review for the Sociology of Sport* 35 (2), 131-48.

King, R. 2004. This is not an Indian. *Journal of Sport and Social Issues* 28 (1): 3–10.

Kingsway International Christian Centre. 2012. KICC provides control centre for LWFCI Olympic team for "Bridging the Gap, UK Outreach 2012". www.kicc.org.uk/Features/LAYWITNESSESFORCHRISTINTERNATIONAL/tabid/213/Default.aspx. Accessed January 11, 2015.

Kissel, R. 2014. CBS, NFL Network combine to draw 20.8 million for "Thursday Night Football." http://variety.com/2014/data/ratings/cbs-nfl-network-off-to-strong-ratings. Accessed December 24, 2014.

Klafs, C., and Lyon, J. 1978. *The female athlete*. 2nd ed. St. Louis: Mosby.

Klein, A. 1991. Sport and culture as contested terrain: Americanization in the Caribbean. *Sociology of Sport Journal* 8: 79–85.

Klein, S. 2012. Violence and Football. The Sports Ethicist. http://sportsethicist.com/2012/08/20/violence-and-football. Accessed May 20, 2014.

Knight Commission on Intercollegiate Athletics. 2001. A call to action: Reconnecting college sports and higher education. www.knightcommission.org/images/pdfs/2001_knight_report.pdf. Accessed October 19, 2010.

Kondolojy, A. 2012. London Olympics on NBC is most-watched television event in U.S. history. http://tvbythenumbers.zap2it.com/2012/08/13/london-olympics-on-nbc-is-most-watched-television-event-in-u-s-history/144780/. Accessed January 25, 2014.

Kretchmar, R.S. 1994. *Practical philosophy of sport*. Champaign, IL: Human Kinetics.

Kretschmann, R., and Benz, C. 2012. God has a plan: Moral values and beliefs of Christian athletes in competitive sports. *Journal of Human Sport Exercise* 7 (2): 495-519.

Kunad, K. 2013. Top 10 most popular sports in the world. www.clicktop10.com/2013/03/top-10-most-popular-sports-in-the-world/. Accessed May 2, 2014.

Kvalsund, P. 2007. Introduction peace and reconciliation. Sport for Development and Peace International Working Group. www.toolkitsportdevelopment.org/html/topic_8C99D814-CFBC-494E-8BAD-8C51BCAEA5BE_6458A396-8CE6-4E87-BD61-6C626363A7AB_1.htm. Accessed September 10, 2010.

Labrozzi, D., Robazza, C., Bertollo, M., Bucci, I., and Bortoli, L. 2013. Pubertal development, physical self-perception, and motivation toward physical activity for girls. *Journal of Adolescence*. www.researchgate.net/publication/249318579_Pubertal_development_physical_self-perception_and_motivation_toward_physical_activity_in_girls. Accessed January 18, 2015.

Ladies Professional Golf Association. 2013. LPGA announces 2014 schedule. www.lpga.com/news/lpga-schedule-to-begin-january. Accessed May 13, 2015.

———. 2015a. Official money/LPGA 2014. www.lpga.com/statistics/money/official-money?year=2014. Accessed January 6, 2015.

———. 2015b. Rankings: Top money lists as of 7/3/2015. www.lpga.com/players. Accessed July 3, 2015.

Laird, S. 2012. 1 in 4 American fans follows sports via social media. http://mashable.com/2012/06/11/1-in-4-american-fans-follow-sports-via-social-media-study/. Accessed July 22, 2013.

———. 2014. Yankees pine tar ejection: A window into baseball's sneaky unwritten rules. http://mashable.com/2014/04/24/pine-tar-in-baseball. Accessed May 20, 2014.

Lajis, R. 1996. The history of drug abuse in sports. www.prn.usm.my/old_website/mainsite/bulletin/sun/1996/sun27.html. Accessed January 15, 2006.

Lambert, C. 2001. Has winning on the field become simply a corporate triumph? *Harvard Magazine*, September-October. www.harvard-magazine.com/on-line/09014.html. Accessed May 23, 2006.

Lapchick, R. 1999. Race, athletes and crime. Special issue, *Sports Business Journal*. www.sportsbusinessdaily.com/Journal/Issues/2000/03/20000306/No-Topic-Name/Celebrate-The-Real-Heroes-Of-Sport.aspx?hl=Richard%20Lapchick&sc=0. Accessed May 13, 2015.

———. 2003. Just do it: Asian American athletes. Asian-Nation: The landscape of Asian America. http://web.bus.ucf.edu/sportbusiness/articles.aspx?y=2000. Accessed December 10, 2004.

———. 2012a. Associated Press sports editors. Racial and gender report card. www.tidesport.org/2012%20RGRC%2011.7.14.pdf. Accessed December 20, 2013.

———. 2012b. The 2012 racial and gender report card: College sport. www.tidesport.org/RGRC/2012/2012_College_RGRC.pdf. Accessed February 13, 2014.

_______2012c. The 2012 racial and gender report card: NFL. www.tidesport.org/RGRC/2012/2012_NFL_RGRC.pdf. Accessed 5/13/2015.

———. 2013a. Academic progress/graduation success rate study of 2013. NCAA Division I women's and men's basketball tournament teams. www.tidesport.org/Grad%20Rates/2013%20Men%27s%20and%20Women%27s%20Basketball%20Tournament%20Teams%20Study.pdf. Accessed January 1, 2015.

———. 2013b. Assessing the 2012–2013 bowl-bound college football teams' graduation rates. www.tidesport.org/Grad%20Rates/2012_Bowl_Study.pdf. Accessed January 1, 2015.

———. 2013c. The 2013 racial and gender report card: Major League Baseball. www.tidesport.org/RGRC/2013/2013_MLB_RGRC_Final_Correction.pdf. Accessed May 15, 2014.

———. 2013d. The 2013 racial and gender report card: Major League Soccer. www.tidesport.org/RGRC/2013/2013_MLS_RGRC.pdf. Accessed May 16, 2014.

———. 2013e. The 2013 racial and gender report card: National Basketball Association. www.tidesport.org/RGRC/2013/2013_NBA_RGRC.pdf. Accessed May 15, 2014.

———. 2013f. The 2013 racial and gender report card: National Football League. www.tidesport.org/RGRC/2013/2013_NFL_RGRC.pdf. Accessed May 15, 2014.

———. 2013g. The Women's National Basketball Association racial and gender report card. www.tidesport.org/RGRC/2013/2013_WNBA_RGRC.pdf. Accessed May 20, 2014.

———. 2014. The 2014 racial and gender report card: Major League Baseball. www.tidesport.org/MLB%20RGRC%202014%20Revised.pdf. Accessed May 13, 2015.

Laskow, S. 2014. The Olympics are the closest to coverage parity female athletes get. www.cjr.org/full_court_press/women_olympics_coverage.php?page=all. Accessed April 10, 2014.

Lavigne, P. 2008. Pro sports figures more invested in this presidential campaign. *ESPN Outside the Lines*, September 4. http://sports.espn.go.com/espn/otl/news/story?id=3565666. Accessed October 19, 2010.

———. 2012. Youth coaches face gambling charges. *ESPN Outside the Lines,* October 30, 2012. http://espn.go.com/espn/print?id=8568724&type=HeadlineNews&ima. Accessed May 27, 2014.

LaVoi, N. 2009. Mother-coach generated strategies for increasing the number of female coaches in youth sport. Tucker Center for Research on Girls & Women in Sport, University of Minnesota. www.cehd.umn.edu/tuckercenter/library/docs/research/Mother-Coach%20Generated%20Strategies.pdf. Accessed May 13, 2015.

LaVoi, N.M. 2013. The decline of women coaches in collegiate athletics: A report on select NCAA Division-I FBS institutions, 2012–13. Minneapolis: Tucker Center for Research on Girls & Women in Sport.

———. 2014. The status of women in collegiate coaching: A report card, 2013–14. Minneapolis: Tucker Center for Research on Girls & Women in Sport.

Leadership for Healthy Communities. 2014a. Overweight and obesity among African-American youths. Fact sheet, May 28. www.leadershipforhealthycommunities.org/resource/overweight-and-obesity-among-african-american-youths/. Accessed November 26, 2014.

———. 2014b. Overweight and obesity among Latino youths. Fact sheet, May 28. www.leadershipforhealthycommunities.org/resource/overweight-and-obesity-among-latino-youths. Accessed November 26, 2014.

Le Batard, D. 2013. Violent NFL players should not surprise us, as problem goes beyond football. *Miami Herald*. http://miami.icito.com/uncategorized/dan-le-batard-violent-nfl-players-should-not-surprise-us-as-problem-goes-beyond-football/. Accessed May 23, 2014

Lederman, D. 2012. College sports reform: Now? Never? *Inside Higher Ed*. www.insidehighered.com/news/2012/01/10/calls-major-reform-college-sports-unlikely-produce-meaningful-change. Accessed January 14, 2014.

Lee, R., McAlexander, K., and Banda, J. 2011. *Reversing the obesogenic environment*. Champaign, IL: Human Kinetics.

Le Fevre, D. 2012. *Best new games*. Updated edition. Champaign, IL: Human Kinetics.

Leibowitz, B. 2010. Football hazing sex assault: Convicted N.M. high school players get sued for sodomizing teammates. *CBS News*, July 2. www.cbsnews.com/news/football-hazing-sex-assault-convicted-nm-high-school-players-get-sued-for-sodomizing-teammates/. Accessed January 16, 2015.

Leigh, B. 2013. *USA Today* reveals college football head coaches' salaries for every FBS school. http://bleacherreport.com/articles/1840036-usa-today-reveals-college. Accessed December 15, 2013.

Leonard, L. 2000. The decline of the black athlete. ColorLines. www.arc.org/C_Lines/CLArchive/story3_1_03.html. Accessed December 4, 2005.

Leonard, W. 1980. *A sociological perspective of sport*. Minneapolis: Burgess.

Levenson, E. 2014. How much will Tiger Woods' absence affect the Masters TV ratings? www.thewire.com/entertainment/2014/how-much-will-tiger. Accessed December 16, 2014.

Lin, Z., Jui-Chia, C., and Esposito, E. 2005. Successful leadership in sport. http://thesportdigest.com/article/successful-leadership-behavior-sport. Accessed October 19, 2010.

Litsky, F. 2002. Mike Webster, 50, dies; Troubled football Hall of Famer. *New York Times*. www.nytimes.com/2002/09/25/sports/mike-webster-50-dies-troubled-football-hall-of-famer.html. Accessed January 14, 2015.

Litsky, F., and Branch, J. 2010. John Wooden, who built incomparable dynasty at U.C.L.A., dies at 99. *New York Times*, June 5. www.nytimes.com/2010/06/05/sports/ncaabasketball/05wooden.html?_r=2&adxnnl=. Accessed July 29, 2010.

Little League. 2015a. History: About our organization. www.littleleague.org/Little_League_Big_Legacy/About_Little_League/Who_We_Are.htm. Accessed 5/13/2015.

Little League. 2015b. State laws on background checks for Little League. www.littleleague.org/learn/programs/childprotection/state-law-bg-checks.htm. Accessed June 3, 2015.

Llorens, I. 2012. Meghan Vogel, Ohio track star, carries runner across finish line at state competition. *Huffington Post*, June 5. www.huffingtonpost.com/2012/06/05/meghan-vogel-ohio-track-star-carries-runner-video_n_1570857.html. Accessed February 14, 2014.

Lombardo, B. 1999. Coaching in the 21st century: Issues, concerns and solutions. *Sociology of Sport Online*. http://physed.otago.ac.nz/sosol/v2i1/v2i1a4.htm. Accessed September 5, 2005.

Lone Star Gridiron. 2014. Texas high school football all-time highest attendance. http://lonestargridiron.com/history-records/all-time-highest-attendance. Accessed December 1, 2014.

Long, J.G. 2012. *Public-private partnerships for major league sports facilities.* New York: Routledge.

Longman, J. 2000. Football: No more football, lots of questions. www.nytimes.com/2000/12/05/sports/football/no/more-football. Accessed April 26, 2015.

Longman, J. 2013. A push to invigorate women's basketball. *New York Times.* www.nytimes.com/2013/06/18/sports/ncaabasketball/official-offers-ways-to-invigorate-womens-basketball.html?_r=0. Accessed May 25, 2015.

Lopiano, D. 1994. Equity in women's sports: A health and fairness perspective. *Athletic Woman* 13 (2): 281–96.

———. 2001. Gender equity and the Black female in sport. www.womenssportsfoundation.org/Content/Articles/Issues/Equity-Issues/G/Gender-Equity-and-the-Black-Female-in-Sport.aspx. Accessed October 19, 2010.

Lowe, P., and Sandreczki, M. 2013. Why was the Maryville rape case dropped? http://kcur.org/post/why-was-maryville-rape-case-dropped. Accessed January 14, 2015.

Lowitt, B. 1999. Terrorists turn '72 Munich Olympics into bloodbath. *St. Petersburg Times,* December 29. www.sptimes.com/News/122999/news_pf/Sports/Terrorists_turn__72_M.shtml. Accessed July 22, 2010.

Loy, J., and Booth, D. 2004. Functionalism in sport and society. In *Handbook of sports studies,* ed. J. Coakley and E. Dunning, 8–25. London: Sage.

Luckerson, V. 2014. Fewer people than ever are watching TV. *Time.* http://time.com/3615387/tv-viewership-declining-nielsen/. Accessed December 17, 2014.

Lumpkin, A. 2010. Teachers and coaches as leaders demonstrating character and competence. *JOPERD* 81 (8): 49–52.

Luschen, G. 2000. Doping in sport as deviant behavior and its social control. In *Handbook of sports studies,* ed. J. Coakley and E. Dunning, 461–76. London: Sage.

Luther, J. 2013. A list of college football sexual assault investigations and cases. *Power Forward,* December 2. http://pwrfwd.net/2013/12/02/updated-a-list-of-college-football-rape-cases/. Accessed May 23, 2014.

Lyons, V. 2013. Moral reasoning of collegiate athletes and intramural sport athletes: An investigation of the influence of religiosity, gender and type of sport played. Doctoral dissertation, Ohio State University.

MacLeod, C. 2007. Chinese sports schools feel an urgency to find gold. *USA Today,* June 14.

Madden, B. 2014. Baseball's most famous "foreign substance" abuser Gaylord Perry says pine tar is definitely a "performing enhancing substance" . . . Tony La Russa agrees. www.nydailynews.com/sports/baseball/madden-gaylord-perry-pine-tar-performance-enhancing-substance-article-1.1767845. Accessed January 13, 2015.

Major League Baseball. 2015. About reviving baseball in inner cities (RBI). http://mlbcommunity.org/programs/rbi.jsp?content=facts. Accessed June 4, 2015.

Maguire, J. 1999. *Global sport: Identities, societies, civilizations.* Cambridge, UK: Polity Press/Cambridge Press.

Maguire, J., Jarvie, G., Mansfield, L., and Bradley, J. 2002. *Sport worlds: A sociological perspective.* Champaign, IL: Human Kinetics.

Malina, R., and Cumming, S. 2003. Current status and issues in youth sports. In *Youth sports: Perspectives for a new century,* ed. R. Malina and M. Clark, 7–25. Monterey, CA: Coaches Choice.

Mancini, M. 2013. 11 Fun facts about hockey pucks. http://mentalfloss.com/article/32285/11-fun-facts-about-hockey-pucks. Accessed December 24, 2014.

Mandell, N. 2014. "Ice Warriors" documentary captures heroism, drama of gold-medal winning American sled hockey team. http://ftw.usatoday.com/2014/11/us-sled-olympics-pbs-documentary. Accessed January 9, 2015.

Marar, M., Mallika, N., McIlvain, S., Fields, D., and Comstock, R. 2012. Epidemiology of concussions among United States high school athletes in 20 sports. *American Journal of Sports Medicine* 40 (4): 747–55.

Marikar, S. 2009. Tiger Woods plus four more sports stars to fall from grace. *ABC News,* December 4. http://abcnews.go.com/print?id=9240643. Accessed July 27, 2010.

Marta, S. 2008. Dallas Cowboys seat license holders hope for a big return. www.strmarketplace.com/en-us/news/71/Dallas-Cowboys-Seat-License-Holders-Hope-for-a-Big-Return.aspx. Accessed May 14, 2015.

Martens, R., Flannery, T., and Roetert, P. 2002. The future of coaching education in America. www.nfhs.org/scriptcontent/va_Custom/vimdisplays/contentpagedisplay.cfm?content. Accessed January 9, 2006.

Martens, R., and Seefeldt, V., eds. 1979. *Guidelines for children's sports.* Reprint. Washington, DC: American Alliance for Health, Physical Education, Recreation and Dance.

Martin, B. 1996. Ten reasons to oppose all Olympic Games. *Freedom* 57 (15): 7.

Matheson, V. 2010. Sports and the economy: Boon or burden? *International Council of Sport and Physical Education,* Bulletin 60 (October): 14–17.

———. 2014. "Hard talk forum: Do mega sports events contribute to the economic development? No." *America's Quarterly* 8 (2): 23, 25.

McBride, K. 2011a. Can a sports network known for its male brand serve the female fan? www.poynter.org/latest-news/top-stories/157096/can-a-sports. March 29, 2014.

———. 2011b. With its "W" initiative, ESPN tries to solve the equation of serving women sports fans. http://espn.go.com/espn/story/_id/7379853/espn-tries-solve-equation. Accessed January 4, 2015.

McClusky, M. 2014. *Faster, higher, stronger: How sports science is creating a new generation of superathletes—and what we can learn from them.* New York: Hudson Street Press.

McFarland, K. 2013. *Frontline*: "League of Denial: The NFL's Concussion Crisis." www.avclub.com/tvclub/frontline-league-of-denial-the-nfls-concussion-cri-103868. Accessed May 22, 2014.

McIntyre, J. 2013. The NFL is entering the golden age of black quarterbacks. http://thebiglead.com/2013/09/13/the-nfl-is-entering-the-golden-age-of-black-quarterbacks/. Accessed January 2, 2014.

McNamara, T. 2000. You're a dumb broad—and that's progress. *Columbia Journalism Review* 38 (5): 43.

Mellinger, S. 2014. Royals are cashing in by the millions, what they do with the money is critical. *Kansas City Star,* October 12.

Messner, M. 2002. *Taking the field: Women, men and sports.* Minneapolis: University of Minnesota Press.

Messner, M., and Cooky, C. 2010. *Gender in televised sports, news and highlights shows, 1989–2009.* Center for Feminist Research, University of Southern California.

Meylan, A. 2014. IOC awards Olympic Games broadcast rights to NBCUniversal through to 2032. www.olympic.org/news/ioc-awards-olympic-games-broadcast-rights-to-nbcuniversal-through-to-2032/230995. Accessed December 20, 2014.

Michener, J. 1987. *Sports in America*. Greenwich, CT: Fawcett.

Mihoces, G. 2015. NFL claims four-year low for concussions in 2014. www.usatoday.com/story/sports/nfl/2015/01/29/concussions-player-safety/22554075/. Accessed June 9, 2015.

Miller, R., and associates. 2005. Sports business market research handbook. www.rkma.com. Accessed November 10, 2005.

Mills, R. 1997. Tapping innate resilience in today's classrooms. Research/practice. Center for Applied Research and Educational Improvement, University of Minnesota. www.cehd.umn.edu/CAREI/Reports/Rpractice/Spring97/tapping.html. Accessed October 19, 2010.

Mirabella, L. 2014. Under Armour surpasses Adidas to become No. 2 sports brand. http://articles.baltimoresun.com/2014-09-08/business/bs-bz-under-armour-beats-adidas-20140908_1_armour-ceo-kevin-plank-market-leader-nike. Accessed January 6, 2015.

Miracle, A., and Rees, C. 1994. *Lessons of the locker room: The myth of school sports*. New York: Prometheus Books.

Moltz, D. 2010. Griner's punch: The rise of bad behavior in women's sports? http://usatoday30.usatoday.com/news/education/2010-03-08-IHE-Griner-punch-women-sports08_ST_N.htm. Accessed January 13, 2015.

MomsTeam. 2014. Youth sports concussion safety laws: Washington state. www.momsteam.com/washington/washington-state-sports-concussion-law-takes-lead-in-concussion-safety. Accessed May 21, 2014.

Money. 2014. No way Under Armour! Nike swooshes in with $300 million to keep Kevin Durant. http://money.cnn.com/2014/09/02/news/companies/durant-nike-under-armour/. Accessed November 17, 2014.

Mooney, A. 2012. The bodies of champion gymnasts. www.boston.com/sports/blogs/stasdriven/2012/08/the_bodies_of_champion_gymnasts.html. Accessed June 16, 2015.

MSNBC. 2006. A look at the NHL's new rules. www.msnbc.msn.com/id/8672777/. Accessed January 2, 2006.

Mughal, K. 2013. Top 10 most popular sports in the world. http://sporteology.com/top-10-popular-sports-world/. Accessed May 2, 2015.

———. 2014. Highest paid athletes 2014 ranked by Forbes. http://sporteology.com/highest-paid-athletes-2014-ranked-by-forbes/. Accessed April 24, 2015.

Murphy, P., Sheard, K., and Waddington, I. 2004. Figurational sociology and its application to sport. In *Handbook of sports studies*, ed. J. Coakley and E. Dunning, 92–105. London: Sage.

Murray, C. 2012. Olympic Games set to break $8bn revenues barrier in four-year cycle ending with London 2012. *Sportcal*, issue 26 (July). www.sportcal.com/pdf/gsi/Sportcal_Issue26_6-9.pdf. Accessed December 19, 2014.

Muse, W. 2000. Commentary: Who is responsible for learning in our society? *Auburn University News*, January 11. www.auburn.edu//administration/univrel/news/archive/1_00news/1_00brooks.html. Accessed May 18, 2006.

Myers, G. 2012. *Coaching confidential: Inside the fraternity of NFL coaches*. New York: Random House.

Napikoski, L. 2015. Goals of the feminist movement. http://womenshistory.about.com/od/feminism/a/feminist_movement_goals_in_the_60s_and_70s.htm. Accessed April 23, 2015.

Nathanson, J. 2014. Gambling is the next wave in mobile gaming. www.slate.com/articles/business/the_bet/2014/03/when_will_gambling_be_legal_in_the_u_s_by_the_end_of_this_decade.html. Accessed December 14, 2014.

National Academies. 2013. Extensive study on concussions in youth sports finds "culture of resistance" for self-reporting injury (press release). www8.nationalacademies.org/onpinews/newsitem.aspx?RecordID=18377. Accessed March 20, 2015.

National Alliance for Youth Sports (NAYS). 2008. National standards for youth sports. www.nays.org/CMSContent/File/National_Standards08FINAL(2).pdf. Accessed November 27, 2014.

National Association of Intercollegiate Athletics. 2014. About the NAIA. www.naia.org/ViewArticle.dbml?DB_OEM_ID=27900&ATCLID=205323019. Accessed December 8, 2014.

National Association for Sport and Physical Education (NASPE). 2008. *National coaching report*. Reston, VA: AAHPERD (now SHAPE America).

National Association of State Boards of Education. 2008. Fit, healthy and ready to learn: Chapter D—policies to encourage physical activity. www.nasbe.org/wp-content/uploads/FHRTL_Physical-Activity-NASBE-Nov20121.pdf. Accessed August 2, 2010.

National Coalition Against Racism in Sports and Media. 2014. Education. www.coalitionagainstracism.org#!blank/c16up. Accessed January 1, 2015.

National Collegiate Athletic Association (NCAA). 2007a. Native American mascot policy—status list. http://fs.ncaa.org/Docs/PressArchive/2007/Announcements/Native%2BAmerican%2BMascot%2BPolicy%2B-%2BStatus%2BList.html. Accessed July 13, 2010.

———. 2007b. Sports wagering (*news* release). March 16. http://fs.ncaa.org/Docs/PressArchive/2007/Miscellaneous/2007%2BNCAA%2BBackgrounder%2B--%2BSports%2BWagering.html. Accessed July 27, 2007.

———. 2012a. Behind the blue disk: Student-athlete benefits. www.ncaa.org/sites/default/files/91618%2BBTBD%2BStudent%2BAthlete%2BBenefits%2BWEB.pdf. Accessed December 10, 2014.

______. 2012b. Median subsidy for all subdivisions is $10 million, reports also released for Divisions II and III. http://fs.ncaa.org/Docs/NCAANewsArchive/2012/october/ncaa%2Breport%2Breveals%2Bconsistent%2Bfinancial%2Ballocation%2Bamong%2Bdi%2Bschoolsdf30.html. Accessed November 24, 2013.

———. 2012c. Revenues and expenses: 2004–2011—NCAA Division II intercollegiate athletics programs report. https://www.ncaapublications.com/p-4299-revenues-and-expenses-2004-2011-ncaa-division-ii-intercollegiate-athletics-programs-report.aspx. Accessed April 22, 2014.

———. 2012d. Revenues and expenses: 2004–2011—NCAA Division III intercollegiate athletics programs report. www.ncaapublications.com/p-4298-revenues-and-expenses-2004-2011-ncaa-division-iii-intercollegiate-athletics-programs-report.aspx. Accessed April 22, 2014.

———. 2012–2013a. Race and gender demographics report. www.ncaa.org/sites/default/files/Final%2B2012%2BCollege%2BRGRC.pdf. Accessed January 1, 2015.

———. 2012–2013b. Student-athlete participation: 1981-1982–2012-2013 NCAA sports sponsorship and participation rates report. www.ncaapublications.com/productdownloads/PR1314.pdf. Accessed April 22, 2014.

———. 2013a. Division I, II, & III: Facts and figures. www.ncaa.org/division-I-facts-and-figures. Accessed April 22, 2014.

———. 2013b. Division II winter festival. www.ncaa.com/news/ncaa/article/2012-12-06/dii-championship-festival-tap. Accessed December 8, 2014.

———. 2013c. NCAA student-athlete gambling behaviors and attitudes: 2004–2012. www.ncaa.org/sites/default/files/ncaa_wagering_prelim_may2013_0.pdf. Accessed January 15, 2015.

———. 2013d. NCAA takes first step to simplify, deregulate complex rulebook. www.ncaa.com/news/ncaa/article/2013-01-20/ncaa-takes-first-step-simplify-deregulate-complex-rulebook. Accessed January 13, 2015.

———. 2013e. Probability of competing beyond high school. www.ncaa.org/about/resources/research/probability-competing-beyond-high-school. Accessed November 15, 2014.

———. 2013f. Revenues and expenses: 2004–2012—NCAA Division I intercollegiate athletics programs report. www.ncaapublications.com/productdownloads/2012RevExp.pdf. Accessed November 22, 2014.

———. 2013–2014. Student-athlete participation: 1981-1982–2013-14 NCAA sports sponsorship and participation rates report. www.ncaapublications.com/productdownloads/PR1314.pdf. Accessed April 22, 2014.

———. 2014a. Divisional differences and the history of multidivisional classification. www.ncaa.org/about/who-we-are/membership/divisional-differences-and-history-multidivision-classification. Accessed November 23, 2014.

———. 2014b. Football: 2013 and 2014 rules and interpretations. www.ncaapublications.com/productdownloads/FR14.pdf. Accessed December 20, 2014.

———. 2014c. Student-athletes continue to achieve academically. www.ncaa.org/about/resources/media-center/news/student-athletes-continue-achieve-academically. Accessed May 14, 2015.

———. 2014d. Mind, body and sport. Understanding and supporting student-athlete mental wellness. www.ncaapublications.com/p-4375-mind-body-and-sport-understanding-and-supporting-student-athlete-mental-wellness.aspx. Accessed December 1, 2014.

———. 2014e. NCAA.com debuts new version of sports app with exclusive live streaming video. March 3. www.ncaa.com/news/ncaa/article/2014-03-03/ncaacom-debuts-new-version-sports-app-exclusive-live-streaming-video. Accessed December 23, 2014.

———. 2014f. NCAA national study of substance use habits of college student-athletes. www.ncaa.org/sites/default/files/Substance%20Use%20Final%20Report_FINAL.pdf. Accessed January 11, 2015.

National Council for Accreditation of Coaching Education (NCACE). 2013. The value of sport coaching education (position statement). www.qualitycoachingeducation.org/benefits/. Accessed January 21, 2014.

National Council of Youth Sports (NCYS). 2010. www.ncys.org. Accessed June 28, 2010.

National Eating Disorders Association. 2014. Coach and athletic trainer toolkit. www.nationaleatingdisorders.org/coach-trainer. Accessed May 20, 2014.

National Federation of State High School Associations. 2004. The case for high school activities. www.nfhs.org/media/885812/2014_case_for_hs_activities.pdf. October 19, 2010.

———. 2006. Sexual harassment and hazing: Your actions make a difference! www.doe.in.gov/sites/default/files/safety/and-hazing.pdf. Accessed October 19, 2010.

———. 2009. *High school today*: Pay to play sports. www.nfhs.org/search.aspx?searchtext=Pay%20to%20play%20sports. Accessed October 19, 2010.

———. 2010. NFHS coaches code of ethics. www.misshsaa.com/coaches_code_of_ethicsathle.htm. Accessed July 29, 2010.

———. 2013-2014. Athletics participation summary. www.nfhs.org/ParticipationStatics/PDF/2013-14_Participation_Survey_PDF.pdf. Accessed December 1, 2014.

______. 2014a. Coaches Code of Ethics. www.nfhs.org/nfhs-for-you/coaches/coaches-code-of-ethics/. Accessed April 30, 2015.

———. 2014b. Learn: Coaching requirements and courses. http://nfhslearn.com. Accessed November 28, 2014.

———. 2014c. NFHS launches second level of national coach certification program. www.nfhs.org/articles/nfhs-launches-second-level-of-national-coach-certification-program/. Accessed November 28, 2014.

National Senior Games Association. 2010. History of the NSGA. www.nsga.com/history.aspx. Accessed July 20, 2010.

———. 2014. Personal best athlete profile, Ethel Lehmann. www.nsga.com/media/documents/personal-best-tour/elehmann-2014pb.pdf. Accessed January 9, 2015.

National Sporting Goods Association. 2009. Women increase market clout in 2009 athletic footwear purchases. http://connection.ebscohost.com/c/articles/37292497/women-increase-market-clout-athletic-footwear-purchases. Accessed July 16, 2010.

National Women's Law Center. 2012. The battle for gender equity in athletics in elementary and secondary schools. January 30. www.nwlc.org/resource/battle-gender-equity-athletics. Accessed 12/30, 2014.

Native American Sports Council (NASC). 2009. Native American professional athletes and Olympic athletes. www.nascsports.org. Accessed September 16, 2009.

Native Drive Network (NDN). 2015. Native American professional athletes and college athletes. www.ndnsports.com. Accessed May 14, 2015.

Ness, B. 2012. Boomers: 26 percent of the population, 40 percent of the economy. www.55places.com/blog/baby-boomers-26-percent-of-population. Accessed January 8, 2015.

Neuman, R. 2005. Adventures in cybersound. www.acmi.net.au/AIC/ENC_BROADCASTING.html. Accessed November 10, 2005.

Newport, F. 2012. In U.S., 77% identify as Christian. Gallup. www.gallup.com/poll/159548/identify-christian.aspx. Accessed May 11, 2014.

New York Post. 2010. 700M watched World Cup final. nypost.com/2010/07/12/700m-watched-world-cup-final/. Accessed July 15, 2010.

New York Street Games. 2010. A crash course for the essential urban games. Book and DVD. www.newyorkstreetgames.com/home.html. Accessed October 10, 2010.

NFL Evolution. 2013. Youth concussion FAQ. www.nflevolution.com/article/youth-concussion-faq?ref=0ap1000000228346. Accessed May 21, 2014.

Nichols, K. 1997. What is the relationship between eating disorders and female athletes? www.vanderbilt.edu/AnS/psychology/health_psychology/sport.htm. Accessed September 5, 2005.

Nielsen. 2012. Nielsen tops of 2012: Television. www.nielsen.com/us/en/insights/news/2012/nielsen-tops-of-2012-television.html. Accessed December 29, 2013.

———. 2013a. Nielsen top TV programs of 2013—Single telecast. www.nielsen.com/us/en/newswire/2013/tops-of-2013-tv-and. Accessed December 23, 2013.

———. 2013b. Year in sports media report—2013. http://talentleague.com/wp-content/uploads/2014/02/year-in-sports-media-report-2013.pdf. Accessed December 17, 2014.

———. 2014a. Super Bowl XLVIII draws 111.5 million viewers, 25.3 million tweets. www.nielsen.com/us/en/insights/news/2014/super-bowl-xlviii-draws-111-5-million-viewers-25-3-million-tweets.html. Accessed December 23, 2014.

______. 2014b. Top TV programs of 2013: TV and social media. www.nielsen.com/us/en/insights/news/2013/tops-of-2013-tv-and-social-media.html. Accessed April 26, 2015.

Nohlgren, S. 2013. How much do the Tampa Bay Rays boost the local economy? *Tampa Bay Times*, March 30. www.tampabay.com/news/localgovernment/how-much-do-the-tampa-bay-rays-boost-the-local-economy/2112236. Accessed July 23, 2013.

North American Indigenous Games Council. 2014. The 2014 NAIG numbers are in! www.naigcouncil.com/news_details.php?news_id=29. Accessed January 2, 2015.

Novy-Williams, E. 2013. Serena Williams proves as big for black athletes as being no. 1. www.bloomberg.com/news/2013-09-26/serena-williams-proves-as-big-for-black-athletes-as-being-no-1.html. Accessed January 5, 2015.

Nuckols, B. 2014. APNewsBreak: Ex-players: NFL illegally used drugs. news.yahoo.com/apnewsbreak-ex-players-nfl-illegally-used-drugs-161812644--spt.html. Accessed May 27, 2014.

NYConvergence. 2012. Major League Baseball's advanced media is a hit. May 5. http://nyconvergence.com/2012/05/major-league-baseballs-advanced-media-is-a-hit.html. Accessed January 12, 2014.

O'Day, K. 2007. Volleyball spectator guide. www.sonic.net/drturner/WebTurner/volleyball_spectator_guide.htm. Accessed May 22, 2015.

O'Keefe, B. 2012. Leadership lessons from Nick Saban. *Fortune*. http://fortune.com/2012/09/07/leadership-lessons-from-alabama-football-coach-nick-saban/. Accessed January 28, 2014.

Olympic Charter. 2004. Fundamental principles of Olympism. #1. www.olympic.org/Documents/olympic_charter_en.pdf. Accessed May 14, 2015.

Olympics Fanhouse. 2010. Visnovsky reprimanded after doping test, February 22. http://olympics.fanhouse.com/2010/02/28/visnovsky-reprimanded-after-doping-test/. Accessed July 27, 2010.

Onslow, J. 2013. Robin Roberts deserves recognition for her contributions to women's athletics. http://bleacherreport.com/articles/1707607-robin-roberts-deserves-recognition. Accessed January 1, 2014.

Oppenheimer/MassMutual Financial Group. 2002. Successful women business executives don't just talk a good game . . . They play(ed) one. www.prnewswire.com/news-releases/new-nationwide-research-finds-successful-women-business-executives-dont-just-talk-a-good-game-they-played-one-75898622.html. Accessed May 14, 2015.

Orlick, T. 1974. The sports environment: A capacity to enhance, a capacity to destroy. Paper presented at the 6th Canadian Symposium of Sports Psychology, September, Halifax, Nova Scotia.

Osborne, B. 2010. NCAA On Demand website breaks single day record. http://geek.com/articles/news/ncaa-on-demand-website-breaks-single-day-record-2010. Accessed June 18, 2010.

Otani, A. 2014. For women, athletic ability could determine corporate advancement. *Business Week*. www.businessweek.com/articles/2014-10-14/women-who-played-sports-get-further-in-the-corporate-world. Accessed January 4, 2015.

Overman, S.J. 1997. *The influence of the Protestant ethic on sport and recreation*. Aldershot, UK: Avebury Press.

Owens, S. 2010. Kentucky Derby: Women are bigger viewers of the Kentucky Derby. *Orlando Sentinel*. http://articles.orlandosentinel.com/2010-04-30/sports/os-women-viewers-kentucky-derby_1_churchill-downs-viewers-nbc. Accessed July 15, 2010.

Oz, M. 2013. Biogenesis scandal—MLB suspends 13 players, including A-Rod, Nelson Cruz, and Jhonny Peralta. August 5. http://sports.yahoo.com/blogs/mlb-big-league-stew/biogenesis-scandal-mlb-suspends-13-players-including-rod-190720911.html. Accessed May 27, 2013.

Ozanian, M. 2012. Dallas Cowboys lead NFL with $2.1 billion valuation. www.forbes.com/sites/mikeozanian/2012/09/05/dallas-cowboys-lead-nfl-with-2-1-billion-valuation/. Accessed November 23, 2013.

———. 2013. The most valuable NFL teams. www.forbes.com/sites/mikeozanian/2013/08/14/the-most-valuable-nfl-teams/. Accessed November 22, 2013.

———. 2014. Baseball team values 2014 led by New York Yankees at $2.5 billion. March 26. www.forbes.com/sites/mikeozanian/2014/03/26/baseball-team-values-2014-led-by-new-york-yankees-at-2-5-billion/. Accessed May 10, 2014.

Pace, E. 1994. Christy Henrich, 22, gymnast who suffered from anorexia. www.nytimes.com/1994/07/28/obituaries/christy-henrich-22-gymnast-who-suffered-from-anorexia.html. Accessed May 28, 2014.

Pagliarini, R. 2013. Why athletes go broke: The myth of the dumb jock. www.cbsnews.com/news/why-athletes-go-broke-the-myth-of-the-dumb-jock/. Accessed January 5, 2015.

Panja, T., and Biller, D. 2014. Rio Olympic infrastructure costs of $2.3 billion are set to rise. www.bloomberg.com/news/2014-01-28/rio-olympic-infrastructure-costs-of-2-3-billion-are-set-to-rise.html. Accessed December 15, 2014.

Papper, R. 2012. 2012 TV and radio news staffing profitability survey. Radio Television Digital News Association. www.rtdna.org/article/2012_tv_and_radio_news_staffing_and_profitability_survey#.VQ3bI-GrFEM. Accessed December 25, 2014.

Paprocki, T., and Paprocki, J. 2013. *Holy goals for body and soul: Eight steps to connect sports with God and faith*. Notre Dame, IN: Ave Maria Press.

Payne, E., and Isaacs, L. 2008. *Human motor development*. 7th ed. New York: McGraw-Hill.

Peralta, K. 2014. Native Americans left behind in the economic recovery. November 27, 2014. www.usnews.com/news/articles/2014/11/27/native-americans-left-behind-in-the-economic-recovery. January 2, 2015.

Peretti-Watel, P., Guafliardo, V., Vergeris, P., Mignon, P., Pruvost, J., and Obadia, Y. 2004. Attitudes toward doping and recreational drug use among French elite student-athletes. *Sociology of Sport Journal* 21 (1): 33-40.

Perform Sports Media. 2014. The global sports media consumption report 2014. http://sportsvideo.org/main/files/2014/06/2014-Know-the-Fan-Study_US.pdf. Accessed April 26, 2015.

Petchesky, B. 2013. Payrolls and salaries for every MLB team. http://deadspin.com/2013-payrolls-and-salaries-for-every-mlb-team-462765594. Accessed April 24, 2015.

———. 2014. Nobody wants to host the 2022 Olympics. http://deadspin.com/nobody-wants-to-host-the-2022-olympics-1582151092. Accessed December 15, 2014.

Pew Research Center. 2012a. "Nones" on the rise. www.pewforum.org/2012/10/09/nones-on-the-rise. Accessed January 10, 2015.

———. 2012b. The global religious landscape. www.pewforum.org/2012/12/18/global-religious-landscape-exec/. Accessed January 10, 2015.

———. 2013a. A portrait of Jewish Americans. www.pewforum.org/2013/10/01/chapter-1-population-estimates. Accessed January 10, 2015.

———. 2013b. Ranking Latino populations in the states. www.pewhispanic.org/2013/08/29/ii-ranking-latino-populations. Accessed December 29, 2014.

———. 2013c. The state of the news media 2013. www.stateofthemedia.org/2013/newspapers-stabilizing-but-still-threatened/. Accessed 12/24/2013.

Phillips, B. 2013. Soccer's new match-fixing scandal. Grantland, February 7. http://grantland.com/features/match-fixing-soccer/. Accessed May 27, 2015.

Pillion, D. 2011. Nick Saban to youth football camp: Pay attention, don't play Xbox, be like Freddy Krueger. July 28. www.al.com/sports/index.ssf/2011/07/nick_saban_to_youth_football_c.html. Accessed June 30, 2013.

Pishardy, A. 2013. The future of television: Will broadcast and cable television networks survive the emergence of online streaming? Honors Thesis, Stern School of Business, New York University. www.stern.nyu.edu/sites/default/files/assets/documents/con_042968.pdf. Accessed December 23, 2014.

Plunkett Research. 2014. Sports industry overview. www.plunkettresearch.com/statistics/sports-industry/. Accessed November 23, 2014.

Pomerantz, D. 2013. Madonna tops Forbes 2013 list of the top-earning celebrities. August 26, 2013. www.forbes.com/sites/dorothypomerantz/2013/08/26/madonna-tops-2013-list-of-top-earning-celebrities/. Accessed August 29, 2013.

Porter, K. 2012. Final Four rousing success. www.ncaa.com/news/basketball-women/article/2012-04-05/final-four-rousing-success. Accessed December 25, 2014.

Porter, T. 2014. Journey to Paralympic glory captured in documentary "Ice Warriors." http://news.mpbn.net/post/journey-paralympic-glory-captured-documentary-ice-warriors. Accessed January 9, 2015.

Posnanski, J. 2014. The Super Bowl is crazy and over the top, and that's the point. www.nbcsports.com/joe-posnanski/super-bowl-crazy-and-over-top-and-thats-point. Accessed December 23, 2014.

Powell, S. 2008. *Souled out: How blacks are winning and losing in sports.* Champaign, IL: Human Kinetics.

Powers, C. 2010. *Making Sense of Social Theory.* 2nd ed. Lanham, MD: Rowman & Littlefield.

President's Council on Fitness, Sports, and Nutrition. 2013. Effective education and development of youth sport coaches. *Research Digest* 14 (4), December. https://www.presidentschallenge.org/informed/digest/docs/201312digest.pdf. Accessed January 15, 2014.

———. 2015. Facts and statistics. www.fitness.gov/resource-center/facts-and-statistics. Accessed May 15, 2015.

———. n.d. Our mission and vision. www.fitness.gov/about-pcfsn/our-mission-and-vision/. Accessed January 11, 2015.

Pribut, S., and Richie, D. 2002: A sneaker odyssey. www.drpribut.com/sports/sneaker_odyssey.html. Accessed June 7, 2006.

Price, S.L. 1997, December. Is it in the genes? *Sports Illustrated,* 52 ff.

Prince, L. 2014. Inclusive fitness means fitness for everyone. www.ihrsa.org/home/2014/8/21/inclusive-fitness-means-fitness-for-everyone.html. Accessed January 11, 2015.

Prisbell, E. 2014. Blame emerges like cracks in Texas high school stadium. *USA Today.* www.usatoday.com/story/sports/highschool/2014/06/09/allen-texas-eagle-high-school-football-stadium-cracks-closed/9903781/. Accessed December 4, 2014.

ProCon. 2011. *Doping cases at the Olympics, 1968–2012.* http://sportsanddrugs.procon.org/view.resource.php?resourceID=004420. Accessed December 20, 2014.

Public Religion Research Institute. 2013. On eve of Super Bowl XLVII, survey finds nearly 3-in-10 Americans say God plays a role in outcomes of sport events. http://publicreligion.org/newsroom/2013/01/january-2013-rtp-release-2/#.VZFJGEbzM6E. Accessed July 22, 2013.

Publishers Weekly. 2005. http://reviews.publishersweekly.com/bd.aspx?isbn=0060758635&pub=pw. Accessed June 8, 2006.

Pumerantz, Z. 2012. *Ranking the biggest events in sports.* http://bleacherreport.com/articles/1247928-ranking-the-biggest-events-in-sports. Accessed July 6, 2012.

Quijano, E. 2014. Racism at World Cup casts shadow over soccer's big event. www.cbsnews.com/news/world-cup-2014-racism-casts-shadow-over-soccers-big-event/. Accessed December 16, 2014.

Quinn, E. 2005. Eating disorders in athletes: About health and fitness. www.sportsmedicine.about.com/cs/eatingdisorders. Accessed September 5, 2005.

Quinn, T.J., and Fainaru-Wada, M. 2008. U.S. pro sports leagues still trail in drug-testing arms race. ESPN, May 22. http://sports.espn.go.com/espn/print?id=3408399&type=Columnist&imagesPrint=off. Accessed November 1, 2009.

Rainey, D., and Granito, V. 2010. Normative rules for trash talk among college athletes: An exploratory study. *Journal of Sport Behavior* 33: 276–94.

Reader, S. 2012. Map: Is your favorite sports team for Romney or Obama? www.wnyc.org/story/231094-map-your-favorite-sports-team-romney-or-obama/. Accessed January 11, 2015.

Reed, F. 2010. Social media and the future of sports: Sports marketing 2.0. www.marketingpilgrim.com/2010/01/social-media-and-the-future-of-sports.html. Accessed July 30, 2010.

Rees, C., and Miracle, A. 2004. Education and sport. In *Handbook of sports studies*, ed. J. Coakley and E. Dunning, 277–90. London: Sage.

Regional Interfaith Network. 2012. Olympics: Faith leaders launch faith pin badge. www.regionalinterfaith.org.au/home/worldwide-news/736-olympics-faith-leaders-launch-faith-pin-badge.html. Accessed January 11, 2015.

Reinhart, M. 2015. For Brittney Griner and Glory Johnson, a complicated match made on the hard wood. *New York Times.* www.nytimes.com/2015/05/11/fashion/weddings/photographs. Accessed July 5, 2015.

Rev Racing. 2014. About Rev Racing. Drive for Diversity (D4D) program. http://revracing.net/about-3/. Accessed January 1, 2015.

Reynold, M. 2013. Turner's expanded TV everywhere presence should boost delivery of NCAA March Madness live. www.multichannel.com/news/mobile/turners-expanded-tv-everywhere-presence-should-boost-delivery-ncaa-march-madness-live/306162. Accessed December 23, 2014.

Rhoden, W. 2007. *Third and a mile: From Fritz Pollard to Michael Vick—an oral history of the trials, tears, and triumphs of the black quarterback*. New York: ESPN.

Rice, E., Hutchinson, J., and Lee, M. 1958. *A brief history of physical education*. New York: Ronald Press.

Rice, G. 1941. *Only the brave and other poems*. New York: Barnes.

Rice, H. 2011. True sport report—Why we play sport and why we stop. http://truesport.org/resources/publications/reports/why-we-play-sport-and-why-we-stop/. Accessed January 6, 2014.

Riemer, H., and Chelladurai, P. 1995. Leadership and satisfaction in athletics. *Journal of Sport and Exercise Psychology* 17: 276–93.

Rieper, M. 2014. With the Royals raking in revenues this October, they need to increase payroll in 2015. www.royalsreview.com/2014/10/13/6969527/royals-revenues-increase-payroll-2015. Accessed November 24, 2014.

Rigauer, B. 2004. Marxist theories. In *Handbook of sports studies*, ed. J. Coakley and E. Dunning, 28–47. London: Sage.

Ripley, A. 2013. The case against high school sports. *The Atlantic*. www.theatlantic.com/magazine/archive/2013/10/the-case-against-high-school-sports/309447/. Accessed January 4, 2014.

Ritzer, G. 2004. *The globalization of nothing*. Thousand Oaks, CA: Pine Forge Press.

Roberts, D. 2014. Fortunate 50, 2014. 50 highest earning American athletes. *Fortune* and *Sports Illustrated*. http://fortune.com/fortunate50/. Accessed November 22, 2014.

Robinson, M. 2010. *Sport club management*. Champaign, IL: Human Kinetics.

Robinson, R. 1999. *Rockne of Notre Dame: The making of a legend*. New York: Oxford University Press.

Roller Derby Worldwide. 2014. Find a league. www.derbyroster.com/league.php?country=united_states. Accessed May 15, 2015.

Rose, N. 2011. The growing third wave of legal gambling. www.gamblingandthelaw.com/index.php/columns/296-the-growing-third-wave-of-legal-gambling. Accessed January 18, 2015.

Rosenthal, S. 2014. LeBron James meets Prince William and Duchess Kate after Cavaliers–Nets. www.sbnation.com/lookit/2014/12/8/7358575/lebron-james-meets-prince-william-and-duchess-kate-after-cavaliers. Accessed January 8, 2015.

Rothstein, M., and Werder, E. 2014. Ndamukong Suh wins appeal. http://espn.go.com/nfl/playoffs/2014/story/_/id/12099681/ndamukong-suh-detroit-lions-wins-appeal-play-playoff-game-vs-dallas-cowboys. Accessed January 13, 2015.

Rovell, D. 2013. Cowboys worth NFL-best $2.3 billion. http://espn.go.com/nfl/story/_/id/9566558/forbes-dallas-cowboys-top-value. Accessed November 22, 2013.

———. 2014. NFL teams split $6 billion in revenue.http://espn.go.com/nfl/story/_/id/11200179/nfl-teams-divided-6-billion. Accessed December 23, 2014.

Roxborough, S. 2012. London 2012: Ambush ads take on official sponsors as Olympics begins. www.hollywoodreporter.com/news/london-2012-ambush-ads-take-354870. Accessed December 20, 2014.

Rudd, A., and Stoll, S. 2004. What type of character do athletes possess? *Sport Journal*. http://thesportjournal.org/article/what-type-of-character-do-athletes-possess/. Accessed December 20, 2013.

Rushin, S. 2013. SI's Power 50 list: Who sits atop our Throne of Games. *Sports Illustrated*. www.si.com/more-sports/2013/03/06/sis-50-most-powerful-people-sports. Accessed January 6, 2015.

Saban, N. 2013. Press conference before the 2013 BCS National Championship Game. http://community.orangebowl.org/assets/1/7/sabanpresser.pdf. Accessed November 29, 2014.

Sabo, D., Miller, K., Melnick, M., and Heywood, L. 2004. *Her life depends on it: Sport, physical activity, and the health and well-being of American girls*. East Meadow, NY: Women's Sports Foundation.

Sagas, M., and Cunningham, G. 2014. Sport participation rates among underserved American youth. Research brief: The Aspen Institute's Project Play. www.aspeninstitute.org/sites/default/files/content/docs/education/Project_Play_Underserved_Populations_Roundtable_Research_Brief.PDF. Accessed December 29, 2014.

Sage, G. 1973. Occupational socialization and value orientation of athletic coaches. *Research Quarterly*. www.tandfonline.com/doi/abs/10.1080/10671188.1973.10615205?journalCode=urqe17. Accessed May 15, 2015.

———. 1998. *Power and ideology in American sport*. 2nd ed. Champaign, IL: Human Kinetics.

Sanchez, J. 2005. Latino Legends team announced. http://mlb.mlb.com/NASApp/mlb/news/article.jsp?ymd=20051026&content_id=1260107&vkey=news_mlb&fext=.jsp&c_id=mlb. Accessed December 4, 2005.

Sandomir, R. 2010. World cup ratings certify a TV winner. *New York Times*. www.nytimes.com/2010/06/29/sports/soccer/29sandomir.html?scp=1&sq=WorldcupratingscertifyaTVwinner&st=cse. Accessed October 9, 2010.

Santa Fe Independent School District vs. Doe, U.S. Supreme Court. 2000. Ontario Consultants on Religious Tolerance. www.religioustolerance.org/ps_pray.htm. Accessed May 15, 2015.

Santa Fe New Mexican. 2014. UNM lets women's soccer coach go. www.santafenewmexican.com/sports/unm-lets-women-s-soccer-coach-go/article_e990fe7c-c2f3-5479-80b8-001dd33f08e0.html. Accessed January 15, 2015.

Santos, R. 2014. Social media monitoring widespread among college athletic departments. www.splc.org/article/2014/03/social-media-monitoring-widespread-among-college-athletic-departments-public-records-survey-shows. Accessed December 24, 2014.

Sappenfield, M. 2010. Bode Miller bronze: What a difference four years makes. February 15. www.csmonitor.com/World/Olympics/2010/0215/Bode-Miller-bronze-what-a-difference-four-years-makes. Accessed July 27, 2010.

Scheiber, D. 2004. History of Olympic Games. *St. Petersburg Times* (FL), September 8.

———. 2005. Extreme evolution. *St. Petersburg Times* (FL), August 4.

Schoettle, A. 2014. Irsay arrest spurs talk of Colts succession plan. www.ibj.com/articles/print/46762-irsay-arrest-spurs-talk-of-colt-. Accessed November 23, 2014.

Schottey, M. 2014. Possible Adrian Peterson return could undercut NFL's domestic violence message. http://bleacherreport.com/articles/2256926-possible-adrian-peterson-return. Accessed January 15, 2015.

Schrag, M. 2012. The case for peace-building as sport's next great legacy. Master's thesis, University of Illinois, Urbana-Champaign.

Schrotenboer, B. 2013a. Arrests a big test for league's image. *USA Today*, September 5.

———. 2013b. Black NFL players arrested nearly 10 times as often as whites. November 29. www.usatoday.com/story/sports/nfl/2013/11/29/racial-profiling-nfl/3779489/. Accessed May 23, 2014.

———. 2013c. NFL arrests persist after turbulent offseason. *USA Today*, November 5. www.usatoday.com/story/sports/nfl/2013/09/04/arrest-aaron-hernandez-roger-goodell-dui-assault/2764291/. Accessed May 23, 2014.

Schultz, J. 2004. Discipline and push-up: Female bodies, femininity, and sexuality in popular representations of sports bras. *Sociology of Sport Journal* 21 (2): 185-205.

Schwarz, A. 2009. Ex-N.F.L. executive sounds alarm on head injury. *New York Times*, October 28. www.nytimes.com/2009/10/28/sports/football/28football.html?_r=1&pagewanted=p. Accessed November 1, 2009.

Schweber, N., Barker, K., and Grant, J. 2014. Football players in Sayreville, N.J., recall hazing. www.nytimes.com/2014/10/20/nyregion/in-new-jersey-young-players-recall-hazing.html?ref=topics. Accessed January 16, 2015.

Seefeldt, V., Ewing, M., and Walk, S. 1992. *Overview of youth sports programs in the United States*. Washington, DC: Carnegie Council on Adolescent Development.

SHAPE America. 2006. National standards for sport coaches (NSSC). 2006. 2nd ed. www.shapeamerica.org/standards/coaching/coachingstandards.cfm. Accessed May 18, 2015.

———. 2010. Position statement: Guidelines for participation in youth sport programs: Specialization versus multiple-sport participation. www.shapeamerica.org/advocacy/positionstatements/pe/loader.cfm?csModule=security/getfile&pageid=4651. Accessed January 5, 2014.

Sharp, D. 1994. The women who took the jounce out of jogging. *Health Magazine*, September 25.

Shields, D. 2002. Charles Barkley's head fake. *Slate*, November 22. www.slate.com/id/2074459/. Accessed March 15, 2004.

Shields, D. 2005. Bad behavior cited in youth sports study. *USA Today*, November 29.

Shields, D., and Bredemeier, B. 2009. *True competition: A guide to pursuing excellence in sport and society*. Champaign, IL: Human Kinetics.

Shpigel, B. 2014. "A classic case of bullying" on the Dolphins, report finds. www.nytimes.com/2014/02/15/sports/football/investigation-finds-pattern-of-harassment-in-dolphins-locker-room.html. Accessed May 28, 2014.

Siltanen, R. 2014. Yes, a Super Bowl ad really is worth $4 million. *Forbes*. www.forbes.com/sites/onmarketing/2014/01/29/yes-a-super-bowl-ad-really-is-worth-4-million/. Accessed February 25, 2014.

Simon, S. 2011. Public schools charge kids for basics, frills. *Wall Street Journal*. www.wsj.com/articles/SB10001424052748703864204576313572363698678. Accessed December 4, 2014.

Sky Sports. 2014. Sochi 2014: Record number of positive tests. April 29. www1.skysports.com/other-sports/news/12993/9288447/sochi-2014-record-number-of-positive-tests. Accessed December 20, 2014.

Slater, R. 2003. *Great Jews in sport*. Middle Village, NY: Jonathan David.

Sleek, S. 2004. Psychologists help debunk the myth of Michael Jordan. www.umich.edu/~paulball/webpage%20papers/Psychologists_Michael_Jordan.htm. Accessed December 16, 2004.

Smart, R., and Smart, M. 1982. *Children: Development and relations*. 4th ed. New York: Macmillan.

Smit, B. 2008. *Sneaker wars*. New York: HarperCollins.

Smith, A. 2013. Smartphone ownership 2013. Pew Research Center. www.pewinternet.org/2013/06/05/smartphone-ownership-2013. Accessed December 6, 2014.

Smith, C. 2013. College football's most valuable teams 2013: Texas Longhorns can't be stopped. www.forbes.com/sites/chrissmith/2013/12/18/college-footballs-most-valuable-teams-2013-texas-longhorns-cant-be-stopped/. Accessed December 19, 2013.

_______. 2014. College football's most valuable teams 2014. www.forbes.com/sites/chrissmith/2014/12/22/college-footballs-most-valuable-teams-2014/. Accessed April 26, 2015.

Smith, J. 2010. On cue, New York Yankees' Derek Jeter goes into acting mode. *Tampa Bay Times*. www.tampabay.com/sports/baseball/rays/on-cue-new-york-yankees-derek-jeter-goes-into-acting-mode/1121913. Accessed October 12, 2010.

Smith, M. 2011. Athletic budgets continue to climb. *SportsBusiness Journal*, August 22. www.sportsbusinessdaily.com/Journal/Issues/2011/08/22/In-Depth/Budgets.aspx. Accessed November 24, 2013.

Smith, M., and Wynn, A. 2013. *Women in the 2012 Olympic and Paralympic Games: An analysis of participation and leadership opportunities*. Ann Arbor, MI: SHARP Center for Women and Girls. http://irwg.research.umich.edu/pdf/Olympic_Report_2012_FINAL%204.11.13.pdf. Accessed May 15, 2015.

Smith, R. 1986. Toward a cognitive-affective model of athletic burnout. *Journal of Sport Behavior* 18 (1): 3–20.

Solomon, J. 2014. Percentage of Major League African-American players has fallen dramatically. www.huffingtonpost.com/jimmie-lee-solomon/african-american-baseball-players_b_4923689.html. Accessed November 27, 2014.

Spears, B., and Swanson, R. 1978. *History of sport and physical activity in the United States*. Dubuque, IA: Brown.

Special Olympics. 2014. Who we are. www.specialolympics.org/Sections/Who_We_Are/Who_We_Are.aspx. Accessed January 9, 2015.

Splitt, F. 2004. The faculty-driven movement to reform big-time college sports. Drake Group. https://drakegroupblog.files.wordpress.com/2013/01/splitt_sequel.pdf. Accessed May 15, 2015.

Sporting Goods Manufacturers Association. 2005. Extreme-sports: Ranking high in popularity. Press release. May 31, 2005. www.sgma.com/press/2005/1117636042-19826.html. Accessed August 4, 2004.

Sporting Goods Manufacturers Association. 2009. Organized sport play dominates team sport market. www.sfia.org/press/153_Organized-Sport-Play-Dominates-Team-Sports-Market. Accessed May 15, 2015.

Sporting News. 2003. Commission seeks fix for scandal-plagued U.S. Olympic Committee. June 19. www.sportingnews.com/soccer/articles/20030619/479205p.html. Accessed June 10, 2004.

———. 2013. Ndamukong Suh voted dirtiest player in *Sporting News* midseason players poll. www.sportingnews.com/nfl/story/2012-11-08/ndamukong-suh-dirtiest-player-poll-finnegan-sporting-news-sn. Accessed January 13, 2015.

Sports and Fitness Industry Association (SFIA). 2012. SGMA says the Olympics do impact sports participation (press release). March 12. www.sfia.org/press/431_SGMA-Says-The-Olympics-Do-Impact-Sports-Participation. Accessed January 1, 2014.

———. 2013a. 2013 sports, fitness, and leisure activities topline participation report. https://www.sfia.org/reports/301_2013-Sports%2C-Fitness%2C-and-Leisure-Activities-Topline-Participation-Report.

———. 2013b. U.S. trends in team sports: Participation report. Sports Marketing Surveys USA. www.sfia.org/reports/all/ Accessed May 18, 2015.

———. 2014. 2014 sports, fitness, and leisure activities topline participation report. https://www.sfia.org/reports/308_2014-Sports%2C-Fitness%2C-and-Leisure-Activities-Topline-Participation-Report.

Sports Doctor. 2000. Women's issues. The female athlete. www.sportsdoctor.com/articles/female9.html. Accessed June 8, 2006.

Sports Illustrated for Women. 2000. Top 100 female athletes of the 20th century. www.topendsports.com/world/lists/greatest-all-time/women-si100.htm. Accessed May 15, 2015.

Sports Marketing Surveys USA. 2013. Pilates training and yoga training: Single sport participation reports. Silver Spring, MD: Sports and Fitness Industry Association.

Sports Venues. 2014. Revenues from sports venues: List of naming rights deals. www.sportsvenues.com/rsv.php?menu=names. Accessed November 20, 2014.

Srakocic, K. 2010. NHL players' union approves ban on head shots. www.usatoday.com/sports/hockey/nhl/2010-03-25-head-shot-rule_N.htm. Accessed October 19, 2010.

Staples, A. 2012. How television changed college football—and how it will again. www.si.com/college-football/2012/08/06/tv-college-football. Accessed December 30, 2013.

Starkman, D. 2013. ESPN's journalism problem. *Columbia Journalism Review*. www.cjr.org/the_audit/espns_journalism_problem.php?page=all.

Statistics Portal, The. 2013. Average percentage of U.S. population engaged in sports and exercise per day from 2010 to 2013. www.statista.com/statistics/189562/daily-engagement-of-the-us-poppulation-in-sports-and-exercise/. Accessed May 24, 2015.

Steele, M. 2012. WNBA players cash in overseas. http://espn.go.com/espnw/news-commentary/article/7538075/wnba-players-cash-overseas. Accessed January 25, 2014.

Steinberg, B. 2013. Super Bowl ads: Fox seeks $4M for 30-second slot in big game. variety.com/2013/tv/news/super-bowl-ads-fox-seeks-4m-for-30-second-slot-in-big-game-1200586371/. Accessed December 24, 2014.

Stephan, E. 1994. For love, for money, for real money. www.edstephan.org/webstuff/es.19thBB.html. Accessed May 15, 2015.

Stevens, T. 2005. Ted Stevens Olympic and Amateur Sports Act. http://videos.usoc.org/legal/TedStevens.pdf. Accessed October 19, 2010.

Stevens, T. 2015. Ted Stevens Olympic and Amateur Sports Act. www.teamusa.org/About-the-USOC/Inside-the-USOC/History. Accessed May 15, 2015.

Stewart, C. 2005. Should boys and girls be coached the same way? www.coachesinfo.com/category/becoming_a_better_coach/13/. Accessed March 2, 2005.

St. Petersburg Times. 2005. Always a diamond jubilee. February 9.

Stoll, S., and Beller, J. 2012. Female student athletes' moral reasoning 1987–2012. Center for Ethics, University of Idaho. www.webpages.uidaho.edu/center_for_ethics/research_fact_sheet.htm. Accessed May 15, 2015.

———. 2009. Male/female student athletes' moral reasoning 1987–2004: Seventeen-year study results and key points. www.webpages.uidaho.edu/center_for_ethics/Measurements/HBVCI/findings.htm. Accessed February 13, 2014.

StopHazing. 2015. Information on hazing. www.stophazing.org/hazing-information/. Accessed May 15, 2015.

Straus, L. 2013. Cheerleading: High rates of catastrophic injuries and concussions. www.momsteam.com/health-safety/cheerleading-high-rates-catas. Accessed January 16, 2015.

Strauss, C. 2014. Chiefs safety Husain Abdullah penalized for post-touchdown prayer. http://ftw.usatoday.com/2014/09/husain-abdullah-penalty-prayer-celebration. Accessed January 10, 2015.

Sundgot-Borgen, J., and Torstveit, M.K. 2004. Prevalence of eating disorders in elite athletes is higher than in the general population. http://journals.lww.com/cjsportsmed/Abstract/2004/01000/Prevalence_of_Eating_Disorders_in_Elite_Athletes.5.aspx. Accessed October 19, 2010.

SuperData Research. 2014. Publishers emphasize eSports in 2014 strategy. eSports: Digital games brief, April. www.slideshare.net/StephanieLlamas/esports-brief-by-superdata-research. Accessed May 15, 2015.

Suttle, R. 2013. How much money do sportswriters make a year? *Demand Media*. http://everydaylife.globalpost.com/much-money-sportswriters-make-yearly. Accessed December 25, 2014.

Tadena, N. 2015. Super Bowl ad prices have gone up 75% over a decade. CMOTODAY. http://blogs.wsj.com/cmo/2015/01/12/super-bowl-ad-prices-have-gone. Accessed April 23, 2015.

Tampa Bay Times. 2012. The signature storyteller. September 19.

———. 2013. NFL's a non-profit? December 15.

Tassi, P. 2014. ESPN boss declares eSports "not a sport." *Forbes*, September 07. www.forbes.com/sites/insertcoin/2014/09/07/espn-boss-declares-esports-not-a-sport/. Accessed December 10, 2014.

Taylor, A. 2014. Why Sochi is by far the most expensive Olympics ever. *Business Insider*. www.businessinsider.com/why-sochi-is-by-far-the-most-expensive-olympics-ever-2014-1. Accessed December 15, 2014.

Team Marketing Report. 2013. Fan cost index. www.teammarketing.com/btSubscriptions/fancostindex/index. Accessed January 15, 2014.

Texas University Interscholastic League. 1998. Benefits of extracurricular activities. www.uil.utexas.edu/admin/benefits.html. Accessed November 14, 2004.

Thompson, D. 2014. Which sports have the whitest/richest/oldest fans? *Atlantic*. www.theatlantic.com/business/archive/2014/02/which-sports-have-the-whitest-richest-oldest-fans/283626/. Accessed January 4, 2015.

Tignor, S. 2013. Esther Vergeer: More than a number. http://espn.go.com/blog/tennis/post/_/id/10/tennis-esther-vergeer-more-number. Accessed May 10, 2014.

Topend Sports. 2013. Top 10 list of the world's most popular sports. www.topendsports.com/world/lists/popular-sport/fans.htm. Accessed January 22, 2014.

Topkin, M. 2004. Provocative poses divide U.S. women. *St. Petersburg Times* (FL), August 25.

Torre, P. 2009. How (and why) athletes go broke. www.si.com/vault/2009/03/23/105789480/how-and-why-athletes. Accessed January 8, 2015.

Tough Mudder. 2014. Corporate sponsors. https://toughmudder.com/content/sponsorship-opportunities. Accessed January 10, 2014.

Tracy, M. 2015. College football is powerful: The proof is in the alcohol. www.nytimes.com/2015/01/11/sports/ncaafootball/signs-of-college-footballs-clout-beer-sales-and-travel-aid-.html?_r=0. Accessed January 13, 2015.

Travis, C. 2013. What's the future of *Sports Illustrated*? March 7. www.foxsports.com/college-football/outkick-the-coverage/whats-the-future-of-sports-illustrated-030713. Accessed December 29, 2013.

Tsiokos, C. 2005. Sports as the opiate of the masses. September 4. www.populationstatistic.com/index.php?s=Sports+as+the+opiate+of+the+ masses&submit=search. Accessed May 15, 2006.

Tucker Center for Research on Girls and Women in Sport. 2007. Developing physically active girls. www.cehd.umn.edu/tuckercenter/library/docs/research/2007-Tucker-Center-Research-Report.pdf. Accessed December 4, 2014.

———. 2014. Media coverage & female athletes: A video documentary. www.cehd.umn.edu/tuckercenter/multimedia/mediacoverage.html. Accessed April 3, 2014.

Tufaro, G. 2015. After hazing scandal, football to return to Sayreville for 2015 season. http://usatodayhss.com/2015/after-scandal-football-to-return-to-sayreville-for-2015-season. Accessed January 11, 2015.

Tuggle, C. 2003. Study shows ESPN still not paying much attention to women's sport. www.unc.edu/news/archives/aug03/tuggle080103.html. Accessed October 19, 2010.

Turco, D., and Ostrosky, T. 1997. Touchdowns and fumbles: Urban investments in NFL franchises. *Cyber-Journal of Sport Marketing*. www.ausport.gov.au/fulltext/1997/cjsm/v1n3/turco.htm. Accessed November 3, 2005.

United Cerebral Palsy. 2004. Americans with Disabilities Act: An overview. www.ucp.org/ucp_generaldoc.cfm/1/8/32/32-11218/3905. Accessed October 19, 2010.

United Nations. 2011. Report on 2nd International Forum on Sport for Peace and Development. Geneva. www.un.org/wcm/webdav/site/sport/shared/sport/pdfs/Reports/10-11.05.2011_UN-IOC_Forum_Geneva_ REPORT_EN.pdf. Accessed June 4, 2014.

United States Adventure Racing Association. 2014. What is adventure racing? www.arpathfinder.com/custompages/articles/GettingStartedGuide.pdf. Accessed May 15, 2015.

United States Equestrian Team Foundation. 2010. www.uset.org/contact.php. Accessed July 19, 2010.

United States Lacrosse Association. 2012 participation survey. www.uslacrosse.org/Portals/1/documents/pdf/about-the-sport/2012-participation-survey.pdf. Accessed January 20, 2014.

United States Olympic Committee. 2010. About the USOC: General information. www.teamusa.org/about-usoc/usoc-general-information. Accessed October 22, 2010.

University of Utah. 2015. Utah gymnastics: A tradition of excellence. www.universityofutahgymnastics.com/history/excellence.html. Accessed August 26, 2015.

USA Coaching. 2010. United States Olympic Committee: Coaching ethics code. www.teamusa.org/USA-Karate/Officials-and-Coaches/Coaches-Resources/USOC-Coaching-Ethics-Code. Accessed 5/15/2015.

U.S. Anti-Doping Agency. 2010. What sport means in America: A study of sport's role in society. www.truesport.org/library/documents/about/what_sport_means_in_america/what_sport_means_in_america.pdf. Accessed February 10, 2013.

———. 2012. What we stand to lose in our obsession to win. www.truesport.org/library/documents/about/true_sport_report/True-Sport-Report.pdf?. Accessed December 4, 2014.

USA Today. 2012. College football coaches continue to see salary explosion. November 20. www.usatoday.com/story/sports/ncaaf/2012/11/19/college-football-coaches-contracts-analysis-pay-increase/1715435/. Accessed February 10, 2014.

———. 2013. List of schools that changed Native American nicknames. www.usatoday.com/story/sports/2013/09/12/native-american-mascot-changes-ncaa/2804337/. Accessed January 1, 2015.

———. 2014. Selig says MLB revenue could top $9 billion. www.usatoday.com/story/sports/mlb/2014/03/28/selig-says-mlb-revenue-could-top-9-billion/7022245/. Accessed July 11, 2014.

U.S. Bureau of Labor Statistics. 2012a. Employment status of the population by sex, marital status, and presence and age of own children under 18, table 5. www.bls.gov/news.release/famee.t05.htm. Accessed January 6, 2014.

———. 2012b. Current population survey: Community survey: 2012. www.census.gov/cps/. Accessed April 14, 2012.

———. 2012c. Nearly 1 in 5 people have a disability in the U.S., Census Bureau reports. www.census.gov/newsroom/releases/archives/miscellaneous/cb12-134.html. Accessed January 9, 2015.

———. 2012d. The 2012 Statistical Abstract: Arts, recreation, and travel. Tables 1244 and 1245. www.census.gov/compendia/statab/2012/tables/12s1245.pdf. Accessed January 6, 2014.

———. 2012e. U.S. census projections show a slower growing, older, more diverse nation a half century from now. www.census.gov.newsroom/releases/archives/population/cb12. Accessed May 24, 2015.

———. 2013a. Child population in United States for 2013. POP1 Child population: Number of children (in millions) ages 0–17 in the United States by age, 1950–2013 and projected 2014–2050. www.childstats.gov/americaschildren/tables/pop1.asp?popup=true. Accessed January 3, 2014.

———. 2013b. Occupational employment and wages, May 2013: 27-2021 athletes and sports competitors. www.bls.gov/oes/current/oes272021.htm. Accessed April 10, 2015.

———. 2013c. Household income: American Community Survey briefs. September 2014. www.census.gov/content/dam/Census/library/publications/2014/acs/acsbr13-02.pdf. Accessed November 22, 2014.

———. 2013d. Income: Families. Table F10. www.census.gov/hhes/www/income/data/historical/families/. Accessed December 20, 2014.

———. 2013e. Percentage of population, ethnicity and race. http://quickfacts.census.gov/qfd/states/00000.html. Accessed February 15, 2014.

———. 2014a. Coaches and scouts. *Occupational Outlook Handbook*, 2014–15 edition. www.bls.gov/ooh/entertainment-and-sports/coaches-and-scouts.htm. Accessed November 28, 2014.

———. 2014b. Women in the labor force: A databook. Report 1052. Dec. 2014. www.bls.gov/opub/reports/cps/women-in-the-labor-force-a-databook-2014.pdf. Accessed January 3, 2014.

———. 2015. Projections of the size and composition of the U.S. population: 2014 to 2066. www.census.gov/content/dam/Census/library/publications/2015/demo/p25-1143.pdf. Accessed 17, 2015.

U.S. Paralympics. 2015. U.S. Paralympics. www.teamusa.org/US-Paralympics. Accessed May 15, 2015.

U.S. Soccer. 2014. All-time records (U.S. Women's National Team). www.ussoccer.com/womens-national-team/records/wnt-records. Accessed January 5, 2015.

Vancouver Sun. 2010. NBC's Vancouver Olympic coverage ousts American Idol from TV ratings throne. February 18. www.vancouversun.com/story_print.html?id=2581974&sponsor=. Accessed July 5, 2010.

VanderZwaag, H., and Sheehan, T. 1978. *Introduction to sport studies*. Dubuque, IA: Brown.

Van Riper, T. 2009. The future of sports. www.forbes.com/2009/03/04/nba-nhl-mlb-nfl-sports-business_future_sports.html. Accessed August 1, 2010.

Van Riper, V. 2011. Women comprise large part of sports audience. http://sports.yahoo.com/top/news?slug=ys-forbes-sports_women_watch_most_093011. Accessed January 4, 2015.

Vare, R. 1974. *Buckeye: A study of coach Woody Hayes and the Ohio State football machine*. New York: Harper Magazine Press.

Vega, T. 2012. NASCAR seeks to woo Latinos with Fox Deportes agreement. New York Times. http://mediadecoder.blogs.nytimes.com/2012/08/19/nascar-seeks-to-woo-latinos-with-fox-deportes-agreement/?_r=0. Accessed January 1, 2015.

Victor, P. 2014. Counting the cost of being a fan: The NFL's priciest teams to support. http://america.aljazeera.com/articles/2014/2/2/a-day-at-the-gamefoodfanfareandallthatisnflfootball.html. Accessed February 2, 2014.

VidStatsX. 2014. YouTube top 200 most subscribed channels list. http://vidstatsx.com/youtube-top-200-most-subscribed-channels. Accessed December 24, 2014.

Wacquant, L. 2004. *Body and soul: Notebooks of an apprentice boxer*. New York: Oxford University Press.

Waldron, J. 2000. Stress, overtraining and burnout associated with participation in sport. Unpublished thesis. Lansing: Institute for the Study of Youth Sports at Michigan State University.

Waldron, T. 2013. How Kentucky drew a record crowd to its women's basketball game this weekend. http://thinkprogress.org/sports/2013/12/23/3099571/kentucky-duke-set. Accessed January 4, 2015.

Warner, D. 2013. Five companies control nearly all the sports on TV. April 9. www.whatyoupayforsports.com/2013/04/five-companies-control-nearly-all-the-sports-on-tv/. Accessed December 29, 2013.

Warren, L. 2015. Tearful WNBA Brittney Griner says her month-long marriage was a 'huge mistake.' www.dailymail.com/uk/news/article-3117188/Britney-Griner-sobs. Accessed July 5, 2015.

Watson, N., and Bold, B. 2015. Mixed martial arts and Christianity: Where feet, fist, and faith collide. http://theconversation.com/mixed-martial-arts-and-christianity-where-feet-fist-and-faith-collide-34836. Accessed January 11, 2015.

Watson, N., and Czech, D. 2005. The use of prayer in sport: Implications for sport psychology consulting. *Athletic Insight: The Online Journal for Sport Psychology* 7 (4). http://athleticinsight.com/Vol7Iss4/PrayerinSports.htm. Accessed October 19, 2010.

Watson, G. 2014. Group files complaint asking Clemson to separate religion from football. http://sports.yahoo.com/blogs/ncaaf-dr-saturday/group-files-complaint-asking-clemson-separate-religion-from-football-191318852.html;_ylt=A0LEViz_UpFVozIAY9InnIlQ;_ylu=X3oDMTE0djZoZWprBGNvbG8DYmYxBHBvcwMxBHZ0aWQDRkZYVUkyOF8xBHNlYwNzcg--. Accessed January 11, 2015.

Watson, T. 2012. London Olympics: Good will, but not good health. http://usatoday30.usatoday.com/sports/olympics/london/story/2012-06-05/london-olympics-bring-goodwill-but-not-good-health/55723852/1. Accessed January 1, 2014.

Webster's Sports Dictionary. 1976. Springfield, MA: Merriam.

Wechsler, H. 2005. Binge drinking on America's college campuses. Findings from the Harvard School of Public Health College Alcohol Study. www.hsph.harvard.edu/cas/Documents/monograph_2000/cas_mono_2000.pdf. Accessed October 19, 2010.

Week. 2014. Eleven things women in Saudi Arabia can't do. www.theweek.co.uk/middle-east/60339/eleven-things-women-in-saudi-arabia-cant-do. Accessed January 10, 2015.

Weekley, D. 2009. No denying Tiger's effect on television ratings. *Charleston Gazette*, April 11. www.wvgazette.com/Sports/DaveWeekely/200904110289. Accessed August 25, 2009.

Weinberg, R., and Gould, D. 2015. *Foundations of sport and exercise psychology*. 6th ed. Champaign, IL: Human Kinetics.

Weir, T. 2011. London Olympics security costs jump to $1.6 billion. *USA Today*. http://content.usatoday.com/communities/gameon/post/2011/12/london-olympics-security-costs-jump-to-16-billion/1#.VQ9rqmctG00. Accessed January 11, 2015.

Welch, K. 2007. Black criminal stereotypes and racial profiling. *Journal of Contemporary Criminal Justice* 23: 276.

Wells, M. 2014. Carlie Irsay-Gordon is leading the way for Indianapolis Colts. www.espn.go.com/blog/indianapolis-colts/post/_/id/4935/irsay-gordon. Accessed November 23, 2014.

Wendel, T. 2005. When smiles leave the game. *USA Today*. August 23, A-13.

Wharton Alumni Magazine. 2007. Keeping his eye on the digital ball. Spring issue. www.wharton.upenn.edu/125anniversaryissue/bowman.html.

White House, The. 2010. First Lady Michelle Obama launches Let's Move: America's move to raise a healthier generation of kids (press release). www.whitehouse.gov/the-press-office/first-lady-michelle-obama-launches-lets-move-americas-move-raise-a-healthier-genera. Accessed January 11, 2015.

———. 2014. *Not Alone*. The first report of the White House Task Force to Protect Students From Sexual Assault. April. www.whitehouse.gov/sites/default/files/docs/report_0.pdf. Accessed January 15, 2015.

Whitley, D. 2012. Olympics 2012: Women rule London—no cynicism necessary. *Sporting News*. www.sportingnews.com/Olympics/story/2012008-12/Olympics-2. Accessed February 8, 2014.

Williams, O. 2012. London 2012: Aya Medany struggles with sport and religion. www.bbc.com/sport/0/olympics/18274033. Accessed January 11, 2015.

Willmsen, C. 2004. Felons found coaching amateur youth sports: Crimes revealed in Washington, Idaho; background checks considered nationally. *Seattle Times*, March 7. www.thefreelibrary.com/_/print/PrintArticle.aspx?id=113988706. Accessed July 23, 2010.

Wilson, A. 2012. The status of women in intercollegiate athletics as Title IX turns 40. www.ncaapublications.com/productdownloads/TITLEIX.pdf. Accessed December 11, 2014.

Wilson, S. 2013. IOC to spend $20M to fight doping, match-fixing. www.canada.com/olympics/news/ioc-to-spend-20-million-to-fight-doping-and-match-fixing-in-olympics. Accessed May 16, 2015.

Wingfield, N. 2014. E-sports: New field of play. *Tampa Bay Times*, December 15.

Wolff, A. 2011. Sports saves the world. *Sports Illustrated*. Sept. 26, 2011. www.si.com/vault/2011/09/26/106112004/sports-saves-the-world. Accessed May 18, 2014.

Wolverton, B. 2012. The education of Dasmine Cathey. *Chronicle of Higher Education*. http://chronicle.com/article/The-Education-of-Dasmine-Cathey/132065/. Accessed December 18, 2013.

Wolverton, B. 2014. Dasmine Cathey stars in HBO report on academic reform in college sports. http://chronicle.com/blogs/players/dasmine-cathey-stars-in-hbo-report-on-academic-reform-in-college-sports/34411). Accessed April 20, 2015.

Women's Flat Track Derby Association. 2014. Frequently asked questions. http://wftda.com/resources/frequently-asked-questions. Accessed January 6, 2015.

Women's Sports Foundation. 1995. Media—images and words in women's sports: The foundation position. www.womenssportsfoundation.org/home/advocate/foundation-positions/media-issues/images_and_words. Accessed May 15, 2015.

———. 1998. Research report: Sport and teen pregnancy. www.womenssportsfoundation.org/home/research/articles-and-reports/mental-and-physical-health/sport-and-teen-pregnancy. Accessed May 15, 2015.

———. 2001a. Research report: Health risks and the teen athlete. www.womenssportsfoundation.org/home/research/articles-and-reports/mental-and-physical-health/health-risks-and-the-teen-athlete. Accessed May 15, 2015.

———. 2001b. The female athlete triad. www.womenssportsfoundation.org/en/home/get-inspired/body-and-mind/nutrition/the-female-athlete-triad. Accessed May 15, 2015.

———. 2007. Addressing the issue of verbal, physical and psychological abuse of athletes: The foundation position. www.womenssportsfoundation.org/home/advocate/title-ix-and-issues/title-ix-positions/verbal_psychological_physical_abuse. Accessed May 15, 2015.

———. 2008. Go out and play: Youth sports in America. www.womenssportsfoundation.org/home/research/articles-and-reports/mental-and-physical-health/go-out-and-play. Accessed May 15, 2015.

———. 2009a. *Her life depends on it: Sport, physical activity, and the health and well-being of American girls and women*. www.womenssportsfoundation.org/home/research/articles-and-reports/mental-and-physical-health/her-life-depends-on-it-ii. Accessed January 12, 2014.

———. 2009b. Women's sports and fitness facts and statistics. Updated March 26, 2009. www.womenssportsfoundation.org/home/research/articles-and-reports/athletes/womens-sports-facts. Accessed May 15, 2015.

———. 2013. Statement on Biediger v. Quinnipiac. www.womenssportsfoundation.org/en/home/media-center-2/statements-and-media-responses/the-womens-sports-foundation-applauds-the-new-legal-precedents. Accessed May 16, 2015.

———. 2014. About us. www.womenssportsfoundation.org/home/about-us/. Accessed January 3, 2015.

Wooden, J. 2015. The pyramid of success. www.coachwooden.com/pyramid_of_success. Accessed January 10, 2014.

Woods, R. 2004. *Coaching tennis successfully*. Champaign, IL: Human Kinetics.

World Anti-Doping Agency. 2010. A brief history of anti-doping. www.wada-ama.org/en/who-we-are/a-brief-history-of-anti-doping. Accessed October 19, 2010.

World Anti-Doping Agency. 2015. The code. www.usada.org/wp-content/uploads/wada-2015-world-anti-doping-code.pdf. Accessed June 11, 2015.

World Health Organization. 2003. Health and development through physical activity and sport. www.goforyourlife.vic.gov.au/hav/admin.nsf/Images/WHO_statement_on_health_and_PA.pdf/$File/WHO_statement_on_health_and_PA.pdf. Accessed May 22, 2010.

———. 2014. Global strategy on diet, physical activity and health. www.who.int/dietphysicalactivity/en/. Accessed January 12, 2015.

World of Sports Science. 2009. Mature athletes. www.faqs.org/sports-science/Je-Mo/Mature-Athletes.html. Accessed October 19, 2010.

World Squash Federation. 2014. Healthy Lifestyle. Squash is "the world's healthiest sport." http://squash2016.info/healthy_lifestyle. Accessed January 5, 2015.

World Team Tennis. 2010. Billie Jean King. www.wtt.com/page.aspx?article_id=1252. Accessed October 19, 2010.

Wyatt, E. 2013. Most of U.S. is wired, but millions aren't plugged in. www.nytimes.com/2013/08/19/technology/a-push-to-connect-millions. Accessed December 24, 2013.

Yglesias, M. 2014. Green Bay Packers' financial data shows how an NFL team can make money in any market. *Vox*. www.vox.com/2014/7/14/5899139/green-bay-packers-financial-data-shows-how-an-nfl-team-can-make-money. Accessed November 20, 2014.

Young, K. 2004. Sport and violence. In *Handbook of sports studies*, ed. J. Coakley and E. Dunning, 382–408. London: Sage.

Zamyatina, T. 2014. Sochi Olympics draw record number of TV viewers worldwide. http://itar-tass.com/en/opinions/763189. Accessed December 20, 2014.

Zillgitt, J. 2013. Nets face $70 million luxury tax next year. *USA Today Sports*, July 10.

Zirin, D. 2013a. *Game over: How politics has turned the sports world upside down*. New York: New Press.

———. 2013b. How jock culture supports rape culture, from Maryville to Steubenville. www.thenation.com/blog/176846/how-jock-culture-supports-rape-culture-maryville-steubenville. Accessed January 14, 2015.

Zona Latina. 1998. Watching soccer on television in Latin America. www.zonalatina.com/Zldata117.htm. Accessed May 16, 2015.

Zremski, J. 2014. How to pay for a new Bills stadium? *Buffalo News*, November 21. www.buffalonews.com/city-region/how-to-pay-for-a-new-bills-stadium-20140920. Accessed November 21, 2014.

INDEX

Note: Page numbers followed by an italicized *f* or *t* refer to the figure or table on that page, respectively.

ABOUT THE AUTHOR

Courtesy of Ron Woods

Ronald B. Woods, PhD, is an adjunct professor of health science and human performance at the University of Tampa. He was a professor of physical education and men's tennis coach at West Chester University in Pennsylvania for 17 years and was inducted into their athletic Hall of Fame. He has more than 40 years of experience as a professor, coach, and sport administrator.

Woods also spent 20 years with the United States Tennis Association and was the first director of player development, a program that assisted in the development of top junior players into successful playing professionals. He was also honored by the International Tennis Hall of Fame with their Educational Merit Award in 1996.

He has been honored by the United States Professional Tennis Association as National Coach of the Year in 1982 and named a Master Tennis Professional in 1984. A lifelong member of SHAPE America, Woods was a member of the U.S. Olympic Coaching Committee for eight years and the Coaches' Commission of the International Tennis Federation.